THE
ENGLISH ESSAYS
OF
Edward Gibbon

THE
ENGLISH ESSAYS
OF
Edward Gibbon

EDITED BY
PATRICIA B. CRADDOCK

OXFORD
AT THE CLARENDON PRESS
1972

Oxford University Press, Ely House, London W. 1

GLASGOW NEW YORK TORONTO MELBOURNE WELLINGTON
CAPE TOWN IBADAN NAIROBI DAR ES SALAAM LUSAKA ADDIS ABABA
DELHI BOMBAY CALCUTTA MADRAS KARACHI LAHORE DACCA
KUALA LUMPUR SINGAPORE HONG KONG TOKYO

*Printed in Great Britain
at the University Press, Oxford
by Vivian Ridler
Printer to the University*

PREFACE

THE admirer of the works of Edward Gibbon enjoys many advantages. All of Gibbon's letters and journals are now available in excellent modern editions (cited below in full). His *Memoirs*, as recently edited by Georges A. Bonnard, are available in as full and careful an edition as one could dream of; Miss J. E. Norton's bibliography and Mr. D. M. Low's biography guide the reader easily among the events of Gibbon's literary and personal life. Though the text of the *Decline and Fall* has suffered corruption and though its last full edition—J. B. Bury's—was last revised 1909–16, that edition permits us to relate Gibbon's great work to subsequent scholarship, to see where he has been superseded and where he has not.

But Gibbon also wrote a surprising number and variety of shorter pieces, not connected with his personal life, that have been available to the reader only in manuscript, or only in the editions of Gibbon's friend and literary executor, John Baker Holroyd, Lord Sheffield. In addition to piecing together a coherent account of Gibbon's life from the several drafts of his memoirs and to publishing a number of letters to and from Gibbon, Sheffield published several excerpts from Gibbon's journals and commonplace books and some of his miscellaneous essays in both French and English in the second volume of his edition of Gibbon's *Miscellaneous Works* (in quarto, 1796).

The public reaction was so favourable that in 1814 he published more of them. As he put it,

> The great satisfaction evinced on the publication of the former Edition of Mr. Gibbon's Miscellaneous Works, and the strong wish repeatedly expressed, that I should give to the public several of the pieces in my possession, mentioned in the Advertisement to that Edition, have much lessened my apprehension of indulging too far my partiality for the compositions of my friend, and have induced me to include in a new Edition such Articles as seem likely to reflect credit on his memory. (Preface)

Sheffield's editions were not further expanded, however, and except for the separate editions of the personal papers mentioned above, the materials Sheffield printed have not been re-edited, or, for the most part, even reprinted. The present edition is intended to make available all the remaining English writings of Gibbon, not in the 'improved' form that Sheffield, quite naturally, thought he ought to give them, but exactly as Gibbon left them, and without excepting those that might not 'reflect credit on his memory'.

I should remark, however, that I do not think the previously unpublished papers or passages that are included in this edition will reflect any discredit upon Gibbon. The modern reader can easily make allowances for an incomplete or unpolished draft, for a youthful effort, for an occasional ribald passage or instances of unconcealed self-satisfaction.

This edition differs from Sheffield's not only in what it includes, but also in what it does not include. The personal papers are omitted here, of course. More significantly, Gibbon's French essays, whether published by Sheffield or not, are omitted from this edition. The reasons for this omission are largely pragmatic: there is so much work in French that the edition would have become almost double its present size, and I lack the knowledge of eighteenth-century Swiss-French usage that would be of great benefit to an editor of the French works. The omission seems justified also, however, on other grounds. The French works, though numerous, are largely the product of Gibbon's youth, and hence do not have the range, either material or chronological, of the English works. And English, after all, is the language of Gibbon's masterpieces, and of his 'unique' style.

Whether writing in English or in French, Gibbon was a master historian and a sensitive, if sometimes imprecise, student of the classics. The editor of his English essays, therefore, should ideally be both a historian and a classicist. I, unfortunately, am neither. But I can provide, and have provided, the materials that will permit, perhaps encourage, today's historians and classicists to consider Gibbon's views at their convenience.

It was tempting to try to become chronologist, geographer, naturalist, classicist, economist, jurist, theologian, historian . . ., to meet Gibbon on his own ground. It was tempting, but hopeless. Yet my very ignorance permits me to recommend Gibbon's essays to the general reader, not just to his fellow specialists. The fragments, notes, and drafts give illuminating insight into the techniques and processes of a fascinating mind, for those who enjoy such things. The completed or nearly completed essays and comments have the irony and wisdom familiar to the reader of Gibbon's larger works. They speak for themselves, so I need not speak for them.

The introductory comments to each set of editor's notes identify the text(s) and previous publication(s), if any, of the piece in question. My editorial notes are intended (1) to identify persons and allusions; (2) to specify, where possible, Gibbon's editions of the works he cites that were not listed in Geoffrey Keynes's *The Library of Edward Gibbon*; and (3) (perhaps most importantly) to relate the materials, views, subjects, and so on, of these essays to each other and to Gibbon's other works, particularly to the *Decline and Fall*. Works cited by Gibbon and listed in Keynes will be found in the Appendix, with such additional information about editors and the like as I have been able to add; ambiguous or elliptical references in Gibbon may be located in this Appendix with the aid of the editor's notes or the cross-references in the Index. Dates of all persons mentioned by Gibbon, even if not discussed in the editor's notes, are given in the Index.

The final respect in which this edition differs from those of Lord Sheffield is arrangement. His first edition was not arranged according to any particular system. In 1814 he arranged the materials by subject matter. The first two volumes contained the autobiography and letters. The third was 'Historical and Critical'; the fourth, 'Classical and Critical'; and the last, 'Miscellaneous'. Within each category, the arrangement was loosely chronological. The present edition is essentially chronological. A reader can, if he wishes, retrace Gibbon's development as stylist, critic, historian, from his early youth to the last year of his life.

Part I contains Gibbon's English notes and essays written prior to the conception of the *Decline and Fall*. Part II contains everything he wrote in English from 1765, when he returned from his tour of the Continent, to 1776, when he published the first volume of his history, except letters, journals, and the history itself. Part III, devoted to the *Decline and Fall* years, extends past the publication of the last three volumes in 1788, because he considered some additions and revisions in 1790–1. It therefore overlaps slightly with Part IV, the last works.

Many teachers, scholars, friends, and relatives have helped me in the preparation of this edition. My late father and late grandfather, Dr. French Hood Craddock, Jr., and Dr. French Hood Craddock, Sr., especially encouraged me by their unfailing pride, confidence, and enthusiasm, and with occasional welcome cash and advice. My mother provided companionship in England and privacy at home, as well as patience and understanding. Master David Huff and Miss Patricia Huff, my nephew and niece, helped by sorting copies, attaching photocopies to manuscript paper, putting pages in order, and understanding why their aunt could not play with them.

I am particularly grateful to Professors Emeritus F. A. Pottle of Yale, who introduced me to Gibbon, taught me about modern editorial standards, and directed my dissertation on Gibbon's autobiographies, and Georges A. Bonnard of Lausanne, who took the time and interest to write a kind note of encouragement when I first thought of this edition; and to Irvin Ehrenpreis, Commonwealth Professor of English in the University of Virginia, without whose judicious combination of bullying and confidence, advice and praise, I probably would never have attempted and certainly would never have completed this edition.

I am also grateful for the encouragement of many friends. I am indebted to the astute criticism of Joan E. Hartman, who read part of the editorial matter in draft, and to the capable assistance of Barbara Simons, Assistant Librarian of the Goucher College Library, who has not only tracked down occasional names and dates for me, but also helped generously in the drudgery of copying and copy-reading the typescript. A student assistant, Miss Patricia Potter, helped with the preliminary typing and dating. Most of all, my friend and sister, Margaret Craddock Huff, has helped with the typing, copying, copy-reading, date-verification, and other tasks with more than sisterly persistence, kindness, and astuteness. I am also indebted to the Copy-Preparation department of the Clarendon Press.

These people, and Gibbon, deserve the credit for the merits of this edition. The faults, however, are all my own.

CONTENTS

ACKNOWLEDGEMENTS

I WISH to thank John Murray, for permission to use the previously unpublished material in the Gibbon manuscripts; the Master and Fellows of Trinity College, Cambridge, for permission to print the annotations in Gibbon's copy of Herodotus (folio, Amsterdam, 1763), now in their Library; the Pierpont Morgan Library, for permission to consult Gibbon's manuscript notebook in that collection; Goucher College and the Ford Foundation, for a Humanities Faculty Development Grant, which facilitated my completion of this edition.

ABBREVIATIONS

AUTHORITIES

REFERENCES to the *Decline and Fall* (*DF*) have the following form and information: chapter number; volume and page of the quarto edition, i.e. the first edition, except for Volume I, where the page reference is to the third and following editions, though the text, if quoted, is that of the first edition; note number, if any. Then 'Bury', volume, page, and note number, i.e. the reference as located in the editions of J. B. Bury.

Dates and biographical information are obtained from the *Dictionary of National Biography* (for Englishmen), the *Biographie Universelle* (for persons of other nationalities), and the *Oxford Classical Dictionary* (for classical writers), without comment. Other sources are noted. Many of the classical writers and scholars are also discussed in Sir John Edwin Sandys's *History of Classical Scholarship*, which I, as a non-classicist, have found invaluable in identifying editions, distinguishing among writers of the same or similar names, tracking down full references from an abbreviation or fragment, and so forth. Similarly indispensable, especially for medieval and non-European historical sources, have been the appendices to J. B. Bury's great edition of Gibbon's history.

ABBREVIATIONS

Add. MSS.	additional manuscripts (British Museum).
Autobiographies	John Murray, ed., *The Autobiographies of Edward Gibbon*, London, 1896.
B.M.	British Museum.
BU	*Biographie universelle* (Michaud) *ancienne et moderne*, nouvelle edition, Paris, 1843–65.
Bury	J. B. Bury, ed., Edward Gibbon, *The History of the Decline and Fall of the Roman Empire*, new edition, 7 vols., London, 1901–6: my copy, i (4th edn.), 1906; ii (3rd edn.), 1901; iii (3rd edn.), 1906; iv (2nd edn.), 1901; v (2nd edn.), 1901; vi (2nd edn.), 1902; vii (2nd edn.), 1902.
Chevalier	Ulysse Chevalier, *Répertoire des Sources Historiques du Moyen Age: Bio-Bibliographie, Topo-Bibliographie*, nouvelle edition, rpt. New York, 1959–60.

DBF	*Dictionnaire de biographie française* (J. Balteau *et al.*) Paris, 1933– .
DF	Edward Gibbon, *The History of the Decline and Fall of the Roman Empire*, 6 vols., London, 1777–88.
DNB	*Dictionary of National Biography*, London, 1885–1901.
Journal A	D. M. Low, ed., Edward Gibbon, *Journal to January 28, 1763*, London, 1929.
Journal B	Georges A. Bonnard, ed., *Le Journal de Gibbon à Lausanne*, Lausanne, 1945.
Journey	Georges A. Bonnard, ed., *Gibbon's Journey from Geneva to Rome*, London, 1961.
Keynes	Geoffrey Keynes, *The Library of Edward Gibbon*, Oxford, 1940.
Letters	J. E. Norton, ed., *The Letters of Edward Gibbon*, London, 1956.
Low	D. M. Low, *Edward Gibbon 1737–1794*, London, 1937.
Memoirs	Georges A. Bonnard, ed., Edward Gibbon, *Memoirs of My Life*, London, 1966.
Misc.	*Miscellanea Gibboniana*, ed. G. R. de Beer, G. A. Bonnard, L. Junod, Lausanne, 1932.
MW 1796	*The Miscellaneous Works of Edward Gibbon*, 2 vol. 4°, London, 1796.
MW 1814	same, 5 vol. 8°, London, 1814 (actually appeared 1815).
NBG	*Nouvelle biographie générale*, Paris, 1852–6 (photographic reprint).
OCD	*Oxford Classical Dictionary.*
OED	*Oxford English Dictionary.*
om.	omitted.
Sandys	Sir John Edwin Sandys, *A History of Classical Scholarship*, 3 vols., 3rd edn. (1920), rpt., New York, 1958.

EXPLANATION OF APPARATUS CRITICUS

I HAVE attempted to reproduce Gibbon's manuscripts exactly, except for the modernization of long *s*. The apparatus criticus records all legible variants in the manuscripts, except Gibbon's corrections of his own mis-spellings and repeated words. It records all changes introduced by Lord Sheffield except: (*a*) changes in spelling of English words; (*b*) changes in mechanics (I silently restore Gibbon's usage); (*c*) changes in method of making note references: Gibbon usually uses numbers for a series of notes; Sheffield invariably uses typographical symbols; (*d*) changes from author's name to 'ibid.' or 'idem' and vice versa that arise from Gibbon's and Sheffield's practice of always using the author's name in the first reference on a page only—I retain Gibbon's word(s), regardless of my page changes, which is a practice different from Gibbon's but which eliminates the possibility of erroneously interpreting his ibid. or idem, as Sheffield and his helpers occasionally did; (*e*) variants, if any, between Sheffield's editions.

Where there is no manuscript, I have used the first printed edition as my copy text, introducing corrections from Gibbon's Errata list, if any, and substantive changes from later editions printed in his lifetime and with his knowledge, if any. The notes record his earlier versions, but do not record changes in punctuation or capitalization introduced in a later edition, unless the change suggests a substantially different interpretation of the passage. In the textual notes, *I.* means 'Gibbon first wrote' or 'In Gibbon's first edition, he printed' (whatever follows); *II.* means 'Sheffield printed' (what follows). It will be seen that I am following approximately the model of Georges A. Bonnard's edition of Gibbon's *Memoirs*, except that I do not distinguish between Sheffield's two editions.

The apparatus criticus will be found at the foot of the page, but *below* Gibbon's own notes, where those are located at the foot of the page in the only authoritative texts, i.e. in *Critical Observations on . . . the Aeneid* and in the *Vindication*. Otherwise Gibbon's notes are listed at the end of the piece to which they pertain; the editor's notes will be found at the end of the volume.

Cues to notes represent one further instance in which liberties had to be taken with Gibbon's practice. All cues are now superscript, but Gibbon sometimes used cues in round brackets set level with his text, i.e. in the 'Hints', in *Critical Observations on the Aeneid*, and (for the first note only) in the entry on Mexico in the Second Commonplace Book.

More often Gibbon used superscript numbers not in brackets, though sometimes followed by a full stop. To distinguish his cues from mine, his have been provided with round brackets. Thus in any remaining instances (other than those just listed) where Gibbon's cues appear in round brackets, they appeared in the manuscripts or early editions as superscript numbers without brackets.

Where Gibbon either did not provide or did not number his cues, either because he provided the reference in a margin or on a facing page, or because he failed to notice his oversight, cue numbers in square brackets have been supplied. Cue numbers without brackets refer to the editor's notes.

One final anomaly: Gibbon sometimes used empty brackets, round or square, to signal a reference. When he did so, the bracket frequently enclosed the nearest punctuation mark. No attempt to reproduce this idiosyncrasy has been made.

Gibbon's hand is remarkably clear and legible, especially as he grows older, but certain ambiguities may be assumed. (1) Some letters, especially those used in Roman numerals, are identical, except for size, in upper and lower case; Gibbon's Arabic 1 and his Roman i or I are all represented by the same simple stroke. My interpretation of these symbols may well err. (2) In the earlier manuscripts, punctuation symbols are sometimes obscure. (3) I have never silently corrected Gibbon's spelling, use of accent marks, omission of end or internal punctuation. The end of a line or page often seemed to him an adequate end punctuation, without a period. Unlike most of his previous editors, I have decided to follow him in this, introducing any additions of punctuation necessary for clarity within square brackets. My reason for this practice is that I think the purpose of an edition that includes rough notes and juvenilia is best served by as exact an indication of the state of the manuscript as possible, so that the reader can judge for himself where errors and ambiguities were likely in the finished works. It is easy, however, to be mistaken in recording or interpreting such minutiae. (4) Variants from modern spelling and punctuation standards, though not followed by '*sic*', are Gibbon's, not the editor's. In particular, he often spells 'honour', 'colour', etc., without the *u*; such readings are not introduced by the oversight of an American editor. (5) Peculiarities of accent, quantity, etc., in Gibbon's quotations from Latin, Greek, French, and Italian have not been corrected.

Further information that applies only to a particular article will be supplied in the notes to that article.

Part I

BOYHOOD–1762

INTRODUCTION

In the summer of 1752, Gibbon tells us in his *Memoirs*, 'Unprovided with original learning, unformed in the habits of thinking, unskilled in the arts of composition, I resolved—to write a book' (p. 55).[1] The young Gibbon—he was just fifteen—attempted to settle an abstruse question of chronology in this first essay, which he called *The Age of Sesostris*. Twenty years later, Gibbon found and destroyed the manuscript of this premature venture (*Memoirs*, p. 56). But it seems probable that we possess a still earlier, if somewhat less ambitious, product of his precocious interest in chronology, in the elaborate comparative list of dates of events for the years 6000–1590 B.C., here printed for the first time.

It is true that Gibbon's interest in chronology continued to be strong until at least the period when he was writing his *Essai sur l'étude de la littérature*, i.e. until the end of February 1759, with revisions in the spring of 1761; in fact, in discussing the *Essai* in his autobiography, Gibbon considers that 'the defence of the early history of Rome and the new Chronology of Sir Isaac Newton form a specious argument' (*Memoirs*, pp. 100–1, 104). And he added works on chronology to his library throughout his life.[2] But I incline to think that this list is the one referred to by Gibbon as having been made before he entered Oxford, after the moment in the summer of 1751 when his thirst for historical reading became so intense that he 'exhausted all that could be learned in English, of the Arabs and Persians, the Tartars and Turks', and managed also to struggle through d'Herbelot in French and Pocock's Abulpharagius in Latin:[3]

Such vague and multifarious reading could not teach me to think, to write or to act; and the only principle that darted a ray of light into the indigested Chaos was an early and rational application to the order of time and place. The maps of Cellarius and Wells imprinted in my mind the picture of ancient Geography: from Strauchius I imbibed the elements of Chronology: the tables of Helvicus and Anderson, the annals of Usher and Prideaux distinguished the connection of events, and I engraved the multitude of names and dates in a clear and indelible series. (*Memoirs*, p. 43)

If this chronology is indeed that 'clear and indelible series', it is of course Gibbon's earliest surviving historical study.

One argument against the proposed dating of this chronological table is the clarity of the hand, but as all the other extant early materials are rough drafts, while this is a fair copy, perhaps that difficulty is not insuperable. Another argument against this dating is that Gibbon refers to Krishna as Kishen (item xii), adding 'or Kreeshna' in the margin, while the only book known to have been in Gibbon's library that gives the name as Kishen was not published until 1768.[4] On the other hand, it is obviously possible that the name was so given in a book that Gibbon read but did not own or is not known to have owned.

In favour of an early date, it may be added that when Gibbon wrote his *Essai*, he had become less dubious about Newton's chronology than he had been at fifteen,[5] but the list differs from Newton in the only event dated by both.[6] In another context, moreover, Gibbon says, 'at a riper age I no longer presume to connect the Greek, the Jewish, and the Egyptian antiquities which are lost in a distant cloud' (*Memoirs*, p. 56), but which are very much connected in this chronological list.

It is quite possible, then, that this chronology dates from 1751–2. Perhaps Lord Sheffield did not print it because Gibbon later disapproved of his youthful presumptuousness:

But in the discussion of the first ages I overleaped the bounds of modesty and use. In my childish balance I presumed to weigh the systems of Scaliger and Petavius, of Marsham and Newton which I could seldom study in the originals;[7] the Dynasties of Assyria and Egypt were my top and cricket-ball: and my sleep has been disturbed by the difficulty of reconciling the Septuagint with the Hebrew computation. (*Memoirs*, p. 43)

The first dated writing that survives in English, apart from letters, is contained in the commonplace book Gibbon began at Lausanne in

1755, when he was almost eighteen years old. It is interesting to see him concentrating his notes on his *historical* readings—he changes his mind as he writes his title-page—and interesting too that his first selections are neither critical of his sources nor remarkable in anything other than colourfulness, while in later entries, even in this first book, he begins to compare and question conclusions of his authors. In the *Memoirs* he tells us about this commonplace book:

> This various reading which I now conducted with skill and discretion was digested according to the precept and model of Mr Locke into a large Commonplace book, a practice however which I do not strenuously recommend. The action of the pen will doubtless imprint an idea on the mind as well as on the paper: but I much question whether the benefits of this laborious method are adequate to the waste of time; and I must agree with Dr Johnson (Idler Nº 74) 'that what is twice read is commonly better remembered than what is transcribed.' (p. 79)

The range of Gibbon's historical reading is not fully represented by the passages in English in this commonplace book, however, for some of the notes, even in the first twenty-six pages, are entirely in French or Latin, while the remaining 130 pages have only five short notes in English and belong rather to a collection of Gibbon's writing in French and Latin. The Latin notes are almost inevitably direct quotations, but the French ones show that in his third year of exile in Switzerland, Gibbon was at least as capable of 'digestion' in French as in English.

Indeed, if we did not know that he was consciously imitating Locke, we might be surprised at his even beginning in English, especially as most of the books he is reading are not in English. Lord Sheffield, in fact, found all but one of these notes (that on Giannone's history of Italy) 'too full of Gallicisms for Publication'.[8] Still, the English entries, and the subjects of the other entries that interrupt them, can give us an idea of how Gibbon began the English records of his historical studies.

Before Gibbon has filled a quarter of this first notebook, however, French, not English, is his preferred language. Similarly, his first extant sustained literary effort, the journal of his travels in Switzerland (autumn 1755), was, although he wrote it for his father, written in French.[9] Next he undertook learned disputation (by letter) in Latin,[10] and even after his return to England (1758), he composed his *Essai sur l'étude de la littérature*, the first of his published works, in French.

While working on the *Essai*, and at other periods in the years between his return to England and the decision to write about the decline of Rome (15 October 1764), Gibbon did occasionally write in English, however. His journal, begun 24 August 1761, with its notes on his reading, was kept in English until he was allowed to return to the Continent in January 1763.[11] On 1 April 1761, when, urged by his father, he had made a reluctant attempt to enter Parliament, but had had 'an opportunity of giving it up with honor', he 'in a set speech, thanked my friends, abused Barnard [his opponent] and declined a poll' (*Journal A*, pp. 23-4). After Gibbon's death a speech purporting to be the one he had made to the electors of Petersfield was issued by Minchin, a Petersfield printer. There is no earlier copy of this speech, and though the style is Gibbonesque, there is no external evidence that the speech Minchin printed is the speech Gibbon made. A printed copy is in B.M. Add. MSS. 34881, f. 251, and it was reprinted in *Journal A* (Appendix II, pp. 242-4). I include it for the convenience of the reader, without being certain of its authenticity.

Gibbon dated only one English essay of this period, the 'fifty[12] close written pages in folio' that contain his 'full and free discussion of the sense of the master [Horace] and the pedantry of the servant [Hurd]' on the 'composition and imitation of Epic and Dramatic Poetry' (*Memoirs*, p. 119); it was begun on 8 February 1762, and completed 18 March of the same year.

Sheffield assigned the 'Outlines of the History of the World' (see below, Part II) to the period 1758-63, on the basis that it was 'in Mr. Gibbon's early handwriting'.[13] Certainly Lord Sheffield had reason to be familiar with his friend's hand, but other evidence suggests that this essay was written in 1771, as I will show below. Sheffield also placed the essay 'On the Character of Brutus' (undated by either Gibbon or Lord Sheffield) between essays dated 1758 and 1762, but interval evidence shows that the Brutus essay must have been written at a later period.

It therefore seems probable that these few pieces are all that remain of young Gibbon's English writing before his second return from the Continent, with the exception of letters and his first journal. Much more remains in French, from 1755 on, and even after he returned to England in 1765, much of his writing was in French. For further materials in his native language, however, we must wait until 1765.

[Chronology] 1rst Period

6000. i	Creation of the World according to an old tradition of the Jews and Christians
5508 ii.	Creation of the World, according to the Septuagint Version.
4749 iii.	Creation of the World according to the Samaritan text.
4700 iv.	The arts and sciences of a primitive people in the north of Asia
4004. v.	The Creation of the World according to the Hebrew text[1]
3955 vi.	The reign of Menes, and foundation of the Monarchy of Egypt[2]
3507 vii	The foundation of the city and palace of Persepolis
3468 viii	The ancient dominion of the Scythians over Asia.
3461.[b] ix.	The reign of Fohi, first founder of the Chinese Empire
3460. x.	The foundation of the Pyramids of Egypt.
3362. xi.	The second Thoth or Hermes, a native of Chaldæa, and the inventor of Alphabetical writing
3287 xii.	The birth of Kishen or Kreeshna[c] a prophet and Legislator the Indian Hercules.
3212. xiii	The Mahabharat or great Indian War of the Kooroos and Pandoos
3207. xiv.	The great Cycle or Astronomical period of the Persians.
3162. xv.	Death of Kishen, and the Pandoo Conquerors of the Mahabharat.

---

[a] *In margin of MS.*   [b] *I.* ix. The foundation of the Pyrami   [c] *I. om.*
or Kreeshna

Years
Before the
Christian Æra

3102.	xvi.	The beginning of the Caluyoog, the fourth period, or Iron age of the Hindoos. or Indians[3]
3074.	xvii.	Death of Adam at the age of 930 years.
2782.	xviii.	The beginning of a Canicular or Sothic period in Egypt.
2750	xix.	The foundation of the temple of Hercules at Tyre.
2637.	xx.	The first Cycle of sixty years, from[a] the sixtieth year of the reign of Hoang-ti Emperor of China[4]
2463.	xxi.	Dynasty of the Chaldæan Kings of Babylon
2446.	xxii	A great conjunction of four or five Planets observed by the Astronomers of China.
2357[b]	xxiii	The reign of Yao Emperor and Lawgiver of China.
2348	xxiv.	Noah's flood, an universal Deluge according to the Hebrew text
2247.	xxv.	The tower of Babel, confusion of languages, and dispersion of Mankind
2238	xxvi.	The Arabian Dynasty of the Kings of Babylon
2234	xxvii	The beginning of a series of Astronomical observations at Babylon[5]
2206	xxviii	The reign of Yu and first hereditary Dynasty (the Hia) of the Emperors of China.
2155	xxix.	An Eclipse of the Sun observed by the Astronomers of China
2082.	xxx.	The invasion and conquest of Egypt by the Hycsos or Arabian Shepherds.
2023	xxxi.	The conquest of Babylon by Belus King of Assyria
1998	xxxii.	The death of Noah
1996	xxxiii.	The birth of Abraham, father of the Hebrews
1968	xxxiv.	The reign of Ninus and foundation of the Assyrian Empire.
1921	xxxv.	The passage of Abraham over the Euphrates, from Mesopotamia into Palestine
1916	xxxvi	The reign of Semiramis in Assyria

[a] *I.* in   [b] *I. om. this entry.*

Years
Before the
Christian Æra

1897 xxxvii. Destruction of the cities of the Asphaltite lake.

1896 xxxviii. The birth of Isaac

1892. xxxix. First voyages of the Phœnicians to Europe, and rape of Io on the banks of the river Inachus[a]

1878 xl. Victory of Aliphragmuthosis King of Thebes over the Hycsos or Arabian shepherds of Memphis

1874 xli. The reign of Ninyas son of Ninus in Assyria

1871 xlii. The sacrifice of Isaac

1856 xliii The marriage of Isaac and Rebecca

1842. xliv. Phoroneus the son of Inachus and founder of Argos: the first *man* among the Greeks.

1836 xlv. The birth of Esau and Jacob, sons of Isaac

1830 xlvi. Deliverance of Egypt by Tethmosis—Retreat of the Hycsos or Arabian shepherds into the isles and morasses of the Delta.

1821 xlvii. The death of Abraham.

1796 xlviii. The old Greek flood; the deluge of Ogyges in Bæstia and Attica

1765 xlix. The second Dynasty (the *Chang*) of the Emperors of China

1759 l. The flight of Jacob from Palestine to Haran in Mesopotamia; and his service in the family of Laban.

1739 li. The return of Jacob with his family, and riches from Mesopotamia to Palestine

1730 lii. The most probable date of the life, or the book of Job.

1728 liii. The captivity of Joseph the son of Jacob in Egypt

1716 liv. The death of Isaac

1715. lv. The administration of Joseph over the Kingdom of Egypt.

---

[a] *I.* Inachus near Argos

Years
Before the
Christian Æra

1706 Lvi.   The migration of Jacob or Israel[a] and his family
             into Egypt and their establishment in the land of
             Goshen

1689 Lvii   The death of Jacob in Egypt

1635 Lviii. The death of Joseph and the servitude of the
             Hebrews or children of Israel in Egypt.

1590. Lix.   The rebellion of the Hycsos or shepherds and the
             flight of Amenophis King of Egypt into Æthiopia

[a] *I. om.* or Israel

Common Place
Book

In which I propose to write what
I find most remarkable
in my Historical[a]
Readings
Begun at Lausanne. March. 19. 1755

Recueil
dans lequel je me propose d'ecrire
ce que je trouverai de remarquable[b]
dans mes lectures Historiques
Commencé a Lausanne. 19 de Mars. 1755.

Nihil legit quod non excerperet, dicere enim solebat.
nullum esse librum tam malum, ut non aliquâ parte prodesset
Plinius Junior[1] ita
loquitur de avunculo suo

Highness[c]

Formerly (says Amelot de la Houssaye)[2] the title of Highness was given only to Crowned Heads. At present tis so common that all the great families take it. All the Grandees (says a Modern[])[1] are ready to be confounded with the Princes and to attack the privileges of the royal majesty. Philip ii sending his brother Don Juan[3] to the War of Grenada ordered him to take only the title of Excellence, but Don Juan[d] suffered[e] the City of Grenada to give him the title of Highness[.][2] Sebastian was the first King of Portugal who

---

[a] *I. om.* Historical   [b] *I.* remarkable   [c] *In margin of MS. Similarly*
all subtitles in this commonplace book, unless centred.   [d] *I. om.* Don Juan
[e] *MS.* suffereded

had the title of Majesty. Philip ii gave it him in their interview of Guadalupe in 1576; choosing Rather to do it than to give him his daughter in marriage. The Cardinal Henry his successor was content with the title of Highness and when the Fidalquas proclaimed Don Antonio King at Santarem they took the oath of fidelity to him by Highness as unwilling to have any obligation to Philip.

Ferdinand King of Arragon and his wife Isabella Queen of Castile were only treated as Highnesses in their audiences; their son in law Philip i. King of Castile never was a Majesty. Charles v was the first who took that title not as King of Spain but as Emperor.

Formerly the Kings of England had only the title of Grace[.] Henry VIII. was the first who had that of Majesty, which Francis I began to give him in their Interview of 1520.

In 1590 Philip II. offered the title of Highness to the Duke of Mantua for a loan of 300,000 Crowns. Philip v gave the same title to the Dukes of Tuscany and Parma, in 1702 on his arrival in Italy.

Victor Amadeus Duke of Savoy was the first who made use of the title of Royal Highness in his interview with the Cardinal Infant Don Fernando which happened at Villefranche in the month of May 1654. This he did to obtain the title of Highness from the Infant who was resolved to treat him only as Excellence[.] About the End of the same year the Duke founding himself on his pretensions to the kingdom of Cyprus; took the title of Royal Highness, which the Jesuit Monod has defended in a Treatise of the Royalty of the Dukes of Savoy.[4] and this he did to spite the Venetians who had been masters of Cyprus, but this difference was terminated by a Decisive treaty in which the Duke renounced to the title of King of Cyprus in all his negociations with the Republic of Venice[.] [3]

[1] Don[a] Diego de Mendoca guerra de Grenada[5] Lib 2.
[2] Histoire de Philippe ii. par Cabrera[6] Lib 9.
[3] Lenglet de Fresnoy: Methode d'Etudier l'Histoire[7] Tom: vii. p. 785 Vide. Amelot de la Houssaye. Memoires Historiques Tom. i. p 53–61.

DUELS

The duels were so frequent in the first years of Lewis XIII that the first news one asked in the morning was who fought yesterday? and in the Evening who fought this morning. [4]

It was not necessary to have had a quarrel with Bouteville[8] to be obliged to fight him; if any one told him by chance or by design,

[a] *This and all subsequent references appear in margins of MS., unnumbered.*

Such a one is brave; he went directly to seek him & when he had found him; Sir (said he) I have heard you are brave; you must fight me. And you were obliged to do it or suffer his affronts.

He lived near the Church of S[t] Eustache in a house belonging to the Abbey of Royaumont: but as he never paid the rent of it (which was a part of the revenue of the abbay). The Archbishop of Bourdeaux N.—— d'Escoubleau de Sourdis Then Abbot put him out of it in giving him a gratuitous quittance for two years he owed him. Nota this Prelate was he who was surnamed the Admiral because he understood well the Marine and that he was of a warlike character. Tis astonishing that two persons who were equally impatient and piquing themselves on their bravery, did not cut one another's throats having some difference together.

Every morning The braves met at Bouteville's in a great hall, where they found always bread and wine on a table placed a purpose with foils[a] to fence with. This hall was the school of the duels and as one may say[b] the Council of war of the Duellists. The Commander de Valencay kept the upper end as a tryed brave. He was afterwards made Cardinal by Pope Urban VIII. He had such an itch for fighting that one day he wou'd have called out his best friend Bouteville for not having taken him for his second in a duel happened some days before. And This quarrel was only appeased by another which Bouteville took for nothing with the Marquis des Portes in which Valencay served for second against Cavois father of him who is now Great Quarter Master of The King's houshold and this last received a wound of Valencay which almost killed him. Nota before the Combat The Marquis having told Valencay that he would find a shoe that would fit him, since he brought him the best scholar of du Perche (a famous fencing master): Valencay said to Cavois in piercing him; That blow my dear friend is not one of du Perche's but you will own tis a good one. Valencay and Cavois were not less good friends afterwards: on the contrary when the Cardinal de Richelieu had a mind to raise a compagny of Gendarmes Valencay recommended him Cavois so strongly that his Eminence gave it him. Twas by that the fortune of that poor Gentleman begun.

Plus enim fati valet hora benigni, quam si nos Veneris commendet epistola Marti

It appears that the Cardinal de Richelieu liked Bouteville by the difficulty with which he consented to his execution[.]

---

[a] I. om. ?foils; *insert in MS. blurred by blot.*   [b] I. om. say

Till The reign of Henry III.[9] The seconds never fought in the
duels but were only simple spectators. But in the duels of Quelus
and d'Entraguas. Livarrot and Maugiron seconds of the first and
Schomberg and Ribeyrac[10] companions of the second would fight
too, and this bad example has continued ever since[.]

[4] Memoires Historiques d'Amelot de la Houssaye Tom. ii. p 259. 60. 61. 65.

KNIGHTS

There is a great difference between a Knight and a Gentleman.[5]
The birth makes a Gentleman, the virtue alone a Knight. The
Princes do not affect the title of Gentleman, but often that of
Knight— — —Tis for that reason that of old the young Gentleman
bore a white sheild till by some feat of arms he had acquired the
right to have on it some painted figure as a monument of their
valour. Like the Catti who as Tacitus tells us[11] wore a ring of iron
till they had broke that shameful band by the death of an enemy.
William Count of Holland[12] having been chose Emperor wou'd be
knighted before his coronation. Lewis XI. before his Sacrè was
made knight by the[a] Duke of Burgundy and made 117 before the
end of the ceremony.[13] Francis I. after the battle of Marignan[14] was
knighted by the hand of the Chevalier Bayard, and Henry II. in his
father's life time by the Marechal de Biez.[15] all this shews that
formerly the title of Knight was not affected to the birth[.]

How great Lord soever one was it was not allowed to wear the
algate before one was knighted.

The Princes and Lords who were not yet Knights were called
simply by their Christian name; followed by the title of Monsieur
as we read in our historians, Antoine Monsieur de Bourgogne,
Charles Monsieur de Bourbon &c but after their baptism they took
the title[b] of Monseigneur which they put before their names. The
same title was also given to the Ancient knights who were called
Bannerets as having other knights under their banner.

The Bannerets who possessed several direct fiefs on which others
depended were called Double Bannerets and their vassals were[c]
called Batchelors. Let me remark here that the word Miles in Latin
is the same as Chevalier in French and the word Miles Militum
which we sometimes meet with in our Historians signifies the
Vassals of the Bannerets.

[a] *I.* Otho   [b] *I.* name   [c] *I.* and their (*repeated*).

The Damoisdaux (in Latin Domicilli diminutif of Domini) were inferior to the Knights but superior to the squires[a]; they were properly the Novices who became Knights by their age and services.

The Golden Spurs and a Golden String round the Bonnet were the marks of Knight[h]ood for properly none but the Knights could wear them. The Squires wore White spurs. The Bishops wear still[b] the girdle and string because they were formerly members of the body of the Knights and Barons.

[5] Amelot de la Houssaye. Memoires Historiques Tom ii. p 78–84.

(ANTONIO) DON. PRIOR OF CRATO

Don Antonio was the natural son of Don Lewis Infant of Portugal and of a Jewess named Violanta Gomez; which was the reason why the Jews gave themselves so great mouvements to obtain his legitimation after the death of the Cardinal King Henry. Antonio having been declared Bastard by a sentence of the Cardinal Henry found means to obtain of Pope Gregory XIII a bref which anulled the sentence and summoned the cause to Rome a procedure which very much checked Philip II who prooved the bastardize of Antonio by two invincib[l]e acts.

After the death of the King Cardinal, treating with Philip he demanded for a renunciation of his pretensions; a Revenue of 200.000 Ducats, The Government of Portugal, for life, the Great Mastership of the Order of S[t] Iago, the nomination of the Viceroy of Brasil and the Capitain General of Afric and the power of disposing at his death of 100.000 Ducats a year. Philip who was afraid least Antonio made himself proclaimed King by the people, received patiently these exorbitant proposals. In effect Antonio was proclaimed King at Santarem. but being unable to sustain himself was abandoned at the approach of the Duke of Alva's army and so saw the accomplisment of a prediction that had been made on him; that he should reign, but a very short time[.]

Either the address or the luck of Antonio was very great. for having been taken prisoner by the Moors in the Battle of Alcazar, he was the first prisoner delivered, tho' naturally (considering his quality) he ought to have been the last. but he concealed so well who he was[c] that he was never even suspected[.]

---

[a] *I. om.* to the squires   [b] *I.* wore formerly   [c] *I. om.* was

After his dethronement he was concealed in the Kingdom from the month of October 1580 to that [of]^a June 1581; without being ever discover[ed] by Philip's officers, notwithstanding the great reward set on his head, and the vast number of hands he was forced to pass thro'[.]

He died at Paris August the 26th 1595 aged 64 years. his body is in the Church of the Cordeliers and his heart in the Rue Maria, where are at the left hand of Altar the two following Epitaphs

> Inter[16] concillos magni præcordia regis
> Invenies, quibus hæc urbs decorata fuit.
> Expulsus regno sed non e cordibus unquam,
> Condidi[17] in tenero plurima corda suo

The other Epitaph was in prose with this eloge "Illud non parvum "Regiæ magnimitatis[18] argumentum est, quod secto post mortem "corpore, omnia ejus viscera tabida ac corrupta inventa sunt præter "cor quod quia in manu dei erat, ab eo incorruptum & illæsum "semper servatum fuit.["] The author of these two Epitaphs who gives him the title of King was a Portuguese Cordelier named Diego Carlos his cousin-german by the mother's side.

Don Antonio left two natural sons Don Christovam and Don Manuel, the latter of which was married clandestinely to Amelia de Nassau sister of Count Maurice. [6]

[6] Amelot de la Houssaye. Memoires Historiques Tom i. p. 110–118.

ALGONKIN.

The Algonkin language is much esteemed, [7] and tis so much more useful as all the nations a thousand leagues round understand it, except the Hurons and the Iroquois: This language differs from those of the nei[gh]bouring people as the Portuguese from the Spanish. Thus Tis not very difficult.

[7] De la Hontan. Voyages en Amerique Tom i. p 22.

ARRAGON^b

Formerly the Kings of Arragon could not be crowned till they^c had been married or at least knighted. Pope Innocent III dispensed them from that con[s]traint.

---

^{a} MS. has caret for insertion, but no insertion. ^{b} Centred and in margin of MS.
^{c} MS. they they

In Arragon the law is above the King; in Castile the King is above the law. S[t] George is the Patron of the kingdom, his standard is the Palleum of their liberties and is never raised but when it is question to defend them against the Prince.

The Arragonese have a Fuero which they call The Privilege of the Manifestation. In vertue of which whoever has been ill judged by any Tribunal of the Kingdom may present himself before the Justicia and demand reparation in deposing a sum of 500 Crowns. If his complaint is founded the judges who condemned him are obliged to pay him the sum deposed, and other proportionable punisments without being able to appeal from the sentence of the Justicia who is sovereign judge of all the others both Ecclesiastical and Civil as Conservator of the Rights and privileges of the nation[.]

In Arragon the States are composed of four Arms, the Arm of the Clergy, the Arm of the Nobility the Arm of the People, and the Arm of the Nobles, which is different from the Arm of the Nobility and is composed of Persons to whom the King gives the title of Nobles, to distinguish them from the other Gentlemen; so that the former Class may be called Nobles of the King[a] and the Second Nobles of the Kingdom[.] [8]

[8] Amelot de la Houssaye. Memoires Historiques Tom. i. p 118–121

(Austria)

DON JUAN DE[b]

Charles V. left a natural son whom he had not owned during his reign but after his abdication he declared him and recomended him to his son Philip ii. to make an ecclesiastic of him. He had intrusted a Spanish Gentleman named Lewis Quijada Lord of Villagarcia, with the care of his Education, who the better to conceal who he was dressed him like a peasant and accustomed him to suffer hardship & labour. Never was bastard of so high a birth both on his father's and his mother's side.[19] Both were of the House of Austria, and the Emperor only hid him so privately to hide from posterity the mother's fault.

There is no appearance that Don Juan ever formed the design to dispossess Queen Elizabeth and deliver Mary Queen of Scots. There is more appearance he aspired to the Sovereignty of the Low Countries. According to Cabrera he dyed of a purple fever a first

[a] I. Kingdom   [b] Also in margin of MS.

of October, aged 33 years. His entrails were found all black, and as it were roasted, and his lungs so dryed that a touch made them fall into pieces: which made his domestics imagine he had been poisoned. In dying he reccomended two things to his Confessor; one to beg the King his brother to pay his debts, and the second to suffer that his body was buried in the Church of St Lawrence of the Escurial and placed near that of the Emperor his father. Cabrera says that Philip granted his demand and that Don Juan having been brought secretly to the Monastery of our Lady of Parazza and was brought from thence to that of St Lawrence by the Bishop of Avila and buried with a royal pomp in the place he had desired. The Same Historian says that Pope Pius V had promised him the investiture of the first Kingdom he should conquer over the Turks[a] and Andrew Morosini[20] says in his history of Venice that Philip had promised his brother the Kingdom of Tunis and all he could conquer[b] in the Levant. But this is not probable considering Philip's character. [9]

[9] Amelot de la Houssaye Memoires Historiques Tom i. p. 193–199.

Philip II.[c] King of Spain [10]

The Spaniards have compared his father Charles V to David on account of his reign entirely military, and himself to Solomon for his peaceful reign, and for the construction of the Magnificent Temple of the Escurial which (says Cabrera) is the Eight wonder of the world, but the first for the dignity the grandeur and the majesty.

[10] Amelot de la Houssaye Mem[.][d] Hist. Tom i. p 192

CONSTANCE [Council of][e]

Sigismond arrives at Constance Christmas-Day (1414). The Duke of Saxony bearing before him the Sword of the Empire naked, and the Burgrave of Nuremberg whom he had made Administrator of Brandenburg the Sceptre. The Golden Globe was carried by his father-in-law the Count of Cillai. This is not an Electoral function. The Pope waits for him in the Cathredral. The Emperor does the office of Deacon in the Mass, and reads the Gospel but no feet

---

[a] *I.* Moors   [b] *I. om.* conquer   [c] *Also in margin of MS.*   [d] *MS. has sign for word division, but word is not continued on succeeding line.*   [e] *Centred in MS. Also in margin of MS. but with round brackets.*

kissed, no stirrup held, no mule lead by the bridle. There were three Thrones in the Church. one for the Pope, one for the Empress, and a third for the Emperor in the middle.

John XXIII. (in 1416) promises to resign the Pontificate in case the Antipopes would do as much, and in all the cases where his deposition should be judged for the interest of the Church. this last clause ruined him. Either he was forced to this declaration or else, the profession of Pirate had not rendered him a very Politic Pope. Sigismond kissed John's feet as soon as John had read the formula which deprived him of the Papacy.

Sigismond is easily master of the Council in surrounding it with his soldiers. He appears there in all his glory.[21] There were there, The Electors Palatin of Saxony and of Mentz; The Administrator of Brandenburg; The Dukes of Bavaria, of Austria and of Silesia; A Hundred and twenty eight Counts; Two Hundred Baron, (who were then of some consequence) Twenty Seven Embassadors representing their Sovereigns. They disputed there in Luxury and magnificence[.] We may judge of it by the number of fifty Goldsmiths who came to establish themselves at Constance. The number of musicians was reckoned at Five Hundred. And what the customs of the age render very Credible there were Seven Hundred and Eighteen Courtisans under the protection of the Magistrates of the town.

The Pope fled disguised like a postillion on the territories of John of Austria Count of Tirol. This Prince is obliged to deliver him and to demand pardon of the Emperor on his knees.

While the Pope is prisoner in the Castle of the Duke of Austria his protector. His process is made. He is accused of all the crimes and is deposed May 29, and by the sentence the Council reserves itself the right of punishing him. [11]

[11] Annales d'Empire par Voltaire.[22] Tom ii. p. 63. 64. 65.

POPE[a23]

The Roman Diurnal of the VII. and VIII Centuries precious monument a part of which is printed, shows in an authentic manner what the Sovreign Pontif was then. He was called Vicar of S[t] Peter Bishop of the city of Rome. As soon as he was elected by the Citizens, The Clergy in body gave notice of it to the Exarch and the formula was,

a _Centred and in margin of MS._

"We beseech you charged with the Imperial minestery to order the "consacration of our father and pastor.["] They informed also the Metropolitan of Ravenna of the new election and wrote to him "Holy "Father we beg your Beatitude to obtain of the Lord Exarch the "ordination in question.["] They were also obliged to write to the judges of Ravenna, whom they stiled Your Eminences.

The new Pope was then obliged to pronounce two professions of faith and in the second, he condemned among the Heretics Pope Honorius I because at Constantinople that Pope passed to have owned but one will in Jesus Christ.

Tis far from this to the Tiara; But tis far too from the first monk who preached on the banks of the Rhine to the Electoral Bonnet, or from a chief of wandering Salians to a Roman Emperor. Every grandeur is formed by little and little and every origine is inconsiderable.[a]

The Pontife of Rome in the avillessment of the city established his grandeur insensibly. The Romans were poor but the church was not so. Constantine had given the Church of the Latran alone, above a thousand marks of gold and about Thirty Thousand marks of Silver, and had assigned it Fourteen Thousand Sous of rent (Solidi). The Popes who fed the poor and who sent missions into all the West had need of secours more considerable and obtained them without difficulty. The Emperors and even the Lombard Kings had granted them lands. They possessed near Rome revenues and Castles called the Justices of St Peter. Many Citizens had contributed with pleasure by testament or donation to enrich a Church the Bishop of which was regarded as the father of his country. The Credit of the Popes was very much superior to their riches. It was impossible not to revere a succession almost uninterrupted of Pontifes, who had comforted the Church, defended the religion, and softened the manners of the Heruli, the Goths, Vandals, Francs and Lombards.

Altho the Pontifs of Rome extended their jurisdiction Metropolitan (in the time of the Exarchs) only[b] over the Suburbican cities that is the cities subject to the government of the Præfect of Rome; however they had the title of Universal Pope given them on account of the grandeur and dignity of their see. Gregory the Great refused that title but deserved it by his virtues and his successor extended their credit in the West. We must not then be surprized when we see Boniface Bishop of Mentz. (the same who consecrated Pepin)

[a] I. considerable   [b] I. om. only

express him thus in the formula of his oath. I promise to S[t] Peter
and to his Vicar the Blessed Gregory &c.[a] [12]

The House of Toscannella [13] had always the principal authority
at Rome she had bought the Pontificate for a child of twelve years
old of this family, two others having also bought it The Three
Pontifs divided the revenues between them and agreed to live
peaceably together abandoning the temporal affairs to the Chiefs of
the house of Toscanella.

This singular triumvirat lasted as long as they had any money
left. when they had no more, each of them sold his portion of the
papacy to the Deacon Gratian whom Maimburg calls a very holy
priest, a man of quality and very rich. But as young Benedict IX.
had be[en] chose a great while before the others, they left him by a
mutual consent the enjoyment of the tribute which England then
payed to Rome and which was called Peter's pence.

The Pope (Adrian IV) wrote in all his letters that he had conferred
the Benefice of the Roman Empire. [14] The word Benefice then
signified a fief.[24] Besides that he exposed a picture in which Lothaire
II.[b] was represented on his knees before Pope Alexander, holding
his hands joined between the hands of the Pontif which was a distinctive mark of Vassalage[.] The inscription of the picture was

> Rex venit ante fores, jurans prius urbes honores Post homo
> fit Papæ, mit[c] quæ dante coronam

Frederic complained of this very much, without being able to obtain
the least satisfaction.

[12] Annales de l'Empire par Voltaire: Tom I. p. 8. 9. 10
[13] Idem. p 167.
[14] Idem. 223. 224.

DESPOTISM[d]

Otho. i[25] endeavours to render himself Despotick, the Lords of[e] the
Great Feifs to become independant. This great quarrel, sometimes
open sometimes Concealed subsists in the minds of men, above
Eight Hundred years as well as[f] that of Rome and the Empire. [15]

---

[a] *MS. has &*[et]   [b] *I. the Pope was*   [c] *First part of word illegible in MS.*
[d] *Centred and in margin of MS.*   [e] *I. to*   [f] *I. of*

This struggle of royal power which will encrease and of the liberty which not yeild has long agitated the Christian Europe. It subsisted in Spain as long as the Christians had the Moors to combat after which the royal autority got the upper hand. Tis that which has troubled France till the middle of the reign of Lewis XI and which established in England the mixt government to which she owes her greatness; that which has Cimented the liberty of the Gentleman and the slavery of the peasant in Poland. The same spirit has troubled the Kingdoms of Denmark and Sweden, and founded the republics of Holland and Switzerland. The same cause produced every where contrary effects.

[15] Voltaire. Annales de l'Empire Tom. i.

GUELFS[a]

The factions of the Gibelins and Guelfs divided and desolated Italy. [16] They had begun by the quarrels of the Popes & Emperors; These names had been every where as watch words in the time of Frederic ii. Those who pretended to acquire the feifs and titles which the Emperors give, declared themselves Gibelins[.][26] The Guelfs appeared to be more partisans of the Italic[b] liberty. The Roman Guelfs were indeed partisans of the Popes when it was question to reunite against the Emperor, but the same partie turned against the same Pontife when delivered from a master, he had a mind to be so himself. These Parties subdivised themselves into several others and served for aliment to the discords of cities and families. Some ancient Captains of Frederic II employed these names of faction, which heat the spirits, to draw people under their banner, and authorized their ravages by the pretence of Sustaining the rights of the Empire. Enemy bands of Robbers pretended to serve the Pope who had not commissioned them and ravaged Italy in his name. Among the robbers who rendered themselves[c] il-lustrious, There was in particular one Ezzolino partisan of Frederic II who[d] was on the point of changing the face of affairs. He is still famous by his ravages; the booty gave him an army and had fortune always seconded his designs, he became a conqueror. But at last he was taken in an embuscade, and Rome who feared him was delivered. The factions Guelf and Gibelin did not dye with him. They always subsisted and were violent; in the times when Germany without

---

[a] *Centred and in margin of MS.*   [b] *I.* Germanic.   [c] *I.* himself
[d] *I. om.* who

Emperor after the death of Conrad IV,[27] could no longer serve as pretext to these troubles.

[16] Voltaire. Annales de l'Empire. Tom ii

FRIZELAND[a]

The East and west Frizeland should have formerly been but one Continent till divided by the sea: for in the time of Tacitus no other distinction was known but that of Greater and Lesser Frisii and that only from the measure of our numbers and forces, and tho' they are said to have had great lakes among them yet the word seem to import that they were of Fresh water which is made yet plainer by the word Ambiunt, that shews those lakes to have been inhabited round by these nations; from all this I may guess, that the more inner parts of the Zudder see was one of the lakes there mentioned, between which and the Ulie and Tessel islands[28] there anciently lay great tracts of land (where the sands are still of so shallow and so continued as seems to make it evident:) but since covered by some great irruptions of waters, which joined those of the sea and the lake together made that great bay called the Zudder Sea by the favour of which the town of Amsterdam is grown to be the most frequented harbour in the world. [17]

The Provinces of Groningen, of Overijssel, and of Friezeland were the seats of the ancient Frisons who under the name of Saxons conquered our island.[29] A reading of the Stories of that time, and the ancient language of the Frizons's having so great an affinity with our old English as to appear easily to have been the same; most of their words still retaining the same signification and[b] sound very different from the language of the Hollanders, will convince any one of it. This is most remarkable in a little town named Malcuera upon the Zuider Sea in Friezland, which is built after the fashion of the old German villages described by Tacitus; without any observation or use of lines or angles, but as if every man had built in a common field just where he had a mind, so as a Stranger who goes in must have a guide to find his way out again.

Sir William Temple draws a paralel between the goverment of England and of Friezeland (so entirely different from that of the other provinces. He finds a great resemblance between the Greatmans of Friezland and our Sherifs, their Twelve Cousellors for the

---

[a] *Centred and in margin of MS.*   [b] *I.* of

justice, and our Circuits, and between the deputies to their states chosen two from each balliage and two from each town, by the votes of all possessed of a certain quantity of land; to the elections of English members of Parliament, especially since those deputies resolve with an intire independance on their principals a circumstance in which they agree with us but differ from all their neig[h]bours.

[17] Observations of Sir William Temple on the United Netherlands,[30] p. 150

IROQUOIS[a]

These Barbarians (the Iroquois) make but one nation and one public interest. One might name them, for the distribution of the lands the Swiss of their continent. The Iroquois are divided into five cantons viz the Isononlouans, the Goyogoans, the Ounotagues, the Onoyouls and the Agniès. Every Canton is properly a village; There is thirty leagues from one to another. They are all situated on the Southern side of the Lake Ontario or Frontenac, and the language is much the same. When we speak of a Canton or Caban of Iroquo[is],[b] we mean a town often considerable. There is at least Twelve thousand souls; sometimes the number reaches fourteen thousand, and that number was calculated by Two Thousand Warriors, Two Thousand Old men, Four Thousand women, Two Thousand Girls and Four Thousand Children—— The Five Cantons visit one another by turns every year by their deputies; Tis then that they make the feast of the Union, and smoke the great pipe of Calumet of the five nations. These[c] people has been a long while allies of the English and by the trade of skins they make with New York they have arms, munitions & every thing they have occasion for, cheaper than the[y] could from the French.—— —— These people are very free in all the extent of the Natural rights, and it seems as if the liberty banished from almost all the rest of the Earth has chose her retreat here. Nothing diverts them so much as to hear talk of obeying the King or fearing the menaces and chastisements of Governors. That makes them laugh: they cannot adjust the idea of submission with that of a real man, and the very name of subjection fills them with horror. Every Iroquois thinks himself sovereign and pretends to be subordinate of none, but of God whom he calls the Great Spirit. [18]

[18] De la Hontan Voyages en Amerique Tom. i p. 33. 34, 35.
   [a] *Centred and in margin of MS.*   [b] *Blot in MS.*   [c] *Possibly* This *over* These

MARSHAM

Sir John Marsham author of the Canon Chronicus dyed in the year 1685 aged 83 years. Histoire d'Angletterre par Rapin Tom x p 44

BOCHAT.

Mons: Charles Loys de Bochat,[31] Lieutenant Ballioal at Lausanne and[a] formerly Professor in Law and Ecclesiastical History in the Academy there; celebrated by the Dissertations pour les services militaires dyed at Lausanne, April 3. 1754. aged 59 years[.]

BELLARMIN

Cardinal Bellarmin's [19] controversial works are very scarce in Italy. some people assign assign for reason the fear of the Catholics least their enemies arguments however mangled should make impression. That Cardinal would infallibly have been chosen Pope had he not been a Jesuite. had that happened he had made a vow to enrich none of his relations. Conclave di Paolo V. p. 512 Fulgattus in vita Bellarmini.[32]

[19] *Dictionaire de Bayle Art Bellarmin* E. Sandis Relation de l'Eglise et de l'etat p. 224. . . . Jacobus I in protestatione. Anti-Vorstiana apud Mayerum de fide Bellarmini. p. 133.

BEZA

Beza [20] was accused by the P. Garasse, (Doctrine Curieuse p. 283. & 4) to have said that the words of Jesus Christ, hoc est corpus meum ought to be read hoc non est corpus meum, and those of the Confession of Augsburg, Domini corpus adesse, ought to be Domini corpus abesse. he was for that refuted by Mons. Ogier (Jugement et Censure de la doctrine Curieuse p 95) and excused himself only by saying that he could not find the book from which he had extracted that particularity.[33]

[20] Dictionaire de Bayle. Art. Beza

(PAOLO) FRA. [21]

Fra Paolo of the order of the Servites, author of the History of the Council of Trent and of several other works dyed at Venice in the year 1623 aged 71 years. He was one of the most learned men of his time Besides divinity which his kind of life obliged him to study, he

[a] *I.* & and

possessed perfectly Philosophy, History, Mathematics and Physic.
Many attribute to him the famous discovery of the circulation of the
blood which is commonly given to Harvey or Aquapendente. He
was very favourably disposed for a Reformation in General, tho' he
dissaprooved of the violent proceedings of many who bore that
name. In the famous difference between Paul V. and the republic of
Venice, Fra Paolo was well disposed for an entire[a] rupture with the
Church of Rome, which had it not been for the folly of James I.
King of England would have probably been effected.

[21] *Bibliotheque Raisoneè. Tom XVII. P. i. p.* 119.[34] Vita del P. Paolo par P Fulgencio.
Vie de Fra Paulo par le Pere Courayer, avant sa traduct: de Hist: du Conc: de Trente
Welwood's Memoirs p. 29. London. 1710. Bedell's life. 15

GIANONE.

M[b] Gianone[35] asserts that Naples did not become a Roman Colony
before the reign of Vespasian or at most before Augustus: [22] a
passage of Cicero well considered will convince us that Naples lost[c]
the state of an Allied City before the Consulat of Cicero or AUC.
690. Cicero [23] speaking against the Agrarian law of Rullus, says
that[d] "Lege permitti (to the Decemvirs of that law) ut quæ velint
"municipia, quas velint veteres colonias, suis colonis occupent.
"Calenum municipium complebunt: Theanum oppriment Attelam,
"Cumas, NEAPOLIN Pompeios, Nuceriam suis præsidiis devincient.
"Putulos[e] vero qui nunc in sua potestate sunt, suo jure libertataque
"utuntur. totos novo populo et adventitiis copiis occupabunt[.]" By
this passage, we see that as power was only granted to the Decemvirs
over the Municipal towns, and the Colonies; that Naples was one
of the two[f] but we know that Naples was never a Municipal city
she must then have been a Colony in that time.

[22] Hist. Civ: du Royaume de Naples Tom i. p 29
[23] Cicero[36] in Orat. ii. de lege Agrar- contra Rullum C. 31

---

[a] *I.* entirely	[b] *II. added* Naples.—	[c] *I.* changed	[d] *I. om.* that
[e] *II.* Puteolos	[f] *I. om.* that . . . two		

The
SPEECH
of
The Late Illustrious Historian
EDWARD GIBBON, Esq.

On the Day of Election of Members to serve in Parliament
for the Borough of Petersfield,
In the Year 1761.

Gentlemen,

I appear here in a Situation very different from my Expectations,
I hoped to have stood here the Asserter of our Common Independency, I can only lament with you a Yoke it is impossible for
us to shake off.

The most considerable part of the still remaining Independent
Freeholders of this Borough addressed themselves some time
ago to my Father, as a Gentleman, whose past conduct had
deserved their esteem, and desired he would offer himself a
Candidate. They were justly provoked with so many Nominations,
with the Mockery of Elections, where Gentlemen were returned for
the Borough, who hardly knew in what County it was situated.

My father accepted their offer with thanks, but soon afterwards
(I fear out of an ill grounded partiality) desired they would transfer
the Honor of their choice upon me. I had the satisfaction of
receiving that Mark of their Approbation.

From that time I had the greatest reason to hope for Success.
Without Threats, without Promises, by no Methods I should blush
to acknowledge in this place, I could without presumption promise
myself the Majority of the real Independent Freeholders in opposition to that unknown Candidate,[1] with whose name we are but just
made acquainted.

One Man[2] disappointed all these hopes; a man who after every
Engagement which could bind a Gentleman or an Honest Man,

infamously abandoned me. This treachery, and the consequences it hath had, leaves me nothing else to do, than to express my most grateful sense of my Obligations to my Friends, Obligations unconnected with Success, and which (were every nobler Principle wanting) my Pride would never suffer me to forget.

Had I succeeded I should have used my utmost endeavours to have acted up to the great Trust reposed in me. I should have considered a Seat in Parliament neither as a Title of Honor, nor as an Instrument of Profit; but a laborious and important Duty, to which the greatest Parts joined to the severest application are scarcely equal. I should have endeavoured to follow the path of Moderation and Impartiality; Loyal to my King without Servility, Zealous for my Country without Faction, attached to the general welfare of Great Britain, but not inatentive to the particular Interests of the Borough I had the Honor to represent.

Excluded from this agreeable Prospect, I must confine my Ambition within the Duties of a Private Life: and I hope my behaviour as a Man, and a neighbouring Gentleman, will never make my Friends repent their having thought me worthy of an Higher Character.

———————

Minchin, Printer, Petersfield.

Q. HORATII FLACCI EPISTOLÆ; AD PISONES ET AUGUSTUM; WITH AN ENGLISH COMMENTARY AND NOTES

To which are added two Dissertations;
The one on the Provinces of the Drama;
The other on poetical imitation: with a
letter to Mr Mason.
in two Volumes. 12°
The second Edition. Cambridge. 1757.

MR Hurd the supposed author of this performance, is one of those valuable authors who cannot be read without improvement. To a great fund of well digested reading[b], he adds a clearness of judgement and a niceness of penetration, capable of taking things from their first principles and observing their most minute differences. I know few writers more deserving of the great, tho' prostituted name of Critic. But like many Critics he is better qualified to instruct, than to execute. His manner appears to me harsh and affected, and his style clouded with obscure metaphors, and needlessly perplexed with expressions exotic, or technical. His excessive praises (not to give them a harsher name) of a certain living Critic and Divine[1] disgust the sensible reader as much as the contempt affected for the same person by many who are very unqualified to pass a judgment upon him.

Horace's art of poetry esteemed by most Critics to be an[c] unconnected set of precepts, without unity of design, or method, appears under Mr Hurd's hands an attempt to reform the Roman Stage, conducted with an artfull plan and carried on thro' the most delicate transitions. This plan is unravelled[d] in Mr Hurd's commentary. If ever those transitions appear too finely spun, the

---

ᵃ *In lefthand margin of MS., parallel to title*   ᵇ *II.* reasoning   ᶜ *II.*
generally deemed an   ᵈ *II.* unrivalled

concealed art of Epistolary freedom will sufficiently account for it. The least Mr Hurd must convince us of, is that if Horace had any plan it was that which he has laid down. Every part of Dramatic poetry is treated of[a] even to the Satyrs and the[b] Attellanes, its metre, subject, characters[,] chorus, explained, and distinguished. The rest of the Epistle contains those precepts of unity of[c] design, acuracy of composition &c., which tho not peculiar to the Dramatic poet are yet as necessary to him as to any other.

I shall say little more of the Epistle[d] to Augustus than that the subject matter is much plainer than in the other but the connection of parts far more perplexed. In the two lines from 30 to 32 a Critic must be very sharp sighted to discover[e] so complicated an argument as Mr Hurd finds out there. However his own Commentary is far superior to that on the art of poetry and rises here into a very elegant paraphrase. As my business lies more with Mr Hurd than with Horace I shall only select one of the numerous beauties of this Epistle; it is that elegant encomium upon the modern poets which extends from V. 118 to 139. Every one must observe that fine gradation which from describing the poet as a happy, innofensive creature, exalts him at last into a kind of mediator between the Gods and men: but an art more refined and nicely attentive to its object, only employs those praises which belong equally to good and to bad poets. Every one complained of the multitude of bad poets. Even these, replies Horace, are not to be despised. Such poetry is an employment which makes it possessor good and happy by abstracting him from the cares of men; he may turn it to the usefull purposes of a virtuous[f] education, and the Gods who attend more to the piety than[g] the talents of the bard will listen with pleasure to his hymns.

I shall now consider some of Mr Hurd's notes upon these Epistles, and then pass to his larger discourses.

Upon v 94. (Vol. i. p 68–77.) He starts a new train of thought upon the use of poetical Expressions in Tragedy. The herd of Critics allow them to the Hero in his calmer moments and forbid them in his more passionate ones. On the contrary (says Mr Hurd and I think with reason) it is that very passion that calls them forth, by rouzing every faculty & exciting images suitable to the grandeur of his situation. Anger indeed which exalts the mind inspires more

---

[a] I. explained   [b] II. om. the   [c] II. and   [d] I. matter of the
[e] I. om. to discover   [f] I. good   [g] I. and

bold and daring images, those of grief are more weak, humble and broken. But when passion sleeps, it is fancy alone that can create[a] figures and fancy is a very improper guide for the severe genius of Dramatic poetry.

Perhaps the natural correspondency between passion & the poetical figures may be more exactly ascertained by defining what is properly meant by poetical figures. It is (if I am not mistaken) a Comparison either expressed or understood between two objects about one of which the mind is particularly engaged, and which it perceives, bears some affinity to another. The Comparison properly so called expresses every feature of that resemblance at full length, the allusion points it out in a more slight and general manner, and the metaphor disdaining that slow deduction of Ideas boldly substitutes to the object of the comparison, that to which it is compared. In the instance Mr Hurd has taken from Tacitus, "Ne "vestis Serica viros *fædaret*, ["]] we may note this difference between the three species of figures. In a comparison he might have said, "That a silken garment was so disgracefull to a man that [it][b] was "like a pollution to his body. ["]] Had he said, That a silken garment, like a pollution was to be avoided by[c] a man, it would have [been] an allusion. But dropping every intermediate idea, He reports the law by which no silken garment was to pollute a man. This is a metaphor and of his own creation. But there are many, especially those where Spiritual[d] faculties and operations, are expressed[e] by material images, which tho' figurative in their origin are by time and use, almost become litteral. These are the figures of poetry. I am sensible there are Rhetorical ones also, but those I believe relate rather to the expression and distribution of the[f] former.

Let us now from these principles investigate the workings of passion. It has been often observed that the highest agitation of the mind is such as no language can describe since language can only paint Ideas, and not that sentimental, silent, almost stupid excess of rage or grief which the soul feels[g] with such energy that it is not master of itself enough to have any distinct perceptions. Such passion baffles all description. But when this storm subsides, passion is as fertile in ideas as it was at first barren. When some striking interest collects all our attention to one object, we consider it under every light it is susceptible of; even that rebel[h] attention,

---

[a] *I.* pro   [b] *So. II*; *MS.* is   [c] *I.* like   [d] *I.* the *II. om.* especially those
[e] *I.* which tho' s   [f] *I. om.* the   [g] *I.* itself feels   [h] *I.* very

chained down with difficulty to any range of ideas endeavours as
much as possible to enlarge the sphære of them. And as the agitation
of our mind crouds them upon us almost at the same instant instead
of presenting them slowly and singly we cannot avoid being struck
with many comparisons suitable to our situation. The past, the
present, the future, our misfortunes, those of other men, our friends
our ennemies[a] our ancestors, our posterity form within us number-
less combinations of ideas either to assuage or irritate the reigning
passion [1]. But those of the first species tho' they strike us with
force we reject as much as is[b] in our[c] power, and therefore the
poet who expresses them in words ought rarely to go farther than
an allusion or a metaphor: these indeed are in general the darling
figures of passion as it loves to pass with rapidity from one idea to
another. However in those conjunctions of ideas which feed and
irritate the passion she will sometimes[d] dwell with complacency
upon them & pursue them to the minutest resemblances of a
simile. I appeal to the breast of every one for the evidence of these
positions and as to the last I shall instance the noble speech with
which Juno opens the Æneid[e] and rousing herself to vengeance
from the comparison of her behavior with that of Pallas, collects
every circumstance of it which could stimulate her more strongly to
the execution of it.[f]

To return to Mr Hurd's notes, he employs several pages[g] to
prove (Vol. i p 81–87) what, I fancy no one would have disputed him,
that tho' the words "Pulchrum, Beau, Beautifull are often used
to express the general conception of beauty[h] they are sometimes[i]
made to signify that particular sort of beauty which pleases the
imagination opposed to that which affects the heart.

Aristotle had blamed the Iphigenia of Euripides as a[j] character
ill supported; so timid at first afterwards so determined. The
general opinion had extended the same reproach to his Electra.
Mr Hurd undertakes (Vol. 1. p 96–105) their vindication if Electra
feels so much remorse after the murder of her mother[k] tho' the
principal[l] author of it, We must consider that she is no[m] where

---

[a] *I.* enemies   [b] *II. om.* is   [c] *I. om.* our   [d] *I. om.* sometimes
[e] *I.* I think however that passion will always find its resemblances in sensible
objects never in inanimate ones. The reason is plain. As ourselves and the affections
of our mind will be the ultimate [*last word illegible*]   [f] *Brackets in MS.*
indicate line reference here, but none given.   [g] *II.* passages   [h] *I. om.* of beauty
[i] *I. om.* sometimes   [j] *I. om.* a   [k] *I. om.* of her mother   [l] *I.* principle
[m] *I.* now w

described as devoid of natural tenderness tho' the thirst of revenge
supported by the maxims of her times such as the doctrine of
remunerative justice, of fate and of the heinousness of adultery had
for a time subdued it. Besides her hatred was chiefly pointed at
Ægisthus and her remorse is greatly exagerated. As to Iphigenia
her timidity when acquainted she was to be sacrificed is easily
accounted for, as she was surprised and at that time ignorant of
the reasons which required it. Even to the last her constancy is yet
mixed with some regret and repining.

Upon v 148, Mr Hurd attempts to account for and establish
one of the most important rules of Epic poetry. (Vol. i p 110–112)
A poet may either tell his story in the natural historical order, or
rushing at once into the middle of his subject he may afterwards
introduce by way of Episode the events previous to it. Which
method should he observe? Homer, at least in one of his poems
has preferred the last [2] and in that as well as in most other things
has been followed by his successors by Virgil by Milton, by Voltaire,
& (in this instance I may call him an Epic poet) by Fenelon.[2] But
as many things which[a] have stood the test of time cannot endure
that of reason, I shall venture to start some objections to this[b]
method, and to consider in a few words, Mr Hurd's defence
of it.

1[rst] Supposing the rule founded on reason it is too vague to be
easily reduced into[c] practice. Since the greatest part of the poem
is to consist in a recital, where the poet himself, speaks; when is
that recital to begin? with the principal action? But in those great
tho simple subjects that alone are worthy of the Epic muse, such
for example as the establishment of Æneas in Italy, there are a great
number of prævious events, which either hasten or retard the
Catastrophe. Are *they* part of the subject? They are intimately
connected with it, and no Critic ever required Unity of place in
the Epopæa. Are they not? how then can the loves of Æneas and
Dido be justified? and if they can, why may not Æneas's meeting
Andromache in Epirus be as much a part of the principal subject
as his meeting Dido at Carthage? I might in this manner follow
the thread of the Episodical[d] story perhaps to the beginning of the
second, but[e] certainly to the beginning of the third book of the
Æneid (and were I to take the Odyssey or any other Epic poem it

---

[a] *II.* that   [b] *I.* that   [c] *II.* to reduce to   [d] *I.* story [*i.e., marked out*
in favour of "Episodical story"   [e] *I.* & pe r

would be the same) and ask at every pause why the bard might not[a] begin his Invocation from thence. Like Horace himself[,]

> —— Demo unum, demo et item[b] unum,
> Dum cadat elusus ratione ruentis acervi

But enough has been said on this head.

ii[ndly].[c] When, without any preparation, we are thrown at once into the midst of the subject Unacquainted with the Characters or situation of the Hero, such a conduct can be productive only of a surprize and perplexity to the reader, which if they are any beauties are at least beauties of a very[d] inferior species of poetry. Nor is this all, this very ignorance and perplexity of the reader, diminishes the interest of that part of the poem, for how can we love virtues[e] we are yet ignorant of, or tremble for misfortunes of which we have a very faint idea. Nor can it be said that the nature of an Epic subject preserves it from this inconveniency, since it always is[f] or ought to be some story already famous. It may be so; but We are not yet acquainted with the alterations it may have suffered, under the hands of the poet. Nor can the similar example of Dramatic poetry be alledged. It is there an unavoidable defect, but we ought not therefore voluntarily to transfer it to another species[g].

iii[rdly]. When this objection begins to vanish and the reader interested in the present misfortunes of the Hero has little or no curiosity to enquire into his past ones it is then the poet chuses to tell them I suppose We[h] have read the first Book of the Æneid; it is impossible to read it as it deserves, without taking the greatest part in the important scene[i] which begins to disclose itself; so romantic a meeting of a Trojan Chief and a Tyrian princess upon the shores of Africa, & the gods themselves, employing every artifice to inspire them with a mutual passion, and prevent the establishment of the Roman Empire. At the instant we are impatient to know the event, and expect the poet should hasten to it, we are entertained with a long recital of the sack of Troy and the Voyages of Æneas. After this is at last ended and we return to Dido we have almost forgot who she was. Is this consulting the pleasure of the reader? and that pleasure ought to be the great[j] aim of every writer. I do not know whether I may not have expressed myself

---

[a] *I. om.* not   [b] *II.* etiam   [c] *Arabic numerals in II.*   [d] *II.* an
[*i.e., om.* 'very']   [e] *II.* beauties   [f] *I.* is always   [g] *II. adds of* poetry
[h] *I.* who   [i] *I* in the important part   [j] *II. om.* great

too strongly in saying, we have little or*a* no curiosity to learn the past fortunes of the hero, but however let it be considered, i.[rst] That before they are told us in a regular narration a thousand hints of them must have been dropped which betray the secret, so that we only come to it with that languid curiosity of learning the particulars of what we have already a general idea. ii[dly] *b* That we are not to consider*c* our positive degree of curiosity to know the events previous to the beginning of the poem, but to compare it with the desire we feel of pursuing the sequel of which we must find far superior to it;*d* For in every operation of the mind there is a much higher delight in descending*e* from the cause to the effect than in ascending from the effect to the cause. In the perusal of a fable it is the event we are anxious about, & our anxiety encreases or diminishes as that event is known or unknown to us. It is easy to apply this to the present argument.

iv[thly] *f* and lastly, (for tho' I endeavour to be concise, I am frightened when I look back) The style of the poet will suffer as much by this inversion as his plan. Bold figures and poetical imagery are the essence of the Epopœa. But with what propriety can they be introduced in that Episode, where it is the Hero, not the poet that speaks. There are two sources of these figures, strong*g* passion and a fine imagination. The first can operate in any strong degree, only during the actual influence of the misfortune which gives*h* birth to it; and tho' the recollection of the latter*i* may call forth some sparks of the former,*j* yet it will be a faint*k* reflected heat, very unequal to that great effect of transporting both the speaker & the hearer[.] On the other hand, a fine imagination is no essential part of a Hero. Homer and Achilles are very different characters. Nay should the chief personnage like Ulysses happen to*l* be a celebrated Orator, [3]*m* even that will not authorize his employing the beauties of poetical language, since his recital to be properly introduced must be unpremeditated and occasional: Not like the poet, who besides the fire of natural genius is indulged with every advantage of time labor, and a particular inspiration of the Gods. [3]*m* The Episodical story must therefore be simple, unadorned and far inferior as to style, to the rest of the poem. I am

a So II; MS. of   *b Arabic numerals in II.*   *c I.* considered   *d II.* which must be far more ardent   *e I.* remounting ascen   *f Arabic numerals in II.*   *g I.* a fine imag warm   *h II.* gave   *i I.* first   *j I.* latter *k I.* very faint   *l II. om.* happen to   *m MS. has two references to this note, as shown.*

sensible the Æneas of Virgil is as great a poet as Virgil himself but either the principles I have laid down are false, or this example is a strong proof of the inconveniences of the method; since it obliged so correct a writer to offend either the judgement or the imagination of his readers.

I cannot pass to Mr Hurd's arguments without mentioning a difficulty which seems to affect my second objection; viz this ignorance & perplexity is an objection only to the first perusal. It is true; but[a] if precepts are to direct the composition of the writer it is certainly that first perusal and the effects it may produce that he should principally consider; especially as to what relates to the clearness of his plot. And should it be said that in my third objection, our[b] curiosity to know the event can be likewise only baulked in[c] the first perusal, to the preceding answer, I must add, that whoever considers the power of imagination will find that reply by no means exact. Altho' when we can coolly reflect, we are acquainted with the event, yet the true poet by interesting our passions chains us down to the present moment & prevents our seeing any thing beyond it. When I read the tragedy of Iphigenia for the twentieth time, I know Iphigenia will not be sacrificed, but the struggles of Agamemnon, the rage of Achilles, the despair of Clytemnestra make me ignorant, and tremblingly anxious for the event.

Let us now hear Mr Hurd, who employing the particular example of the Æneid justifies this common method from two reasons 1 The nature of an Epic poem, & 2 the state & expectations[d] of the reader.

1.[rst e] The nature of an Epic poem obliges the poet to relate at full length every event he himself relates. Now the destruction of Troy related in this manner must have taken up several books. By that time it would have taken such hold of the imagination of the reader, that the remainder of the poem would have appeared little more than an[f] appendix to it. The conclusion is certain; but on what is the principle founded? upon an assertion advanced without the least proof. I should rather think that as an Epic poem must preserve an Unity of hero, and of action Every event instead of being related at full length, need only occupy a space proportionable to[g] it's importance and degree of connection with the principal[h] subject. This is at least the rule of history, and if poetry should only deviate from it, for the sake of making the fable, one, connected, marvellous,

---

[a] *I. om.* but   [b] *I.* the   [c] *II.* on   [d] *II.* expectation   [e] *II.* 1.
[f] *MS.* and   [g] *II.* proportionate with   [h] *I.* principle

heroic and answering to our notions of justice [4], I do not see how the poet is dispensed from it in this instance. If from reason we go to authority, does not Virgil himself dispatch in sixty lines, the state of Italy at the arrival of the Trojans, with the ancestors, history & character of Latinus (Æneid. L vii. V. 45–105)

2.$^{\text{dly}\,a}$ I do not see^b any material difference between this & the last argument. To find any I must suppose Mr Hurd means that, had Virgil begun the poem with the taking of Troy, that story however Concisely told would have engrossed too much of the reader's attention. I believe it would; but no rule can be founded upon this particular instance, where the preliminaries of the poem happen to be incomparably more important than the subject matter of it. When a poet finds himself under such a difficulty, I think the common method may be very serviceable to him.

I flatter^c myself, I have now proved this rule never essential to the Epopœa, & in general hurtfull to it. But has it no advantages? The only one I can discover is that making the hero tell part of his own story, gives the poem a more varied and dramatic air, brings the reader more familiarly acquainted with the chief personnages & furnishes the writer with unaffected strokes, rather indeed of manners & character^d, than of passion. To these ends it may be serviceable. Let it however be remembered^e that^f poet who has obtained them the most^g compleatly, has done it in one of his poems, without the assistance of this method.

Mr Hurd, tho a very rational admirer of antiquity, looks upon the Chorus as essentially necessary to Tragedy, & blames the Moderns for having rejected it. The subject is curious, & I think never well considered^h, but as such a discussion would lead me too far, I shall defer it till another opportunity, and only report here the substance of Mr Hurd's commentary.

The Chorus rejected by us notwithstanding the authority of Aristotle & Horace joined to the example of the ancient Tragedians, and of our own Milton, and Racine, has many advantages to recommend it. the principal are (Vol. i. p 116–119) 1$^{\text{rst}\,i}$ The Chorus interposing in the action & bearing a part in^j it, gives it an air of probability, and real life, and fills up that vacuity, which is so sensibly felt upon the modern stage. 2$^{\text{dly}\,k}$ The Chorus is as

---

^{a} *II.* 2. ^{b} *I.* seeing ^{c} *I.* th[*ink?*] ^{d} *II.* of character
^{e} *I. om.* be remembered ^{f} *II. inserts* the *here, before* poet ^{g} *I. om.* most
^{h} *II.* has never been well considered ^{i} *II.* 1. ^{j} *II.* of ^{k} *II.* 2.

usefull to the Ethics as to the poetry of the stage, It is a perpetual
moral commentary upon the Drama, enforcing every virtuous
sentiment rectifying every vicious one, and[a] pointing out the
important lessons which may be drawn from the catastrophe. Nor
can it be said that the audience do not want this assistance; A
sharp-sighted Athenian audience, even with the help of the chorus,
could not distinguish between the real sentiments of Euripides, and
those he was obliged to suit to his characters.

These advantages[b] of the Chorus explain[c] the laws of it. 1rst[d]
Its songs must be animated with a spirit of virtue and morality, &
2.dly[e] Their subject matter must be relative to & connected with
the plot of the play and the actual situation of the personnages. The
Greek Tragœdians who invented the Chorus have scarce ever
deviated from the spirit of it; but Seneca who seems to have
endeavoured, by his faults to illustrate the admonitions of Horace,—
has often mistaken it in the grossest manner (Vol. i. p 120–127).
Mr Hurd selects his Hippolytus, one of his best plays, and examines
it act by act upon these principles. Every where, his Chorus bears
a most idle and uninteresting part. The Example of the third[f] act,
which contains the falsse accusation of Hippolytus, & the too easy
deception of Theseus, may suffice. What had the Chorus to do here,
but to warn against a[g] too great credulity, and to commiserate the
case of the deluded father? Yet it declaims in general, upon the
unequal distribution of good and ill. Mr Hurd traces the source of
these blunders, to an injudicious imitation of some passages of
Euripides, without any attention to character or situation.

The second[h] law of the Chorus is without exception but several
things may be said to explain or modify the first.[i] 1rst[j] The use of
moral[k] sentences is not only necessary but peculiar to the Chorus.[l]
That is their proper place. If they were frequently put into the
mouths of the speakers, it would only give the Drama an air of
stifness & pedantry very opposite to real life. If the Greeks (especially
Euripides) have acted otherwise, they are[m] only to be justified
from the manners of their age (Vol. i. p 155–163). That age was
peculiarly addicted to moral sentences, from a singular mixture of
simplicity and refinement. Their simplicity inspired them, as it does

---

  a *I.* which   *b* *II.* uses *II. failed to paragraph*   *c* *II.* naturally ascertain
its laws   *d II.* 1.   *e II.* 2.   *f I.* fourth   *g II.* the   *h I.*
first   *i I.* second   *j II.* 1.   *k II.* modern   *l I.* Drama. It is
there the   *m II.* were.

always, with a spirit of moralizing, expressed in short, proverbial, sentences. At the same time Moral Philosophy, was never more universal, and even fashionable. Both these causes, operating upon the manners and conversation[a] of the Greeks, could allow the poet, without offending against probability, to extend those maxims, to the personnages of the Drama, which succeeding times should confine to the Chorus. Accius & Pacuvius indeed, & after them Seneca, injudiciously copied the Greeks in this instance; tho writing to a nation whose manners were very different. 2dly[b] Tho the Chorus should always take the side of Morality, it must not be so much that of a pure, philosophical morality, as of the popular system of Ethics of that age & country (Vol. i. p 131–139). This restriction will be a reply to many cavils. We are shocked in[c] the Medea, when we see, a virtuous Chorus not only conceal, but even abett the cruel designs of that princess, against her husband, her rival, & the tyrant Creon; designs most[d] justly repugnant to the purer lights of modern religion and philosophy. But we must consider, that in the pagan world, the severest revenge for such injuries as the violation of the marriage-bed, so far from being a crime[e] was almost an act of duty; and that since positive[f] laws allowed it to the husband, a Chorus of women might very well think, no natural law forbad it to the wife. 3.^{rdly}[g] Great allowance must be made for bad politics, as well as bad Ethics. A Chorus of free citizens will be virtuous, and independent. But should they (as in the Antigone) be composed of the servile ministers of a tyrant; Their words, and even their thoughts, will be slavish; and the will of their master, the[h] only rule of right & wrong. Their depravity will be the fault of the subject, not the[i] poet. Nay this depravity will convey a fine moral lesson, of the balefull influence of arbitrary power. (Vol. i. p 127–131).

Mr Hurd thinks the verses from 202–220, which are generally considered, as[j] a censure[k] on the corruption of the modern music, are in fact an encomium, on it's improvement, couched under an irony, by which he sneers at the too great austerity, of those who blamed it, without a sufficient attention to the alteration of manners, and the mixed company, a public assembly is made up of. (Vol. i p 139–155).[l]

---

[a] *I.* conversations   [b] *II.* 2   [c] *I. om.* in   [d] *MS.* must   [e] *I. om.* a crime   [f] *I.* the   [g] *II.* 3.   [h] *II.* masters, their   [i] *II.* of the   [j] *I. om.* as   [k] *MS.* censured   [l] *II. om. this reference.*

The account, our commentator gives of the Satyrs, mimes, and Attellanes is as curious, as it is new. I shall only report the substance 1. The Attellanes were originally a Roman entertainement; so called from Attella, a town of the Osci, in Campania; for which reason, both the language, and characters, were Oscan, & the introduction of an old provincial dialect, was a source of[a] pleasantry, very apposite to the unpolished taste of those ages. 2. In the seventh[b] century of Rome Pomponius began to write Latin Attellanes; preserving however, an antique cast of expression. This reformation & a more moral turn, which he gave his Attellanes, procured him, the name of inventor of them, and the honor of being imitated,[c] by the dictator Sylla. 3. Soon after, and before Horace wrote, the Oscan characters, now become absurd, had disappeared, & made way for the Greek Satyrs. 4. Horace finding this entertainement established & even necessary for the populace of Rome, undertook to regulate it, and to substitute to the gross ribaldry of the Attellanes, the poignant wit of the Greek Satyrs. 5. If it is asked in what that wit consisted, it may be answered; principally, in the double character, of the Satyrs themselves; who, tho rustick and grotesque personnages, were supposed in antient mythology, to be great masters of civil and moral wisdom.[d] Should[e] Horace be censured, as he has been, for preferring these Attellanes, to the elegant mimes of Laberius, it may be replied, that we rate too high, the merit of these mimes. Cicero despised them, & the best ancients, represent them, as a confused medley of comic drollery, on a variety of subjects; without any order or design; delivered by one actor, and heightened with all the licence of obscene gesticulation. (Vol. i. p. 165–184)

This inelegancy, (to pass to another remark of Mr Hurd), was the general character of ancient wit, which consisted rather, in a rude illiberal satyr, than in a just and temperate ridicule, restrained within the bounds, of decency and good manners. Cicero and Horace themselves, tho' masters of every other part of elegant composition, joke with a very ill grace. A favorite topic of ancient raillery, was corporal defects, a decisive proof[f] of the coarsness of their humor. And this practice was recommended by rule, & enforced by the authority of their greatest masters. (Cicer. de Orator. L. ii C. 59 & 66). After this we must not be surprized, if they

---

[a] *MS.* or   [b] *I.* sixth   [c] *MS.* imitatated   [d] *I.* knowledge knol
[e] *MS.* b Should; *II.* but should   [f] *I.* proofs

preferred those authors, whose wit was like their own; rough and coarse: Plautus to Terence, Aristophanes to Menander. We must follow Mr Hurd for a few moments, into his enquiry into the causes of this defect. 1. The free and popular governments of Antiquity. These by setting all the citizens on a level, took of[f]*a* those restraints of civility, which arise, from a fear of displeasing, & which can alone curb the licentiousness*b* of ridicule. The only court to be paid, was from the Orators to the people. These were to be entertained With the coarse banter, proper to please them; and design passing into habit[,] these orators, & after them the Nation, accustomed themselves to it, at all times. The Old Comedy was therefore an excellent school for an orator, and always recommended as such. But when arbitrary power had moulded the Roman manners, to more obsequiosness, and decency*c* Terence and Menander, began to receive a deserved applause. Tho even then ancient wit was never thoroughly refined; for 2^{dly d} The old festal entertainements still subsisted, the Panathenæa and Dionysiæ of the Greeks, the Bacchanalia and Saturnalia of the Romans; and preserved always, an image, as well, of the frank libertine wit, of their old stage, as of the original equality and independency, of their old times. Upon this subject (V. i p 186–203)*e*, I agree with Mr Hurd, but I think this influence of governement, upon the manners and litterature of a nation, might be the*f* subject of a very original enquiry. I have a good many ideas myself, tho' as the Abbé Trublet calls it *"Je n'ai pas achevé de les penser."*

Upon V. 404. Mr Hurd explains his author*g*, differently from his predecessors. They extended that encomium, to all poetry, which Horace meant only for the Lyric. In fact it is only adequate to that species, which is besides so particularly pointed at,*h* by *"Musa Lyræ solers, et cantor Apollo"* This a*i* delicate stroke of Horace, after his panegyric upon Dramatic poetry, to show the Lyric, had also it's merit, & to prevent the Piso's from despising the choice he had made. (V. i p 234–237)

These are the principal notes, upon the art of poetry. On the Epistle to Augustus I find but two worthy much notice.

The first is the explanation of a magnificent allegory, which opens the third Georgic. Virgil after apologizing, for the meanness

---

a II. off   *b So II. MS.* licentiousless   *c I. om.* and decency   *d II.* 2.
e II. om. this reference.   *f I. om.* the   *g I.* authors   *h II.* out   *i II.* is a

of his subject,[a] breaks away with a poetic[b] enthusiasm, to foretell his successes, in the future great work of the Æneid. He shadows it under the idea of a triumph in which he is lead captive, all the Græcian Muses; The monument of the Triumph, is to be the usual one, a temple; consecrated by games, and sacrifices; and every ornament of which, alluded to the tutelary Divinity, Augustus. Thus under the popular authorized veil, of the apotheosis of that prince, He lets us at once, into the whole secret of his plan (Vol. ii. p 30–50). This explanation is exquisitely fine, but if my memory is good, the P. Catrou[3] had started it, before Mr Hurd.

2.[dly] The other remark is to explode a practice familiar to Ovid, and not unknown to more correct writers. "That of coupling two substantives to a verb, which does not strictly govern both, or which at least, must be taken in two different significations.["] He proves very copiously, against the Professor d'Orville, that such a practice breaks the natural connection, of our ideas & turns the attention of the reader, from the subject, to a discovery and admiration, of the art of the writer. He therefore pronounces it unworthy of serious poetry. (Vol. ii. p 61–75).

As yet I have only spoke,[c] of Mr Hurd's notes. His Discourse upon the several provinces of the Drama, is a truly critical performance; I may even say, a truly philosophical one (Vol. i. p 247–308). From simple definitions of each species, he deduces a very extensive Theory. To touch the heart, by an interesting story, is the end of Tragedy; to please our curiosity, and perhaps our malignity, by a faithfull representation of manners, is the purpose of Comedy. To excite laughter, is the sole and contemptible aim of farce.

These enquiries are delicate. Sometimes we[d] imagine[e] we are reasoning upon things, when in fact, we are only cavilling about words. It is more especially so, with regard to those ideas, which do not represent substances, but only modes of thinking, and moral combinations. There we can be only guided, by practice and experience. They are out of the province of reason. If Plautus & Aristophanes, have given the name of Comedy, to a species of entertainement, of which the essence was ridicule, they had a right to do it. If their successors Terence and Menander, have given the same name, to their more serious drama, we must either, prove these definitions not incompatible, or give some other appellation,

---

[a] *I. om.* subject   [b] *II.* poetical   [c] *II.* spoken   [d] *I.* when we   [e] *II.* think

to the object of the last. All that reason can do upon this head, is dropping names to investigate the sources of our pleasures, to class them, and to see how far, they agree or interfere with each other.

It is very natural that the contemplation of human life, should be the favourite amusement of man. It is his easiest and yet least mortifying method of studying himself. This contemplation can be only considered, in two different lights, manners and actions. We must allow, tho' we cannot explain it, that our humanity, makes us hurt and yet pleased, with the misfortunes of our fellow creatures, and that the recital of a story, terrible[a] or pathetic, rouzes every faculty in the human breast.[b] On the other hand, daily experience convinces us that our reflections and conversations, never turn upon any subject, so often, and with so much pleasure, as the various characters of mankind. It is to give us these pleasures, less strongly perhaps but thro' the means of fiction, more compleatly; that two entertainements have been invented; to the first of which, we may hypothetically give the name of Tragedy, and to the second, that of comedy. The laws of each species, are to be deduced from their ends. But in following Mr Hurd, I shall only mention those, particular to what we have just now called Comedy.

The first law of comedy, must relate to the choice of character. They must be mixt ones: human nature never deals, in manners perfectly good, or compleatly bad. But the poet is not confined, to those characters only, which excite contempt and ridicule. Virtuous aimiable persons, who inspire us with sentiments of love and approbation, may be properly introduced,. Since all probable domestic manners, lie within the province of comedy. These characters will not indeed, occur so often as those of another Kind, not only, because they are less frequent in real[c] life, but because they admit of less variety: For reason and virtue pursue a steady uniform course, while the extravagant wanderings of vice and folly are infinite. However, when properly brought upon the stage, they will occasion more pleasing sensations there, than in society, wheuras, the ridicule of a scenical character, is much weaker, than that of a real one. Perhaps our malignity may furnish a reason, for this difference. 2d [1]ly Another rule of comedy, relates to the management of characters; they are to be displayed, in a natural manner,[d] and as much as may be, the personnages[e] are to give

---

[a] *I.* great   [b] *II.* heart   [c] *I.* the   [d] *I.* manner possible   [e] *I.* they

their own characters; but that, by undesigned actions or[a] expressions, by which they lay themselves open, without knowing it. Nor is that character always to appear; since it cannot always exist, but as the ruling passion is modified by others, or called forth by circumstances. A contrary method, tho too common, is turning a man into a single passion; a man such as nature never made, since those who are the most under the dominion of a ruling passion, act[b] and talk upon many occasions, like the rest of mankind.

Since actions are the province of Tragedy, and manners that of comedy, *That* must form their distinctive difference.[c] However even there,[d] they cannot avoid running a good deal, into each other. Without manners, no action could[e] be carried on since we act according to our passions: nor could it affect us much, since our terror or our pity, depend[f] chiefly upon our love and hatred. On the other hand, how could manners be represented, without a probable series of events, contrived to call them forth in a natural manner. We can only say therefore that in Tragedy, the action is the principal, manners an accessory circumstance; in Comedy, manners are the principal, action the accessory circumstance. In both, the poet must take care, that the end be not lost in the means. For this reason, the complicated plots of the Spanish writers, have been justly laid aside, as contrary to the true genius of comedy. It may be worthy[g] some notice, in speaking of characters, that tho'[h] most natural ones are comic, many highly so, are unfit for Tragedy. Tragedy requires characters, good or bad, but of a power and energy equal to the greatest effects. But many[i] passions, (the passions of weak minds) such as Vanity,[j] can never with truth be[k] raised to that dramatic importance, their[l] actions will be always like themselves, puny and insignificant. But the energy of the stronger passions, may be softened, and reduced to the level of common life. Cruelty and ill nature, may disturb, either a family, or a nation[.] Besides, there are other passions, the power of[m] which tho' great, is vilified by their object. The various species of avarice, have produced the most tragic events; but the love of money is of so vile and groveling a nature, that it would degrade the most pathetic tragedy, that turned upon it.

   [a] *I.* of   [b] *I.* act upon   [c]*II.* Actions are the province of tragedy, and manners that of comedy; this forms their distinctive difference. *II. Failed to paragraph.*
[d] *II. om.* even there   [e] *II.* can   [f] *II.* depends   [g] *II.* worthy of
[h] *II.* the   [i] *I.* as *or* al   [j] *I.* vanity, love of play &c.   [k] *I.* retained
[l] *II.* the actions produced by such passions   [m] *I.* the effects of

This difference of the two species, cannot well be disputed; but it has been asked whether they are not[a] distinguished, by the rank as well as the character, of the personnages; or in other words, whether Tragedy, is confined to the public, and exalted characters of Kings and generals, and comedy to the humbler stations of private life. Without any regard to authority, I shall examine this question, mixing indifferently, my own reasons and[b] Mr Hurd's.

As to Tragedy; it may indeed be said, that we are the most affected, by those misfortunes which might happen to ourselves, and that therefore the distresses of a private family, must touch us more nearly, than[c] those of a Monarch. But to counter balance[d] that advantage, we may remark that the Story of those, whom we are accustomed, to look upon with awe and veneration, attaches us in the strongest manner, and awakes our terror and pity, much more than the wretchedness of private men. These indeed are popular notions; but the poet's business, lies in complying with those notions, not in reforming them. Besides the misfortunes of the great, tho' not superior in themselves, to those of the people,[e] are yet far more important, in their consequences; which heighten the distress, by extending the influence of it, to the whole community. To these general remarks, I may add a particular one, that in the noblest subjects, those founded upon ambition, love of our country, &c the rank of the personnages, cannot be too exalted; since upon that, depends the greatness of the prize for one,[f] and of the sacrifices in the other, and consequently, great part of the importance of the action, and strength of passion.

But cannot comedy admit of Monarchs? they have their private life, and may not the ridicules of it be displayed upon the stage? I think not. But I must give my reasons.

1 The first will be taken from the Spectators. We love Comedy because it offers us[g] a faithfull representation of what we meet with in life. It must be therefore, the life of the most considerable part of the audience, that the poet should represent. But what is that[h] part? The question is easily resolved, by looking thro' human society, and observing that insensible gradation, from the man of quality, to that degree immediately above the mechanic and the labourer, every link from the highest to the lowest, enough connected with the[i] others to have some acquaintance with their

---

^a II. have not been   ^b I. with   ^c So II. MS. that   ^d II. counteract
^e II. multitude   ^f II. the one   ^g II. to us   ^h I. the   ⁱ I. each

manners, and enough improved by education, to laugh at theirs, and[a] their own follies. These then are the manners, a poet should copy in their different appearances: Should he touch those of the prince or peasant, they must either, be the same, or different. If the same, why go out of the way for them? if different who will he find,[b] to understand or relish them? This is particularly true, of the manners of princely life. Those of the lowest, we are better acquainted with and he[c] may find, some archetypes, amongst[d] the spectators. But the grossness of them, will disgust every one, whom the poet[e] can desire to please.

2. But are the[f] manners of princes[g] different from those of their subjects? Are there any qualities[h] peculiarly royal? I know but of[i] one; that is, the thinking there[j] are such. In other words, I mean, a fondness for flattery. That ridicule can, I confess, be no where so well represented, as upon[k] the throne; since those will always receive and love, the most extravagant adulation, who have it most in their power, to reward and punish. But still, I think it a better subject for Satyre than Comedy. It would be difficult to put in action, the follies of a Monarch; the great Theatrical ressource, is the opposition and contrast of characters, to[l] display each other. The severity of Demea, and the easiness of Micie, throw a light upon one another. Should We be half so well acquainted, with the misanthropy of Alceste, were it not for the fashionable, complaiant character of Philinte? But the poet, would be almost destitute of this ressource, if he laid his scene in courts; which offer[m] one uniform set of manners, moulded upon the example of the prince. What contrast could be found, to set of[f][n] _his_ character? None; since such a contraste, supposes freedom and equality. This I take to be the true reason; not merely that politeness which in high life, obliges even equals, to conceal from each other, their real characters. This is rather an advantage. We pursue with pleasure, the various arts of concealment, which it inspires, &[n] when as it must often happen, chance, familiarity, passion, interest, throw it of[f][o] it's guard, and display the man in his true colours, the long constraint gives them a new vivacity, and the discovery gives a higher relish, to our entertainement.

_a_ _II. om._ theirs, and   _b_ _II._ be found   _c_ _II._ With those of the lowest we are better acquainted; and the poet   _d_ _II._ among   _e_ _II._ he   _f_ _I._ those
_g_ _I._ princely life   _h_ _I._ follies   _i_ _II. om._ of   _j_ _II._ that there   _k_ _II._ on
_l_ _II._ that   _m_ _I._ offers   _n_ _I. om._ &   _o_ _So II. MS._ of

3. But the most important objection, to these characters still remains. They can have no private life. They[a] have doubtless, many things ridiculous and insignificant in themselves; hardly any thing, that is so in it's consequences. Every action of theirs is important, by the[b] influence, it has upon the community; and if we paint their follies, those follies, rendered vices by their Tragical effects, would excite contempt themselves, indignation[c] for their consequences, and as the first of these passions, is as repugnant to tragedy, as the second is improper for comedy; could produce only[d] a very motley, and disagreable composition. Therefore when M. de Fontenelle asks, whether Augustus in his last sickness, surrounded by Aruspices, who promise him a speedy recovery, by Parthian Embassadors, who restore[e] him standards, he is mighty indifferent about,[f] fawned upon by Livia, who is impatient for his, death; whether all this, would not make as good a comedy, as the *Malade imaginaire*; the answer, will not be difficult. No. Because the follies and weakness[g] of the last, as they are innocent, divert us: while the fawning of Livia, and her power with[h] her husband, fill us with horror and indignation; when we reflect that by setting Tiberius[i] on the throne, they made the world unhappy, for three and twenty years, & finished the ruin, of the liberty, and nobility of the republic.

The practice of M de Fontennelle tho' very happy, is rather a confirmation of this theory. In his Comedies, he endeavours to reconcile us, to those great personnages, but he is continually reduced, to shifts of lowering[j] our idea of their importance,[k] and divesting them of their power and majesty, before he can make them real comic characters.[l] His common expedients, are making them, of mean extraction, tho raised to the throne; not putting them in possession of the crown, till the end of the play; and laying his scene in Greece, in order to fill their courts,[m] with simple Citizens instead of nobles.[n]

I cannot help thinking, that Farce (the third species of Mr Hurd's) is rather a corruption of comedy,[o] than a distinct species of itself.[p] Is not his own definition of it,[q] a proof of this? That as Comedy is a faithfull, so Farce is an exagerated, picture, of human life? If

---

[a] *I.* Nothi   [b] *So II; MS.* the the   [c] *II.* would in themselves excite contempt and indignation   [d] *I. om.* only   [e] *I.* bring   [f] *II.* standards about which he is totally indifferent;   [g] *II.* weaknesses   [h] *II.* over   [i] *I.* Aug
[j] *I.* reducing   [k] *I. om.* importance   [l] *I.* per   [m] *II.* court   [n] *II.* with nobles   [o] *I.* Mr Hurd's comedy   [p] *II.* corruption, than a distinct species of comedy.   [q] *II. om.* of it,

they are distinct, there is little occasion to fear any encroachments, into the province of Comedy, from Farce; But many comic writers, to please the corrupt taste of the multitude, have descended to the extravagancies*a* of Farce. There is another subject, which Farce has preserved from the old Comedy. This is, the painting personal individual characters: But that practice seldom followed,*b* and never authorized upon the modern stage, rather deserves the animadversion of the magistrate, than of the Critic. As to follies not confined to a man but to an age or country, I think Mr Hurd too severe, in banishing them into Farce; He seems sensible of it himself, and in*c* the instance of the Alchymist, attempts to soften his sentence, by a distinction rather chimerical[.]

I have, tho without design,*d* extended this extract so much already,*e* that I shall abridge the other discourse of Mr Hurd, far more than it's merit would otherwise make me do.*f* The subject of it is extremely curious. Poetical imitation, examined upon very original principles; a question, in which the reputation of all the great writers since Homer, is vitally concerned. It is thus stated by Mr Hurd. "Whether that conformity of phrase or sentiment, "between two writers of different times, which we call *imitation*, "may not with probability enough, for the most part, be accounted "for, from general causes, arising from our common nature; that is "from the exercise of our natural faculties, upon such objects as lie "common to all observers. ["] (Vol. ii. p 105–207)

It has often been observed with truth, that as our capacities are narrow, and the materials of observation, the same to all men; it is impossible, that*g* in so great a number, as*h* those who have thought, and published their thoughts, some should not have coincided,*i* in the same opinions, without any knowledge of each other. I believe I*j* may appeal to every man of letters, whether sometimes he has not met with things*k* in books, which he had observed, before he ever saw those books; and that even, things*l* of an uncommon, and particular nature. Even in those sublimer mathematics, so different by*m* their evidence and universality, from our other speculations, the same discoveries, have been made by different men, Who seem to have met, not*n* followed each other. Is not that the decision, of

---

a II. all the extravagance   *b I.* practice   *c I. om.* in   *d I. om.* design
e II. already so much extended this extract,   *f II.* justify   *g I.* for so
h II. of   *i So II. MS.* coincideded   *j II.* that I   *k I.* notions
l II. before he had ever seen those books; and things too   *m MS.* for by
n II. rather to have coincided with, than to have

the moderate part of mankind, upon the celebrated dispute[4] of Sir Isac Newton and Leibnitz, in the beginning of this century? (V Fontenelle in the Eloge of Leibnitz, Tom. v. p. 520–531). If this is the case, in those general abstracted branches, which contain such amazing combinations of ideas, it is surely probable, that in works of imagination, which contain much fewer, this ought oftener to happen. Besides the most original poetry, is in fact imitation; imitation of nature, & in those images, which are confessedly natural, it seems difficult to say, why two[a] genius[e]s[b] may not have seen them, without any knowledge[c] of each other. From these reasons, the candid critic will readily allow, that there may be similitude, without imitation[.]

But a slight glance on the history of the sciences, and a few reflections on mankind, will reduce this candor within it's due limits. Let us remember. that[d] 1. Since the time of Homer, who perhaps was without models to imitate, that author has been introduced, into the earliest part of our education; that succeeding times added to his lessions, those of the other Greeks, that the Romans studied them with care, and that since the revival of letters, we are made acquainted, as soon as possible, with the Greeks and Latins. That those impressions, engraved in[e] our minds, before we reflect, grow up with us afterwards, and that[f] when we look abroad, into the Moral and natural world, which these companions, often prevent us from doing, we see it only with the eyes of the ancients. 2. If habit was not sufficient, to dispose us[g] to imitate the ancients, authority founded on reason, would oblige us to do it.[h] The ancient compositions, have stood the test of time and examination, and the veneration, that is paid them,[i] is enough to engage a modern, to endeavour to associate himself to it, by transfusing into his own writings, the spirit, the thoughts, and even the expressions of these admired models, and 3[j] Inclination will[k] direct him, to the imitation of some particular model; of some writer whose soul is most congenial to his own, and whom he can read with the greatest delight, and imitate with the most ease. All[l] these reasons, bring us back to our first suspicion, that where there is a striking similitude, there[m] is imitation, since, where there are two ways of bringing it

[a] *I.* they   [b] *II.* men of genius; *MS.* genius s   [c] *II.* previous knowledge
[d] *I. om.* that   [e] *II.* on   [f] *II.* afterwards grow up with us, and when
[g] *I. om.* us   [h] *II.* ancients. Authority, founded on reason, would oblige us to
act in this way.   [i] *II.* to them   [j] *II.* 2.   [k] *I. om.* will   [l] *II. om.*
All   [m] *I.* and

about, it is natural to prefer the easiest, especially, when it is
confessedly a very common one.[a]

Mr Hurd found it was[b] necessary, to go further, if he intended to
clear his authors, from the charge of imitation; accordingly he
endeavours to prove, by a very elaborate deduction, that both the
ideas, and the methods employed by[c] the ancients, were *not only
natural ones*, but the *sole[d] natural ones*; so that if succeeding poets,
endued with judgement, looked abroad into nature, they not only
might, but *must* meet with them[e]; while men of irregular fancies,
could *only* avoid *them*,[f] by avoiding truth and probability. This
theory accounts for resemblances of works, by resemblances of
things; and forbids any suspicion of imitation, unless we are guided
to it, by particular circumstances.

In[g] a matter of such vast extent, it is as difficult, to refute as to
prove. There would indeed be a very short method, of overthrowing
at once Mr Hurd's doctrine. Could I write[h] a work of imagination, full
of beauties, formed upon[i] the model of nature, and yet different
from those of the ancients, I should demonstrate[j], they have
not exhausted it. But such a confutation is far beyond my power;
without aspiring to genius, I shall think myself very happy, if[k] I can
frame my opinions according to the dictates of good sense.

If we examine this question, a posteriori, from practice and
experience of what *has* been done, tho we shall meet with[l] nothing
very decisive, I think[m] however, the[n] advantage will not be of[o]
Mr Hurd's side. He will indeed, quote many striking similarities of
this kind, from writers, who could have[p] no knowledge of one
another. But he will be answered. 1. That such writers can hardly
be found; that the sacred writings should not be mentioned, nor
compared with Homer, since we are talking, of human not divine
compositions[q], and that Shakespeare,[r] the modern who appears
freest from exception, tho' ignorant himself, lived in a learned age.
2.[s] That *their* example, can be only quoted against such, as should[t]
think every similarity *must* be an imitation, without any regard, to
the circumstances of the writers. That as such a coincidency[u] is
possible, we must employ it, to explain a Phænomenon we could

[a] *II.* accomplishing it, it is natural . . . confessedly very common   [b] *II. om.* was
[c] *I. om.* by   [d] *I.* only   [e] *I. om.* them   [f] *II.* could avoid *them only*
[g] *II. failed to paragraph*   [h] *I.* point out   [i] *II.* on   [j] *II.* then demonstrate
that   [k] *I. om.* if   [l] *I.* without   [m] *I. om.* think   [n] *II.* that the
[o] *II.* on   [p] *II.* have had   [q] *I.* writings   [r] *I.* the   [s] *I.* They
[t] *II.* can only be quoted against those who   [u] *II.* concidence

not otherwise account for;[a] but that when the more easy and probable one[b] may be recurred to, we ought to employ it. On the other hand an antagonist of Mr Hurd's, would have[c] occasion for no great compass of reading, to discover in the most modern writers, many original images and sentiments. He would select them, particularly from those very writers, who from an apprehension, that every thing had been already said, had cramped their natural genius, by an open, perpetual imitation of the ancients; and he would infer with some plausibility, that had they wrote, more from their own feelings[d] & observations, they would have been still more original. He would desire Mr Hurd, to reconcile this with his principles; and even press him for a precise answer, at what period of the history of Letters, the scene had been closed, nature exhausted, and, succeeding writers reduced to the hopes of imitating successfully. Wherever he chose to fix it, the critic would bring against him, so many later original images, that the ressource of disputing their claim, and hunting for some distant allusion, or general resemblance, would be hardly sufficient.

Without following minutely our author, thro' his copious deductions a priori, in[e] which, he has certainly shewn great learning and ingenuity; I shall only make two or three general observations, which may given an idea, both of his method of reasoning, and of my objections to it.

1.[f] He enters upon a task, in my opinion far above human abilities. To examine the origin of our ideas, is the business of Metaphysics, and the greatest philosophers, have failed in the attempt. But it is perhaps still more difficult to embrace them all, at one view, &[g] to class them according to their different objects, in so accurate a manner, as to assure ourselves, we[h] have suffered no material species to escape. This is however what Mr Hurd attempts. He divides the world of ideas, which can enter into Poetry into three[.][i] 1. The vast Compages of corporeal forms, of which this universe is compounded. 2 The internal workings and movements, of our own mind, under which is comprehended[j] the manners, sentiments, and passions. 3. The outward operations, which are made objective to sense, by the means, of speech gesture and action. These are

[a] *II.* for which we . . . account;   [b] *I. om.* one   [c] *I.* ask   [d] *II.* written more from their own natural feelings   [e] *I.* I sh   [f] *II. om.* 1.   [g] *II.* and   [h] *II.* that we   [i] *II.* undertakes. He makes three divisions of the world of ideas which can enter into poetry.   [j] *II.* which the manners . . . passions are comprehended.

again by him subdivided, with an exactness, in which I shall not pursue him. I shall only remark, that his smallest species, are yet too general to prove any thing. That Milton,[a] for instance must like Homer, have made use of moral, religious and œconomical sentiments, and could not invent any new species, I shall readily allow, nor is it upon such general resemblances, that a charge of imitation is ever founded. It is upon more particular similarities, where Mr Hurd can never attain to shew that *those* ideas, were the *only ones*. The[b] only method, Mr. Hurd can there follow, is a sort of vicious reasoning, in a circle; to look for the images upon every subject, he can meet with in the oldest authors, and then to conclude they[c] are the only ones existing.

2. Even supposing, he[d] had exhausted the whole stock of nature, and had shewn that every image singly, had been so obvious, as to be seen and employed, by the first writers, a much larger field would still remain, their different combinations, which are infinite. With regard only to human manners, the great sources of character passion, and situation may be combined, in such a variety of ways as no Algebra would[e] reach. Let us for a moment, abandon fiction and enter into historic truth. Consult the annals of any nation, observe the various effects, of the modifications of those three principles, upon their history; and then say whether the operations of human nature, are easily classed or circumscribed.

3. This consideration of the shifting picture of mankind, as an illustration, leads us to consider it in itself: We shall find it a most extensive and infinite range of ideas, almost alone sufficient,[f] to preserve Genius from imitation, since to the writers of every age or[g] country, it appears in a different shape. It is the manners, the government, the religion of that age and country, he is to study, and whether the nature of his subject, allows him to introduce them at full length, whether he can only, adorn his works with distant allusions to them, whether he[h] can only catch the general spirit of them, they will always make him an original. I shall quote one instance of what I mean, and that from an authority Mr Hurd will hardly dispute (Warburton's Divine Legation). When Milton conceived[i] the glorious plan of an English Epic, he soon saw, the most striking subjects had been taken from him, that Homer had

---

[a] *I.* Hom   [b] *I.* In a word his gener divisions are too general. The   [c] *II.* that they   [d] *II.* that he   [e] *II.* could   [f] *II.* almost sufficient of itself [g] *II.* and   [h] *I.* last   [i] *I.* form

taken all Morality, for his province, & Virgil exhausted the subject of politics. Religion remained; but as Paganism, tho' it furnished very agreable scenes of machinery, took too slight a hold on men's minds, to build the story of the Epopœa upon it, he had recourse to Christianity and taking his story from an article of our faith, struck out a new species of Epic poetry. But he could never have done it, with success,[a] had not the manners of that age, attached to religion in general, and to that[b] tenet in particular, warmed his imagination, and given it a dignity and importance, which he could never have trans[f]used[c] into his poem, if he had not first felt it himself. Nor is this observation repugnant to another, I have made elsewhere, (Essai sur l'etude de la Litterature p. 19)[5] that the manners of the ancients, were more favorable to[d] poetry than ours. I think so still; of their manners, as well as their languages. Yet I would have our poets employ, our own, not only for the sake of variety, but because we shall always make the best use of those, we are the most intimately acquainted with[.][e]

From these Observations, I must decline subscribing, to Mr Hurd's Theory; or circumscribing the poet's images, within such narrow limits. It is however, without running into the other extreme, or condemning immeditiately[f], every resemblance as a designed formal imitation. I take the exact difference, between Mr Hurd and myself to be this: I look upon imitation, to be the most natural and general cause, of any striking resemblance, between two writers; and therefore assign[g] it, without particular reasons to the contrary. Mr Hurd on the other hand, thinks it may generally be[h] accounted for, by a resemblance of mental operations, and therefore never suspects an imitation, without particular circumstances, which lead to the detection of it.

He employs another discourse in the[i] review of these circumstances (Vol. ii. p. 1–76), but as every one, is accompanied with examples, taken from the ancients and moderns, and criticised with great taste, I can only reduce the great number, he alledges to three, drawn from the different lights, in which we may consider, every resemblance, and fix the probability,[j] of it's happening by chance or by design. 1. How close is the resemblance? Is the thought

---

[a] *II. om.* with success   [b] *I. om.* to that   [c] *So II. MS.* transused
[d] *I. om.* to   [e] *II.* shall make the best use of those with which . . . acquainted.
[f] *II. om.* immeditiately   [g] *I.* two; and there assigning   [h] *I. om.* be *and* for
[i] *II.* with a   [j] *I.* degree of probability

exactly the same, is it introduced upon the same occasion, is it expressed in the same manner, the same words or words nearly the same. Is it a short passage or one of a considerable length? 2. What degree of acquaintance can the second poet, be supposed to have had with the first? Did he live in a learned or a[n]*[a]* ignorant age, was he himself a man of letters, or without education? did he affect the fame of originality, or did he modestly profess a desire and habit of imitating the ancients? Was the first author, an acknowledged favourite of his. 3. What appearance is there that the Idea should have naturally struck the second? was it common or*[b]* particular, did it agree with the style and design of his work, with his own character, with the real appearances*[c]* of nature, with manners*[d]* and opinions of his age country,*[e]* and profession, or at least with those he describes? Is it introduced and expressed, in a natural*[f]* unnaffected manner, or brought in without any occasion, and cloathed in uncommon obsolete language. Mr Hurd thinks these circumsances, all or some, necessary to form a suspicion, I allow they are very usefull to confirm one.

I have at last finished Mr Hurd's performance. I reckoned upon six or seven pages, I am now writing the thirtieth. Another time I hope to confine my abstracts*[g]*, within proper limits.[6]

Blandford March the 18th 1762*[h]*.

[1] When Marius proscribed by*[i]* the party of Sylla,*[j]* was obliged after a thousand dangers to take refuge upon*[k]* the coast of Africa the Prætor of that province sent him an order to leave it immediately: the Lictor found him plunged in thought and sitting on some stones on the beach. When he asked him what answer he should carry back to the Prætor "Tell him (replied Marius) that thou hast seen Marius sitting upon the ruins of "Carthage." This implied comparison between his fall & that of a once powerfull city displayed on the same spot is poetically bold. Yet passion & real misfortune joined to the coincidency of place could sugget it to Marius a rough illiterate soldier. Is not this a striking illustration of Mr Hurd's theory?

[2] In the Odyssey. As to the Iliad, properly speaking he has followed neither. The events previous to the subject, the anger of Achilles; he neither relates himself, nor throws into an Episode; but as they were few & simple, he leaves the reader to collect them, from occasional hints, dispersed thro' the poem.

[3] When Antenor in the 3ᵈ Iliad points out to Priam, Ulysses among the Græcian Chiefs he describes the nature of his eloquence.

Αλλ' οτε δη πολυμητις αναϊξειεν Οδυσσευς,
Στασκεν, υπαι δε ιδεσκε κατα χθονος ομματα πηξας:

---

[a] So II.   *[b]* I. obselete or   *[c]* II. appearance   *[d]* II. the manners
[e] I. and country   *[f]* II. introduced in a general   *[g]* II. extracts   *[h]* In
margin of MS.   *[i]* I. was able   *[j]* I. om. of Sylla   *[k]* II. on

Σκηπτρον δ' ουτ' οπισω, ουτε προπρηνες ενωμα
Αλλ' αστεμφες εχεσκεν, αϊδρει φωτι εοικως
Φαιης κεν ζακοτον τινα εμμεναι, αφρονα θ' αυτως
Αλλ' οτε δη ρ' οπα τε μεγαλην εκ στηθεος ιει,
Και επεα, νιφαδεσσιν εοικοτα χειμεριησιν
Ουκ' αν επειτ' Οδυσηι, γ' ερισσειε βροτος αλλος.

(Iliad iii. v 216–223)[a]

Out of the several testimonies to the eloquence of Ulysses collected by Dr Clarke, I shall only subjoin that of Quintilian: "Sed summam adgressus (*Homerus*), ut in Ulysse "facundiam, magnitudinem illi junxit; cui orationem nivibus hybernis, et copia verborum "atque impetu parem tribuit. Cum hoc igitur nemo mortalius[b] contendet." (Quintil. L. xii. C 10.)[c]

[4] Lord Bacon and Mr Hurd himself, agree that poetry, is an imitation of history, deviating however from it, so as to answer the above-mentioned ends. (Mr Hurd. vol. ii. p. 160–162.)[d]

---

[a] *MS. marginal ref. begins* (1)   [b] *II.* mortalium   [c] *MS.* (2) *and in margin*
ref. begins (2)   [d] *MS.* (1). *MS. marginal ref. begins* (1)

Part II

1765–1775

INTRODUCTION

THE period between Gibbon's return from Italy in June 1765 and
the publication of the first volume of the *Decline and Fall* (February
1776) was of course one of intense literary activity for him, but
relatively few traces of that activity remain. In the first four years
Gibbon continued to devote much of his energy to writing in
French. With the help of his Swiss friend Georges Deyverdun, who
knew German, he planned and actually began a history of the Swiss
republics, in French (summer 1767). Hume, who saw the manuscript, urged Gibbon to go on writing history, but in English.[1]
Nevertheless, Gibbon's next publications were also in French: his
contributions to the journal he and Deyverdun edited, *Mémoires
littéraires de la Grande-Bretagne* for 1767 (issued in 1768) and 1768
(issued in 1769). Thereafter, however, all Gibbon's important works
were written in English.[2]

His 'first serious production in [his] native language', a 'copious
and critical abstract' of Blackstone's first volume of *Commentaries
on the Laws of England* (*Memoirs*, p. 148), has never been published,
except for the second paragraph and some of Gibbon's notes (*MW*
1814, v. 545–7). It must have been written in 1765, when Blackstone's first volume had appeared but not his second (1766), for
Gibbon remarks that 'we have only the first Volume'.[3] To the
same period, i.e. 1765–70, we may attribute two collections of
assorted notes, one called by Gibbon 'Hints' and the other 'Index
Expurgatorius'.

The consistency of the quality of the hand and of the numbering
of the sheets suggests that Gibbon wrote all the 'Hints' at much
the same period; if so, that period must have been 1765 or later,
because Gibbon refers to Mably's *Observations sur l'histoire de*

France, which was first published in 1765, in Hints No. 3. They might have been written at any later date, of course, but I think they belong to this period of Gibbon's life. 1. Their varied subjects reflect the varied interests of the period before he concentrated his studies on preparations for the writing of the *Decline and Fall*. 2. In No. 9, Gibbon's view of the relation between the secular games and the religious Jubilees is different from that suggested in the *Decline and Fall* (chapter vii), i. 234, n. 56 (Bury i. 193, n. 72). 3. Hints No. 2, point 3, seems echoed in the 'Outlines of the History of the World' below, p. 193.

The set of hints on the 'Character and conduct of Brutus' (Nos. 14 and 15) is clearly a preliminary outline for the 'Digression on the Character of Brutus' (below, pp. 96–106). I have therefore assumed an approximate date of 1766 for that essay, of which there are two copies. Neither is holograph, but one has autograph corrections. Gibbon employed a copyist with a similar hand in or after 1774 (to copy the essay on the man in the iron mask, below, pp. 204–8), but of course the date of the transcription, even if established, need not be that of composition.

The 'Index Expurgatorius' was written on both fronts and backs of sheets not only numbered by Gibbon, but also provided by him with an alphabetical index. Both sheets and entries are numbered. Again, the consistency in numbering makes it likely that all these notes are the product of the same period; if so, that period must have been during or after August 1767, since in No. 35 Gibbon refers to 'Mr Christopher Smart a new and very indifferent translator of Horace (See Monthly Review August, 1767)'. References to Buffon's index (in No. 40), published 1767, but not to any of his supplementary volumes, which began to appear in 1770 and which Gibbon both owned and read, suggest 1768–9 (Sheffield's opinion) for the date of the 'Index Expurgatorius'. Furthermore, the earlier of the two editions of Voltaire's *Œuvres* (referred to in four entries) that are listed in Keynes was published in Geneva, 1768–77. Thus we have at least an approximate *terminus a quo* for the 'Index Expurgatorius', though not a *terminus ad quem*, except perhaps Voltaire's death (1778)—see No. 25, where Gibbon speaks of Voltaire as if he were alive.

In any event, Gibbon's *Critical Observations on the Sixth Book of the Aeneid* was certainly sent to the press 'in the beginning of the year 1770' (*Memoirs*, p. 145), so it must have been written in 1769.

It was his first and only English publication before the *Decline and Fall*.

Both study and writing now became very difficult for Gibbon. His father was in his final illness, and died 10 November 1770. Then, in Gibbon's words, 'near two years (November 1770–October 1772) were suffered to elapse before I could disentangle myself from the management of the farm, and transfer my residence from Buriton to . . . London' (*Memoirs*, p. 151). Nevertheless, to the period beginning in 1768 and ending with his settlement in London, Gibbon attributes his 'preparatory studies' for his history, his exploration especially of the 'darkness of the middle ages': 'I almost grasped the ruins of Rome in the fourteenth Century, without suspecting that this final chapter must be attained by the labour of six quartos and twenty years' (*Memoirs*, p. 147). This reference, and that pointed out by J. W. Swain[4] to a 'rough draught of the present History' which was 'as early as 1771' (*DF* [chapter xxx] iii. 169, n. 86 [Bury iii. 268, n. 88]), suggest that the 'Outlines of the History of the World', which deals with the years 800–1500, considered by Sheffield an early work on the basis of the handwriting, was actually written in 1771. As Gibbon originally conceived his history, the third division began in the year 800 and ended approximately six and a half centuries later (*DF* Preface, i). This essay begins and ends abruptly, contains a sketch of the events of that third period, but does not contain, as the last chapter of the *Decline and Fall* does, any account of the ruins of the city of Rome in the fourteenth and fifteenth centuries. Furthermore, the hand of the manuscript, though not so admirable as that of Gibbon's last works, is quite different from the cramped and difficult hand of the works that can definitely be dated before 1763. There seems no objection, therefore, to accepting Swain's hypothesis that these 'Outlines' are the surviving part of a 1771 draft of the *Decline and Fall*.[5]

Although the composition of the first sixteen chapters of the history might seem to require all Gibbon's time from October 1772, to June 1775, when volume i was ready for the press (*Memoirs*, p. 157), a small commonplace book with several entries from Raynal's *Histoire politique et philosophique des deux Indes*, first published in 1770, exists, as does a formal essay on the identity of the man in the iron mask, which is dated 27 May 1774. Gibbon's own copy of Raynal was the edition of 1774; perhaps his notes were made before he owned the work, or when he first acquired it. Sheffield attributed these notes to the period 1755–64, but that is obviously impossible. With these brief excursions, in any case, Gibbon's English works prior to the *Decline and Fall* are complete.

Commentaries on the Laws of England Book the 1[rst]; by William Blackstone Esq[re] Vinerian Professor &c. Oxford. 1765. in 4°. pp. 473

Introduction

[Ch. 1. p. 3–38][a] The first Chapter[1] which was read at the opening of the Vinerian Lectures, 25 October 1758 is employed in proving the use and importance of the study of the Laws, and in explaining how so necessary a branch of learning was so long neglected in the University of Oxford. The first of these points is too self evident to require much argument. It concerns every man to be acquainted with the rule to which he must conform his actions and to have a clear idea of the whole system of duties which he is to perform and of rights which he may exact. The various relations which an English Gentleman may support either in the execution or formation of laws only serve to make his Knowledge of them of greater consequence or his ignorance more scandalous

Unfortunately for this usefull science, the foreign Clergy[2] who poured in shoals into England after the Norman conquest had little relish for[b] the old Common law of this Country; they had formed the design of erecting upon it's ruins the new System of Civil and Canon Law which had just began[c] to revive in the Court of Rome and the Italian Universities. The artfull designs of these Ecclesiastics were however constantly disapointed by the steady opposition of the Nobility and Laity who supported the Municipal Law of England against these innovations; till at last despairing of sucess the Clergy affected to despise what they were unable to destroy & withdrew almost entirely from the secular tribunals. The Court of Chancery of which they retained the direction adopted many of the forms of the Civil Law, and as they were the sole masters of the two Universities, they easily proscribed a science which they abhorred, and reduced the Students of the Common Law to the necessity of erecting peculiar Schools, in London and within the neighbourood of the Courts of Justice. Altho' two hundred years

---

[a] *In margin of MS.*   [b] *I.* of   [c] *II.* begun

have now elapsed since the reformation, yet the reverence for established customs will easily account for so material a defect in our Academical education not having been sooner corrected.[a] [3]

[Ch. ii. p. 38–63] All Municipal laws may be comprehended under one general character, that of "A Rule of civil conduct "prescribed by the supreme power in the state; commanding what "is right and prohibiting what is wrong." Mr B illustrates this definition with great acuracy, but perhaps with somewhat too-great prolixity. [4] I shall only select one member of it which leads him into a just and natural encomium of the British Constitution. "by "the Supreme power in a state" The power of Legislation contains within itself the foundation of every other power, which must be delegated by it's superior authority. The idea of a perfect[b] Legislator seems to represent him as virtuous enough to make the publick happiness his only aim, wise enough to discover the means of procuring it, and powerfull enough to carry those means into immediate execution The first of these qualifications is oftenest to be found in democraties. Aristocratical governments seem with reason to claim the second; and the last is peculiar to Monarchy. Our happy constitution by blending these three several powers into one united Legislature, enjoys[c] at once the Vigour of a Monarch, the wisdom of the few, and the honesty of the many. Such at least are the flattering prospects which Theory holds out[d] to our hopes and admiration

It is almost unnecessary to add that every prohibitory law must be armed with the terrors of punishment, and that[e] in the interpretation of these rules of Civil conduct we should never lose sight of the precepts of equity, Grammar, and rational Logick.

[C. iii. p. 63–93.] This rule of conduct may be authorized by the positive declaration, or by the tacit consent and allowance of the Legislature. It is this difference which constitutes the essential distinction between the written and unwritten our Statute and our Common Law.

The common law [5] is supposed to have been formed from the most ancient customs of the nations who formerly inhabited this island; collected and published in the Code of the Great Alfred and afterwards restored by Edward the Confessor. To these we may perhaps add many institutions introduced by the Normans, and

---

[a] *I.* correction   [b] *I.* perfected   [c] *I.* has   [d] *I.* up   [e] *I. om.* that

which easily amalgamated with those of the Britons and Saxons. But the written monuments of this law have long since perished, and the Common law receives it's authority from custom, so much the more venerable as the memory of man cannot reach the first origin of it. It extends it's important influence over the proceedings of our Courts, the different[a] methods[b] of acquiring and transferring property, and a vast variety of other objects both civil and criminal. In short it's authority is equal to that of the Statute Law; unless in those cases, where the former has been particularly altered by the latter.

The existence & validity[c] of these traditional customs is determined by the Judges of the several courts of Justice who must decide in all cases of doubt and who are bound to decide according to the Law of the Land; Their Knowledge of the Law is derived from experience and study, and from being long personally accustomed to the Judicial decrees of their predecessors: and indeed these Judicial decisions are the principal[d] and most authoritative evidence that can be given of the existence of such a custom as shall form a part of the common law. Such rule and precedent once established can no longer be deviated from nor sacrificed to the private opinion of a Judge who is not the Maker but the expounder of the Law. The Memory of these legal customs is preserved in the Records of the Courts of Justice, the Reports which are extracted from them, and which form an uninterupted chain of authorities since the reign of Edward the second, and in the supplemental writings of the Sages of the Law, whose opinions are supposed to be founded on the evidence of ancient facts; of these Sages Sir Edward Coke is the last

Besides the general customs of the realm there are[e] some particular customs which are allowed to form legal exceptions; such as the law of Gavelkind in Kent, the traditional priviledges of the City of London &c. After the existence validity and reason of these partial laws have been proved to the satisfaction of the Court; the rule is, to interpret them as strictly as possible in prejudice of the Common law.

The Civil and Canon law are received in some particular courts, but they are so strictly controulled that[f] they seem rather tolerated than authorized. An Act of parliament may however be pleaded in

---

[a] *I.* differents   [b] *I. om.* methods   [c] *I. om.* & validity   [d] *I.* most principal   [e] *I. om.* are   [f] *I. om.* that

favor of the Canon laws, which gives them a temporary sanction untill a revision which has never taken place

With regard to the Statute law, I shall only take notice of a rule or two observed by all our courts in the expounding them. A Court of Justice considers[a] ex officio all general laws; particular ones must be formally alledged. Penal statutes are to be interpreted strictly, laws to prevent frauds and which consider the offence[b] rather than the offender are to be construed in the most liberal and beneficial light.

[Ch. IV p. 93–117] The distinction just laid down between the Common and Statute law, will easily point out; to[c] what parts of the British dominions they respectively extend themselves. The authority of the one is created by Parliament, the validity of the other is determined by the Courts of Justice. All parts may be equally subjected to the uncontroulable power of the Legislature which is only confined by those articles which united two Independant nations. But this power is not always exerted; Scotland and Wales who are parts of the representative Body of Great Britain, are subject to every act of that body from which they are not formally excepted Ireland and the Plantations are[d] bound only by those in which they are particularly named. Their own Representative assemblies enjoy under various[e] restraints a provincial and subordinate right of Legislation

The Common Law has submitted to times and Circumstances. 1. The Union of Wales with England is now compleat, but it naturally carryed along with it a total sacrifice of the priviledges of the Vanquished nation, which adopted all the laws and customs of their new masters. 2. Scotland treated as an independent Kingdom; and preserved their ancient courts of Judicature directed by their own Common law; which tho' different from ours; appears to have sprung from the same root. 3. When Ireland became subject to the Crown of England, it was found necessary to soften the manners of the Barbarous inhabitans by the introduction of our national customs and to secure their dependency by opening an appeal from their Courts to our own. 4. The great distance of the American Colonies from the seat of Empire made it necessary to vest a supreme authority in their Courts of Judicature who consequently became the Interpreters of their own Common Law, which is however naturally borrowed from that of the Mother Country.

[a] *I.* tak   [b] *I.* offender   [c] *I.* out to us   [d] *I.* is   [e] *I.* vary

[parallel to Gibbon's first paragraph]

[1] This excellent work, of[a] which, we have only the first Volume is extracted which Mr. B.[b] read as Vinerian Professor, and[c] may be considered as a rational System of the English Jurisprudence digested into a natural method, & cleared of the pedantry the obscurity and the superfluities which rendered it the unknown horror of all men of taste

[parallel to the second paragraph]

[2][d] Perhaps Mr B might have shewn the reasons of the preference which the Clergy gave to the Civil and Canon, and have given us some instances how well they suited the Views and Interest of the Ecclesiastical Order.

[3][d] Mr. B. touches upon this neglect, with the becoming tenderness of a pious son who would wish to conceal the infirmities of his parent.

[beginning opposite 'too-great prolixity']

[4] I have entirely omitted a Metaphysical enquiry upon the nature of Laws in General, Eternal and positive laws and a number of sublime terms which I admire as much as I can without understanding them. Instead of following this high priori road, Would it not be better humbly to investigate the desires fears, passions and opinions of the human being; and to discover from thence what means an able Legislator can employ to connect the private happiness of each individual, with the observance of those laws which secure the well being of the whole.

[beginning opposite 'The common law is supposed']

[5] Mr Blackstone speaks with uncommon respect of the Old Common Law, which the generality of Lawyers highly prefer to the Statute Law. He will find it however difficult to persuade an impartial reader; that old customs (begun in barbarous ages and since continued from a blind reverence to Antiquity) deserve[e] more respect than the positive decrees of the Legislative power. I can indeed suspect that a general rule which is gathered only from a rude and prodigious mass of particular examples and opinions will easily acquire an obscurity, a prolixity and an uncertainty which will at last render the priests of Themis the sole interpreters of her oracles. I think the Clergy of all religions have as constantly preferred the traditional to the written law; and perhaps too from the same motives.[f]

Book the first.

[C. i. p. 117–142] The general object of Law, is to enforce rights and to prevent wrongs, rights are relative[g] either to persons or to things; wrongs are either of a private or a publick nature; These Commentaries will fall into four[h] above-mentioned divisions.

The first chapter upon the absolute rights[i] of individuals is rather perplexed from a method which seems inverted. All societies

---

[a] *II. om.* of . . . extracted   [b] *II.* Blackstone   [c] *II. om.* and   [d] *II. om. this note*   [e] *II. om.* deserve   [f] *II. om. this sentence*   [g] *I.* either relative   [h] *I.* t   [i] *I.* writ w

must retrench from the natural liberties of each individual. Free societies retrench as little as possible. The restrictions imposed by the laws of England will be diffused throughout the whole work and this chapter would I think have appeared with more propriety as an appendix than as a preface.

The securities given by our laws to the natural rights of the subject seem to consist in a representative legislature, and a judicial power independant without being arbitrary. Those very delicate trusts of life liberty and property can scarcely be comitted to[a] safer hands.

Those patriots who, (from the Barons of the Magna Charta, to the Parliaments of the Revolution,) have formed a glorious chain of assertors of freedom considered how easily the wisest provisions have been defeated by the arts of power and that unless arbitrary and tedious imprisonments can[b] be guarded against, laws and tribunals are without[c] efficacy This is the great object of the Habeas Corpus bill.[1] No gaoler can receive a prisoner without a legal warrant specifying the particular cause of his comittment; the prisoner must receive a copy of it within six hours & may instantly (by himself or friends) apply for an order to be produced in court. The Judges are obliged to allow him to find Bail or if his offence does not admit of it; he is again remanded to prison, and his tryal cannot be deferred longer than the next term. The whole method of proceeding is easy and expeditious and severe penalties are enacted against all such as shall obstruct any part of it; and as prisoners[d] might be sent to such distances as the eye of the law cannot reach,[e] they are never to be transported out of the Kingdom of England.

As to more extraordinary securities, every subject has a right of petitioning (in a respectfull manner; any branch of the Legislature; and arms are allowed him for his defence, (at least,) against private injuries.

These natural rights are common to all; but there are many more that[f] vary with the different characters and relations, which we acquire or support in civil society. Of these the most universal is the public distinction of Magistrates and subjects, those who command and those who obey

[C. ii. p. 142–183] The supreme power in our constitution is

---

[a] *I.* entrusted in   [b] *I.* g   [c] *I.* withouts   [d] *I.* often prisoners
[e] *I. om.* reach   [f] *I.* which

lodged in a great council, the essential parts of which consist[a] of
1 An hereditary King, 2 An assembly of Hereditary Nobles,
originally appointed by the King, of 26[b] Bishops who are constantly
nominated by the same authority and of sixteen Peers elected from
and by the body of the Scotch Nobility, and 3 of the Representatives
of the Commons of Great Britain chose by themselves in their
respective divisions of Counties, Cities and boroughs. In the joint
consent of these three branches of the legislature exists that supreme
absolute power which is essential to Civil Society, and their will
declared in the Legal forms is considered as the will of the whole.
The peculiar authority of the King in this respect is rather negative
than positive. He may reject but he can never propose. The house
of Peers lies under the same restraint in the particular instance of
taxes of all denominations, which the lower house have ever claimed
as their peculiar province

But tho' destitute of legislative activity himself, the Supreme
Magistrate and he alone gives life and activity to the whole machine
by his exclusive power of summoning, proroguing and dissolving
Parliaments. This prerogative was attacked during the reign of
Charles I, & was suspended by the spontaneous meetings of the
two Conventions. But excepting such extraordinary and eccentric
cases, it seems calculated to serve many usefull purposes without
threaghtening in the least public Liberty especially since the laws
which fix the duration of each parliament at seven years,[2] and
confine the legal intervall between them to three[c].

When the King assembles the Parliament [6] he issues with[d] the
advice of his privy council and thro the Channel of his Chancellor
a writ directed to the Sheriff of each county and dated at least forty
days before the time appointed for the meeting. The Sheriff proceeds himself to the election of the Knights of the Shire, and directs
his precepts to the proper returning officers to elect members for
their several cities and boroughs. I shall mention the essential
requisites of these elections. 1. The twelve Judges, the Clergy,
Aliens, Minors, Non-Conformists, all returning officers and all
officers of the Revenue, except the Commissioners of the treasury
are incapable of being elected 2. The qualifications both of Candidates and Voters are exactly fixed with regard to the Counties. The
former must be possessed of a freehold or Copy-hold estate of £600
per annum, the latter of a freehold of forty Shillings. (Many

[a] *I.* have consisted   [b] *I. om.* 26   [c] *I. om.* to three   [d] *I.* without

(perhaps useless) provisions have been made to exclude all fraudu-
lent and temporary conveyances. 3. The laws of boroughs are as
various and uncertain as their creation has been different and
accidental. The Right of election depends solely on the several
charters, customs and constitutions of the different places. A landed
qualification of £300 per annum has however been made necessary
for the elected; a just and proper weight thrown into the scale of
the landed interest 4. All undue influence either of the crown or the
Candidates is carefully guarded against. No troops can remain
within two miles of any place of Election. But it is far easier to
exclude open violence than the silent pleasing power of interest.
Severe penalties are enacted but it is found very difficult to inflict
them. Religion has been called in to the assistance of Law; but oaths
when too frequent soon lose their efficacy. These indeed against
bribery and corruption might be more usefull if they were administered to the Candidates instead of the Electors. 5. When the
Sheriffs &c have returned the Members elected, they have a right to
take their seats and can only be removed from them by an[a] appeal
to the house of Commons the sole and absolute Judge of all matters
relating to their own elections.

The priviledges of Parliament are so large and indefinite that they
can scarcely be determined but by their own resolutions The most
notorious priviledges of the members of either house are liberty of
speech and freedom from arrests. This last is of a very extensive
nature during the actual sitting of Parliament. It secures his person,
his domesticks, his goods and his Lands from any legal process of
a court of Justice. During the recess of Parliament a Member enjoys
personal security, the Peer from a perpetual right the Commoner
from the shortness of those recesses which at present never exceed
the fourscore days during which his person is legally protected. The
right of proxies and protests is peculiar to the Lords.

This our Gothic Constitution seems[b] to have never been without
some great council. The form which I have described has subsisted
five hundred years, with some alterations however as time experience
and circumstances have suggested them. I shall conclude with one
of them. The bills were presented in form of petitions; when they
had received the royal assent, the[y] were digested by the Judges
into the form of acts. In the reign of Henry vi, the Parliament chose
to dictate the expressions as well as the substance of their own Laws

---

[a] *I*. the   [b] *I*. seems never

[opposite the beginning of Gibbon's third paragraph re C. ii]

[6]a N.B. when the house of commons actually exists, the Speaker issues out the writs, to fill up particular vacancies.

When the parliament exists, but in a state of prorogation, the King may (when constrained by the exigency of invasion or rebellion,) assemble it, at only fourteen days notice.

[C. iii. p. 183–212 *King's Title*] The executive power of the English nation being by immemorial custom vested in one single person; it is of utmost consequence to have that person acurately described. Such is the origin and foundation of the laws relative to the succession

Setting therefore aside the incomprehensible absurdity of a divine Right, this seems to be the fundamental maxim of our legal Succession. "That the crown is by common Law and Constitutional "custom, hereditary; and this in a manner peculiar to itselfᵇ; but "that the right of inheritanceᶜ may from time to time be changed "and limited by act of Parliament; under which limitations the "Crown still continues Hereditary"

The proofs of the most important of these propositions, the 1ʳˢᵗ and the 3ᵈ, appear dispersed thro' the whole course of our Laws and history: but they are may found at once inᵈ that fierce Parliamentary contest of the exclusion bill.[3] The Commonsᵉ acknowledged the Crown to be hereditary: the Lords who rejected it confessed the succession might be altered by authority of Parliament. The second observation is explained by saying that the Crown follows the general rules of feudal inheritance [7], except in the particular instance of not dividing the succession amongst the daughters; in default of male issue as such divisions would be productive of the greatest inconveniences. Such were the rules according to which the British Monarchs claimed from the original stock of William the Conqueror till the time of the Revolution. In the single instance of the Lancaster family (the only legal alteration,) the Parliament confirmes the rule, as soon as they had made the exception and settled anew the old hereditary right among the descendants of Henry iv.

The revolution presented a singular and uncommon scene. The Convention parliament declaredᶠ that King James the second by his endeavours to subvert the constitution and by his abdication had left the throne vacant. They then proceeded to a new settlement in

ᵃ *II. om. this note*   ᵇ *I.* ourself   ᶜ *I.* succession   ᵈ *I. om.* in
ᵉ *I.* Whighs   ᶠ *I. om.* declared

the persons of King William, Queen Mary and Queen Anne, postponing however the children of the former to those of the two latter. Some years afterwards[4] they found it necessary to provide new heirs in the default of these: they had already enacted as a fundamental law, that the profession of the Popish religion should immediately extinguish all right[a] either in next heir or in the actual possessor. In consequence of this principle the posterity of James ii was of course excluded; the protestant offspring of Charles i was likely to fail They therefore settled the crown upon the nearest protestant descendant of James 1, the Princess Sophia, and her posterity; being protestants, and married to protestants. This is the hereditary but parliamentary and conditional title of our present King; a title produced at first by a deviation from established rules; but which is now supported by the plea of necessity and reason, the weight of legal authority and a national consent of seventy years

[opposite the second-to-last paragraph in the summary of C. iii]

[7][b] I wish Mr B. had talked a little less of Egbert, and of a right suspended from Edward the Confessor to James I.[5] Such a suspension must be equivalent to a total extinction, in the opinion of all, but Jure-divino men.

[C. iv. p. 212–220 *His family*] The King's consort is the partner of his bed, but not of his throne. She is in every respect his subject and may be guilty of high treason against him. A just regard for her dignity has however allowed her many privileges. She does not (like other married women[c], lose her separate existence, but is still capable of performing every legal act. A portion of all fines voluntary offerings &c made to the King was formerly considered as a part of her revenue. But when her life and chastity were made sacred by rendering it High treason to contrive the one or violate the other, the law had a much higher object in view. The Queen was considered, not as the companion of the King but as the mother of future princes

The heir apparent who is born Duke of Cornwall and usually created Prince of Wales and Earl of Chester enjoys the same security for his life; which is also extended to the chastity of his wife, and of the Princess Royal the King's eldest daughter The rest of the Sovereign's are no further regarded by the laws, than to give them precedence before all Peers Spiritual or Temporal

---

[a] *I. om.* all right   [b] *II. om. this note*   [c] *I. om.* women

[C. v. p. 220–226, *His Councils*] In a country where the Counsellors are answerable for the advice they give; it is necessary they should be clearly [defined.][a] Besides the Parliament which is, perhaps improperly styled the King's great council, he used formerly to assemble upon emergencies a convention of the Peers alone. But of this custom nothing seems to remain except the privilege which each peer seems entitled to; of demanding an audience, whenever he thinks proper. The Courts of Law are likewise considered as the King's natural council in matters relative to their province. But it is[b] the privy council coæval with monarchy tho'[c] new-modelled by Charles ii which is considered as the legal and perpetual council in all publick affairs. Every part of it's constitution is arbitrary and depends solely upon the King's pleasure. The laws have indeed a security for the person of a Privy Counsellor, by making it felony to attempt his life, when in the execution of his office

[C. VI p. 226–230, *His Duties*] The King's duties toward his people[d], implied by[e] the original contract, more precisely pointed out at the Revolution, and expressed in the Coronation Oath; oblige him, to govern according to law; to execute Justice in Mercy; and to maintain the established religion. But this oath is only declaratory of the comprehensive duty of protection, which becomes incumbent upon the supreme Magistrate, from the first instant of his government, and which alone entitles him, to claim from his subjects, the reciprocal duty of allegiance.

[C. vii. p[f]. 230–271 *His Prerogative*] The powers of the first Magistrate of a free constitution are bounded by known limits He has none but those which the[g] laws of the Community have imparted to one for the good of the whole. This distinct view of the prerogative so favorable to liberty is very different from those Mysterious clouds which the old Lawyers chose to cast around it. To consider so extensive a subject with some order we may divide it into, 1 The King's Royal Character 2 his Royal Authority, and 3 His Royal Revenue.

1. The good of Society is interested in every institution which tends to inspire reverence and awe for the supreme Magistrate. The Laws of England have not only vested their King with very[h] extensive powers, but they likewise attribute to him, several high

---

[a] *A line ends here in MS.; Gibbon did not complete the sentence.*   [b] *I. om.* it is   [c] *I.* but   [d] *I.* realm   [e] *I.* in   [f] *I.* His   [g] *I. om.* the
[h] *I.* several very

perfections[a] and attributes inherent to his political character tho' often very foreign to his personal one. *He is Sovereign and acknowledges no superior jurisdiction upon earth.* This will readily be allowed in regard to every foreign authority but it has been thought and the tryal of Charles 1 was founded upon that supposition, that his people have a right to resist his tyranny by force of arms to depose, and even to punish him: but the laws of England enacted with his consent and administered[b] in his name, cannot[c] suppose such a case, much less could they find an adequate remedy. Such cases are out of reach of legal provisions. Should they unfortunately happen[d], the wisdom of the times must provide new remedies for new emergencies, by exerting those inherent (tho' latent) powers of society which no climate, no Time, no Constitution, no contract can ever destroy or diminish: We are however, from the case of the revolution, authorized to say[e] that should a prince "endeavour to "subvert the Constitution, by breaking the original contract, "between King and People: should violate the fundamental laws "and should withdraw himself out of the Kingdom," that such a conjunction of circumstances would amount to an abdication: and that the throne would be thereby vacant. *He is absolutely perfect. He can neither do nor think any wrong* Which maxim properly explained, flows only from the reverence which the constitution entertains for him, and which not suffering the thought that he can design or execute a wilfull injury, imputes whatever may be exceptionable to his being deceived by evil Counsellors. The Common law never supposes him a minor, and whatever necessary provisions have been made upon those occasions, have been the peculiar and temporary acts of the Legislature. *He is eternal.* He never dies. Upon the natural death of George or Edward, the King still survives in the person of his successor.

I shall run over slightly the principal branches of his legal power. 1[rst] He is an essential part of the Legislature: his assent is necessary to every Law: This prerogative gives a proper balance to the constitution and secures a just independency to the Executive power which can never be limited or weakened but by it's own consent. 2. He is the sole representative of the Society in their intercourse with other nations and in all such foreign transactions, He enjoys a supreme and unlimited power. He alone can send or receive

---

[a] *I.* perpetual perfections   [b] *I.* exer   [c] *I.* are   [d] *I. om.* happen
[e] *I. om.* authorized to say

Ambassadors, grant letters of protection or reprizals, declare peace or war, and conclude alliances and treaties with foreign powers. His acts are the acts of the nation. without him, the acts of the whole nation are only those of individuals. The Common Law considered all these matters as so foreign to their province that till the reign of Queen Anne no provision made for the privileges of Ambassadors, or other ministers. They now enjoy a compleat protection and independency, which is extended to their Household 3. Since the King alone can declare War he alone must be General of that Military force, by which it is supported. Altho this prerogative is somewhat limited by the alteration of manners and some late acts of the legislature, yet he has still the sole and supreme command*a* of all forces both by land*b* and of all forts &c All commissions run in his name and no other person or power can claim any part of the same. It is conjectured that the power of prohibiting his subjects to leave the Kingdom or of recalling from foreign parts*c* those who have already left it, is founded upon the military service which he had a right to exact from every member of the Community. 4. He is supreme Head of the Church of England; which title is vested in him since the reign of Henry viii. In this capacity, he convenes and dissolves Synods; rejects or confirms their constitutions, appoints Bishops and other dignitaries, and receives in his Court of Chancery appeals from all Ecclesiastical Courts. 5 He is the fountain of Justice and the General Conservator of peace throughout the Kingdoms. All Courts of Justice act in his name and by his authority and he he is supposed to present in all. Indeed he has in this province, little more than a nominal superiority He can neither erect new courts, alter the form of the ancient ones, nor displace the Judges; whom he has once appointed. This separation of the Judicial from the executive power, has been finally compleated in our own time, and may be considered as one of the strongest securities of our liberties. 6 He is the fountain of honor, office and privilege, which are all created, or alotted to individuals according to his Wisdom. 7. As Arbiter of Commerce, he seems to have an inspection of some domestick concers. He appoints marts and fairs, regulates weights and measures and coins money. This general measure requires the stamp and sanction of the Sovereign to answer for its value, and as such this right has ever been considered, as his peculiar province.

[C. VIII. p. 271–326 *His Revenue*] The Fiscal prerogatives form

a I. om. command   *b Line ends in MS.*   *c I. om.* parts

the third and last division of the Regal title. These were formerly
very numerous; the Various branches of hereditary Revenues which
were formerly inherent to the Royal dignity gave him a Constitutional independency that he no longer enjoys. Some of these
branches have been retrenched by Parliament, many more granted
away by different Monarchs, and the remainder would now produce
scarce any thing considerable. Mr B. however examines them with
great learning and perhaps too great acuracy, for subjects many of
which are become obsolete. I shall however follow him thro' the
principal heads.

1. The King enjoyed a very considerable share of property,
denominated the Crown or Demesne Lands, consisting of various
Manors, Lordships &c, of which scarce any thing now remains, by
the improvident liberality of former Kings and especially of William
III. Some provision has been lately made for futurity. A Grant of
Crown lands cannot now exceed three lives or thirty one years; a
rent must likewise be reserved. 2. By the feudal tenures, the King
was considered as Lord Paramount of all the lands of England; this
was a most extensive prerogative. The waste grounds which he
converted into forests, afforded him profit as well as pleasure. It
was by this prerogative that he was the general owner of all things
which seemed without one; Estates confiscated for capital offences,
or left without an heir. Shipwrecks which the humanity of modern
ages has interpreted such ships only as come to land, without any
living creature on board; mines which their equity has confined to
those of gold and silver, treasures that were discovered, (*treasure
trove*), goods thrown away by a thief (*Waifs*) valuable animals that
strayed without an owner (*Estrays*), inanimate things or[a] personal
chattels which had been the occasion of the death of a reasonable
creature (*,Deodands*) All these flowed from the feudal ideas, and are
most of them, now appropriated to particular Manors. 3. The King
had many perquisites, for the pains He took in administering
justice to his subjects, which under the names of fines &c, the
Subject still pays, altho' few of them, are now returned into the
exchequer. The custody of Idiots, was formerly considerable as he[b]
enjoyed the profits of their lands during their life. But this is
reduced to nothing as the courts seldom find a man, an idiot or
natural fool, but only a Lunatic or accidental one: in which case the
Chancellor (as representing the King) names a trustee, who is

[a] *I.* which   [b] *I.* a person was

accountable for all the profits, he receives. 4. As Head of the Church, the King receives the first fruits, or Annates, tenths &c; which were formerly paid to the Pope. They are now appropriated to the encrease. The King has likewise (thro' from a very mixed title) the Custody of the temporalities of all Bishopricks; which our ancient Monarchs made rather scandalous use of. 5. To support the King's household, custom had given him many rights of purveyance and preemption, To buy provisions at a price, generally fixed below the value; in preference of^a any other purchaser; and even without the consent of the owner. This right was given up at the Restoration, in lieu of the Wine licences, which were again changed into an annuity upon the Stamp duties

As the expences have been encreasing, whilst the revenue has decreased, It has been found necessary to assist the Supreme Magistrates; by temporary contributions out of the general stock. The first Vote of all such aids & supplies, proceeds from the Commons. they regulate the quantum and mode of raising it, and the other two branches of the Legislature have only a negative.

The Extraordinary taxes at present are either annual or perpetual; the Annual taxes are the land tax and the Malt tax

1. The land tax has now superseded all other methods, of taxing either property or persons in proportion to their property; such as tenths, fifteenths Scutages, Hydages, Tailliages.

The tenths, (which were more usually fifteenths) were a tax upon personal property, invented by Henry ii under the pretence of the Croisades, but afterwards applied to every emergency. This fifteenth of the Moveable of every individual, was at first occasionally determined by new assessments, upon each^b grant of the Commons; till at last a new taxation was made in the reign of Edward iii, and recorded in the Exchequer by which a fifteenth was constantly valued at £29.000

The same Henry ii in his foreign wars received a pecuniary consideration, from his Vassals to be excused, from the military service which they owed him. This contribution, under the name of Scutage soon grew very frequent; and as it seemed rather a favor than a tax; our Kings imposed it without the Consent of Parliament; till they were restrained by Magna Charta. At the same time^c that Scutages were laid upon Knight's feee, another tax, (Hydage^d) were laid upon other lands, and a third (tailliages) upon towns[.]

^{a} *I.* witho ^{b} *I.* every ^{c} *I.* At the times ^{d} *I.* tailliages

These all fell into disuse; upon the introduction of subsidies about
the time of Richard 11,[a] and Henry IV. These were a tax not
immediately upon property; but upon persons, in respect of their
reputed property, at the nominal rate, of 4s in the pound for lands[b]
and 2 s 6 d for goods. But the nominal rate[c] was or became so inferior
to the true one, that in Sir Edward Coke's time a subsidy on a fifth
of the landed property, was only valued at £70000. The Clergy
always granted their subsidies separately. They were set at £20000.
It was not till after the restoration,[d] that they were comprized with
the laity in one universal mode of taxation.

The Assessments invented by the long parliament, and occasionally continued till the Revolution were properly a Land tax; since
a specific sum was imposed upon every county; to be levied by a
pound rate upon lands and personal estates. King William iii is
indeed often considered as the inventor[e] of the Land-tax; it is 1
Because since that time, it has been perpetual tho' annual. 2 Because
we still follow the assessment made in 1692, which has determined
the rate one shilling in the pound, to be equal to £500,000. This
sum is invariably divided amongst the Counties, but the distribution
of each county-proportion upon individuals, is annually settled by
the Commissioners; who are themselves the principal Landholders
of the County. This tax has varied from 4 to 1 Shilling in the pound.
The[f] Medium since the revolution, may be calculated at 3 Shillings,
or £.1.500.000 per annum.

2. The other annual tax is that upon malt. It is under the direction
of the Excise-Office, and produces about £.750.000 per annum.

The various branches of the perpetual revenual are.

1. *The Customs*. which is a duty paid by the Merchant upon
certain[g] merchandises imported or exported. Some of those customs
were formerly hereditary, as a duty upon wool exported, which sunk
to nothing, upon the encrease of our own Manufactures. butlerage
or prisage upon wines exported &c. Others (such as the Tonnage
and poundage, so fatal to Charles 1) were granted by Parliament,
to the King either for his life or for a limited term. They are now
all comprized under the general name of customs. All customs as
they are ultimately paid by the Consumer; who confounds them
with the price of the commodity, are very easy to the people; but
when they are too heavy they encourage[h] smuggling, cramp trade,

---

[a] *I.* the 11   [b] *I.* good   [c] *I. om.* rate   [d] *I.* reformation
[e] *I.* founder   [f] *I.* 2. The other   [g] *I.* every   [h] *I.* increase

and being laid upon the first stages of the commodity; raise the price of it to the ultimate Consumer, who pays not only the duty, itself but the interest of it from the time of the importation.

2. *The Excise* being a[a] duty laid upon the Last stage of any commodity either foreign or domestic, viz upon the ultimate consumer or at least upon the retailer, does not raise the price to the same degree. The Mode of collecting it is not very expensive. These advantages, are counterbalanced (at least in the eye of a free people) by the arbitrary powers necessary to the support of the Excise. The power of searching houses, and the summary proceedings of three Justices; who decide without any appeal to the total exclusion both of Juries, and of the Common Law. The Excise was first introduced by the long Parliament, to support the charges of the Civil war; and though this tax was never popular, it has been[b] continued ever since, and is often extended to new articles. 3. The Salt. duty:[c] tho' under the direction of particular commissioners is only a branch of the excise.

4. The Post-Office was first set up, by the long Parliament, and raises a great sum of money; with the singular advantage; that this tax is as convenient to the people, as it is beneficial to the Crown. It has been lately much improved by a strict limitation of the right of Franking.

5. The Stamp duty is a revenue arising from papers and parchments which are employed in any legal transactions, cards dice advertisements &c. The rates of which vary extremely. The chief advantage of this tax is, that by authenticating deeds, it renders it much more difficult to counterfeit them.

6. The duty upon houses and Windows, is very ancient under the name of Hearth Money. At the revolution it was abolished, as a badge of slavery: but revived six years afterwards under a new appellation.[d]

7. 8. The two last branches of the perpetual revenue consist in the duty upon the licenses of Hackney chairs & coaches, and the tax of 1[s] in the pound upon places & pensions. I need not say that the last is a most popular tax.

The Clear produce of the several branches, after paying the charges of collecting them amount annually, to about seven millions and three quarters; besides the two millions and a quarter,[e] raised

---

[a] *I.* la   [b] *I.* been of   [c] *I.* officer   [d] *I.* appellation. The 7th
[e] *I.* three quarters

annually upon an average by the Land and Malt tax: The whole*a*
forming an ordinary revenue of ten Millions Sterling per annum.

The first and great call upon the perpetual revenue is to discharge
the interest of the national debt; an incumbrance scarce heard of
before the revolution. An unsettled government, expensive wars and
a desire natural enough to our ancestors, rather to load their
posterity than themselves were the chief springs which gave rise to
this new and complicated system, which has been pursued with so
much constancy that the national debt now amounts to the enormous
sum of £145.000.000; the annual interest of which is about four
millions and three quarters[.] Some reasons may be alledged in
favor of a publick debt; a certain proportion of it may connect the
people to the present government, and even afford some conveniences for trade. It is difficult to fix that proportion; but our
enormous taxes which raise the price of all our manufacture; the
ruin of the landed interest, and the anticipation of those resources,
which should be reserved for the greatest emergencies, shew that
we have long since exceeded it.

The produce of the several duties were formerly appropriated to
the payment of particular debts. They are now made mutual
securities for each, and distinguished only into three capital funds.
1 The Agregate fund, 2 The General fund, and 3 The South Sea
fund. The surplus of the whole, (particularly of the first, is collected
under the name of the sinking fund, and remains at the disposal of
parliament, either to supply the deficiences of the annual taxes; or
(if possible to diminish the principle [*sic*] of the debt. This Surplus,
(from the encrease of trade and the reduction of interest amounted
in 1764, to two millions & a quarter

The Sinking fund is charged*b* with an annuity for the King's life,
designed for the support of his houshold, and to defray the civil
expences of government. It is called the Civil list and now consists
of a Clear sum of £800.000 per annum.; which is somewhat less
than the more complex establishment which was given George 11.
Charles 11, and James 11 enjoyed indeed a much greater revenue;
but then they supported out of it the fleet and army: which, since
the revolution the parliament has chose to provide for annual.

We have now finished this vast title of law, *The King*; the result
of which seems to be that the Crown has lost much within this
century by having at present no independent property, nor any

---

a I. om. whole   *b I.* ti

arbitrary or mysterious prerogative. A vast revenue of which he is the sole manager, and a regular standing army of which he is the perpetual general have made ample amends for these losses. The reign of interest, is less odious than that of fear & more solid than that of prejudice.

[C. ix. p. 327–354 *Of subordinate Magistrates*] Those subordinate magistrates who are the proper object of law, are such as have a jurisdiction & authority dispersedly throughout the Kingdom; and first of *Sheriffs*; so called from the Saxon Shire-Reeve, Bailif of the County.

When the Earls, the ancient Guardians of the Counties, became meer Titulars; their deputies the Sheriffs (Vice-Comites) succeeded to the custody of these districts[.] From a demotractical principle of our constitution which did not even expire in the storms of the Norman Conquest[a]; the Sheriffs were chosen by the people, till the reign of Edward 11, when it was transferred by Parliament to the Chancellor, Treasurer, Judges &c. This regulation[b] still subsists. Every year the twelve Judges, with some great officers of state, nominate three persons for each county; out of whom, the King appoints one to be Sheriff.

In his Judicial capacity the Sheriffs authority is as confined, as in his ministerial one it is extensive. 1. As the King's Minister "he "represents his person, collects his casual revenues" preserves the peace of his county, and (if necessary) can assemble the power of it (posse Comitatus.) either against foreign or domestick enemies. 2. As Minister of the Laws, he arrests both Criminals & debtors, is answerable for their persons, summons the Jury, and is obliged to execute their sentence, either by himself or by some other person. 3.[c] As Minister of the people, he assembles the Freeholders for the election of their members, decides the qualifications of the voters, and returns the persons elected. The greatest part of the business is now left to the Under Sheriff—who is usually a Lawyer.

The Coroner (Coronator) of whom there are several in each county, is charged to enquire into the cause of all violent deaths, and to commit the murderer; (if he and his jury have found any) to prison for further tryal. This employment is now exercised by very mean persons.

The Justices (formerly Conservators) of the peace were formerly elected by the people, till the minority of Edward iii; when the Queen Regent desirous of preserving peace in her yet unsettled

[a] *I.* Conquests   [b] *I.* alteration   [c] *I.* Th

government, issued the[a] King's commission to her friends in every county. Their number is indefinite and at present very great; and their functions have been so multiplied, by many acts of parliament as to require a separate treatise.

The High Constables in every hundred & the petty constables of each town or parish, are to keep the King's peace; and for that purpose, they are armed with very large powers of, arresting, breaking open houses &c; the extent of which, luckily very few of them are acquainted with[.]

The Surveyors of the Highways are to call together all the inhabitants of their parish in order to mend them, six days in the years. Those who *Keep* occupy lands, send a team,[b] for every draught, or every fifty pounds a year. The others owe their personal labour, or another man in their room.

The Overseers of the poor, (appointed in Queen Elizabeth reign) raise a tax upon the inhabitants of the parish in order to support the helpless, and employ the idle part of it. As this brings a burden upon a parish, regulations to prevent a stranger from too easily acquiring a dew settlement. The legal means may be reduced to forty days residence, after having given publick notice. But several circumstan[ces][c] may supply the place of such notice; as serving any parish office, any estate, a tenement of 10 pounds per annum, an annual service &c. All these poor-laws are now as intricate as ineffectual[.]

[C. x p. 354-364. *Of the People*] This most natural division of the people is into Natives and Aliens. According to the common principles, (which seem rather drawn from utility than from nature) the former has contracted by his birth an obligation of an indelible[d] character; which[e] for ever submits him to the laws of his native country, & which is known by the name of Allegiance. The duties which it imposes are comprized in the oaths of Allegiance, Supremacy, and abjuration, which must be taken by every servant of the government, and may by two Justices be tendered to any dissafected person.

The Alien become a legal by an [Act] of the Legislature only; in which his exclusions from all places of trust or profit under the Crown, or from the body of the people must be particularly specified. The King may grant some privileges of naturalization (under the

---

[a] *I.* her   [b] *I.* dr   [c] *Word left uncompleted at line end in MS.*   [d] *I.* e
[e] *I.* & which

appellation of Denizen; particularly that of acquiring landed property by purchase, tho' not by inheritance. The Children of Natives born abroad are considered as Natives; as well as those of Aliens born in England. Some other more indirect means of naturalization are allowed of; but all suppose and demand a communion with the Church of England.

[C xi. p. 364–384. *Of the Clergy*] The Ecclesiastical order is now very properly subjected to the Civil; tho' they still enjoy some privileges both as individuals and as a body. The King recovered at the reformation his ancient right of appointing the Governors of this order: the Archbishops & Bishops. There is indeed the shadow of an election still left, but reduced to nothing by the following powers of the Crown. 1. A permission is necessary to enable the chapter to proceed to an election. 2. It is always accompanied by a recommendatory letter in favor of a person to be chose. 3. He cannot be consecrated without letters patent, directed to the Archbishop &c. 4. He must receive his temporalities from the King; who by his election acquires a right of presenting, to whatever benefices, he was in possession of.

The most numerous part of the Clergy, and certainly the most usefull are the parish priests. These are distinguished[a] into, Rectors or Parsons, & Vicars. The former represent the *person* of the Church, and have a property for their lives in the parsonage tithes, glebe and all other dues. The latter are only perpetual curattes, with a regular stipend, usually consisting of certain small tithes[b] and a portion of the glebe; whilst the benefice it is annexed to the patron of the living, who becomes properly the Parson or Spiritual corporation. These are called impropriations and were originally a refinement of Monastic policy. The Convents, by various means, and with the consent both of Kings and bishops, acquired the property of a great number of benefices; and allowed something to the Monk whom they sent to serve them. But abuses soon arising, A statute was made (4 Henry iv) to ordain that the Vicar (a secular priest) should be perpetual, with an independant stipend. The[c] dissolution of monasteries would have disapropriated all these parsonages (amounting to a third of the parishes[d] in England;) had not an act of parliament vested them in the Crown; who has since granted many of them away, and to lay persons, whose families now enjoy them[.]

[a] *I.* the p   [b] *I.* th   [c] *I.* A   [d] *I.* parished

The method of becoming a parson or Vicar is by, 1. Holy orders.
2. Presentation of the patron to the Bishop. 3. Institution, which is
the Bishop's approbation & gives him the spiritualities of the living.
4. Induction. By which He takes possession of the temporalities.

[C. xii. p. 384–394. *Of the Civil State*] The Civil State is divided
into, the Nobility and Commonalty. The first which is composed
only of the peerage of great Britain, has been already considered as
an agregate body; their several degrees or titles of honor are now
to be taken notice of.

The Norman conquest introduced or at least confirmed among us
the idea of a feudal nobility. All Lords of manors, who held their
lands immediately from the King, were by that title his Barons and
the hereditary members of his great council: seve[ral]*a* of these
with the name of Earl, enjoyed*b* likewise the Hereditary government
of a particular county. A distinction began to be made towards the
reign of King John; the more considerable Barons only were*c*
personally summoned to Parliament, and with this right the title
likewise was confined only to them. Succeeding Kings, conferred
the new honours of Duke, Marquiss and Viscount, and at last all
these dignities from territorial, became gentilitial; the family not
the land became the object of them. Peers are now created either
by writ or patent; their nobility (except one extraordinary instance
of a parliamentary degradation) can be lost only by death, or
attainder.

The Commonalty (the rest of the nation) are not so nicely
distinguished. Their principal legal divisions are those of Knights,
Esquires, Gentlemen Yeomen, artificers and labourers. In all
tryals these are all considered as peers, viz equal, to each other; in
the same manner as the Nobility; with this difference that the
Nobleman is tryed by the whole body of his peers; and the commoner by a select number of his.

[Ch. xiii. p. 394–410 *Of the Military State*] It is needless to repeat
that under the Feudal System, the King's tenants held their lands
by Knight's service and were both intrusted and charged with the
defence of the Kingdom. When their personal service began to be
commuted into money the able bodied men of every county*d* were
trained & exercised in the manner directed by the several statutes
of armour. This Militia supported by our ancient princes laid aside

---

a Word uncompleted at line end in MS.   *b I.* enjoys   *c I.* were only
d I. country

by James i, & revived after the restoration has at length in our days ripened into a more regular, and usefull form: *Esto perpetua!*

As to those standing armies which the ambition of some have rendered necessary to all: our laws consider them rather as temporary excrescencies than as natural parts of our constitution; their*a* legal existence which we date only from the revolution is founded upon the following principles.

1. The King (as has been said) has the sole right of the sword, and all orders and commissions relative to the levying, training, or employing any military forces can proceed only from him. This right was solemnly recognized after the restoration; but was somewhat doubtfull at the time, the long parliament assumed it[.]

2. The consent of Parliament is indispensably necessary to give exercise and activity to the King's prerogative. It was declared at that memorable Æra of our liberties it has been declared "that the "Keeping a standing army in this Kingdom without the consent of "parliament is contrary to law"*6* This consent and the necessary supplies to maintain it, must be reiterated every year. Thus our army tho' grown perpetual, is only annual; and may every year be anihilated by the negative vote of any branch of the legislature

3. This consent is always accompanied by an act for the better payment of the army; and their quarters; & for preventing mutiny and desertion. By this act a new form of judicature is introduced into the army. Court martials are substituted to Juries, and in case of mutiny, desertion, cowardice, treachery, or disobedience to lawfull orders are even impowered (with the King's approbation) to punish the offender with death.

4. As armies require the direction of a pretty absolute authority; the parliament has invested the Crown with a discretionary power of forming articles of war trying crimes by those articles and inflicting such penalties as those articles shall direct; with the proviso only that such penalties shall not extend either to life or limb. Mr B laments the condition of the unhappy soldiers, the only slaves in a free country. But when as in modern institutions, the defence of the nation is entrusted to the vilest part of it: such wild beasts must either*b* tremble themselves; or else they will soon make their masters tremble.

The Condition of the sailor is somewhat more liberal: their articles of war are enacted by parliament not framed by the crown.

a I. the   *b I. om.* either

But the[a] power or rather license of pressing is contrary to reason, humanity and every principle of freedom, and is suffered only from the still more powerfull plea of necessity.

[C. xiv p. 410–421 *Of Master & Servant*] Besides the publick relations of which we have already treated; there are some others of as general, but of a more private nature. Such are those, of Master and servant, Husband and wife, parent and child, and guardian & ward.

The laws of England are unacquainted with strict and absolute slavery: tho' in order to accomodate themselves in some degree to the modern institution of negro Slaves they allow the master a kind of right to the perpetual service of John or Thomas. The right is indeed scarce reconciliable with any notions of equity: since it is founded upon no voluntary contract, nor compensated by any just equivalent. Notwithstanding this irregular complyance with the interests of commerce, the humanity of our laws still protects the slave and restrains the cruelty or injustice of the masters. It is easily conceived the our laws do not become more favorable to the slave upon his receiving Baptism and that his embracing a new faith, makes makes no alteration as to his civil rights.

As all other services are founded upon those voluntary contracts, the particular conditions of them are left to the discretion of the parties; except in the case of Servants for husbandry whose wages and term of service are[b] regulated by authority, and apprentices whose contract is of a more solemn nature as well as longer duration, and tends not only to the advantage of the master but likewise, to the instruction of the servant, who is a kind of pupil.

The duties of this relation are the natural consequences of protection on one side and obedience on the other. They have a mutual right and obligation to defend and support each other. The master is answerable for whatever is done by his Servant with his consent either declared or implied; and according to a very equitable Rule he may be a loser, but never can be a gainer by the trust reposed in his Servant: but if the action be in itself illegal the person that ordered and he that executed it, are equally liable to punishment.

[C. xv p. 421–434 *Of Husband & Wife*] Our laws consider[c] Matrimony only as a Civil contract. The holiness of that tye is left entirely to the Ecclesiastical law. The sole conditions which constitute the validity of the engagement are that the parties were, 1[d]

---

[a] *I.* their   [b] *I.* is   [c] *I.* considere   [d] *I.* w

Willing to contract, 2 Able to contract, and 3 that they actually did contract in the proper forms & solemnities required by law. The first of these requisite conditions needs no explanation. The second is always supposed except either of the parties labour under any legal disabilities, viz the having already contracted a prior marriage; which (besides the punishment incident to Polygamy) renders void[a] any subsequent marriage; the not[b] enjoying the use of reason; the being under the legal age which is fixed at fourteen for males and twelve for females: any engagement contracted before that term may be rejected by either of the parties. From that age to the compleat period of twenty one years, the consent of parents or[c] guardians is still so indispensably required that the want of it annulls whatever engagement the minor may have entered into. This last clause was[d] superadded by the last Marriage act; and has been considered in very various lights. All marriages must be celebrated by[e] a person in orders in a parish church or chapel, (unless by particular dispensation) after having been preceeded by publication of banns; or license from the spiritual judge.

When any of these requisites have been wanting, our laws do not annull the Marriage; (for that is a practice unknown to them, but they consider it as never having had an existence, the union as meretricious, and the children as bastards. There are some other disabilities which have the same effect in the spiritual courts, such as consanguinity, affinity, some corporal infirmities, and perhaps a prior contract. When any of these occur the marriage is not ipso facto void (as in the case of civil impediments, but only voidable by a sentence which must be obtained during the life of the parties. An absolute separation a vinculo Matrimonii is the consequence of such a sentence. There is milder separation a Thoro et Mensa, which operates only on the consequences of the Matrimonial union; not on the essence of it. And this is the sole redress which our laws afford to the complaints of ill temper or even adultery; unless the Legislature should interpose (as it has frequently done of late, and by an act of supreme power dissolve the contract.

The matrimonial union is so intimate[f] according to our laws; that the very legal existence of the wife is lost in that of the husband, with whom in general she composes but one person. From this principle flow almost all the[g] legal rights, duties and disabilities of

---

[a] *I.* voids   [b] *I. om.* not   [c] *I.* of   [d] *I.* is   [e] *I.* in a pub
I. so very intimate   [g] *I. om.* the

either of them, such as their mutual inability to covenant with, or bear evidence for or against each other; as well as the obligation of the husband to maintain his wife & to pay her debts contracted either before their marriage; or afterwards for necessaries only. She is however sometimes considered as a separate but inferior being; and as her husband still*[a] enjoys a right of chastising her; so his constraint or authority excuses her from the punishment of some inferior crimes; but not of either felony or murder.

[C. xvi p. 434–448 *Of Parent & Child*] This universal relation is divided by all Civil laws into Spurious and legitimate: and our laws define a legitimate child to be one, born at a time, when his parents are actually married

Marriage has been encouraged by every civilized Society; in order to ascertain the father of each particular child, and to make him answerable to the community, for the protection, maintenance and education of those infants he has brought into the world. Such is the spirit which ought to animate the laws of every Society. Ours seems rather imperfect in that respect. They are almost totally silent on the last head: and a father is at liberty to regulate or neglect the education of his children, as he thinks fit. The obligation of allowing them a necessary maintenance is likewise circumscribed[b] to the absolute necessaries of life, and even to the case where the Children either thro' infancy, disease or accident are unable to procure them by their own labour. This provision tho' perhaps sufficient for the lower classes of mankind is almost equivalent to a total desertion, where the unavoidable consequences of a softer education has formed both the mind and body to habits of ease and delicacy. Our laws seem to have reposed a entire confidence in the powers of natural affection; at least when they[c] are not checked by religious zeal; since a Popish or Jewish Parent may be legally compelled to allow his Christian or Protestant child a fit and decent maintenance. Our laws indulge[d] the parent in the unrestrained disposal of his fortune; which he may totally deprive his children of; unless he is restrained by particular family compacts: a dreadfull power indeed: since the momentary caprice of old age may by a rash but irrevocable sentence make an indiscreet perhaps an innocent youth for ever miserable. A Medium might surely be discovered: and the Child tho' not liable to want from the tyranny of his parent might yet find it his interest as well as his duty to

---

a I. om. still   *b I.* extremely circumscribed   *c I.* they the   *d I.* al

deserve his favor. The absolute power which the Roman father enjoyed over the life of his child in a virtuous state, it might be a usefull supplement to publick justice, and nature which may often be too careless or injust towards her offspring, would always start with horror at the thoughts of destroying it. In this case contrary to general rules, the greater trust seems of less dangerous consequence, than the lesser. In our laws the strict paternal power is very confined. It extends only to moderate correction for the benefit of the child's education, and to approving or preventing his marriage. He has no right over his son's estate, than as guardian or trustee, and his authority entirely ceases at the age of twenty one. Till that period however he may delegate it to another, either during his life or after his decease

A Bastard, in our law, is a child born out of lawfull[a] and he is not legitimated, as in the civil and canon law, by the subsequent marriage of his parents. Each of these methods has it's advocates. In general it may be asked since the end of law is the prevention of a Vague commerce between the sexes[b], whether it is better to deter them by severity, or to recover them from it by gentleness. Children[c] born too long after the husband's death are likewise bastards; but if the Widow marries so soon that it may be doubtfull to which of the husbands, the child belongs, he may chuse his father when he arrives at years of discretion. A Bastard is entitled to maintenance and protection, and enjoys every priviledge of a man and a subject. His chief incapacity consists in his having no ancestors nor relation. Every thing, his very[d] name must be of his own acquiring. He can inherit from no one; and can have no heirs but of his own body.

[C. xvii p. 448-454 *Of Guardian & Ward*] The Guardian is a kind of temporary parent, appointed to take of the Infants person and estate during his minority. These are of several sorts. 1 Guardians by nature; these are the father and, (in some cases) the mother of an infant who is possessed of an independant estate. 2. Guardians by soccage or common law and this trust always devolves to the next of kin to whom the inheritance can never descend: The reason of this last restriction is obvious and natural. Both these sorts of guardians continue only till the Minor is fourteen years of age: 3 Guardians by statute. Every parent may by will dispose of the custody of his child till the age of[e] twenty one to any

---

[a] *At end of line in MS.* [b] *I. om.* between the sexes [c] *I.* The [d] *I.* ever
[e] *I. om.* of

person, not a Popish recusant. When the minor has attained that
age, the Guardian must give him an account, of all^a that he has
transacted on his behalf, and must answer for all losses by his
wilfull default or negligence. Of late years, many Guardians have
chose to indemnify themselves by accounting to the court of
chancery, the general and supreme guardian of all infants

An infant is incapable of any legal act, deed or contract; with
some few exceptions, such in particular as that of presenting to an
ecclesiastical benefice. There are however several periods of his
minority. A male at *twelve*^{b} may take^c the oath of allegiance; at
fourteen he is at years of discretion, may chuse his Guardian, and
dispose of his personals,: he then becomes liable to capital punishment. At *seventeen* he may be an executor, and at *twenty one* he is
at his own disposal and may aliene^d his lands goods and chattels

[C xviii p. 455–473 *Of Corporations*] Corporations are a kind of
artificial persons who enjoy a legal immortality, by maintaining a
perpetual succession of individuals^e invested with the same rights
and priviledges. Mr B. attributes the invention to the Roman and
the improvement of it to our own laws; tho' for my part I can see
nothing so wonderfull in either. Since Kings or councils, priests
or Magistrates have existed, there must always have been Corporations both sole and agregate; which is first general division of them
They are likewise distinguished into. 1 Ecclesiastical; as Bishops,
Chapters, Parsons &c. 2. Civil; which are designed for a variety of
temporal purposes, and 3 Eleemosynary such as all hospitals and
colleges. The King's consent is necessary for the erection of any
corporation.

All corporate Bodies have many natural & inseparable rights,
either formally or tacitly annexed to them a perpetual succession,
the power of purchasing or granting lands, except in the cases,
which are very many where they are restrained by statute; a common
seal to manifest their intentions, and a right of making bye laws to
regulate the conduct of the members. The consent of the Corporation must always be signified by that of the greater number. The
Sages of the law^f have been very jocular upon some particular
privileges and disabilities incident to a Corporation agregate and
Sir Edward Coke has condescended to remark that a Corporation
agregate cannot be hanged because it has no body, nor be excommunicated because it has no soul.

^{a} *I*. th ^{b} *I*. f ^{c} *I*. cho ^{d} *I*. dispose ^{e} *I*. indesti ^{f} *I*. laws

The Visitation of these bodies with a coercive jurisdiction over them, varies according to their different nature and is still a point of great obscurity. It is held that the Ordinary or Bishop is the visitor of all Ecclesiastical corporations, that in all Eleemosynary one this right belongs to the founder & his heirs, or the persons he may substitute in their room: that the King is the sole founder of all civil corporations; which can be only visited by his Judges of the court of King's bench

A Corporation may be dissolved, by an act of Parliament, by the natural death of all the members, and by the surrender or forfeiture of their Charter. This last was the foundation of the famous Quo Warranto's of Charles II, which at that time were rather contrary to liberty, than to law; but succeeding times have better secured the rights and privileges of these necessary bodies.

The End of the First Book

Hints. N°. I

Historians friends to Virtue? yes—with exceptions.
1. Allow great Latitude in the means.
2. Incline more to personal than Social virtues.
3. Moderns if religious, pervert their natural Ideas.[a]

Difference of the Civil Wars[1] in France and England.
1. The English caused by riches and long[b] peace. The French by long wars and impatience of Ease. Union of the House of Commons. Power & discords of the Guises Bourbons &c. |

Hints. N°. II

2. The English chiefly used the axe; the French the dagger.— Contraste, Mary Q[c] of Scots beheaded, the Marshal d'Ancre murdered. Cause of this difference. the[d] superior corruption of the French? equity[e] of the English? Fanaticism?[f]—independency[g] of the French Nobles?——The Custom borrowed from the Italians, & communicated to the Scotch.
3. The English left to themselves The Pope, Spain, England &c took part in the French Wars. The Duke of Mayenne preferred to the Admiral de Coligny.[2] |

Hints. N°. III.

Davila's[3] general Errors.

1. The election and even Existence of Pharamund[4] doubtfull. The assembly and resolution of the Franks chimerical.
2. The Stability of their government ridiculous. It varied every age.[(1)h]

---

[a] *II. om. this third point*   [b] *I. om.* long   [c] *II.* Queen   [d] *I.* not the
[e] *I.* nor equity   [f] *I.* nor Fanaticism   [g] *I.* nor independency *II.* Independence
[h] *Cued by* (.) *in MS.*

3. The Salic Law[5] not fundamental. established by accidents in the xiv[th] Century

4. The first Prince had no inherent right to the regency. The point is yet undetermined.

[1] See Mably's[6] Observations sur l'histoire de France &c.

Henry iii[7] studied Politicks with an Italian Abbè. Vanity |

Hints. N°. IV

of that Science.—Ignorance why *we* have have acted——how *we* shall act—how *others* will act. Our sense, eloquence secrecy &c the only principles. assisted by the confidence of others—Example of Henry iii, his inactivity, his violence—of Henry iv.——The proper time for changing his religion how very nice——If too soon the Catholics[a] would be suspicious if too late, grown desperate

---

The effect of Civil Wars on the minds of Men——A general ferment of fanaticism, discord, and faction

Two singular exceptions. Montagne in his retirement |

Hints. N°. V

Henry iv[8] on the Throne—He loved and trusted Mankind—How different from Charles ii!

France little altered by 40 years civil War. The same limits— The succession attacked but preserved.—The regal Authority unempaired. Violent principles detested & forgotten—

Power of the Governors of Provinces, direct and absolute over the Military; their Levies expeditions disposal of offices strong places, gentlemen & guards——indirect over the Finances and Justice; only checked by the Parliaments.

The Duke of Mayenne &c wanted to[b] make them Hereditary.—— The followers of Henry iv |

[a] *I.* his Enemies   [b] *I. om.* to

Hints. N°. VI

made the same demand: had he consented, the Feudal System was
again established

---

1. French Cavalry famous in the xvi[th] Century—All Noblesse, 5000
Gentlemen at once in the army of Henry iv——Brave but impatient
of labour & fatigue.—Laid aside their Lances, and fought with
pistols & Carabines—The custom blamed but at last adopted.
2. The Spanish Infantry well disciplined- Walloons, -Italians. The
Duke of Parma—Retreat from before Amiens. Saying of Henry iv
3. Swiss Phalanx. March from Meaux[a]
4. English & Germans brave but undisciplined |

Hints N°. VII

Religious Wars.

1. Persecution inspires union obstinacy, and at last resentment.—A
sect becomes a party—Why Christianity suffered so long——
Greeks & Asiatics—Objection from Martyrs—Difference of Active
& passive Courage.—Chinese.
2. Connection of Religion and politics. The Leaders seldom free
from enthusiasm, or the followers from ambition.
3. Other[b] passions mix with these——Massacre of Paris owing to
revenge—of Charles ix.——of Guise—of the Parisians

The Ruling passion?. very rare. most passions confined to times |

Hints N°. VIII

places, persons, circumstances—Love, Hatred, revenge envy
jealousy, Vanity &c—Patriotism seldom even a passion.—Ambition
generally mixed with other passions, often subservient to them—
when pure as in Cæsar or Richelieu must succeed or perish——
Avarice perhaps the only permanent[c] ruling passion.

---

[a] *I.* Dreux   [b] *I.* Others   [c] *II.* ruling permanent passion

Search then the ruling passion, there alon[e]
The fools are constant, & the wise are Know[n] & [c] Pope.[9]

Bobinet in the Comtesse d'Escarbagnas, and Sir Hugh in the merry
Wives of Windsor[10]—ridiculous resemblance without probability
of imitation

The Popish Worship like the Pagan? Certainly. Huetius's |

Hints N° IX

ode will serve for either Mary or Diana.—But this[a] resemblance
probably without imitation.—Reasons

1. Images, ornaments, garlands lights odors, music affect the
   senses of all Men—are found in the worship of the Indians
   Chinese, Americans &c.
2. Images opposed whilst the Pagans subsisted, received as soon
   as they were extinct
3. The Jubilee invented by Priests who had scarcely heard of
   the Secular games.
4. Monks & relicks of Martyrs the favorite superstitions of the
   iv[th] Century, detested by the Pagans. Middleton,[11] elegant &
   just in facts[b] car|ries

Hints N°. X

his paralel too far.—the Sacerdotal order on quite different principles
from that of old Rome—Warburton dogmatic,—just in his inference, weak in his argument.
See Huetii Commentarius p 258–262

Freedom of thought.

1. Infallible Authority allows not the faculties of the Mind fair
   play.—May be just & happy but is a Yoke—Grace and Faith—
   Various degrees of Slavery[c]—Faith of the Pagan light and easy—of

[a] I. But rather   [b] I. om. in facts   [c] II. om. Grace . . . Slavery

the Christian binding & comprehensive—of the Papist variable—
Plutarch Tillotson[a] & Bellarmin.[12]
2. Authority of Doctors—a voluntary slavery under the name |

Hints. N°. XI

of reason—how common! how pernicious![b]—the ancient Sects—
professed[c] Philosophers how bigotted—Romans &c more liberal,
heard several before they chose—Obstinate in their choice yet
sometimes changed.
3. Authority of our own Systems. Men of imagination.[d]—
Bolingbroke—dogmatic.—True freedom & Scepticism[e]——
Ease and pleasantry—Bayle and a Student of Salamanca.[13]
    A Freethinker may be rational or wild, superficial or profound——
However the road is open before him, & his sight clear.
    Freedom of individual relative to general Slavery—

Hints N°. XII

An Englishman may reject with | contempt what an Italian examines
with caution—yet the Italian the Freethinker—
Il Voto Sanguinario of Muratori.——The tenets of Atterbury &
Courayer nearly the same, their manner of thinking how different—
The one tended to slavery the other to Liberty.

    Maxim of la Bruyere of Governments; when quiet how ever
disturbed! when disturbed how ever quiet! very just.—Supported
by the interest of a few, Courtiers Priests Soldiers——real power
of the Latter—honor and attachment[f]—despotic government more
secure in large states—Indolence, prejudices &c of the |

Hints N°. XIII

Multitude—chain of imitation—power of habit—necessity of order
—Every conspiracy a new Society——Danger of each Individual—

---

[a] *I. om.* Tillotson   [b] *II. om.* how pernicious!   [c] *I.* ancient   [d] *I.* genius.
om. — Bolingbroke— *II.* dogmatic.—Bolingbroke.   [e] *I.* just Scepticism
[f] *I om.* honor & attachment

Extreme danger[a] Strong passions and great talents—When the charm is once broke[b] every man feels his real strength and despises the Idol——Hopes[c] succeed to fears—The bond of faction grows stronger, that of government weaker——Vicissitude

---

Character and conduct of Brutus.[14]

Obstinate patriotism of Scipio and Cato after the battle of Pharsalia—collect a formidable force in Africa.[(1)d] |

Hints. N°. XIV

second Civil war—Brutus the nephew and Disciple of Cato.—remained quiet in Italy—studied eloquence with Cicero.—Their panygerics on Cato[(2)]—attended with no danger

The more moderate Patriots had submitted to Cæsar,——Cicero, Varro, Marcellus &c—Their motives, horror of Civil War, despair of success, cruelty of the Pompeian party, Cæsar[']s mildness, hopes that he would restore the Republic—Their private life, melancholy complaints, Cicero's boldness.[(3)]

Brutus submitted immediately after the battle—made the first advances,—revealed |

Hints. N°. XV

Pompey's designs.[(4)], was admitted into friendship and confidence. —Proconsul[e] of the Cisalpine Gaul(.)[f]—his equity & mildness.[(5)]—importance of the Province, military force.[(6)]—had the War been transferred to Italy, Brutus must have betrayed Cæsar or the Republic.

His further honors, first Prætor, and Consul Elect.[(7)g]—præferred to Cassius——No freedom of election.[(8)]—Voluntary engagements —to obey the decrees[(9)]——to defend the Person of Cæsar[(1)]—no faith with Tyrants[(2)]—excuse rather than motive.

---

[a] *I. om.* Extreme danger *II.* extreme danger of   [b] *II.* broken   [c] *I.* The bond   [d] *Cued by* (.) *in MS.*   [e] *I.* Governor   [f] *II.* (5) *Other numbers altered consistently*   [g] *II.* (1) *New page; other numbers altered consistently*

Respect for Brutus.[3]——Tyrannicide, hatred of Kings——
greatness of Rome—Fame of Cæsar, humanity of Brutus |

[1] Lucan. Pharsal. ix. 18 &c magni post funera, partes Libertatis erunt.
Hirt. de bello Afr. C. 1, 2 &c & M. Guichardt's Military Commen.
[2] Cic. Orator. C. 10. ad Attic. xiii 46, xii 21.
[3] See Cicero to Atticus, Varro Papirius Pætus Cæcina[a] &c. pro Marcell.[b] 8, 9. pro
Ligario. 3. et passim
[4] Plut. in Brut. Bayle au mot *Brutus*. (.) Plut. Aurel Victor de VI. C. 82. Cic. ad
Fam. vi. 6. XIII. 10 &c
[5] Cic. Orator. C. 10. Plut
[6] Montesq: grand. des Roma C xi. Cic. Philipic. iii. C 5.
[7] Vell. Pat. L ii. C 56, 58. Plut
[8] Sueton in Cæsar. C. 41, 76 Lucan. v. 381. &c.

> Fingit solemnia campi;
> et non admissæ *dirimit* suffragia plebis
> leg. *diribet* meo periculo

[9] Appian. de bell. Civ. L ii[c] p 494.
[1] Cic. pro Marcell. C. 10.
[2] Appian de B. C. L ii. p 515
[3] Vell. Pater. L ii. C 72. M. Anto & August. ap. Plut. in Brut

---

Hints. N°. XVI

---

[d]In scelus it Pharium Romani pœna Tyranni:
Exemplumq: perit[4]—— ————
L'exemple, que tu dois, periroit avec toi.[5]

Fine imitation—The sentiment itself truly Roman—great in
Lucan's mouth—far greater in Pompey's Widow.—has a sublime
effect in the Tragedy, as it engages Cornelia to discover the conspiracy, and save the life of her enemy.

[4] Lucan. x. 343.
[5] Le Pompèe de Corneille.[15] Act. iv. Scen. 4.

---

[e]Thucydides and Guicciardini[16] in the true Station for historians
of their own times——mistake of Mr Warton[17] as to the latter[1]——
Both acquainted with business[f] of peace and war——Their
characters procured them every information— |

[a] *I. om.* Cæcina *II.* Cecinna   [b] *II.* Mariell   [c] *I. om.* L ii   [d] *II. treats*
this as part of "Brutus" hints   [e] *II. treats this as part of preceding item*   [f] *II. the*
business

Hints N°. XVII

—had studied the greatest men of their times—better acquainted with them all, than each of them was with the others—Personal knowledge of great men, the chief advantage of their personal Memoirs——Disapointed in those of Cæsar—we perceive the Scholar and the Soldier, we lose the man—except in the simplicity with which he relates his greatest actions——The Memoirs of Xenophon much more characteristic—Those of de Retz still more so, pity the events are so little interesting |

(1) Adventurer. N°. 123

Digression on the Character
of Brutus.

The Memory of Cæsar, celebrated as it is, has not been transmitted down to posterity with such uniform and encreasing applause as that of his PATRIOT ASSASSIN. Marc Antony acknowledged the rectitude of his Intentions. Augustus refused to violate his Statues. [1] All the great Writers of the succeeding Age, enlarged on his Praises, [2] and more than two hundred Years after the Establishment of the Imperial Government the Character of Brutus was studied as the Perfect Idea of Roman Virtue. [3] In England as in France, in modern Italy as in ancient Rome, his name has always been mentioned with Respect by the Adherents of Monarchy, [3] and pronounced with Enthusiasm by the Friends of Freedom. It may seem rash and invidious to appeal from the Sentence of Ages; yet surely I may be permitted to enquire, in what consisted THE DIVINE VIRTUE OF BRUTUS?

The few Patriots, who by a bold and well concerted Enterprize, have delivered their Country from foreign or domestic Slavery, Timoleon, and the elder Brutus, Andrew Doria, and Gustavus Vasa, the three Peasants of Switzerland, [4] and the four princes of Orange, excite the warmest Sensations of Esteem and Gratitude in those breasts which feel for the interest of Mankind.[1] But the Design of the younger Brutus was vast and perhaps impracticable, the Execution feeble and unfortunate. Neither as a Statesman nor as a General did Brutus ever approve himself equal to the arduous task he had so rashly undertaken, of restoring the Commonwealth; instead of restoring it, the Death of a mild and generous Usurper produced only a series of Civil Wars, and the Reign of three Tyrants whose union and whose discord were alike fatal to the Roman People.

The sagacious Tully often laments that he could be pleased with nothing in the Ides of March, except the Ides themselves; that the Deed was executed with a manly Courage, but supported by childish counsels; that the Tyranny survived the Tyrant; as the Conspirators satisfied with Fame and Revenge, had neglected every Measure that might have restored public Liberty. [5] Whilst Brutus and Cassius contemplated their own Heroism with the most happy Complacency, Marc Antony who had preserved his Life, and the first Magistracy of the State by their injudicious clemency, seized the Papers and Treasure of the Dictator, inflamed the People and the Veterans, and drove them out of Rome and Italy, without any other Opposition than some grave Remonstrances which the patriots vainly addressed to the Consul.[6]

The[a] eloquence of Cicero, and the dangerous aid of young Cæsar awakened, in the Senate a spirit of freedom and resistance. Brutus and Cassius had time to seize on Macedonia and Syria, whilst the Forces of Antony were diverted and almost destroyed in the memorable Siege of Modena. The Legions stationed in those Provinces acknowledged them as lawfull Proconsuls, the Wealth of the East fell into their Hands, and they had collected an Army of one hundred thousand men,[7] before the Triumvirs had cemented their Union with the noblest blood of Rome, and were prepared to lead their veteran Legions against the last Defenders of the Public Liberty. Cassius was of Opinion, that they should protract their military Operations into the approaching Winter; but though Cassius was the older and the better Soldier,[8] had been the first Author of the Conspiracy and was the principal Support of the War, he yielded, with a Sigh, to the authority of Brutus, whose Mind, oppressed with laborious Anxiety, wished impatiently for an immediate decision[b].[9] The decision was unfavorable; and both the Chiefs, relinquishing all their remaining Hopes, and withdrawing themselves from the Calamities, which they had brought on their Country, put an End to their Lives by a hasty Act of Déspair: "Brutus and Cassius (says the President Montesquieu) killed them-"selves, with a precipitancy that cannot be excused; and it is "impossible to read this part of their History, without pitying the "Republic, which was thus abandoned. The Death of Cato was the "Catastrophe of the Tragedy; but these Men, in some Measure "opened the Tragedy by their own Deaths.["][10]

The Justice of the memorable Ides of March has been a Subject of Controversy above eighteen hundred Years; and will so remain, as long as[c] the interests of the Community, shall be considered by different Tempers in different Lights. Men of high and active

---

[a] *I.* A new spirit which the Eloquence of Cicero, and the dangerous aid of young Cæsar awakened, in the senate, gave Brutus and Cassius time   [b] *II.* division
[c] *I. om.* as

Spirits, who deem the Loss of Liberty, or sometimes in other Words the Loss of Power, the worst of misfortunes, will approve the use of every Stratagem and every Weapon in the Chace of the common Foe of Society. They will ask how a Tyrant who has raised himself above the Laws and usurped the Forces of the State, can be punished except by an Assassination; and whether the circumstance that most aggravates his Crime, ought to secure his Person and Government. On the other hand, the Lovers of Order and Modera-tion, who are swayed by the Calm of Reason, rather than by the impetuosity of Passion, will never consent to establish every private Citizen the Judge and Avenger of the public Injury, or to purchase a temporary Deliverance by the severe Retaliation, that will surely be exercised on those, who have first violated the Laws of War. The fate of Cæsar was alledged to colour the Edict of Proscription;[11] and perhaps the generous Ambition of the younger Guise would have been startled at the Massacre of Paris, had it not satisfied his great Revenge against the Admiral de Coligny[2] and other Leaders of a Party, whom not without Reason he accused of his Fathers Murder.[12] We may observe that the Assassination of Tyrants has been generally applauded by the Ancients. The Fate of a great Empire is[a] usually decided by the Sword of War; but against the petty Usurper of a Greek or Italian City, the Dagger of Conspiracy had been often found as efficacious an Instrument. The same Doctine is as gener-ally condemned by the present Nations of Europe; influenced by a milder System of Manners and impressed with a deep Sense of the bloody Mischiefs perpetrated both by the Catholics and the Calvinists during the Alliance of religious and political Fanaticism.

Whilst the Merit of Brutus's GODLIKE STROKE, (for such it has been called[13]) is at least doubtfull, we can only allow in his Favor that by acting up to the established Standard of Roman Virtue he is entitled to our Indulgence and in some Measure to our Esteem. But in these nice Cases, where the Esteem is bestowed on the INTENTION, rather than on the ACTION, we ought to be well assured that the Intention was pure from any interested or passionate Motive; that it was not the hasty Suggestion of Resent-ment or Vanity, but the calm Result of consistent and well grounded Virtue, impatient of Slavery and tender of the Rights of Mankind. The praises of Antiquity and the noble Spirit that breathes in the Epistles of Brutus,[14] may indeed præpossess us

_a_ "is usually" _for I._ can be decided only

in favor of his moral Character; but it is the uniform Tenor of his Life, private as well as public which must in a great Degree, acquit or condemn the Conspirator.

Plutarch singles out of the whole Life of Brutus, one exceptionable Action; his promising the Plunder of Lacedæmon and Thessalonica to his Troops.[15] But had Plutarch been better acquainted with the Epistles of Atticus, he would have seen in that faithfull Mirror of the Times, some Instances of Avarice and Inhumanity, which the philosophic Brutus could not have excused by the sad Necessity of Civil War.

When Cicero was appointed Proconsul of Cilicia, his first Object was to relieve the Cities of his Government, almost ruined by the heavy Debts, which they had been obliged to contract in Order to satisfy the Rapaciousness of his Predecessors. The Case of Salamis in Cyprus deserved peculiar Compassion. One Scaptius, a Roman Money Broker strongly recommended by Brutus claimed very large Sums as due to him from that City. The Deputies of Salamis acknowledged the Debt, and made a Tender of the Money with legal Interest, as[a] it was fixed by Cicero's Edict at twelve per Cent and compound Interest at the End of every Year. But Scaptius demanded Forty eight per Cent according to the Condition of his usurious Bond; and to enforce his Demand by military Execution he had obtained from the former Proconsul a Troop of Horse with which he kept the Senate House of Salamis closely[b] besieged, till five of the most obstinate Senators were actually starved to Death. This Proconsul was Appius Claudius the Father in Law of Brutus, and when the Province of Cilicia devolved upon Cicero, the same Brutus recommended with more than common Earnestness, the Affairs of Scaptius to the Favor of the[c] new governor. Cicero was at first surprised at finding so intimate a Connection between a Man of Merit and an[d] infamous Usurer, but he was still more astonished, when the shamefull Secret was disclosed. The wretched Agent disappeared, and the virtuous Brutus without a Blush avowed HIMSELF the Creditor of the Salamians. As soon as he threw off the Mask, instead of commiserating the Ruin of a City under his immediate Patronage he insisted on the utmost Rigour of his iniquitous Demands, and requested of Cicero in the most haughty Terms, that he would send the same Scaptius into Cyprus

---

[a] *I.* which Cicero's edict had fixed at   [b] *I.* so closely   [c] *I.* a   [d] *I.* so infamous an usurer

at the Head of a second Troop of Horse to exact the extravagant Amount of the accumulated Principal and Interest. On this Occasion the Virtue of Cicero was supported by a noble Firmness. "I should "be desirous (he repeats it in several Places) to oblige Brutus, but I "cannot sacrifice to his Interest, the Feelings of Humanity, the "Principles of Justice, the Uniformity of my Character and the "Approbation of all good Men. I shall be concerned to lose his "Friendship, but I shall be still more concerned to lose the Esteem "I have ever entertained for him."[16]

The numerous Crimes of Verres, exagerated as they most probably have been, by the strongest Powers of Eloquence, scarcely furnish such an Instance of unrelenting Avarice as this Transaction of Brutus, which is related by Cicero, with the candid Simplicity of a private Correspondence. The Money due from the City of Salamis amounted to about twenty thousand Pounds; a small Part of the immense Sums which Brutus appears to have lent out on similar Securities.[17] We cannot forbear enquiring, by what Arts a private Citizen the Son of a proscribed Father, and who had never commanded Armies, or governed Provinces could accumulate so ample a Fortune; the Enquiry would lead to some Suspicions severe but not unreasonable.

In the Beginning of the Civil War we find young Brutus in the Camp of Pompey, by whose Order his Father had been put to Death about thirty Years before.[18] This Sacrifice of filial Piety to a superior and public Duty has been highly applauded. But was it in Brutus's Power either to remain inactive or to enlist in the Army of Cæsar? Was it in his Power to refuse to follow the General of the Republic, his Uncle Cato, the Consuls, ten Consulars, the greatest Part of the Senate and the Flower of the Equestrian Order.[19] The Defeat of Pharsalia, and the Death of Pompey removed the general Constraint, and displayed the genuine Views and Characters of the principal Men of his Party.

There were some very respectable Senators; Men of an advanced Age, moderate Tempers, and cool Penetration; who had never entertained a favorable Opinion of the Hopes or even of the Designs of their own Party. Cicero, Marcellus, Sulpicius, Varro had been driven by a Sense of[a] Honor into Scenes of War and Tumult, as little suited to their Talents as to[b] their Inclination. They resolved to consider the Decision of Pharsalia as final; and not to aggravate

[a] *MS. of of*   [b] *I. om.* to

by a vain Resistance the Miseries of their Country. When Cicero returned to Rome, he avoided the Forum and the Senate, and devoted his Leisure and Abilities to the noble Design of explaining the Græcian Philosophy in the Latin Language. Yet his Retirement was sometimes invaded by his own Reproaches and by those of the World; by the Comparison of his tame Acquiescence with the glorious Struggle of Cato, Scipio, Labienus, and their Followers who had anew erected the Standard of Liberty in Africa.[20]

These[a] Patriots, of more active Spirits and more sanguine Hopes, thought it even yet a Crime to déspair of the Republic. Fifteen Months, wasted by Cæsar in the Arms of Cleopatra, the romantic Campaign of Alexandria and the rapid Conquest of Pontus, gave them Time to assemble a new Army of twelve Legions; disciplined by Misfortune, and deriving fresh Courage from Déspair. Fertile Africa afforded every Supply for carrying on the War. The Alliance of Juba filled the Roman Camp with an innumerable Host of Moors and Numidians. Spain was in Arms, and Italy expected her Deliverers with a Mixture of Terror and Impatience.[21] Cæsar again fought and triumphed; but the unconquered Soul of Cato easily escaped from Life and from the Usurper. Such was the Constancy of that Patriot, and such the Lessons, which he had ever inculcated to his Nephew Brutus: let us next examine what Fruits they produced.

After the Battle of Pharsalia Brutus lay concealed in the Marshes of Thessaly. He made the first Advances to the Conqueror; experienced his Clemency, and was immediately admitted into his Confidence. The latter was obtained by revealing, I will not call it betraying whatever he had been able to learn of Pompey's Designs.[22] He then left Cæsar to follow the Pursuit he had pointed out, and entertained himself with an agreable Tour through the Cities of Greece and Asia. In a few Months he returned to Rome, resigned himself to the calm Studies of History and Rethoric, and passed many of his leisure Hours in the Society of Cicero, and Atticus. Their Litterary Conversations were sometimes interrupted by Complaints of the melancholy Situation of Public Affairs.[23]

At a Time when Cicero was in Retirement, Marcellus in voluntary Exile,[24] and Cato in Arms; we might at least expect that the Nephew of Cato would have declined any political Connection with the Usurper. When Cæsar set out for the African War, Brutus

[a] I. The

accepted at his Hands the Government of the Cisalpine Gaul;[25] a Command of infinite Importance from its Vicinity to the Capital, and from the Legions always stationed in that Province to protect the Frontiers of Italy from the unconquered Rhætians. The same Legions gave the Governor of the Cisalpine Gaul an almost decisive Weight in every civil Commotion, as a March of a few Days brought him to the Gates of Rome.[26] Experience had already acquainted Cæsar with this Advantage, and by thus appointing Brutus his Lieutenant during his Absence, he shewed the most implicit Confidence in his Fidelity. Suppose that Rome had attempted to break her Chains; suppose the Sons of Pompey from Spain, or Cato from Africa had made a Diversion in Italy, what could have been the Conduct of the Patriot Brutus? His Station must have forced him into Action, and by his Action he must have betrayed either his Trust or his Country. Into this fatal Dilemma had he wantonly thrown himself.

When Cæsar, on his Return from the Conquest of Africa, visited a Part of Gaul, his obsequious Governor went out to meet him with the respectfull Attention of an experienced Courtier, and attended him on his Way to the Triumph, in which a Picture of Cato tearing out his own Bowels was exposed to the Eyes of the Roman People.[27] I wish not however to conceal that, about the same time, Brutus gave some Proofs of Regard for his Uncles Memory, by marrying his Cousin Portia,[28] and by composing a Treatise on the Life and Character of Cato; an honorable rather than a dangerous Undertaking: Since even the prudence of Cicero permitted him to publish a Work on the same Subject. The Dictator disdained to employ the Arms of Power, when those of Eloquence were sufficient. He appealed to the Tribunal of the Public, and in a severe and masterly Censure of the Conduct of Cato, he treated the Persons of his two litterary Antagonists, Cicero and Brutus with every Expression of Regard and Esteem.[29]

This polite Controversy was so far from leaving any unfavorable Impressions in Cæsar's Mind, that a few Months afterwards, he named Brutus the first of the sixteen Prætors with the honorable Department of the City Jurisdiction and with a Promise of the Consulship for one of the ensuing Years.[30] Could Brutus accept, could he solicit the Honors of the State; from a Master who had abolished the Freedom, and who scarcely preserved the Forms of Elections.

—— Tinget solennia campi,[a]
Et non admissæ, diribet[31] suffragia plebis
Decantatque Tribus, et vanâ versat in Urnâ;
Nec Cœlum servare licet; tonat Augure Surdo;
Et lætæ jurantur aves, bubone sinistro.[32]

I have heard much of the heroic Spirit of Brutus; of his glorious Sacrifice of Gratitude to Patriotism. True Patriotism would have instructed him not to cancel but to refuse Obligations of such a Nature from the declared Enemy of Cato and the Liberty of Rome.

Nay more, by soliciting these Honors, Brutus solicited a public Occasion of engaging his Fidelity to the Person and Government of Cæsar by a solemn and voluntary Oath of Allegiance.[33] "A few "Days before the Execution of their fatal Purpose, these Patriots "all swore Fealty to Cæsar, and protesting to hold his Person ever "sacred, they touched the Altar with those Hands which they had "already armed for his Destruction."[34] Antiquity has not preserved the Oath, but we may suppose that it was not very different from the warm but faithless Professions of Cicero. "We exhort, we "beseech you to guard your Safety against the secret Dangers, "which you seem to suspect. We all promise (that I may express for "others what I feel for myself) not only to watch over your precious "Life with the most anxious Vigilance, but to oppose our own "Bodies, our own Breasts to the impending Stroke.[35]" Relying on these Assurances the Dictator dismissed his Spanish Guards,[36] and neglected every Precaution. He could not persuade himself that those whom he had conquered would be brave enough, or those whom he had pardoned base enough, to shorten a Life already sufficient either for Nature or for Glory.[37] By those Men he was flattered and assassinated. Such solemn Perjury cannot be justified except by the dangerous Maxim that no Faith is to be kept with Tyrants.[38]

It was only for usurping the Power of the People that Cæsar could deserve the Epithet of Tyrant. He used the power with more Moderation and Ability than the People was capable of exerting; and the Romans already began to experience all the Happiness and Glory compatible with a Monarchical Form of Government.[39] To this Government Brutus had yielded his Obedience and Services during three Years before he lifted his Dagger against Cæsar's Life. What *new* Crime had Cæsar committed, which so suddenly[40]

[a] I. campo

transformed his Minister into an Assassin? He aspired to the Title
of King, and that odious Name called upon the Descendant of
Junius Brutus to assert the Glories of his Race? Such a Regard to
a Word, and such Insensibility to the Thing itself may be excused
in the Populace of Rome; but to a Philosopher of an enlarged Mind
it was surely of little Moment under what Appellation public
Liberty was oppressed.

Such are the Reflections, which an accurate Examination of the
Character of Brutus has suggested to an Enemy of Tyranny, under
every Shape: who will neither be awed by the Frown of Power, nor
silenced by the hoarse Voice of popular Applause. The Monarch
and the Patriot are alike amenable to the severe but candid
Inquisition of Truth.

Notes[a]

1 Plutarch in Antonio p. 925, in Brut: p 1011. Among these were the Statues
which the Athenians had erected to Brutus and Cassius; by the Side of their own
Deliverers, Harmodius and Aristogiton.

2 Under the jealous Tyranny of Tiberius, Cremutius Cordus was arraigned before
the Senate for the Encomiums which he bestowed, in his History on Brutus and Cassius.
He justified himself by the Toleration of Augustus and the Example of Asinius Pollio,
Messalla and Livy: nor was it within the Tyrants Power to suppress his Writings, or
the general Sense of Mankind. Tacit. Annal. iv. 34. 35.

3 M. Antonin de Rebus suis. L. i.

3b Velleius Paterculus, (an elegant writer, but servilely devoted to the Imperial
Family and most probably one of the Judges who condemned Cremutius) can only say
of Brutus. Corrupto animo ejus in[c] diem quo[d] omnes *Virtutes* unius facti *temeritate*
abstulit. II. 72.

4 Who in the Year 1308 delivered their Country from the Austrian Yoke. See Simlerus
de Republica Helvetica. Guillimannus de Rebus Helveticis, and the great Chronicle of
Tchudi.[e3]

5 See the XIVth, XVth and XVIth Books of the Epistles to Atticus.

6 See Epistol. ad Famil. XI. 2. 3. The Spirit of these Letters is finely tempered by the
Politeness with which Brutus and Cassius address the Consul. They respect the Magistrate whilst they defy the Tyrant.

7 Appian. L. iv. p 640.

8 Fuit autem Dux Cassius melior quanto Vir Brutus. Velleius Paterculus II. 72.

9 This Anecdote was preserved by Messalla, who in the Court of Augustus was always
proud of remembering Cassius as his General. Plutarch. in Brut. Tacit. Annal. IV. 34.

10 Considerations sur la Grandeur des Romains Chap. XII.

11 Appian. IV. p. 593.

12 See the XXXIVth Book of the History of Thuanus.

13   Tho' Cato liv'd, tho' Tully spoke
                              Tho' Brutus dealt the *Godlike Stroke;*
                              Yet perish'd fated Rome.[4]

---

a II. lists notes at foot of each page and therefore omits this heading.   *b* Gibbon
clearly indicates two locations for note 3 and numbers two notes "3".   *c I. om. in*
d II. quae illi   *e II. (correctly)* Tschudi

[14] He declares (Epist. 16. or 22. in Middleton's Edition) that were his Father alive again he would not suffer *him* to possess a Power above the Laws and the Senate. Pity it is that this whole Correspondence and particularly this celebrated Epistle should be liable to the Suspicion of a Forgery committed in those Ages when Latin had ceased to be a living Language. See Tunstal and Markland on one Side of the Question and Dr. Middleton on the other.[5]

[15] Plutarch in Brut.

[16] Brutus says Cicero has not sent me one Letter, in which there was not something singular and arrogant. His Style gives me little uneasiness; but indeed he forgets *what* and to whom he is writing. For this whole Transaction see the Epistles to Atticus, L. V. 21. VI. 1, 2, 3.

[17] Brutus by Cicero's Interest had received from Ariobarzanes King of Cappadocia, an[a] hundred Talents upon Account of a much larger Sum that was due to him. The Concerns of Brutus in Asia which he recommended to the Care of the proconsul filled a whole Volume of Requests or rather Mandates as they are called by Cicero.

[18] Plutarch in Brut. The Father was one of the Lieutenants of the weak and wicked Lepidus, who raised a Rebellion in Italy after the Death of Sylla.

[19] *Decem* fuimus *Consulares* &c[a]—Qui vero *Prætorii*? quorum Princeps M. Cato, &[b]—ut magna excusatione opus iis sit, qui in illa castra non venerunt. Philipp. XIII. 13, 14.

[20] See the Epistles to Atticus XI. 7; where he unbosoms himself to his Friend with a very wonderfull or rather a very natural Mixture of Spirit, and Meanness, of Patriotism and Selfishness.

[21] Hist. de Bello African. 18. 40.
    Sueton: in Cæsar. 66.
    Dio. Cassius L XLII. p 338.
    Cicero ad Attic. XI. 7.

[22] Plutarch in Brut. Some Casuists Spaniards and others, have attempted to justify this Conduct. (See Bayle Dictionaire à l'Article BRUTUS). The Feelings of a Man of Honor are the best Confutation of such Sophistry.

[23] See Cicero's two Treatises De *Claris Oratoribus* and on[c] *Orator* both which he dedicated to Brutus about this Time. The latter gave Rise to a celebrated Controversy between them.

[24] He retired to Mytilene and refused to accept the Victor's Clemency. His Letters (see ad Familiar L. IV.) are full of noble Sentiments, and his Behaviour does not appear to have disgraced them.

[25] Plutarch in Brut. Appian de B. C L. II. p 477.
    Cicer. ad Famil XIII. 10 &c[a].

[26] Montesquieu has already remarked the Importance of that Province. Considerations sur la Grandeur &c[a] C. XI.

[27] Plutarch in Brut. Appian L. II p 491.

[28] Plutarch. Cicer. ad Attic. XIII. 9.

[29] Cicer. ad Attic. XII. 21. XIII. 46. Cæsar paid a Compliment to these two pieces in Favor of Cato: but his Compliment is obscure and equivocal. He probably meant it should be so.

[30] Plutarch. in Brut. Vellicus Paterculus. II. 56.

[31] The Common Editions read *Dirimit*, which puzzles all the Commentators. *Diribere* was a Term peculiar to the Comitia and signifies to poll the Votes in the regular *Divisions*.

[32] Lucan. Pharsal. V. 391.

[33] Appian L. II. p 494.

[34] Humes Dialogue on the Principles of Morals[6]

---

[a] *I. and II.* a   [b] *II.* &c.   [c] *II. De*

³⁵ Cicer. pro Marcello C. 10.

³⁶ Sueton. in Cæsar. C. 86

³⁷ Cicero pro Marcel. C. 8.

³⁸ Appian L. II. p 515. This Maxim is introduced in a Speech of Brutus to the people; but the Speech is evidently manufactured by the Historian.

³⁹ See some of Cæsars vast and beneficial Designs in Suetonius (C. 44). The Reformation of the Calender*a* still remains a small Specimen of them.

⁴⁰ Brutus took the Oath of Allegiance, about seventy five Days before the Execution of the Conspiracy.

------

a II. corrects to calendar

INDEX EXPURGATORIUS

1. Mr Hurd (English commentary upon[a] Horace[1] Tom. ii. p 38 &c) represents himself as the first discoverer of the Allegory in the third Georgic; and as such receives the Compliments of his friend Warburton (Divine Legation Vol. i. p 295.). The Jesuit Catrou had however explained it upon the same principle many years before. (Virgile de Catrou. Tom. ii. p. 452 &c.)

2. Mr Dacier. (V. Horace de Dacier. sur le $\mathscr{V}$ 67. de la 1re Satire du Livre ii.) is doubly mistaken in supposing that the Metellus of Lucilius was Metellus Numidicus; between whom, and Scipio Africanus some jealousy had arisen from their several African exploits. 1. The sense of Horace supposes that Scipio was an impartial judge; consequently no adversary of Metellus. 2. Scipio had never an opportunity of being jealous of the other's African glory. Scipio died in the Consulship of M. Aquilius and C. Sempronius. (Vell. Patercul. L. ii. C 4) A.UC. 624. (V. Pigh. Annal ad annum[b]). Metellus was Consul with the province of Numidia in 644. (Pigh. ad ann.) M. Dacier might also have considered that the intimacy which the Satyrist enjoyed with Scipio, supposes him much older than twenty when that Hero died, and consequently that Eusebius brings his birth too low (to the 158th Olympiad [)] M. Bayle (Dictionnaire. au mot Lucilius Not. 9[c]) drew the same conclusion, though from less decisive circumstances.

3. Mr Hume would infer from the list of the Belgic army in Cæsar (de bello Gallico. L. ii. C. 4). the number of inhabitants in all Gaul. He justly enough considers Belgium (more properly the Belgic Gaul) as one fourth of the whole; (at least with regard to population [)]: but he forgot that not above half the Belgic nations entered into the Alliance; which circumstance must double the Calculation. ($\mathscr{V}$ Hume's Essays in 4° 1758. p. 247.) It is wonderfull that Mr Wallace (Numbers of Mankind p. 71 &c. Appendix. p. 312 &c [)]

---

[a] *II.* on   [b] *II.* ann.   [c] *II.* G

should rather chuse to refute him by the most improbable conjectures than by so plain a fact. In the same place Mr Hume observes that the numbers in Cæsar are to be depended upon; as the Greek translation Checks the original. Mr Hume must know that this version (which is a very indifferent one) is attributed by the learned to Gaza or Planudes; and consequently is not older than our most recent MSS.[2]

---

*4. M. de Beaufort (Republique Romaine Tom ii. p. 220) talks & quotes so very idly about the Consulars & Correctors of Italy; as to shew, he had mighty little idea of the Constantinean Scheme. I am afraid, his quotations from the Code and Notitia are only second-hand.[3]

---

5. In the Notitia of the Western Empire we meet among the officers of the City of Rome with the Consularis Aquarum I believe that this employ[b] no longer subsisted in the Theodosian Age. 1. Because it appears here out of it's rank and amongst the subalterns. 2. Because we find no commission for it among the Formulæ of Cassiodorus. 3. Because the functions of this place are exactly the same with the Comes Formarum who is very well known in those times. I therefore suspect that the Consularis Aquarum was lost in the Comes Formarum about the age of Constantine.

---

6. Abbè Mongault[c] had decided, that the Nice where Brutus pleaded before Cæsar for King Dejotarus was the Italian & not the Bithynian City of that name (Epitres de Ciceron à Atticus. L. xiv. 1) Dr Middleton. (Life of Cicero. V. ii p. 407) has echoed it from him with a severe censure upon the Jesuits Catrou & Rouillè.[4] Both Leader and follower are mistaken 1. Nice in Italy was a wretched town among the Alpes where Cæsar upon his return from Spain would never have stopped to try a cause which he could as easily try a few days afterwards at Rome. Nice in Bithynia was a great City (in the neighbourood of Galatia) thro' which Cæsar must have passed in his progress when, "Jura in Tetrarchas, Reges, "civitates distribuit" Hirt de bell. Alex. C. 78. nay we are told in the

---

same chapter that he actually decided a cause against Dejotarus. Brutus appears to have been in Asia about that time 2. Cicero's dialogue de Claris Oratoribus was wrote[a] after Brutus's oration for Dejotarus. (V̇ C. 3.) It was likewise wrote[a] before the death of Marcellus. (C. 71), who was killed A. UC. 707 (V̇ Fabric in Vit. Ciceron ad ann)[5] Therefore the oration was[b] in 706; when Cæsar was in Asia; not in 708 when he was returning from Spain. Altho the dialogue of Cicero may be feigned; yet we know how very attentive the ancients were in preserving the Chronology of these kind of fictions (C 60) The only foundation of Mongault's opinion seems to be some obscure places. (Epist. ad Attic. L. xiii. 39. 40) where Cicero hints at a journey, Brutus made to meet Cæsar, but without any relation either to Nice or Dejotarus.

---

7. Cicero (pro lege Maniliâ. C. 4) speaks of Ecbatana, as the royal seat of Mithridates. I suppose it is not necessary to prove, that Ecbatana was the Capital of Media, or that Media was[c] never a part of that prince's empire. Tully[d] was probably but an indifferent Geographer, and the celebrated name of Ecbatana, sounded extremely well. A lesson for Criticks!

---

8. Mr Guthrie (English translation of Cicero's letters to Atticus L. ix. 10) translates Getæ by Goths; a barbarous name which was first heard of 250 years after Cicero's death. V. Cluverii German. L. iii.[6]

---

9. Hirtius must be mistaken when he says (De bell. Gall. L. viii. C 46) that Q Cicero was sent into winter quarters in Belgium: when it appears that he was serving under his brother in Cilicia, the 13th of October. (Cicer. ad Attic. L. v. 20) of the same year AUC. 702 (V. Pigh. ad annum)

---

10. M. Guichardt (Memoires Militaires sur les Grecs et les Romains, Tom. ii. p 220) attributes the stay of Cæsar in Egypt not to Cleopatra, but to the Etesian winds; which Hirtius seems to Confirm. But this reason or pretence could only relate to a very inconsiderable part of the nine months (Appian de bell Civil. L. ii. p 484) which he

---

[a] *II.* written   [b] *I. om.* was   [c] *I. om.* was   [d] *I.* But Tully

8124961   E

spent there; since the season of the Etesian winds is over some time before the autumnal equinox; (V. Plin Hist. Natur. L. ii. C 47.) and Cæsar did not land in Egypt before the middle of August. The proof of this depends upon an acurate survey of the then irregular Roman Calendar. I adopt the system of M. de la Nauze. (V. Memoires de Litterature. Tom. xxvi.) as it appears to me far more probable than that of Archbishop Usher. In general some light may be thrown upon Cæsar's transactions in Egypt[7]

11. Sallust is no very correct historian. I blame. 1. His Chronology. Let any[a] one consider the context of his history from the siege of Numantia to the Consulship of Calphurnius Bestia ($\stackrel{\vee}{V}$ Bell. Jugurth C. 5–29) A fair reader can never imagine, a space of more than five or six years. There were really 22 ($\stackrel{\vee}{V}$. Pigh. ad ann. U C. 620 et 642) 2 His Geography. Notwithstanding his laboured description of Africa, nothing can be more confused than his Geography without either division of provinces or fixing of towns. We scarce perceive any distance, between Capsa and the river Mulucho.[b] [(] Bell. Jugurthin. C. 94 97 &c.) situated at the two extremities of Numidia, perhaps 500 miles from each other. 3 Having undertaken a particular history of the Jugurthine War[c]; he neither informs us of the fate of the conquered province nor of the Captive King.

12. M. de Montesquieu quotes the famous inscription of the Rubicon; as ancient and authentick. (Considerations sur la Grandeur des Romains. C xi. p. 123.) We may excuse Blondus, and Leander Alberti for having been deceived by so very gross an imposition; which carries it's own condemnation along with it; has been regurlarly confuted by Cluverius. (Ital. Antiq. L. i. C. 28. p. 297. [)] and must be rejected by every scholar in Europe[8]

13. M. Muratori is grosly mistaken in the interpretation of a passage of Olympiodorus preserved by Photius (V. Annali d'Italia, Tom iv. p 83). The[d] historian speaks of several rich Senators who enjoyed an annual income of forty Centenaries of Gold[e], others of 15, others

---

a I. om. any   *b II.* Mulucha   *c I.* manner   *d I.* He   *e I. om.* of Gold

of ten &c. The Annalist understands by a Centenary of Gold 100,000 pieces of Gold, which he supposes nearly equivalent to the Crowns or Ducats of our time. But the real signification of Centenary κεντηναριαν,[a] means only one hundred pounds weight of Gold; (which was the[b] general and legal computation under the lower Empire). I owe Salmasius the justice of observing, that he has given the true explanation of this word. (V. Comment. ad Script. Hist. August. p. 418. [)] Muratori's erroneous reckoning would increase the fortunes of these wealthy Senators in the enormous proportion of at least seven to one[9]

---

14. M. Freret justifies the common reading of Pliny the Naturalist (L. iii. 5)[c] which allows 13,200 paces for the circuit of Rome; by an ingenious calculation drawn from the measure of the surfaces of the xiv Regions as set down in the Notitia. The Circumference deduced from them is 13549 paces. This seeming agrement is a real contradiction. Pliny only speaks of the narrower boundaries of Servius Tullius. The Rome of the Notitia (the xiv Regions) comprized all that was contained within the more extensive walls of the Emperor Aurelian. V. Mem. de Litterature Tom. xxiv. p. 531 &c.

---

[d]15. Dr Warburton, Bishop of Glocester in explaining the Moral sense of Apuleius, supposes that the Ass Lucius was shocked at the thoughts of the unnatural crime, he was about to perpetrate, and that he[e] made his escape to avoid it. This unnatural crime (which was no other than a bestial commerce with a Messalina of Corinth) is elegantly described in the xth (not the ix[th] [)] book of Metamorphoses, and might perhaps be qualified less severely by a Casuist who should reflect on the peculiarity of Lucius's supposed situation. (V. the Divine Legation Vol. i. p. 312) Let that be as it will, the Bishop does Lucius more honor than he deserves; the crime had been already perpetrated; perpetrated with great pleasure, & without the least scruple or remorse (Apuleii Metamorphos. L. x. p. 225, 226 Edit. Pricæi). Indeed when he was to repeat the same ceremony upon a condemned criminal; he was then shocked both at the thoughts of a publick enjoyment in the Amphitheatre, and of the wickedness of his partner whose life was sullied (p. 227–232)

---

[a] II. κεντηνάριον   [b] I. its   [c] MS. possibly 3   [d] II. om. entry 15 and renumbers others accordingly   [e] I. om. that he

with the most monstrous crimes. (V. p 232 234.) The fear of the wild beasts which surrounded them was however[a] his principal concern, & when he made his escape he was "Non de pudore jam, sed de salute ipsâ sollicitus" (p. 235) Lucian attributes the same character & feelings to the little hero of his tale (.V. Lucian Oper. Edit Bourdelot. p. 667. 668.) The Bishop is ridiculously enough mistaken but it may perhaps be rather a credit to his character: that he is not so very acurately acquainted with the amours of the Ass Lucius.[10]

---

16. Sir William Temple. (V. his Works in folio, Tom i. p. 223) has discovered a fundamental law in the Mamluk Empire; which the Mamluks themselves were totally unacquainted with [.] "The son "of a Sultan might inherit his father's private fortune, but he was "for ever excluded from the succession The throne was elective, and "the election confined to the native Circassians, who had been "brought slaves into Egypt, and had served as private soldiers in "the Mamluk Bands." The throne was indeed elective like the Roman Empire in the third Century; but the Army elected, deposed or murdered their Sovereigns according to their own[b] wild caprices, which were unrestrained by either law, or principle. As prosperity is seldom the school of manly virtue it is not surprising, that a Soldier of fortune was often preferred by his fellow soldiers to the son of a Monarch; or a hardy Scythian to the native of that effeminate country; where every race of animals is observed to degenerate (V. Maillet. Description de l'Egypte, Tom. ii. p. 222). Sir W[c]. T.'s notion is as contrary to fact, as to reason. The Scepter[d] of the Mamluks was above a century in the hands of the same family. Kelasun[e] was elected Sultan of Egypt in the year 1279, and was succeeded[f] (with only two or three temporary usurpations) by fourteen of his descendants; two in the first generation, eight in the second, two in the third and two in the fourth. (V. Pocock, Supplem. ad Abulpharag: dynast. p. 6–32; Hist. Generale des Huns &c par M. de Guignes Tom. i. p. 266, 267 Tom. v. p. 155–246). It is unfortunate for letters, that the Knowledge of facts, and the art of making use of them are so[g] very seldom united. I pass over several other mistakes of Sir W.[h] T. that I may not seem to treat a polite scholar,

---

[a] *I. om.* however   [b] *I. om.* own   [c] *II.* William Temple's   [d] *I.* Crown
[e] *II.* Kelaoun   [f] *I.* succeeding   [g] *II. om.* so   [h] *II.* Sir William Temple

with the critical severity, which he justly enough complained of,
(Tom. 1 p. 299); but I can scarce refrain from smiling at his
Almanzor the most accomplished of the Western Caliphs who
reigned over Arabia Egypt Africa and Spain; but in fact an[a]
imaginary Hero of an imaginary Empire. S[r] W[b]. T was deceived
by some Spanish Romances, which he took for Arabian history.
(.V. Ockley's preface to the Second Volume of his history of the
Saracens, p. xxiii)[11]

---

17. M. Maillet (author of the Descriptio[c] de l'Egypte in 2 Vol. 12°
À la Haye 1740) seems to have been a curious and acurate observer
of whatever fell within his reach during a sixteen years Consulship
in that country. His account of the Physical, moral, commercial and
political state of Egypt is clear, copious, and entertaining. But his
book has some considerable defects. 1. Tho' a sensible man the
Consul was no Scholar; He affects to despise the ancients; seldom
quotes them and often mistakes them This ignorance betrays him
into many very gross errors &[d] deprives us of all the lights which he
might have extracted from or reflected upon the writings of those
ingenious nations who were so long masters of Egypt. It would be
endless to enumerate particulars. Let any one compare his sixth
letter with the Pyramidographia of the learned Mr Greaves (V his
works Vol. 1. p. 1–164.) 2. He was well versed in Arabian litterature,
and followes as his oracles those writers, even in respect to the[e]
earlier ages, which were to them (as they truly styled it) the time of
ignorance; &[f] upon which indeed they can offer us nothing better
than traditions, fables or conjectures. He is even far from acurate
in his use of them. His considering the Mamluk princes till the
conquest of the Turks as so many descendants of the great Saladin.
(V Tom ii, p. 287 &[f] elsewhere) may serve as a specimen. 3. The
Consul entrusted his materials to a french Abbè (Mascrier) to be
revised and fitted for the press. The Editor (who tho' an affected is
no contemptible writer) seems to have considered amusement as the
only end of writing, and idle tales &[f] *ambitious* ornaments as the
only source of amusement. Nay I am well assured that he has
improved or rather spoiled the honest Consul's memoirs by many
additions drawn from his own imagination; &[f] what is unfortunate

[a] *I*. the   [b] *II*. Sir William Temple   [c] *II*. Description   [d] *II*. and   [e] *I*.
those   [f] *II*. and

for us, is, that it*a* is impossible to clear the native soil from these noxious weeds.

---

18. M de Voltaire accuses the author of the Lettres Provinciales of having imputed to the Jesuits "un dessein forme de corrompre les "mœurs des hommes["] Compare this accusation with the fifth letter, and you will be astonished that any man could advance it "Sachez donc que leur objet n'est pas de corrompre les mœurs; ce "n'est past leur dessein., ["] (Vol. 2. p. 5). When I meet Voltaire upon Grecian Roman or Asiatic ground, I treat him with the indulgence he has so much occasion for; but we might have expected to have found him better acquainted with one of the finest writers of his own country. V. Oeuvres de Voltaire Tom. xvi p. 322, et Lettres Provinciales. Tom ii, p. 1–36. in 12° à Leyde 1761*b*

---

19. M. de Voltaire, speaking of the many instances which seemed to justify *Mademoiselle's* marriage with a private Gentleman; alledges the examples of the daughters of the Roman Emperors, and those of the Sovereigns of Asia. (Oeuvres de Voltaire. Tom xvi. p 124 [)] Both are very unhappily chosen; as the circumstances are totally different. The only Kings in the time of the Roman Empire were vassals or ennemies to it: All barbarians and all considered with reason as very inferior to a Roman Senator. The Eastern maxims of domestick government make those unequal alliances the most suitable and the most eligible for a Sultan s daughter. She must marry a Slave, to avoid the being one herself

---

20 The Example of Quadratus may give us an idea of the blind or perhaps artfull Credulity, with which Mr Addison composed his admired little treatise of the Christian Religion. He describes this Apologist as a famous Philosopher, a Convert, and a martyr. (Addison's work's Vol. iii. p. 290) Dr Cave was not half so well acquainted with him. (V. Hist. Litterar. p. 32. 33) I do not find the least trace of his conversion; his martyrdom is founded only upon the modern Martyrology of the Greeks and I see no other proof of his Philosophy than his being an Athenian; and that Mr Addison might suppose that every athenian was of course a famous Philo-

a *I. om.* it   *b* *II.* 1767

sopher. There is scarce a prejudice or a legend, that this popular writer has not condescended to adopt as the strongest arguments

---

21. Pope's verses to Addison upon his treatise of medals have certainly great beauties; but I think, I discover two faults in them. 1 I scarce know a more compleat piece of tautology than the Verses 6, 7, and 8. There cannot be any the most minute difference, between *hostile fury, barbarian blindness,* and *Gothick fire: religious rage, Christian zeal,* and *Papal piety,* express one and the same idea 2. I hardly know a stronger impropriety; than complimenting the author of a Didactic work by trangressing one of his principal rules. If Mr Pope had considered how severely his friend[a] condemned all inscriptions in verse; especially when they run into any length; he would never have[b] given a legend of six Heroick verses for Mr Cragg's medal. (V. Addison's works. Vol. 3, p. 155, 156)

> And round the orb in lasting notes be read
> Statesman, yet friend to truth &c—[12]

---

22. Mr Addison boldly asserts that there never was a single Martyr amongst the primitive Hereticks; &[c] even draws inferences from this undoubted fact, in favor of the truth of pure, Orthodox Christianity (Vol iii p 301) To connect different degrees of persuasion with different modes of opinion appeared to me highly unphilosophical; however I consulted my ingenious friend Dr Middleton who[d] (I recollected) had placed the Christian martyrs in a very new and curious light (See, Free Enquiry &c in his works Vol 1. p 162– 173) He immediately informed me from the authority of all history and particularly that of Eusebius (Hist. Ecclesiast. v. 16) that the Hereticks had their Martyrs, as well as the Orthodox: upon verifying the quotation, I even found that the Sectaries boasted of the great number of their Martyrs, and that their antagonists did not pretend to deny the fact.

---

23. Dr Lardner (Jewish and Heathen Testimonies. Vol ii, p 18, 28, 63) and the celebrated Mosheim. (Ecclesiastical History translated by Maclaine Vol 1. p 76) have both imagined, that as all Domitian's laws had been repealed by the Senate, Pliny the younger was at loss

[a] *I.* friends   [b] *I. om.* have   [c] *II.* and   [d] *I.* whom

what rule of conduct to observe in respect to the Christians. (V Epist. X 97) It may be[a] allowed from the author[it]y of Suetonius (in Dom C 23,) and Lactanctius[b] (de mortib Persec. C. [2][c] that the Senate in the first fury of a just revenge attempted to abolish every memorial of the tyrant; but it should have been recollected from a still better authority (Plin. Epist x 66) that his prudent successor soon settled the general administration of the Empire by restoring the constitutions and rescripts of Domitian to their former validity. "Epistolis etiam Domitiani standum est". It is evident from thence, that Domitian enacted no laws relative to the Christians; and that till Pliny thought it necessary to consult the Emperor upon a case which grew daily more important, the Governors of the provinces had no rule of conduct but their own discretion. This observation might lead to some important consequences in regard to the history of the first age of Christianity[13]

---

24. M. de Voltaire has given us, among many other ingenious trifles, a dialogue between Marcus Aurelius, and a Recolet fryar. The latter accuses the former of having persecuted the Christians to whom he had such obligations. The Emperor assures him, that he never persecuted any one (V. Oeuvres de Voltaire. Tom iv. p 384). The poet[d] forgot the characters of his speakers. 1. It is very natural that the fryar, a friend to miracles and legends should adopt the story of the Thundering legion; but he would likewise have adopted the catastrophe of the fable, which exalts to the highest degree the gratitude of Marcus towards his benefactors. (Tertull. Apolog. C 5 Lardner's Jewish and Heathen testimonies Vol. ii. p 226 &c). 2 The Emperor was too sincere to deny that many martyrs suffered during his reign &[e] that he himself added to the severity of the laws already in force against the Christians. (V. Lardner Vol. ii, p. 179–221, and Mosheim's Ecclesiastic History. Vol. i. p. 78

---

25 M. de Voltaire rejects with a magisterial Haughtiness the famous Chinese inscription which relates the origin of Christianity in that country &[e] asserts with as de[cis]cive[f] a Confidence that Christianity was absolutely unknown in China in the time of Charlemagne. If he will take the trouble of reading a very curious disserta-

---

[a] I. om. be   [b] II. Lactantius   [c] Thus II; number now lost in binding
[d] I. poets   [e] II. and   [f] I. Magisterial; II. decisive

tion in the Estratto della Letteratura Europea[a] per l'anno 1761. P. 1 2 & 4, and which is perfectly agreable to the principles of M de Guignes (V Mem de l'Acad Tom 30[)] he may see the two following positions established upon the most convincing proofs. 1. It is certain from the Chinese Historians[b], the Nestorian Writers, and the Arabian and European travellers, that a very considerable Christian Church subsisted in China from the vii[th] to the xiv Century which at first flourished very much under the peculiar protection of the Emperors. 2. That the inscription carries every mark of authenticity &[c] is perfectly agreable to the history of those times and to[d] even to the character and doctrines of the Nestorian sect. I am not insensible that before this question was so acurately examined, some Learned men have had doubts concerning the inscription; but where they doubted, Voltaire decided. Tho his objections are very contemptible, yet I am still more offended at the haughtiness of his[e] unbelief, than at his unbelief itself.[14]

---

26. M de Fontenelle, in that elegant piece of history and Philosophy which he has extracted from the learned rubbish of Vandale, discovers many ingenious reasons which account for Porphyry's producing or even inventing oracles that were favorable to the Christians (Oeuvres de Fontenelle. Tom ii, p 239 &c) Perhaps if he had attended to the well grounded suspicions of his own author, he might have concluded with still more reason that Porphyry never did produce them, and that the work in question is spurious. Is not this a[f] little too like, the story of the Golden tooth?

---

27. M. de Fontenelle (Tom ii. p 383)[g] is mistaken when he thinks the Romans prohibited the Carthiaginians[h] by treaty, from offering any more human sacrifices. The Original treaties between those powerfull Republicks are still extant in Polybius and Livy. I need only refer to them. Gelon Tyrant of Syracuse is indeed reported (though not upon the very best authority) to have imposed that humane condition after the battle of Himera (.V Diodor Sicul. L. xi. 21 et Wesseling ad loc) M de Fontenelle is pleased to accuse the Romans of contradicting their own practice; since they sacrificed a man every year to Jupiter Latiatis. But I shall not[i] believe upon

[a] *I. om.* Europea [b] *I.* writers [c] *II.* and [d] *II. om.* to [e] *I. om.* his [f] *I.* the [g] *I. om.* (Tom ii. p 383) [h] *II.* Carthaginians [i] *I. om.* not

the words only of Porphyry, Lactanctius,[a] and Prudentius[15] that human sacrifices were ever a regular part of the Roman worship.

---

28. I think M. de Fontenelle has very injudiciously called Homer and Hesiod the first Grecian Philosophers. Reason and Inspiration are widely different. The first poets were the Prophets and Theologians of their time; not the Philosophers.[b] Several great sects of Philosophy who from either inclination or policy chose to connect their System with the established Theology were obliged to consult the most approved Interpreters of it; which scheme of conciliation has often betrayed them into absurdities. Thus in more modern ages the great Descartes has attempted to explain Transubstantiation; and the greater Newton to expoun the Revelations. Fontenelle might have spared his satyrical exclamation "Voila les raisonnemens "de cette Antiquitè si vantèe. (Oeuvres de Fontenelle. Tom ii. p 251[)]

---

29. Lord Shaftesbury has observed that after despotism was fully established at Rome, not a statue picture or medal not a tolerable piece of Architecture afterwards appeared. Mr Addison adopted his remark with great complacency &[c] Mr Warton received it too easily (Essay on the Genius &[c] writings of Pope p. 176). However if we take the period of the reigns of Vespasian &[c] Commodus; which is certainly a very fair one, we must confine this observation to painting alone. For the state of Architecture I need only appeal to the Coliseum and Trajan's column; The Statues of Antinous and Marcus Aurelius will give us an idea of the taste of Sculpture. Every connoisseur knows that the highest perfection of the Roman medals is to be sought for in the time of Trajan and Hadrian.

---

30. The Epistles of Phalaris have been pronounced spurious after a much fuller hearing than they deserved (See the Controversy between Boyle and Bentley. [)] Let me however discover another mark of their being so. Phalaris enlarges very much (See Epistle LXX &c) upon the glory the honors and the rewards that awaited the murderers of Tyrants. This was I acknowledge a general law of nations amongst the Grecian Republicks, but I think it highly improbable that it could have been so ancient as the age of Phalaris,[d] who (if he was not as Pliny reports the first Tyrant[e] known[f] in the

---

[a] *II.* Lactantius   [b] *I.* Philosophers of their time.   [c] *II.* and   [d] *I.* the world   [e] *I.* Tyrants   [f] *II. om.* known

world) may be proved to have flourished about 600 years before Christ. (Bentley against Boyle p. 29–91) Such a custom supposes many revolutions of freedom and servitude in the several Grecian Republicks; who were willing to intimidate future Tyrants by arming and encouraging every private citizen to destroy them. Such was the conduct of the Athenians when they recovered their liberty in 512; and the honors which were paid to the memory[a] of Harmodius and Aristogiton became a model for the rest of Greece.[16]

---

31. I am surprized that during that long and sharp controversy concerning the Epistles of Phalaris, neither party should have paid the least attention to the time of the foundation of Agrigentum; since the tyrant could[b] have no existence before his City. This last was built according to the authentic accounts of Thucydides (L vi sub init) 153 years later than Syracuse founded according to the Chronicle of Eusebius in the second year of the xiv.th Olympiad. (Ant. Ch. 735.); or according to the more accurate computation which Sir John Marsham has formed upon the Arundel Marbles A.C. 769. (Canon. Chron. p. 490, 495.) These two Epochas will give us 582, or 616: Either of them are[c] sufficient to refute the earlier date which Eusebius himself has given us for the age of Phalaris; and to reduce that controversy within narrower bounds

---

32. The Author of the Adventurer. Nº 127. (Mr Joseph Warton concealed under the signature of Z) concludes his ingenious paralel of the ancients and moderns by the following remark. "That age "will never again return: when a Pericles after walking with Plato[d] "in a Portico built by Phidias & painted by Appelles, might repair "to hear a pleading of Demosthenes or a tragedy of Sophocles." It will never return because it never existed. Pericles (who died in the 4th year of the LXXXIXth Olympiad. Ant. Chr. 429. Diodor.[e] Sicul. L. xii. 46) was confessedly the patron of Phidias, &[f] the cotemporary[g] of Sophocles but he could enjoy no very great pleasure in the conversation of Plato who was born the same year that he[h] himself died (Diogenes[i] Laertius in Platone V. Stanley's history of Philosophy. p. 154). The error is still more extraordinary with

---

[a] *I.* model   [b] *I.* was founded   [c] *II.* is   [d] *I. om.* with Plato   [e] *II.* Dio. Sic.   [f] *II.* and   [g] *II.* contemporary   [h] *I.* Pericles   [i] *I.* Plato in Diogenes

regard to Appelles and Demosthenes since both[a] the Painter and the Orator survived Alexander the great whose death is above a century posterior to that of Pericles (in 323). And indeed tho' Athens was the seat of every liberal art from the days of Themistocles to those of Demetrius Phalareus, yet no particular Æra will afford Mr W[b] the compleat synchronism he seems to wish for; as Tragedy was deprived of her famous triumvirate, before the arts of Philosophy and eloquence had attained the perfection[c] which they soon after received from the hands of Plato, Aristotle, and Demosthenes

---

33. Dr Mosheim supposes that the Koran, collected by the successors of Mahomet, and which is now extant; was[d] different from the law, which the Prophet gave the Arabians during his life time because in the former he appeals to &[e] extols the latter. This fact or rather conjecture is founded only on a reason evidently groundless. The 114 Chapters which compose that extraordinary book[f] were brought down by the Angel Gabriel upon[g] as many different occasions; and it is no ways absurd that in his later revelations, Mahomet should appeal to those he had already received Mr Sale whom, Dr Mosheim in the same place (Ecclesiastical History. Vol. 1 p. 314) celebrates with reason as the Ablest Expositor of the Koran, would have informed him[h] of that particularity. (See Preliminary Discourse to the English translation of the Koran. p. 63, 64

---

34. Dr Mosheim represents the Norman Pirates as absolutely devoid of any religion whatsoever. (Ecclesiastical History Vol. 1 p. 432). It is however certain that these Pirates who were the bravest &[e] the noblest adventurers of the Scandinavian nations, worshipped the Gods of their fathers believed in the immortality of the soul, and received with religious faith the System of doctrine laid down in their Edda; which book M. Mallet (see Introduction à l'histoire du Dannemarc) has since introduced to the general acquaintance of the publick; but which was even then accessible to the curiosity of a German Scholar. D[r] Mosheim's proposition is at once groundless, and dangerous

---

[a] *I.* it i	[b] *II.* Warton	[c] *I.* perfections	[d] *I.* to be	[e] *II.* and
[f] *I. om.* book	[g] *I.* at	[h] *I. om.* him		

35. Mr Christopher Smart a new and very indifferent translator of Horace (See Monthly Review August, 1767) conjectures, that the first lines of the art of Poetry, not only condemn an[a] affected and vitiated taste in writing; but are particularly levelled against the Metamorphoses of Ovid, which are[b] so often infected by it. The Conjecture is ingenious &[c] supported by some appearances; but it is totally repugnant to Ovid's own Chronology of his works. Horace died AUC. Cap. 745; Ovid was banished AUC. 761. At that very time he was writing the Metamorphoses, and as he was leaving Rome he attempted to commit them to the flames:[d] as a rude and imperfect work. Paternal love prevailed: Ovid finished the Poem at Tomi and sent it to a friend at Rome with a short Elegy which may be considered as a preface to it (Trist. L. 1. Eleg. 7)[e] It is therefore imposible that Horace could satyrize a work which still[f] remained unfinished and in the Author's hands sixteen years after Horace's death. Even in the Augustan Age there was more than one poet who had occasion for the Critick's advice, and the Satyrist's correction

---

36. M. de Buffon speaks of compleat vessels being found in the heart of mountains at a great distance from the sea. A[g] fact indeed of a very extraordinary nature[h]; which shews us a lively glimpse of a former world and of arts cultivated by men who inhabited some country now overwhelmed by the sea, in[i] ages when the modern Alps were buried under the waters; It ought therefore to be supported by some better authority than Gordon's Geographical Grammar, or an Obscure Commentator of Ovid's Metamorphoses. It is often to be lamented that Natural Philosophers are too little acquainted with History or the laws of historical evidence. Their ignorance of them sometimes deprives them of the[j] knowledge of facts highly essential to their Systems, and at other times deceives them by fables in the dress of truth. Facts either moral or natural are related by men. The value of the evidence must be determined by the character of the witness, and yet all M. de Buffon's witnesses appear levelled by an undiscriminated equality. (Buffon. Histoire Naturelle Tom. 1. p. 592

---

[a] *I.* and [b] *I. om.* are [c] *II.* and [d] *I. om.* as . . . work [e] *I. om.* (Trist. L. 1. Eleg. 7) [f] *I. om.* still [g] *I.* But a fact of so [h] *I.* which s [i] *I.* at [j] *I. om.* them *and* the

37. Angora is famous for the long, beautifull and silky hair of several sorts of animals, and particularly of it's goats. M. de Buffon as the General historian of all those animals, has often occasion to speak of so curious a distinction; but he as constantly supposes Angora, to be a City of Syria, and even deduces consequences after his method, from the happy Climate of that country, so congenial to those animals (V Histoire Naturelle. aux articles de la Chevre du Chat, et du Lapin Tom. v, et vi). This supposed Syrian City, is however in reality one of the most considerable towns of Asia Minor, which at present contains 100,000 Souls, &^{a} is the seat of a Turkish Pasha; and which was formerly under the name of Ancyra, the Capital of the province of Galatia. This breed of Goats is even confined to about thirty miles round Ancyra, &^{a} easily degenerates when carried to any distance (V Pococke's Description of the East. Vol. ii. P. ii. p. 86–90) M. de Buffon was not betrayed into this error by any præconceived System. On the contrary, the latitude of Spain agrees still more strictly with Asia Minor, than with Syria[17]

---

38. M. de Voltaire (V. Le Corneille de Voltaire Tom ix. p. 153)[18] praises Racine and Corneille for having, both of them, very judiciously avoided shewing the contempt which the Romans &^{a} indeed all Mankind entertained for the Jewish nation. Berenice was^b the Heroine of their Tragedy and the Reader might possibly have thought too much like a Roman. Voltaire might have added, that those poets were equally in the right in representing her as a young princess; altho at the time of her separation from Titus, she was above fifty. History *must* receive &^{a} *can* only explain the most improbable facts when they are properly averred. Poetry ought always to prefer agreable probablities to harsh &^{a} unlikely truths. The proof of Berenice's age is clear &^{a} easy. Her father Agrippa died. AC. 44. She was then 16 and already married to her uncle Herod King of Calcis: Titus succeeded his father Vespasian in the year 79, 35 years after the death of Agrippa (.V. Tillemont Histoire des Empereurs. Tom. 1. p. 839 de l'edit in 12° et toutes les autoritès qu'il cite)[19]

---

39. That ingenious trifler, Mr Horace Walpole has given us. (Royal and Noble authors Vol. 1. p 67–81)[20] a very curious article of the

^{a} *II.* and ^{b} *I.* wh

brave and learned Earl Rivers. He is however inacurate in the account of a tournament in Smithfield between the Earl and the great Bastard of Burgundy. 1 The tournament which was held just[a] before the death of Philip Duke of Burgundy, that is to say in the beginning of the summer 1467 (V. Memoires dOlivier de la Marche p. 489 &c in 4° à Gand 1566 et Chronique de Bourgogne dans le second Volume de Philippe de Comines p 189) could have no relation with the nuptials of Duke Charles and the Princess of England which were celebrated in July 1468. From this mistaken date Mr W[b] extracts a very puerile reflection. The Hero &[c] the Virago might think the combat of their near relation a proper compliment to their union; but the brother of Edward iv.[thsd] wife can[e] scarcely be deemed a near relation[f] of Edward's sister. 2. Mr W[b] draws his account[g] of the combat from an Englishman, who thought that[h] when the champions were parted, the superiority was clearly on Earl Rivers side Olivier de la Marche was of a different opinion, but he viewed the whole affair with the partial eyes of a subject of Burgundy Mr W[b] shews at least an equal partiality to the English Knight, when he extolls Earl Rivers generosity, for disdaining[i] the first day to make use of the advantage he had gained by killing the Bastard's horse. The advantage itself was a contravention of the laws of Chivalry, the Earl was forced to excuse himself both to the King who expressed great anger, and to his adversary who readily accepted his excuses and his assurances that the blow was purely accidental (V.[j] Oliv. de la Marche p. 91. Memoires sur la Chevalerie par M. de S[te] Palaye &c.) I am sorry Mr W.[b] never met with Olivier de la Marche. He might have added to his article of Earl Rivers a multitude of those little anecdotes[k] he is so fond of.[21]

---

40. M de Buffon often sacrifices truth to eloquence, and consistency to variety. In the fourth Vol[l] of his Natural history. (V. Discours sur la Nature des Animaux p. 13–34) the brain is the general sensorium of the animal; &[c] the center of the whole nervous system, with which it communicates by an universal action and reaction; in a word the seat of sentiment and the spring of action in every creature destitute of an intellectual soul. Such is[m] the basis of

[a] *I. om.* just   [b] *II.* Walpole   [c] *II.* and   [d] *II.* the Fourth's   [e] *I. om.* can   [f] *I.* account   [g] *I.* relation   [h] *I. om.* that   [i] *I.* who disdained   [j] *I.* I am   [k] *I.* articles   [l] *I. om.* Vol; *II.* volume   [m] *I.* are

M. de B's[a] profound tho' obscure metaphysics. But in the seventh Volume (Discours sur les animaux Carnassiers p. 13, 16 &c) this basis is entirely overturned. The brain is degraded into dead matter insensible, &[b] scarcely organized, which serves only to transmit to the nerves the nourishment it has received from the arteries. The Diaphragma succeeds to all[c] the former powers of the brain; at least to many of them; for M. de Buffon disdains to acquaint us, either with the defects he discovered in his old System, or with the parts of it he still chuses to retain, and the manner he connects them with his new principles. Instead of a candid confession that he had been seduced by a delusive tho' brilliant Hypothesis, he endeavours to make the world[d] forget it, by observing a profound silence on that head, in the copious and curious index he has drawn up himself for[e] his great work.

---

41. M de Buffon seems to be a very poor Classical scholar. He always cites Aristotle in Latin &[b] most of his quotations from the ancients appear borrowed from Gesner &[b] Aldrovandus.[22] It is a great pity, as this ignorance has deprived him of many curious materials. His admirable history of the Elephant. (Histoire Naturelle. Tom. xii. p. 1–93) might have been still more curious &[b] equally authentic; since I think the testimony of a Pliny &c who[f] appeal[g] to the whole Roman people as to what they saw in the Amphitheatre, deserves as much credit, as the stories a traveller brings back from Congo or Siam. M. de Buffon might perhaps have determined with less confidence that the Climate of Europe is too cold for Elephants (V. p. 30, 47.) I am sensible that there are no examples of that animal's multiplying or even subsisting in a state of nature beyond the limits of Asia &[b] Africa. But there are many, of the Elephant's being employed in war, in Spain, Sicily, &[b] the southern parts of Italy, of their going thro' all the fatigues of a campaign, &c. Those of Hannibal perished indeed in the severe winter marches, that General made over the Alps &[b] Apennines. A curious passage of Juvenal (Satir. xii. 102) informs us that droves of Elephants belonging to the Emperor were kept in the fields around Ardea. They were probably maintained for the publick shews; and it is to[h] other droves of the same nature, that we are to refer the Elephant's bones found in

[a] *II.* Buffon's [b] *II.* and [c] *I.* th [d] *I. om.* world [e] *I.* of *I.* whole [g] *I.* appeals [h] *I.* probably to

Tuscany and other parts of Italy. (V. Dissertazioni del Cavalier Guazzeri. p. 68 &[c]

---

42. Father Pagi to whom good letters have many obligations shews (in his Dissertatio Hypatica p. 368) that he read history like a monk A writer or two of his own complexion had made use of the words *Consulatus, Fasces &c* in speaking of the Saracen Kings of Corduba (The Khalifs of Spain of the house of Ommiyah) Now as the Kings of France, Italy, &c of those ages, really took the title of Consul, Father Pagi very sagaciously concludes that the Arab Khalifs imitated their example without ever reflecting on the enormous difference there was between them. The Northern Chiefs had adopted the religion and manners of the conquered nations &^{a} still revered the power they had overturned. The Musulmans detested that religion, were strangers to those manners &^{a} despised that power. The Successors of the Prophet would have disdained a title which levelled them with the servants of the Christian Dog. In them the imitation of the Roman style would have been absurd; in the authors^b of those times it was easy &^{a} natural. Salust was a more correct writer, than Eulogius or the Abbot Samson of Cordova; yet Salust (Bell. Jugurth. C. 12) speaks of the *Lictor proxumus* of a Numidian prince, who had Guards &^{a} officers, but who certainly had no lictors. This translation of ideas is common in all languages

---

43 Olearius as quoted by M. de Buffon (Histoire Naturelle. Tom xi. p 241) rejects with scorn the antipathy which the ancients have supposed between the horse and the Camel, &^{a} of which they have related such celebrated instances. Every caravan &^{a} ever[y]^c stable in Persia is according to Olearius a proof of the contrary. But this reasoning is very fallacious The instances mentioned by the ancients suppose those animals unacquainted with each other, meeting for the first time, &^{a} left entirely to their natural impressions. But it is not the least proof of the empire of man over^d the animals, that by habit and education he can subdue those impressions, and can establish a degree of harmony and even of familiarity between the most discordant natures. The Dog and the Cat are domestick evidences of this assertion[23]

---

^{a} *II*. and ^{b} *I*. writers ^{c} *II*. every ^{d} *I*. of

44. Pliny speaking of an animal. (Machlis) supposed to be the Rain-deer, says the creature was only to be found in Scandinavia[a] Cæsar describes[b] the same animal as a native of the Hercynian Forrest in Germany M. de Buffon is struck with this contradiction, (Histoire Naturelle. Tom xii p. 82) which is indeed only apparent. Our author who is a better Naturalist, than an Antiquarian, did not know that the vast island or peninsula of Scandinavia was considered by most of the ancients as a part of Germany (V. Cluver. German. Antiq. L. iii. p. 159 &c.) that the ocean was the northern boundary of Germany. (Tacit. de morib. German. C. 1. &c) &[c] that the Hercynian forrest lost itself in the most remote parts of that un-known country. (Cæsar. de bell. Gallic. L. vi. C. 25

---

45. M. de Buffon asserts (Hist. Natur. Tom xi. p. 229, [)] that the camel has been so compleatly subdued by man that there remains no individuals of the species in a state of nature &[c] freedom. This may be true enough in our times, but it was not so in those of Diodorus Siculus. That curious traveller says there were wild Camels in Arabia. (Bibliot. L. iii. C. 44. Edit. Wesseling) The fact seems probable in itself, and it confirms M. de B's[d] opinion that the Camel was originally a native of Arabia, for whose sandy deserts he and he alone seems formed

---

46. M. Marmontel has made a singular mistake in his elegant translation of Lucan That poet had said of the Gallic Druids (Lucan. Pharsal. L. 1 ℣ 452).

> Solis nosse Deos, et cœli numina vobis
> Aut solis nescire datum—

In the French version of the Pharsalia, this exclamation is turned into a panygerick of the doctrine of the Gallican Church. "Vous "seuls, avez le privilege de choisir entre tous les Dieux, ceux qu'on "doit adorer, ceux qu'on doit meconnoitre.["] But the poet was admiring not the truth but the singularity of the Druidical System of[e] Theology. Observing how much it disagreed with that of other nations; he cries out "The knowledge of the Gods has been granted

---

[a] *I.* the   [b] *I.* describing   [c] *II.* and   [d] *II.* Buffon's   [e] *I.* in the

"or has been refused to you alone.["] (V. le Lucaèn de Marmontel. Tom. i. p. 32)

---

47. The King of Prussia appears throughout his writings an enemy to the English. His description of the battle of Blenheim is a glaring instance of his partiality (.V l'Art de la Guerre. Chant. vi)

> Ainsi le grand Eugene, à ce fameux village
> Où Tallard et Marsin s'etoient très mal postès
> D'un effort general donna de tous cotès &c.

The history contained in these lines is as erroneous as the poetry of them is indifferent. The great Eugene, to whom the sole glory of the day is ascribed, commanded the right wing of the Allied army, and was so well opposed by Marsin and the Elector of Bavaria, that his repeated attacks made no impression on them. It was his Collegue the Duke of Marlbouroug,[a] who improved the many blunders of Tallard, passed the rivulet, broke the center of the French army, took the flower of their troops in the Village of Blenheim, and in a word obtained a compleat victory. (V. Memoires de Feuquieres, Tom. iii p. 357–387 Kane's Campaigns p. 57–61, Histoire Generale par Voltaire. Tom. vme. p. 277

---

48. The translator of M de Haller's poems has inserted a note which is to me incomprehensible. The poet (p. 112) had exclaimed with indignation "Ou coule aujourdhui le sang des Muhleren et des "Bubenberg? *Bubenberg* (adds the translator) famille d'une ancienne "noblesse à Berne . . . . *Muhleren* un officier de cette famille, qui etoit "aussi d'une ancienne noblesse fit paroitre son courage dans la "defense de Morat contre Charles le hardi en 1476.["] 1. If the family was noble[b] (as it certainly was,) it seems superfluous to add that each individual of it was so likewise. 2. I am perfectly well acquainted with the Bubenberg who defended Morat so gallantly against Charles the hardy. His hame was Adrian, and neither Schilling a Cotemporary[c] historian, nor that indefatigable Collector M. Leu (in his Helvetic dictionary [)] make the least mention of that extraordinary name of Muhleren which I never heard of, but which

---

[a] *II*. Marlborough   [b] *MS. marked as if quotation continued*   [c] *II*. contemporary

M. de Haller himself seems clearly to separate from that of Bubenberg. This passage is more singular as I have some reason to believe
that the translator is M. de Tscharner of one of the best families of
Berne; and who has wrote[a] with applause a history of his own country in the German language. (V. Choix des Poesies Allemandes par
M Huber. Tom. iii. p. 242)[24]

ALPHABETICAL. LIST[b].

		N[os].
1.	Addison. —	20, 22
2.	Beaufort— — —	4.
3	Boyle & Bentley—	31
4.	Buffon — —	36, 37, 40, 41, 44, 45
5	Cicero — —	7
6	Corneille and Racine —	38
7.	Dacier —	2
8.	Fontenelle —	26, 27, 28
9	Freret —	14.
10	Guichardt	10
11	Guthrie —	8
12	Hirtius —	9
13	Hume —	3
14	Hurd — —	1
15	Lardner & Mosheim —	23
16	Maillet.[c]	17
17	Marmontel	46
18	Mongault & Middleton.	6
19.	Montesqieu[d] —	12.
20	Mosheim	33[e]
21.	Mosheim[f] —	34
22	Muratori —	13
23.	Notitia U[g] J.	5
24.	Olearius —	43
25.	Pagi — —	42.
26.	Phalaris —	30

[a] II. written   [b] II. alters all numbers necessary owing to its omissions
[c] I. Montesqieu   [d] II. Montesquieu   [e] Page ends. MS. repeats N[os] at head
of column on next page.   [f] II. lists the Mosheim entries together.   [g] II. W

		Nos.
27	Pope —	21
28.	Prussia (King of)	47.
29.	Salust.	11
30	Shaftsbury &c	29
31	Smart. — —	35
32.	(Temple (Sir William).	16
33	Tscharner —	48
34.	Voltaire —	18, 19, 24, 25[a]
35	Walpole —	39
36.	Warburton —	15
37	Warton — —	32

[a] *II. adds* 36, *i.e.* 38

CRITICAL OBSERVATIONS

ON THE

SIXTH BOOK

OF THE

Æ N E I D.

As the reasonable De La Bruyere observes, "*Qui ne sait
être un* ERASME, *doit penser à être un* EVEQUE."

POPE's WORKS, vol. IV. p. 321. with the Commentaries
and Notes of Mr. WARBURTON.

LONDON:

Printed for P. ELMSLEY, Successor to Mr. Vaillant,
in the Strand.

MDCCLXX.

CRITICAL OBSERVATIONS

ON THE

D E S I G N

OF THE

SIXTH BOOK of the ÆNEID.

THE Allegorical Interpretation which the Bishop of Glocester[1] has given of the Sixth Book of the Æneid, seems to have been very favourably received by the Public. Many writers, both at home and abroad, have mentioned it with approbation, or at least with esteem; and I have more than once heard it alledged, in the conversation of scholars, as an ingenious improvement on the plain and obvious sense of Virgil. As such, it is not undeserving of the notice of a candid critic; nor can the enquiry be void of entertainment, whilst Virgil is our constant theme. Whatever may be the fortune of the chace, we are sure it will lead us through pleasant prospects and a fine country.

That I may escape the imputation as well as the danger of mis-representing his Lordship's Hypothesis, I shall expose it in his own words. "The purpose of this Discourse is to shew that Æneas's "adventure to the INFERNAL SHADES, is no other than a figurative "description of his INITIATION INTO THE MYSTERIES; and "particularly a very exact one of the SPECTACLES of the ELEU-"SINIAN[1]." This general notion is supported with singular in-genuity, dressed up with an easy yet pompous display of Learning, and delivered in a style much fitter for the Hierophant of Eleusis, than for a Modern Critic, who is observing a remote object through the medium of a glimmering and doubtful light:

Ibant obscuri, solâ sub nocte, per umbram.

[1] See Warburton's Dissertation, &c. in the third volume of Mr. Warton's Virgil. I shall quote indifferently that Dissertation or the Divine Legation itself.

His Lordship naturally enough pursues two different methods which unite, as he apprehends, in the same conclusion. From general principles peculiar to himself, he infers the propriety and even necessity of such a Description of the Mysteries; and from a comparison of particular circumstances he labours to prove that Virgil has actually introduced it into the Æneid. Each of these methods shall be considered separately.

×   ×   ×   ×

As the learned Prelate's Opinions branch themselves out into luxuriant Systems, it is not easy to resume them in a few words. I shall, however, attempt to give a short idea of those general principles, which occupy, I know not how, so great a share of the *Divine Legation of Moses demonstrated.*

"The whole System of Paganism, of which the Mysteries were an "essential part, was instituted by the Antient Lawgivers for the "support and benefit of Society. The mysteries themselves were a "School of Morality and Religion, in which the vanity of Polythe-"ism[2], and the Unity of the First Cause, were revealed to the "Initiated. Virgil, who intended his immortal Poem for a Republic "in action, as those of Plato and Tully were in precept, could not "avoid displaying this first and noblest art of Government. His perfect "Law-giver must be initiated, as the antient Founders of States had "been before him; and as Augustus himself was many ages after-"wards."

What a crowd of natural reflections must occur to an unbiassed mind! Was the civil magistrate the mover of the whole machine; the sole contriver, or at least the sole support of Religion? Were antient laws ALWAYS designed for the benefit of the people, and NEVER for the private interest of the Lawgiver? Could the first fathers of rude societies instruct their new-made subjects in philosophy as well as in agriculture? Did they all agree, in Britain as in Egypt, in Persia as in Greece, to found these secret schools on the same common principle; which subsisted near*a* eighteen hundred years at Eleusis[3]

---

[2] At least of the vulgar polytheism, by revealing that the *Dii Majorum Gentium* had been mere mortals.

[3] From their institution, 1399 years before the Christian æra (Marm. Arundel. Ep 14),[2] till their suppression, towards the end of the fourth century.

---

a II. nearly

in its primæval purity? Can these things be? Yes, replies the learned prelate; they are: "Egypt was the mysterious mother of Religion and "Policy; and the arts of Egypt were diffused with her colonies over "the antient World. Inachus carried the Mysteries into Greece, "Zoroaster into Persia[4], &c. &c."——I retire from so wide a field, in which it would be easy for me to lose both myself and my adversary. THE ANTIENT WORLD, EIGHTEEN CENTURIES, and FOUR HUNDRED AUTHORS GENUINE AND APOCRYPHAL[5], would, under tolerable management, furnish some volumes of controversy; and since I have perused the two thousand and fourteen pages of the unfinished *Legation*, I have less inclination than ever to spin out volumes of laborious trifles.

I shall, however, venture to point out a fact, not very agreeable to the favourite notion, that Paganism was entirely the Religion of the magistrate. The Oracles were not less antient, nor less venerable than the Mysteries. Every difficulty, religious or civil, was submitted to the decision of those infallible tribunals. During several ages no war could be undertaken, no colony founded, without the sanction of the Delphic Oracle; the first and most celebrated amongst[b] several hundred others[6]. Here then we might expect to perceive the

---

[4] Though I hate to be positive, yet I would almost venture to affirm, that Zoroaster's connection with Egypt is no where to be found, except in the *D.L.*

[5] See a list of four hundred Authors, quoted, &c. in the *D.L.* from St. Austin and Aristotle, down to Scarron and Rabelais. Amongst these authors we may observe Sanchoniatho, Orpheus, Zaleucus, Charondas, the Oracles of Porphyry, and the History of Jeffrey of Monmouth.[3]

The bishop has entered the lists with the tremendous Bentley, who treated the laws of Zaleucus and Charondas as the forgeries of a sophist. A whole section of mistakes or misrepresentations is devoted to this controversy: But Bentley is no more, and W——n may sleep in peace.

I shall, however, disturb his repose, by asking him on what authority he supposes that the old language of the Twelve Tables was altered for the conveniency[a] of succeeding ages. The fragments of those laws, collected by Lipsius, Sylburgius, &c. bear the stamp of the most remote antiquity. Lipsius himself (tom. i. p. 206) was highly delighted with those *Antiquissima Verba*: But what is much more decisive, Horace (L. II. Ep. i. Ver. 23), Seneca (Epistol. 114), and Aulus Gellius (XX. 1), rank those laws amongst the oldest remains of the Latin tongue. Their obsolete language was admired by the lawyers, ridiculed by the wits, and pleaded by the friends of antiquity as an excuse for the frequent obscurities of that code.

Had an adversary to the *Divine Legation* been guilty of this mistake, I am afraid it would have been styled an *egregious blunder*.

[6] See Vandale de Oraculis, p. 559. That valuable book contains whatever can now be known of Oracles.[4] I have borrowed his facts; and could with great ease have borrowed his quotations.

---

[a] *II.* convenience   [b] *II.* among

directing hand of the magistrate. Yet when we study their history with attention, instead of the Alliance between Church and State, we can only discover the antient Alliance between the Avarice of the Priest and the Credulity of the People. For my own part, I am very apt to consider the Mysteries in the same light as the Oracles. An intimate connection subsisted between them[7]: Both were preceded and accompanied with fasts, sacrifices, and lustrations; with mystic sights and preternatural sounds: But the most essential preparation for the ASPIRANT, was a general confession of his past life, which was exacted of him by the Priest. In return for this implicit confidence, the Hierophant conferred on the Initiated a sacred character; and promised them a peculiar place of happiness in the Elysian fields, whilst the souls of the Profane (however virtuous they had been) were wallowing in the mire[8]. Nor did the Priests of the Mysteries neglect to recommend to the brethren a spirit of friendship, and the love of virtue; so pleasing even to the most corrupt minds, and so requisite to render any society respectable in its own eyes. Of all these religious societies, that of Eleusis was the most illustrious. From being peculiar to the inhabitants of Attica, it became at last common to the whole Pagan world. Indeed, I should suspect that it was much indebted to the genius of the Athenian writers, who bestowed fame and dignity on whatever had the least connection with their country; nor am I surprised that Cicero and Atticus,[6] who were both initiated, should express themselves with enthusiasm, when they speak of the sacred rites of their beloved Athens.

But our curiosity is yet unsatisfied; we would press forwards into the sanctuary; and are eager to learn, WHAT was the SECRET which was revealed to the Initiated, and to them alone. Many of the Profane, possessed of leisure and ingenuity, have tried to guess, what has been so religiously concealed. The SECRET of each is curious and philosophical; for as soon as we attempt this Enquiry, the honour of the Mysteries becomes our own[9]. I too could frame

---

[7] The prophet Alexander, whose arts are so admirably laid open by Lucian, instituted his Oracle and his Mysteries as regular parts of the same plan. It is here we may say, with the learned Catholic, "Les nouveaux Saints me font douter des Anciens."[5]

[8] See Diogen. Laert. vi. 39. &[a] Menag. ad loc.

[9] I shall sum them up in a curious passage of the celebrated Freret. "Les sectes "philosophiques cherchoient à diviner le Dogme caché sous le voile des Ceremonies; &[b]

---

[a] II. and   [b] II. et

an hypothesis, as plausible perhaps, and as uncertain as any of theirs, did I not feel myself checked by the apprehension of discovering what never existed[10]. I admire the discretion of the Initiated; but the best security for discretion is, the vanity of concealing that we have nothing to reveal.

The examples of great men, when they cannot serve as models, may serve as warnings to us. I should be very sorry to have discovered, that an ATHEISTICAL HISTORY[1] was used in the celebration of the Mysteries, to prove the Unity of the First Cause, and that an ANTIENT HYMN[2] was sung, for the edification of the devout Athenians, which was most probably A MODERN FORGERY of some Jewish or Christian Impostor. Had I delivered THESE TWO DISCOVERIES, with an air of Confidence and Triumph, I should be still more mortified.

After all, as I am not apt to give the name of Demonstration to what is mere conjecture, his Lordship may take advantage of my Scepticism, and still affirm, that his favourite Mysteries were Schools of Theism, instituted by the Lawgiver. Yet unless Æneas is the Lawgiver of Virgil's Republic, he has no more business with the Mysteries of Athens, than with the laws of Sparta. We will,

"tachoient de le ramener chacune à leur doctrine. Dans l'hypothése des Epicuriens, adoptée de nos jours par M.M. Leclerc & Warburton," (Leclerc *adopted* it in the year 1687;[7] Mr. Warburton *invented* it in the year 1738) "tout ce qu'on révéloit aux "adeptes après tant de préparatifs &[a] d'épreuves, c'est que les Dieux adorés du Vulgaire, "avoient été des hommes, &c. Les Stoiciens & les Hylozoistes supposoient qu'on en- "seignoit aux Initiés, qu'il n'y avoit d'autres Dieux que les élémens &[a] les parties de "l'univers materiel. Enfin suivant les nouveaux Platoniciens, ces Symboles servoient à "couvrir les dogmes d'une Théologie &[a] d'une Philosophie sublimes, enseignées autrefois "par les Egyptiens &[a] les Chaldéens." Mr.[b] Freret inclines, though with great diffidence, to the last opinion. *Mem. de l'Academie des Inscriptions, &c. tom.* xxi. *p.* 12. *Hist.*

[10] Je ne suis pas si convaincu de nôtre ignorance par les choses qui sont, & dont la raison nous est inconnuë; que par celles qui ne sont point & dont nous trouvons la raison. *Oeuvres de Fontenelle, tom.* xi. *p.* 229.

[1] *The Fragment of Sanchoniatho's Phœnician History.* Eusebius and bishop Cumberland have already observed, that the formation of the world is there attributed to the blind powers of Matter, without the least mention of an Intelligent Cause.

[2] *Orpheus's Hymn to Musæus,* quoted by Justin Martyr, and several other Fathers, but rejected as spurious by Cudworth (Intellectual System, p. 300), by Leclerc (Hist. Eccl. p. 692), and by Dr. Jortin (Remarks on Ecclesiastical Hist. vol. I. p. 199). The first of these, the *immortal Cudworth,* is often celebrated by the Bishop of Gloucester; Leclerc's literary character is established; and with respect to Dr. Jortin, I will venture to call him a learned and moderate Critic. The few who may not chuse to confess, that their objections are unanswerable, will allow that they deserved to be answered.

[a] *II.* et   [b] *II.* M.

therefore, reflect a moment on the true nature and plan of the Æneid.

An Epic Fable must be important as well as interesting: Great actions, great virtues, and great distresses, are the peculiar province of Heroic Poetry. This rule seems to have been dictated by nature and experience, and is very different from those chains in which Genius has been bound by artificial Criticism. The importance I speak of, is not indeed always dependant on the rank or names of the Personages. Columbus, exploring a new world with three sloops and ninety sailors, is a Hero worthy of the Epic Muse; yet our imagination would be much more strongly affected by the image of a virtuous Prince saved from the ruins of his country, and conducting his faithful followers through unknown seas and through hostile lands. Such is the Hero of the Æneid. But his peculiar situation suggested other beauties to the Poet, who had an opportunity of adorning his subject with whatever was most pleasing in Grecian fable, or most illustrious in Roman history. Æneas had fought under the walls of Ilium; and conducted to the Banks of the Tyber a Colony from which Rome claimed her origin.

The character of the Hero is expressed by one of his friends in a few words; and, tho'[a] drawn by a friend, does not seem to be flattered:

> Rex erat Æneas nobis; quo justior alter,
> Nec pietate fecit,[b] nec bello major &[c] armis. [3]

These three virtues, of JUSTICE, of PIETY, and of VALOR, are finely supported throughout the Poem. [4]

1. I shall here mention one instance of the Hero's justice, which has been less noticed than its singularity seems to deserve.

After Evander had entertained his Guests, with a sublime simplicity, he lamented, that his age and want of power made him a very useless Ally. However, he points out auxiliaries and a cause worthy of a Hero. The Etruscans, tired out with the repeated tyrannies of

---

[3] Æneid, i. 548.

[4] M. de Voltaire condemns the latter part of the Æneid, as far inferior in fire and spirit to the former. As quoted in the *Legation*, he thinks that Virgil

—s'épuise avec Didon & rate à la fin Làvinie;[8]

a pretty odd quotation for a Bishop; but I most sincerely hope, that neither his Lordship nor Mrs. W——n are acquainted with the true meaning of the word *Rater*.

---

[a] *II*. though   [b] *II*. fuit   [c] *II*. et

Mezentius, had driven that monarch from his throne, and reduced him to implore the protection of Turnus. Unsatisfied with freedom, the Etruscans called loudly for revenge; and, in the Poet's opinion, revenge was justice.

> *Ergo omnis* furiis *surrexit Etruria* justis:
> Regem *ad* supplicium *præsenti*ᵃ *Marte reposcunt*[5].

Æneas, with the approbation of Gods and men, accepts the command of these brave rebels, and punishes the Tyrant with the death he so well deserved. The conduct of Æneas and the Etruscans may, in point of justice, seem doubtful to many; the sentiments of the Poet cannot appear equivocal to any one. Milton himself, I mean the Milton of the Commonwealth, could not have asserted with more energy the daring pretensions of the people, to punish as well as to resist a Tyrant. Such opinions, published by a writer, whom we are taught to consider as the creature of Augustus, have a right to surprize us; yet they are strongly expressive of the temper of the times; the Republic was subverted, but the minds of the Romans were still Republican.

2. Æneas's piety has been more generally confessed than admired. St. Evremond laughs at it, as unsuitable to his own temper. The Bishop of Gloucester defends it, as agreeable to his own System of the Lawgiver's Religion. The French wit was too superficial, the English scholar too profound, to attend to the plain narration of the Poet, and the peculiar circumstances of antient Heroes. WE believe from faith and reason: THEY believed from the report of their senses. Æneas had seen the Grecian Divinities overturning the foundations of fated Troy. He was personally acquainted with his mother Venus, and with his persecutor Juno. Mercury, who commanded him to leave Carthage, was as present to his eyes as Dido, who strove to detain him. Such a knowledge of Religion, founded on sense and experience, must insinuate itself into every instant of our lives, and determine every action. All this is, indeed, fiction; but it is fiction in which we chuse to acquiesce, and which we justly consider as the charm of Poetry. If we allow, that Æneas lived in an intimate commerce with superior Beings, we must likewise allow, his love or his fear, his confidence or his gratitude, towards those Beings, to

[5] Æneid, viii. 495.

ᵃ *II.* presenti

display themselves on every proper occasion. Far from thinking Æneas too pious, I am sometimes surprized at his want of faith. Forgetful of the Fates, which had so often and so clearly pointed out the destined shores of Latium, he deliberates, whether he shall not sit down quietly in the fields of Sicily. An apparition of his father is necessary to divert him from this impious and ungenerous design.

3. A Hero's valor will not bear the rude breath of suspicion; yet has the courage of Æneas suffered from an unguarded expression of the Poet:

> *Extemplò Æneæ solvuntur frigore membra^a*
> *Ingemit*[6].

On every other occasion, the Trojan chief is daring without rashness, and prudent without timidity. In that dreadful night, when Troy was delivered up to her hostile Gods, he performed every duty of a Soldier, a Patriot, and a Son.

> *Moriamur &^{b} in media arma ruamus.*
> *Una salus victis, nullam sperare salutem.*[7]
> *Iliaci cineres, &^{b} flamma extrema meorum,*
> *Testor, in occasu vestro, nec tela, nec ullas*
> *Vitavisse vices Danaûm; &,^{b} si fata fuissent*
> *Ut caderem, meruisse manu*[8].

To quote other proofs of the same nature, would be to copy the six last books of the Æneid. I cannot, however, forbear mentioning the calm and superior intrepidity of the Hero, when, after the perfidy of the Rutuli, and his wound, he rushed again to the field, and restored Victory by his presence alone.

> *Ipse neque aversos dignatur sternere morti;*
> *Nec pede congressos æquo, nec tela ferentes*
> *Insequitur: solum densa in caligine Turnum*
> *Vestigat lustrans, solum in certamina poscit*[9].

At length, indignant that his victim has escaped him,^{c} his contempt gives way to fury:

> *Jam tandem invadit medios, &^{b} Marte secundo*
> *Terribilis, sævam nullo discrimine cædem*
> *Suscitat, irarumque omnes effundit habenas*[10].

---

[6] Æneid, i. 96.   [7] Æneid, ii. 353.   [8] Idem, ii. 431.
[9] Idem, xii. 464.   [10] Idem, xii. 497.

---

^{a} *II.* membra; ^{b} *II.* et ^{c} *II. om.* him

The Heroic character of Æneas has been understood and admired by every attentive reader. But to discover the LAWGIVER in Æneas, and A SYSTEM OF POLITICS in the Æneid, required the CRITICAL TELESCOPE[1] of the great W——n. The naked eye of common sense cannot reach so far. I revolve in my memory the harmonious sense of Virgil: Virgil seems as ignorant as myself of his political character. I return to the less pleasing pages of the *Legation*: So far from condescending to proofs, the Author of the *Legation* is even sparing of conjectures.

"Many political instructions may be drawn from the Æneid." And from what book which treats of MAN, and the adventures of human life, may they not be drawn? His Lordship's Chymistry (did his Hypothesis require it) would extract a SYSTEM OF POLICY from the ARABIAN NIGHTS ENTERTAINMENTS.

"A System of Policy delivered in the example of a great prince, "must shew him in every public occurrence of life. Hence, Æneas "was of necessity to be found voyaging, with Ulysses, and fighting, "with Achilles[2]."

There is another public occurrence, at least as much in the character of a LAWGIVER, as either voyaging or fighting; I mean, GIVING LAWS. Except in a single line[3], Æneas never appears in that occupation. In Sicily, he compliments Acestes with the honour of giving laws to the colony, which he himself had founded.

> *Interea Æneas urbem designat aratro,*
> *Sortiturque domos: hoc, Ilium; &ᵃ hæc loca, Trojæ*
> *Esse jubet; gaudet regno Trojanus Acestes,*
> *Indicitque forum, &ᵃ patribus dat jura vocatis[4].*

In the solemn treaty, which is to fix the fate of his posterity, he disclaims any design of innovating the laws of Latium. On the contrary,

---

[1] Others are furnished by Criticism with a *Telescope*. They see with great clearness whatever is too remote to be discovered by the rest of mankind; but are totally blind to all that lies immediately before them. They discover in every passage some secret meaning, some remote allusion, some artful allegory, or some occult imitation, which no other reader ever suspected: But they have no perception of the cogency of arguments, the contexture of narration, the various colours of diction, or the flowery embellishments of fancy. Of all that engages the attention of others they are totally insensible; while they pry into the worlds of conjecture, and amuse themselves with phantoms in the clouds. *Rambler.*9

[2] D.L. vol. I. p. 212.   [3] Æneid, iii. 137.   [4] Idem, v. 755.

ᵃ *II.* et

he only demands a hospitable seat for his Gods and his Trojans; and professes to leave the whole authority to king Latinus.

> *Non ego, nec Teucris Italos parere jubebo,*
> *Nec mihi regna peto: paribus se legibus ambæ*
> *Invictæ gentes æterna in fœdera mittant.*
> *Sacra Deosque dabo: socer arma Latinus habeto,*
> *Imperium solemne socer: mihi mœnia Teucri*
> *Constituent, urbique dabit Lavinia nomen*[5].

"But after all, is not the fable of the Æneid the establishment "of an empire?" Yes, in one sense, I grant it is. Æneas had many external difficulties to struggle with. When the Latins were defeated, Turnus slain, and Juno appeased, these difficulties were removed. The Hero's labor was over, the Lawgiver's commenced from that moment; and, as if Virgil had a design against the Bishop's System, at that very moment the Æneid ends. Virgil, who corrected with judgment, and felt with enthusiasm, thought perhaps, that the sober arts of peace could never interest a reader, whose mind had been so long agitated with scenes of distress and slaughter. He might perhaps say, like the Sylla of Montesquieu, "J'aime à remporter des victoires, "à fonder ou détruire des états, à faire des ligues, à punir un usur-"pateur; mais, pour ces minces détails de gouvernement, où les "Génies médiocres ont tant d'avantages, cette lente exécution des "loix, cette discipline d'une milice tranquille, mon ame ne sçauroit "s'en occuper[6]."

Had Virgil designed to compose a POLITICAL INSTITUTE, the example of Fenelon,[10] his elegant Imitator, may give us some notion of the manner in which he would have proceeded. The preceptor of the Duke of Burgundy professedly designed to educate a prince for the happiness of the people. Every incident in his pleasing Romance is subservient to that great end. The Goddess of Wisdom, in a human shape, conducts her pupil thro'[a] a varied series of instructive adventures;[b] and every adventure is a lesson or a warning for Telemachus. The pride of Sesostris, the tyranny of Pygmalion, the perfidy of Adrastus, and the imprudence of Idomeneus, are displayed in their true light. The innocence of the inhabitants of Bœtica, the commerce of Tyre, and the wise laws of Crete and Salentum, instructed the prince of the various means by which a people may be

---

[5] Æneid, xii. 189.   [6] Oeuvres de Montesquieu, tom. iii. p. 555.

---

[a] *II.* through   [b] *II.* adventure

made happy. From the Telemachus of Fenelon, I could pass with pleasure to the Cyropœdia of Xenophon. But I should be led too far from my subject, were I to attempt to lay open the true nature and design of that philosophical history. We must return from Fenelon and Xenophon to the Bishop of Glocester.

His Lordship props the legislative character of Æneas with an additional support: "Augustus, who was shadowed in the person of "Æneas, was initiated into the Eleusinian Mysteries[7]. *Ergo, &c.*" This doctrine of types and shadows, though true in general, has on this, as well as on graver occasions, produced a great abuse of reason, or at least of reasoning. To confine myself to Virgil, I shall only say, that he was too judicious to compliment the Emperor, at the expence of good sense and probability. Every age has its manners; and the poet must suit his Hero to the Age, and not the Age to his Hero. It is easy to give instances of this truth. Marc Antony, when defeated and besieged in Alexandria, challenged his competitor to decide their quarrel by a single combat. This was rejected by Augustus with contempt and derision, as the last effort of a desperate man[8]; and the world applauded the prudence of Augustus, who preferred the part of a General to that of a Gladiator. The temper and good sense of Virgil must have made him view things in the same light; yet, when Virgil introduces Æneas in similar circumstances, he gives him a quite different conduct. The Hero wishes to spare the innocent people, provokes Turnus to a single combat, and, even after the perfidy and last defeat of the Rutuli, is still ready to risk his person and victory, against the unhappy life and desperate fortunes of his Rival. The Laws of Honor are different in different Ages; and a behaviour which in Augustus was decent, would have covered Æneas with infamy.

We may apply this observation to the very case of the Eleusinian Mysteries. Augustus was initiated into them, at a time when Eleusis was become the COMMON TEMPLE OF THE UNIVERSE. The Trojan Hero could not with the smallest propriety set him that example; as the Trojan Hero lived in an age when those rites were confined to the natives of Greece, and even of Attica[9].

[7] D.L. p. 228.*a*   [8] Plutarch, in Vit. M. Anton. tom. i. 950. Edit. Wechel.[11]
[9] Plutarch, in Vit. Thesei, tom. i. p. 16. Herodot. viii. 65. Cicero de Nat. Deor. i. 42. The gradation of Athenians, Greeks, and mankind at large, may be traced in these passages.

a II. vol. i. p. 228

I have now wandered through the scientific maze in which the Bishop of Gloucester has concealed his first and general argument. It appears (when resumed) to amount to this irrefragable demonstration, "THAT IF THE MYSTERIES WERE INSTITUTED BY LEGIS-"LATORS (which they probably were not) ÆNEAS (who was no "Legislator) MUST OF COURSE BE INITIATED INTO THEM BY THE "POET."

And here I shall mention a collateral reason assigned by his Lordship, which might engage Virgil to introduce a description of the Mysteries: the PRACTICE OF OTHER POETS. This proof is so exceedingly brittle, that I fear to handle it; and shall report it faithfully in the words of our ingenious Critic[10].

"Had the old Poem under the name of Orpheus been now extant, "it would perhaps have shewn us, that no more was meant than "Orpheus's Initiation; and that the hint of this Sixth Book was "taken from thence."

As nothing now remains of that old Poem, except the title, it is not altogether so easy to guess what it would or would not have shewn us.

"But farther, it was customary for the poets of the Augustan age "to exercise themselves on the subject of the Mysteries, as appears "from Cicero, who desires Atticus, then at Athens, and initiated, to "send to Chilius, a poet of eminence, an[a] account of the Eleusinian "Mysteries; in order, as it would seem, to insert them into some "poem he was then writing."

The Eleusinian Mysteries are not mentioned in the original Passage. Cicero using the obscure brevity of familiar Letters, desires that Atticus would send their friend Chilius, $EYMOΛΠΙΔΩΝ$ $ΠΑΤΡΙΑ$[1], which may signify twenty different things, relative either to the worship of Ceres in particular, or to the Athenian Institutions in general; but which can hardly be applied to the Eleusinian Mysteries[2].

[10] D.L. vol. I. p. 233.

[1] Chilius te rogat, & ego ejus rogatû; ευμολπιδων πατρια. *Cicero ad Attic.* i. 9.

[2] As the B. of G.[b] alledges the authority of Victorius, I shall shelter myself under the names and reasons of Grœvius and the Abbé Mongault, and even transcribe the words of the former. "Non est ut hic intelligantur ritus illi secretiores, qui tantùm "Mystis noti erant, &[c] sine Capitis periculo vulgari non poterant, sed illa sacra &[c] cere-"moniæ, quibus in Eleusiniis celebrandis utebantur in omnium oculis Eumolpidæ; "quasque Poetæ &[c] prisci Scriptores alii commemorant passim: aut fortè per Eumolpidas

[a] *II.* on   [b] *II.* Bishop of Gloucester   [c] *II.* et

"Thus it appears that both the antient and modern poets afforded "Virgil a pattern for this famous episode."

How does this appear? From an old Poem, of whose contents the Critic is totally ignorant, and from an obscure passage, the meaning of which he has most probably mistaken.

×   ×   ×   ×

Instead of conjecturing what Virgil might or ought to do, it would seem far more natural to examine what he has done. The Bishop of Gloucester attempts to prove, that the Descent to Hell is properly an Initiation; since the Sixth Book of the Æneid really contains the secret Doctrine as well as the Ceremonies of the Eleusinian Mysteries.

What was this SECRET DOCTRINE? As I profess my ignorance, we must consult the Oracle. "The secret Doctrine of the Mysteries "revealed to the Initiated, that JUPITER . . . AND THE WHOLE "RABBLE OF LICENTIOUS DEITIES, WERE ONLY DEAD MOR- "TALS[3]." Is any thing like this laid open in the Sixth Book of Virgil? Not the remotest hint of it can be discovered throughout the whole Book; and thus, to use his Lordship's own words, SOME- THING (I had almost written EVERY THING) is still wanting "to "complete the IDENTIFICATION[4]."]

Notwithstanding this disappointment, which is cautiously con- cealed from the reader, the learned Bishop still courses round the Elysian Fields in quest of a Secret. Once he is so lucky as to find Æneas talking with the Poet Musæus, whom tradition has reckoned among the founders of the Eleusinian Mysteries. The Critic listens to their conversation; but, alas! Æneas is only enquiring, in what part of the garden he may find his Father's shade; to which Musæus returns a very polite answer. Anchises himself is our last hope. As that venerable shade explains to his son some mysterious doctrines, concerning the Universal Mind and the Transmigration of Souls, his Lordship is pleased to assure us, that these are THE HIDDEN DOCTRINES OF PERFECTION revealed only to the Initiated. Let us for a moment lay aside Hypothesis, and read Virgil.

It is observable, that the three great Poets of Rome were all

"intelligt tectè ipsos Athenienses: ut petierit Chilius, Atheniensium leges &[a] disciplinam "sibi describi &[a] mitti."

[3] D.L. vol. I. p. 154.   [4] Idem, p. 277

---

[a] *II*. et

addicted to the Epicurean philosophy; a System, however, the least
suited to a Poet; since it banishes all the genial and active Powers
of Nature, to substitute in their room a dreary void, blind atoms,
and indolent Gods. A Description of the Infernal Shades was in-
compatible with the ideas of a Philosopher, whose disciples boasted,
that he had rescued the captive World from the Tyranny of Religion,
and the Fear of a Future State. These ideas, Virgil was obliged to
reject: But he does still more; he abandons not only the CHANCE of
Epicurus, but even these Gods, whom he so nobly employs in the
rest of his Poem, that he may offer to the Reader's imagination a far
more specious and splendid sett of Ideas.

> *Principio cœlum, ac terras, camposque liquentes,*
> *Lucentemque globum Lunæ, Titaniaque astra*
> *Spiritus intus alit, totamque infusa per artus.*
> *Mens agitat molem, &ᵃ magno se corpore miscet.*[5]

The more we examine these lines, the more we shall feel the sublime
Poetry of them. But they have likewise an air of Philosophy and
even of Religion, which goes off on a nearer approach. The mind
which is INFUSED[6] into the several parts of Matter, and which
MINGLES ITSELF with the mighty mass, scarce retains any Property
of a Spiritual Substance; and bears too near an affinity to the
Principles, which the impious Spinoza revived rather than invented.

I am not insensible, that we should be slow to suspect, and still
slower to condemn. The poverty of human language, and the
obscurity of human ideas, makes it difficult to speak worthily of
THE GREAT FIRST CAUSE. Our most religious Poets, in striving
to express the presence and energy of the Deity, in every part of the
Universe, deviate unwarily into images, which are scarcely distinguished from Materialism. Thus our Ethic Poet:

> "All are but parts of one stupendous Whole,
> "Whose body Nature is, and God the soul[7];"

and several passages of Thomson[12] require a like favourable construction. But these writers deserve that favour, by the sublime

---

[5] Æneid, vi. 724.
[6] Quomodo porro Deus iste si nihil esset nisi animus, aut infixus aut *infusus* esset
in mundo. *Cicero de Naturâ Deor.* l. i. c. 11.
[7] Pope's Essay on Man, Epistle^b I. ver. 267.

ᵃ *II.* et   ᵇ *II.* Epist. i.

manner in which they celebrate the great Father of the Universe, and by those effusions of love and gratitude, which are inconsistent with the Materialist's System. Virgil has no such claim to our indulgence. THE MIND of the UNIVERSE is rather a Metaphysical than a Theological Being. His intellectual qualities are faintly distinguished from the Powers of Matter, and his moral Attributes, the source of all religious worship, form no part of Virgil's creed.

Yet is this creed approved[8] by our Orthodox Prelate, as free from any mixture of Spinozism. I congratulate his Lordship, on his indulgent and moderate temper. His Brethren (I mean those of former times) had much sharper eyes for spying out a latent Heresy. Yet I cannot easily persuade myself, that Virgil's notions were ever the creed of a religious Society, like that of the Mysteries. Luckily, indeed, I have no occasion to persuade myself of it; unless I should prefer his Lordship's mere authority to the voice of Antiquity, which assures me, that this System was either invented or imported into Greece by Pythagoras; from the writings of whose disciples Virgil might so very naturally borrow it.

Anchises then proceeds to inform his son, that the souls both of men and of animals were of celestial origin, and (as I understand him) parts of the Universal Mind; but that by their union with earthly bodies they contracted such impurities as even Death could not purge away. Many expiations, continues the venerable shade, are requisite, before the soul, restored to its original Simplicity, is capable of a place in Elysium. The far greater part are obliged to revisit the upper world, in other characters and in other bodies; and thus by gradual steps to reascend towards their first perfection.

This moral Transmigration was undoubtedly taught in the Mysteries. As the Bishop asserts this from the best authority, we are surprized at a sort of diffidence, unusual to his Lordship, when he advances things from his own intuitive knowledge. In one place, this Transmigration is part of the hidden Doctrine of Perfection[9]; in another, it is one of those principles, which were promiscuously communicated to all[10]. The truth seems to be, that his Lordship was afraid to rank among the secrets of the Mysteries, what was professed and believed by so many Nations and Philosophers. The pre-existence of the human soul is a very natural idea; and from that idea speculations and fables of its successive revolution through various bodies will arise. From Japan to Egypt, the Transmigration

[8] D.L. vol. I. p. 278.   [9] D.L. vol. I. p. 279.   [10] Idem, p. 142.

has been part of the popular and religious creed[1]. Pythagoras[2] and Plato[3] have endeavoured to demonstrate the truth of it, by facts, as well as by arguments.

Of all these visions (which should have been confined to the Poets) none is more pleasing and sublime, than that which Virgil has invented. Æneas sees before him his posterity, the Heroes of antient Rome; a long series of airy forms

"Demanding life, impatient for the skies,"[14]

and prepared to assume, with their new bodies, the little passions and transient glories of their destined lives.

Having[4] thus revealed the secret Doctrine of the Mysteries, the learned Prelate examines the Ceremonies. With the assistance of Meursius[5], he pours out a torrent of Erudition to convince us, that the scenes thro'[a] which Æneas passed in his descent to the Shades, were the same as were represented to the Aspirants in the Celebration of the Eleusinian Mysteries. From thence, his Lordship draws his great conclusion, That the Descent is no more than an emblem of the Hero's Initiation.

A staunch Polemic will feed a dispute, by dwelling on every accessary circumstance, whilst a candid Critic will confine himself to the more essential points of it. I shall, therefore, readily allow, what I believe may in general be true, that the Mysteries exhibited a theatrical representation of all that was believed or imagined of the lower world; that the Aspirant was conducted through the mimic scenes of Erebus, Tartarus, and Elysium; and that a warm Enthusiast, in describing these awful Spectacles, might express himself as if he had actually visited the infernal Regions[6]. All this I can allow, and yet allow nothing to the Bishop of Gloucester's Hypothesis. It is not surprising that the COPY was like the ORIGINAL; but it still remains undetermined, WHETHER VIRGIL INTENDED TO DESCRIBE THE ORIGINAL OR THE COPY.

Lear and Garrick, when on the stage, are the same; nor is it possible to distinguish the Player from the Monarch.[15] In the Green-

---

[1] See our modern Relations of Japan, China, India, &c. and for Egypt, Herodotus, l. ii.[13]   [2] Ovid. Metamorph. xv. 69, &c. 158, &c.

[3] Plato in Phædro & in Republic. l. x.

[4] I shall mention here, once for all, that I do not always confine myself to the ORDER of his Lordship's PROOFS.   [5] Meursii Eleusinia, sive de Cereris Eleusinæ sacro.

[6] See D.L. vol. I. particularly p. 280.

---

[a] *II.* through

room, or after the representation, we easily perceive, what the
warmth of fancy and the justness of imitation had concealed from
us. In the same manner it is from extrinsical circumstances, that we
may expect the discovery of Virgil's Allegory. Every one of those
circumstances persuades me, that Virgil described a real, not a mimic
world, and that the Scene lay in the Infernal Shades, and not in the
Temple of Ceres.

The singularity of the Cumœan Shores must be present to every
traveller who has once seen them. To a superstitious mind, the thin
crust, vast cavities, sulphureous steams, poisonous exhalations, and
fiery torrents, may seem to trace out the narrow Confine*a* of the two
Worlds. The lake Avernus was the chief object of religious horror;
the black Woods which surrounded it, when Virgil first came to
Naples, were perfectly suited to feed the superstition of the People[7].
It was generally believed, that this deadly flood was the entrance of
Hell[8]; and an Oracle was once established on its banks, which pretended, by magic rites, to call up the departed Spirits[9]. Æneas, who
revolved a more daring enterprise, addresses himself to the Priestess
of those dark Regions. Their conversation may perhaps inform us,
whether an Initiation, or a descent to the Shades, was the object of
this enterprize. She endeavours to deter the Hero, by setting before
him all the dangers of his rash undertaking:

> *Facilis descensus Averni*:
> *Noctes atque dies patet atri janua Ditis*;
> *Sed revocare gradum, superasque evadere ad auras*,
> *Hoc opus, hic labor est*[10].

These particulars are absolutely irreconcileable with the idea of
Initiation, but perfectly agreeable to that of a real descent. That
every step, and every instant, may lead us to the grave is a melancholy truth. The Mysteries were only open at stated times, a few
days at most in the course of a year. The mimic descent of the
Mysteries was laborious and dangerous, the return to light easy and
certain. In real death, this order is inverted:

> *Pauci, quos æquus amavit*
> *Jupiter, aut ardens evexit ad æthera virtus*,
> *Diis geniti, potuere*[1].

---

[7] Strabo, l. v. p. 168.   [8] Silius Italicus, l. xii.
[9] Diod. Sicul. l. iv. p. 267. edit. Wesseling.   [10] Æneid, vi. 126.   [1] Idem, vi. 129.

---

a *II.* confines

These Heroes, as we learn from the speech of Æneas, were Hercules, Orpheus, Castor and Pollux, Theseus, and Pirithous. Of all these, Antiquity believed, that before their death they had seen the habitations of the dead; nor, indeed, will any of the circumstances tally with a supposed Initiation. The adventure of Eurydice, the alternate life of the brothers, and the forcible intrusion of Alcides, Theseus, and Pirithous, would mock the endeavours of the most subtle Critic, who should try to melt them down into his favourite Mysteries. The exploits of Hercules, who triumphed over the King of Terrors,

> *Tartareum ille manu custodem in vincla petivit,*
> *Ipsius à solio regis traxitque trementem*[2],

was a wild imagination of the Greeks[3]. But it was the duty of antient Poets, to adopt and embellish these popular Traditions; and it is the interest of every man of taste, to acquiesce in THEIR POETICAL FICTIONS.

After this, we may leave ingenious men to search out what, or whether any thing, gave rise to those idle stories. Diodorus Siculus represents Pluto as a kind of undertaker, who made great improvements in the useful art of funerals[4]. Some have fought for the Poetic Hell in the mines of Epirus[5], and others in the Mysteries of Egypt. As this last notion was published in French[6], six years before it was invented in English[7], the learned author of the *D.L.* has been severely treated by some ungenerous Adversaries[8]. Appearances, it must be confessed, wear a very suspicious aspect: But what are appearances, when weighed against his Lordship's declaration, "That this is a point of honor in which he is particularly delicate; "and that he may venture to boast, that he believes no Author was

---

[2] Æneid, vi. 395.

[3] Homer, Odyss. l xi. ver. 623. Apoll. Biblioth. l. ii. c. 5.

[4] Diodor. Sicul. l. v. p. 386. Edit. Wesseling.

[5] Leclerc Biblioth. Universelle, tom. vi. p. 55.

[6] By the Abbé Terasson, in his Philosophical Romance of Sethos, printed at Amsterdam in the year 1732. See the Third Book, from beginning to end. The author was a Scholar and a Philosopher. His book has far more variety and originality than Telemachus. Yet Sethos is forgotten, and Telemachus will be immortal. That harmony of style, and the great talent of speaking to the heart and passions, which Fenelon possessed, was unknown to Terasson. I am not surprized that Homer was admired by the one, and criticized by the other.

[7] See D.L. vol. I. p. 228, &c. The first edition was printed in London, in the year 1738.

[8] Cowper's Life of Socrates, p. 102.

"ever more averse to take to himself what belonged to another[9]?"
Besides, he has enriched this mysterious discovery with many collateral arguments, which would for ever have escaped all inferior
Critics. In the case of Hercules, for instance, he demonstrates, that
the Initiation and the descent to the Shades were the same thing,
because an Antient has affirmed that they were different[10]; and that
Alcides was initiated at Eleusis, before he set out for Tænarus, in
order to descend to the Infernal Regions.

There is, however, a single circumstance, in the narration of Virgil,
which has justly surprized Critics, unacquainted with any, but the
obvious sense of the Poet; I mean the IVORY GATE. The Bishop of
Glocester seizes this, as the secret mark of Allegory, and becomes
eloquent in the exultation of Triumph[1]. I could, however, represent to him, that in a work which was deprived of the Author's last
revision, Virgil might too hastily employ what Homer had invented,
and at last unwarily slide into an Epicurean idea[2]. Let this be as it
may, an obscure expression is a weak basis for an elaborate System;
and whatever his Lordship may chuse to do, I had much rather
reproach my favourite Poet with want of care in one line, than with
want of taste throughout a whole Book[3].

Virgil has borrowed, as usual, from Homer, his Episode of the
Infernal Shades, and, as usual, has infinitely improved what the
Grecian had invented. If, among a profusion of beauties, I durst
venture to point out the most striking beauties of the Sixth Book,
I should perhaps observe, 1. That after accompanying the Hero
through the silent realms of Night and Chaos, we see with astonishment and pleasure a new Creation bursting upon us; 2. That we
examine, with a delight which springs from the love of Virtue, the
just empire of Minos; in which the apparent irregularities of the
present System are corrected; where[a] the Patriot who died for his

---

[9] Letter from a late Professor of Oxford[16], &c. p. 133.
[10] D.L. vol. III. p. 277.
[1] Idem, vol. I. p. 229.   [2] Idem, vol. I. p. 283.
[3] Horace seems to have used as unguarded an expression:

> Et adscribi *quietis*
> Ordinibus patiar Deorum.   *Od. l.* iii. 3.

The word and idea of *Quietis* are perfectly Epicurean; but rather clash with the active
passions displayed in the rest of Juno's speech.

His Lordship (D.L. vol. II. p. 140) accuses Virgil himself of a like inattention; which,
with his usual gentleness, he calls an *absurdity*.

---

[a] *II.* and where

Country is happy, and the Tyrant who oppressed it is miserable. 3. As we interest ourselves in the Hero's fortunes, we share his feelings: The melancholy Palinurus, the wretched Deiphobus, the indignant Dido; the Grecian Kings, who tremble at his presence, and the venerable Anchises, who embraces his pious son, and displays to his sight the future glories of his race; all these objects affect us with a variety of pleasing sensations.

Let us for a moment obey the mandate of our great Critic, and consider these awful scenes as a mimic shew, exhibited in the Temple of Ceres, by the contrivance of the Priest, or, if he pleases, of the Legislator. Whatever was animated (I appeal to every reader of taste), whatever was terrible, or whatever was pathetic, evaporates into lifeless Allegory:

tenuem sine viribus umbram.

Dat inania verba,
Dat sine mente sonum, gressusque effingit euntis.

The end of Philosophy is Truth; the end of Poetry is Pleasure. I willingly adopt any interpretation which adds new beauties to the Original; I assist in persuading myself, that it is just; and could almost shew the same indulgence to the Critic's as to the Poet's fiction. But should a grave Doctor lay out fourscore pages, in explaining away the sense and spirit of Virgil, I should have every inducement to believe, that Virgil's soul was very different from the Doctor's.

×   ×   ×   ×

I have almost exhausted my own, and probably my reader's patience, whilst I have obsequiously waited on his Lordship, through the several stages of an intricate Hypothesis. He must now permit me to alledge two very simple reasons, which persuade me, that Virgil has not revealed the Secret of the Eleusinian Mysteries; the first is HIS IGNORANCE, and the second HIS DISCRETION.

1. As his Lordship has not made the smallest attempt to prove that Virgil was himself initiated, it is plain that he supposed it, as a thing of course. Had he any right to suppose it? By no means: That ceremony might naturally enough finish the education of a young Athenian; but a Barbarian, a Roman, would most probably pass through life without directing his devotion to the foreign rites of Eleusis.

The Philosophical sentiments of Virgil were still more unlikely to inspire him with that kind of devotion. It is well known that he was a determined Epicurean[4]; and a very natural Antipathy subsisted between the Epicureans and the Managers of the Mysteries. The Celebration opened with a solemn excommunication of those Atheistical Philosophers, who were commanded to retire, and to leave that holy place for pious Believers[5]; the zeal of the people was ready to enforce this admonition. I will not deny, that curiosity might sometimes tempt an Epicurean to pry into these secret rites; and that gratitude, fear, or other motives, might engage the Athenians to admit so irreligious an Aspirant. Atticus was initiated at Eleusis; but Atticus was the Friend and Benefactor of Athens[6]. These extraordinary exceptions may be proved, but must not be supposed.

Nay, more; I am strongly inclined to think that Virgil was never out of Italy till the last year of his life. I am sensible, that it is not easy to prove a negative proposition, more especially when the materials of our knowledge are so very few and so very defective[7]; and yet by glancing our eye over the several periods of Virgil's life, we may perhaps attain a sort of probability, which ought to have some weight, since nothing can be thrown into the opposite scale.

Altho'[c] Virgil's father was hardly of a lower rank than Horace's, yet the peculiar character of the latter afforded his son a much superior education: Virgil did not enjoy the same opportunities, of observing mankind on the great Theatre of Rome, or of pursuing Philosophy, in her favourite shades of the Academy.

> *Adjecêre bonæ paulò plus artis Athenæ:*
> *Scilicet ut possem curvo dignoscere rectum,*
> *Atque inter silvas Academi quærere verum*[8].

[4] See the Life of Virgil by Donatus,[17] the Sixth Eclogue, and the[a] Second Georgic, ver.[b] 490.

[5] Lucian in Alexandro, p. 489.

[6] Cornel. Nepos, in Vit Attici, c. 2, 3, 4.

[7] The Life of Virgil, attributed to Donatus, contains many characteristic particulars; but which are lost in confusion, and disgraced with a mixture of absurd stories, such as none but a Monk of the darker ages could either invent or believe. I always considered them as the interpolations of some more recent writer; and am confirmed in that opinion, by the life of Virgil, pure from those additions, which Mr. Spence lately published, from a Florence MS. at the beginning of Mr. Holdsworth's valuable observations on Virgil.

[8] Horat. l. II. ep. ii. ver. 43.

---

[a] *II. om.* the   [b] *II.* v.   [c] *II.* Although

The sphere of Virgil's education did not extend beyond Mantua, Cremona, Milan, and Naples[9].

After the accidents of civil war had introduced Virgil to the knowledge of the Great, he passed a few years at Rome, in a state of dependance, the JUVENUM NOBILIUM CLIENS[10]. It was during that time that he composed his Eclogues, the hasty productions of a Muse capable of far greater things[1].

By the liberality of Augustus and his courtiers, Virgil soon became possessed of an affluent fortune[2]. He composed the Georgics and the Æneid, in his elegant Villas of Campania and Sicily; and seldom quitted those pleasing retreats even to come to Rome[3].

After he had finished the Æneid, he resolved on a journey into Greece and Asia, to employ three years in revising and perfecting that Poem, and to devote the remainder of his life to the study of Philosophy[4]. He was at Athens, with Augustus, in the summer of A V C[a] 735; and whilst Augustus was at Athens, the Eleusinian Mysteries were celebrated[5]. It is not impossible, that Virgil might then be initiated, as well as the Indian Philosopher[6]; but the Æneid could receive no improvement from his newly-acquired[b] knowledge. He was taken ill at Megara. The journey encreased his disorder, and he expired at Brundusium, the twenty-second of September of the same year 735[7].

Should it then appear probable, that Virgil had no opportunity of learning the SECRET of the Mysteries, it will be something more than probable, that he has not revealed what he never knew.

His Lordship will perhaps tell me, that Virgil might be initiated into the Eleusinian Mysteries, without making a Journey to Athens: since those Mysteries had been brought to Rome long before[8]. Here indeed I should be apt to suspect some mistake, or, at least, a want of precision in his Lordship's Ideas; as Salmasius[9] and

[9] Donat. in Virgil.   [10] Horat. l. IV. od. xii.   [1] Donat. in Virgil.

[2] Prope *Centies Sestertium*, about eighty thousand pounds.

[3] Donat. in Virgil.   [4] Id. ibid.

[5] They always began the fifteenth of the Attic month Boedromion, and lasted nine days. Those who take the trouble of calculating the Athenian Calendar, on the principles laid down by Mr. Dodwell (de Cyclis Antiquis) and by Dr. Halley, will find, that A V C.[a] Varr. 735, the 15th of Boedromion coincided with the 24th of August of the Julian year. But if we may believe Dion Cassius, the Celebration was this year anticipated, on account of Augustus and the Indian Philosopher. L. LIV. p. 739. edit. Reimar.

[6] Strabo, l. xv. p. 720.   [7] Donat. in Virgil.   [8] D.L. vol. I p. 188.[c]

[9] Salmasius ad Scriptores[d] Hist. August. p. 55.

---

[a] *II*. A.U.C.   [b] *II*. newly acquired   [c] *II*. 118   [d] *II*. Sriptores

Casaubon[10], men tolerably versed in Antiquity, assure me, that indeed some Grecian Ceremonies of Ceres had been practised at Rome from the earliest Ages; but that the Mysteries of Eleusis were never introduced into that Capital, either by the Emperor Hadrian, or by any other; And I am the more induced to believe, that these rites were not imported in Virgil's time, as the accurate Suetonius speaks of an unsuccessful attempt for that purpose, made by the Emperor Claudius, above threescore years after Virgil's death[1].

II. None but the Initiated COULD reveal the secret of the Mysteries; and THE INITIATED COULD NOT REVEAL IT, WITHOUT VIOLATING THE LAWS, AS WELL OF HONOR AS OF RELIGION. I sincerely acquit the Bishop of Glocester of any design; yet so unfortunate is his System, that it represents a most virtuous and elegant Poet, as equally devoid of taste, and of common honesty.

His Lordship acknowledges, that the Initiated were bound to Secrecy by the most solemn obligations[2]; that Virgil was conscious of the imputed impiety of his design; that at Athens he never durst have ventured on it; that even at Rome such a discovery was esteemed not only IMPIOUS BUT INFAMOUS: and yet his Lordship maintains, that after the compliment of a formal Apology,

Sit mihi fas, audita loqui[3].

Virgil lays open the whole SECRET of the Mysteries under the thin Veil of an Allegory, which could deceive none but the most careless readers[4].

An Apology! an Allegory! Such artifices might perhaps have saved him from the sentence of the Areopagus, had some zealous or interested Priest denounced him to that court, as guilty of publishing A BLASPHEMOUS POEM. But the Laws of Honor are more rigid, and yet more liberal, than those of Civil Tribunals. Sense, not words, is considered; and Guilt is aggravated, not protected, by artful Evasions. Virgil would still have incurred the severe censure of a Contemporary, who was himself a man of very little Religion.

> *Vetabo, qui Cereris sacrum*
> *Vulgârit arcanæ, sub iisdem*
> *Sit trabibus, fragilemque mecum*
> *Solvat phaselum*[5].

[10] Casaubon ad Scriptor. Hist. August. p. 25.
[2] D.L. vol I. p. 147.
[4] D.L. vol. I. p. 277.

[1] Sueton. in Claud. c. 25.
[3] Idem, p. 240.
[5] Horat. l. III. od. ii.

Nor can I easily persuade myself, that the ingenuous mind of Virgil could have deserved this Excommunication.

These lines belong to an Ode of Horace, which has every merit, except that of order. That Death in our Country's cause is pleasant and honourable; that Virtue does not depend on the caprice of a popular Election; and that the Mysteries of Ceres ought not to be disclosed, are ideas which have no apparent connection. The beautiful disorder of Lyric Poetry, is the usual Apology made by Professed Critics on these occasions:

> *Son style impetueux, souvent marche au hazard;*
> *Chez elle, un beau desordre est un effet de l'art*[6].

An insufficient Apology for the few, who dare judge from their own feelings. I shall not deny, that the irregular notes of an untutored Muse have sometimes delighted me. We can very seldom be displeased with the unconstrained workings of Nature. But the Liberty of an Outlaw is very different from that of a Savage. It is a mighty disagreeable sight, to observe a Lyric Writer of Taste and Reflection striving to forget the Laws of Composition, disjointing the order of his Ideas, and working himself up into artificial Madness,

> *Ut cum Ratione insaniat.*

I had once succeeded (as I thought) in removing this defect, by the help of an Hypothesis which connected the several parts of Horace's Ode with each other. My Ideas appeared (I mean to myself) most ingeniously conceived. I read the Ode once more, and burnt my Hypothesis. But to return to our principal subject.

The Date of this Ode may be of use to us; and the date may be fixed with tolerable certainty, from the mention of the PARTHIANS, who are described as the enemies against whom a brave youth should signalize his valor.

> Parthos *feroces*
> *Vexet eques metuendus hastâ*, &c.

Those who are used to the LABOURED HAPPINESS of all Horace's expressions[7] will readily allow, that if the Parthians are mentioned rather than the Britons or Cantabrians, the Gauls or the Dalmatians,

[6] Boileau, Art Poetique, l. ii. v. 72.

[7] *Curiosa Felicitas.* The ingenious Dr. Warton has a very strong dislike to this celebrated character of Horace. I suspect that I am in the wrong, since, in a point of Criticism, I differ from Dr. Warton. I cannot however forbear thinking, that the expression *is itself* what Petronius[18] wished to describe; the happy Union of such Ease as seems the gift of fortune, with such justness as can only be the result of care and labor.

it could be only at a time when a[a] PARTHIAN WAR engaged the public attention. This reflection confines us between the years of Rome 729 and 735. Of these six years, that of 734 has a superior claim to the Composition of the Ode.

Julius Caesar was prevented by death from revenging the defeat of Crassus[8]. This glorious task, unsuccessfully attempted by Marc Antony[9], seemed to be reserved for the prudence and felicity of Augustus; who became sole master of the Roman World in the year 724; but it was not till the year 729, that, having changed the civil administration, and pacified the Western provinces, he had leisure to turn his Views towards the East. From that time, Horace, in compliance with the Public wish, began to animate both Prince and People to revenge the manes of Crassus[10]. The cautious Policy of Augustus, still averse to war, was at length roused in the year 734, by some disturbances in Armenia. He passed over into Asia, and sent the young Tiberius with an army beyond the Euphrates. Every appearance promised a glorious war. But the Parthian monarch, Phrahates, alarmed at the approach of the Roman Legions, and diffident of the fidelity of his subjects, diverted the storm, by a timely and humble submission:

> *Jus, imperiumque Phraates[b]*
> *Cæsaris accepit gentibus[c] minor[1].*

Cæsar returned in Triumph to Rome, with the Parthian Hostages, and the Roman ensigns, which had been taken from Crassus.

These busy scenes, which engage the attention of Contemporaries, are far less interesting to posterity, than the silent labours, or even amusements of a man of Genius.

> *Cæsar dum magnus ad altum*
> *Fulminat Euphraten bello, victorque volentes*
> *Per Populos dat jura, viamque adfectat Olympo.*
> *Illo Virgilium me tempore dulcis alebat*
> *Parthenope, studiis florentem, ignobilis otî.*

[8] S[u]eton.[d] in Cæsar. c. 44.
[9] Plut. in Vit. Anton Julian in Cæsar. p. 324. edit. Spanheim
[10] Horat. l. I. od. ii. L. III od. v. L. II. serm. i. v. 15, &c.
[1] Horat. l. I. epist. xii. Vell.[e] Pater. l. II. c. xciv. Tacit. Annal. l. II. c. i. Sueton. in Octav. c. xxi. and in Tiber. c. xiv. Justin, l. XLII. c. v. Dion Cassius, l. LIV. p. 736. edit. Reimar. Joseph, Ant. l. XV.[f] c. v. Ovid. Fast. v. ver. 551, &c.

---

[a] *II.* the   [b] *II.* Phrahates   [c] *II.* genibus   [d] *1770* Sneton   [e] *II. thus; correction of 1770* Vall.   [f] *II.* v.

Whilst Cæsar humbled the Parthians, Virgil was composing the
Æneid. It is well known, that this noble Poem occupied the Author,
without being able to satisfy him, during the twelve last*a* years of
his life, from the year 723 to the year 735[2]. The public expectation
was soon raised, and the modest Virgil was sometimes obliged to
gratify the impatient curiosity of his friends. Soon after the death of
young Marcellus[3], he recited the second, fourth, and SIXTH books
of the Æneid, in the presence of Augustus and Octavia[4]. He even
sometimes read parts of his work to more numerous companies;
with a desire of obtaining their judgment, rather than their applause.
In this manner, Propertius seems to have heard the SHIELD OF
ÆNEAS, and from that specimen he ventures to foretell the approaching birth of a Poem, which will surpass the Iliad.

> *Actia Virgilium Custodis litora Phœbi,*
> *Cæsaris &b fortes dicere posse rates*
> *Qui nunc Æneæ Trojani suscitat Arma*
> *Jactaque Lavinis mœnia litoribus.*
> *Cedite Romani scriptores, cedite Graii,*
> *Nescio quid majus nascitur Iliade[5].*

As a friend and as a Critic, Horace was entitled to all Virgil's confidence, and was probably acquainted with the whole progress of the
Æneid, from the first rude sketch, which Virgil drew up in Prose, to
that harmonious Poetry, which the author alone thought unworthy
of posterity.

   To resume my Idea, which depended on this long deduction of
Circumstances; when Horace composed the second Ode of his third
Book, the Æneid, and particularly the Sixth Book, were already
known to the Public. The detestation of the Wretch who reveals the
Mysteries of Ceres, though expressed in general terms, must be
applied by all Rome to the Author of the Sixth Book of the Æneid.
Can we seriously suppose, THAT HORACE WOULD HAVE BRANDED
WITH SUCH WANTON INFAMY, ONE OF THE MEN IN THE WORLD
WHOM HE LOVED AND HONOURED THE MOST[6]?

---

(2) Donat. in Virgil.
(3) Marcellus died in the latter end of the year 731. *Usserii Annales, p.* 555.
(4) Donat. in Virgil.   (5) Propert l. II. el. xxv. v. 66.
(6) Horat. l. I. od. iii. L. I. serm. v. ver. 39. &c.

---

   a II. last twelve   *b II.* et

Nothing remains to say, except that Horace was himself ignorant of his friend's allegorical meaning, which the Bishop of Glocester has since revealed to the World. It may be so; yet, for my own part, I should be very well satisfied with understanding Virgil no better than Horace did.

It is perhaps some such foolish fondness for Antiquity, which inclines me to doubt, whether the BISHOP OF GLOCESTER has really united the severe sense of ARISTOTLE with the sublime imagination of LONGINUS. Yet a judicious Critic (who is now, I believe, ARCHDEACON OF GLOCESTER)[19] assures the Public, that his Patron's mere amusements have done much more than the joint labours of the two Grecians. I shall conclude these Observations with a remarkable passage from the Archdeacon's Dedication[7]: "It was not enough, in YOUR ENLARGED VIEW OF THINGS, to "restore either of these models (ARISTOTLE or LONGINUS) to "their original splendor. They were both to be revived; or rather "A NEW ORIGINAL PLAN OF CRITICISM to be struck out, WHICH "SHOULD UNITE THE VIRTUES OF EACH OF THEM. This Experi-"ment was made on the two greatest of our own Poets (Shakespeare "and Pope), and by reflecting all the LIGHTS OF THE IMAGINATION "on THE SEVEREST REASON, every thing was effected which the "warmest admirer of antient art could promise himself from such a "union. BUT YOU WENT FARTHER: By joining to these powers A "PERFECT INSIGHT INTO HUMAN NATURE; and so ennobling the "exercise of literary, by the justest moral censure, YOU HAVE NOW "AT LENGTH ADVANCED CRITICISM TO ITS FULL GLORY?"

POSTSCRIPT.

I WAS not ignorant, that, several years since, the Rev. Dr. Jortin had favoured the Public, with a DISSERTATION ON THE STATE OF THE DEAD, AS DESCRIBED BY HOMER AND VIRGIL[1]: But the Book is now grown so scarce, that I was not able to procure a sight of it till after these Papers had been already sent to the press. I found Dr Jortin's performance, as I expected, moderate, learned, and critical. Among a variety of ingenious observations, there are two or three which are very closely connected with my present subject.

[7] See the Dedication of Horace's Epistle to Augustus, with an English Commentary and Notes.
[1] Six Dissertations on Different Subjects, published in a Volume in Octavo, in the year 1755, It is the Sixth Dissertation, p. 207-324.

I had passed over in silence one argument of the Bishop of Glocester, or rather of Scarron and the Bishop of Glocester; since the former found the Remark, and the latter furnished the Inference.

Discite justitiam moniti, &ᵃ non temnere Divos,

cries the unfortunate Phlegyas. In the midst of his torments, he preaches Justice and Piety, like Ixion in Pindar. A very useful piece of advice, says the French Buffoon, for those who were already damned to all Eternity:

Cette sentence est bonne &ᵃ belle:
Mais en enfer, de quoi sert elle?[20]

From this judicious piece of Criticism his Lordship argues, that Phlegyas was preaching not to the Dead, but to the Living; and that Virgil is only describing the Mimic Tartarus, which was exhibited at Eleusis for the instruction of the Initiated.

I shall transcribe one or two of the reasons, which Dr. Jortin condescends to oppose to Scarron's Criticism.

"To preach to the Damned, says he, is labour in vain. And what "if it is? It might be part of his punishment, to exhort himself and "others, when exhortations were too late. This admonition, as far "as it relates to himself and his companions in misery, is to be looked "upon not so much as an admonition to amend,ᵇ but as a bitter "sarcasm, and reproaching of past iniquities.

"It is labour in vain. But in the poetical system, it seems to have "been the occupation of the Damned to labour in vain, to catch at "meat and drink that fled from them, &c.

"His instruction, like that of Ixion in Pindar, might be for the use "of the living. You will say, *how can that be?* Surely nothing is more "easy and intelligible. The Muses hear him——The Muses reveal "it to the Poet, and the inspired Poet reveals it to mankind. And so "much for Phlegyas and Monsieur Scarron."

It is prettily observed by Dr. Jortin, "That Virgil, after having "shone out with full splendor through the Sixth Book, sets at last "in a cloud." The IVORY GATE puzzles every Commentator, and grieves every lover of Virgil: Yet it affords no advantages to the Bishop of Glocester. The objection presses as hard on the notion of an Initiation, as on that of a real Descent to the Shades. "The

ᵃ *II.* et   ᵇ *II.* mend

"troublesome conclusion still remains as it was; and from the manner
"in which the Hero is dismissed after the Ceremonies, we learn, that
"in those Initiations, the Machinery, and the whole Shew, was (in
"the Poet's opinion) a representation of things, which had no truth
"or reality.

> "*Altera candenti perfecta nitens elephanto*:
> "Sed F ALSA *ad cœlum mittunt* INSOMNIA *manes.*

"Dreams in general, may be called *vain* and *deceitful*, *somnia vana*,
"or *somnia falsa*, if you will, as they are opposed to the *real* objects,
"which present themselves to us when we are awake. But when *false*
"dreams are opposed to *true* ones, there the Epithet *falsa* has another
"meaning. True dreams represent what is real, and shew what is
"true; false dreams represent things, which are not, or which are not
"true. Thus Homer and Virgil, and many other poets, and indeed
"the nature of the thing, distinguish them."

Dr. Jortin, though with reluctance, acquiesces in the common
opinion, that by six unlucky lines, Virgil is destroying the beautiful
System, which it had cost him eight hundred to raise. He explains
too this preposterous conduct, by the usual expedient of the Poet's
Epicureism.[a] I only differ from him in attributing to haste and indiscretion, what he considers as the result of design.

Another reason, both new and ingenious, is assigned by Dr. Jortin,
for Virgil explaining away his Hero's descent into an idle dream.
"All communication with the Dead, the infernal powers, &c. be-
"longed to the Art [of][b] Magic, and Magic was held in abomination
"by the Romans." Yet if it was held in ABOMINATION, it was supposed to be real. A writer would not have made his court to James
the first, by representing the stories of Witchcraft as the Phantoms
of an over-heated Imagination.[21]

Whilst I am writing, a sudden thought occurs to me, which, rude
and imperfect as it is, I shall venture to throw out to the Public. It is
this. After Virgil, in imitation of Homer, had described the two
Gates of Sleep, the Horn and the Ivory, he again takes up the first in
a different sense:

QUA VERIS FACILIS DATUR EXITUS UMBRIS.

The TRUE SHADES, VERÆ UMBRÆ, were those airy forms which
were continually sent to animate new bodies, such light and almost

---

[a] *II.* epicurism   [b] *1770 om.* of (Magic *begins new line*).

immaterial Natures as could without difficulty pass through a thin transparent substance. In this new sense, Æneas and the Sybill, who were still incumbered with a load of flesh, could not pretend to the prerogative of TRUE SHADES. In their passage over Styx,[a] they had almost sunk Charon's boat.

> *Gemuit sub pondere cymba*
> *Sutilis, &[b] multam accepit rimosa paludem.*

Some other Expedient was requisite for their return; and since the Horn Gate would not afford them an easy dismission, the other passage, which was adorned with polished Ivory, was the only one that remained either for them, or for the Poet.

By this explanation, we save Virgil's judgement and religion, though I must own, at the expence of an uncommon harshness and ambiguity of expression. Let it only be remembered, that those, who, in desperate cases, conjecture with modesty, have a right to be heard with indulgence.[c]

FINIS.[d]

[a] *II.* the Styx   [b] *II.* et   [c] *II. A note reference follows* indulgence. *Note is* "It appears from the Memoirs that this work was sent to the press early in 1770."
[d] *II. om.* Finis.

Outlines of the History
of the World

The ixth Century. [800–900]^a

THE more civilized part of the Globe was divided between the Christians and the Mahometans; the former under two Emperors, the latter under two Khalifs. 1. The new^b erected Empire of the Franks extended over France, Germany and Italy, and even the Christian Princes of Britain and the mountains of Spain respected the power and dignity of Charlemagne. 2. The Empire of the Greeks or as they vainly styled it of the Romans had^c only preserved^d Macedonia, Thrace and Asia Minor. 3. The Khalifs of the House of Ommiyah reigned in Spain. 4. Africa, Egypt Syria, Arabia, and Persia were subject to the Abassides. Whatever lay beyond the limits of these four Empires was still Pagan, and, excepting China, still barbarous.

The overgrown Monarchy[1] of the Abassides soon declined. The powerfull Viceroys of great and distant Provinces gradually usurped the prerogatives, though they still respected the dignity of the Khalif. The reigns of Al Rashid [776–809],[2] Al Mamûn [813–833], and Al Motassem [833–841] were however wise and prosperous: but their feeble Successors immersed in the Luxury of the Seraglio resigned the Guard of their Throne and Person, to a body of Turkish Mercenaries who, as their interest or passions might dictate, deposed [866], massacred [869], and created the Lieutenants of the Prophet [870].[3] At length they began to experience the dire effects of the Enthusiasm to which they owed their Grandeur. A Sect of desperate Fanatics, called Karmathians[4] disturbed Irak and Arabia [892]. The Assassins of Syria so much dreaded, during the Crusades were the last remains of them.

The ruin of the French Empire was more precipitate and attended with greater calamities. It is chiefly to be ascribed to the fierce spirit of the Franks,[5] unable to support either an arbitrary or a legal Government; to the incapacity of Lewis the Debonnaire [814–840],

---

^a *In margin of MS., unbracketed.*   ^b *II.*[newly   ^c *I. om.* had   ^d *II.* preserved only

and to the ambition of his four sons, who, in one battle [841], destroyed a hundred thousand of their Subjects. The dignity of the throne and blood of Charlemagne was eclipsed, as every Prince divided his Dominions among his Children; and the spirit of Union was irrecoverably lost. Charles the Bald[a] disgraced the Imperial Purple by acknowledging [875] that he held it from the favour of his Subject the Bishop of Rome. Another[b] Charles, as unworthy as the former, was deposed by his Subjects, and the Vacant Empire usurped [888] by the Kings of France, of Burgundy, of Arles, of Germany and of Italy, all strangers to the family of Charlemagne. The Dukes and the[c] Counts who had served their Ambition, converted their Goverments into hereditary Possessions, which they shared among their Barons, and these again among their Followers[d]; the Superior still reserving the Faith, Hommage and Military service of his Vassal. The People both of the Cities and Country was reduced to a state of Slavery. The Clergy sometimes imitated, and sometimes moderated the Tyranny of the Military Order.

In the mean while the Normans from the North, the Hungarians from the East and the Arabs or Saracens from the South, assaulted this defenceless Empire on every side [849]. Rome and Paris [885] were besieged, and these Invaders[e] often met each other in the Center of the Ruined Provinces. The Normans especially, animated by the Saxons, great numbers of whom had retired[f] into Scandinavia, to escape the bloody Baptism of Charlemagne, inflicted a dreadfull revenge on the persons and property of the Christian Priests.

The Union of the Saxon Heptarchy [827] was effected[g] by Egbert King of the West-Saxons, who had been trained to arms and Policy in the school of Charlemagne but[h] it was scarcely yet cemented [840], when England experienced the same Calamities as the Continent[i] from the Danes or Normans. They were with much difficulty expelled or subdued by the victories[j] of Alfred [872–900]. Amidst the deepest gloom of Barbarism, the virtue of Antoninus, the Learning and valour of Cæsar, and the Legislative Genius of Lycurgus shone forth united in that Patriot King. Several of his institutions have survived the Norman Conquest, and contributed to form the English Constitution.

---

[a] *I.* Fat   [b] *I.* That Unworthy Prince soon lost his Empire, which was
[c] *I. om.* the   [d] *I.* Knights   [e] *I.* Formidable Barbarians   [f] *I.* escaped
[g] *I.* was sacrcely formed . . . not yet cemented   [h] *II.* for   [i] *I. om.* as the
Continent   [j] *I.* arms

The Arabs, whether subject to the House of Abbas, or to that of Ommiyah formed but one People. The Christians of the Western and Eastern Empires had*a* scarce*b* any common resemblance, except of Religious Superstition. The Franks had almost forgot*c* to read or write in the most litteral sense of those Words. The Greeks preserved their ancient Authors, without attempting to imitate them. But the Arabs were Poets and Philosophers; bewildered themselves very ingeniously in the maze of Metaphysics, and improved the more usefull Sciences of Physic, Astronomy and the Mathematics.[6] The Arts, which minister to the conveniency*d* and Luxury of Life, were known only in the East, and at Constantinople.[7]

From these Arts, the Arabs derived their splendor and the Greeks their existence. A People, without valour or discipline, and a Throne perpetually stained with blood, and occupied by weak Princes, could not long have withstood the numerous Enemies which on every side surrounded them. Constantinople alone, attracting by its situation and industry the commerce of Europe and Asia, supplied the absolute Monarch with an inexhaustible source of Wealth and Power.[8]

The xth Century [900–1000]

Out of respect for*e* Charlemagne's memory, Charles the Simple and his descendants to the third Generation [898–987] were permitted to hold the crown of France:[9] but it was a Crown without either power or splendor. Italy with the Imperial dignity, Germany with the neighbouring provinces of Lorraine, Alsace, Franchecomtè, Dauphinè and Provence were separated from the French Monarchy. The last Carlovingian Princes reduced to the City of Laon, beheld the misery of their Country, and the Wars among their great Vassals. Of these the most powerfull were the Dukes of France, of Normandy, of Burgundy and of Aquitain; the Counts of Flanders, of Champagne and of Tholouse. Rollo the first Duke of Normandy,[10] acquired that fertile Province by Conquest and by treaty [912]: his barbarian followers readily adopted the French Manners, Religion and Language. Hugh Capet Duke of France and Count of Paris, and Orleans [987–996] wrested [987] from the last of the Carlovingians,

---

a I. bore   *b II.* scarcely   *c II.* forgotten   *d II.* convenience
e II. to

the Scepter, which still remains in the hands of his Posterity: but his new Regal title scarcely gave him any authority over his *Peers*, and his ample Fiefs composed a very inconsiderable Kingdom.

The Germans, freed from the French Yoke, elected for their King Conrad Duke of Franconia [912], and after him a line of Saxon Princes. Henry the Fowler [918–936] chastised the Hungarians, civilized his rude Subjects, and was the first founder of Cities in the Interior parts of Germany. His son Otho the Great [936–973][11] passed the Alps, gave laws to Italy and to the Popes, and for ever fixed the Imperial Dignity in the German Nation [962]. He imposed a tribute on the Vanquished Danes and Bohemians; and since that time the King of Bohemia has acknowledged himself the first Vassal of the German Empire, which was treated with contempt by the Greeks, reluctantly submitted to by the Italians, but respected by the rest of Europe. The second [973–983] and third Otho [983–1002.], son and grandson to the first, supported though with less vigour and Capacity, the Claims which he transmitted to them.

Spain flourished under the happy Government of the Ommiades[12] more than in any former or later Period. Their Capital, Cordova is said to have contained two hundred thousand houses, and the adjacent Country twelve thousand Villages. The active Genius of the Arabs was at once employed in War, Science, Agriculture, Manufactures and Commerce. The annual revenue of the Khalif Abdoubrahman III [912–961], exceeded six Millions sterling, and probably surpassed that of all the Christian Kings united. Under the reign of his Grandson [976–1006], the Vizirs became Masters of the Palace and the Governors of their Provinces. The Christian Princes, of Gothic or Gascon Extraction who had maintained their Independance in the Pyrenæan and Asturian Mountains and of whom the King of Leon was the most considerable, prepared to take advantage of the intestine divisions of the Mahometans.

A new Empire arose in Africa [909]. Obeidollah who styled himself the descendant and Avenger of Ali, reduced under his obedience the whole Country from the Atlantic Ocean to the frontiers of Egypt, together with the Island of Sicily, and founded the Dynasty of the Fatimite Khalifs.[13] Moez Ledinillah, the fourth in descent and succession from him, conquered [969] Egypt and Syria, and built Grand Cairo on the Banks of the Nile, which soon became one of the first Cities of the World. But in proportion as the Fatimite Khalifs extended their conquests towards the East, their Western dominions of Africa escaped from their Yoke. In the mean while the Arabs of Mauritania, who still retained their Pastoral life, spread the terror of their arms and the Law of Mahomet among the Negroe Nations in the interior parts of Africa[.]

The Empire of Abbassides was dismembered[a] [936] by twenty Dynasties, Arabs Turks and Persians. The Khalif[14] of Bagdad a prisoner in his Palace enjoyed the vain honour of being named first in the public prayers; and of granting the investiture of his Provinces to every Fortunate Usurper. The Greeks[15] seized the favourable opportunity, recovered Antioch [969], and once more extended their power as far as the banks of the Euphrates.

As[b] England formed a separate World, which maintained very little intercourse with other nations, it may be reserved for the last place. Edward the Elder [900–924], and Athelstan [924–940] inherited the military virtues of Alfred. The great grandson of that Prince, Edgar [959–975], is celebrated by the Monks for his profuse devotion to their Order, and by rational Men, for the attention he gave to the natural strength of his Kingdom, a maritime Power. The Danes, who since the time of Alfred, had respected the Coasts of England, renewed their attacks, as soon as they discovered the weakness of young Ethelred the son of Edgar [978–1016.].

While the Musulmans, notwithstanding their intestine troubles, preserved the light of Science, Europe sunk still deeper into Ignorance, Barbarism and Superstition. The Benedictine Abbeys though they nursed the last of these Monsters, opposed some faint resistance against[c] the two former. They transcribed ancient Books, improved their lands, and opened an azylum for the slaves of Feudal tyranny, which had every where erected fortified Castles on the ruins of Cities and villages.[16] The inhabitants of the rocks of Genoa, and of the Marshes of Venice began to seek first a subsistence, and soon afterwards wealth and power, in the usefull employments of Trade and Navigation[.]

The xi[th] Century [1000–1100]

The general history of this Age may be comprehended under four Great Events. 1. The Empire of the Turks in Asia. 2. The Disputes between the Emperors and the Popes. 3. The Conquest of England

---

[a] *I*. at an end,   [b] *I*. The   [c] *I*. to

and Naples[a] by the Normans. and, 4 The Crusades against the Mahometans.

1. Mahmud of Gazna, was the first Prince, who, under the Empire of the Khalifs, assumed the title of Sultan. He reigned over the Eastern parts of Persia, and invaded the rich and peacefull nations of Hindostan several of which bowed to his Yoke and to that of the Alcoran. As he had occasion for great armies, he invited into his service the Tribe of Seljuk, one of the bravest and most numerous among the Turks.[17] They served the Father, but rebelled against the son [1031]. The several Dynasties of Persia fell successively before the sword of Togrul Beg their first Sovereign [1038–1063]. The feeble Khalif of Bagdad was obliged to grant him the investiture of his Conquests [1055], and to receive a Turk for his Protector and his son in law. Alp Arslan [1063–1072], the successor of Togrul, took the Emperor Romanus Diogenes prisoner in a great Battle [1071], and treated him with a generous Courtesy, that would have done honour to the most civilized Nations. Asia Minor, a part of the Greek Empire; and Syria and Palestine, then subject to the Khalifs of Egypt were subdued by the victorious Turks [1080]. The Empire of Malek Shâh [1072–1092] extended from India to the Hellespont: his Court was the seat of Learning, Justice and Magnificence. The Turks who had adopted the Religion and Manners of the Arabs, studied to conceal from the Nations[b] of Asia, that they had changed their Masters.

2. The Emperor Otho iii was succeeded by his cousin Henry ii [1002–1024] surnamed the Saint because he chose to be the last of his family. The Franconian Princes, Conrad the Salic [1024–1043], Henry iii [1043–1056] and Henry iv [1056–1106] succeeded to the house of Saxony. These Emperors possessed as much power as was compatible with the Feudal System. Their great Vassals were more accustomed to order and obedience than those of France. They enjoyed a large Domain and Revenue in Germany. Italy once the Mistress and since the Slave of the Nations was treated as a Conquered Country. The Right of granting the Investiture of Benefices, and even of the See of Rome, became in their hands a[c] inexhaustible source either of Power or of profit. Gregory vii. [1073–1085][18] a Monk of a daring and obstinate Spirit, embraced the pretence of abolishing Simony, and the opportunity of delivering himself and his successors from an odious Yoke. The Emperor was excommunicated and deposed; and these Spiritual Arms were seconded

[a] *I. om.* and Naples   [b] *I.* People   [c] *II.* an

either from interested or pious Motives by the Normans, by the Countess Matilda, by the Princes of Germany, and even by the sons of Henry. Though he defended himself with Vigour and was victorious in sixty six Battles[a]; the Church still maintained the War with new ressources and inflexible resolution; and the Roman Pontif exalted his Mitre above all the Crowns in[b] Europe.

3. In this Century England was twice Subdued by foreign Invaders. Sueno[c] the Dane ravaged the Country; but his son Canute [1016–1036], who had embraced Christianity was acknowledged King by the Nation, and shewed himself as mild in Peace as he had been terrible in War. The Dominion of the Danes expired with the Sons of Canute; and Edward the Confessor [1042–1066] ascended, without opposition the vacant Throne. The[d] more than doubtfull Testament of this weak Prince the last of the Saxon Line, was however the best Pretence, with which William the Bastard Duke of Normandy, could colour his Invasion of England [1066]. In the decisive Battle of Hastings [14 October], the Valour of the English was unable to withstand the Flower of Europe's Chivalry, led on by an experienced General, and supported by the thunder of a Papal Excommunication. William [1066–1087] secured his Conquest, at first by the most gentle, afterwards by the most violent measures. He attempted to abolish the Laws and Language of the Anglo-Saxons, and divided their Country among the Companions of his Victory. Fourteen hundred Manors, which he reserved for the Crown formed an ample and independant Revenue. Sixty Thousand Knights were bound by duty and interest to support the throne of their Benefactor. The Government was military; and a Military Government always verges towards Despotism. The only compensation, which England received for so many Calamities, was a system of Manners somewhat more polished; and a more extensive influence on the Continent. The power of William the Conqueror and of his son William Rufus [1087–1100] eclipsed their sovereigns the Kings of France. Robert [996–1031], Henry I [1031–1060] and Philip I [1060–1108], the successors of Hugh Capet in Lineal Descent, wanted both talents and opportunity to wrest the Prerogatives and Provinces of their Crown from the great Vassals, on whose usurpations, Time had almost bestowed a legal Sanction.

The Normans were at that time renowned in arms beyond all the European Nations. A few private Gentlemen of Normandy, who[e]

---

[a] I. sixty six, the Chur   [b] I. of   [c] II. Sweyn   [d] I. From   [e] I. whose

visited the southern parts of Italy [1016] as Pilgrims, and served there as Mercenaries, soon formed themselves into a little army of Conquerors [1043], and erected a formidable power on the ruins of the Greeks, the Arabs and the Lombards. Robert Guiscard [1057–1085],[19] the greatest of their Chiefs, who passed the Alps with only six Horsemen and thirty foot, attained the honour of protecting Gregory vii, and of seeing both[a] Emperors, of the West, and of[b] East successively fly before him. His vast projects against the latter of these Empires were interrupted[c] only by an untimely Death. The devotion or the policy of the Normans engaged them to put their Conquests under the protection of S[t] Peter; and, since that time, the Kingdom of Naples has been a Fief of the Church of Rome.[d]

4. As soon as the Khalifate of Spain was destroyed, the Christians emerged from obscurity, and in their turn attacked the Moors or Arabs [1038], now divided into twenty petty Sovereignties. While each Mahometan Prince defended himself separately, all were vanquished but the Victory was long doubtfull and bloody. Every district cost a battle: every city a siege. The Siege of Toledo [1085] lasted a year, and the reputation of the Spanish General, celebrated in History and Romance under the name of the Cid attracted the bravest Knights of Italy and France to his standard. The Dominions of his Master Alfonso vi [1065–1109] comprehended both the Castilles, Leon, Biscay, Astureas, and Gallicia. The Spanish Princes of Navarre Arragon, and Catalonia, were still confined between the Ebro, and the Pyrenees[.] About the same time [1072] Count Roger the Norman, brother of Robert Guiscard expelled the Arabs from the Island of Sicily, and pursued them to the coasts of Africa[.]

These advantages were preludes to the great enterprize of the Crusades [1094.].[20] When we recollect that Arms and Devotion were the ruling passions of the independant Barons and their numerous Followers; and that Fame Riches, and Paradise were[e] held forth as the sure rewards of this Holy Warfare, we shall be the less surprized that more than a Million of Men enlisted under the Banner of the Cross. Of this undisciplined multitude the far greater part perished in Hungary and Asia Minor. Godfrey of Bouillon, and the other Christian Leaders arrived on the banks of the Jordan, with only twenty thousand Foot, and fifteen hundred Horse; but even this handfull of Warriors was sufficient to recover the Holy Sepulchre,

---

[a] II. both the   [b] II. of the   [c] I. pre   [d] I. om. this sentence
[e] I. were the

and to establish a feeble and transitory Dominion over Jerusalem, Antioch, Tripoli, and Edessa [1099]. The French and Normans had the greatest share in the folly and Glory of the first Crusade, which rouzed Europe from it's long and profound Lethargy, and was productive of much unforeseen benefit to the Popes, the Kings of France and the commercial States of Italy.

Denmark, Norway, Sweden, Poland Bohemia, and Hungary[21] adopted the Christian or rather Popish faith, a more civilized life and the first rudiments of Feudal Policy. The Conversion of Russia was the work of the Greek Church. The Slavonian Tribes on the coasts of the Baltic from the Elbe to the Gulf of Finland still preserved their ancient Religion and savage Independance.

The xii[th] Century [1100–1200]

The Popes[22] prevailed against their ancient Sovereigns, the Emperors of Germany, and deprived the unfortunate Henry iv. of his dominions, his reputation his life, and the last honours of a grave [1106]. To escape a similar fate, Henry v [1106–1125] resigned the long contested Right of Investitures [1121] which was gradually usurped by the Roman Pontif. The Clergy, instead of regaining their liberty, soon experience[d][a] a Yoke still heavier, when imposed by one of their own order. The Fictitious Donation of Constantine, and the Will of Matilda were likewise asserted by the Popes, but with less success; and they found it easier to shake the thrones of other Princes, than to establish their own temporal Dominion. A jealous truce subsisted between the Church and Empire during the reigns of Lothaire ii [1125–1137] and Conrad iii [1137–1152.]; the latter of whom, was the first of the House of Swabia. The War was renewed between the Emperor Frederic i surnamed Barbarossa [1152–1190], and Pope Alexander iii, each of whom pretended that the other was his Creature and Vassal. The Cities of Lombardy enriched by commerce and aspiring to liberty, ranged themselves under the Papal Banner. Though Frederic maintained his lofty claims with the greatest resolution and ability, though he set up an Anti-Pope, marched six times into Italy besieged Rome, and levelled Milan with the ground; yet he was at last obliged to bend before the throne of Alexander, and to[b] confirm all the immunities of the Italian Confederacy [1177].[c]

[a] So in II; MS. experience   [b] II. om. to   [c] II. 1117

This Emperor, and his successor Henry vi [1190–1198], were however dreaded and obeyed in Germany, now enlarged by the forced Conversion of the Vandals of Mecklenburgh, and Pomerania. In the north of Italy the Imperial Authority was almost lost: but in the south Henry vi acquired the Kingdom of the two Sicilies by marrying Constantia the daughter of Roger i who had united the Norman Conquests and assumed the Regal title [1130]. A powerfull Party was unable to resist the Right and the Arms of Henry but he sullied his Victory with cruelty and avarice [1194].

The Kings of France still remained the feeble Heads of a great Body. In private quarrels the most inconsiderable Baron was able to wage War against his Sovereign: but when Lewis vi [1108–1137] assembled the national force against a foreign Enemy two hundred thousand Men appeared under the banner of the Oriflamme [1124]. Lewis vii. [1137–1180] was a Prince of slender abilities, who lost the great Dutchy of Aquitain, by divorcing his Wife Eleanor on a jealous suspicion. His Minister Suger, and his son Philip Augustus [1180–1223] deserve to be considered as the Founders of the French Monarchy. The former was an honest Statesman, and a Monk without the prejudices of the^a Convent. The fortune of the latter was equal to his Genius.

In England, the weak title of Henry I [1100–1135] youngest^b son of the conqueror^c, his marriage with a Saxon Princess, and above all the hand of time, gradually uniting^d the Normans and the English into one People; contributed to abolish the memory of the Conquest, and to relax the chains of Despotism. After the death of Henry, England was^e afflicted with a Civil War [1135–1154], between his daughter Matilda and his nephew Stephen; till at length the contending Parties acknowledged Henry II [1154–1189.], the son of Matilda, an active powerfull and fortunate Monarch. From his mother he^f inherited England and Normandy; from his father, Fulk Plantagenet, the Counties of Anjou, Maine and Touraine. By the marriage, which he most eagerly contracted with the repudiated Eleanor, he obtained^g the provinces of Aquitain and Poitou. He disposed of the Dutchy of Brittanny in favour of his third son Jeffrey. The King of Scotland did him hommage, the Welsh dreaded his power; and to the adventurous valour of some Subjects, he was indebted for the Sovereignty of Ireland [1171]; a conquest at that

^{a} II. a ^{b} I. om. youngest ^{c} I. om. son of the conqueror ^{d} I. united
^{e} I. was long ^{f} I. his ^{g} MS. ob = [line ends] obtained

time of little value, but which now contains more wealth and industry, than the extensive Empire of Henry ii. His reign was however disturbed by the ambition and still more by the murder of Becket [1170]; by the intrigues of the French King and by the ingratitude of his sons. Richard i [1189–1199], the second of them, possessed only the personal courage of a Soldier. John [1199–1216], the youngest (who[a] usurped the Crown, in prejudice to his nephew Arthur, the son of Jeffrey) was even devoid of that vulgar merit. The Crusade and Captivity of Richard exhausted England, and impov[er]ished[b] the Crown.

The Christians of Spain acquired a manifest superiority over the Infidels. The Kingdom of Castile was already a considerable power, and Alfonso viii vainly styled himself Emperor of Spain [1135]. The little Kingdom of Navarre still remained among the Pyrenees: but the Kings of Arragon (one of whom married the heiress of Catalonia [1162]) descended from the mountains into the plain, took Saragossa [1118], and carried their arms to the frontiers of Castile, and Valentia. The progress of the Kingdom of Portugal was still more rapid. A prince of the House of France had received from Alfonso vi the city of *Porto-Calle*, with the title of Count; his successor assumed that of King [1139], took Lisbon [1148], with the assistance of some English and Flemish Crusaders, and subdued the Western Coast of Spain from Gallicia to the Algarves. All these Victories were attended with the greater difficulty and glory, as the Moors both of Spain and Africa were united under the Empire of the Miramolins; in whom were revived the Zeal, the valour, the learning and the magnificence of the Khalifs. Their Capitals Fez and Morocco were superior to any Cities in Christendom.

Each state, unconnected with it's neighbours[c] had it's own Revolutions, but the Expeditions to Palestine were[d] the common business of Europe. Though the sermons of S[t] Bernard excited a second Crusade [1147] more formidable than the first, the far greater part of the numerous Armies which followed the Emperor Conrad and Lewis vii of France perished by the artifices of the Greeks, and the arms of the Turks, and those Monarchs appeared in the Holy Land, rather as Pilgrims than as Conquerors. The most dangerous Enemy of the Christians was Saladin, who abolished the Fatimite Khalifs [1171], and raised himself from a private station to the

[a] *I.* youngest of them (whom   [b] *So II. MS.* impovished   [c] *I.* with the
neighbouring   [d] *I.* was

Sovereignty of Egypt and Syria. Zeal and Policy forbade him to suffer a Christian Kingdom in the heart of his Dominions. Jerusalem yielded to his arms [1187], and the Christians experienced a generous treatment as*a* unexpected as it was undeserved. The News of this loss filled Europe with shame grief and indignation. Suspending their domestic quarrels, the military force of Germany, France and England marched into the East under their respective Monarchs [1189]. Frederic Barbarossa died in Asia Minor, in a career of useless victories. Philip Augustus and Richard i, who preferred the safer*b* but more expensive method of transporting their troops by sea, took the inconsiderable town of S*t* John d'Acre after a siege of two*c* Years [1191]. This third Crusade was followed by the death of Saladin [1193], who left a name admired in Asia, dreaded and esteemed in Europe.

The provinces beyond the Tigris no longer obeyed the house of Seljuk. New Princes (to use the Eastern expression) had arisen from the dust before their throne. A race of Slaves (the Governors afterwards Sultans of Carizme)*d* enriched by their favour, and spared by their clemency, deprived the last of these Monarchs of his scepter, and life [1192]. The Khalifs of Bagdad, with a juster title had recovered their independance and the adjacent*e* province of Irak [1136–1160]. Two younger branches of the house of Seljuk still reigned in Kerman, and Asia Minor.

Under the Feudal System the rights, natural as well as civil, of Mankind, were enjoyed only by the Nobles and Ecclesiastics who scarcely formed the thousanth part of the Community. In this Century they were gradually diffused among the Body of the People. The Cities of Italy acquired full Liberty: the great*f* towns of Germany, England France and Spain became legal Corporations, and purchased Immunities more or less considerable; even the Peasant began to be distinguished from the rest of the Cattle on his Lord's estate.

With the Liberty of Europe, it's Genius awoke; but the first efforts of it's growing strength were consumed in vain and fruitless pursuits. Ignorance was succeeded by error. The Civil and Canon Jurisprudence were blindly adopted, and laboriously perverted. Romances of Chivalry, and Monkish Legends still more fabulous, supplied the place of History. The dreams of Astrology were dignified with the

a *I.* which   *b* *I.* fa   *c* *I.* three   *d* *I. om.* (the . . . Carizme)   *e* *So*
II. MS. adjancent   *f* *II.* greater

name of Astronomy. To discover the Philosopher's stone was the
only end of Chymistry. Superstition, instead of flying before the light
of true Philosophy, was involved in thicker darkness by the Scholastic Phantom which usurped it's honours. The two great sources of
Knowledge, Nature and Antiquity, were neglected and forgotten.

The xiiith Century [1200–1300]

We may now contemplate two of the greatest powers, that have
ever given laws to Mankind; the one founded on force, the other[a]
on opinion: I mean the Tartar Conquerors, and the Roman Pontifs.

[*The Moguls.*][23] Birth-right, Election, Personal merit, force of
Arms, and some claims to a Divine Mission invested Zingis[b] Khan,
with the absolute command of all the Tartar and Mogul Tribes
[1203]. As soon as he had introduced a degree of order and discipline
among his Barbarous Host; he invaded the Empire of China, took
Pekin, and subdued the Northern Provinces [1211]. From thence he
marched into Persia against Mohammed Sultan of Carizme, who,
by putting to death the Mogul Embassadors, drew ruin on himself,
his family, and his Dominions [1218]. From the Jaxartes to the
Tigris, nothing could withstand the numbers and fury of the Moguls.
Carizme, Bocara, Samarcand, &c were levelled with the ground, and
the rich Provinces to the East and to the South of the Caspian Sea
were changed from a Garden to a Desert. Zingis[b] died [1227],
loaded with the spoils and curses of Asia. His Successors troad in
the same paths of Rapine and Conquest. About the same time [1234],
one Army of Moguls compleated the reduction of[c] the Northern
Empire of China, and penetrated to the farthest point of Corea,
almost within sight of the shores of Japan; a second over-ran Russia
Poland and Hungary, threatened Constantinople, and won the Battle
of Lignitz in Silesia; a third Army took Bagdad[d] [1258] destroyed
the Empire of the Khalifs, and laid waste Asia Minor and Syria. The
Mogul Princes of Persia and the Western Tartary long hesitated
between the Gospel and the Alcoran. Their conversion would have
been of greater benefit to the Church, than all the Crusades; but at
length they preferred the faith of Mahomet [1292], and renounced
all intercourse with the Great Khan [1278], who[e] still adhered to the

---

[a] *I. om.* other on   [b] *I.* Jengiz   [c] *I.* reduction of China; a second
[d] *I.* Bagdad and   [e] *I.* who had adopted the Laws and Religion of China, then first
known in Europe, under the name of Cathay.

worship of the Dalai Lama. Cublai Khan the grandson and fourth successor of Zingis, united by the extinction of the Dynasty of the South the whole Chinese Monarchy, with Eastern Tartary, adopted the laws and manners of the Conquered people encouraged the arts and artists of every Nation and is reckoned by the Chinese themselves among their best Emperors.[a]

[*The Popes.*][24] The Roman Pontifs claimed a[b] Universal Monarchy, Temporal as well as Spiritual; and maintained that all inferior Powers, Emperors, Kings, and Bishops, derived from the Chair of S[t] Peter their delegated Authority. Of all the Popes, none asserted these lofty pretensions with more spirit and success than Innocent iii [1198–1216]. By establishing the Doctrine of Transubstantiation, and the Tribunal of the Inquisition, he obtained the two most memorable Victories over the common Sense, and common Rights of Mankind[.] He reduced the Schismatic Greeks, exterminated the Albigeois Heretics, despoiled Raymond count of Thoulouse of his Dominions, excommunicated two Emperors, a King of France, and a King of England; the last of whom confessed himself the Vassal and Tributary of the see of Rome. Innocent reigned in Rome as the successor of Constantine, and in Naples, as the natural Guardian of young Frederic, the son of Henry the sixth; who, after Philip of Suabia and Otho iv, was acknowledged Emperor of Germany.

[*The Empire*] The superior abilities of Frederic ii [1215–1250],[25] his Italian Education, the Imperial Scepter, the Kingdom of the two Sicilies and the vast Possessions of the house of Swabia rendered him formidable[c] to the Popes, who, unmindfull of their accustomed Policy, had rather assisted, than checked his Elevation. This fatal error could only be retrieved[d] by the destruction of the House of Swabia, and the design was prosecuted during more than forty years [1227–1268], with a Constancy worthy[e] of the ancient Senate. The Roman Pontifs seized the first ground of dispute, rejected all terms of Peace, and convinced both their friends and their Enemies, that they were resolved either to perish or to conquer. The Parties of the Church, and of the Empire, under the names of Guelfs and Ghibelins, divided and desolated Italy. Amidst this confusion, Innocent iv solemnly deposed Frederic in the Council of Lyons [1245], and pursued that unfortunate Monarch to the grave. After his death[f]

---

[a] *I. om. this sentence*   [b] *II.* an   [c] *I.* a formidable   [d] *II.* could be retrieved only   [e] *I.* th   [f] *II.* decease

[1250], the name of Emperor was assumed, for a short time, by his son Conrad iv; and the Kingdom of Naples was defended by his bastard Mainfroy, till the Papal arms were entrusted [1266] to Charles Count of Anjou, the brother of Lewis ix. Followed by the bravest and most pious Warriors of Christendom, that active Prince passed the Alps, and in a single battle deprived Mainfroy of his scepter and his life. Conradin, the grandson of Frederic, and the last of that unhappy line, lost his head on a scaffold at Naples [1268], after a brave but unsuccessfull attempt to recover the throne of his Ancestors. His blood was soon revenged by the blood of 8000 French in the Sicilian Vespers [1282]; who fell the[a] just Victims of their licentious Insolence. A long and bloody Quarrel commenced between the House of Arragon, which was called by the oppressed people to the throne of Sicily, and the House of Anjou, which still remained in possession of Naples.

[*Italy*] The Free Cities of Italy now delivered from the German yoke, began to enjoy and to abuse the blessings of Wealth and Liberty. Of a hundred independant Republics, every one, except Venice, was destitute of a regular Government, and torn by civil dissensions. The Guelfs and the Ghibelins, the Nobles and the Commons contended for the sovereignty of their Country. The most trifling incident was sufficient to produce a Conspiracy, a Tumult, and a Revolution. Among these troubles[b], the dark insidious, vindictive spirit of the Italians was gradually formed.

[*Germany.*] In Germany, the death of Frederic ii, was succeeded by a long Anarchy [1250–1272]. The Prerogatives and Domains of the Emperor[c] were usurped by the great Vassals. Every Gentleman exercised round his Castle a licentious Independance; the Cities were obliged to seek protection from their Walls and Confederacies; and from the Rhine and Danube to the Baltic, the names of Peace and Justice were unknown. It was at length discovered, that without an appearance of Union, the Germanic Body could not subsist. The Great Princes, who began to assume the title of *Electors*, agreed to invest a first Magistrate with the dignity, but not with the power, of their ancient Emperors. Their jealous caution successively fixed on Rodolph Count of Hapsburgh [1272–1291], and Adolph Count of Nassau [1292–1298]; whose fortune was far inferior to their birth and personal merit. The former, however, who was Father of the House of Austria, transmitted to his son Albert [1298–1308], such

---

[a] *II. om.* the   [b] *I.* civil troubles   [c] *II.* emperors

ample Hereditary Dominions, as enabled him to form a Party against the Emperor Adolph to wrest from him the Scepter, and to display that ambitious Pride, which has ever since been the Characteristic of that family.

[*France*] The Agrandisement of the French Monarchy bore the appearance of an act of Justice. Philip Augustus [1180–1223.] summoned John, King of England and Peer of France, before the Parliament of Paris [1203], to justify himself of the murder of his*a* nephew Arthur. The Parliament punished the contumacious Vassal, by the confiscation of his Fiefs; and the King executed the sentence, before the indignation of the other Peers, could subside into a sense of their common interest. Normandy, Anjou, Maine, and Poitou were united to the crown [1204]. Aquitain or Guyenne still remained in the hands of the English. The victory of Philip over the Empire was more splendid, but less usefull: In the decisive and well fought Battle of Bovines [1214], he defeated Otho iv, at the head of two hundred thousand Germans. His Navy threatened England [1213], and his son Lewis, afterwards Lewis viii, was for a time, acknowledged King by the English Nation [1216]. The reign of that Prince was short and inglorious [1223–1226]: but France owes as much to the Laws of Lewis ix [1226–1270],[26] as to the arms of Philip Augustus his grandfather. Lewis ix, notwithstanding he has been disgraced by the title of Saint, possessed uncommon virtues and abilities. To abolish private hostilities and judicial combats; to introduce an uniform and equitable Jurisprudence; to receive appeals from the Barons Courts; to protect, and extend the Liberties of the People; to acquire the esteem and confidence of his Neighbours; were the honest arts of his wise policy[.] Notwithstanding his mad passion for the Crusades, (the only blemish of this accomplished Character), he left his son Philip iii [1270–1285] surnamed the bold, the most flourishing Kingdom in*b* Europe; which was*c* soon augmented by the re-union of the rich County of Thoulouse [1271]. Philip iii was succeeded by his son Philip iv [1285–1315] surnamed the Fair.

[*England.*] To break the fetters which had been forged at the Norman Conquest, was the great business of the English Barons. John, whose misfortunes deserve no pity, lost his reputation and foreign power by his contests with Rome and France; and his domestic Authority by signing Magna Charta [1215], which contains the rude outlines of British freedom. The fifty six years of his

<hr>

a I. the   *b II.* of   *c I.* under

son Henry iii [1216–1272] were a long Minority; during which the reins of Government were successively resigned to foreign favourites, and usurped by the turbulent Barons under their leader Simon de Montfort Earl of Leicester [1258]. Edward i [1265], then only the Heir Apparent, rescued his Father, vanquished[a] Montfort and his Adherents in the field, and restored the Royal Authority [1272–1307]; but his good sense soon taught him to respect the new Barriers raised against it to confirm Magna Charta, and to desist from a rash attempt to resume the alienated Crown Lands. Amidst these troubles, the House of Peers became less numerous and more powerfull, the Commons were admitted to a share of the Legislature, the Common Law and Courts of Justice received their present form, and the[b] first Statutes were enacted against the avarice of Rome. Edward i, to whose wisdom we owe many of those advantages, conceived and almost executed the great design of uniting the whole Island under one Dominion. The Welsh lost their ancient independance [1283], but for several Ages preserved their savage Manners. The Throne of Scotland was disputed [1291], almost with equal claims by several Candidates. Edward who was acknowledged as Umpire, awarded the Crown to Baliol [1292] the most obsequious of the Competitors, treated him first as a Vassal, and soon after[c] as a Rebel [1296], endeavoured by every expedient to break the spirit of a haughty Nation, and sullied his glorious End, by the injustice and cruelty of the means, which he used to attain it [1298].

[*Spain.*] The Empire of the Miramolins was destroyed by the greatest Battle ever fought between the Moors and the Christians [1212.]. The latter pursued their advantage; Seville [1236.] and Cordova [1248] were taken and, the provinces of Estramadura, Andalusia, and Murcia, were, in about forty years, annexed to the Crown of Castile. The Kings of Arragon were not less successfull. They wrested from the Moors the fertile Kingdom of Valencia [1238], and established a naval power, by the conquest of the Islands of Majorca, and Minorca [1229]. The bravest of the Moors took refuge in the Kingdom of Grenada, and displayed as much industry in the improvement, as they exerted valour in the defence of this last remnant of their extensive Conquests. The Kings of Castile who acquired the greatest reputation were Ferdinand iii [1217–1252], and Alphonso the Astronomer [1252–1284], the former for his political[d] wisdom, the latter for his speculative knowledge.

[a] *I.* w   [b] *I.* wise   [c] *II.* afterwards   [d] *I.* wisdom of his admi

[*The Crusades*] Four Great Crusades, besides many smaller expeditions, were undertaken in this Century; but though Palestine was still the object of the War, it was no longer the scene of Action. The French and Venetians of the iv[th] Crusade turned their arms against the Schismatic Greeks, took Constantinople [1204], and divided the Empire. Constantinople was indeed recovered by the Greeks [1261], but the trade and dominions which had once belonged to that Capital, were irretrievably lost. John de Brienne a soldier of Fortune, and titular King of Jerusalem invaded Egypt [1218], took Damietta (the old Pelusium) after a siege of two years; but soon thought himself happy to purchase a safe retreat by surrendering that important place. The Crusade of Lewis ix [1248] was more splendid at first; but in the end more unfortunate. It seemed impossible that Egypt subdued as often as it had been attacked, should withstand a young Hero at the head of sixty thousand valiant Enthusiasts. The Army was however destroyed [1250] and the French Monarch remained a prisoner among the Infidels. Rather from a vague passion of combating the Mahometans, than from any rational prospect of recovering the Holy Land, Lewis IX led another Crusade to Africa[a] [1270], and died of the plague under the walls of Tunis. The few places yet held by the Christians on the coast of Syria were swept away [1291] by the Sultans the successors but no longer the descendants of Saladin. The Mamalukes, a body of Circassian and Tartar Slaves, had dethroned their masters [1250], usurped the Sovereignty of Egypt and Syria, and established a military Government, oppressive at home, but formidable abroad.

Of these seven Great Armaments which shook Asia, and depopulated Europe, nothing remained except the Kingdom of Cyprus in the House of Lusignan, and the three Military Orders. The Templars, by their luxury and pride hastened their dissolution [1307]. The Hospitaliers, and Teutonick Knights preserved themselves by their Valour. The[b] former conquered Rhodes [1310] and are still settled at Malta. The latter formed a great dominion in Prussia [1227], and Courland [1309], at the expence of the Idolaters whom they compelled to become Christians and subjects. A great part of the old Nobility of Europe perished in the Crusades; their fiefs reverted to their Lords and their place was supplied by new Men, raised by wealth, merit or favour, and who soon imbibed the Vanity though not the independance of their Predecessors.

[a] *I.* the coast of Africa   [b] *I.* They

[*Learning*] The numerous Vermin of Mendicant Fryars, Franciscans, Dominicans Augustins, Carmelites, who swarmed in this
Century, with habits and institutions variously ridiculous, disgraced
Religion, Learning and Common sense. They seized on Scholastic
Philosophy, as a science peculiarly suited to their minds, and, excepting only Fryar Bacon, they all preferred words to things. The subtle,
the profound, the Irrefragable, the Angelic, and the Seraphic Doctor
acquired those pompous titles, by filling ponderous Volumes with
a small number of Technical terms, and a much smaller number of
Ideas. Universities arose in every part of Europe, and thousands of
Students employed their lives upon these grave follies. The Love
songs of the Troubadours, or Provençal Bards were follies of a more
pleasing nature, which amused the leisure of the greatest Princes,
polished the southern Provinces of France, and gave birth to the
Italian Poetry.

The xiv[th] Century [1300–1400]

[*The Popes*] Both the Popes and the Emperors, the Conquerors
and the Vanquished withdrew from Italy, their field of Battle. The
former, invited by the Kings of France and disgusted with the rebellious spirit of the Romans, established the Papal residence at
Avignon [1305] during more than seventy years. These French
Pontifs were more strongly possessed by the love of money, than
by[a] the love of power. John XXII [1316–1334] by the sale of benefices, indulgencies, and absolutions, accumulated a treasure of
twenty five millions of Gold Florins. At the repeated sollicitations
of the Romans, who felt their error; when it was too late; Gregory
xi returned to his Capital [1377]; but his eyes were scarcely closed
when the enraged People surrounded the Conclave, threatening the
Cardinals with instant death, unless they chose an Italian Pontif
[1378]. The affrighted Frenchmen yielded[b] to their fury, but were
no sooner at liberty than they protested against their first Election
and nominated one of their own Countrymen. Europe was divided
between the two Rivals. Italy, Germany, and England acknowledged
the Pope of Rome; France, and Spain sided with the Pope of
Avignon. Each[c] had his adherents his Doctors, his Saints and his
Miracles, but their mutual Excommunications, which at another
time might have produced a Battle of Swords, only occasioned a
War of Pens.

[a] *II. om.* by   [b] *I.* Co   [c] *I. om.* Each . . . Miracles,

[*The Emperors*][a] Emperors, whose authority in Germany was so much circumscribed, could not invade, with any success, the confirmed liberty of the Italians. Henry vii, of Luxemburgh [1308–1313], and Lewis v of Bavaria [1314–1347], entered Rome in triumph; but their triumph was not attended with any[b] solid or permanent advantages. The grand-son[c] of Henry of Luxemburgh Charles iv [1347–1378], Emperor and King of Bohemia, was invited, by the eloquent Petrarch, to assume the station and character of the ancient Cæsars. The Bohemian Cæsar marched into Italy; but it was only to see himself excluded from every fortified City as an Enemy[d], or cautiously received as a Prisoner. He was crowned at Rome; but quitted it very day of his Coronation, meanly, or perhaps wisely, resigning to the Popes, all the ancient Rights which he derived from Charlemagne and Otho. His son Wenceslaus [1378–1400], would gladly, to use his own expression, have relinquished the Empire with it's remaining prerogatives, for a few Hogsheads of Rhenish or Florence Wine.

[*Italy*] Although neither leisure, independance, nor ingenuity were wanting to the Italians; they were never able to connect themselves into a System of Union and Liberty. Naples flourished under the administration of Robert [1309–1343], the grandson of Charles of Anjou, but was almost ruined by his grand-daughter[e] Joan [1343–1382]. By the murder of her first husband Andrew, she drewn[f] down the vengeance of his brother the stern King of Hungary; by adopting Lewis Duke of Anjou, the brother of Charles v entailed on her dominions a Civil War of which she was herself the first victim. *Rome* saw for a moment [1347] her Tribunes, her freedom and her dignity restored by Nicholas Rienzi, whose extraordinary character was a compound of the Heroe and the Buffoon. *Florence*, like Athens, experienced all the evils incident or rather inherent to a wild Democracy. The *Venetians* and the *Genoese*, wasted each other's strength in Naval Wars [1350–1355], [1377–1381], which allowed not[g] the latter a moment's respite from their intestine[h] dissentions. The Free Cities of Lombardy and Romagna were oppressed by domestic Tyrants under the specious titles of Vicars of the Church or of the Empire; but these petty Usurpers were gradually swallowed up in the power of the Visconti, first Lords [1317] and afterwards Dukes [1395.] of *Milan*

---

[a] *I. Germany*   [b] *I. om.* any   [c] *I.* son   [d] *I. om.* as an Enemy
[e] *I.* daughter   [f] *II.* drew   [g] *I. om.* not   [h] *I.* dom

[*Germany*.] The more phlegmatic Germans, though poor and Barbarous, maintained and even improved the form of their Constitution. Whatever concerned the Election and Coronation of the Emperors, the most fruitfull source of Civil discord was finally regulated by the Golden Bull [1356], published by Charles iv in a general Diet. The title and power of Electors[a] were confined to seven great Princes; The Archbishops of Mentz Treves and Cologne, The King of Bohemia, the Duke of Saxony the Margrave of Brandenburgh and the Count Palatin. These Electors soon asserted over the Emperor Wenceslaus their right of deposing an unworthy Sovereign [1400].

[*Switzerland*] The Swiss owe their reputation to their freedom, and their freedom to their valour. The Peasants of three Vallies among the Alps, Uri, Schwitz and Underwald oppressed by the Officers of the Emperor Albert entered into a strict Alliance [1308] at first for seven Years and afterwards for ever. Leopold Duke of Austria and son of Albert marched against them at the head of twenty thousand Men; but was overthrown in the Battle of Morgarten by 1300 Swiss [1315]. The little Communities of Zug and Glaris, and the Cities of Lucerne, Zurich and Bern gradually acceded to the Confederacy, which was cemented with the blood of another Duke Leopold, who fell, with the flower of the Austrian Nobility in the Battle of Sempach [1386]. Zurich and Bern were allowed the first rank among the eight Cantons; the former for it's wealth, the latter for it's military power. In the five rustic Communities, the government was a pure Democracy; in the three Cities, it was tempered with[b] a small mixture of Aristocracy, which time and circumstances have very much strengthened. The whole Commonwealth, disclaiming the tyranny of the House of Austria, retained their ancient Allegiance to the German Empire.

[*France*] The Constitution of the French Monarchy, received new strength and harmony from the following events. 1. In the memorable quarrel [1303] between Pope Boniface viii. and Philip the Fair, the greater part of the French Clergy remembered that they were subjects as well as Priests. *The Liberties of the Gallican Church* were asserted with spirit and success; and the Crown was, in some degree, delivered from a servile dependance on a foreign Prelate [1301]. 2. *The States General*, composed of the Clergy, the Nobility and the Commons were assembled by Philip the Fair, for the first time since the decline of the Carlovingian Race. As their Meetings were short

[a] *I.* P   [b] *I.* whi

and irregular they never acquired the authority of Legislators; and their tumultuous opposition commonly subsided into an obsequious compliance with the demands of the Court. 3. *The Parliament of Paris* was styled the Court of Peers and should have been composed of the great Vassals of the Crown but as they disdained the humble office of Judicature, their place was supplied by the Bishops, the Barons and the principal Officers, whose *noble* ignorance was directed by some Plebeian Assessors. The servants gradually supplanted their Masters, combated the violence of the Nobility, with the subtilities of Law, and laboured to erect a pure Monarchy on the ruins of the Feudal System. For a long time, these Magistrates[a] held their places only during the King's pleasure 4. *The Salic Law*, though of the most lasting benefit to the Monarchy, occasioned the long and[b] destructive Wars between France and England. After a series of Eleven Kings, in lineal and male descent from Hugh Capet, Lewis x [1314–1317], Hutin, was succeeded by his brothers Philip v [1317–1322], and Charles iv[c] [1322–1328], and afterwards by his first Cousin Philip vi of Valois [1328–1350], on the acknowledged Principle, that Females were incapable of inheriting the crown of France. Whether that principle be admitted or rejected the claim of Edward iii of England is equally indefensible. The[d] quæstion was not however[e] decided by arguments but by arms. Both Nations signalized their valour in the battles of Crecy [1346] and Poitiers [1356], but the discipline of the English triumphed over the numbers of the French. The Captivity of John [1350–1364], who had succeeded to the Crown and misfortunes of his Father Philip, exposed France to a total dissolution of Government with all it's attendant calamities: However[f] though Edward was able to ruin, he was unable to conquer, that great Kingdom. By the Treaty of Bretigny [1360] he accepted[g] three millions of Gold Crowns, the City of Calais, and seven Provinces adjacent to Guyenne: but the last[h] were soon [1369] wrested from him by the arms and policy of Charles v [1364–1380], whose wise administration healed the wounds of his Country. They bled afresh under his unhappy son Charles vi [1380–1422]: first a minor and afterwards deprived of his senses, he was ever the[i] victim of the ambition and avarice of his Uncles. In this Century, Champagne, and Dauphinè, the first by inheritance and treaty; the second by donation, were re-united to the Crown.

---

[a] *I.* places   [b] *I.* d   [c] *I.* the iv,   [d] *I.* But the   [e] *I. om.* however
[f] *I.* but   [g] *II.* accepted of   [h] *I.* latter   [i] *II.* a

[*England*.] The iron fetters, in which Edward i seemed for ever to have bound Scotland, were broke[a] [1306] by the valour and fortune of Robert Bruce, a descendant of the ancient Kings. To resist the Heroic Leader of a brave Nation, combating[b] for freedom and a Throne, required all the powerfull Genius of Edward I, and was a task by[c] far too arduous for his feeble son [1307–1327]. The Victory of Bannocks Boarn [1315] secured to Robert a scepter, which by the marriage of his daughter, was transmitted to the House of Stuart [1371]. Edward ii,[d] Vanquished by his Enemies, despised by his subjects, governed by his favourites, betrayed by his brother, his wife and his son, descended from a throne to a prison, and from a prison to an untimely Grave. The English dwell with rapture on the Trophies of Edward iii [1327–1377] and his gallant Son the Black Prince; on the fields of Cressy and Poitiers; and on the Kings of France and Scotland at the same time prisoners in London. To a thinking mind, Edward's encouragement of the Woollen Manufacture is of greater value than all these Barren laurels. Richard ii [1377–1399], son of the Black Prince affords the second instance, in this Century, of an English King deposed and murdered by his subjects. The House of Commons acquired it's present form, and a dignity unknown to the third Estate, in any other Country, by the junction of the Knights of Shires or Representatives of the Lesser Nobility, who about this time separated themselves from the Peers. After the deposition of Richard [1399], Henry IV, son of John of Gaunt Duke of Lancaster, the third son of Edward iii, usurped the Crown. The posterity of the second son Lionel of Clarence was disregarded, but still existed[e] latent in the House of York[.]

[*Spain*.] The Mahometan Kingdom of Grenada, and the four Christian Monarchies of Castile, Arragon, Navarre and Portugal, preserved their respective Laws and limits. The Constitution of the Christian States was suited to the haughty and generous temper of the People. The Justiciary of Arragon, a name dreadfull to Royal ears possessed the noble but dangerous privilege of declaring, *when* the Subjects were justified in taking arms against their Sovereign. The Castilians, without waiting for the sentence of a Magistrate, knew how to resist a Tyrant either in the *Cortez* or in the field. The Civil War [1366–1368] between Peter the Cruel King of Castile and his brother Henry,[f] occasioned a great Revolution, in which France

---

[a] *II.* broken   [b] *I.* struggling   [c] *I. om.* by   [d] *I. om.* Edward ii,
[e] *I.* remained   [f] *II. om.* Henry,

and England took the opposite sides rather from a wild love of Enterprize, than from any rational motives of Policy. After[a] several turns of fortune the Bastard was victorious, transmitted the Crown to his posterity, and ratified a strict Union[b] with his French Allies; binding France and Castile to each other, King to King, People to People, and Man to Man.

Africa, relapsing into it's native Barbarism, no longer merits our attention. Egypt and Syria continued to groan under the tyranny of the Mamalukes, although some of those Sultans corrected, by their personal virtues, the defects of their institution. In the East two formidable powers arose. The greatness of the Othman Turks was gradual and permanent; the Conquests of Timur, were rapid and transitory.

[*The Turks.*][27] During the anarchy, which overspread Asia Minor, on the fall of the Seljukian Dynasty, the Greeks recovered many of the maritime places, and every Turkish Emir made himself independant within his Jurisdiction. Othman [1300–1326] first erected his standard near[c] Mount Olympus in Bithynia, and as he commanded only a small tribe of Shepherds and Soldiers, he was branded with the name[d] of Robber. A more numerous Army, and the reduction of Nice, Nicomedia, and Prusa, bestowed on his son Orcan [1326–1360] the appellation of Conqueror. The imprudent Greeks, in the madness of civil discord, invited the Turks, opened the Hellespont, and betrayed Christendom. Adrianople became the Capital of the Othman Power in Europe, and the Eastern Empire, reduced to the suburbs of Constantinople, was pressed on either side by the arms of Amurath 1 [1360–1389]. That Sultan instituted the Janizaries; a body of Infantry, from their arms, discipline, and Enthusiasm, almost invincible. The flower of the Christian Youth, torn in Infancy from their Parents, were gradually agregated to the Turkish Nation, after they had lost, in the severe Education of the Seraglio, all memory of their former Country and Religion. Bajazet I. [1389–1402] deserved his surname[e] of *Ilderim* or Lightening, by the rapid impetuosity with[f] which he flew from the Euphrates to the Danube. He triumphed by turns over the Mahometans of Asia Minor, and the Christians of Bulgaria, Servia, Hungary, and Greece; and the total defeat of an Army of French in the battle[g] of Nicopolis [1396], spread the terror of his name to the most remote parts of Europe.

[*Timur*][28] Timur, or Tamerlane raised himself from a private, though not a mean condition to the throne of Samarcand [1369–1405]. His first dominions lay between the Jaxartes and the Oxus, in the Country, called Sogdiana by the ancients, Maurenahar by modern Persians, and by the Tartars Zagatay from one of the sons of Zingis. The lawfull[a] successor of Zagatay, rather mindfull of his situation, than of his descent, served with humble fidelity in the Army of the Usurper. After reducing the adjacent provinces of Carizme and Khorasan, Timur invaded Persia, and extinguished all the Petty Tyrants [1335.], who had started up since the decline of the house of Zingis. The Khan of the Western Tartary, (who ruled the Kingdoms of Cazan, and Astracan, and exacted a tribute from the Grand Duke of Muscovy,) was unable to elude the pursuit, or to resist the arms of Timur. From the deserts of Siberia, he marched to the Banks of the Ganges, and returned from Dehli to Samarcand, laden with the treasures of Hindostan. He knew how to reign, as well as how to conquer. Although very profuse of the blood of his Enemies, he was carefull of the lives and property of his Subjects. He loved magnificence and society, encouraged the arts, and was versed in the Persian and Arabian Litterature. His Zeal for the Musulman Faith, inflamed his natural Cruelty, against the Gentoos of India, and the Christians of Georgia. The Empire of the Moguls in China, founded on violence, and maintained by Policy, was at length dissolved by it's own weakness. The Chinese placed a dynasty of their Countrymen on the throne [1370]; whilst the Tartars returning to the Pastoral life of the desert, gradually recovered, the martial spirit, which they had lost amidst the Arts and luxury of the conquered Provinces[.][b]

[*Commerce*.] A more diffusive Commerce began to connect the European Nations by their mutual wants and conveniences. The discovery of the Compass inspired Navigators, with greater boldness and security. The Hanseatic Cities of Prussia[c] and[d] Saxony formed a powerfull Association, engrossed the Fishery, Iron Corn, timber, Hides, and furs of the North; and contended for the sovereignty of the Baltic, with the Kings of Denmark and Sweden. The Exchange of Money, the finer Manufactures, and the trade of the East were in the hands of the Italians. The Merchants of Venice and of Dantzic met at the common mart of[e] Bruges; which soon became

---

[a] *I. om.* lawfull   [b] *I. om. two sentences:* The Empire . . . Provinces.
[c] *I.* Polish   [d] *I.* and the   [e] *II.* at

the Warehouse of Europe. The Flemings,[a] animated by the spectacle of Wealth and Industry, applied themselves with great ardour to the usefull arts, and particularly to the making broad Cloth[b], linnen and tapestry.

[*Litterature*][29] The advantages of trade were common to several Nations: but the pleasures and Glory of Litterature were confined to the Italians; or rather to a few men of Genius, who emerged from an ignorant and superstitious Multitude. The writings of Dante, Boccace, and Petrarch for ever fixed the Italian language. The first displayed the powers of a wild but original Genius. The Decameron of the second contains a just and agreable picture of Human life. A few stanzas on[c] Laura and Rome, have immortalized the name of Petrarch; who was a Patriot, a Philosopher, and the first Restorer of the Latin Tongue, and of the study of the Ancients. If any Barbarian on this side the Alps, deserves to be remembered, it is our countryman Chaucer, whose Gothic Dialect often conceals natural humour, and Poetical[d] Imagery.

The xv[th] Century [1400–1500]

[*Timur*] After breaking the power of the Mamalukes, and ruining the Cities of Bagdad, Aleppo, and Damascus, Timur advanced towards the frontiers of Bajazet. The situation and character of the two Monarchs rendered a War inevitable. The Armies met in the plains of Angora [1402], and the contest was decided in the Tartar's favour, by the total defeat, and captivity of his Rival. After this victory the Empire of Timur extended from Moscow to the Gulf of Persia, and from the Hellespont to the Ganges; but his ambition was yet unsatisfied: Death surprized him [1405] as he was preparing to invade China, to assert the cause of his Nation and of his Religion. His feeble successors far from meditating new conquests, saw province after province gradually escape from their dominion, till a few Cities near the Oxus, were the only Patrimony that remained to the House of Timur [1470].

[*The Turks*][30] The Turks had been defeated but not subdued. As soon as Timur was no more, they collected their scattered forces, re-placed their Monarchy on it's former basis and, under the conduct of Mahomet i [1413[e]–1421] were[f] again victorious both in

---

[a] *I.* Flemings themselves   [b] *So in II; MS.* Clock   [c] *I.* (amon   [d] *I.* pleasi
[e] *II.* 1418   [f] *I. om.* were

Europe and Asia. Amurath ii [1421-1451.] swayed the Othman Scepter with the abilities of a great Monarch, and twice resigned it with the moderation of a Philosopher. He was forced from his retreat to chastise the perfidy of Ladislaus King of Hungary, who at the instigation of the Court of Rome, had violated a solemn truce. That act of Justice was most compleatly executed in the decisive Battle of Warna [1444.], which was fatal to the King, to the Papal Legate, and to the whole Christian Army. The easy but important conquest of Constantinople [1453.] was reserved for Mahomet ii [1451-1481]. The little[a] Empire of Trebizond, and the other independant provinces of Greece and Asia Minor soon experienced the same fate [1462]. Though Mahomet was obliged to raise the sieges of Belgrade and Rhodes, though he was, for a long time, stopped by Scanderbeg in the Mountains of Albania, yet his arms were generally successfull from the Adriatic to the Euphrates[b]; on the banks of which he vanquished Uzun Hassan; a Turcoman Prince who had usurped Persia from the posterity of Timur. The Conquest of Rome and Italy was the great object of Mahomet's ambition; and[c] a Turkish Army had already[d] invaded the Kingdom of Naples; when[e] the Christians were delivered from this imminent danger by the seasonable death of Mahomet, and the inactive disposition of his son Bajazet ii [1481-1512.]. But the valour and discipline of the Turks were still[f] formidable to Christendom, and the passion for Crusades was[g] ceased at the very time when[h] it might have been approved by reason and justice.

[*Popes and Councils*][31] The Council of Pisa [1409.], by the election of a third Pontif, multiplied instead of extinguishing the evils of the Great Schism. The Council of Constance [1414-1418], in[i] which the five great Nations of Europe were represented by their Prelates and Embassadors, acted with greater vigour and effect. They rejected the defective title of two Pretenders, and judicially deposed the third by whose authority they were assembled. The Election of Martin V restored peace to the Church, but the spirit of independance which had animated the Fathers of Constance, revived in the Council of Basil [1432-1443]. The assembled Bishops of Christendom attempted to limit the despotic power which the Bishop[j] of Rome had usurped over his Brethren; but the treasures of the Church

---

[a] *I*. Phantom of the [b] *I*. Europe [c] *I. om.* and [d] *I. om.* had already
[e] *I*. but [f] *So II. MS.* still still [g] *II*. had [h] *I. om.* when [i] *I*. to
[j] *I*. Bishops

distributed with a skilfull hand silenced the Opposition; and nothing remains of those famous Councils, but a few decrees revered at Paris, detested and dreaded at Rome. Amongst these disorders, the Laity of some Countries discovered as much discontent at the riches of the Clergy, as the Clergy expressed at the power of the Popes. John Huss and Jerom of Prague, two Bohemian Doctors, who taught principles not very different from those of the Protestants, were committed to the flames [1415.] by the Council of Constance, before which they appeared under the sanction of the Public faith. From their ashes arose a Civil War; in which the Bohemians inflamed by revenge and enthusiasm for a long time, inflicted and suffered the severest Calamities.

[*Italy*] Italy, undisturbed by foreign invasions, maintained an internal balance, thro' a series of artfull Negociations, and harmless Wars, attended with scarcely any[a] effusion of blood. The sword, which had fallen from the hands of the Italian Sovereigns, was taken up by troops of independent Mercenaries who acknowledged no tie but their interest, nor any allegiance except to Leaders of their own choice. The five principal Powers, were the Popes, The Kings of Naples, The Dukes of Milan, and The Republics of Florence, and Venice.[b] 1. The *Popes*, after the Councils[c] of Constance and Basil, applied themselves to reconcile the Roman People to their Government, and to extirpate the petty Usurpers of the Ecclesiastical State. 2 Their great Fief, the *Kingdom of Naples*, was the Theatre of a long civil War between the Houses of Anjou and Arragon. It flourished under the administration of Alphonso the wise [1442–1458], who[d] preferred Italy to his Spanish Dominions. Ferdinand [1458–1494], his natural son, succeeded him in Naples only, oppressed the Barons, protected the People, and was delivered by a seasonable death from the arms of Charles viii King of France. 3. After the death of the last of the Visconti [1448], the Dutchy of Milan, superior in value to several Kingdoms, was claimed by the Duke of Orleans in right of his mother; but was usurped by Francis Sforza [1450–1466], the bastard of a peasant and one of the most renowned Leaders of the Mercenary Bands, who, with a policy[e] equal to his valour, left Milan the peaceable inheritance of his family. 4. The Elevation of the Medici[f] was the more gradual effect of prudence and industry.

---

[a] *I. om.* any   [b] *I.* 1 The Popes, 2 The Kings . . . 3 The Dukes . . . 4 The Republic of Florence, and 5 The Republic of Venice.   [c] *II.* council   [d] *I.* p
[e] *I.* prudence   [f] *I.* Medici at Florence

Cosmo [1433–1464] the Father of his Country, and Lorenzo [1472–1492] the Father of the Muses, in the humble station of Citizens and Merchants revived Learning; governed Florence, and influenced the rest of Italy. The old forms of the Commonwealth were preserved and it was only by an unusual tranquillity, that the Florentines could be sensible of the loss of their freedom. 5. The Wisdom of the Venetian Senate the arts and opulence of Venice, an extensive commerce, a formidable navy, the possession of a long tract of sea Coast in Dalmatia, with the Islands of Candia Cyprus &c, formed the natural strength of a Republic, respected in Europe as the firmest bulwark against the Turkish arms. The imprudent Conquests in Lombardy, from[a] which the Venetians were not able to refrain; the Friul, Padua, Vicenza Verona, Brescia, and Bergamo, drained the Treasury of S[t] Mark, and excited the jealousy of the Italian Powers.

[*Germany.*] The reign of the[b] Emperor Robert [1400–1410], Count Palatin, was obscure and inglorious. Though Sigismund of Luxemburgh [1410–1438] presided with some dignity at the Council of Constance, his administration was rather busy than active. After his death the Imperial Crown returned, for ever to the House of Austria, first in the person of Albert ii [1438–1440], and then of Frederic iii [1440–1493].[32] The latter possessed the title of Emperor above half a Century, without either authority or reputation. Germany was without influence in Europe, but judicious foreigners began to discover the latent powers of that great Body; when once rouzed into action, by the necessity of it's own defence. The Levity of Maximilian I [1493–1519], engaged him in perpetual Wars and Treaties, which commonly ended in his disapointment and confusion. However he may be considered as the Founder of the Austrian Greatness, by his marriage with Mary of Burgundy; and as the Founder of the *Public Law*, by his usefull, institutions of the Circles, and of the Imperial Chamber.

[*England[c]*] The Usurpation of the House of Lancaster was supported by the fortune and abilities of Henry iv. His warlike son Henry v, asserted by the Victory of Azincour the claim of the Plantagenets to the French Monarchy. The Conquest of it was[d] a task much too difficult for a Prince, whose revenue did not exceed a[e] hundred and ten thousand Pounds, of our present money, and whose

---

[a] *I.* whic   [b] *I. om.* the   [c] *So in II. Not in MS.*   [d] *For remainder of this sentence, in I*: would have required more preserving efforts, than England was either able or willing to exert, had not   [e] *II.* an

subjects were neither able nor willing to make any extraordinary efforts to render[a] England in the end a province of France. The[b] vindictive Spirit of Queen Isabella and of Philip Duke of Burgundy, betrayed their Country and posterity. The English Monarch was *sollicited* to sign the Treaty of Troyes and to accept, with the hand of the Princess Catharine the quality of Regent and Heir of France. His infant son Henry vi was proclaimed at Paris as well as at London. His reign was a series of weakness and misfortunes. The French[c] conquests were gradually lost, and the English Barons returned into their Island, exasperated against each other, habituated to the power and licence of War, and as much discontented with the monkish Virtues of Henry, as with[d] the masculine spirit, and foreign connections of his Queen Margaret of Anjou. The pretensions of Richard Duke of York, and of his son Edward iv, inflamed the discontent into Civil War. Hereditary right was pleaded against long possession; the banners of the White and Red Roses met in many a bloody field, and the Votes of Parliament varied with the chance of arms.[e] Edward of York assumed the title of King revenged the death of his father, and triumphed over the Lancastrian Party: but no sooner was the imprudent Youth seated on the Throne, than he cast away the friendship of the great Earl of Warwick and with it the English Scepter. That warlike and popular Nobleman impatient of indignities drove Edward into exile, and brought back Henry (scarcely conscious of the change) from the Tower to the Palace. Edward's activity soon retrieved his indiscretion. He landed in England with a few followers, called an Army to his standard, obtained the decisive Victories of Barnet and Tewksbury, and suffered no Enemy[f] to live, who might interrupt the security and pleasures[g] of his future Reign. The Crimes of Richard iii, (who ascended the throne by the murder of his two nephews (Edward V and his brother,) reconciled the parties of York and Lancaster. Henry Tudor Earl of Richmond was invited over from Brittany, as the common Avenger, vanquished and slew the Tyrant in the field of Bosworth and, uniting[h] the two Roses, by his marriage with the eldest Daughter of Edward iv gave England a prospect of serener

---

[a] *I*. make   [b] *I*. the   [c] *I*. Eng   [d] *I*. with much as   [e] *For next four sentences, in I*: War. The Rival Princes were successively [*deleted*] alternately on the Throne, in prison, and in exile, till the decisive Victories of Barnet and Tewksbury, followed by the death of Henry fixed the crown on the head of Edward iv, an active, cruel and a voluptuous Monarch.   [f] *I*. live Enemy   [g] *II*. pleasure   [h] *I*. by uniting

days. The Kingdom had however suffered less, than might be expected from the calamities of Civil War. The frequent Revolutions were decided by one or two battles; and so short a time was consumed in Actual hostilities as allowed not any foreign Power to interpose his dangerous Assistance: No cities were destroyed, as none were enough fortified to sustain a siege. The Churches and even the privilege of Sanctuaries were respected, and the revenge of the Conquerors was commonly confined to the Princes and Barons of the adverse Party, who all died in the field or on the Scaffold. The Power and Estates of this old Nobility were gradually shared by a multitude of new families enriched by Commerce, and favoured by the wise Policy of Henry vii; but between the depression of the Aristocracy and the rise of the Commons, there was an interval of unresisted Despotism.

[*France*[a]] The Factions of Burgundy and Orleans, who disputed the Government of Charles vi, filled France with Blood and Confusion. The Duke of Orleans was treacherously murdered in the streets of Paris, and John[b] Duke of Burgundy who avowed and justified the deed, was, some years afterwards assassinated in the presence and probably with the consent of the young Dauphin. That[c] Prince persecuted by his mother, disinherited by the Treaty of Troyes, and on every side pressed and surrounded by the victorious English, assumed the title of Charles vii on his father's death, and appealed though with little hopes of success to God and his Sword. The French Monarchy was on the brink of ruin, but like the Othman Empire in the same Century, rose more powerfull from it's fall. A Generous Enthusiasm first revived the National spirit, and awakened the young Monarch from his indolent despair. A Shepherdess declared a divine Commission to raise the siege of Orleans, and to crown him in Rheims. She performed her promises; and the consternation of the English was still greater, than their real loss. The Genius of Charles, seconded by his brave and loyal Nobility, seemed to expand with his fortune. The Duke of Burgundy was reconciled to his Kinsman and Sovereign. Paris opened it's Gates, with willing submission; and at length, after[d] some years of languid Operations, or imperfect truces, the French recovered Normandy and Guyenne, and left the English no footing in their Country, beyond the walls of Calais. The last years of Charles vii's reign were employed in reforming and regulating the state of the

a So II. Not in MS.   *b I.* th   *c I.* After   *d I.* the

Kingdom. He is[a] the first modern Prince, who has possessed a
Military force in time of peace, or imposed[b] taxes by his sole
authority. The former was[c] composed of 1500 Lances, who with
their followers made a body of 9000 Horse. The latter did not exceed
360,000 Pounds Sterling. This great alteration was introduced without opposition and felt only by it's consequences, which gradually
affected all Europe.

The Feudal System, weakened in France by these innovations
was anihilated by the severe despotism of Lewis xi, into whom the
soul of Tiberius might seem to have passed. As it was his constant
policy to level all distinctions among his subjects, except such as
were derived from *his* favour, the Princes and Great Nobility took up
arms, and[d] besieged him in Paris: but their Confederacy surnamed
of the *Public Good*, was soon dissolved by the jealousy and private
views of the Leaders few of whom afterwards escaped the revenge
of a Tyrant, alike insensible to the sanctity of oaths, the laws[e] of
Justice or the dictates of humanity. The Gendarmerie of the Kingdom was encreased to 4000[f] Lances: besides a disciplined Militia[g]
a large body of Swiss Infantry, and a considerable train of Artillery,
the use of which had[h] already altered the Art of War. The revenue
of France was raised to near[i] a Million Sterling, as well by extraordinary impositions, as by the Union of Anjou, Maine, Provence,
Roussillon, Burgundy, Franche-Comte and Artois to the body of the
French Monarchy, which under this wise Tyrant, began to improve
in domestic Policy, and to assume the first station in the great
Republic of Christendom.

The Revolution, which restored Burgundy to the French Monarchy, merits more than common attention. Charles the Bold, of the
house of France, Duke of Burgundy and Sovereign of the Netherlands was the natural and implacable Enemy of Lewis XI. His
subjects of Burgundy were brave and Loyal; those of Flanders rich
and industrious; his revenue was considerable; his Court[j] magnificent; his troops numerous and well disciplined and his dominions
enlarged by the acquisition of Guelders, Alsace and Lorrain:[k] but
his vain projects of ambition were far superior either to his power
or[l] his abilities. At one and the same time, he aspired to obtain the
Regal Title, to be elected King of the Romans, to divide France with

---

[a] *I.* was   [b] *I.* raised   [c] *II.* were   [d] *I.* against him   [e] *II.* law
[f] *I.* 4500   [g] *I. om.* a disciplined Militia   [h] *I.* began to alter the former Art
[i] *II.* nearly   [j] *I.* household   [k] *I. om.* and his dominions . . . Lorrain: [l] *I.* of

the English, to invade Italy, and to lead a Crusade against the Turks. The Swiss Cantons, a name till then unknown in Europe, humbled his pride. Many writers more attentive to the moral precept than to historic truth, have represented the Swiss as a harmless people attacked without justice or provocation. Those rude mountaineers were on the contrary the Aggressors, and it appears by authentic documents that French intrigues and even French Money had found a way into the Senate of Bern. Lewis xi, who, in his youth had experienced the valour of the Swiss, inflamed the quarrel till it became irreconcilable and then sat down; the quiet Spectator of the Event.[a] The Gendarmerie of Burgundy was discomfited in three great Battles, by the firm Battalions of Swiss Infantry, composed of Pikemen and Musqueteers. At Granson, Charles lost his honor and treasures, at Morat, the flower of his troops and at[b] Nancy his life. He left only an orphan Daughter, whose rich Patrimony Lewis might perhaps have secured by a Treaty of Marriage. Actuated by passion rather than sound policy, he chose to ravish it by Conquest. Burgundy and Artois submitted without much difficulty; but the Flemings exasperated by the memory of ancient injuries, disdained the French Yoke, and married their young Princess Mary to Maximilian son of the Emperor Frederic iii. The Low[c] Countries became[d] the inheritance of the House of Austria, and the subject as well as Theatre of a long series of Wars, the most celebrated that have ever disturbed Europe.

Such was the growing prosperity of France, that even the disturbances of a Minority proved favourable to it's greatness. Brittany the last of the Great Fiefs, escaped a total Conquest, only by[e] the marriage of Anne Heiress of that great Dutchy, with Charles viii son and successor of Lewis xi. The Expedition of Charles viii into Italy, displayed his character, and that of the Nation, which he commanded. In five Months, he traversed affrighted Italy as a Conqueror, gave laws to the Florentines and the Pope, was acknowledged King of Naples and assumed the title of Emperor of the East. Every thing yielded to the first Fury of the French; every thing was lost by the imprudence of their Councils. The Italian Powers, recovered from their astonishment, formed a League with Maximilian and Ferdinand, to intercept the return of Charles viii[f][.] The Kingdom of Naples escaped from his hands, and the Victory of Fernova, only

---

[a] *I. om. this sentence*   [b] *I. om.* at   [c] *I.* Net   [d] *I.* wer   [e] *I. om.* by
[f] *I.* his return. The Kingdom of Naples escaped the hands of Charles viii

served to secure his retreat. He died soon afterwards, leaving his Kingdom exhausted by this rash Enterprize, and weakened by the imprudent Cession of Roussillon to the Spaniards and of Franche-Comtè and Artois to the House of Austria.

[*Spain*[a]] Spain was hastening to assume the form of a powerfull Monarchy. Castile and Arragon were first united under the same Family, and not long afterwards under the same Sovereigns. Henry iv King of Castile a Prince odious[b] for his vices and contemptible for his weakness, was solemnly deposed in a great Assembly of his subjects; who, despising the suspicious birth of his daughter Juanna, placed the crown on the head of Isabella,[c] his sister. The marriage of that Princess with Ferdinand of Arragon, compleated the salutary Revolution. The Spaniards celebrate with reason the united Administration of those Monarchs; the manly virtues of Isabella, and the profound policy of Ferdinand the Catholic, always covered with the veil of Religion, though often repugnant to the principles of Justice. After a ten years War they executed the great Project of delivering Spain from the[d] Infidels. The Moors of Grenada, defended that last possession with obstinate valour, and[e] stipulated by their[f] Capitulation, the free Exercise of the Mahometan Religion. Public faith, gratitude, and policy ought to have maintained this treaty and it is a reproach to the memory of the great Ximenes, that he urged his Masters to violate it. The severe Persecutions of the Mahometans, and the expulsion of many thousand[g] of Jewish families inflicted a deep but secret Wound on Spain in the midst of it's glory. The prosperity of Ferdinand and Isabella was embittered by the death of their only son. Their daughter Juanna, married the Archduke Philip (son[h] of the Emperor Maximilian and of Mary of Burgundy) and the great successions of the houses of Austria, of Burgundy of Arragon and of Castile were gradually accumulated on the head of Charles the Fifth[i], the fortunate Offspring of that Marriage.

The Dominion of Spain was extended into a new Hemisphære, which had never yet been visited by the Nations placed on our side of the Planet.[j] Christopher Columbus a Genoese obtained from the Ministers of Isabella, after long solicitations and frequent repulses, three small Barks and ninety Men with which he trusted himself to

---

   a So II. Not in MS.   *b I.* of the   *c I.* the   *d I.* the yoke of the
e I. at   *f II.* that   *g II.* thousands   *h I.* Philip (and of Mary of Burgu
i II. V.   *j I. om.* which had never yet . . . Planet.

the unknown Atlantic. His timid and ignorant[a] Sailors repeatedly exclaimed that he was carrying them beyond the appointed limits of Nature, from[b] whence they could never return. Columbus resisted their clamours, and at the end of thirty three days from the Canaries, shewed them the Island of Hispaniola, abounding in Gold, and inhabited by a gentle Race of Men. In his subsequent Voyages, undertaken with a more considerable force, he discovered many other Islands, and saw the great Continent of America, of whose existence, he was already convinced from Speculation[.]

The discoveries of Columbus were the effort of Genius and courage; those of the Portuguese, the slow effect of time and industry. They sailed round the Continent of Africa; found, by the Cape of Good Hope, a new and more independent Route to the East Indies, and soon diverted the Commerce of the East from Alexandria and Venice, to Lisbon.

[*Italy*[c]] A[d] New World was opened to the studious as well as to the active Part of Mankind. It was scarcely possible for the Italians to read Virgil, and Cicero, without a desire of being acquainted with Homer, Plato and Demosthenes. Their wishes were gratified by the assistance of many learned Greeks who fled from the Turkish Arms[.] The Manuscripts, which they had saved, or which were discovered in old Libraries, were quickly diffused and multiplied by the usefull invention of Printing: which so much facilitated the acquisition of Knowledge. For some time however the Genius of the Italians seemed overpowered by this sudden accession of Learning[e]. Instead of exercising their own Reason, they acquiesced in that of the Ancients: instead of transfusing into their native tongue, the Taste and spirit of the Classics, they copied with[f] the most aukward servility the language and ideas suited to an age so[g] different from their own.

If we turn from Letters to Religion[h], the Christian must grieve and the Philosopher will smile. By a propensity natural to Man, the Multitude had easily relapsed into the grossest Polytheism. The existence of a Supreme Being was indeed acknowledged; his Mysterious Attributes were minutely and even indecently canvassed in the Schools; but he was allowed a very small share in the Public Worship or the administration of the Universe. The Devotion of the

[a] *I. om.* and ignorant   [b] *II. om.* from   [c] *So II. Not in MS.*   [d] *I.* It was scarcely poss   [e] *I.* Knowl   [f] *I.* th   [g] *I.* and Country so   [h] *I.* Philosophy

People was directed to the Saints and the Virgin Mary, the Delegates and almost the Partners of his Authority. From the extremities of Christendom, thousands of Pilgrims laden with rich offerings, crowded to the Temples and statues the*a* most celebrated for their miraculous powers. New Legends and new practices of Superstition were daily invented by the interested diligence of the Mendicant Fryars; and as this Religion had scarcely any connection with Morality, every sin was expiated by Pennance, and every Pennance *indulgently* commuted into a fine. The Popes, Bishops, and rich Abbots, careless of the public Esteem were Soldiers, Statesmen, and Men of Pleasure; yet even *such*b* dignified Ecclesiastics blushed at the grosser vices of their inferior Clergy.

a I. of the   *b I.* these

[Second Commonplace Book]

Mexico.[a]

The ancient Empire was said to contain ten Millions of Souls: at present about one. [1][b]

The City once 200.000, now 50000,—afflicted by inundations.[c]— Los Angelos, near Tlascala, has gained by it's loss. [2] From the Mines, 65.000.000 (of Livres) are annually coyned[3] at Mexico. The King has a fifth on the Silver, an[d] tenth on the Gold, as those Mines are more casual. The Gold coyned is about a fifth of the Silver

Mexico is highly taxed yet the net Revenue returned to Europe is only £ 6.300.000[e] [4] Las Casas[1] persuaded the Court of Spain to restore liberty but not property to the [5] Mexican Indians. They are no where so happy, noble and ingenious as in his Diocese of Chiapa.[f]

/1/.[g] Hist Philosophique des deux Indes. Tom iii. p 76[h]   [2][i] Id. p 117
[3] p. 108. 109.   [4] p. 114.   [5] p. 77&c.

Spain.

Contained thirteen or fourteen Millions before the discovery of America [1]

In the year 1747 only 7.423.590 Souls. including 180.046 head of Clergy. [2]

Her Manufactures flourished till the Expulsion of the Moors. Segovia Cloths the best in Europe—60000 silk looms at Seville [3]

About fifty Millions (French) of Merchandizes are sent annually from Cadiz to America. About an eighth part is Spanish property. [4]

---

[a] *MS. has titles and references in margin; II. put all titles in this commonplace book in the text, not in margin.*   [b] *Not superscript in MS.*   [c] *II. inundation*
[d] *II. a*   [e] *II. 6, 300, 800 l.*   [f] *Here II. adds a list of notes about Mexico that were not in this commonplace book. See Part III.*   [g] *Slant lines are Gibbon's.*
[h] *II. p. 75*   [i] *My number, Gibbon's note. Lord Sheffield supplied 'Id.' at the beginning of all references in each of the items in this book for which Gibbon gave no title in the note, except that for the first note of a new page Sheffield repeats the title, as usual. In some cases, the 'Id.' is an obvious error, e.g. Gibbon's notes 4 and 5 under Hercules.*

About seventeen Millions of Piasters (Ł 89.250.000)[a] arrive annually at Cadiz from America in gold and silver. The account seems particular and exact. [5]

[1] Hist Philosop des deux Indes p 392.   [2] p 418.
[3] p 388.   [4] p. 401.   [5] p. 431.

Portugal

The number of it's Inhabitants has sunk from 3.000.000. to 1.800.000. [1]

[1] Hist. Philos Tom iii.

Brasil

It's gold Mines (under the Tropic of Capricorn) were discovered about the year 1730. [1]

The Portuguese content themselves with the quantity, which the Torrents wash down into the Vallies. It amounts annually to about Ł 45.000.000[b]. The King has one fifth. The importation diminishes the proportion of Gold to Silver.

The Mine of Diamonds was discovered about the year 1730— Given to an exclusive Company, and the Country round it dispeopled.[2]—The Government, who is the Agent in Europe under articles to sell no more annually than Ł 1.250.000[c].—Bought and cut by the Dutch and English, chiefly sold in France—are 10 per Cent inferior to East India Diamonds.

	Carats.
Great Mogul s.	279 1/16
The Great Duke's.	139.
The Sancy	106
The Pitt.	136
⎰ The K. of Portugal s.	1280
⎱ inestimable if not a Topaze	

[1] Hist. Philosophiq des deux Indes. Tom iii. p 528
[2] Id. p 534.

Severus[d] (Cornelius)

The Poem of Ætna, though it's author is praised by Ovid and Quintilian, discovers very little taste or invention.[1] The Philosophy is

[a] II. (89,250,000 l)   [b] II. 45,000,000 l.   [c] II. 1,250,000 l.   [d] II. places this item after those on Russia and Hercules.

narrow, and probably erroneous (see the long descant on the Virtues of the Millstone). The Style languid, harsh, and perplexed. Instead of the ornaments of Nature and propriety, the barren Writer consumes a fourth of his Poem in Mythological stories which he affects to despise. The prettiest passages are the Complaint of the preference given to the lucrative over the curious Arts ($\mathbb{V}$ 250–283) and the power of fire (533–561).

[1] See le Clerc (G[or]lus)'s[a] Edition[2] Amsterdam[b] 17[03]

Russia

To what causes may we ascribe the abject slavery of the Russians, the brethren of those hardy Poles and Bohemians, who so long[c] asserted and abused the rights[d] of freedom? Perhaps to the following causes. 1. The Russians derived the knowledge of Christianity and the rudiments of a civil education from a servile and superstitious people, the Greeks of Constantinople. 2. The Tartar Conquerors broke and degraded the spirit of the Russian nation. 3. After the Russians had lost all communication with the Euxine and the Baltic, they were wholly separated and in a great measure secluded from the rest of Europe, and the civilized[e] part of the human race. 4. The accidental advantage of fire-arms enabled the Czars to extend their Empire over the north of Asia; and the power of prejudice was enforced by that of the sword.

Hercules[3]

   —— Qualemque vagæ post crimina noctis
  Thestius obstupuit, *toties* socer.
       Statius in Sylv.[4] L iii. Ep. i V. 42.

The question is therefore *quoties*, and according to the three different tales which prevailed among the Greeks, the amorous prowess of Hercules will excite the idea of a *man*, of a *Hero*, or of a *God*.

i. When Young Hercules was six feet high and only eighteen years of age, he hunted the Lyon on Mount Cithæron in Bœotia, and was hospitably entertained by Thestius Prince of Thespiæ. Every night, by the command of their father, one of the fifty daughters of Thestius shared the bed of Hercules; and the young Hero embraced all[f]

---

 [a] *II.* (Gorlus)'s *-or- and 03 (in date) are now lost in binding.* [b] *II.* of Amsterdam
 [c] *I.* often [d] *II.* right [e] *I.* civil part [f] *I.* them all

these *Virgins* with such undistinguishing and irresistible[a] vigour, that at the expiration of fifty prolific nights he was still persuaded of the identity of his companion. Such is the modest and perhaps the original account of the first of the labours of Hercules; as it is given by Apollodorus.[1]

ii According to another relation the conversion of the fifty virgins into wives and mothers was effected by the indefatigable Hercules within the space of *seven days*. Athenæus[2] has extracted this anecdote from the writings of Herodotus or rather Herodorus[b] the Lycian who, as it appears by[c] another quotation[3] had composed at least seventeen books on the actions of Hercules.

iii. But the popular opinion which at length prevailed ascribed to Hercules the singular honour of consummating in one and the same night his fifty or at least his forty nine marriages. This miracle which seems to be insinuated by Diodorus Siculus,[4] is positively affirmed by Pausanias,[5] and that diligent traveller has recorded the virtue of one of the daughters of Thestius, who refusing to submit to the common fate of her sisters, was invested[d] by Hercules with the sacerdotal dignity, and condemned to a life of perpetual celibacy. The Christian Apologists have adopted this third account, which according to their ideas of merit, was the least honourable to the son of Jupiter. "Hercules, sanctus Deus natas quinquaginta de "Thestio, *nocte unâ* perdocuit, et nomen Virginitatis exponere et "genetricum pondera[e] sustinire"[6]

The vigour of a demigod can be matched only by that of a Prophet. In the space of a single hour, each of[f] the eleven wives of[g] Mahomet successively[h], acknowledged him as[i] a tender and active husband. This anecdote is related by Belon on the faith of an Arabic book entitled "des bonnes Coutumes de Mahomet."[7]

[1] Hist Poet. L ii C 4. p 96.5   [2] Deipnosophist L xiii p 556.
[3] Id. L ix p 410   [4] L iv. p 274–Edit. Wess.   [5] L ix. p 763. Ed. Kuhn[i]
[6] Arnobius. L iv. p 145. His commentator Elmenhorst. p 144 quotes several of the Fathers on this interesting topic
[7] Observations dans ses Voyages. L iii C x p 179.

Παιδεραστια

Herodotus[6] observes with the most placid indifference that the

[a] *I. om.* and irresistible   [b] *II.* Herodotus   [c] *I.* fr   [d] *I.* honoured
[e] *I.* nomina   [f] *I. om.* each of   [g] *I.* whom   [h] *I a.* was to marry, *I b.*
was deservedly permitted to possess,   [i] *I.* with pleasure as   [j] *II.* Kuhr.

Persians fond[a] of adopting new customs and new pleasures. From the Medes they borrowed their dress, from the Egyptians their breast-plates. By the Greeks they were taught to forget the distinction of sexes. απ' Ελληνων μαθοντες, παισι μισγονται.[1]

[1.] L i. C 135

Noue (de la)

The situation and behaviour of de la Noue at the siege of La Rochelle is perhaps without paralel in history. i. Such was his established reputation for honour and virtue, that in the heat of the civil wars of France immediately after the Massacre of St Bartholemy[b], Catherine of Medicis and her son intrusted this zealous Protestant to negociate with the Rochellois. ii By the election of the people, and with the consent of the court he accepted the military command in the revolted City. iii During the siege of la Rochelle, he performed with admirable courage and conduct all the duties of a Soldier, and a Mediator. iv. When the fanaticism of the Rochellois had rejected equitable conditions of peace, he obeyed the summons of the Duke of Anjou, repaired to the Royal standard, and afterwards retired to his own house, with the esteem and confidence of Both parties.

Such wonders require much[c] stronger evidence, than[d] the partial authority of a biographer: and it is almost as singular that they are attested in all the material circumstances, by D'Aubigny a violent protestant,[1] by Thuanus a moderate Philosopher,[2] and by Davila a bigotted Catholic[3.]

The testimony of Davila is the more valuable as he betrays some inclination to *suspect* the *intentions* of de la Noue, in his return to the Royal Camp.

[1.] Hist. Universelle. Tom ii p. 34. 45.[7]
[2.] Hist sui Temporis. L iii. 12. L vi. 5.
[3.] Istoria delle Guerre Civile di Francia. Tom i p 326–330. Edit Londra.

Shoes

The practice of nailing shoes to the hoofs of horses &[e] was unknown to the ancients; who occasionally tyed them with strings round the feet of those animals.[1]

[1] Gesner. Lexicon ad Script. de Re rusticâ. p 132. 133.

[a] *II.* were fond   [b] *II.* Bartholomew   [c] *I.* very strong   [d] *I.* and
[e] *II.* &c.

[A Dissertation on the Subject of l'Homme au Masque de Fer]*a*

The Mysterious History of the famous French Prisoner, known by the Appellation of *l'homme au Masque de fer*, is related by Monsieur de*b* Voltaire in the *Siécle de Louis XIV*.[1] and in the *Quæstions sur l'Encyclopedie*.[2] That Writer the most Sceptical and Lively of his Age never attempts either to contest the Truth or to reveal the secret of that wonderful Affair. *"Je ne connois point de fait ni plus "extraordinaire ni mieux constatè"* is the just conclusion of his first Account. In his subsequent additions, he refutes with force and contempt, the idle suppositions that this unknown Prisoner was the Duc de Beaufort,[3] the Count de Vermandois,[4] or the Duke of Monmouth.[5] At length, breaking off abruptly he throws out a dark intimation, [*"]qu'il en sait peut-etre plus que le Pere Grifet,*[6] *et qu'il "n'en dira pas davantage."*

If we are disposed to exercise our Curiosity and Conjectures on*c* this historical Anecdote, we must steadily remember, that no Hypothesis can deserve the least credit, unless it corresponds with, and explains the following Circumstances.

1. The Prisoner who passed his melancholy life in the Isles de S*te* Marguerite and the Bastille, was called *Marchiali*. As the name was most assuredly fictitious, this Circumstance seems, and indeed is, of small importance. However in case an Italian was either the Author of his birth, or the Guardian of his Infancy, a name drawn from that language would most naturally present itself.

2. Marchiali was buried secretly and by night in the Parish Church of S*t* Paul's, on the 3*d* of March in the year 1703, as is proved by the Journal of the Pere Grifet, who was entrusted with the very delicate Employment of Confessor to the Bastille. A few days before his death, the unknown Prisoner told his Physician that he believed himself about sixty years of Age. If he reckoned with precision he was born in the Spring of the year 1643, about the time of the death of Louis the thirteenth. But the dreary Hours of a prison move slowly, and the infirmities of Age are hastened by grief and

---

a II. supplies title; none in MS.   *b II.* M. Voltaire   *c II.* upon

solitude. Marchiali could speak only from conjecture; nor is it unlikely that he might be somewhat younger than he supposed himself.

3. He was conducted to the Isles de Ste Marguerite on the Coast of Provence, some Months after the death of Cardinal Mazarin, that is to say about the end of the year 1661 or the beginning of 1662. This is the first among the few events of his Life. M. de Voltaire mentions in one place, a previous confinement at Pignerol; but without being perfectly clear or even consistent on that head.

4. Marchiali, whoever he was, had never acted any distinguished part on the public Theatre of the World. The sudden absence of such a person in any part of Europe would infallibly have occasioned much wonder and enquiry, some traces of which must have reached our knowledge. But in this instance, using the amplest latitude of time, we cannot discover any one important *Death*, that leaves the minutest opening for our most licentious suspicions.

5. An illustrious birth was therefore the only advantage by which the Prisoner could be distinguished, and his birth must indeed have been illustrious, since when Monsieur de Louvois made him a visit, he spoke to him standing, and, *avec une consideration qui tenoit du respect*. We must ascend very high ere we can attain a rank which that proud and powerful Minister of the French Monarchy could think it his duty to *respect*.

6. The most extraordinary precautions were employed not only to secure but to conceal this Mysterious Captive, and his Guards were ordered to kill him if he made the least attempt to discover himself. That order as well as the silver plate which he threw out of the Prison Window after writing something upon it, and which fell into the hands of an illiterate Fisherman, sufficiently prove that he was acquainted with his own name and condition. The Mask, which he never was permitted to lay aside, shews the apprehension of the discovery of some very striking resemblance.

7. Prisoners of such alarming importance are seldom suffered to live. Of all precautions the dagger or the bowl are undoubtedly the surest. Nothing but the most powerful motives, or indeed the tenderest ties could have stopped the Monarch's hand, and induced him rather to risk a discovery, than to spill the blood of this unfortunate Man. He was lodged in the best apartment of the Bastille, his table was served in the most delicate manner, he was allowed to play

on the Guitar, and supplied with the finest laces and linen, of which
he was passionately fond. Every kind attention was studiously
practised that could in any wise alleviate the irksomeness of his
perpetual Imprisonment.

8. When Monsieur de Chamillard in the year 1721 was on his
deathbed, his Son in Law the Marèchal de la Feuillade, begged on
his knees that he would disclose to him that mysterious transaction.
The dying Minister refused to gratify this unseasonable Curiosity.
"It was the Secret of the State, he said, and he had taken an Oath
"never to divulge it." The Prisoner had then been dead eighteen
Years, and Louis the fourteenth almost six. It must have been a
Secret of no common magnitude that could still affect the peace
and welfare of future Generations.

Before we proceed to a probable solution of these strange circumstances, let us try to connect them with some facts of a more public
and general Nature.

1. The doubtful birth of Louis XIV. often occurs in Conversation, as the Subject of Historical Scepticism. The first grounds of
the Suspicion are obvious. He was born after a sterile union of
twenty three years between Louis XIII and Anne of Austria. But as
such an Event, however unfrequent, is neither destitute of possibility nor even of example, the scandalous rumour would long since
have died away in oblivion had it not derived additional strength
from the Character and situation of the Royal Pair.

2. Though Louis XIII. wanted not either parts or Courage, his
Character was degraded by a coldness and debility both of mind and
body, which had little affinity with his heroic Father. Had his
indifference towards the Sex, been confined to the Queen it might
have been considered as the mere effect of personal dislike; but his
chaste Amours with his female Favorites betrayed to the laughing
Court that the King was less than a Man.

3. Without reviving all the obsolete scandal of the *Fronde*, we
may respectfully insinuate that Anne of Austria's reputation of
Chastity was never so firmly established as that of her husband. To
the Coquetry of France, the Queen united the warm passions of
a Spaniard. Her friends acknowledge that she was gay, indiscreet,
vain of her Charms, and strongly addicted at least to Romantic
Gallantry. It is well known that she permitted some distinguished
favorites to entertain her with soft tales of her beauty and their
Love; and thus removed the distant Ceremony which is perhaps the

surest defence of Royal Virtue. Anne of Austria passed twenty eight years with a Husband alike incapable of gratifying her tender or her sensual inclinations. At the Age of forty three, she was left an independent Widow, mistress of herself and of the Kingdom.

4. The Civil Wars which raged during the Minority of Louis XIV, arose from the blind and unaccountable attachment of the Queen to Cardinal Mazarin, whom she obstinately supported against the universal Clamor of the French Nation. The Austrian Pride perhaps and the useful Merit of the Minister might determine the Queen to brave an insolent Opposition; but a connection formed by Policy might very easily terminate in Love. The necessity of business would engage that Princess in many a secret and midnight Conference with an Italian of an agreable Person, vigorous Constitution, loose Morals and artful Address. The amazing Anecdote hinted at, in the honest Memoirs of La Porte sufficiently prove[a] that Mazarin was capable of employing every expedient to insinuate himself into *every part* of the Royal Family.

5. If Anne of Austria yielded to such opportunities and to so artful a Lover; if she became a Mother after her Husband's death, Her weakness and the consequences of it would have been carefully screened from the Eye of curious Malignity. When Louis XIV succeeded to the possession of the Kingdom and of the fatal Secret, he was deeply interested in the guard of his own and of his Mothers Honor. Had her frailty been revealed to the World, the living proof would have awakened and confirmed all the latent Suspicions, diffused a spirit of distrust and division among the People and shaken the Hereditary claim of the Monarch. If the strong grasp of Louis XIV retained the French Scepter, the doubt and the danger were entailed on future Ages. In some feeble or infant Reign, an ambitious Condé might embrace the fair pretence to assert the right of[b] his genuine branch and to exclude from the Succession, the spurious posterity of Louis the thirteenth.

In a Word the Child of Anne of Austria and of Cardinal Mazarin would have been at once the brother and the most dangerous Enemy of his Sovereign. The humanity of Louis XIV might have declined a brother's murder; but pride policy and even patriotism must have compelled that Prince to hide his face and his existence with an Iron Mask and the Walls of the Bastille.

It is scarcely necessary to add that I suppose the unfortunate

[a] II. proves   [b] II. to

Marchiali to have been that Child. If the several facts, which I have drawn together blend themselves without constraint into a consistent and natural System, it is surely no weak argument in favor of the Truth or at least of the probability of my Opinion.

May the 27ᵗʰ 1774.

Part III

DECLINE AND FALL YEARS, 1776–1791

INTRODUCTION

THE available materials connected with the *Decline and Fall* are of two kinds: preliminary notes, and plans or materials for revisions. The *Vindication of the Fifteenth and Sixteenth Chapters* was the only part of this material published in its present form during Gibbon's lifetime, and Lord Sheffield chose not to include much of the rest in his editions of Gibbon's miscellaneous works.

The earliest material is what I have called 'Notes on Modern Europe'. It contains much information obtained not from books, but from persons whom Gibbon would have seen in Paris in his visit of May–October 1777. Some of this information is incorporated in chapter xvii of the *Decline and Fall*, which Gibbon wrote, according to his record in a Pocketbook for 1776 (Morgan Library), between June 4 and August 4, except for the notes. The apparent contradiction is resolved, however, by the *Memoirs*: '1777 December &c—Near two years had elapsed between the publication of my first, and the commencement, of my second, Volume; and the causes must be assigned of this long delay. . . . 3. It is difficult to arrange with order and perspicuity the various transactions of the age of Constantine: and so much was I displeased with the first Essay that I committed to the flames above fifty sheets' (pp. 158–9).

The next remnants are called by Gibbon 'Materials for corrections and improvements for the 1ʳˢᵗ Vol. of my History'. This material must be later than 1777, because it uses the pagination of the third and subsequent quarto editions.[1] But it is probably prior to the *Vindication*, for Jerome's testimony about the size of Palestine (p. 228) is used in the *Vindication* (p. 247).

The *Vindication* itself, published 14 January 1779, is the next surviving item. As it was published during Gibbon's lifetime, and Gibbon seems never to have kept manuscripts of his published works, there is no manuscript of the *Vindication*. In it, Gibbon avers a desire to make one change in the text of the *Decline and Fall*, though *not* one proposed by his attackers; it may, therefore, be counted among the materials for revising the history. Its real merit and interest, however, are its superb annihilation of the pretensions of his opponents and its brilliant defence of his own historical views and methods. Gibbon had it printed in octavo, so that it could not be bound with his history, and hoped that his readers, when convinced of his innocence, 'would forget [his] *Vindication*'. But as Professor Trevor-Roper has remarked, 'if he seriously hoped for such oblivion, he should have written differently: with less irony, less appearance of relish, fewer of those majestic, devastating phrases'.[2]

The next materials are from 1781, some comments on editions of Procopius, dated 8 November 1781 and used in *DF*, iv (chapter xl), and an account of Cosmas, an Egyptian merchant and monk. Much of the material about Cosmas is also in *DF*, iv, and it can therefore be dated 1781-4, unless it is thought to be a draft of a supplemental note. That hypothesis is unlikely because of exact repetitions of words in this essay and in the history, as indicated in my notes below.

To the same period belongs a loose sheet of notes on Mexico. It contains a reference to Warton's *Essay* on Pope, volume ii, and the second volume was first published in 1782.

In 1783 Gibbon kept a notebook which he called 'Notes/Gibbon' and which is now in the Pierpont Morgan Library. Sheffield published most of these notes, but he did not show, as Gibbon's manuscript clearly does, that some of them were intended for insertion in the *Decline and Fall*, i and ii, and that others are used later in the history.

The next item, 'Miscellanea', can be assigned to the *Decline and Fall* period because of the reference to 30 Aout 1786 within it. But not all the materials seem to have been used in the history—not surprising, perhaps, in view of the title Gibbon gave them.

The 'Fragmentary Notes to Vol. V and Vol. VI' were made while the last three volumes of the *Decline and Fall* were being printed, August 1787-April 1788. 'The length of the operation, and the leisure of the Country allowed some time to review my manuscript: several rare and useful books, the Assises de Jerusalem, Ramusius de bello C.P^ano, the Greek acts of the Synod of Florence, the Statuta Urbis Romæ &c were procured, and I introduced in their proper places the supplements which they afforded' (*Memoirs*, pp. 181–2).

Finally, there are several items which must have been written after the publication of volumes iv–vi (8 May 1788). The notes from Airoldi are not referred to a page in the *Decline and Fall*, but the book was not published until 1790. It seems probable that all these items were written in the winter of 1790–1, when Gibbon proposed to his publisher a 'seventh, or supplemental Volume to my History':

The materials of which it will be composed will naturally be classed under the three following heads: 1. A series of fragments, disquisitions, digressions, &c more or less connected with the principal subject. 2. Several tables of geography, chronology, coins, weights and measures, &c; nor should I despair of obtaining from a gentleman at Paris some accurate and well-adapted maps. 3. A critical review of all the authors whom I have used and quoted. I am convinced such a supplement might be rendered entertaining, as well as useful; and that few purchasers would refuse to *complete* their Decline and Fall. (*Letters*, iii. 209.)

These materials include 'Supplement to the History of the decline and fall of the Roman Empire', '1^rst Period From the accession of Nerva to the death of Marcus Antoninus' (a chronology), some substantive changes made in a copy of the history, a revision of 'Vol vi p 200 Not 51', 'The Sabatic year and the Jubilees', and 'Memoranda [and] Supplemental Notes to the six Volumes of the History of the decline and fall of the Roman Empire'. There is no reason, except Gibbon's plan to annotate his authors, to attribute his remarks on Busbequius to this period, but there is equally no reason to attribute them to any other.

Gibbon had abandoned this plan within two months, but what he produced in that brief time, with perhaps the beginnings of Draft E of his memoirs as well,[3] suggests that he could indeed have filled a seventh volume.

[Notes on Modern Europe]

GEHAN OU DGIHAN NAMA

c'est a dire *Miroir du Monde*

L'auteur de cet ouvrage se nommoit Kiatib. Tchelibi; il a*a* ete compilè et augmentè par un Cordelier Polonois Renegat, qui etoit Mutefaraka. L'ancien fonds de l'ouvrage se bornoit à la description de l'Asie: à la sollicitation de M. d'Anville la partie de l'Empire Turc, l'Arabie, la Perse, l'Inde ont etè traduits en Francois par M. Armain Interprete attachè à la Bibliothèque du Roi. On trouve à la fin de ce Volume un morceau qu'on a trouvè à propos d'appeller *Harmonie universelle de l'Univers*; et qui est une exposition des Systemes de Ptolomèe et des autres Astronomes. Le Continuateur ou l'auteur a dediè son ouvrage à Mahomet v. Il*b* paroit que l'auteur au moins le dernier est bien versè dans la langue Latine, et qu'il a profitè des livres ecrits en cette langue, ainsi que de ceux des Arabes, des Turcs et des Persans. Ce Volume imprimè a CP en 1732, contient 40 petites cartes et toutes les figures de Mathematique, d'Astronomie et de Trigonometrie qui appartiennent à la Geographie.

The printed Copy of the Turkish original is in the noble library of the *Marquis de Paulmy* at the Arsenal and the preceding note was written in it by the Marquis himself. His collection consists of at least 60.000 Volumes.

About two Millions are taken annually at the three Spectacles[1] of which the Opera has rather the largest share. After deducting the ordinary expences, the interest of a debt of L[2] 400000, and a tax of L 60000 p*r* annum for the poor, the profits of the Comedie Francoise are divided into 23 parts, which are held either entire or in Fractions by the principal performers who are in a great measure managers Judges of new plays &c. Each part is worth 16 or 17000 Livres a year. Molè has two, for himself and his wife.

a *I.* etoit   *b* *I.* L'auteur

From the *Marèchal Duc de Duras* who as premier Gentilhomme de la Chambre has the inspection of the Spectacles.

The Emperor[3] saw in the Chambre des Comptes the revenue of last year; four hundred and thirteen millions.

Le Comte de Stainville

The farmed revenue amounts by this *bail* to Ł 174. Millions. *M. de Monttion.*[4] Conseiller d'Etat and Intendant of several provinces.

The Gabelle of Salt and the Tobacco amount to above sixty millions.

The principal grievance consists in the price which is unequally 24 or 40 Livres per Minot. In the provinces where the quantity is imposed, a Minot is assigned for 14 persons, which answers to about nine pounds for each individual[.] But in the provinces where it is *merchandise*, experience has shewn that seven persons consume a Minot.

M. de la Reyniere. Fermier General[5]

The amount of the two *vingtiemes* is forty millions, that of the *Taille* sixty millions; so that the whole Land tax of France is one hundred millions. As the two vingtiemes are very lightly assessed they do not constitute[a] above *one* twentieth of the rental. In that case the whole Rental would be about eight hundred Millions and the French may be said to pay two shillings and six pence in the pound. M. Necker.[b6]

But the *President Cotte*[7] who has been much employed in the Finances assures me that the two *vingtiemes* amount to a seventeenth part of the Rental which would then be six hundred and eight millions, and the land tax three shillings and about three pence in the pound. The two *vingtiemes* are paid by the Landlord, the taille by the tenant or Cultivator but if he is noble he is exempt from the taille for as much as he can cultivate with one plough. The assessment of the two vingtiemes varies in the different provinces: and *M. de St Lambert* the friend of the Prince de Beauvau tells me from

---

[a] *I.* continue   [b] *I.* Necker. The Taille two vingtiemes

his own knowledge that for an estate in Lorraine of Ł 120.000 a year the Prince pays no more than Ł 4000. But it is a general complaint that the rich are favoured while the poor are oppressed

---

It is computed that the medium value of Arable land in France is about eleven Livres per Arpent: seven shillings and six pence per English Acre. *Le Chevalier de Chastelleux.*

In the neighbourhood of Paris land lets for about a Louis per arpent. ˢ16.9ᵈ per Acre. Their course of crops is wheat, oats and fallow

Every peasant, exclusive of what he may possess pays thirty sous, for the *premier* pied de taille. His limbs are considered as a kind of property and he pays for the use of them

The President de Cotte

The actual population of Spain exceeds ten millions I[a] hear, 10.600.000. and is not far short of eleven according to the returns which were made by order of Count d'Aranda from the Curès of all the Parishes in the Kingdom. The military Establishment was not comprized, and there was great reason to suspect that the fear of being enlisted prevented[b] many of the young men from giving in their names. From his own knowledge of his estates in Arragon (80 or 100 parishes) he was convinced that the numbers on the returns were considerably below the truth. *The Count d'Aranda* himself now Spanish Ambassador at Paris. He added that since the States of Arragon and their free gifts have been abolished 1707,[c] that Kingdom pays a land tax of about one thirtieth, according to a fixed Cadastre. A similar one is now making for the crown of Castille.

In Spain there are in all 147.805 Ecclesiastical persons, men and[d] women, of the secular and of the Regular Clergy. *From the Count d'Aranda.* He is convinced that the Jesuits were not guilty of the sedition of Madrid, though he acknowledges that the public discontents to which by their discourses they had contributed were the occasion of an Enquiry into their institute.

The people of Arragon enjoyed their states and independent privileges till the year 1707 when they were abolished by Philip v.

[a] *I. om.* I hear. 10,600.00. and   [b] *I.* occasioned   [c] *I. om.* 1707   [d] *MS.* and

The Count d'Aranda speaks of the loss like a man sensible of the value of freedom.

The following is a general idea of the military establishment of France.

Gendarmerie and Maison du Roi.	3000.
French and Swiss Guards.	6000.
200 Bataillons of Infantry	120.000.
each of about 600 men	
52 Regiments of Cavalry and	26000
Dragoons each of 500 men.	
	155.000.

Besides about 60000 Militia. 16.000. Gardes-Cotes, Marines &c.

Le Marquis de Castries. Lt General and Commandant of the Gendarmerie.

Peter the third was incapable of having children, and the father of the present heir apparent of Russia was Count Soltikow[8] a young Nobleman appointed for that singular function by the Empress Elizabeth and her Council. The Chancellor[a] Bestucheff proposed him to the Grand Dutchess Catherine. She heard him with indignation. He insisted on the necessity of an heir and the danger of a refusal . . . "Amenez le moi[b] ce soir" was her only answer and Soltikow was admitted as the first of a long list of Lovers.

[c]Peter iii. was poisoned in a glass of brandy. On his refusing a second glass he was forcibly thrown down and strangled with a handkerchief by Orlof le balafrè,[9] Teplow Potenkin,[d] and the youngest of the Princes Baratinski.[10] When the body was exposed the marks of violence on the neck &c were evident. Orlof instantly returned to Petersburgh,[e] and appeared at the Empress's dinner in the disorder of a Murderer. She caught his eye rose from table, called him into her Closet, sent for Count Panin to whom she imparted the news, and returned to dinner with her[f] usual ease and chearfulness.

These particulars are taken from a history of the Revolution in 1762 composed by M. Rulhiere a French Officer[g] who was an

[a] I. Grand Chancellor   [b] I. om. moi   [c] Published MW 1814 v. 528
[d] II. Potemkin   [e] II. Petersburg   [f] I. their   [g] I. Gen

attentive spectator, and who afterwards conversed with the principal actors. Prudence prevents him from publishing; but he reads his Narrative to large Companies, and I have already heard it twice. It is an entertaining spirited piece of historical composition not unworthy of being compared with*a* Vertot's conspiracy of Portugal. But I find that Rulhiere's fidelity is impeached by persons perhaps partial but certainly well informed, by the *Baron de Goltz*[11] the Prussian Minister, by the *Count de Swaloff*[12] Elizabeth's favourite and by the *Princess d'Askoff* herself.

The library of the Duke de*b* la Valiere contains 50000 Volumes and is distinguished by expensive luxury and curious vanity: 2000 Editions of the xvth Century, of which 600 are principes, primarice &c; 300 printed on Vellum. The most valuable room cost 600.000 Livres. *The Abbè Rive*^{c} who prepares a Catalogue Raisonnè of it.[13]

According to M. de Rulhiere, Poniatowski[14] (the present King of Poland) had been the Ganymede of Sir Charles Hanbury Williams who afterwards introduced him as a lover to the Grand Dutchess of Russia. Rulhiere asserts that it was at least the general report of the North[.]

A rough sketch of the Finances of France.

The whole amount of the Revenue may be reckoned at about three hundred and eighty or ninety millions. About*d* one hundred and seventy or eighty millions must be allowed for the necessary deductions; for the payment of the interest of the national debt, and of the infinite number of useless offices which at different times have been created and sold by the Crown. The expence of the military establishment in time of peace is sixty eight millions besides nine or ten millions for the maintenance of the fortifications. The ordinary expence of the Navy is thirty millions, but as the French are building a great many ships it amounted last year to forty five Millions. The Court and Royal family require at least thirty two millions but they commonly exceed that sum. The system of foreign affairs Ambassadors &c is supported at the expence of about ten millions. From this superficial view it appears that the French gover[n]ment receives seventeen, and may spend, nine, millions sterling. Of these about five are expended for

I. the ^{b} *I.* of ^{c} *I. de la Rive* ^{d} *I.* The

the national defence in the great articles of army navy and fortifications. two*a* millions more are assigned for the domestic splendor and foreign negociations of the Crown. About two millions should therefore remain for roads, public buildings, establishments and all the various expences incidental to Civil government; and whenever*b* any part of the public debt is discharged the money must be taken from this fund.—It is generally supposed that the expence of France has hitherto exceeded the receipt from two reasons. 1 The *Extraordinaries* are never provided for*c* beforehand, and the accounts of every year are perplexed by this accumulation of vague demands for services already incurred. 2. *The Anticipations.* As money*d* is always wanted before it becomes due, Government has*e* borrowed it of the bankers at five per Cent with a premium of 1 per Cent for every six months which made a considerable deduction. We may observe a most essential difference between the administration of the Finances in England and in France. In the former it is accountable and public; in the latter it is secret and unaccountable.

Le Chevalier de Chastellux. Author of *the Felicitè publique.*

The following is the general result of the lists of population (births, marriages and deaths) transmitted to Government by the Intendants of the thirty three Generalities of the Kingdom, comprehending the Island of Corsica, from the year 1770 to the year 1774, both inclusive: from whence may be deduced the total number of subjects of France, reckoning one birth for twenty six persons alive [1] according to the medium proportion between Cities, towns and country parishes

The number of births taken at a medium during those five years. is 928.918

$$\left.\begin{array}{l}\text{479.649 boys}\\\text{449.269 girls.}\end{array}\right\}\text{928.918.}$$

This number of births according to the above-mentioned proportions gives us a total of 24.151.868.

$$\left.\begin{array}{l}\text{12.470.874. males}\\\text{11.680.994. females.}\end{array}\right\}\text{24.151.868.}$$

---

a I. The supreme magistrat r   *b I.* if   *c I. om.* for   *d I.* the money
e I. om. has

We may observe that a still greater number of persons are comprized within the dominions of France, the lists of population taking in a very small portion of those who do not profess the established Religion, and none of those who inhabit the possessions of the Crown out of Europe. *From the originals in the depot of the Controle General, which[a] were shewn me by order of M. Necker.* The Clerk particularly intrusted with that department is M. Garnier,[15] a very laborious and intelligent man.

[1][b] In order to be assured that the proportion of 1 birth to 26 persons is accurate we should be in possession of the actual *denombrement* of a large and various tract of country, which we might compare with the result of the calculation. We can give this comparaison as far as it relates to French Hainault and the annexed territories.

The annual[c] number of births taken on an average of the years 1770. to 1776 inclusivement amounted to.

$$\left.\begin{array}{l}5102 \text{ boys}\\4804 \text{ girls}\end{array}\right\} \ 9.906$$

Total. 9.906

and consequently the whole population (after multiplying by 26 [)] to

$$\left.\begin{array}{l}132.652 \text{ males}\\124.904. \text{ females}\end{array}\right\} \ 257.556.$$

Total. 257.556.

The average of the *effective* denombrement annually taken from the year 1773 to the year 1776 inclusively amounts to

$$\left.\begin{array}{l}133.545 \text{ males.}\\123\ 552 \text{ females}\end{array}\right\} \ 257.097.$$

The difference between the calculation and the actual *denombrement* of Hainault is 459 persons more in the former than in the latter: but this trifling difference is equivalent only to the proportion of 18 births, of both sexes taken[d] without choice on a period of seven years.

---

[e]The deaths of Religious persons of both sexes is about 1800 per annum, and as there is some reason to believe that about one out of thirty dye every year, the whole number of persons in France engaged in the monastic life is about 54.000. of whom we may reckon 24.000 men and 30.000 women.

M. Garnier and the originals of the Controle General

---

[f]The allowance of each person in France may be reckoned at two Septiers (one English quarter) of wheat per annum which give

[a] *I.* to which   [b] *MS. on Add. MSS. 34882, ff. 237v and 238v.*   [c] *I. om.* annual   [d] *I.* indis in   [e] *Published MW 1814, v. 529*   [f] *I.* M. Neck

them per diem one pound and a half of bread. This is the soldier's allowance; and if labouring men eat more the excess is compensated by women children and sick persons. M. Necker. in his traitè *sur la Legislations des Grains.*

During the last ten years, one hundred and ten or One hundred and twenty millions of Livres in gold and silver have been annually received from America, of which about one hundred remain in Europe. During that time France has coined forty three millions a year; and as long as she receives, it is impossible that she should export with an expence of two per cent. Allowing seven millions more for the encrease of plate &c, France alone receives half the gold and silver which remains in Europe. The specie of France is computed at two thousand millions.

The same

The annual sum issued from the treasury for the highways and bridges may be estimated at four Millions of Livres; and the work performed by the oppressive duty of Corvies is computed at twelve millions more; so that the whole of the annual expence amounts to about seven hundred thousand pounds.

M le Clerc[16] formerly premier Commis de tresor Royal

---

[a]Since the year 1756, Russia has been engaged almost without interruption in the Prussian, the Polish and the Turkish wars[.] During the last mentioned war, the Empress at the same time employed *seven armies* (on the Danube, in Crim Tartary, in Georgia in Grece[b], in Poland, in Ingria, and against the rebel Pugascheff). and four fleets on the Baltic, the Archipelago, the Black sea, and the Danube. Whilst she was making these extraordinary efforts she supported the splendor of her Court, encouraged the arts of England France and Italy by her[c] expensive orders, which were most punctually paid; and encreased onethird the salaries of almost all her officers. As soon as the War was at an end, she suppressed some

---

[a] *All of the following note on Russia was published in MW 1814, v. 525–8.*
[b] *II.* Greece   [c] *I.* their

taxes (about seven or eight millions of French Livres); and she is now paying off about ten millions which she borrowed in Holland, and which forms the whole national debt of Russia.

The army at present consists; of four Regiments of Guards, one cavalry and three infantry that compose the formidable body of about 10000 men which has so often disposed of the throne; of one hundred and five regiments of Infantry (1600 men each) making about 170.000 men; to these we must add, the artillery between 20. and 30.000 and the Cavalry, Dragoons &c between 40 and 50.000. Upon the whole we may compute the establishment of regular forces at about 250.000.[a]: and had the Turkish war continued, both men and money were provided[b] for an augmentation of 50 000 more. To this establishment we must add the stationary garrisons of the remote provinces, and the numerous bodies of Irregulars, Cossacks, Calmucks &c which are always ready to obey the commands of the Russian Monarch

There is not any direct land tax in Russia and the revenue arises. from the Capitation the Consumption[c], and the Customs. 1. The Clergy and Nobility are exempt from the Capitation which is assessed chiefly on the Peasants, but as these are all *Villains* the[d] tax ultimately falls on their masters, and must be tolerably proportioned to their landed property. The master who enjoys the fruit of his slave's labour is obliged to give him a piece of land to cultivate, sufficient not only for his own subsistence but likewise for the payment of the tax; which is[e] estimated at about four livres, on the head of every male, from the moment of his birth to the age of sixty. Not less than ten millions of persons are rated to the Capitation which consequently must amount to about forty millions. 2. The Nobles have the exclusive privilege of making salt and distilling spirituous liquors on their estates, but they can dispose of them only to the Empress

On the other hand the licensed venders of those necessary articles can purchase them only in the Imperial magazines. By this double Monopoly the Crown gains two or three hundred per Cent and raises an indirect Excise. 3. The Customs, both on exports and imports are excessively high; but they are exacted only on the frontiers of the Empire, and the interior commerce is perfectly free. To these great articles we must add the mines, the tribute of furs

---

[a] *I.* 250.000. men   [b] *I.* prepared   [c] *I.* Excise and Consumption   [d] *I.* their   [e] *I.* am

&c, which in the whole form a Revenue of one hundred and fifty millions of French Livres.

The population of Russia, without including the Savages of the North, or the *wandering* Tartars, whose allegiance is voluntary and precarious, has been computed at twenty two millions.

From the Prince Bariatinski[17], *Minister from Russia at Paris.*

The population of Poland is computed at about seven or eight millions, of which near three millions have been transferred to the three great powers who have dismembered Poland.[18] As the trading towns of Prussia are compensated by the wastes of Lithuania, this number of subjects may give us some idea of the extent of territory which they have usurped.

M. de Glaire.[19] *Agent from the King of Poland at Paris*

According to actual denombremens made and published by public authority, the whole population of Sweden with Finland amounted in the year 1751 to 2.229.661 persons. In the year 1769. it was found to consist of 2.571 800 persons. Consequently in eighteen years it had encreased above 342.000[a] persons.

Memoires sur la Suede in 2 Vol in 4° published at London (Leipsic) 1776.[20]

At the death of Charles xii[21] the population was reduced to 500.000 exclusive of the three principal cities.

The Count de Creutz[22] *Ambassador from Sweden at Paris*

In the time of Gustavus Vasa, the population of Sweden has been computed from ancient documents at nine millions of inhabitants.

The Count de Creutz

The Revenue of France consists of.

1. *La Ferme Generale* which comprehends what we should call the excise and customs; the *Aides* the Gabelle le Tabac[b] the *Tailes* &c. besides many smaller duties such as a tax of about 1 1/2 per cent on the sale of Estates. The present *Bail* is one hundred and fifty Millions besides fourteen millions which from the uncertainty of the produce the Farmers have taken in *regie*.

[a] *I.* 3.42   [b] *I. om.* le Tabac

2. The *recette Generale*, which comprehends the *taille*, the two *vintiemes*, the *Capitation* and may amount to one hundred and forty millions.

3. To these two great articles of three hundred millions, we must add the *Dons gratuits* of all the *pays d'Etats*: Bretagne Bourgogne Languedoc, Provence, Artois and Bearn which are given in lieu of land tax and Capitation. The Don gratuit of the Clergy once every five years, the Posts, the Crown lands or[a] Domain. &c. which in the whole make the French Revenue above four hundred millions.

M. le Clerc formerly *premier Commis du Tresor Royal*

In the year 1726, when there [was] a general recoinage, the gold and silver called into the treasury amounted to eighteen hundred millions.

M. Le Clerc

The Capitation of the whole Kingdom amounts to about thirty four or thirty five millions: of which Ł500.000 is paid at court by person who have titles——The assessment is determined according to a fixed proportion for all those who have titles employments or a decided rank. No one except the Dauphin is exempt. The Duke of Orleans pays Ł 3600: a Duke, or Fermier General Ł 2400. With regard to private persons, a[b] conjecture is made of their fortune by their expence. A Man who keeps a coach can scarcely be rated at less than Ł 150 and if he has a house with a number of servants, at five or six times as much.

The expence of the Recette generale is about five per Cent from which we must deduct the interest of thirty millions which the Receivers General have advanced to the King. The expence of[c] the Ferme is about fifteen per cent which is owning to the infinite number of Officers they are obliged to employ.

The farmers who were formerly forty are now sixty. They advance a million to the King at nine per Cent and Ł 560.000 at five per Cent: this[d] makes the sum of 93.600 000. Ł. of which the King generally reimburses one third during the Bail of six years. [2]

The necessary stock of salt, Tobacco &c which they are obliged to lay in, and the payments which become due before they are collected

[a] *I.* of   [b] *I.* the   [c] *I.* from   [d] *I. om.* this

require a prævious fund of forty millions, and they are allowed to issue notes to that amount.

The accounts are kept in the Italian bookeeping. When the last bail was made the Abbè Terray on[a] the one[b] hand employed several intelligent persons to calculate the amount of the different duties and on the other he called on the Farmers for their books. They tallied with the most surprizing accuracy.

The residue after paying the expences and the rent is left in the[c] Caisse of the *Ferme* (a million or[d] two may sometimes be borrowed) till the end of the Bail. The King then deducts three tenths of the profit for himself and leaves the rest to the Farmers. If on the contrary there is a deficiency, the Farmers are allowed to prove it, and receive a discharge with the interest of their money. They treat le Clerc à Maitre[e] Reckoning the extraordinary interest of their first million at four per Cent: a place of farmer General does not at present exceed Ł 100.000 a year. Formerly in Cardinal de Fleury's time[23] it was 100000 Crowns.

M. le Clerc.

[2][f] He reimburses every year Ł 3.600.000: which encreases the sinking fund of interest for the ensuing years.

The assembly of the Clergy of France meets at Paris every five years, and is composed of one Bishop or Archbishop, and one representative of[g] the inferior Clergy (who is commonly a Grand Vicar) from each of the eighteen provinces of France. Every tenth year (1780 will be the next) the assembly is more solemn, and the number of members is doubled. They are chosen, by their respective orders, in provincial assemblies, and these (with regard to the inferior[h] clergy are formed by a prævious election in each Diocese. A very compleat model of representation! In the general assemblies they vote by provinces and if the Bishop and the representative do not agree the vote of the province is dormant. The assembly names the President at the *recommendation* of the King.

The principal business is to grant their *Don gratuit*, which has insensibly risen from five to fourteen or fifteen millions. It was Cardinal Fleury's policy to reserve the supplies of the Clergy for the emergencies of state and he frequently dismissed their ordinary

---

[a] *I.* one   [b] *I. om.* one   [c] *I. om.* the   [d] *I.* of   [e] *This sentence* ('They . . . à Maitre') *inserted between two regular lines of text in MS. Add. MSS. 34882, f. 247[v].*   [f] *MS. on*   [g] *I.* from each of the eighteen provi   [h] *I.* provincia

assemblies without making any demand. Succeeding ministers have been less tender,[a] they have convoked extraordinary assemblies, and about the close of the last War the Comptroller General Laverdy[24] exacted from the Clergy in two years near thirty millions.

Even when the demand was moderate the Clergy more careful of themselves than of their Successors chose rather to borrow than to pay the principal. Their debt[b] has insensibly accumulated to one Hundred and thirty millions, for which they once paid 5 and now only 4 per Cent: the interest at present far exceeds the tax, and they are obliged to pursue this same method

The money required for these purposes, with a surplus which goes towards keeping down the debt is assessed by the Assembly. A Bishop pays about the sixth part of his Revenue a dignitary about a fourth, and a poor Curate only a thirtieth.

About the year 1751, M. de Machault offended the prejudices of the Clergy by claiming a right of taxation instead of accepting a free gift. A controversy was excited. The Assembly asserted their freedom by an absolute refusal. They were exiled (thirty six Bishops at once) to their Dioceses. They persisted, the Minister was disgraced. They maintained their privilege, and gave their money.

The Bishop of Orleans, the favourite of Lewis xv, and who had the feuille des Benefices during the whole ministry of the Duke *de Choiseul*.[25] He had the merit of refusing a cardinal's hat, with the richest preferrments

---

The debts of the Crown of Naples amount to eighty millions of Crowns (about eighteen millions Sterling. Several branches of the Revenue have been alienated for the payment of the interest, and the creditors (except a few Genoese) are chiefly Neapolitan subjects The clear revenue is about 6.000.000 of Crowns (£ 1.325.000).

The Roman debt which has been insensibly accumulated by twenty successive Popes now amounts to sixty millions of Crowns, thirteen millions and a quarter, chiefly to foreigners

The Marquis Carraciole[26] *Ambassador from the King of the two Sicilies at Paris*

When the King of Prussia examined the accounts of the last war, he found that the whole expence amounted to one hundred and twenty millions of German crowns: twenty millions sterling, in

[a] *I.* sparing   [b] *I.* debts

seven years. He had supported this expence by his own revenues, the subsidies of England and the contributions of Saxony without incurring any debt, and without touching the treasure left by his father

M. d'Alembert. from the King of Prussia himself[27]

Materials for corrections and improvements for the 1ʳˢᵗ Vol. of my History

1ʳˢᵗ Dynasty of the Medes. see Diodorus Siculus L ii p 146. authority of Ctesias. Nicol. Damasc. in Eccerpt. Vales.[2] p 426–437. Manners of an oriental Court. The Dynasty of Ctesias which began AD. 910. reigned in the East. The Dynasty of Herodotus[3] rose on it's ruins in the West, lasted longer, and was more familiar to Greek Travellers.

The Medes reigned 350 years. Justin. i. 6. Justin or at least Trogus Pompeius[4] had read Ctesias. The Magi in their speech to Astyages (Herodot L i C 120) consider themselves as Medes and expect to fall with thier King and Nation.

Zoroaster was born at Irmia, Urmia or Arimat, an ancient large and pleasant City of Adirbijan, to the south of a lake and 40 Parasangs to the East of Mosul. Schultens in Indic. Geogr. ad vit Saladin. Voce *Irmia*.[5] He quotes a Geographical Dictionary and Abulfeda: and the opinion is countenanced by the Zendavesta—see D'Anquetil. xxxi p 375.[6]

Miracle of Mahraspand Hyde de VRP. C. xxi p 280. He was the 30ᵗʰ from Zoroaster Foucher.[b] xxxix. p 725., who consequently lived 750 years before Christ;[c] the date is probable, and if the Genealogy is fictitious, it would be adapted to the age of the Prophet.

Temples and human Statues of Anaitis the Assyrian Venus erected by Artaxerxes Moremons. Plutarch in Artax. Clement. Alex. in protrept.[7]

M. d'Anquetil. (xxxi p 339–443) has given a very curious treatise on the ancient languages of Persia: the *Zend* and the two Derivatives the *Pehlvi*, and the *Parsi*. 1 The Zend was the ancient language of the Medes and Zoroaster; has forty eight letters, which express thirty five sounds; and bears a remarkable affinity to the Armenian

---

[a] *In margin of MS. Repeated at beginning of each MS. page.*   [b] *I. om.* Foucher. xxxix. p. 725.   [c] *I.* Christian

and especially the Georgian: is written from right to left. 2 The
Pehlvi was the language of the Eastern provinces from Aderbijan
to Khorasan. It was spoken at the Court of Balch, and the use of it
did not cease till the Dynasty of the Sassanides. It has five vowels
and twenty one Consonants: and is still studied for the sake of the
translations of the Avesta and some old books. 3. The Parsi or
Persian has now received a great mixture of Turkish and Arabic;
yet the original language still remains and supplies etymologies for
the Persian words, which have been preserved by Greek writers.
For the authenticity of the writings of Zoroaster see Foucher (xxix.
p 308 &c xxxix. p 711 &c). He justly[a] treats the translation of
d'Anquetil as an ancient Liturgy, a Missal of the Guebres, occasionally interspersed with some chapters of the Avesta, and filled up
with superstitious nonsense Unless the works of Zoroaster have
been strangely exagerated by the Greeks, the best and largest
part has long since perished—

Hermippus, qui de totâ ea arte diligentissime scripsit; et vicies
centum millia versuum a Zoroastre condita indicibus quoque
voluminum ejus positis explanavit &c Plin. Hist Natur. xxx. 2.
Hermippus was a disciple of Callimachus and lived about two
hundred years before Christ. see Index Auctor. Harduin p 56. 60.

See a fine passage of Zoroaster in Eusebius (Præpar Evangel. L i.
C 10. and a[b] sublime idea of the Persian Theology in Dion Chrysostom Orat xxxvi Barysthenie.[8]

In the Memoires of the Academie, from xxv to xxxix there are two
series of Dissertations, the one by the Abbè Foucher the other by
M. d'Anquetil. the former is too much a Theologian the latter too
much a Traveller. The former degrades[c] the latter exalts the
Magian Religion. We are indebted to d'Anquetil for some[d] fragments
of the Avesta, but Foucher[e] (see Tom xxxix [)] has made a much
more judicious use of them. They have convinced him that Zoroaster was ignorant of Moses, and ruined a part of his System,
without weakening his proof of the Idolatry of the Guebres.

Chardin (Voyages en Perse Tom ii p 179–187) is almost the only
traveller who was capable of observing manners and religions.

The Guebres (Contes Arabes Tom iii p 365 387) were accused of
annually sacrificing a Musulman at the imaginary mountain of fire.[9]

---

[a] I. judges   [b] I. an   [c] I. despises   [d] I. the   [e] I. th

p 30*a*

Utique a Dan usque Bersabee quæ vix centum sexaginta milium in longum.*b* spacio tenditur . . . Pudet dicere latitudinem terræ Repromissionis, ne Ethnicis occasionem blasphemandi dedisse videamur[.] Ab Joppe usque ad viculum nostrum Bethlehem quadraginta sex milia sunt, cui succedit vastissima Solitudo plena ferocium Barbarorum. . . . Hæc est Judiætuarum longitudo et latitudo terrarum. Hieronym ad Dardanum. Tom iii p 66. Edit Basil. 1536[10]

Whatever might be the motives of Jerom (and they were foolish enough) his scale of distances is just and accurate. see Reland. Palest L ii*c* C 5. p 421.

a In margin of MS.   *b I.* sp   *c I.* L iii

A

VINDICATION

O F

SOME PASSAGES

IN THE

Fifteenth and Sixteenth Chapters

OF THE

HISTORY of the DECLINE and FALL of
the ROMAN EMPIRE.

BY THE AUTHOR.

LONDON:

PRINTED FOR W. STRAHAN; AND T. CADELL,
IN THE STRAND.
MDCCLXXIX.

A
VINDICATION,

&c. &c.

PERHAPS it may be necessary to inform the Public, that not long since an Examination of the Fifteenth and Sixteenth Chapters of the History of the Decline and Fall of the Roman Empire was published by Mr. Davis. He styles himself a Bachelor of Arts, and a Member of Baliol College in the University of Oxford. His title-page is a declaration of war,[1] and in the prosecution of his religious crusade, he assumes a privilege of disregarding the ordinary laws which are respected in the most hostile transactions between civilized men or civilized nations. Some of the harshest epithets in the English language are repeatedly applied to the historian, a part of whose work Mr. Davis has chosen for the object of his criticism. To this author Mr. Davis imputes the crime of betraying the confidence and seducing the faith of those readers, who may heedlessly stray in the flowery paths of his diction, without perceiving the poisonous snake that lurks concealed in the grass. *Latet anguis in herbâ.* The Examiner has assumed the province of reminding them of "the "unfair proceedings of such an insidious friend, who offers the "deadly draught in a golden cup, that they may be less sensible of "the danger[1]. In order to which, Mr. Davis has selected several of "the more notorious instances of his misrepresentations and errors; "reducing them to their respective heads, and subjoining a long "list of almost incredible inaccuracies: and such striking proofs of "servile plagiarism, as the world will be surprised to meet with in "an author who puts in so bold a claim to originality and extensive "reading[2]?" Mr. Davis prosecutes this attack through an octavo volume of not less than two hundred and eighty-four pages with the same implacable spirit, perpetually charges his adversary with

---

[1] Davis, Preface, p. ii.   [2] Ibid. Preface, p. iii.

perverting the ancients, and transcribing the moderns; and inconsistently enough imputes to him the opposite crimes of art and carelessness, of gross ignorance and of wilful falsehood. The Examiner closes his work[3] with a severe reproof of those feeble critics who have allowed any share of knowledge to an odious antagonist. He presumes to pity and to condemn the first historian of the present age, for the generous approbation which he had bestowed on a writer who is content that Mr. Davis should be his enemy, whilst he has a right to name Dr. Robertson[2] for his friend.

When I delivered to the world the First Volume of an important History, in which I had been obliged to connect the progress of Christianity with the civil state and revolutions of the Roman Empire, I could not be ignorant that the result of my inquiries might offend the interest of some and the opinions of others. If the whole work was favourably received by the Public, I had the more reason to expect that this obnoxious part would provoke the zeal of those who consider themselves as the Watchmen of the Holy City. These expectations were not disappointed; and a fruitful crop of Answers, Apologies, Remarks, Examinations, &c. sprung up with all convenient speed. As soon as I saw the advertisement, I generally sent for them; for I have never affected, indeed I have never understood, the stoical apathy, the proud contempt of criticism, which some authors have publicly professed. Fame is the motive, it is the reward, of our labours; nor can I easily comprehend how it is possible that we should remain cold and indifferent with regard to the attempts which are made to deprive us of the most valuable object of our possessions, or at least of our hopes. Besides this strong and natural impulse of curiosity, I was prompted by the more laudable desire of applying to my own, and the public, benefit, the well-grounded censures of a learned adversary; and of correcting those faults which the indulgence of vanity and friendship had suffered to escape without observation. I read with attention several criticisms which were published against the Two last Chapters of my History, and unless I much deceive[a] myself, I weighed them in my own mind without prejudice and without resentment. After I was[b] clearly satisfied that their principal objections were founded on misrepresentation or mistake, I declined with sincere and

(3) Davis, p. 282, 283.

---

[a] *II.* deceived   [b] *I.* After I had clearly satisfied myself

disinterested reluctance the odious task of controversy, and almost formed a tacit resolution of committing my intentions, my writings, and my adversaries to the judgment of the Public, of whose favourable disposition I had received the most flattering proofs.

The reasons which justified my silence were obvious and forcible: the respectable nature of the subject itself, which ought not to be rashly[a] violated by the rude hand of controversy; the inevitable tendency of dispute, which soon degenerates into minute and personal altercation; the indifference of the Public for the discussion of such questions as neither relate to the business nor the amusement of the present age. I calculated the possible loss of temper and the certain loss of time, and considered, that while I was laboriously engaged in a humiliating task, which could add nothing to my own reputation, or to the entertainment of my readers, I must interrupt the prosecution of a work which claimed my whole attention, and which the Public, or at least my friends, seemed to require with some impatience at my hands. The judicious lines of Dr. Young[3] sometimes offered themselves to my memory, and I felt the truth of his observation, That every author lives or dies by his own pen, and that the unerring sentence of Time assigns its proper rank to every composition and to every criticism, which it preserves from oblivion.

I should have consulted my own ease, and perhaps I should have acted in stricter conformity to the rules of prudence, if I had still persevered in patient silence. But Mr. Davis may, if he pleases, assume the merit of extorting from me the notice which I had refused to more honourable foes. I had declined the consideration of their *literary Objections*; but he has compelled me to give an answer to his *mischievous[b] Accusations*. Had he confined himself to the ordinary, and indeed obsolete charges of impious principles, and criminal intentions, I should have acknowledged with readiness and pleasure that the religion of Mr. Davis appeared to be very different from mine. Had he contented himself with the use of that style which decency and politeness have banished from the more liberal part of mankind, I should have smiled, perhaps with some contempt, but without the least mixture of anger or resentment. Every animal employs the note, or cry, or howl, which is peculiar to its species; every man expresses himself in the dialect the most congenial to his temper and inclination, the most familiar to the

---

[a] *I.* lightly   [b] *I.* criminal (*corrected to* mischievous *in Errata*)

company in which he has lived, and to the authors with whom he is conversant; and while I was disposed to allow that Mr. Davis had made some proficiency in Ecclesiastical Studies, I should have considered the difference of our language and manners as an unsurmountable bar of separation between us. Mr. Davis has overleaped that bar, and forces me to contend with him on the very dirty ground which he has chosen for the scene of our combat. He has judged, I know not with how much propriety, that the support of a cause, which would disclaim such unworthy assistance, depended on the ruin of my moral and literary character. The different misrepresentations, of which he has drawn out the ignominious catalogue, would materially affect my credit as an historian, my reputation as a scholar, and even my honour and veracity as a gentleman. If I am indeed incapable of understanding what I read, I can no longer claim a place among those writers who merit the esteem and confidence of the Public. If I am capable of wilfully perverting what I understand, I no longer deserve to live in the society of those men, who consider a strict and inviolable adherence to truth, as the foundation of every thing that is virtuous or honourable in human nature. At the same time, I am not insensible that his mode of attack has given a transient pleasure to my enemies, and a transient uneasiness to my friends. The size of his volume, the boldness of his assertions, the acrimony of his style, are contrived with tolerable skill to confound the ignorance and candour of his readers. There are few who will examine the truth or justice of his accusations; and of those persons who have been directed by their education to the study of ecclesiastical antiquity, many will believe, or will affect to believe, that the success of their champion has been equal to his zeal, and that the *serpent* pierced with an hundred wounds lies expiring at his feet. Mr. Davis's book *will* cease to be read (perhaps the grammarians may already reproach me for the use of an improper tense); but the oblivion towards which it seems to be hastening, will afford the more ample scope for the artful practices of those, who may not scruple to affirm, or rather to insinuate, that Mr. Gibbon was publickly convicted of falsehood and misrepresentation; that the evidence produced against him was unanswerable; and that his silence was the effect and the proof of conscious guilt. Under the hands of a malicious surgeon, the sting of a wasp may continue to fester and inflame, long after the vexatious little insect has left its venom and its life in the wound.

The defence of my own[a] honour is undoubtedly the first and prevailing motive which urges me to repel with vigour an unjust and unprovoked attack; and to undertake a tedious vindication, which, after the perpetual repetition of the vainest and most disgusting of the pronouns, will only prove that *I* am innocent; and that Mr. Davis, in his charge, has very frequently subscribed his own condemnation. And yet I may presume to affirm, that the Public have some interest in this controversy. They have some interest to know whether the writer whom they have honoured with their favour is deserving of their confidence, whether they must content themselves with reading the History of the Decline and Fall of the Roman Empire as a *tale amusing enough*, or whether they may venture to receive it as a fair and authentic history. The general persuasion of mankind, that where *much* has been positively asserted, *something* must be true, may contribute to encourage a secret suspicion, which would naturally diffuse itself over the whole body of the work. Some of those friends who may now tax me with imprudence for taking this public notice of Mr. Davis's book, have perhaps already condemned me for silently acquiescing under the weight of such serious, such direct, and such circumstantial imputations.

Mr. Davis, who in the last page of his[4] Work appears to have recollected that modesty is an amiable and useful qualification, affirms, that his plan required only that he should consult the authors to whom he was directed by my references; and that the judgment of riper years was not so necessary to enable him to execute with success the pious labour to which he had devoted his pen. Perhaps before we separate, a moment to which I most fervently aspire, Mr. Davis may find that a mature judgment is indispensably requisite for the successful execution of *any* work of literature, and more especially of criticism. Perhaps he will discover, that a young student who hastily consults an unknown author, on a subject with which he is unacquainted, cannot always be guided by the most accurate reference to the knowledge of the sense, as well as to the sight of the passage which has been quoted by his adversary. Abundant proofs of these maxims will hereafter be suggested. For the present, I shall only remark, that it is my intention to pursue

---

[4] Davis, p. 284.

---

[a] *II. om.* own

in my defence the order, or rather the course, which Mr. Davis has marked out in his Examination; and that I have numbered the several articles of my impeachment according to the most natural division of the subject. And now let me proceed on this hostile march over a dreary and barren desert, where thirst, hunger, and intolerable weariness, are much more to be dreaded, than the arrows of the enemy.

I.

QUOTATIONS IN GENERAL.

"The remarkable mode of quotation which Mr. Gibbon adopts "must immediately strike every one who turns to his notes. He "sometimes only mentions the author, perhaps the book; and often "leaves the reader the toil of finding out, or rather guessing at the "passage. The policy, however, is not without its design and use. "By endeavouring to deprive us of the means of comparing him "with the authorities he cites, he flattered himself, no doubt, that "he might safely have recourse to *misrepresentation*[5]." Such is the style of Mr. Davis; who in another place[6] mentions this mode of quotation "as a good artifice to escape detection;" and applauds, with an agreeable irony, his own labours in turning over a *few*[a] pages of the Theodosian Code.

I shall not descend to animadvert on the rude and illiberal strain of this passage, and I will frankly own that my indignation is lost in astonishment. The Fifteenth and Sixteenth Chapters of my History are illustrated by three hundred and eighty-three Notes; and the nakedness of a few Notes, which are not accompanied by any quotation, is amply compensated by a much greater number, which contain two, three, or perhaps four distinct references; so that upon the whole my stock of quotations which support and justify my facts cannot amount to less than eight hundred or a thousand. As I had often felt the inconvenience of the loose and general method of quoting which is so falsely imputed to me, I have carefully distinguished the *books*, the *chapters*, the *sections*, the *pages* of the authors to whom I referred, with a degree of accuracy and attention, which might claim some gratitude, as it has seldom been

[5] Davis, Preface, p. ii.   [6] Id. p. 230.

[a] *II. om. italics*

so regularly practised by any historical writers. And here I must confess some obligation to Mr. Davis, who, by staking my credit and his own on a circumstance so obvious and palpable, has given me this[a] early opportunity of submitting the merits of our cause, or at least of our characters, to the judgment of the Public. Hereafter, when I am summoned to defend myself against the imputation of misquoting the text, or misrepresenting the sense of a Greek or Latin author, it will not be in my power to communicate the knowledge of the languages, or the possession of the books, to those readers who may be destitute either of one or of the other, and the part which *they* are obliged to take between assertions equally strong and peremptory, may sometimes be attended with doubt and hesitation. But in the present instance, every reader who will give himself the trouble of consulting the First Volume of my History, is a competent judge of the question. I exhort, I solicit him to run his eye down the columns of Notes, and to count *how many* of the quotations are minute and particular, *how few* are vague and general. When he has satisfied himself by this easy computation,[4] there *is* a word which may naturally suggest itself; an epithet, which I should be sorry either to deserve or use; the boldness of Mr. Davis's assertion, and the confidence of my appeal will tempt, nay, perhaps, will force him to apply that epithet either to one or to the other of the adverse parties.

I have confessed that a critical eye may discover *some* loose and general references; but as they bear a very *inconsiderable* proportion to the whole mass, they cannot support, or even excuse a false and ungenerous accusation, which must reflect dishonour either on the object or on the author of it. If the examples in which I have occasionally deviated from my ordinary practice were specified and examined, I am persuaded that they might always be fairly attributed to some one of the following reasons. 1. In some *rare* instances, which I have never attempted to conceal, I have been obliged to adopt quotations which were expressed with less accuracy than I could have wished. 2. I may have accidentally recollected the sense of a passage which I had formerly read, without being able to find the place, or even to transcribe from memory the precise words. 3. The whole tract (as in a remarkable instance of the second Apology of Justin Martyr)[5] was so short, that a more particular description was not required. 4. The form of the composition

[a] *I.* so early an opportunity

8124961 I

supplied the want of a local reference; the preceding mention of the *year* fixed the passage of the annalist, and the reader was guided to the proper spot in the commentaries of Grotius, Valesius or Godefroy, by the more accurate citation of their original author. 5. The idea which I was desirous of communicating to the reader, was sometimes the general result of the author or treatise that I had quoted; nor was it possible to confine, within the narrow limits of a particular reference, the sense or spirit which was mingled with the whole mass. These motives are either laudable or at least innocent. In two of these exceptions my ordinary mode of citation was superfluous; in the other three it was impracticable.[6]

In quoting a comparison which Tertullian had used to express the rapid increase of the Marcionites, I expressly declared that I was obliged to quote it from memory[7]. If I have been guilty of comparing them to *bees* instead of *wasps*,[7] I can however most sincerely disclaim the sagacious suspicion of Mr. Davis[8], who imagines that I was tempted to amend the simile of Tertullian from an improper partiality for those odious Heretics.

A rescript of Diocletian, which declared *the* old law (not *an* old law[9]), had been alleged by me on the respectable authority of Fra-Paolo. The Examiner, who thinks that he has turned over the pages of the Theodosian Code, informs[1] his reader that it may be found, l. vi. tit. xxiv. leg. 8.; he will be surprised to learn that this rescript could not be *found* in a code where it does not exist, but that it may distinctly be read in the same number, the same title, and the same book of the CODE OF JUSTINIAN. He who is severe should at least be just: yet I should probably have disdained this minute animadversion, unless it had served to display the general ignorance of the critic in the History of the Roman Jurisprudence. If Mr. Davis had not been an absolute stranger, the most treacherous guide could not have persuaded him[a] that a rescript of Diocletian was to be found in the Theodosian Code, which was designed only to preserve the laws of Constantine and his successors. Compendiosam (says Theodosius himself) Divalium Constitutionum scientiam, ex D. Constantini temporibus roboramus. (Novell. ad calcem Cod. Theod. l. i. tit. i. leg. i.)

(7) Gibbon's History, p. 551. I shall usually refer to the third edition, unless there are any various readings.
(8) Davis, p. 144.   (9) Gibbon, p. 593.   (1) Davis, p. 230.

a I. om. him

II.

ERRORS OF THE PRESS.

Few objects are below the notice of Mr. Davis, and his criticism is never so formidable as when it is directed against the guilty corrector of the press, who on some occasions has shewn himself negligent of my fame and of his own. Some errors have arisen from the omission of letters; from the confusion of cyphers, which perhaps were not very distinctly marked in the original manuscript. The *two* of the Roman, and the *eleven* of the Arabic, numerals have been unfortunately mistaken for each other; the similar forms of a 2 and a 3, a 5 and a 6, a 3 and an 8, have improperly been transposed; A*n*tolycus for A*u*tolycus, Idolatria for Ido*l*olatria, Holste*r*ius for Holste*n*ius, had escaped my own observation, as well as the diligence of the person who was employed to revise the sheets of my History. These important errors, from the indulgence of a deluded Public, have been multiplied in the numerous impressions of three different editions; and for the present I can only lament my own defects, whilst[a] I deprecate the wrath of Mr. Davis, who seems ready to infer that I cannot either read or write. I sincerely admire his patient industry, which I despair of being able to imitate; but if a future edition should ever be required, I could wish to obtain, on any reasonable terms, the services of so useful a corrector.

III.

DIFFERENCE OF EDITIONS.

Mr. Davis had been directed by my references to several passages of Optatus Milevitanus[2], and of the Bibliotheque Ecclesiastique of M. Dupin[3]. He eagerly consults those places, is unsuccessful, and is happy. Sometimes the place which I have quoted does not offer any of the circumstances which I had alleged, sometimes only a few; and sometimes the same passages exhibit a sense totally adverse and repugnant to mine. These shameful misrepresentations incline Mr. Davis to suspect that I have never consulted the original (not even of a common French book!) and he asserts his right to censure my presumption. These important charges form

---

[2] Davis, p. 73.   [3] Id. p. 132–136.

[a] *II.* while

two distinct articles in the list of *Misrepresentations*; but Mr. Davis has amused himself with adding to the slips of the pen or of the press, some complaints of his ill success, when he attempted to verify my quotations from Cyprian and from Shaw's Travels[4]. The success of Mr. Davis would indeed have been somewhat extraordinary, unless he had consulted the same *editions*, as well as the same places. I shall content myself with mentioning the editions which I have used, and with assuring him, that if he renews his search, he will not, or rather, that he will be, disappointed.

Mr. Gibbon's Editions.	Mr. Davis's Editions.
Optatus Milevitanus, by Dupin, fol. Paris, 1700.	Fol. Antwerp, 1702.
Dupin, Bibliotheque Ecclesiastique, 4to. Paris, 1690.	8vo. Paris, 1687.
Cypriani Opera, Edit. Fell, fol. Amsterdam, 1700.	Most probably Oxon. 1682.
Shaw's Travels, 4to. London, 1757.	The folio Edition.

IV.

JEWISH HISTORY, TACITUS,

The nature of my subject had led me to mention, not the real origin of the Jews, but their first *appearance* to the eyes of other nations; and I cannot avoid transcribing the short passage in which I had introduced them. "The Jews, who under the Assyrian and "Persian monarchies had languished for many ages the most "despised portion of their slaves, emerged from their obscurity "under the successors of Alexander. And as they multiplied to a "surprising degree in the East, and afterwards in the West, they "soon excited the curiosity and wonder of other nations[5]." This simple abridgment seems in its turn to have excited the wonder of Mr. Davis, whose surprise almost renders him eloquent. "What a "strange assemblage," says he, "is here. It is like Milton's Chaos, "without bound, without dimension, where time and place are lost. "In short, what does this display afford us, but a deal of boyish "colouring to the prejudice of much good history[6]." If I rightly understand Mr. Davis's language, he censures, as a piece of confused declamation, the passage which he has produced from my history;

[4] Id. p. 151. 155.   [5] Gibbon, p. 537.   [6] Davis, p. 5.

and if I collect the angry criticisms which he has scattered over twenty pages of controversy[7], I think I can discover that there is hardly a period, or even a word, in this unfortunate passage, which has obtained the approbation of the Examiner.

As nothing can escape his vigilance, he censures me for including the twelve tribes of Israel under the common appellation of JEWS[8], and for extending the name of ASSYRIANS to the subjects of the Kings of Babylon[9], and again censures me, because some facts which are affirmed or insinuated in my text, do not agree with the strict and proper limits which he has assigned to those national denominations. The name of *Jews* has indeed been established by[a] the scepter of the tribe of *Judah*, and, in the times which precede the captivity, it is used in the more general sense with some sort of impropriety; but surely I am not peculiarly charged with a fault which has been consecrated by the consent of twenty centuries, the practice of the best writers, ancient as well as modern (see Josephus and Prideaux, even in the titles of their respective works), and by the usage of modern languages, of the Latin, the Greek, and, if I may credit Reland, of the Hebrew itself (see Palestin, l. i. c. 6.). With regard to the other word, that of Assyrians, most assuredly I will not lose myself in the labyrinth of the Asiatic monarchies before the age of Cyrus; nor indeed is any more required for my justification, than to prove that Babylon was considered as the capital and royal seat of Assyria. If Mr. Davis were a man of learning, I might be morose enough to censure his ignorance of ancient geography, and to overwhelm him under a load of quotations, which might be collected and transcribed with very little trouble: But as I *must* suppose that he has received a classical education, I might have expected him to have read the first book of Herodotus, where that historian describes, in the clearest and most elegant terms, the situation and greatness of Babylon: Της δε Ασσυριης τα μεν κου και αλλα πολισματα μεγαλα πολλα, το δε ονομαστοτατον και ισχυροτατον και ενθα σφι, Νινου αναστατου γενομενης, τα βασιληια κατεστηκεε,[b] ην Βαβυλων. (Clio, c. 178.) I may be surprised that he should be so little conversant with the Cyropœdia of Xenophon, in the whole course of which the King of Babylon, the adversary of the Medes and Persians, is repeatedly mentioned by the style and title of THE ASSYRIAN, ῾Οδε

---

[7] Id. p. 2–22.   [8] Id. p. 3.   [9] Id. p. 2.

[a] *II.* with   [b] *II.* κατεστηκες

Ασσυριος,[a] ὁ Βαβυλωνα τε εχων και την αλλην Ασσυριαν. (l. ii. p. 102, 103, Edit. Hutchinson.) But there remains something more: and Mr. Davis must apply the same reproaches of *inaccuracy*, *if not ignorance*, to the Prophet Isaiah, who, in the name of Jehovah, announcing the downfal of Babylon and the deliverance of Israel, declares with an oath; "And as I have purposed the thing shall "stand: to crush the ASSYRIAN in my land, and to trample him on "my mountains. Then shall his yoke depart from off them; and "his burthen shall be removed from off their shoulders." (Isaiah, xiv. 24, 25. Lowth's new translation. See likewise the Bishop's note, p. 98.) Our[b] old translation expresses, with less elegance, the same meaning; but I mention with pleasure the labours of a respectable Prelate, who in this, as well as in a former work, has very happily united the most critical judgment, with the taste and spirit of poetry.

The jealousy which Mr. Davis affects for the honour of the Jewish people will not suffer him to allow that they were *slaves* to the conquerors of the East; and while he acknowledges that they were tributary and dependent, he seems desirous of introducing, or even inventing, some milder expression of the state of vassalage and *subservience*[1]; from whence Tacitus assumed the words of *despectissima pars servientium*. Has Mr. Davis never heard of the distinction of civil and political slavery? Is he ignorant that even the natural and victorious subjects of an Asiatic despot have been deservedly marked with the opprobrious epithet of slaves by every writer acquainted with the name and advantage of freedom? Does he not know that under such a government, the yoke is imposed with double weight on the necks of the vanquished, as the rigour of tyranny is aggravated by the abuse of conquest. From the first invasion of Judæa by the arms of the Assyrians, to the subversion of the Persian monarchy by Alexander, there elapsed a period of above four hundred years, which included about twelve ages or generations of the human race. As long as the Jews asserted their independence, they repeatedly suffered every calamity which the rage and insolence of a victorious enemy could inflict; the throne of David was overturned, the temple and city were reduced to ashes, and the whole land, a circumstance perhaps unparalleled in

[1] Davis, p. 6.

---

[a] I. Ασσυριης; *corrected in Errata*   [b] *I. om. this sentence.*

history, remained three-score and ten years without inhabitants, and without cultivation. (2 Chronicles, xxxvi. 21.) According to an institution which has long prevailed in Asia, and particularly in the Turkish government, the most beautiful and ingenious youths were carefully educated in the palace, where superior merit sometimes introduced these fortunate *slaves* to the favour of the conqueror, and to the honours of the state. (See the book and example of Daniel.) The rest of the unhappy Jews experienced the hardships of captivity and exile in distant lands, and while individuals were oppressed, the nation seemed to be dissolved or annihilated. The gracious edict of Cyrus was offered to all those who worshipped the God of Israel in the temple of Jerusalem; but it was accepted by no more than forty-two thousand persons of either sex and of every age, and of these about thirty thousand derived their origin from the Tribes of Judah, of Benjamin, and of Levi. (See Ezra, i. Nehemiah, vii. and Prideaux's Connections, vol. i. p. 107. fol. Edit. London, 1718.) The inconsiderable band of exiles, who returned to inhabit the land of their fathers, cannot be computed as the hundred and fiftieth part of the mighty people, that had been numbered by the impious rashness of David. After a survey, which did not comprehend the Tribes of Levi and Benjamin, the Monarch was assured that he reigned over *one million five hundred and seventy thousand men* that drew sword ([a] Chronicles, xxi. 1–6), and the country of Judæa must have contained near seven millions of free inhabitants. The progress of restoration is always less rapid than that of destruction; Jerusalem, which had been ruined in a few months, was rebuilt by the slow and interrupted labours of a whole century; and the Jews, who gradually multiplied in their native seats, enjoyed a servile and precarious existence, which depended on the capricious will of their master. The books of Ezra and Nehemiah do not afford a very pleasing view of their situation under the Persian Empire; and the book of Esther exhibits a most extra-ordinary instance of the degree of estimation in which they were held at the Court of Susa. A Minister addressed his King in the following words, which may be considered as a Commentary on the *despectissima pars servientium* of the Roman historian; "And "Haman said to King Ahasuerus, there is a certain people scattered "abroad, and dispersed among the people in all the provinces of "thy kingdom; and their laws are diverse from all people, neither

[a]*I.* 2 Chronicles

"keep they the King's laws; therefore it is not for the King's profit "to suffer them. If it please the King let it be written that they may "be destroyed; and I will pay ten thousand talents of silver to the "hands of those that have the charge of the business to bring it to "the King's treasuries. And the King took his ring from his hand, "and gave it to Haman, the son of Hammedatha the Agagite, the "Jews enemy. And the King said unto Haman, The silver is given "unto thee: the people also, to do with them as it seemeth good to "thee." (Esther, iii. 8–11.) This trifling favour was asked by the Minister, and granted by the Monarch, with an easy indifference, which expressed their contempt for the lives and fortunes of the Jews; the business passed without difficulty through the forms of office; and had Esther been less lovely, or less beloved, a single day would have consummated the universal slaughter of a submissive people, to whom no legal defence was allowed, and from whom no resistance seems to have been dreaded. I am a stranger to Mr. Davis's political principles; but I should think that the epithet of *slaves*, and of *despised* slaves, may, without injustice, be applied to a captive nation, over whose heads the sword of tyranny was suspended by so slender a thread.

The policy of the Macedonians was very different from that of the Persians; and yet Mr. Davis, who reluctantly confesses that the Jews were oppressed by the former, does not understand how long they were favoured and protected by the latter[2]. In the shock of those revolutions which divided the empire of Alexander, Judæa, like the other provinces, experienced the transient ravages of an advancing or retreating enemy, who led away a multitude of captives. But in the age of Josephus, the Jews still enjoyed the privileges granted by the Kings of Asia and Egypt, who had fixed numerous colonies of that nation in the new cities of Alexandria, Antioch, &c. and placed them in the same honourable condition (ἰσοπολίτας, ἰσοτίμους) as the Greeks and Macedonians themselves. (Joseph. Antiquat. l. xii. c. 1. 3. p. 585. 596. Vol. i. edit. Havercamp.) Had they been treated with less indulgence, their settlement in those celebrated cities, the seats of commerce and learning, was enough to introduce them to the knowledge of the world, and to justify my *absurd* proposition, that they emerged from obscurity under the successors of Alexander.

The Jews remained and flourished under the mild dominion of

[2] Davis, p. 4.

the Macedonian Princes, till they were compelled to assert[a] their civil and religious rights against Antiochus Epiphanes, who had adopted new maxims of tyranny, and the age of the Machabees is perhaps the most glorious period of the Hebrew annals. Mr. Davis, who on this occasion is bewildered by the subtlety of Tacitus, does not comprehend why the historian should ascribe the independence of the Jews to three *negative* causes, "Macedonibus invalidis, "Parthis nondum adultis, et Romani procul aberant."[8] To the understanding of the critic, Tacitus might as well have observed that the Jews were not destroyed by a plague, a famine, or an earthquake; and Mr. Davis cannot see, for his own part, any reason why they might[b] not have elected Kings of their own two or three hundred years before[(3)]. Such indeed was not the reason of Tacitus; he probably considered that every nation, depressed by the weight of a foreign power, naturally rises towards the surface, as soon as the pressure is removed; and he might think that, in a short and rapid history of the independence of the Jews, it was sufficient for him to shew that the obstacles did not exist, which, in an earlier or in a later period, would have checked their efforts. The curious reader, who has leisure to study the Jewish and Syrian history, will discover that the throne of the Asmonæan Princes was confirmed by the two great victories of the Parthians over Demetrius Nicator, and Antiochus Sidetes (See Joseph. Antiquitat. Jud. l. xiii. c. 5, 6. 8, 9. Justin, xxxvi. 1. xxxviii. 10. with Usher and Prideaux, before Christ 141 and 130); and the expression of Tacitus, the more closely it is examined, will be the more rationally admired.

My Quotations[(4)] are the object of Mr. Davis's criticism[(5)], as well as the Text of this short, but obnoxious passage. He corrects the error of my memory, which had suggested *servitutis* instead of *servientium*;[9] and so natural is the alliance between truth and moderation, that on this occasion he forgets his character, and candidly acquits me of any malicious design to misrepresent the words of Tacitus. The other references, which are contained in the first and second Notes of my Fifteenth Chapter, are connected with each other, and can only be mistaken after they have been forcibly separated. The silence of Herodotus is a fair evidence of the obscurity

---

[(3)] Davis, p. 8.   [(4)] Gibbon, p. 537. Note 1, 2.   [(5)] Davis, p. 10. 11. 20.

[a] *I. for this sentence so far had* Under the reign of those princes who occupy the interval between Alexander and Augustus, the Jews asserted   [b] *II.* may

of the Jews, who had escaped the eyes of so curious a traveller. The Jews are first mentioned by Justin, when he relates the siege of Jerusalem by Antiochus Sidetes; and the conquest of Judæa, by the arms of Pompey, engaged Diodorus and Dion to introduce that singular nation to the acquaintance of their readers. These epochs,[10] which are within seventy years of each other, mark the age in which the Jewish people, emerging from their obscurity, began to act a part in the society of nations, and to excite the curiosity of the Greek and Roman historians. For that purpose only, I had appealed to the authority of Diodorus Siculus, of Justin, or rather of Trogus Pompeius, and of Dion Cassius. If I had designed to investigate the Jewish Antiquities, reason, as well as faith, must have directed my inquiries to the Sacred Books, which, even as human productions, would deserve to be studied as one of the most curious and original monuments of the East.

[a]I stand accused, though not indeed by Mr. Davis, for profanely depreciating the *promised* Land, as well as the *chosen* People. The Gentleman without a name has placed this charge in the front of his battle[(1)], and if my memory does not deceive me, it is one of the few remarks in Mr. Apthope's[11] book, which have any immediate relation to my History. They seem to consider in[b] the light of a reproach, and of an unjust reproach, the idea which I had given of Palestine, as of a territory scarcely superior to Wales in extent and fertility[(2)]; and they strangely convert a geographical observation into a theological error. When I recollect that the imputation of a similar error was employed by the implacable Calvin, to precipitate and to justify the execution of Servetus, I must applaud the felicity of this country, and of this age, which has disarmed, if it could not mollify, the fierceness of ecclesiastical criticism (see Dictionnaire Critique de Chaffeupié, tom. iv. p. 223).[12]

As I had compared the narrow extent of Phœnicia and Palestine with the important blessings which those celebrated countries had diffused over the rest of the earth, their minute size became an object not of censure but of praise.

> Ingentes animos angusto in pectore versant.

[(1)] Remarks, p. 1.   [(2)] Gibbon, p. 30.

---

[a] *Next three paragraphs, headed* PAGE 29., *added at end of first edition; inserted here in second.*   [b] *I.* consider as a reproach, and as an unjust reproach,

The precise measure of Palestine was taken from Templeman's Survey of the Globe: he allows to Wales 7011 square English miles, to the Morea, or Peloponnesus, 7220, to the Seven United Provinces 7546, and to Judæa or Palestine 7600.[13] The difference is not very considerable, and if any of these countries has been magnified beyond its real size, Asia is more liable than Europe to have been affected by the inaccuracy of Mr. Templeman's maps. To the authority of this modern survey, I shall only add the ancient and weighty testimony of Jerom, who passed in Palestine above thirty years of his life. From Dan to Bershebah, the two fixed and proverbial boundaries of the Holy Land, he reckons no more than one hundred and sixty miles (Hieronym. ad Dardanum, tom. iii. p. 66), and the breadth of Palestine cannot by any expedient be stretched to one half of its length (see Reland, Palestin. l. ii. c. 5. p. 421).[14]

The degrees and limits of fertility cannot be ascertained with the strict simplicity of geographical measures. Whenever we speak of the productions of the earth in different climates, our ideas must be relative, our expressions vague and doubtful; nor can we always distinguish between the gifts of Nature and the rewards of Industry. The Emperor Frederick II. the enemy and the victim of the Clergy, is accused of saying, after his return from his Crusade, that the God of the Jews would have despised his promised land, if he had once seen the fruitful realms of Sicily and Naples (see Giannone Istoria Civile del Regno di Napoli, tom. ii. p. 245). This raillery, which malice has perhaps falsely imputed to Frederick, is inconsistent with truth and piety; yet it must be confessed, that the soil of Palestine does not contain that inexhaustible, and as it were spontaneous principle of fecundity which under the most unfavourable circumstance has covered with rich harvests the banks of the Nile, the fields of Sicily, or the plains of Poland. The Jordan is the only navigable river of Palestine: a considerable part of the narrow space is occupied, or rather lost, in the *Dead Sea*, whose horrid aspect inspires every sensation of disgust, and countenances every tale of horror. The districts which border on Arabia partake of the sandy quality of the adjacent desert. The face of the country, except the sea-coast and the valley of the Jordan, is covered with mountains, which appear for the most part as naked and barren rocks; and in the neighbourhood of Jerusalem there is a real scarcity of the two elements of earth and water (see Maundrel's Travels, p. 65, and Reland Palestin. tom. i. p. 238–395). These disadvantages, which now operate in their fullest extent, were formerly corrected by the labours of a numerous people, and the active protection of a wise government. The hills were cloathed with rich beds of artificial mould, the rain was collected in vast cisterns, a supply of fresh water was conveyed by pipes and aqueducts to the dry lands, the breed of cattle was encouraged in those parts which were not adapted for tillage, and almost every spot was compelled to yield some production for the use of the inhabitants. (See the same testimonies and observations of Maundrel and Reland).

> – – – – – Pater ipse colendi
> Haud facilem esse viam voluit, primusque per artem
> Movit agros; curi acuens mortalia corda
> Nec torpere gravi passus sua Regna veterno.

Such are the useful victories which have been atchieved by Man on the lofty mountains of Switzerland, along the rocky coast of Genoa, and upon the barren hills of Palestine; and since Wales has flourished under the influence of English freedom, that rugged country has surely acquired some share of the same industrious merit and the same artificial fertility. Those Critics who interpret the comparison of Palestine and Wales as a tacit libel on the former, are themselves guilty of an unjust satire against the latter of those countries. Such is the injustice of Mr. Apthorpe and of the anonymous *Gentleman*: but if Mr. Davis (as we may suspect from his name) is himself of Cambrian origin, his patriotism on this occasion has protected me from his zeal.

V.

I shall begin this article by the confession of an error which candour might perhaps excuse, but which my Adversary magnifies by a pathetic interrogation. "When he tells us, that he has carefully "examined all the original materials, are we to believe him? or is it "his design to try how far the credulity and easy disposition of the "age will suffer him to proceed unsuspected and undiscovered[6]?" *Quousque tandem abuteris Catilina patientiâ nostrâ?*

In speaking of the danger of idolatry, I had quoted the pictoresque expression of Tertullian, "Recogita sylvam et quantæ latitant spinæ," and finding it marked c. 10 in my Notes, I hastily, though

[6] Davis, p. 25.

naturally, added *de Idololatria*, instead of *de Corona Militis*,[15] and referred to one Treatise of Tertullian instead of another[7]. And now let me ask in my turn, whether Mr. Davis had any real knowledge of the passage which I had misplaced, or whether he made an ungenerous use of his advantage, to insinuate that I had invented or perverted the words of Tertullian? Ignorance is less criminal than malice, and I shall be satisfied if he will plead guilty to the milder charge.

The same observation may be extended to a passage of Le Clerc,[16] which asserts, in the clearest terms, the ignorance of the more ancient Jews with regard to a future state. Le Clerc lay open before me, but while my eye moved from the book to the paper, I transcribed the reference c. i. sect. 8. instead of sect. i. c. 8. from the natural, but erroneous persuasion, that *Chapter* expressed the larger, and *Section* the smaller division[8]: and this difference, of such trifling moment and so easily rectified, holds a distinguished place in the list of Misrepresentations which adorn Mr. Davis's table of Contents[9]. But to return to Tertullian.

The *infernal* picture, which I had produced[1] from that vehement writer, which excited the horror of every humane reader, and which even Mr. Davis will not explicitly defend, has furnished him with a few critical cavils[2]. Happy should I think myself, if the materials of my History could be always exposed to the Examination of the Public; and I shall be*a* content with appealing to the impartial Reader, whether my Version of this Passage is not as fair and as faithful as the more literal translation which Mr. Davis has exhibited in an opposite column. I shall only justify two expressions which have provoked his indignation. 1. I had observed that the zealous African pursues the infernal description in a long variety of affected and unfeeling witticisms; the instances of Gods, of Kings, of Magistrates, of Philosophers, of Poets, of Tragedians introduced*b* into my Translation. Those which I had omitted relate to the Dancers, the Charioteers, and the Wrestlers; and it is almost impossible to express those conceits which are connected with the language and manners of the Romans. But the reader will be *sufficiently* shocked, when he is informed that Tertullian alludes to

[7] Gibbon, p. 553. Note 40. [8] Gibbon, p. 560, Note 58.
[9] Davis, p. 19. [1] Gibbon, p. 566. [2] Davis, p. 29–33.

a I. content myself with *b* II. were introduced

the improvement which the agility of the Dancers, the *red^a* livery of the Charioteers, and the attitudes of the Wrestlers, would derive from the effects of fire. "Tunc histriones cognoscendi solutiores "multo per ignem; tunc spectandus Auriga in flammea rota totus "ruber. Tunc Xystici contemplandi, non in Gymnasiis, sed in igne "jaculati." 2. I cannot refuse to answer Mr. Davis's very particular question, Why I appeal to Tertullian for the condemnation of the wisest and most virtuous of the Pagans? *Because* I am inclined to bestow that epithet on Trajan and the Antonines, Homer and Euripides, Plato and Aristotle, who are all manifestly included within the fiery description which I had produced.

I am accused of misquoting Tertullian ad Scapulam[3], as an evidence that Martyrdoms were lately introduced into Africa[4]. Besides Tertullian, I had quoted from Ruinart (Acta Sincera, p. 84.)[17] the Acts of the Scyllitan Martyrs; and a very moderate knowledge of Ecclesiastical History would have informed Mr. Davis, that the two authorities thus connected establish the proposition asserted in my Text. Tertullian, in the above-mentioned Chapter, speaks of one of the Proconsuls of Africa, Vigellius Saturninus, "qui *primus hic* gladium in nos egit;" the Acta Sincera represent the same Magistrate as the Judge of the Scyllitan Martyrs, and Ruinart, with the consent of the best Critics, ascribes their sufferings to the persecution of Severus. Was it my fault if Mr. Davis was incapable of supplying the intermediate ideas?

Is it likewise necessary that I should justify the frequent use which I have made of Tertullian? His copious writings display a lively and interesting picture of the primitive Church, and the scantiness of original materials scarcely left me the liberty of choice. Yet as I was sensible, that the Montanism of Tertullian is the convenient screen, which our orthodox Divines have placed before his errors, I have, with peculiar caution, confined myself to those works which were composed in the more early and sounder part of his life.

As a collateral justification of my frequent appeals to this African Presbyter, I had introduced, in the third edition of my History, two passages of Jerom and Prudentius, which prove that Tertullian was the master of Cyprian, and that Cyprian was the master of the

---

[3] Davis, p. 35, 36.   [4] Gibbon, p. 609, Note 172.

---

a II. om. italics.

Latin Church[5]. Mr. Davis assures me, however, that I should have done better not to have "added this note[6], as I have only "accumulated my inaccuracies." One inaccuracy he had[a] indeed detected, an error of the press, Hieronym. de Viris illustribus, c. 53 for 63;[18] but this advantage is dearly purchased by Mr. Davis. Επιδος τον διδασκαλον, which he produces as the original words of Cyprian, has a braver and more learned sound, than *Da magistrum*; but the quoting in Greek a sentence which was pronounced, and is recorded in Latin, seems to bear the mark of the most ridiculous pedantry; unless Mr. Davis, consulting for the first time the Works of Jerom, mistook the Version of Sophronius, which is printed in the opposite column, for the Text of his original Author. My reference to Prudentius, Hymn. xiii. 100. cannot so easily be justified, as I presumptuously believed that my critics would continue to read till they came to a full stop. I shall now place before them, not the first verse only, but the entire period, which they will find full, express, and satisfactory. The Poet says of St. Cyprian, whom he places in Heaven,

> Nec minus involitat terris, nec ab hoc recedit orbe:
> Disserit, eloquitur, tractat, docet, instruit, prophetat;
> Nec *Libyæ populos* tantum regit, exit usque in ortum
> Solis, et usque obitum; *Gallos* fovet, imbuit *Britannos*,
> Presidet *Hesperiæ*, Christum serit ultimis *Hibernis*.

VI.

SULPICIUS SEVERUS AND FRA-PAOLO.

On the subject of the imminent dangers which the Apocalypse has so narrowly escaped[7], Mr. Davis accuses me of misrepresenting the sentiments of Sulpicius Severus[19] and Fra-Paolo[8], with this difference, however, that I was incapable of reading or understanding the text of the Latin author; but that I wilfully perverted the sense of the Italian historian. These imputations I shall easily wipe away, by shewing that, in the first instance, I am probably in the right, and that in the second, he is certainly in the wrong.

1. The concise and elegant Sulpicius, who has been justly styled the Christian Sallust, after mentioning the exile and Revelations of

---

[5] Gibbon, p. 566. N. 72.   [6] Davis, p. 145.   [7] Gibbon, p. 563, 564. N. 67.
[8] Davis, p. 40–44.

[a] *II.* has

St. John in the Isle of Patmos, observes (and surely the observation
is in the language of complaint), "Librum sacræ Apocalypsis, qui
"quidem *a plerisque* aut stulte aut impie non recipitur, conscriptum
"edidit." I am found guilty of supposing *plerique* to signify *the
greater number*; whereas Mr. Davis, with Stephens's Dictionary in
his hand, is able to prove that *plerique* has not *always* that extensive
meaning, and that a classic of good authority has used the word in
a much more limited and qualified sense. Let the Examiner therefore try to apply his exception to this particular case. For my part,
I stand under the protection of the general usage of the Latin
language, and with a strong presumption in favour of the justice
of my cause, or at least of the innocence and fairness of my intentions; since I have translated a familiar word according to its
acknowledged and ordinary acceptation.

But, "if I had looked into the passage, and found that Sulpicius
"Severus there expressly tells us, that the Apocalypse was the work
"of St. John, I could not have committed so unfortunate a *blunder*,
"as to cite this Father as saying That the greater number of Chris-
"tians denied its Canonical authority[9]." Unfortunate indeed would
have been my blunder, had I asserted that the same Christians who
denied its Canonical authority, admitted it to be the work of an
Apostle. Such indeed was the opinion of Severus himself, and his
opinion has obtained the sanction of the Church; but the Christians
whom he taxes with folly or impiety for rejecting this sacred book,
must have supported their error by attributing the Apocalypse to
some uninspired writer; to John the Presbyter, or to Cerinthus the
Heretic.

If the rules of grammar and of logic authorise, or at least allow
me to translate *plerique* by the *greater number*, the Ecclesiastical
History of the fourth century illustrates and justifies this obvious
interpretation. From a fair comparison of the populousness and
learning of the Greek and Latin Churches, may I not conclude that
the former contained the *greater number* of Christians qualified to
pass sentence on a mysterious prophesy composed in the Greek
language? May I not affirm, on the authority of St. Jerom, that the
Apocalypse was generally rejected by the Greek Churches? "Quod
"si eam (the Epistle to the Hebrews) Latinorum consuetudo non
"recipit inter Scripturas Canonicas; nec Græcorum Ecclesiæ
"Apocalypsim Johannis eadem libertate suscipiunt. Et tamen nos

[9] Davis, p. 270.

"utramque suscipimus, nequaquam hujus temporis consuetudinem, "sed veterum auctoritatem sequentes." Epistol. ad Dardanum, tom. iii. p. 68.

It is not my design to enter any farther into the controverted history of that famous book; but I am called upon[1] to defend my Remark that the Apocalypse was tacitly excluded from the sacred canon by the council of Laodicea (Canon LX.) To defend my Remark, I need only state the fact in a simple, but more particular manner. The assembled Bishops of Asia, after enumerating all the books of the Old and New Testament which should be read in churches, omit the Apocalypse, and the Apocalypse alone; at a time when it was rejected or questioned by many pious and learned Christians, who might deduce a very plausible argument from the silence of the Synod.

2. When the Council of Trent resolved to pronounce sentence on the Canon of Scripture, the opinion which prevailed, after some debate, was to declare the Latin Vulgate authentic and *almost* infallible; and this sentence, which was guarded by formidable Anathemas, secured all the books of the Old and New Testament which composed that ancient version, "che si dichiarassero tutti "in tutte le parte come si trovano nella Biblia Latina, esser di Divina "è ugual autorita." (Istoria del Concilio Tridentino, l. ii. p. 147. Helmstadt (*Vicenza*) 1761.) When the merit of that version was discussed, the majority of the Theologians urged, with confidence and success, that it was absolutely necessary to receive the Vulgate as authentic and inspired, unless they wished to abandon the victory to the Lutherans, and the honours of the Church to the Grammarians. "In contrario della maggior parte dè Teologi era detto . . . . "che-questi nuovi Grammatici confonderanno ogni cosa, e sarà "fargli giudici e arbitri della fede; e in luogo dè Teologi e Canonisti, "converrà tener il primo conto nell' assumere a Vescovati e Cardin-"alati dè pedanti." (Istoria del Concilio Tridentino, l. ii. p. 149.) The sagacious Historian, who had studied the Council, and the judicious Le Courayer, who had studied his Author (Histoire du Concile de Trente, tom. i. p. 245. Londres 1736) consider this *ridiculous* reason as the most powerful argument which influenced the debates of the Council: But Mr. Davis, jealous of the honour of a Synod which placed tradition on a level with the Bible, affirms that Fra-Paolo has given another more substantial reason on which

[1] By Mr. Davis, p. 41. and by Dr. Chelsum, Remarks, p. 57.

these Popish Bishops built their determination, That after dividing the books under their consideration into three classes; of those which had been always held for divine; of those whose authenticity had formerly been doubted, but which by use and custom had acquired canonical authority; and of those which had never been properly certified; the Apocalypse was judiciously placed by the Fathers of the Council in the second of these classes.

The Italian passage which, for that purpose, Mr. Davis has[a] alleged at the bottom of his page, is indeed taken from the text of Fra-Paolo: but the reader who will give himself the trouble, or rather the pleasure, of perusing that incomparable historian, will discover that Mr. Davis has *only* mistaken a motion of the opposition for a measure of the administration. He will find that this critical division, which is so erroneously ascribed to the public reason of the Council, was no more than the ineffectual proposal of a temperate minority, which was soon over-ruled by a majority of artful Statesmen, bigotted Monks, and dependent Bishops.

"We have here an evident proof that Mr. Gibbon is equally expert "in misrepresenting a modern as an ancient writer, or that he "wilfully conceals the most material reason, with a design, no doubt, "to instil into his Reader a notion, that the authenticity of the "Apocalypse is built on the slightest foundation[2]."

VII.

Clemens.

I had cautiously observed (for I was apprised of the obscurity of the subject) that the Epistle of Clemens does not lead us to discover any traces of Episcopacy either at Corinth or Rome[3]. In this observation I particularly alluded to the republican form of salutation, "The Church of God inhabiting Rome, to the Church of "God inhabiting Corinth;" without the least mention of a Bishop or President in either of those ecclesiastical assemblies.

Yet the piercing eye of Mr. Davis[4] can discover not only traces, but evident proofs of Episcopacy, in this Epistle of Clemens; and he actually quotes two passages, in which he distinguishes by capital letters the word Bishops, whose institution Clemens refers

---

[2] Davis, p. 44.   [3] Gibbon, p. 592[20]. N. 110.   [4] Davis, p. 44, 45.

[a] *I.* had; *corrected in Errata*

to the Apostles themselves. But can Mr. Davis hope to gain credit by such egregious trifling? While we are searching for the origin of Bishops, not merely as an ecclesiastical title, but as the peculiar name of an order distinct from that of Presbyters, he idly produces a passage, which, by declaring that the Apostles established in every place *Bishops* and *Deacons*, evidently confounds the *Presbyters* with one or other of those two ranks. I have neither inclination nor interest to engage in a controversy which I had considered only in an historical light; but I have already said enough to shew, that there are more traces of a disingenuous mind in Mr. Davis, than of an Episcopal Order in the Epistle of Clemens.

VIII.

EUSEBIUS.

Perhaps, on some future occasion, I may examine the historical character of Eusebius; perhaps I may enquire, how far it appears from his words and actions that the learned Bishop of Cæsarea was averse to the use of fraud, when it was employed in the service of Religion. At present I am only concerned to defend my own truth and honour from the reproach of misrepresenting the sense of the Ecclesiastical Historian. Some of the charges of Mr. Davis on this head are so strong, so pointed, so vehemently urged, that he seems to have staked, on the event of the trial, the merits of our respective characters. If his assertions are true, I deserve the contempt of learned, and the abhorrence of good, men. If they are false, *******

1. I had remarked, without any malicious intention, that one of the seventeen Christians who suffered at Alexandria was likewise *accused* of robbery[5]. Mr. Davis[6] seems enraged because I did not add that he was *falsely* accused, takes some unnecessary pains to convince me that the Greek word εσυκοφαντηθη signifies *falso accusatus*, and "can hardly think that any one who had looked into the original, "would dare thus absolutely to contradict the plain testimony of "the author he *pretends* to follow." A simple narrative of this fact, in the relation of which Mr. Davis has *really* suppressed several material circumstances, will afford the clearest justification.

[5] Gibbon, p. 654, N. 75.
[6] Davis, p. 61, 62, 63. This ridiculous charge is repeated by another *Sycophant* (in the Greek sense of the word), and forms one of the *valuable* communications, which the learning of a Randolph suggested to the candour of a Chelsum. See Remarks, p. 209.

Eusebius has preserved an original letter from Dionysius Bishop of Alexandria to Fabius Bishop of Antioch, in which the former relates the circumstances of the persecution which had lately afflicted the capital of Egypt. He allows a rank among the martyrs to one Nemesion, an Egyptian, who was falsely or maliciously accused as a companion of robbers. Before the Centurion he justified himself from this calumny, which did not relate to him: but being charged as a Christian, he was brought in chains before the Governor. That unjust magistrate, after inflicting on Nemesion *a double measure of stripes and tortures*, gave orders that he should be *burnt with the robbers*. (Dionys. apud Euseb. l. vi. c. 41.)

It is evident that Dionysius represents the religious sufferer as innocent of the criminal accusation which had been falsely brought against him. It is no less evident, that whatever might be the opinion of the Centurion, the supreme magistrate considered Nemesion as guilty, and that he affected to shew, by the measure of his tortures, and by the companions of his execution, that he punished him, not only as a Christian, but as a robber. The evidence against Nemesion, and that which might be produced in his favour, are equally lost; and the question (which fortunately is of little moment) of his guilt or innocence rests solely on the opposite judgments of his ecclesiastical and civil superiors. I could easily perceive that both the Bishop and the Governor were actuated by different passions and prejudices towards the unhappy sufferer; but it was impossible for me to decide which of the two was the[a] most likely to indulge his prejudices and passions at the expence of truth. In this doubtful situation, I conceived that I had acted with the most unexceptionable caution, when I contented myself with observing that Nemesion was *accused*; a circumstance of a public and authentic nature, in which both parties were agreed.

Mr. Davis will no longer ask, "what possible evasion then can "Mr. Gibbon have recourse to, to convince the world that I have "*falsely* accused *him* of a gross misrepresentation of Eusebius?"

2. Mr. Davis[7] charges me with falsifying (*falsifying* is a very serious word) the testimony of Eusebius; because it suited my purpose to magnify the humanity and even kindness of Maxentius towards the afflicted Christians[8]. To support this charge, he

[7] Davis, p. 64, 65.   [8] Gibbon, p. 693, N. 168.

a *II. om.* the

produces some part of a chapter of Eusebius, the English in his text, the Greek in his notes, and makes the Ecclesiastical Historian express himself in the following terms: "Although Maxentius at "first favoured the Christians with a view of popularity, yet after-"wards, being addicted to magic, and every other impiety, HE "exerted himself in persecuting the Christians, in a more severe and "destructive manner than his predecessors had done before him."

If it were in my power to place the volume and chapter of Eusebius (Hist. Eccles. l. viii. c. 14.) before the eyes of every reader, I should be satisfied and silent. I should not be under the necessity of protesting, that in the passage quoted, or rather abridged, by my adversary, the second member of the period, which alone contradicts my account of Maxentius, has not the most distant reference to that odious tyrant. After distinguishing the mild conduct which *he* affected towards the Christians, Eusebius proceeds to animadvert with becoming severity on the general vices of his reign; the rapes, the murders, the oppression, the promiscuous massacres, which I had faithfully related in their proper place, and which the Christians, not in their religious, but in their civil capacity, must occasionally have shared with the rest of his unhappy subjects. The Ecclesiastical Historian then makes a transition to *another tyrant*, the cruel Maximin, who carried away from his friend and ally Maxentius the prize of superior wickedness; for HE was addicted to magic arts, and was a cruel persecutor of the Christians. The evidence of words and facts, the plain meaning of Eusebius, the concurring testimony of Cæcilius or Lactantius, and the superfluous authority of Versions and Commentators, establish beyond the reach of doubt or cavil, that Maximin, and not Maxentius, is stigmatized as a persecutor, and that Mr. Davis alone has deserved the reproach of *falsifying* the testimony of Eusebius.

Let him examine the chapter on which he founds his accusation. If in that moment his feelings are not of the most painful and humiliating kind, he must indeed be an object of pity.

3. *A gross blunder* is imputed to me by this polite antagonist[9], for quoting under the name of Jerom, the Chronicle which I ought to have described as the work and property of Eusebius[1]; and Mr. Davis kindly points out the occasion of my blunder, That it was the consequence of my looking no farther than Dodwell for this remark, and of not rightly understanding his reference. Perhaps the

[9] Davis, p. 66.   [1] Gibbon, p. 673, N. 125.

Historian of the Roman Empire may be credited, when he affirms that he frequently consulted a Latin Chronicle of the affairs of that Empire; and he may the sooner be credited, if he shews that he knows something more of this Chronicle besides the name and the title-page.

Mr. Davis, who talks so familiarly of the Chronicle of Eusebius, will be surprised to hear that the Greek original no longer exists. Some chronological fragments, which had successively passed through the hands of Africanus and Eusebius, are still extant, though in a very corrupt and mutilated state, in the compilations of Syncellus and Cedrenus. They have been collected, and disposed by the labour and ingenuity of Joseph Scaliger; but that proud Critic, always ready to applaud his own success, did not flatter himself, that he had restored the hundredth part of the genuine Chronicle of Eusebius. "Ex eo (*Syncello*) omnia Eusebiana excerpsimus quæ "quidem deprehendere potuimus; quæ, quanquam ne centesima "quidem pars eorum esse videtur quæ ab Eusebio relicta sunt, "aliquod tamen justum volumen explere possunt." (Jos. Scaliger Animadversiones in Græca Eusebii in Thesauro Temporum, p. 401. Amstelod. 1658.) While the Chronicle of Eusebius was perfect and entire, the second book was translated into Latin by Jerom, with the freedom, or rather licence, which that voluminous Author, as well as his friend or enemy Rufinus, always assumed. "Plurima in "vertendo mutat, infulcit, præterit," says Scaliger himself, in the Prolegomena, p. 22. In the persecution of Aurelian, which has so much offended Mr. Davis, we are able to distinguish the work of Eusebius from that of Jerom, by comparing the expressions of the Ecclesiastical History with those of the Chronicle. The former affirms, that, towards the end of his reign, Aurelian was moved by some councils to excite a persecution against[a] the Christians; that his design occasioned a great and general rumour; but that when the letters were prepared, and as it were signed, Divine Justice dismissed him from the world. *Ηδη τισι βουλαις ως αν διωγμον καθ' ήμων εγειρειεν ανεκινειτο. πολυς τε ην ὁ παρα πασι περι τουτου λογος. μελλοντα δε ηδη και σχεδον ειπειν τοις καθ' ήμων γραμμασιν υποσημειουμενον, θεια μετεισιν δικη.* Euseb. Hist. Eccles. l. vii. c. 30. Whereas the Chronicle relates, that Aurelian was killed after he had excited or moved a persecution against the Christians, "cum "adversum nos persecutionem movisset."

[a] *I.* gainst

From this manifest difference I assume a right to assert; first, that[a] the expression of the Chronicle of *Jerom*, which is always proper, became in this instance necessary; and secondly, that the language of the Fathers is so ambiguous and incorrect, that we are at a loss how to determine how far Aurelian had carried his intention before he was assassinated. I have neither perverted the *fact*, nor have I been guilty of *a gross blunder*.

IX.

JUSTIN MARTYR.

"The persons accused of Christianity had a convenient time "allowed them to settle their domestic concerns, and to prepare "their answer[1]." This observation had been suggested, partly by a general expression of Cyprian (de Lapsis, p. 88. Edit. Fell. Amstelod. 1700.) and more especially by the second Apology of Justin Martyr, who gives a particular and curious example of this legal delay.

The expressions of Cyprian, "dies negantibus præstitutus, &c.", which Mr. Davis most prudently suppresses, are illustrated by Mosheim in the following words: "Primum qui delati erant aut "suspecti, illis certum dierum spatium judex definiebat, quo "decurrente, secum deliberare poterant, utrum profiteri Christum "an negare mallent; *explorandæ fidei præfiniebantur dies*, per hoc "tempus liberi manebant in domibus suis; nec impediebat aliquis "quod ex consequentibus apparet, ne fugâ sibi consulerent. Satis "hoc erat humanum." (De Rebus Christianis ante Constantinum, p. 480.) The practice of Egypt was sometimes more expeditious and severe; but this humane indulgence was still allowed in Africa during the persecution of Decius.

But my appeal to Justin Martyr is encountered by Mr. Davis with the following declaration[2]: "The reader will observe, that "Mr. Gibbon does not make any reference to any section or division "of this part of Justin's work; with what view we may shrewdly "suspect, when I tell him, that after an accurate perusal of the "whole second Apology, I can boldly affirm, that the following "instance is the only one that bears the most distant similitude to

---

[1] Gibbon, p. 663.   [2] Davis, p. 71, 72.

[a] *I. om.* that; *corrected in Errata*

"what Mr. Gibbon relates as above on the authority of Justin. What
"I find in Justin is as follows: "A woman being converted to
"Christianity, is afraid to associate with her husband, because he
"is an abandoned reprobate, lest she should partake of his sins. Her
"husband, not being able to accuse *her*, vents his rage in this manner
"on one Ptolemæus, a teacher of Christianity, and who had con-
"verted her, &c." Mr. Davis then proceeds to relate the severities
inflicted on Ptolemæus, who made a frank and instant profession
of his faith: and he sternly exclaims, that if I take every opportunity
of passing encomiums on the humanity of Roman magistrates, it is
incumbent on me to produce better evidence than this.

His demand may be easily satisfied, and I need only for that
purpose transcribe and translate the words of Justin, which *immediately* precede the Greek quotation alleged at the bottom of my
adversary's page. I am possessed of two editions of Justin Martyr,
that of Cambridge, 1768, in 8vo, by Dr. Ashton, who only published
the two Apologies; and that of all his works, published in fol.[a] Paris,
1742, by the Benedictines of the Congregation of St. Maar: the
following curious passage may be found, p. 164, of the former, and
p. 89 of the latter Edition. κατηγοριαν πεποιηται, λεγων αυτην χρισ-
τιανην ειναι, και ἡ μεν βιβλιδιον σοι τω αυτοκρατορι αναδεδωκε,
προτερον συνχωρηθηναι αυτῃ διοικησασθαι τα εαυτης αξιουσα. επειτα
απολογησασθαι περι του κατηγορματος, μετα την των πραγματων
αυτης διοικησιν. και συνεχωρησας τουτο. "He brought an accusation
"against her, saying, that she was a Christian. But she presented a
"petition to the Emperor, praying that she might first be allowed to
"settle her domestic concerns; and promising, that after she had
"settled them, she would then put in her answer to the accusation.
"This you granted."

I disdain to add a single reflection; nor shall I qualify the conduct
of my adversary with any of those harsh epithets, which might be
interpreted as the expressions of resentment, though I should be
constrained to use them as the only words in the English language,
which could accurately represent my cool and unprejudiced
sentiments.

[a] II. folio,

X.

LACTANTIUS.

In stating the toleration of Christianity during the greatest part of
the reign of Diocletian, I had observed[3], that the principal officers*a*
of the palace, whose names and functions*b* were particularly specified, enjoyed, with their wives and children, the free exercise of the
Christian religion. Mr. Davis twice affirms[4], in the most deliberate
manner, that this pretended fact, which is asserted on the sole
authority, is contradicted by the positive evidence, of Lactantius. In
both these *affirmations* Mr. Davis is inexcusably mistaken.

1. When the storms of persecution arose, the Priests, who were
offended by the sign of the Cross, obtained an order from*c* the
Emperor, that the profane, the Christians, who accompanied him to
the Temple, should be compelled to offer sacrifice; and this incident
is mentioned by the Rhetorician, to whom I shall not at present
refuse the name of Lactantius. The act of idolatry, which at the
expiration of eighteen years was required of the officers of Diocletian,*d* is a manifest proof that their religious freedom had hitherto
been inviolate, except in the single instance of waiting on their
master to the Temple; a service less criminal, than the profane
compliance for which the Minister of the King of Syria solicited the
permission of the Prophet of Israel.

2. The reference which I made to Lactantius expressly pointed
out this exception to their freedom. But the proof of the toleration*e*
was built on a different testimony, which my disingenuous adversary
has concealed; an ancient and curious instruction, composed by
Bishop Theonas, for the use of Lucian and the other Christian
eunuchs of the palace of Diocletian. This authentic piece was
published in the Spicilegium of Dom Luc d'Acheri; as I had not the
opportunity of consulting the original, I was contented with quoting
it on the faith of Tillemont, and the reference to it immediately
precedes (ch. xvi. note 133.) the citation of Lactantius (note 134).

Mr. Davis may now answer his own question, "What apology can
"be made for thus asserting, on the sole authority of Lactantius,
"facts which Lactantius so expressly denies?"

---

[3] Gibbon, p. 676. N. 133, 134.   [4] Davis, p. 75, 76.

---

a *I*. eunuchs   *b* *I*. offices   *c* *I*. leave of   *d* *I*. Dioletian
e *I*. toleration which they enjoyed, was

XI.

DION CASSIUS.

"I have already given a curious instance of our Author's asserting,
"on the authority of Dion Cassius, a fact not mentioned by that
"Historian. I shall now produce a very singular proof of his en-
"deavouring to conceal from us a passage really contained in him[4]."
Nothing but the angry vehemence with which these charges are
urged, could engage me to take the least notice of them. In themselves they are doubly contemptible: they are trifling, and they are
false.

1. Mr. Davis[5] had imputed to me as a crime, that I had mentioned, on the sole testimony of Dion (l. lxviii. p. 1145.), the spirit of
rebellion which inflamed the Jews, from the reign of Nero to that of
Antoninus Pius[6], whilst the passage of that Historian is confined
to an insurrection in Cyprus and Cyrene, which broke out within
that period. The Reader who will cast his eye on the Note (ch. xvi.
note 1.) which is supported by that quotation from Dion, will discover that it related only to *this* particular fact. The general position
which is indeed too notorious to require any proof, I had carefully
justified in the course of the same paragraph; partly by another
reference to Dion Cassius, partly by an allusion to the well-known
History of Josephus, and partly by *several* quotations from the learned
and judicious Basnage, who has explained, in the most satisfactory
manner, the principles and conduct of the rebellious Jews.

2. The passage of Dion, which I am accused of endeavouring to
conceal, might perhaps have remained invisible, even to the piercing
eye of Mr. Davis, if *I* had not carefully reported it in its proper
place[7]: and it was in my power to report it, without being guilty of
any *inconsiderate contradiction*. I had observed, that, in the large
history of Dion Cassius, Xiphilin had not been able to discover the
name of *Christians*: yet I afterwards quote a passage in which Marcia,
the favourite Concubine of Commodus, is celebrated as the Patron-
ess of the *Christians*. Mr. Davis has transcribed my quotation, but
he has concealed the important words which I now distinguish by
Italics (ch. xvi. note 106. Dion Cassius, *or rather his abbreviator
Xiphilin*, l. lxxii. p. 1206.) The reference is fairly made and cautiously
qualified; I am already secure from the imputations of fraud or in-

[4] Davis, p. 83.   [5] Id. p. 11.   [6] Gibbon, p. 622.
[7] Gibbon, p. 667, n. 107.

consistency; and the opinion which attributes the last-mentioned passage to the Abbreviator, rather than to the original Historian, may be supported by the most unexceptionable authorities. I shall protect myself by those of Reimar (in his Edition of Dion Cassius, tom. ii. p. 1207. note 34.), and of Dr. Lardner; and shall only transcribe the words of the latter, in his Collection of Jewish and Heathen testimonies, vol. iii. p. 57.

"This paragraph I rather think to be Xiphilin's than Dion's. The "style at least is Xiphilin's. In the other passages before quoted, "Dion speaks of *Impiety*, or *Atheism*, or *Judaism*; but never useth the "word *Christians*. Another thing that may make us doubt whether "this observation be entirely Dion's, is the phrase, "it is related "(ιστορειται)." For at the beginning of the reign of Commodus, "he says, "These things, and what follows, I write not from the "report of others, but from my own knowledge and observation." "However, the sense may be Dion; but I wish we had also his style "without any adulteration." For my own part, I must, in my private opinion, ascribe even the sense of this passage to Xiphilin. The *Monk* might eagerly collect and insert an anecdote which related to the domestic history of the church; but the religion of a courtezan must have appeared an object of very little moment in the eyes of a *Roman Consul*, who, at least in every other part of his history, disdained or neglected to mention the name of the Christians.

"What shall we say now? Do we not discover the name of "Christians in the History of Dion? With what *assurance* then can "Mr. Gibbon, after asserting a fact manifestly *untrue*, lay claim to the "merits of diligence and accuracy, the indispensable duty of an "Historian. Or can he expect us to credit his assertion, that he has "carefully examined all the original materials[8]?""

Mr. Gibbon may still maintain the character of an Historian; but it is difficult to conceive how Mr. Davis will support his pretensions, if he aspires to that of a Gentleman.

I almost hesitate whether I should take any notice of another ridiculous charge which Mr. Davis includes in the article of Dion Cassius. My adversary owns, that I have occasionally produced the several passages of the Augustan History which relate to the Christians; but he fiercely contends that they amount to more than *six lines*[9]. I really have not measured them: nor did I mean that loose expression as a precise and definite number. If, on a nicer survey,

[8] Davis, p. 83.   [9] Gibbon, p. 634. n. 24.

those short hints, when they are brought together, should be found to exceed six of the long lines of my folio edition, I am content that my critical Antagonist should substitute eight, or ten, or twelve, lines: nor shall I think either my learning or my^a veracity much interested in this important alteration.

XII.

PLINY, &c.

After a short description of the unworthy conduct of those Apostates who, in a time of persecution, deserted the Faith of Christ, I produced the evidence of a Pagan Proconsul[1], and of two Christian Bishops, Pliny, Dionysius of Alexandria, and Cyprian. And here the unforgiving Critic remaks, "That Pliny has not particularized that "difference of conduct (in the different Apostates) which Mr. Gib- "bon here describes: yet his name stands at the head of those "Authors whom he has cited on the occasion. It is allowed indeed "that this distinction is made by the other Authors; but as Pliny, "the first referred to by Mr. Gibbon, gives him no cause or reason to "use *them*," (I cannot help Mr. Davis's bad English) "it is certainly "very reprehensible in our Author, thus to confound their testimony, "and to make a needless and improper reference[2]."

A criticism of this sort can only tend to expose Mr. Davis's total ignorance of historical composition.[21] The Writer who aspires to the name of Historian, is obliged to consult a variety of original testimonies, each of which, taken separately, is perhaps imperfect and partial. By a judicious re-union and arrangement of these dispersed materials, he endeavours to form a consistent and interesting narrative. Nothing ought to be inserted which is not proved by some^b of the witnesses; but their evidence must be so intimately blended together, that as it is unreasonable to expect that each of them should vouch for the whole, so it would be impossible to define the boundaries of their respective property. Neither Pliny, nor Dionysius, nor Cyprian, mention *all* the circumstances and *distinctions* of the conduct of the Christian Apostates; but if any of them was withdrawn, the account which I have given would, in some instance, be defective.

[1] Gibbon, p. 664. N. 102.   [2] Davis, p. 87, 88.

---

^{a} *II. om.* my ^{b} *I.* some one

Thus much I thought necessary to say, as several of the subsequent *misrepresentations* of Orosius, of Bayle, of Fabricius, of Gregory of Tours, &c.[3], which provoked the fury of Mr. Davis, are derived only from the ignorance of this common historical principle.

Another class of Misrepresentations, which my Adversary urges with the same degree of vehemence (see in particular those of Justin, Diodorus Siculus, and even Tacitus), requires the support of another principle which has not yet been introduced into the art of criticism; *that* when a modern historian appeals to the authority of the ancients for the truth of any particular fact, he makes himself answerable, I know not to what extent, for all the circumjacent errors or inconsistencies of the authors whom he has quoted.

XIII.

IGNATIUS.

I am accused of throwing out a false accusation against this Father[3], because I had observed[4] that Ignatius, defending against the Gnostics the resurrection of Christ, employs a vague and doubtful tradition, instead of quoting the certain testimony of the Evangelists: and this observation was justified by a remarkable passage of Ignatius, in his Epistle to the Smyrnæans, which I cited according to the volume and the page of the best edition of the Apostolical Fathers, published at Amsterdam, 1724, in two volumes in folio. The Criticism of Mr. Davis is announced by one of those solemn declarations which leave not any refuge, if they are convicted of falsehood. "I cannot find any passage that bears the least affinity to "what Mr. Gibbon observes, in the whole Epistle, which I have "read over more than once."

I had already marked the *situation*; nor is it in my power to prove the *existence* of this passage, by any other means than by producing the words of the original. Εγω γαρ και μετα την αναστασιν εν σαρκι αυτον οιδα και πιστευω οντα, και οτε προς τους περι Πετρον ηλθεν, εφη αυτοις, λαβετε, ψυλαφησατε με, και ιδετε οτι ουκ᾽ ειμι δαιμονιον ασωματον. και ευθυς αυτου ἥψαντο, και επιστευσαν. "I have "known, and I believe, that after his resurrection likewise he existed "in the flesh: And when he came to Peter, and to the rest, he "said unto them, Take, handle me, and see that I am not an

[3] Davis, p. 88. 90. 137.   [3] Davis, p. 100, 101.   [4] Gibbon, p. 551, Note 35.

"incorporal dæmon or spirit. And they touched him and believed."
The faith of the Apostles confuted the impious error of the Gnostics,
which attributed only the *appearances* of a human body to the Son
of God: and it was the great object of Ignatius, in the last
moments of his life, to secure the Christians of Asia from the
snares of those dangerous Heretics. According to the tradition of
the modern Greeks, Ignatius was the child whom Jesus received
into his arms (See Tillemont Mem. Eccles. tom. ii. part ii. p. 43.);
yet as he could scarcely[a] be old enough to remember the resurrection of the Son of God, he must have derived his knowledge
either from our present Evangelists, *or* from some Apocryphal
Gospel, *or* from some unwritten tradition.

1. The Gospels of St. Luke and St. John would undoubtedly
have supplied Ignatius with the most invincible proofs of the reality
of the body of Christ, when he appeared to the Apostles after his
resurrection: but neither of those Gospels contain the characteristic
words of ουκ δαιμονιον ασωματον, and the important circumstance
that either Peter, or *those* who were with Peter, touched the body of
Christ and believed. Had the Saint designed to quote the Evangelist
on a very nice subject of controversy, he would not surely have
exposed himself by an inaccurate, or rather by a false reference, to
the just reproaches of the Gnostics. On this occasion, therefore,
Ignatius did not employ, as he might have done, against the Heretics,
the certain testimony of the Evangelists.

2. Jerom, who cites this remarkable passage from the Epistle of
Ignatius to the Smyrnæans (See Catalog. Script. Eccles. in Ignatio,
tom. i. p. 273. edit. Erasm. Basil 1537), is of opinion that it was taken
from the *Gospel* which he himself had lately translated: and *this*,
from the comparison of two other passages in the same Work (in
Jacob. et in Matthæo, p. 264), appears to have been the Hebrew
Gospel, which was used by the Nazarenes of Beræa, as the genuine
composition of St. Matthew. Yet Jerom mentions another Copy of
this Hebrew Gospel (so different from the Greek Text), which was
extant in the library formed at Cæsarea, by the care of Pamphilus:
whilst the learned Eusebius, the friend of Pamphilus and the Bishop
of Cæsarea, very frankly declares (Hist. Eccles. l. iii. c. 36.), that *he*
is ignorant from whence Ignatius borrowed those words, which are
the subject of the present Enquiry.

3. The doubt which remains, is only whether he took them from

[a] *I.* hardly

an Apocryphal Book, or from *unwritten tradition*: and I thought myself safe from every species of Critics, when I embraced the rational sentiment of Casaubon and Pearson. I shall produce the words of the Bishop. "Præterea iterum observandum est, quod de "hac re scripsit Isaacus Casaubonus, *Quinetiam fortasse verius, non* "*ex Evangelio Hebraico, Ignatium illa verba descripsisse, verum* "*traditionem allegasse non scriptam, quæ postea in literas fuerit relata,* "*et Hebraico Evangelio, quod Matthæo tribuebant, inserta.* Et hoc "quidem mihi multo verisimilius videtur." (Pearson. Vindiciæ Ignatianæ, part ii. c. ix. p. 396. in tom. ii. Patr. Apostol.)

I may now submit to the judgment of the Public, whether I have looked into the Epistle which I cite with such a parade of learning, and *how profitably* Mr. Davis has read it over more than once.

XIV.

MOSHEIM.

The learning and judgment of Mosheim had been of frequent use in the course of my Historical Inquiry, and I had not been wanting in proper expressions of gratitude. My vexatious Adversary is always ready to start from his ambuscade, and to harass my march by a mode of attack, which cannot easily be reconciled with the laws of honourable war. The greatest part of the Misrepresentations of Mosheim, which Mr. Davis has imputed to me[5], are of such a nature, that I must indeed be humble, if I could persuade myself to bestow a moment of serious attention on them. *Whether* Mosheim could prove that an absolute community of goods was not established among the first Christians of Jerusalem; *whether* he suspected the purity of the Epistles of Ignatius; *whether* he censured Dr. Middleton with temper or indignation (in this cause I must challenge Mr. Davis as an incompetent judge); *whether* he corroborates the *whole* of my description of the prophetic office; *whether* he speaks with approbation of the humanity of Pliny, and *whether* he attributed the same sense to the *malefica* of Suetonius, and the *exitiabilis* of Tacitus. These questions, even as Mr. Davis has stated them, lie open to the judgment of every reader, and the superfluous observations which I could make, would be an abuse of their time and of my own. As little shall I think of consuming their patience, by examining whether Le Clerc and Mosheim *labour* in the interpretation of some texts of

[5] Davis, p. 95–97. 104–107. 114–132.

the Fathers, and particularly of a passage of Irenæus, which seem to favour the pretensions of the Roman Bishop. The material part of the passage of Irenæus consists of about *four lines*; and in order to shew that the interpretations of Le Clerc and Mosheim are not *laboured*, Mr. Davis abridges them as much as possible in the space of *twelve pages*. I know not whether the perusal of my History will justify the suspicion of Mr. Davis, that I am secretly inclined to the interest of the Pope: but I cannot discover how the Protestant cause can be affected, if Irenæus in the second, or Palavicini in the seventeenth century, were tempted, by any private views, to countenance in their writings the system of ecclesiastical dominion, which has been pursued in every age by the aspiring Bishops of the Imperial city. Their conduct was adapted to[a] the revolutions of the Christian Republic, but the same spirit animated the haughty breasts of Victor the First, and of Paul the Fifth.

There still remain one or two of these imputed Misrepresentations, which appear, and indeed only appear, to merit a little more attention. In stating the opinion of Mosheim with regard to the progress of the Gospel, Mr. Davis boldly declares, "that I have *altered* "*the truth* of Mosheim's history, that I might have an opportunity of "contradicting the belief and wishes of the Fathers[6]." In other words, I have been guilty of uttering a malicious falsehood.

I had endeavoured to mitigate the sanguine expression of the Fathers of the second century, who had too hastily diffused the light of Christianity over every part of the globe, by observing, as an undoubted fact, "that the Barbarians of Scythia and Germany, who "subverted the Roman Monarchy, were involved in the errors of "Paganism; and that even the conquest of Iberia, of Armenia, or of "Æthiopia, was not attempted with any degree of success, till the "scepter was in the hands of an orthodox Emperor[7]." I had referred the curious reader to the fourth century of Mosheim's General History of the Church: Now Mr. Davis has discovered, and can prove, from that excellent work, "that Christianity, not long after "its first rise, had been introduced into the less as well as greater "Armenia; that part of the Goths, who inhabited Thracia, Mæsia,[b] "and Dacia, had received the Christian religion long before this "century; and that Theophilus, their Bishop, was present at the "Council of Nice[8]."

---

[6] Davis, p. 137.   [7] Gibbon, p. 611, 612.   [8] Davis, p. 126, 127.

---

[a] *I.* followed   [b] *II.* Mœsia

On this occasion, the reference was made to a popular work of Mosheim, for the satisfaction of the reader, that he might obtain the general view of the progress of Christianity in the fourth century, which I had gradually acquired by studying with some care the Ecclesiastic[a] Antiquities of the Nations beyond the limits of the Roman Empire. If I had reasonably supposed that the result of our common inquiries must be the same, should I have deserved a very harsh censure for my unsuspecting confidence? Or if I had declined the invidious task of separating a few immaterial errors, from a just and judicious representation, might not my respect for the name and merit of Mosheim, have claimed some indulgence? But I disdain those excuses, which only a candid adversary would allow. I can meet Mr. Davis on the hard ground of controversy, and retort on his own head the charge of concealing a part of the truth. He himself has dared to suppress the words of my text, which immediately followed his quotation. "Before that time the various accidents of war "and commerce might indeed diffuse an imperfect knowledge of the "Gospel among the tribes of Caledonia, and among the borderers of "the Rhine, the Danube, and the Euphrates;" and Mr. Davis has likewise suppressed one of the justificatory Notes on this passage, which expressly points out the time and circumstances of the first Gothic conversions. These exceptions, which I had cautiously inserted, and Mr. Davis has cautiously concealed, are superfluous for the provinces of Thrace, Mæsia,[b] and the Lesser Armenia, which were contained within the precincts of the Roman Empire. They allow an ample scope for the more early conversion of some independent districts of Dacia and the Greater Armenia, which bordered on the Danube and Euphrates; and the entire sense of this passage, which Mr. Davis first mutilates and then attacks, is perfectly consistent with the original text of the learned Mosheim.

And yet I will fairly confess, that after a nicer inquiry into the epoch of the Armenian Church, I am not satisfied with the accuracy of my own expression. The assurance that the first Christian King, and the first Archbishop, Tiridates, and St. Gregory the Illuminator, were still alive several years after the death of Constantine, inclined me to believe, that the conversion of Armenia was posterior to the auspicious Revolution, which had given the scepter of Rome to the hands of an orthodox Emperor. But I had not enough considered the two following circumstances. 1. I might have recollected the dates

---

[a] *II*. Ecclesiastical   [b] *II*. Mœsia

assigned by Moses of Chorene, who, on this occasion, may be regarded as a competent witness. Tiridates ascended the throne of Armenia in the third year of Diocletian (Hist. Armeniæ, l. ii. c. 79. p. 207.), and St. Gregory, who was invested with the Episcopal character in the seventeenth year of Tiridates, governed almost thirty years the Church of Armenia, and disappeared from the world in the forty-sixth year of the reign of the same Prince. (Hist. Armeniæ, l. ii. c. 88. p. 224, 225.) The consecration of St. Gregory must therefore be placed A.D. 303, and the conversion of the King and kingdom was soon atchieved by that successful missionary. 2. The unjust and inglorious war which Maximin undertook against the Armenians, the ancient faithful allies of the Republic, was evidently derived from a motive of superstitious zeal. The historian Eusebius (Hist. Eccles. l. ix. c. 8. p. 448. edit. Cantab.) considers the pious Armenians as a nation of Christians, who bravely defended themselves from the hostile oppression of an idolatrous tyrant. Instead of maintaining "that the conversion of Armenia was not "attempted with any degree of success till the scepter was in the "hands of an orthodox Emperor," I ought to have observed, that the seeds of the faith were deeply sown during the season of the last and greatest persecution, that many Roman exiles might assist the labours of Gregory, and that the renowned Tiridates, the hero of the East, may dispute with Constantine the honour of being the first Sovereign who embraced the Christian religion.

In a future edition, I shall rectify an expression which, in strictness, can only be applied to the kingdoms of Iberia and Æthiopia. Had the error been exposed by Mr. Davis himself, I should not have been ashamed to correct it; but *I am* ashamed at being reduced to contend with an adversary who is unable to discover, or to improve his own advantages.

But instead of prosecuting any inquiry from whence the public might have gained instruction, and himself credit, Mr. Davis chuses to perplex his readers with some angry cavils about the progress of the Gospel in the second century. What does he mean to establish or to refute? Have I denied, that before the end of that period Christianity was very widely diffused both in the East and in the West? Has not Justin Martyr affirmed, without exception or limitation, that it was already preached to *every* nation on the face of the earth? Is that proposition true at present? Could it be true in the time of Justin? Does not Mosheim acknowledge the exaggeration?

"Demus, nec enim quæ in occulos incurrunt infitiari audemus, esse
"in his verbis exaggerationis nonnihil. Certum enim est diu post
"Justini ætatem, multas orbis terrarum geɳtes cognitione Christi
"caruisse." (Mosheim de Rebus Christianis, p. 203.) Does he not
expose (p. 205.) with becoming scorn and indignation, the falsehood and vanity of the hyperboles of Tertullian? "bonum hominem
"æstu imaginationis elatum non satis adtendisse ad ea quæ litteris
"consignabat."

The high esteem which Mr. Davis expresses for the writings of
Mosheim, would alone convince me[a] how little he has read them,
since he must have been perpetually offended and disgusted by a
train of thinking, the most repugnant to his own. His jealousy, however, for the honour of Mosheim, provokes him to arraign the boldness of Mr. Gibbon, who presumes *falsely* to charge such an eminent
man with *unjustifiable assertions*[9]. I might observe, that my style,
which on this occasion was more modest and moderate, has acquired,
perhaps undesignedly, an illiberal cast from the rough hand of Mr.
Davis. But as my veracity is impeached, I may be less solicitious
about my politeness; and though I have repeatedly declined the
fairest opportunities of correcting the errors of my predecessors, yet
as long as I have truth on my side, I am not easily daunted by the
names of the most eminent men.

The assertion of Mosheim, which did not seem to be justified[1]
by the authority of Lactantius, was, that the wife and daughter of
Diocletian, Prisca and *Valeria*, had been privately *baptized*. Mr.
Davis is sure that the words of Mosheim, "Christianis sacris clam
"initiata," need not be confined to the rite of baptism; and he is
equally sure, that the reference to Mosheim does not lead us to discover even the name of Valeria. In both these assurances he is
grossly mistaken; but it is the misfortune of controversy, that an
error may be committed in three or four words, which cannot be
rectified in less than thirty or forty lines.

1. The true and the sole meaning of the Christian initiation,
one of the familiar and favourite allusions of the Fathers of the
fourth century, is clearly explained by the exact and laborious
Bingham. "The baptized were also styled ὅι μεμνημενοι, which the
"Latins call *initiati*, the initiated, that is admitted to the use of

---

[9] Davis, p. 131.   [1] Gibbon, p. 676, Note 132.

[a] I. om. me

"the *sacred* offices, and knowledge of the*a* *sacred* mysteries of the
"Christian Religion. Hence came that form of speaking so fre-
"quently used by St. Chrysostom, and other ancient writers, when
"they touched upon any doctrines or mysteries which the Cate-
"chumens understood not ισασιν ὁι μεμνημενοι, the initiated
"know what is spoken. St. Ambrose writes a book to these *initiati*;
"Isidore of Pelusium, and Hesychius call them μυσται and μυστα-
"γωγητοι. Whence the Catechumens have the contrary names,
"Αμυστοι, Αμυητοι, Αμυσταγωγητοι, the uninitiated or un-
"baptized." (Antiquities of the Christian Church, l. i. c. 4. N° 2.
vol. i. p. 11. fol. edit.) Had I presumed to suppose that Mosheim
was capable of employing a technical expression in a loose and equivocal sense, I should indeed have violated the respect which I have
always entertained for his learning and abilities.

2. But Mr. Davis cannot discover in the text of Mosheim the name
of Valeria. In that case Mosheim would have suffered another slight
inaccuracy to drop from his pen, as the passage of Lactantius,
"sacrificio pollui coegit," on which he founds his assertion, includes
the names both of Prisca and Valeria. But I am not reduced to the
necessity of accusing another in my own defence. Mosheim has
properly and expressly declared that Valeria imitated the pious
example of her mother Prisca, "Gener Diocletiani uxorem habebat
"*Valeriam* matris exemplum pietate erga Deum imitantem et a cultu
"fictorum Numinum alienam.["]¹ (Mosheim, p. 913.) Mr. Davis has
a bad habit of greedily snapping at the first words of a reference,
without giving himself the trouble of going to the end of the page
or paragraph.²²

These trifling and peevish cavils would, perhaps, have been confounded with some criticisms of the same stamp, on which I had
bestowed a slight, though sufficient notice, in the beginning of this
article of Mosheim; had not my attention been awakened by a perora-
tion worthy of Tertullian himself, if Tertullian had been devoid of
eloquence as well as of moderation—"Much less does the Christian
"Mosheim give our *infidel Historian* any pretext for inserting that
"*illiberal malignant insinuation*, "That Christianity has, in every
"age, acknowledged its important obligations to FEMALE devotion;"
"the remark is truly *contemptible*⁽²⁾."

(2) Davis, p. 132.

---

a *I. om.* the

It is not my design to fill whole pages with a tedious enumeration of the many illustrious examples[a] of female Saints, who, in every age, and almost in every country, have promoted the interest of Christianity. Such instances will readily offer themselves to those who have the slightest knowledge of Ecclesiastical History; nor is it necessary that I should remind them how much the charms, the influence, the devotion of Clotilda, and of her great-grand-daughter Bertha, contributed to the conversion of France and England. Religion may accept, without a blush, the services of the purest and most gentle portion of the human species: but there are some advocates who would disgrace Christianity, if Christianity could be disgraced, by the manner in which they defend her cause.

XV.

TILLEMONT.

As I could not readily procure the works of Gregory of Nyssa, I borrowed[3] from the accurate and indefatigable Tillemont, a passage in the Life of Gregory Thaumaturgus, or the Wonderworker, which affirmed that when the Saint took possession of his Episcopal See, he found only SEVENTEEN *Christians* in the city of Neo-Cæsarea, and the adjacent country, "Les environs, la Campagne, "le pays d'alentour." (Mem. Eccles. Tom. iv. p. 677. 691. Edit. Brusselles, 1706). These expressions of Tillemont, to whom I explicitly acknowledged my obligation, appeared synonymous to the word *Diocese*, the whole territory intrusted to the pastoral care of the Wonder-worker, and I added the epithet of *extensive*; because I was apprised that Neo-Cæsarea was the capital of the Polemoniac Pontus, and that the whole kingdom of Pontus, which stretched above five hundred miles along the coast of the Euxine, was divided between sixteen or seventeen Bishops. (See the Geographia Ecclesiastica of Charles de St. Paul, and Lucas Holstenius,[b] p. 249, 250, 251.) Thus far I may not be thought to have deserved any censure; but the omission of the subsequent part of the same passage, which imports that at his death the Wonder-worker left no more than *seventeen Pagans*, may seem to wear a partial and suspicious aspect.

[3] Gibbon, p. 605. N. 156.

---

[a] *I.* examples of female devotions, which *changed in Errata corrected in Errata*

[b] *I.* Hostenius

Let me therefore first observe, as some evidence of an impartial disposition, that I *easily* admitted, as the cool observation of the philosophic Lucian, the angry and interested complaint of the false prophet Alexander, that Pontus was filled with Christians. This complaint was made under the reigns of Marcus or of Commodus, with whom the impostor so admirably exposed by Lucian was contemporary: and I had contented myself with remarking that the numbers of Christians must have been very unequally distributed in the several parts of Pontus, since the diocese of Neo-Cæsarea contained, above sixty years afterwards, only seventeen Christians. Such was the inconsiderable flock which Gregory began to feed about the year two hundred and forty, and the real or fabulous conversions ascribed to[a] that Wonder-working Bishop during a reign of thirty years, are totally foreign to the state of Christianity in the preceding century. This obvious reflection may serve to answer the objection of Mr. Davis[4], and of another adversary[5], who on this occasion is more liberal than Mr. Davis of those harsh epithets so familiar to the tribe of Polemics.

XVI.

Pagi.

"Mr. Gibbon says[6], "Pliny was sent into Bithynia (according to "Pagi) in the year 110."

"Now that accurate Chronologer places it in the year 102. See the "fact *recorded* in his Critica-Historico-Chronologica in Annales "C. Baronii, A. D. 102. p. 99. fæc. ii. § 3."

"I appeal to my reader, Whether this anachronism does not plainly "prove that our Historian never looked into Pagi's Chronology, "though he has not hesitated to make a pompous reference to him "in his note[7]?

I cannot help observing, that either Mr. Davis's Dictionary is extremely confined, or that in his Philosophy all sins are of equal magnitude. Every error of fact or language, every instance where he does not know to reconcile the original and the reference, he expresses by the gentle word of *misrepresentation*.[b] An inaccurate appeal to the sentiment of Pagi, on a subject where I must have been

[4] Davis, p. 136, 137.   [5] Dr. Randolph, in Chelsum's Remarks, p. 159, 160.
[6] Gibbon, p. 605. N. 157.   [7] Davis, p. 140.

---

[a] *I.* by *corrected in Errata*   [b] *I. om. italics*

perfectly disinterested, might have been styled a lapse of memory, instead of being censured as the effect of vanity and ignorance. Pagi is neither a difficult nor an uncommon writer, nor could I hope to derive much additional fame from a *pompous* quotation of his writings which I had never seen.

The words employed by Mr. Davis, of *fact*, of *record*, of *anachronism*, are unskilfully chosen, and so unhappily applied, as to betray a very shameful ignorance, either of the English language, or of the nature of this Chronological Question. The date of Pliny's government of Bithynia is not a fact recorded by any ancient writer, but an opinion which modern critics have variously formed, from the consideration of presumptive and collateral evidence. Cardinal Baronius placed the consulship of Pliny one year too late;[23] and, as he was persuaded that[a] the old practice of the republic still subsisted, he naturally supposed that Pliny obtained his province immediately after the expiration of his consulship. He therefore sends him into Bithynia in the year which, according to his erroneous computation, coincided with the year one hundred and four, (Baron. Annal. Eccles. A. D. 103. N° 1. 104. N° 1), or, according to the true chronology, with the year one hundred and two, of the Christian Æra. This mistake of Baronius, Pagi, with the assistance of his friend Cardinal Noris, undertakes to correct. From an accurate parallel of the Annals of Trajan and the Epistles of Pliny, he deduces his proofs that Pliny remained at Rome several years after his Consulship: by his own ingenious, though sometimes fanciful theory, of the imperial Quinquennalia, &c. Pagi at last discovers that Pliny made his entrance into Bithynia in the year one hundred and ten. "Plinius igitur anno "Christi CENTESIMO DECIMO Bithyniam intravit." Pagi, tom. i. p. 100.

I will be more indulgent to my adversary than he has been to me. I will admit, that he has *looked into Pagi*; but I must add, that he has only looked into that accurate Chronologer. To rectify the errors, which, in the course of a laborious and original work, had escaped the diligence of the Cardinal, was the arduous task which Pagi proposed to execute: and for the sake of perspicuity, he distributes his criticisms according to the particular dates, whether just or faulty, of the Chronology of Baronius himself. Under the year 102, Mr. Davis confusedly saw a long argument about Pliny and Bithynia, and without condescending to read the Author whom he *pompously*

---

[a] *I. om.* that *Supplied in Errata*

quotes, this hasty Critic imputes to him the opinion which he had so laboriously destroyed.

My readers, if any readers have accompanied me thus far, must be satisfied, and indeed satiated, with the repeated proofs which I have made of the weight and temper of my adversary's weapons. They have, in every assault, fallen dead and lifeless to the ground: they have more than once recoiled, and dangerously wounded, the unskilful hand that had presumed to use them. I have now examined all the *misrepresentations* and *inaccuracies*, which even for a moment could perplex the ignorant, or deceive the credulous; the *few* imputations which I have neglected, are still more palpably false, or still more evidently trifling, and even the friends of Mr. Davis will scarcely continue to ascribe my contempt to my fear.

PLAGIARISMS.

The first part of his Critical Volume might admit, though it did not deserve, a particular reply. But the easy, though tedious compilation, which fills the remainder[8], and which Mr. Davis has produced as the evidence of my shameful *plagiarisms*, may be set in its true light by three or four short and general reflexions. I. Mr. Davis has disposed, in two columns, the passages which he thinks proper to select from my Two last Chapters, and the corresponding passages from Middleton, Barbeyrac, Beausobre, Dodwell, &c. to the most important of which he had been regularly guided by my own quotations. According to the opinion which he has conceived of literary property, to *agree* is to *follow*, and to *follow* is to *steal*.[24] He celebrates his own sagacity with loud and reiterated applause, and[a] declares with infinite facetiousness, that if he restored to every author the passages which Mr. Gibbon has purloined, *he* would appear as naked as the proud and gaudy Daw in the Fable, when each bird had plucked away its own plumes. Instead of being angry with Mr. Davis for the parallel which he has extended to so great a length, I am under some obligation to his industry for the copious proofs which he has furnished the reader, that my representation of some of the most important facts of Ecclesiastical Antiquity, is supported by the authority or opinion of the most

_____

[8] Davis, p. 168-274.

a I. om. and *Supplied in Errata*

ingenious and learned of the modern writers. The Public may not, perhaps, be very eager to assist Mr. Davis in his favourite amusement of *depluming* me. They may think that if the materials which compose my Two last Chapters are curious and valuable, it is of little moment to whom they properly belong. If my readers are satisfied with the form, the colours, the new arrangement which I have given to the labours of my predecessors, they may perhaps consider me not as a contemptible Thief, but as an honest and industrious Manufacturer, who has fairly procured the raw materials, and worked them up with a laudable degree of skill and success.

II. About two hundred years ago, the Court of Rome discovered that the system which had been erected by ignorance must be defended and countenanced by the aid, or at least by the abuse, of science. The grosser legends of the middle ages were abandoned to contempt, but the supremacy and infallibility of two hundred Popes, the virtues of many thousand Saints, and the miracles which they either performed or related, have been laboriously consecrated in the Ecclesiastical Annals of Cardinal Baronius. A Theological Barometer might be formed, of which the Cardinal and our countryman Dr. Middleton should constitute the opposite and remote extremities, as the former sunk to the lowest degree of credulity, which was compatible with learning, and the latter rose to the highest pitch of scepticism, in any wise consistent with Religion. The intermediate gradations would be filled by a line of ecclesiastical critics, whose rank has been fixed by the circumstances of their temper and studies, as well as by the spirit of the church or society to which they were attached. It would be amusing enough to calculate the weight of prejudice in the air of Rome, of Oxford, of Paris, and of Holland; and sometimes to observe the irregular tendency of Papists towards freedom, sometimes to remark the unnatural gravitation of Protestants towards slavery.[25] But it is useful to borrow the assistance of so many learned and ingenious men, who have viewed the first ages of the Church in every light, and from every situation. If we skilfully combine the passions and prejudices, the hostile motives and intentions, of the several theologians, we may frequently extract knowledge from credulity, moderation from zeal, and impartial truth from the most disingenuous controversy. It is the right, it is the duty of a critical historian to collect, to weigh, to select the opinions of his predecessors; and the more diligence he has exerted in the search, the more rationally he may hope to add some improvement to the stock of knowledge, the use of which has been common to all.

III. Besides the ideas which may be suggested by the study of the most learned and ingenious of the moderns, the historian may be indebted to them for the occasional communication of some passages of the ancients, which might otherwise have escaped his knowledge or his memory. In the consideration of any extensive subject, none will pretend to have read all that has been written, or to recollect all that they have read: nor is there any disgrace in recurring to the writers who have professedly treated any questions, which in the course of a long narrative we are called upon to mention in a slight and incidental manner. If I touch upon the obscure and fanciful theology of the Gnostics, I can accept without a blush the assistance of the candid Beausobre; and when, amidst the fury of contending parties, I trace the progress of ecclesiastical dominion, I am not ashamed to confess myself the grateful disciple of the impartial Mosheim. In the next Volume of my History, the Reader and the Critic must prepare themselves to see me make a still more liberal use of the labours of those indefatigable workmen who have dug deep into the mine of antiquity. The Fathers of the fourth and fifth centuries are far more voluminous than their predecessors; the writings of Jerom, of Augustin, of Chrysostom, &c. cover the walls of our libraries. The smallest part is of the historical kind: yet the treatises which seem the least to invite the curiosity of the reader, frequently conceal very useful hints, or very valuable facts. The polemic who involves himself and his antagonists in a cloud of argumentation, sometimes relates the origin and progress of the heresy which he confutes; and the preacher who declaims against the luxury, describes the manners, of the age; and seasonably introduces the mention of some public calamity, that he may ascribe it to the justice of offended Heaven. It would surely be unreasonable to expect that the historian should peruse enormous volumes, with the uncertain hope of extracting a few interesting lines, or that he should sacrifice whole days to the momentary amusement of his Reader. Fortunately for us both, the diligence of ecclesiastical critics has facilitated our inquiries: the compilations of Tillemont might alone be considered as an immense repertory of truth and fable, of almost all that the Fathers have preserved, or invented, or believed; and if we equally avail ourselves of the labours of contending sectaries, we shall often discover, that the same passages which the prudence of one of the disputants would have suppressed or disguised, are placed in the most conspicuous light by the active and interested zeal of his adversary. On these occasions, what is the duty of a faithful historian, who derives from some modern writer the knowledge of some ancient testimony, which he is desirous of introducing into his own narrative? It is his duty, and it has been my invariable practice, to consult the original; to study with attention the words, the design, the spirit, the context, the situation of the passage to which I had been referred; and before I appropriated it to my own use, to justify my own declaration, "that I had carefully examined all the original "materials that could illustrate the subject which I had undertaken "to treat." If this important obligation has sometimes been imperfectly fulfilled, I have only omitted what it would have been impracticable for me to perform. The greatest city in the world is still destitute of that useful institution, a public library; and the writer who has undertaken to treat any large historical subject, is reduced to the necessity of purchasing, for his private use, a numerous and valuable collection of the books which must form the basis of his work. The diligence of his booksellers will not always prove successful; and the candour of his readers will not *always*[a] expect, that, for the sake of verifying an accidental quotation of ten lines, he should load himself with a useless and expensive series of ten volumes. In a very few instances, where I had not the opportunity of consulting the originals, I have adopted their testimony on the faith of modern guides, of whose fidelity I was satisfied; but on these occasions[9], instead of decking myself with the borrowed plumes of Tillemont or Lardner, I have been most scrupulously exact in marking the extent of my reading, and the source of my information. This distinction, which a sense of truth and modesty had engaged me to express, is ungenerously abused by Mr. Davis, who seems happy to inform his Readers, that "in ONE instance (Chap. xvi. 164. "or, in the first edition, 163.) I have, by an unaccountable oversight, "unfortunately for myself, forgot to drop the modern, and that I "modestly disclaim all knowledge of Athanasius, but what I had "picked up from Tillemont[1]." Without animadverting on the decency of these expressions, which are now grown familiar to me,

[9] Gibbon, p. 605, N. 156; p. 606, N. 161; p. 690, N. 164; p. 699, N. 178.
[1] Davis, p. 273.

a II. om. italics

I shall content myself with observing, that as I had frequently quoted Eusebius, or Cyprian, or Tertullian, *because* I had read them; so, in this instance, I only made my reference to Tillemont, *because* I had not read, and did not possess, the works of Athanasius. The progress of my undertaking has since directed me to peruse the Historical Apologies of the Archbishop of Alexandria, whose life is a very interesting part of the age in which he lived; and if Mr. Davis should have the curiosity to look into my Second Volume, he will find that I make a free and frequent appeal to the writings of Athanasius. Whatever may be the opinion or practice of my adversary, this I apprehend to be the dealing of a fair and honourable man.

IV. The historical monuments of the three first centuries of ecclesiastical antiquity[a] are neither very numerous, nor very prolix. From the end of the Acts of the Apostles, to the time when the first Apology of Justin Martyr was presented, there intervened a dark and doubtful period of fourscore years; and, even if the Epistles of Ignatius should be approved by the critic, they could not be very serviceable to the historian. From the middle of the second to the beginning of the fourth century, we gain our knowledge of the state and progress of Christianity from the successive Apologies which were occasionally composed by Justin, Athenagoras, Tertullian, Origen, &c.; from the Epistles of Cyprian; from a few *sincere* acts of the Martyrs; from some moral or controversial tracts, which indirectly explain the events and manners of the times; from the rare and accidental notice which profane writers have taken of the Christian sect; from the declamatory Narrative which celebrates the deaths of the persecutors; and from the Ecclesiastical History of Eusebius, who has preserved some valuable fragments of more early writers. Since the revival of letters, these original materials have been the common fund of critics and historians: nor has it ever been imagined, that the absolute and exclusive property of a passage in Eusebius or Tertullian was acquired by the first who had an opportunity of quoting it. The learned work of Mosheim, *de Rebus Christianis ante Constantinum*, was printed in the year 1753; and if I were possessed of the patience and disingenuity of Mr. Davis, I would engage to find all the ancient testimonies that he has alleged, in the writings of Dodwell or Tillemont, which were published before the end of the last century. But if I were animated by any malevolent intentions against Dodwell or Tillemont, I could as easily, and as

[a] *II.* antiquities

unfairly, fix on *them* the guilt of Plagiarism, by producing the same passages transcribed or translated at full length in the Annals of Cardinal Baronius. Let not criticism be any longer disgraced by the practice of such unworthy arts. Instead of admitting suspicions as false as they are ungenerous, candour will acknowledge, that Mosheim or Dodwell, Tillemont or Baronius, enjoyed the same right, and often were under the same obligation, of quoting the passages which they had read, and which were indispensably requisite to confirm the truth and substance of their similar narratives. Mr. Davis is so far from allowing me the benefit of this common indulgence, or rather of this common right, that he stigmatizes with the name of *Plagiarism* a close and literal agreement with Dodwell in the account of some parts of the persecution of Diocletian, where a few chapters of Eusebius and Lactantius, perhaps of Lactantius alone, are the sole materials from whence our knowledge could be derived, and where, if I had not transcribed, I must have invented. He is even bold enough (*bold* is not the *proper* word) to conceive some hopes of persuading his readers, that an Historian who has employed several years of his life, and several hundred pages, on the Decline and Fall of the Roman Empire, had never read Orosius, or the Augustan History; and that he was forced to borrow, at second-hand, his quotations from the Theodosian Code. I cannot profess myself very desirous of Mr. Davis's acquaintance; but if he will take the trouble of calling at my house any afternoon when I am *not* at home, my servant shall shew him my library, which he will find tolerably well furnished with the useful authors, ancient as well as modern, ecclesiastical as well as profane, who have *directly* supplied me with the materials of my History.

The peculiar reasons, and they are not of the most flattering kind, which urged me to repel the furious and feeble attack of Mr. Davis, have been already mentioned. But since I am drawn thus reluctantly into the lists of controversy, I shall not retire till I have saluted, either with stern defiance or gentle courtesy, the theological champions who have signalized their ardour to break a lance against the shield of a *Pagan* adversary. The fifteenth and sixteenth Chapters have been honoured with the notice of several writers, whose names and characters seemed to promise more maturity of judgment and learning than could reasonably be expected from the unfinished studies of a Batchelor of Arts. The Reverend Mr. Apthorpe, Dr. Watson, the Regius Professor of Divinity in the University of

Cambridge, Dr. Chelsum of Christ Church, and his associate Dr. Randolph, President of Christ Church College, and the Lady Margaret's Professor of Divinity in the University of Oxford, have given me a fair right, which, however, I shall not abuse, of freely declaring my opinion on the subject of their respective criticisms.

MR. APTHORPE.

If I am not mistaken, Mr. Apthorpe was the first who announced to the Public his intention of examining the interesting subject which I had treated in the Two last Chapters of my History. The multitude of collateral and accessary ideas which presented themselves to the Author insensibly swelled the bulk of his papers to the size of a large volume in octavo; the publication was delayed many months beyond the time of the first advertisement; and when Mr. Apthorpe's Letters appeared, I was surprised to find, that I had *scarcely* any interest or concern in their contents. They are filled with general observations on the Study of History, with a large and useful catalogue of Historians, and with a variety of reflections, moral and religious, all preparatory to the direct and formal consideration of my Two last Chapters, which Mr. Apthorpe seems to reserve for the subject of a second Volume. I sincerely respect the learning, the piety, and the candour of this Gentleman, and must consider it as a mark of his esteem, that he has thought proper to begin his approaches at so great a distance from the fortifications which he designed to attack.

DR. WATSON.

When Dr. Watson gave to the Public his Apology for Christianity, in a Series of Letters, he addressed them to the Author of the Decline and Fall of the Roman Empire, with a just confidence that he had considered this important object in a manner not unworthy of his antagonist or of himself. Dr. Watson's mode of thinking bears a liberal and philosophic[a] cast; his thoughts are expressed with spirit, and that spirit is always tempered by politeness and moderation. Such is the man whom I should be happy to call my friend, and whom I should not blush to call my antagonist. But the same motives which might tempt me to accept, or even to solicit, a private and amicable conference, dissuaded me from entering into a public

[a] *II.* a philosophic

A VINDICATION

controversy with a Writer of so respectable a character; and I embraced the earliest opportunity of expressing to Dr. Watson himself,
how sincerely I agreed with him in thinking, "That as the world is
"now possessed of the opinion of us both upon the subject in
"question, it may be perhaps as proper for us both to leave it in this
"state[2]." The nature of the ingenious Professor's Apology contributed to strengthen the insuperable reluctance to engage in hostile
altercation which was common to us both, by convincing me, that
such an altercation was unnecessary as well as unpleasant. He very
justly and politely declares, that a considerable part, near seventy
pages, of his small volume are not directed to me[3], but to a set of
men whom he places in an odious and contemptible light. He leaves
to other hands the defence of the leading Ecclesiastics, even of the
primitive church; and without being *very* anxious, either to soften
their vices and indiscretion, or to aggravate the cruelty of the
Heathen Persecutors, he passes over in silence the greatest part of
my Sixteenth Chapter. It is not so much the purpose of the Apologist to examine the facts which have been advanced by the Historian,
as to remove the impressions which may have been formed by many
of his Readers; and the remarks of Dr. Watson consist more properly
of general argumentation than of particular criticism. He fairly owns,
that I have expressly allowed the full and irresistible weight of the
first great cause of the success of Christianity[4], and he is too candid
to deny that the five *secondary* causes, which I had attempted to
explain, operated with *some* degree of active energy towards the
accomplishment of that great event. The only question which remains between us, relates to the *degree* of the weight and effect of
those secondary causes; and as I am persuaded that our philosophy
is not of the dogmatic kind, we should soon acknowledge that this
precise degree cannot be ascertained by reasoning, nor perhaps be
expressed by words. In the course of this enquiry, some incidental
difficulties have arisen, which I had stated with impartiality, and
which Dr. Watson resolves with ingenuity and temper. If in some
instances he seems to have misapprehended my sentiments, I may
hesitate whether I should impute the fault to my own want of clearness or to his want of attention, but I can never entertain a suspicion
that Dr. Watson would descend to employ the disingenuous arts of
vulgar controversy.

[2] Watson's Apology for Christianity, p. 200.   [3] Id. p. 202–268.   [4] Watson's Apology for Christianity, p. 5.

There is, however, one passage, and one passage only, which must not pass without some explanation; and I shall the more eagerly embrace this occasion to illustrate what I had said, as the misconstruction of my true meaning seems to have made an involuntary, but unfavourable, impression on the liberal mind of Dr. Watson. As I endeavour *not* to palliate the severity, but to discover the motives, of the Roman Magistrates, I had remarked, "it was in "vain that the oppressed Believer asserted the unalienable rights of "conscience and private judgment. Though his situation might excite "the pity, his arguments could never reach the understanding, either "of the philosophic or of the believing part of the Pagan world[5]." The humanity of Dr. Watson takes fire on the supposed provocation, and he asks me with unusual quickness, "How, Sir, are the argu-"ments for liberty of conscience so exceedingly inconclusive, that "you think them incapable of reaching the understanding even of "philosophers[6]?" He continues to observe, that a captious adversary would embrace with avidity the opportunity this passage *affords* of blotting my character with the odious stain of being a Persecutor; a stain which no learning can wipe out, which no genius or ability can render amiable; and though he himself does not entertain such an opinion of my principles, his ingenuity tries in vain to provide me with the means of escape.

I must lament that I have not been successful in the explanation of a very simple notion of the spirit both of philosophy and of polytheism, which I have repeatedly inculcated. The arguments which assert the rights of conscience are not inconclusive in themselves, but the understanding of the Greeks and Romans was fortified against their evidence by an invincible prejudice. When we listen to the voice of Bayle, of Locke, and of genuine reason, in favour of religious toleration, we shall easily perceive that our most forcible appeal is made to our mutual feelings. If the Jew were[a] allowed to argue with the Inquisitor, he would request that for a moment they might exchange their different situations, and might safely ask his Catholic Tyrant, whether the fear of death would compel *him* to enter the synagogue,[b] to receive the mark of circumcision, and to partake of the paschal lamb. As soon as the case of persecution was brought home to the breast of the Inquisitor, he must have found

[5] Gibbon, p. 625.   [6] Watson, p. 185.

[a] *I.* was *corrected in Errata*   [b] *I.* syna-/as gogue *corrected in Errata.*

some difficulty in suppressing the dictates of natural equity, which would insinuate to his conscience, that he could have no right to inflict those punishments which, under similar circumstances, he would esteem it as his duty to encounter. But this argument could not reach the understanding of a Polytheist, or of an ancient Philosopher. The former was ready, whenever he was summoned, or indeed without being summoned, to fall prostrate before the altars of any Gods who were adored in any part of the world, and to admit a vague persuasion of the *truth* and divinity of the most different modes of religion. The Philosopher, who considered them, at least in their literal sense, as equally *false* and absurd, was not ashamed to disguise his sentiments, and to frame his actions according to the laws of his country, which imposed the same obligation on the philosophers and the people. When Pliny declared, that whatever was the opinion of the Christians, their obstinacy deserved punishment, the absurd cruelty of Pliny was excused in his own eye, by the consciousness that, in the situation of the Christians, he would not have refused the religious compliance which he exacted. I shall not repeat, that the Pagan worship was a matter, not of *opinion*, but of *custom*; that the toleration of the Romans was confined to nations or families who followed the practice of their ancestors; and that in the first ages of Christianity their persecution of the individuals who departed from the established religion was neither moderated by pure reason, nor inflamed by exclusive zeal. But I only desire to appeal from the hasty apprehension to the more deliberate judgment of Dr. Watson himself. Should there still remain any difference of opinion between us, I shall be satisfied, if he will consider me as a sincere, though perhaps unsuccessful, lover of truth, and as a firm friend to civil and ecclesiastical freedom.

Dr. Chelsum and Dr. Randolph.

Far be it from me, or from any faithful Historian, to impute to respectable societies the faults of some individual members. Our two Universities most undoubtedly contain the same mixture, and most probably the same proportions, of zeal and moderation, of reason and superstition. Yet there is much less difference between the smoothness of the Ionic and the roughness of the Doric dialect, than may be found between the polished style of Dr. Watson, and the coarse language of Mr. Davis, Dr. Chelsum, or Dr. Randolph.

The second of these Critics, Dr. Chelsum of Christ Church, is unwilling that the world should forget that *he* was the first who sounded to arms, that *he* was the first who furnished the antidote to the poison, and who, as early as the month of October of the year 1776, published his *Strictures* on the Two last Chapters of Mr. Gibbon's History. The success of a pamphlet, which he modestly styles imperfect and ill-digested, encouraged him to resume the controversy. In the beginning of the present year, his Remarks made their second appearance, with some alteration of form, and a large increase of bulk; and the author, who seems to fight under the protection of two episcopal banners, has prefixed, in the front of his volume, his name and titles, which in the former edition he had less honourably suppressed. His confidence is fortified by the alliance and communications of a *distinguished* Writer, Dr. Randolph, &c. who, on a proper occasion, would, no doubt, be ready to bear as honourable testimony to the merit and reputation of Dr. Chelsum. The two friends are indeed so happily united by art and nature, that if the author of the Remarks had not pointed out the valuable communications of the Margaret Professor, it would have been impossible to separate their respective property. Writers who possess any freedom of mind, may be known from each other by the peculiar character of their style and sentiments; but the champions who are inlisted in the service of Authority, commonly wear the uniform of the regiment. Oppressed with the same yoke, covered with the same trappings, they heavily move along, perhaps not with an equal pace, in the same beaten track of prejudice and preferment. Yet I should expose my own injustice, were I absolutely to confound with Mr. Davis the two Doctors in Divinity, who are joined in one volume. The three Critics appear to be animated by the same implacable resentment against the Historian of the Roman Empire; they are alike disposed to support the same opinions by the same arts; and if in the language of the two latter the disregard of politeness is somewhat less gross and indecent, the difference is not of such a magnitude as to excite in my breast any lively sensations of gratitude. It was the misfortune of Mr. Davis that he undertook to *write* before he had *read*. He set out with the stock of authorities which he found in my quotations, and boldly ventured to play his reputation against mine. Perhaps he may now repent of a loss which is not easily recovered; but if I had not surmounted my almost insuperable reluctance to a public dispute, many a reader might still be dazzled by the

vehemence of his assertions, and might still believe that Mr. Davis
had detected several wilful and important misrepresentations in my
Two last Chapters. But the confederate Doctors appear to be scholars
of a higher form and longer experience; they enjoy a certain rank in
their academical world; and as their zeal is enlightened by some rays
of knowledge, so their desire to ruin the credit of their adversary is
occasionally checked by the apprehension of injuring their own.
These restraints, to which Mr. Davis was a stranger, have confined
them to a very narrow and humble path of historical criticism; and
if I were to correct, according to their wishes, all the particular facts
against which they have advanced any objections, these corrections,
admitted in their fullest extent, would hardly furnish materials for
a decent list of *errata*.

The *dogmatical* part of their work, which in every sense of the
word deserves that appellation, is ill adapted to engage my attention.
I had declined the consideration of theological arguments, when they
were managed by a candid and liberal adversary; and it would be
inconsistent enough, if I should have refused to draw my sword in
honourable combat against the keen and well-tempered weapon of
Dr. Watson, for the sole purpose of encountering the rustic cudgel
of two staunch and sturdy Polemics.

I shall not enter any farther into the character and conduct of
Cyprian, as I am sensible that if the opinion of Le Clerc, Mosheim,
and myself, is reprobated by Dr. Chelsum and his ally, the difference must subsist, till we shall entertain the same notions of moral
virtue and Ecclesiastical power[7]. If Dr. Randolph will allow that
the primitive Clergy received, managed, and distributed the tythes,
and other charitable donations of the faithful, the dispute between
us, will be a dispute of words[8]. I shall not amuse myself with proving that the learned Origen must have derived from the *inspired*
authority of the Church his knowledge, not indeed of the *authenticity*,
but of the *inspiration* of the *four* Evangelists, *two* of whom are not in
the rank of the Apostles[9]. I shall submit to the judgment of the
Public, whether the Athanasian Creed is not read and received in
the Church of England, and whether the wisest and most virtuous
of the Pagans[1] believed the Catholic faith, which is declared in the
Athanasian Creed to be absolutely necessary for salvation. As little

[7] Gibbon, p. 558, 559. Chelsum, p. 132–139.   [8] Gibbon, p. 592. Randolph
in Chelsum, p. 122.   [9] Gibbon, p. 551. Note 33. Chelsum, p. 39.   [1] Gibbon,
p. 565, Note 70. Chelsum, p. 66.

shall I think myself interested in the elaborate disquisitions with which the Author of the Remarks has filled a great number of pages, concerning the famous testimony of Josephus, the passages of Irenæus and Theophilus, which relate to the gift of miracles, and the origin of circumcision in Palestine or in Egypt[2]. If I have rejected, and rejected with some contempt, the *interpolation* which pious fraud has very aukwardly inserted in the text of Josephus, I may deem myself secure behind the shield of learned and pious critics (See in particular Le Clerc, in his Ars Critica, part iii. sect. i. c. 15. and Lardner's Testimonies, Vol. i. p. 150, &c.), who have condemned this passage: and I think it very natural that Dr. Chelsum should embrace the contrary opinion, which is not destitute of able advocates. The passages of Irenæus and Theophilus were thoroughly sifted in the controversy about the duration of Miracles; and as the Works of Dr. Middleton may be found in every library, so it is not impossible that a diligent search may still discover some remains of the writings of his adversaries. In mentioning the confession of the Syrians of Palestine, that they had received from Egypt the rite of circumcision, I had simply alleged the testimony of Herodotus, without expressly adopting the sentiment of Marsham. But I had always imagined, that in these doubtful and indifferent questions, which have been solemnly argued before the tribunal of the Public, every scholar was at liberty to chuse his side, without assigning his reasons; nor can I yet persuade myself, that either Dr. Chelsum, or myself, are likely to enforce, by any new arguments, the opinions which we have respectively followed. The only novelty for which I can perceive myself indebted to Dr. Chelsum, is the very extraordinary Scepticism which he insinuates concerning the time of Herodotus, who, according to the chronology of some, flourished during the time of the Jewish captivity[3]. Can it be necessary to inform a Divine, that the captivity which lasted seventy years, according to the prophecy of Jeremiah, was terminated in the year 536 before Christ, by the edict which Cyrus published in the first year of his reign (Jeremiah, xxv. 11, 12. xxix. 10. Ezra, i. 1. &c. Usher and Prideaux, under the years 606 and 536.)? Can it be necessary to inform a man of letters, that Herodotus was fifty-three years old at the commencement of the Peloponnesian war (Aulus Gellius, Noct. Attic. xv. 23. from the Commentaries of Pamphila), and consequently that he was born in the year before Christ 484, fifty-two

[2] Chelsum's Remarks, p. 13-19. 67-91. 180-185.   [3] Chelsum, p. 15

years after the end of the Jewish captivity? As this well attested fact is not exposed to the slightest doubt or difficulty, I am somewhat curious to learn the names of those unknown authors, whose chronology Dr. Chelsum has allowed as the specious foundation of a probable hypothesis. The Author of the Remarks, does not seem indeed to have cultivated, with much care or success, the province of literary history; as a very moderate acquaintance with that useful branch of knowledge would have saved him from a positive mistake, much less excusable than the doubt which he entertains about the time of Herodotus. He styles Suidas "a *Heathen* writer, who lived "about the end of the *tenth* century[4]." I admit the period which he assigns to Suidas; and which is well ascertained by Dr. Bentley (See his Reply to Boyle, p. 22, 23.) We are led to fix this epoch by the chronology which this *Heathen* writer has deduced from Adam, to the death of the emperor John Zimisces, A. D. 975: and a crowd of passages might be produced, as the unanswerable evidence of his Christianity. But the most unanswerable of all is the very date, which is not disputed between us. The philosophers who flourished under Justinian (See Agathias, l. ii. p. 65, 66.),[26] appear to have been the last of the Heathen writers: and the ancient religion of the Greeks was annihilated almost four hundred years before the birth of Suidas.

After this animadversion, which is not intended either to insult the failings of my Adversary, or to provide a convenient excuse for my own errors, I shall proceed to select *two* important parts of Dr. Chelsum's Remarks, from which the candid reader may form some opinion of the whole. They relate to the military service of the first Christians, and to the historical character of Eusebius; and I shall review them with the less reluctance, as it may not be impossible to pick up something curious and useful even in the barren waste of controversy.

I.

MILITARY SERVICE OF THE FIRST CHRISTIANS.

In representing the errors of the primitive Christians, which flowed from an excess of virtue, I had observed, *that* they exposed themselves to the reproaches of the Pagans, by their obstinate refusal

[4] Chelsum, p. 73.

to take an active part in the civil administration, or military defence of the empire; *that* the objections of Celsus appear to have been mutilated by his adversary Origen, and *that* the Apologists, to whom the public dangers were urged, returned obscure and ambiguous answers, as they were unwilling to disclose the true ground of their security, their opinion of the approaching end of the world[5]. In another place I had related, from the Acts of Ruinart, the action and punishment of the Centurion Marcellus, who was put to death for renouncing the service in a public and seditious manner[6].

On this occasion Dr. Chelsum is extremely alert. He denies my facts, controverts my opinions, and, with a politeness worthy of Mr. Davis himself, insinuates that I borrowed the story of Marcellus, not from Ruinart, but from Voltaire. My learned Adversary thinks it highly improbable that Origen should dare to *mutilate* the objections of Celsus, "whose work was, in all probability, extant at the "time he made this reply. In such case, had he even been inclined to "treat his adversary unfairly, he must yet surely have been with-held "from the attempt, through the fear of detection[7]." The experience both of ancient and modern controversy, has indeed convinced me that this reasoning, just and natural as it may seem, is totally in-conclusive, and that the generality of disputants, especially in re-ligious contests, are of a much more daring and intrepid spirit. For the truth of this remark, I shall content myself with producing a recent and very singular example, in which Dr. Chelsum himself is personally interested. He charges[8] me with passing over in "silence "the important and unsuspected testimony of a Heathen historian "(Dion Cassius) to the persecution of Domitian; and he affirms, that "I have produced that testimony so far only as it relates to Clemens "and Domitilla; yet in the very same passage, follows immediately, "that on a like accusation MANY OTHERS were also condemned. "Some of them were put to death, others suffered the confiscation "of their goods[9]." Although I should not be ashamed to undertake the apology of Nero or Domitian, if I thought them innocent of any particular crime with which zeal or malice had unjustly branded their memory; yet I should indeed blush, if, in favour of tyranny, or even in favour of virtue, I had suppressed the truth and evidence of historical facts. But the Reader will feel some surprize, when he has convinced himself that, in the three editions of my First Volume,

[5] Gibbon, p. 580, 581.   [6] Id. p. 680.   [7] Chelsum, p. 118, 119.
[8] Id. p. 188.   [9] Gibbon, p. 645.

after relating the death of Clemens, and the exile of Domitilla, I continue to allege the ENTIRE TESTIMONY of Dion, in the following words: "and sentences either of death, or of confiscation, were "pronounced against a GREAT NUMBER OF PERSONS who were "involved in the SAME accusation. The guilt imputed to their charge, "was that of Atheism and Jewish manners; a singular association of "ideas which cannot with any propriety be applied except to the "Christians, as they were obscurely and imperfectly viewed by the "magistrates and writers of that period." Dr. Chelsum has not been deterred, by the fear of detection, from this scandalous mutilation of the popular work of a living adversary. But Celsus had been dead above fifty years before Origen published his Apology; and the copies of an ancient work, instead of being instantaneously multiplied by the operation of the press, were separately and slowly transcribed by the labour of the hand.

If any modern Divine should still maintain that the fidelity of Origen was secured by motives more honourable than the fear of detection, he may learn from Jerom the difference of the *gymnastic* and *dogmatic* styles. Truth is the object of the one, Victory of the other; and the same arts which would disgrace the sincerity of the teacher, serve only to display the skill of the disputant. After justifying his own practice by that of the orators and philosophers, Jerom defends himself by the more respectable authority of Christian Apologists. "How many thousand lines, says he, have been composed "against *Celsus* and Porphyry, by *Origen*, Methodius, Eusebius, "Apollinaris. Consider with what arguments, with what slippery "problems, they elude the inventions of the Devil; and how in their "controversy with the Gentiles, they are sometimes obliged to speak, "not what they really think, but what is most advantageous for the "cause they defend." "Origenes, &c. multis versuum millibus "scribunt adversus Celsum et Porphyrium. Considerate quibus "argumentis et quam lubricis problematibus diaboli spiritu contexta "subvertunt: et quia interdum coguntur loqui, non quod sentiunt, "sed quod necesse est dicunt adversus ea quæ dicunt Gentiles." (Pro Libris advers. Jovinian. Apolog. Tom. ii. p. 135.)

Yet Dr. Chelsum may still ask, and he has a right to ask, why in this particular instance I suspect the pious Origen of mutilating the objections of his adversary. From a very obvious, and, in my opinion, a very decisive circumstance. Celsus was a Greek philosopher, the friend of Lucian; and I thought that although he might support error by sophistry, he would not write nonsense in his own language. I renounce my suspicion, if the most attentive reader is able to understand the design and purport of a passage which is given as a formal quotation from Celsus, and which begins with the following words: Ου μην ουδε εκεινο ανεκτον σου λεγοντος, ως, &c. (Origen contr. Celsum, l. viii. p. 425. edit. Spencer, Cantab. 1677.) I have carefully inspected the original, I[a] have availed myself of the learning of Spencer, and even Bouhereau (for I shall always disclaim the absurd and affected pedantry of using without scruple a Latin version, but of despising the aid of a French translation), and the ill success of my efforts has countenanced the suspicion to which I still adhere, with a just mixture of doubt and hesitation. Origen very boldly denies, that any of the Christians have affirmed what is imputed to them by Celsus, in this unintelligible quotation; and it may easily be credited, that none had maintained what none can comprehend. Dr. Chelsum has produced the words of Origen; but on this occasion there is a strange ambiguity in the language of the modern Divine[1], as if he wished to insinuate what he dared not affirm; and every reader must conclude, from his state of the question, that Origen expressly denied the truth of the *accusation* of Celsus, who had *accused* the Christians of declining to assist their fellow-subjects in the military defence of the empire, assailed on every side by the arms of the Barbarians.

Will Dr. Chelsum justify to the world, can he justify to his own feelings, the abuse which he has made even of the privileges of the Gymnastic style? Careless and hasty indeed must have been his perusal of Origen, if he did not perceive that the ancient Apologist, who makes a stand on some incidental question, admits the accusation of his adversary, that the Christians *refused* to bear arms even at the command of their Sovereign. "και ου συστρατευομεθα "μην αυτω, καν επειγη." (Origen, l. viii. p. 427.) He endeavours to palliate this undutiful refusal, by representing that the Christians had their peculiar camps, in which they incessantly combated for the safety of the emperor and the empire by lifting up their right hands—in prayer. The Apologist seems to hope that his country will be satisfied with this spiritual aid, and dexterously confounding the colleges of Roman priests with the multitudes which swelled the

(1) Chelsum, p. 118.

---

a II. and I

Catholic Church, he claims for his brethren, in all the provinces, the exemption from military service, which was enjoyed by the sacerdotal order. But as this excuse might not readily be allowed, Origen looks forwards with a lively faith to that auspicious Revolution, which Celsus had rejected as impossible, when all the nations of the habitable earth, renouncing their passions and their arms, should embrace the pure doctrines of the Gospel, and lead a life of peace and innocence under the immediate protection of Heaven. The faith of Origen seems to be principally founded on the predictions of the Prophet Zephaniah (See iii. 9, 10.); and he prudently observes, that the Prophets often speak secret things (εν απορρητω λεγουσι, p. 426.) which may be understood by those who can understand them; and that if this stupendous change cannot be effected while we retain our bodies, it may be accomplished as soon as we shall be released from them. Such is the reasoning of Origen: though I have not followed the order, I have faithfully preserved the substance of it; which fully justifies the truth and propriety of my observations.

The execution of Marcellus, the Centurion, is naturally connected with the Apology of Origen, as the former declared by his actions, what the latter affirmed in his writings, that the conscience of a devout Christian would not allow him to bear arms, even at the command of his Sovereign. I had represented this religious scruple as *one* of the motives which provoked Marcellus, on the day of a public festival, to throw away the ensigns of his office; and I presumed to observe, that such an act of desertion would have been punished in any government according to martial or even civil law. Dr. Chelsum[2] very *bluntly* accuses me of misrepresenting the story, and of suppressing those circumstances which would have defended the Centurion from the unjust imputation thrown by me upon his conduct. The dispute between the Advocate for Marcellus and myself, lies in a very narrow compass; as the whole evidence is comprized in a short, simple, and, I believe, authentic narrative.

1. In another place I observed, and even pressed the observation, "that the innumerable Deities and rites of Polytheism were closely "interwoven with every circumstance of business or pleasure, of "public or of private life;" and I had particularly specified how much the Roman discipline was connected with the national superstition. A solemn oath of fidelity was repeated every year in the name of the Gods and of the genius of the Emperor, public and daily

[2] Chelsum, p. 114-117.

sacrifices were performed at the head of the camp, the legionary was continually tempted, or rather compelled to join in the idolatrous worship of his fellow-soldiers, and had not any scruples been entertained of the lawfulness of war, it is not easy to understand how any serious Christian could inlist under a banner which has been justly termed the *rival of the Cross.* "Vexilla æmula Christi." (Tertullian de Corona Militis, c. xi.) With regard to the soldiers, who before their conversion were already engaged in the military life, fear, habit, ignorance, necessity might bend them to some acts of occasional conformity; and as long as they abstained from absolute and intentional idolatry, their behaviour was excused by the indulgent, and censured by the more rigid casuists. (See the whole Treatise *De Coronâ Militis.*) We are ignorant of the adventures and character of the Centurion Marcellus, how long he had conciliated the profession of arms and of the Gospel, whether he was only a Catechumen, or whether he was initiated by the Sacrament of Baptism. We are likewise at a loss to ascertain the particular act of idolatry which so suddenly and so forcibly provoked his pious indignation. As he declared his faith in the midst of a public entertainment given on the birth-day of Galerius, he must have been startled by some of the sacred and convivial rites (Convivia ista profana reputans) of prayers, or vows, or libations, or, perhaps, by the offensive circumstance of eating the meats which had been offered to the idols. But the scruples of Marcellus were not confined to these accidental impurities; they evidently reached the essential duties of his profession; and when before the tribunal of the magistrates, he avowed his faith at the hazard of his life, the Centurion declared, as his cool and determined persuasion, that it does not become a Christian man, who is the soldier of the Lord Christ, to bear arms for any object of earthly concern. "Non enim decebat Christianum hominem molestiis "secularibus militare, qui Christo Domino militat." A formal declaration, which clearly disengages from each other the different questions of war and idolatry. With regard to both these questions, as they were understood by the primitive Christians, I wish to refer the Reader to the sentiments and authorities of Mr. Moyle, a bold and ingenious critic, who read the Fathers as their judge, and not as their slave, and who has refuted, with the most patient candour, all that learned prejudice could suggest in favour of the silly story of the thundering legion. (See Moyle's Works, Vol. ii. p. 84—88. 111—116. 163—212. 298—302. 327—341.) And here let me add, that the passage of Origen, who in the name of his brethren disclaims the duty of military service, is understood by Mr. Moyle in its true and obvious signification.

2. I know not where Dr. Chelsum has imbibed the principles of logic or morality which teach him to approve the conduct of Marcellus, who threw down his rod, his belt, and his arms, at the head of the legion, and publicly renounced the military service, *at the very time* when he found himself obliged to offer sacrifice. Yet surely this is a very false notion of the condition and duties of a Roman Centurion. Marcellus was bound, by a solemn oath, to serve with fidelity till he should be regularly discharged; and according to the sentiments which Dr. Chelsum ascribes to him, he was not released from this oath by any mistaken opinion of the unlawfulness of war. I would propose it as a case of conscience to any philosopher, or even to any casuist in Europe, Whether a particular order, which cannot be reconciled with virtue or piety, dissolves the ties of a general and lawful obligation? And whether, if they had been consulted by the Christian Centurion, they would not have directed him to increase his diligence in the execution of his military functions, to refuse to yield to any act of idolatry, and patiently to expect the consequences of such a refusal? But instead of obeying the mild and moderate dictates of religion, instead of distinguishing between the duties of the soldier and of the Christian, Marcellus, with imprudent zeal, rushed forwards to seize the crown of martyrdom. He might have privately confessed himself guilty to the tribune or præfect under whom he served: he chose on the day of a public festival to disturb the order of the camp. He insulted without necessity the religion of his Sovereign and of his country, by the epithets of contempt which he bestowed on the Roman Gods. "Deos vestros ligneos et "lapideos, adorare contemno, quæ sunt idola surda et muta." Nay more: at the head of the legion, and in the face of the standards, the Centurion Marcellus openly renounced his allegiance to the Emperors. "Ex hoc militare IMPERATORIBUS VESTRIS desisto;" From this moment I no longer serve YOUR EMPERORS, are the important words of Marcellus, which his advocate has not thought proper to translate. I again make my appeal to any lawyer, to any military man, Whether, under such circumstances, the pronoun *your* has not a seditious and even treasonable import? And whether the officer who should make this declaration, and at the same time throw away his sword at the head of the regiment, would not be

condemned for mutiny and desertion by any court-martial in Europe? I am the rather disposed to judge favourably of the conduct of the Roman government, as I cannot discover any desire to take advantage of the indiscretion of Marcellus. The Commander of the Legion seemed to lament that it was not in his power to dissemble this rash action. After a delay of more than three months, the Centurion was examined before the Vice-præfect, his superior Judge, who offered him the fairest opportunities of explaining or qualifying his seditious expressions, and at last condemned him to lose his head; not simply because he was a Christian, but because he had violated his military oath, thrown away his belt, and publicly blasphemed the Gods and the Emperors. Perhaps the impartial reader will confirm the sentence of the Vice-Præfect Agricolanus, "Ita se habent "facta Marcelli, ut hæc *disciplinâ* debeant vindicari."

Notwithstanding the plainest evidence, Dr. Chelsum will not believe that either Origen in Theory, or Marcellus in Practice, could seriously object to the use of arms; "because it is well known, that "far from declining the business of war altogether, whole legions of "Christians served in the Imperial armies[8]." I have not yet discovered, in the Author or Authors of the Remarks, many traces of a clear and enlightened understanding, yet I cannot suppose them so destitute of every reasoning principle, as to imagine that they here allude to the conduct of the Christians who embraced the profession of arms after their religion had obtained a public establishment. Whole legions of Christians served under the banners of Constantine and Justinian, as whole regiments of Christians are now inlisted in the service of France or England. The representation which I had given, was confined to the principles and practice of the Church of which Origen and Marcellus were members, before the sense of public and private interest had reduced the lofty standard of Evangelical perfection to the ordinary level of human nature. In those primitive times, where are the Christian legions that served in the Imperial armies? Our Ecclesiastical Pompeys may stamp with their foot, but no armed men will arise out of the earth, except the ghosts of the Thundering and the Thebæan legions, the former renowned for a Miracle, and the latter for a Martyrdom. Either the two Protestant Doctors must acquiesce under some imputations which are better understood than expressed, or they must prepare, in the full light and freedom of the eighteenth century, to undertake the defence of

[8] Chelsum, p. 113.

two obsolete legends,[a] the least absurd of which staggered the well-disciplined credulity of a Franciscan Friar. (See Pagi Critic. ad Annal. Baronii, A. D. 174. tom. i. p. 168.) Very different was the spirit and taste of the learned and ingenuous Dr. Jortin, who after treating the silly story of the Thundering Legion with the contempt it deserved, continues in the following words: "Moyle wishes "no greater penance to the believers of the Thundering Legion, "than that they may also believe the Martyrdom of the Thebæan "Legion." (Moyle's Works, vol. ii. p. 103): to which good wish, I say with Le Clerc (Bibliotheque A. et M. tom. xxvii. p. 193) AMEN.[27]

Qui Bavium non odit, amet tua carmina Mævi.

(Jortin's Remarks on Ecclesiastical History, vol. i. p. 367. 2d edition. London, 1767.)

[b]Yet I shall not attempt to conceal a formidable army of Christians and even of Martyrs, which is ready to inlist under the banners of the confederate Doctors, if they will accept their service. As a specimen of the extravagant legends of the middle age, I had produced the instance of ten thousand Christian soldiers supposed to have been crucified on Mount Ararat, by the order either of Trajan or Hadrian[(1)]. For the mention and for the confutation of this story, I had appealed to a Papist and a Protestant, to the learned Tillemont (Mem. Ecclesiast. tom. ii. part ii. p. 438), and to the diligent Geddes (Miscellanies, vol. ii. p. 203), and when Tillemont was not afraid to say that there are few histories which appear more fabulous, I was not ashamed of dismissing the *Fable* with silent contempt. We may trace the degrees of fiction as well as those of credibility, and the impartial Critic will not place on the same level the baptism of Philip and the donation of Constantine. But in considering the crucifixion of the ten thousand Christian soldiers, we are not reduced to the necessity of weighing any internal probabilities, or of disproving any external testimonies. This legend, the absurdity of which must strike every *rational* mind, stands naked and unsupported by the authority of any writer who lived within a thousand years of the age of Trajan, and has not been able to obtain the poor sanction of the uncorrupted

---

[(1)] Gibbon, p. 654. note 74.

[a] *II.* legions placed here in 2nd.   [b] *This paragraph, headed* PAGE 121., *added at end, 1st edition;*

Martyrologies which were framed in the most credulous period of Ecclesiastical History. The two Protestant Doctors will probably reject the unsubstantial present which has been offered them; yet there is one of my adversaries, the *annonymous Gentleman*, who boldly declares himself the votary of the ten thousand Martyrs, and challenges me "to discredit a FACT which hitherto by many has been "looked upon as well established[2]." It is pity that a prudent confessor did not whisper in his ear, that, although the martyrdom of these military Saints, like that of the eleven thousand Virgins, may contribute to the edification of the faithful, these wonderful tales should not be rashly exposed to the jealous and inquisitive eye of those profane Critics, whose examination always precedes, and sometimes checks, their Religious Assent.

II.

CHARACTER AND CREDIT OF EUSEBIUS.

A grave and pathetic complaint is introduced by Dr. Chelsum, into his preface[9], that Mr. Gibbon, who has often referred to the Fathers of the Church, seems to have entertained a general distrust of those respectable witnesses. The Critic is scandalized at the epithets of scanty and *suspicious*, which are applied to the materials of Ecclesiastical History; and if he cannot impeach the truth of the former, he censures in the most angry terms the injustice of the latter. He assumes, with peculiar zeal, the defence of Eusebius, the venerable parent of Ecclesiastical History, and labours to rescue his character from the *gross misrepresentation*, on which Mr. Gibbon has openly insisted[1]. He observes, as if he sagaciously foresaw the objection, "That it will not be sufficient here to alledge a few in-"stances of apparent credulity in some of the Fathers, in order to "fix a general charge of *suspicion* on all." But it *may* be sufficient to allege a clear and fundamental principle of historical as well as legal Criticism, that whenever we are destitute of the means of comparing the testimonies of the opposite parties, the evidence of *any* witness, however illustrious by his rank and titles, is justly to be *suspected* in his own cause. It is unfortunate enough, that I should be engaged with adversaries, whom their habits of study and conversation appear

[2] Remarks, p. 65, 66, 67.　　　[9] P. ii, iii.　　　[1] Chelsum and Randolph
p. 220–238.

to have left in total ignorance of the principles which universally regulate the opinions and practice of mankind.

As the ancient world was not distracted by the fierce conflicts of hostile sects, the free and eloquent writers of Greece and Rome had few opportunities of indulging their passions, or of exercising their impartiality in the relation of religious events. Since the origin of Theological Factions, some Historians, Ammianus Marcellinus, Fra-Paolo, Thuanus, Hume, and perhaps a few others, have deserved the singular praise of holding the balance with a steady and equal hand. Independent and unconnected, they contemplated with the same indifference, the opinions and interests of the contending parties; or, if they were seriously attached to a particular system, they were armed with a firm and moderate temper, which enabled them to suppress their affections, and to sacrifice their resentments. In this small, but *venerable* Synod of Historians, Eusebius cannot claim a seat. I had acknowledged, and I still think, that his character was less tinctured with credulity than that of most of his contemporaries; but as his enemies must admit that he was sincere and earnest in the profession of Christianity, so the warmest of his admirers, or at least of his readers, must discern, and will probably applaud, the religious zeal which disgraces or adorns every page of his Ecclesiastical History. This laborious and useful work was published at a time, between the defeat of Licinius and the Council of Nice, when the resentment of the Christians was still warm, and when the Pagans were astonished and dismayed by the recent victory and conversion of the great Constantine. The materials, I shall dare to repeat the invidious epithets of scanty and suspicious, were extracted from the accounts which the Christians themselves had given of their *own* sufferings, and of the cruelty of their enemies. The Pagans had so long and so contemptuously neglected the rising greatness of the Church, that the Bishop of Cæsarea had little either to hope or to fear from the writers of the opposite party; almost all of that *little* which did exist, has been accidentally lost, or purposely destroyed; and the candid enquirer may vainly wish to compare with the History of Eusebius, some Heathen narrative of the persecutions of Decius and Diocletian. Under these circumstances, it is the duty of an impartial judge to be counsel for the prisoner, who is incapable of making any defence for himself; and it is the first office of a counsel to examine with distrust and *suspicion*, the interested evidence of the accuser. Reason justifies the suspicion, and it is confirmed by the constant experience of modern History, in almost every instance where we have an opportunity of comparing the mutual complaints and apologies of the religious factions, who have disturbed each other's happiness in this world, for the sake of securing it in the next.

As we are deprived of the means of contrasting the adverse relations of the Christians and Pagans; it is the more incumbent on us to improve the opportunities of trying the narratives of Eusebius, by the original, and sometimes occasional testimonies of the more ancient writers of his own party. Dr. Chelsum[2] has observed, that the celebrated passage of Origen, which has so much thinned the ranks of the army of Martyrs, must be confined to the persecutions that had already happened. I cannot dispute this sagacious remark, but I shall venture to add, that this passage more immediately relates to the religious tempests which had been excited in the time and country of Origen; and still more particularly to the city of Alexandria, and to the persecution of Severus, in which young Origen successfully exhorted his father, to sacrifice his life and fortune for the cause of Christ. From such unquestionable evidence, I am authorised to conclude, that the number of holy victims who sealed their faith with their blood was not, on this occasion, very considerable: but I cannot reconcile this fair conclusion with the positive declaration of Eusebius, (l. vi. c. 2. p. 258) that at Alexandria, in the persecution of Severus, an innumerable, at least an indefinite multitude ($\mu\nu\rho\iota\iota$) of Christians were honoured with the Crown of Martyrdom. The advocates for Eusebius may exert their critical skill in proving that $\mu\nu\rho\iota\iota$ and $\iota\lambda\iota\gamma\iota\iota$, *many* and *few*, are synonymous and convertible terms, but they will hardly succeed in diminishing so palpable a contradiction, or in removing the suspicion which deeply fixes itself on the historical character of the Bishop of Cæsarea. This unfortunate experiment taught me to read, with becoming caution, the loose and declamatory style which *seems* to magnify the multitude of Martyrs and Confessors, and to aggravate the nature of their sufferings. From the same motives I selected, with careful observation, the more certain account of the number of persons who actually suffered death in the province of Palestine, during the whole eight years of the last and most rigorous persecution.

Besides the reasonable grounds of suspicion, which suggests themselves to every liberal mind, against the credibility of the Ecclesi-

[2] Gibbon, p. 653. Chelsum, p. 204–297.

astical Historians, and of Eusebius, their venerable leader, I had taken notice of two very remarkable passages of the Bishop of Cæsarea. He frankly, or at least indirectly, declares, that in treating of the last persecution, "he has related whatever might redound to "the glory, and suppressed all that could tend to the disgrace, of "Religion[3]." Dr. Chelsum, who, on this occasion, most lamentably exclaims that we should hear Eusebius, before we utterly condemn him, has provided, with the assistance of his worthy colleague, an elaborate defence for their common patron; and as if he were secretly conscious of the weakness of the cause, he has contrived the resource of intrenching himself in a very muddy soil, behind three several fortifications, which do not exactly support each other. The advocate for the sincerity of Eusebius maintains: 1st, That he never made such a declaration: 2dly, That he had a right to make it: and 3dly, That he did not observe it. These separate and almost inconsistent apologies, I shall separately consider.

1. Dr. Chelsum is at a loss how to reconcile,——I beg pardon for weakening the force of his dogmatic style; he declares that, "It is[a] "plainly impossible to reconcile the express words of the charge "exhibited, with any part of either of the passages appealed to in "support of it[4]." If he means, as I think he must, that the *express words* of my text cannot be found in that of Eusebius, I congratulate the importance of the discovery. But was it possible? Could it be my design to quote the words of Eusebius, when I reduced into one sentence the spirit and substance of two diffuse and distinct passages? If I have given the true sense and meaning of the Ecclesiastical Historian, I have discharged the duties of a fair Interpreter; nor shall I refuse to rest the proof of my fidelity on the translation of those two passages of Eusebius, which Dr. Chelsum produces in his favour[5]. "But it is not our part to describe the sad calamities which "at last befel them (the *Christians*), since it does not agree with our "plan to relate their dissentions and wickedness before the persecu- "tion; on which account we have determined to relate nothing more "concerning them than may serve to justify the Divine Judgment. "We therefore have not been induced to make mention either of "those who were tempted in the persecution, or of those who made "utter shipwreck of their salvation, and who were sunk of their own

[3] Gibbon, p. 699.   [4] Chelsum, p. 232.   [5] P. 228. 231.

<hr>

[a] *II.* was

"accord in[a] the depths of the storm; but shall only add those things
"to our General History, which may in the first place be profitable
"to ourselves, and afterwards to posterity." In the other passage,
Eusebius, after mentioning the dissentions of the Confessors among
themselves, again declares that it is his intention to pass over all
these things. "Whatsoever things, (continues the Historian, in the
"words of the Apostle, who was recommending the practice of virtue)
"whatsoever things are honest, whatsoever things are of good report,
"if there be any virtue, and if there be any praise; these things
"Eusebius thinks most suitable to a History of Martyrs;" of *wonderful* Martyrs, is the splendid epithet which Dr. Chelsum had not
thought proper to translate. I should betray a very mean opinion of
the judgment and candour of my readers, if I added a single reflection on the clear and obvious tendency of the two passages of the
Ecclesiastical Historian. I shall only observe, that the Bishop of
Cæsarea seems to have claimed a privilege of a still more dangerous
and extensive nature. In one of the most learned and elaborate works
that antiquity has left us, the Thirty-second Chapter of the Twelfth
Book of his Evangelical Preparation bears for its title this scandalous
Proposition, "How it may be lawful and fitting to use falsehood as a
"medicine, and for the benefit of those who want to be deceived."
Ὅτι δεήσει ποτὲ τῷ ψεύδει ἀντὶ φαρμάκου χρῆσθαι ἐπὶ ὠφελείᾳ τῶν
δεομένων τοῦ τοιούτου τρόπου. (p. 356, Edit. Græc. Rob. Stephani,
Paris 1544.) In this chapter he alleges a passage of Plato, which
approves the occasional practice of pious and salutary frauds; nor
is Eusebius ashamed to justify the sentiments of the Athenian
philosopher by the example of the sacred writers of the Old Testament.

2. I had contented myself with observing, that Eusebius had
violated one of the fundamental laws of history, *Ne quid veri dicere
non audeat*; nor could I imagine, if the *fact* was allowed, that any
question could possibly arise upon the matter of *right*. I was indeed
mistaken; and I now begin to understand why I have given so little
satisfaction to Dr. Chelsum, and to other critics of the same complexion, as our ideas of the duties and the privileges of an historian
appear to be so widely different. It is alleged, that "every writer has
"a right to chuse his subject, for the particular benefit of his reader;
"that he has explained his own plan consistently; that he considers
"himself, according to it, not as a complete historian of the times, but
"rather as a *didactic* writer, whose main object is to make his work

[a] *II*. into

"like the Scriptures themselves, PROFITABLE FOR DOCTRINE;
"that as he treats only of the affairs of the Church, the plan is at
"least excusable, perhaps peculiarly proper; and that he has con-
"formed himself to the principal duty of an historian, while,
"according to his immediate design, he has not particularly related
"any of the transactions which could tend to the disgrace of reli-
"gion[6]." The historian must indeed be generous, who will conceal,
by his own disgrace, that of his country, or of his religion. Whatever
subject he has chosen, whatever persons he introduces, he owes to
himself, to the present age, and to posterity, a just and perfect
delineation of all that may be praised, of all that may be excused,
and of all that must be censured. If he fails in the discharge of
his important office, he partially violates the sacred obligations
of truth, and disappoints his readers of the instruction which
they might have derived from a fair parallel of the vices and
virtues of the most illustrious characters. Herodotus might range
without controul in the spacious walks of the Greek and Barbaric
domain, and Thucydides might confine his steps to the narrow
path of the Peloponnesian war; but those historians would never
have deserved the esteem of posterity, if they had designedly
suppressed or transiently mentioned those facts which could
tend to the disgrace of Greece or of Athens. These unalterable
dictates of conscience and reason have been *seldom* questioned,
though they have been seldom observed; and we must sincerely
join in the honest complaint of Melchior Canus, "that the lives of
"the philosophers have been composed by Laertius, and those of
"the Cæsars by Suetonius, with a much stricter and more severe
"regard for historic truth, than can be found in the lives of saints
"and martyrs, as they are described by Catholic writers." (See Loci
Communes, l. xi. p. 650, apud Clericum, Epistol. Critic. v. p. 136.)
And yet the partial representation of truth is of far more pernicious
consequence in ecclesiastical than in civil history. If Laertius had
concealed the defects of Plato, or if Suetonius had disguised the vices
of Augustus, we should have been deprived of the knowledge of
some curious, and perhaps instructive facts, and our idea of those
celebrated men might have been more favourable than they deserved;
but I cannot discover any practical inconveniencies which could have
been the result of our ignorance. But if Eusebius had fairly and
circumstantially related the scandalous dissentions of the Confessors;

[6] Chelsum, p. 229, 230, 231.

if he had shewn that their virtues were tinctured with pride and obstinacy, and that their lively faith was not exempt from some mixture of enthusiasm; he would have armed his readers against the excessive veneration for those holy men, which imperceptibly degenerated into religious worship. The success of these *didactic* histories, by concealing or palliating every circumstance of human infirmity, was one of the most efficacious means of consecrating the memory, the bones, and the writings of the saints of the prevailing party; and a great part of the errors and corruptions of the Church of Rome may fairly be ascribed to this criminal dissimulation of the ecclesiastical historians. As a Protestant Divine, Dr. Chelsum must abhor these corruptions; but as a Christian, he should be careful lest his apology for the prudent choice of Eusebius should fix an indirect censure on the unreserved sincerity of the four Evangelists. Instead of confining their narrative to those things which are virtuous and of good report, instead of following the plan which is here recommended as *peculiarly proper* for the affairs of the Church, the inspired writers have thought it their duty to relate the most minute circumstances of the fall of St. Peter, without considering whether the behaviour of an Apostle, who thrice denied his Divine Master, might redound to the honour or to the disgrace of Christianity. If Dr. Chelsum should be frightened by this unexpected consequence, if he should be desirous of saving his faith from *utter shipwreck*, by throwing over-board the useless lumber of memory and reflection, I am not enough his enemy to impede the success of his honest endeavours.

The didactic method of writing history was[a] still more profitably exercised by Eusebius in another work, which he has intitled, The Life of Constantine, his gracious patron and benefactor. Priests and poets have enjoyed in every age a privilege of flattery; but if the actions of Constantine are compared with the perfect idea of a royal saint, which, under his name, has been delineated by the zeal and gratitude of Eusebius, the most indulgent reader will confess, that when I styled him a *courtly Bishop*[7], I could only be restrained by my respect for the episcopal character from the use of a much harsher epithet. The other appellation of a *passionate declaimer*, which seems to have sounded still more offensive in the tender ears

[7] Gibbon, p. 704.

---

[a] *I.* is

of Dr. Chelsum[8], was not applied by me to Eusebius, but to Lactantius, or rather to the author of the historical declamation, *De mortibus persecutorum*; and indeed it is much more properly adapted to the Rhetorician, than to the Bishop. Each of those authors was alike studious of the glory of Constantine; but each of them directed the torrent of his invectives against the tyrant, whether Maxentius or Licinus, whose recent defeat was the actual theme of popular and Christian applause. This simple observation may serve to extinguish a very trifling objection of my critic, That Eusebius has not represented the tyrant Maxentius under the character of a Persecutor.

Without scrutinizing the considerations of interest which might support the integrity of Baronius and Tillemont, I may fairly observe, that both those learned Catholics have acknowledged and condemned the dissimulation of Eusebius, which is partly denied, and partly justified, by my adversary. The honourable reflection of Baronius well deserves to be transcribed. "Hæc (the passages "already quoted) de suo in conscribendâ persecutionis historia "Eusebius; parum explens numeros sui muneris; dum perinde ac "si panegyrim scriberet non historiam, triumphos dumtaxat mar- "tyrum atque victorias, non autem lapsus jacturamque fidelium posteris scripturæ monumentis curaret." (Baron. Annal. Ecclesiast. A. D. 302, N° 11. See likewise Tillemont, Mem. Eccles. tom. v. p. 62. 156; tom. vii. p. 130.) In a former instance, Dr. Chelsum appeared to be more credulous than a Monk: on the present occasion, he has shewn himself less sincere than a Cardinal, and more obstinate than a Jansenist.

3. Yet the advocate for Eusebius has still another expedient in reserve. Perhaps he made the unfortunate declaration of his partial design, perhaps he had a right to make it; but at least his accuser must admit, that he has saved his honour by not keeping his word; since I myself have taken notice of THE CORRUPTION OF MANNERS AND PRINCIPLES among the Christians, so FORCIBLY LAMENTED by Eusebius[9]. He has indeed indulged himself in a strain of *loose* and *indefinite* censure, which may generally be just, and which cannot be personally offensive, which is alike incapable of wounding or of correcting, as it seems to have no fixed object or certain aim. Juvenal might have read his satire against women in a circle of Roman ladies, and each of them might have listened with pleasure

[8] Chelsum, p. 234.   [9] Chelsum, p. 226, 227.

to the amusing description of the various vices and follies, from which she herself was so perfectly free. The moralist, the preacher, the ecclesiastical historian, enjoy a still more ample latitude of invective; and as long as they abstain from any particular censure, they may securely expose, and even exaggerate, the sins of the multitude. The precepts of Christianity seem to inculcate a style of mortification, of abasement, of self-contempt; and the hypocrite who aspires to the reputation of a saint, often finds it convenient to affect the language of a penitent. I should doubt whether Dr. Chelsum is much acquainted with the comedies of Moliere. If he has ever read that inimitable master of human life, he may recollect whether Tartuffe[28] was very much inclined to confess his real guilt, when he exclaimed,

> Oui, mon Frere, je suis un mechant, un coupable;
> Un malheureux pécheur, tout plein d'iniquité;
> Le plus grand scelerat qui ait jamais été.
> Chaque instant de ma vie est chargé de souillures,
> Elle n'est qu'un amas de crimes et d'ordures.
> . . . .
> Oui, mon cher fils, parlez, traitez moi de perfide,
> D'infame, de perdu, de voleur, d'homicide;
> Accablez moi de noms encore plus detestés:
> Je n'y contredis point, je les ai merités,
> Et j'en veux à genoux souffrir l'ignominie,
> Comme une honte due aux crimes de ma vie.

It is not my intention to compare the character of Tartuffe with that of Eusebius; the former pointed his invectives against himself, the latter directed them against the times in which he had lived: but as the prudent Bishop of Cæsarea did not specify any place or person for the object of his censure, he cannot justly be accused, even by his friends, of violating the *profitable* plan of his *didactic* history.

The extreme caution of Eusebius, who declines any mention of those who were tempted and who fell during the persecution, has countenanced a suspicion that he himself was one of those unhappy victims, and that his tenderness for the wounded fame of his brethren arose from a just apprehension of his own disgrace. In one of my notes[(1)], I had observed, that he was charged with the guilt of some criminal compliances, in his own presence, and in the

---

[(1)] Gibbon, p. 699, N. 178.

Council of Tyre. I am therefore accountable for the reality only, and not for the truth, of the accusation: but as the two Doctors, who on this occasion unite their forces, are angry and clamorous in asserting the innocence of the Ecclesiastical Historian[2], I shall advance one step farther, and shall maintain, that the charge against Eusebius, though not legally proved, is supported by a reasonable share of presumptive evidence.

I have often wondered why our orthodox Divines should be so earnest and zealous in the defence of Eusebius; whose moral character cannot be preserved, unless by the sacrifice of a more illustrious, and, as I really believe, of a more innocent victim. Either the Bishop of Cæsarea, on a very important occasion, violated the laws of Christian charity and civil justice, or we must fix a charge of calumny, almost of forgery, on the head of the great Athanasius, the standard-bearer of the Homoousian cause, and the firmest pillar of the Catholic faith.[a] In the Council of Tyre, he was accused of murdering, or at least of mutilating, a Bishop, whom he produced at Tyre alive and unhurt (Athanas. tom. i. p. 783. 786.); and of sacrilegiously breaking a consecrated chalice, in a village where neither church, nor altar, nor chalice, could possibly have existed. (Athanas. tom. i. p. 731, 732. 802.) Notwithstanding the clearest proofs of his innocence, Athanasius was oppressed by the Arian faction; and Eusebius of Cæsarea, the venerable father of ecclesiastical history, conducted this iniquitous prosecution from a motive of personal enmity. (Athanas. tom. i. p. 728. 795. 797.) Four years afterwards, a national council of the Bishops of Egypt, forty-nine of whom had been present at the Synod of Tyre, addressed an epistle or manifesto in favour of Athanasius to all the Bishops of the Christian world. In this epistle they assert, that some of the Confessors, who accompanied them to Tyre, had accused Eusebius of Cæsarea of an act relative to idolatrous sacrifice. οὐκ Εὐσέβιος ὁ ἐν Καισερεια τῆς Παλαιστινης ἐπι θυσια κατηγορειτο ὑπο[b] των συν ἡμιν ὁμολογητων; (Athanas. tom. i. p. 728.) Besides this short and authentic memorial, which escaped the knowledge or the candour of our confederate Doctors, a consonant but more circumstantial narrative of the accusation of Eusebius may be found in the writings of Epiphanius (Hæres. lxviii. p. 723, 724.), the learned Bishop of

[2] Chelsum and Randolph, p. 236, 237, 238.

[a] I. orthodox doctrine   [b] I. υπο

Salamis, who was born about the time of the Synod of Tyre. He relates, that, in one of the sessions of the Council, Potamon, Bishop of Heraclea in Egypt, addressed Eusebius in the following words: 'How now, Eusebius, can this be borne, that you should be seated "as a judge, while the innocent Athanasius is left standing as a "criminal? Tell me, continued Potamon, were we not in prison "together during the persecution? For my own part, I lost an eye for "the sake of the truth; but I cannot discern that *you* have lost any "one of your members. You bear not any marks of your sufferings "for Jesus Christ; but here you are, full of life, and with all the parts "of your body sound and entire. How could you contrive to escape "from prison, unless you stained your conscience, either by actual "guilt or by a criminal promise to our persecutors." Eusebius immediately broke up the meeting, and discovered by his anger, that he was confounded or provoked by the reproaches of the Confessor Potamon.

I should despise myself, if I were capable of magnifying, for a present occasion, the authority of the witness whom I have produced. Potamon was most assuredly actuated by a strong prejudice against the personal enemy of his Primate; and if the transaction to which he alluded had been of a private and doubtful kind, I would not take any ungenerous advantage of the respect which my Reverend Adversaries must entertain for the character of a Confessor. But I cannot distrust the veracity of Potamon, when he confined himself to the assertion of a fact, which lay within the compass of his personal knowledge: and collateral testimony (see Photius, p. 296, 297.) attests, that Eusebius was long enough in prison to assist his friend, the Martyr Pamphilus, in composing the first five books of his Apology for Origen. If we admit that Eusebius was imprisoned, he must have been discharged, and his discharge must have been either honourable, or criminal, or innocent. If his patience vanquished the cruelty of the Tyrant's Ministers, a short relation of his own confession and sufferings would have formed an useful and edifying Chapter in his Didactic History of the Persecution of Palestine; and the Reader would have been satisfied of the veracity of an Historian who valued truth above his life. If it had been in his power to justify, or even to excuse, the manner of his discharge from prison, it was his interest, it was his duty, to prevent the doubts and suspicions which must arise from his silence under these delicate circumstances. Notwithstanding these urgent reasons, Eusebius has observed a profound, and perhaps a prudent, silence: though he frequently celebrates the merit and martyrdom of his friend Pamphilus (p. 371. 394. 419. 427. Edit. Cantab.), he never insinuates that he was his companion in prison; and while he copiously describes the eight years persecution in Palestine, he never represents himself in any other light than of a spectator. Such a conduct in a Writer, who relates with a visible satisfaction the honourable events of his own life, if it be not absolutely considered as an evidence of conscious guilt, must excite, and may justify, the suspicions of the most candid Critic.

Yet the firmness of Dr. Randolph is not shaken by these rational suspicions; and he condescends, in a magisterial tone, to inform me, "That it is highly improbable, from the general well-known decision "of the Church in such cases, that had his apostacy been known, "he would have risen to those high honours which he attained, or "been admitted at all indeed to any other than lay-communion." This weighty objection did not surprize me, as I had already seen the substance of it in the Prolegomena of Valesius[29]; but I safely disregarded a difficulty which had not appeared of any moment to the national council of Egypt; and I still think that an hundred Bishops, with Athanasius at their head, were as competent judges of the discipline of the fourth Century, as even the Lady Margaret's Professor of Divinity in the University of Oxford. As a work of supererogation, I have consulted, however, the Antiquities of Bingham (see l. iv. c. 3. f. 6, 7. vol. i. p. 144, &c. fol. Edit.), and found, as I expected, that much real learning had made him cautious and modest. After a careful examination of the facts and authorities already known to me, and of those with which I was supplied by the diligent Antiquarian, I am persuaded that the theory and the practice of discipline were not invariably the same, that particular examples cannot always be reconciled with general rules, and that the stern laws of justice often yielded to motives of policy and convenience. The temper of Jerom towards those whom he considered as Heretics was fierce and unforgiving; yet the Dialogue of Jerom against the Luciferians, which I have read with infinite pleasure (tom. ii. p. 135—147. Edit. Basil. 1536.), is the seasonable and dextrous performance of a Statesman, who felt the expediency of soothing and reconciling a numerous party of offenders. The most rigid discipline, with regard to the Ecclesiastics who had fallen in time of persecution, is expressed in the 10th Canon of the Council of Nice; the most remarkable indulgence was shewn by the Fathers of the same Council to the *lapsed*, the degraded, the schismatic Bishop of Lycopolis. Of the penitent sinners, some might escape the shame of a public conviction or confession, and others might be exempted from the rigour of clerical punishment. If Eusebius incurred the guilt of a sacrilegious promise (for we are free to accept the milder alternative of Potamon), the proofs of this criminal transaction might be suppressed by the influence of money or favour; a seasonable journey into Egypt might allow time for the popular rumours to subside. The crime of Eusebius might be protected by the impunity of many Episcopal Apostates (see Philostorg. l. ii. c. 15. p. 21. Edit. Gothofred.); and the Governors of the Church very reasonably desired to retain in their service the most learned Christian of the Age.

Before[a] I return these sheets to the press I must not forget an anonymous pamphlet, which under the title of *A Few Remarks*, &c. had been published against my History in the course of the last summer. The unknown writer has thought proper to distinguish himself by the emphatic, yet vague, appellation of A GENTLEMAN: but I must lament that he has not considered, with becoming attention, the duties of that respectable character. I am ignorant of the motives which can urge a man of a liberal mind, and liberal manners, to attack without provocation, and without tenderness, any work which may have contributed to the information, or even to the amusement of the public. But I am well convinced, that the author of such a work, who boldly gives his name and his labours to the world, imposes on his adversaries the fair and honourable obligation of encountering him in open day-light, and of supporting the weight of their assertions by the credit of their names. The effusions of wit, or the productions of reason, may be accepted from a secret and unknown hand. The critic who attempts to injure the reputation of another, by strong imputations which may possibly be false, should renounce the ungenerous hope of concealing behind a mask the vexation of disappointment, and the guilty blush of detection.

After this remark, which I cannot make without some degree of concern, I shall frankly declare, that it is not my wish or my intention

---

[a] *I*. Postscript/WHILE the sheets of this Vindication were in the press, I was informed that an anonymous pamphlet, under the title of *A Few Remarks*, &c. had been published etc.

to prosecute with this *Gentleman* a literary altercation. There lies between us a broad and unfathomable gulph; and the heavy mist of prejudice and superstition, which has in a great measure been dispelled by the free inquiries of the present age, still continues to involve the mind of my Adversary. He fondly embraces those phantoms (for instance, an imaginary Pilate[1]), which can scarcely find a shelter in the gloom of an Italian convent; and the resentment which he points against me, might frequently be extended to the most enlightened of the PROTESTANT, or, in his opinion, of the HERETICAL critics. His observations are divided into a number of unconnected paragraphs, each of which contains some quotation from my History, and the angry, yet commonly trifling expression of his disapprobation and displeasure. Those sentiments I cannot hope to remove; and as the religious opinions of this *Gentleman* are principally founded on the infallibility of the Church[2], they are not calculated to make a very deep impression on the mind of an English reader. The view of *facts* will be materially affected by the contagious influence of *doctrines*. The man who refuses to judge of the conduct of Lewis XIV. and Charles V. towards their Protestant subjects[3], declares himself incapable of distinguishing the limits of persecution and toleration. The devout Papist, who has implored on his knees the intercession of St. Cyprian, will seldom presume to examine the actions of the Saint by the rules of historical evidence and of moral propriety. Instead of the homely likeness which I had exhibited of the Bishop of Carthage, my Adversary has substituted a life of Cyprian[4], full of what the French call *onction*, and the English, *canting* (See Jortin's Remarks, Vol. ii. p. 239.): to which I can only reply, that those who are dissatisfied with the principles of Mosheim and Le Clerc, *must* view with eyes very different from mine, the Ecclesiastical History of the third century.

It would be an *endless* discussion (*endless* in every sense of the word), were I to examine the cavils which start up and expire in every page of this criticism, on the inexhaustible topic of opinions, characters, and intentions. Most of the instances which are here produced, are of so brittle a substance that they fall in pieces as soon as they are touched: and I searched for some time before I was able to discover an example of some moment where the *Gentleman* had fairly staked his veracity against some positive fact asserted in

[1] Remarks, p. 100.   [2] Remarks p. 15.   [3] Id. p. 111.   [4] Id. p. 72–88.

the two last Chapters of my History. At last I perceived that he has absolutely denied[5] that any thing can be gathered from the Epistles of St. Cyprian, or from his treatise *De Unitate Ecclesiæ*, to which I had referred, to justify my account of the spiritual pride and licentious manners of some of the Confessors[6]. As the *numbers* of the Epistles are not the same in the edition of Pamelius and in that of Fell,*a* the Critic may be excused for mistaking my quotations, if he will acknowledge that he was ignorant of ecclesiastical history, and that he never heard of the troubles excited by the spiritual pride of the Confessors, who usurped the privilege of giving letters of communion to penitent sinners. But my reference to the treatise *De Unitate Ecclesiæ* was clear and direct; the treatise itself contains only ten pages, and the following words might be distinctly read by any person who understood the Latin language. "Nec quisquam miretur, dilectissimi fratres, etiam de confessoribus quosdam ad ista procedere, inde quoque aliquos tam nefanda tam gravia peccare. Neque enim confessio immunem facit ab insidiis diaboli; aut contra tentationes, et pericula, et incursus atque impetus seculares adhuc in seculo positum perpetuâ securitate defendit: ceterum nunquam in confessoribus, *fraudes*, et *stupra*, et *adulteria* postmodum videremus, quæ nunc in quibusdam videntes ingemiscimus et dolemus." This formal declaration of Cyprian, which is followed by several long periods of admonition and censure, is alone sufficient to expose the scandalous vices of some of the Confessors, and the disingenuous behaviour of my concealed adversary.

After this example, which I have fairly chosen as one of the most specious and important of his objections, the candid Reader would excuse me, if from this moment I declined *the Gentleman*'s acquaintance. But as two topics have occurred, which are intimately connected with the subject of the preceding sheets, I*b* have inserted each of them in its proper place, as the conclusion of the fourth article of my answers to Mr. Davis, and of the first article of my reply to the confederate Doctors, Chelsum and Randolph.

It is not without some mixture of mortification and regret, that I now look back on the number of hours which I have consumed, and the number of pages which I have filled, in vindicating my

---

(5) Remarks, p. 90, 91.   (6) Gibbon, p. 661, Note 91.

---

a II. Fel   *b I.* I shall insert them in this place, and desire that they may be read as the conclusion *etc.*

literary and moral character from the charge of wilful *Misrepresentations*, gross *Errors*, and servile *Plagiarisms*. I cannot derive any triumph or consolation from the occasional advantages which I may have gained over three adversaries, whom it is impossible for me to consider as objects either of terror or of esteem. The spirit of resentment, and every other lively sensation, have long since been extinguished; and the pen would long since have dropped from my weary hand, had I not been supported in the execution of this ungrateful task, by the consciousness, or at least by the opinion, that I was discharging a debt of honour to the Public and to myself. I am impatient to dismiss, and to dismiss FOR EVER, this odious controversy, with the success of which I cannot surely be elated; and I have only to request, that as soon as my Readers are convinced of my innocence, they would forget my vindication.

BENTINCK-STREET,
February 3, 1779.[a]

FINIS.[b]

N.B.[c] If any slips of the pen, or errors of the press, should still remain in this *second* Edition, I must make my appeal, not to the candour of my Adversaries, but to the indulgence of the Public.[c]

---

[a] *I. om. place and date. I. was published 14 January, 1779 (J. E. Norton, A Bibliography of the Works of Edward Gibbon [Oxford, 1940], p. 86).* [b] *I. and II. om. FINIS.* [c] *I. and II. om. material between N.B. and Public I. has Errata list and N.B. If any other errors of the press should be detected, I can only implore the mercy of my Critics, and I must now lament that the name, or rather the provincial appellation of* HOLSTENIUS (Luke of *Holstein*) *should again have been mistaken by the Printer.*

Materials for the fourth Vol of the history of the decline and fall of the Roman Empire. *November 8ᵗʰ 1781*

After Procopius[1] had been strangely disfigured by the Italians of the fifteenth Century, who in their Latin versions used bad copies with bad faith the Greek text was first published (Augsburgh 1607 in 8°) by Daniel Hoeschelius from three MSS one of Augsburgh (*Boicum*), and the two others of Joseph Scaliger and Isaac Casaubon. He gave the viii books, de bellis; with the vi de Edificiis which had been already (Basil 1531) most imperfectly printed from a MS. of Conrad Peutinger. (see Fabricius. B. G. L v. C 5. Tom vi p 250–253). The Anecdotes were first published with learned notes (Lugdan. 1623.) by Nic. Alemannus from a Vatican MS (see his preface in the second Vol. of the Louvre Edition). From an entire MS of the Vatican, the *lacunæ* of the Augsburgh Edition were supplied by Lucas Holstenius, first in the Latin version of Hugo Grotius. (Epist. 645. p 263 prolegom. ad Hist. Goth. p 1. Amstel. 1655), and afterwards in the Greek text published with a new version by the Jesuit Maltret (Paris 1663 2 Vol. in fol. in the Byzantine collection of the Louvre) who declares in his preface that he had not seen the Edition of Grotius. The learning and diligence of Grotius (Græcam primum Editionem quam Hoeschelio curante habemus locis infinitis emendavi, partim ex conjecturâ probabili partim auctoritate librorum e regis Galliæ bibliothecâ . . . et sic Procopium latine verti)[a] give his version the credit of an original. but the Jesuit Maltret, who vainly promised notes and supplements, never consulted any MS himself, and[b] was satisfied with an hasty collation from the Vatican. The Script. rerum Italicarum afforded Muratori[2] a fair occasion which he neglected of publishing a more perfect edition of Procopius (see Maffei Osservazioni letterarie Tom 1 p 84.)

[a] *Ellipsis Gibbon's*   [b] *I.* but

[Cosmas]

The Collectio Nova Patrum published by the P. Montfaucon at Paris 1707. in two Vol. in folio contains (Tom ii p. 113–346). the Topographia Christiana of Cosmas, surnamed Indicopleustes, of which very curious extracts may be found in Photius. (Cod. xxxvi. p. 9. 10. Edit. Hoeschel.) Fabricius[a]. (Bibliot. Græc. L iii. C 25. Tom ii. p 603–617). and the first part of the Relations des Voyages &c of Melchizedek[b] Thevenot.

Cosmas was an Egyptian merchant who afterwards became a Monk. His voyages to the Æthiopian and perhaps to the Indian Coast were performed about the year 522 in the[c] beginning of the reign of the elder Justin, and he composed his Topography at Alexandria between the years 535. and 547. (L ii p. 140–141. Montfaucon præfat. C. 1). He wrote to confute the impious doctrine that the Earth is a Globe, and to maintain the orthodox faith, which represents it as a flat surface 12.000 miles long, and 6000 broad, (L ii. p 138)[d] surrounded by the Ocean and covered by the concave of the Heavens. (see the xii books of Cosmas passim. and Montfaucon præfat C 2.). In the defence of such a cause, which is founded however on the litteral interpretation of scripture, he abundantly deserves the censures of Photius, who styles him, μυθικώτερον μᾶλλον ἢ ἀληθέστερον: yet amidst the nonsense of the monk, the practical knowledge of the merchant and traveller sometimes emerges.[1] 1. It is evident from Cosmas, that in the vi[th] Century, the direct[e] trade of Egypt with India was no longer prosecuted[f], and that[g] the merchants of Alexandria were contented to proceed from Ela down the Red-Sea as far as Adulis. (L ii. p 140) From thence the subjects of Rome might sometimes embark in Barbarian vessels; the commodities of India were still purchased with Roman gold, and the beauty of the coin announced to the inhabitants of Taprobana the wealth and greatness of the Emperor. (L xi. p 338).[2] 2. Adulis the port of the Axomites was about two miles from the Red Sea, sixty

[a] I. and Fabricius   [b] I. The   [c] I. om. the   [d] I. om. (L ii p 138)
[e] I. om. direct   [f] I. practiced   [g] I. om. that

days sail or journey from Alexandria and one hundred and ten from C.P. (L. ii. p 138-140). Cosmas read and copied a proud Greek Inscription, which Ptolemy Euergetes engraved on marble, (L ii. p 140-143). and Fabricius has transcribed.[3] 3. The Axomites traded by sea and land, above fifty days to the south (L ii. p 138, along[a] the Eastern coast of Africa, which they named Barbaria and Zingi. (L ii. p 132). The King of the Axomites or his Governor of Agau (a name still extant near the head of the Nile. Montfaucon. note p 139) sent Caravans[b] of five hundred persons who exchanged oxen salt and iron for the gold of the natives. (L ii. 10 139).[c] The same coast produced Aromatics. (λίβανον, κασίαν, κάλαμον) which were exported from Adulis to the Homerites, Persia, and India. (L ii p 139) The ships of Adulis visited Taprobana (L xi p 338); and the Emeralds collected by the Æthiopians from the neighbouring Blemonyes, were advantageously sold to the white Huns of India. (L xi. p 339).[4] 4. The Persians likewise, whose proximity gave them an irresistible superiority, (Procop. de Bell. Pers. L i. C 20. p 61. Edit Louvre) frequented Taprobana, and vainly celebrated their King, as far more wealthy and powerful than the Roman Emperor (L xi p 338). 5. After a curious description of the animals of India (L xi p 334-336)[d], Cosmas mentions ten seaports, which seem to be situate between the Indus and Cape Comorin are[e] marked by the vernacular terms of *Male* and *Patan*, and are still farther identified by the production of pepper on the *Mala*-bar coast. (L xi. p 337.)[f] The white Huns who reigned in the northern parts of India made extensive conquests and their King sometimes marched at the head of two thousand Elephants. (L xi. p 338-339).[5] 6. The great island of Sielidiva or Taprobana lyes in the Indian Ocean, amidst a cluster of smaller isles, and five days sail beyond the pepper country. It is 300 γαύδια, 900 miles in length and breadth, and is divided between two Kings, one of whom possesses the Hyancinth (perhaps a sort of Garnet or amethyst. Hill's Theophrastus on Stones p 47). and the other the harbour and foreign trade of India, Persia, and Æthiopia. From its convenient situation the Island receives and sends a great number of merchant-ships[g]; καὶ ἀπὸ μὲν τῶν ἐνδοτέρων, λέγω δὴ τῆς τζινίστας, καὶ ἑτέρων ἐμπορίων, δέχεται μέταξιν, ἀλωὴν, καρυόφολλον (Garofolo, Clou de Girofle, Cloves.

---

[a] *I.* and to   [b] *I.* trave   [c] *I. om.* (L ii. p 139)   [d] *I. om.* (L. xi p 334-336)   [e] *I.* and are   [f] *I. om.* (L xi. p 337.)   [g] *I.* merchant ships, and they bring from the inner countries,

Montfaucon præfat. C 3) τζανδάνον (I believe sandal-wood) καὶ ὅσα κατὰ χώραν ἐισί. καὶ μεταβάλλει τοῖς ἐξωτέρω, λέγω δὲ τῇ Μαλέ, ἐν ᾗ τὸ πίπερι γίνεται, καὶ τῇ καλλιάνα. &c. as far as the Indus, Persia, the Homerites, and Adulis, from whence Taprobana receives many articles of trade to export with its own commodities to the *inner* Indians. (L xi p 338. 39. 40). 7. For the sake of wretched[a] gain, the silk merchants travel to the extremities of the Earth (L ii p 137): but it is not clear of what country, those merchants were natives. Tzinista (perhaps Canton in China) was not as[b] distant from Taprobana, as[c] Taprobana itself from the Persian Gulf, (L ii p 138). and this country which produced the silk lay beyond the land of Cloves (L xi p 337) By land Tzinista was somewhat less distant; 150 days journey from the frontier of Persia, 230 from Nisibis and 243 from Seleucia at the mouth of the Orontes (L ii p 138).[6] 8. Christianity was widely diffused in the East and West, as far as the Huns, the Indians &c and every people[d] abounded with Martyrs and Monks. A Bishop was sent from Persia to Calliane; a church was founded at Male in the pepper Country. The Greek Colony settled by the Ptolemies in the island of Dioscurias had embraced Christianity. A Presbyter, a Deacon and the whole Ecclesiastical Liturgy was[e] established by the Christians of Persia at Taprobana (L xi p 337), but Cosmas was ignorant whether the faith had been propagated *beyond* that island. For this general state see L iii. p 178-179.[7]

[a] *I.* a wretched   [b] *I.* less   [c] *I.* than   [d] *I.* country   [e] *I.* had been

Mexico[a].

1. Immortality of the soul, rejected only by the Barbarous Otomites, believed by the Mexicans. *Clavigero* Storia[b] antica del Messico.[1] Tom ii. p 4. *2.* Mictlanteuchlti. God of Hell and his wife—a subterraneous dwelling, black priests, nocturnal sacrifices &c. p 17. *3.* The Hades in the centre of the Earth,—gate of paradise—perilous journey—pleasant abode with the God of Waters.—the supreme heaven in the Sun. p. 4. 5 6–94. *4.* The souls of those who died in War or childbearing held the first place—the second for the drowned, the dropsical, the thunder struck, infants &c.— vulgar deaths in the third. p 5. 5 Noble Tlascalans. 6. A similar life, and body? Utensils arms, gold[c] deposited in sepulchres Their Techichi slain to accompany them (p 94–99.) The same as the Alco, a mute melancholy sort of dog, now extinct. (Tom i. p 73). False criticism on Pope (Warton Vol. ii p 129).[2] 7. Transmigration, of plebeian souls, into vile animals of noble into the humming bird. (p 5). Beautiful image. —Buffon's fine description of 43 species of Oiseaux-mouches and Colibris. (Tom xxi p. 1—64. in 4°)[3]

[a] *II. om. title* Mexico.   [b] *I.* Istoria di M   [c] *I.* money

Notes
Gibbon

There is some Philosophical amusement in tracing the birth and progress of error. Till the beginning of the ix[th] Century the two Dionysii, of Athens, and of Paris, however adorned with imaginary trophies were carefully distinguished[b] from each other in the Greek and in the Latin Churches. Under the reign of Lewis the son of Charlemagne, about the year 824, Hilduin[c] Abbot of S[t] Denys[2] resolved to confound them and to dignify the Gallican Church by assigning it's origin not to an obscure Bishop of the third Century, but to a celebrated Philosopher of Athens who received his Mission from the Apostles themselves. As the genuine writers of Antiquity refused to countenance this opinion, Hildiun[c] though he sometimes quoted and corrupted them found it necessary to *create* the works of Aristarchus of Visbius &c which existed only in his fancy or at the most in the suspicious archives of his convent. The zeal and correspondence of the Benedictine Monks spread[d] the tale as far as Rome and Constantinople. It was published by Anastasius in the Latin, and by Methodius in the Greek tongue.[3] From the East it was reverberated back into France with such an encrease of sound; it was so grateful to the ear of national vanity; that as early as the year 876, the famous Hincmar Archbishop of[e] Rheims[4] could scarcely persuade himself that there still existed[f] any remains of incredulity. In the seventeenth century Sirmond the Jesuit[g] and the indefatigable Launoy ventured to restore the long-lost[h] distinction of the two Dionysii, and the Bigots after some struggle were reduced to silence. See Varia de duobus Dionysiis Opuscula in 8°. Paris 1660.

The two extraordinary circumstances in the Legend of George of Cappadocia are his gradual tran[s]formations from a Heretic to

[a] *II. om.* Vol. i Note p *Entry published MW 1814, v. 489–90*   [b] *I.* diligently
[c] *II.* Hilduia   [d] *I.* soon spread   [e] *I.* could   [f] *I.* re   [g] *I.* Jesuits
[h] *I.* dis   [i] *II. om.* Vol. ii Note. *Entry published MW 1814, v. 490–2*

a Saint and from a Saint to a Knight Errant. 1. It clearly appears from Epiphanius[6] (Hæres. lxxvi) that some persons revered George as a Martyr because he had been massacred[a] by the fury of the Pagans. But as Epiphanius observes with truth that his vices not his faith had been the cause of his death, the Arians disguised the object of their veneration by changing the time and place of his martyrdom, stigmatized his adversary Athanasius under the title[b] of Athanasius the Magician, and when they returned to the Catholic Church, they brought with them a new Saint of whose real character they had insensibly lost the remembrance. At first he was received with coldness and distrust; and in the year 494, the Council of Rome held under Pope Gelasius mentions his acts as composed by the Heretics, and his person as better known to God than to Men.[7] But in the succeeding century his glory broke out with sudden lustre both in the East and in the West. see[c] the contemporary testimonies of Procopius (de Edificiis L iii.) of Venantius Fortunatus (L ii Carm 13) of Gregory of Tours (de gloria Martyram. L i. C 101) and of Gregory of Rome (in libro Sacrament)[8] New legends were invented by the lively fancy of the Greeks which described the stupendous miracles and sufferings of the *great Martyr*: and from Lydda in Palestine (See Glaber L iii C 7. Wilhelm. Tyr. L viii C 22)[9] the supposed place of his burial, devout[d] pilgrims transported the suspicious relicks which adorned the temples erected to his honour in all the countries of Europe and Asia. 2. The Genius of Chivalry and Romance mistook the symbolical representations which were common to St George of Cappadocia and to several other Saints; the Dragon painted under their feet was designed for the Devil, whom the Martyr transpierced with the spiritual lance of faith and thus delivered the Church described under the figure of a Woman, but in the time of the Croisades, the Dragon so common in Eastern Romance was considered a[e] real monster slain near the city of Silena in Libya by the Christian Hero who (like another Perseus) delivered from his fury a beautiful and Royal damsel named St Margaret. In[f] the great battle of Antioch St George fought on the side of the Christians at the head of an innumerable host whose shields banners &c were perfectly white[g]: and the truth of this prodigy so analogous to his character is[h] attested by contemporaries

 a I. put to death   *b* I. character of a   *c* I. om. see . . . Sacrament) *Added on* *facing page in MS.*   *d* I. the devout   *e* MS. a a   *f* I. It was extremely *natural that in*   *g* I. which   *h* I. was

and eye-witnesses. (Robert Hist Hierosolym L v. et vii. Petrus Tudebrod ap. Duchesne Tom iv).[10] The name of St George who on other occasions, in Spain and Italy, is said to have lent a similar aid was invoked by Princes and Warriors as that of their peculiar Patron. Cities and Kingdoms Malta Genoa, Barcelona, Valencia Arragon England &c adopted him as their tutelar[a] Saint; and even the Turks have vied with the[b] Christians in celebrating the martial prowess of their Cælestial Enemy, whom they style the Knight of the white horse (Cotobii in Itinerar. Cantacuzen in Apol. iii. contra Mahametanos).[11] An ample collection of whatever relates to St George may be found in the Bollandists. Acta Sanctorum[12] mens April Tom[c] iii. p 100–163. The first who discovered the Arian persecutor under the mask of sanctity was Isaac Pontanus de Rebus Amstelod. L ii C 4, and though[d] Father Papebroch (Acti SS. Boll. p 112) is extremely angry with him, the more cand:d Abbè de Longuerue[e] (Longueruana Tom.) embraced[f] the opinion of Pontanus with pleasure and assurance. Perhaps our Knights of the Garter would be somewhat astonished at reading this short history of their Patron.

Vol. i. p.   Not.[g]

It would be absurd to quote or even to refute the recent forgeries of Flavius Dexter, Marcus Maximus, Julian Peter, or Luitprand[13] by which the Spaniards have endeavoured to support their favourite tradition that they received the Gospels[h] from the Apostle St James, in the fifteen years which elapsed between the death of Christ and his own Martyrdom. If we except the[i] ambiguous passages[j] of St Jerom (Comment ad Isaiam C 38. 42).[14] the earliest testimonies which can be produced are those of two Spanish Bishops Isidore of Seville, and Julian of Toledo who both flourished in the vii[th] Century. In the ancient liturgy which after the conquest of the Arabs, acquired the title of Mozarabic St James is celebrated as the Apostle of Spain. His pretensions were peaceably admitted into the offices of most of the Latin Churches, and when with the other Arts the art of criticism was restored, he could already boast an uninterrupted possession of 900 years. When the Roman Breviary was

---

[a] *II.* tutelary   [b] *I.* their   [c] *II.* Jan.   [d] *II.* although   [e] *II.* Longuerne (Longuewand) *Om.* Tom. p   [f] *II.* embraces   [g] *II. om.* Vol. i. p. *Not. Entry published MW 1814, v. 492–3.*   [h] *II.* Gospel   [i] *I.* div   [j] *II.* passage

corrected under Clement viii, a serious attention was paid to the doubts of Cardinal Baronius, and the positive[a] assertion of the mission of St James into Spain was exchanged for the qualified expression of "mox Hispaniam adiisse et aliquos discipulos ad fidem convertisse Ecclesiarum illius provinciæ *traditio* est." This national disgrace was obliterated in the year 1635 after forty years negociation, but by the anxious policy of the Court of Rome the new form was composed in such a manner as to guard the pre-eminence of St Peter from the interference of any other Apostle in the West. From that time the Spaniards have triumphed the French critics, Noel Alexandre and Tillemont[15] have been obliged to offer their difficulties with diffidence and respect; and it is pleasant enough to see them stigmatized as free-thinkers by the Bollandists. Acta Sanctorum mens. Julii. Tom vi p 69–114.

About the year 814, one hundred years after the Conquest of Spain by the Arabs, Theodeorier Bishop of Iria Flavia in Gallicia, guided by some nocturnal and præternatural lights, had the good fortune to discover in the adjacent forrest of Compostella, an ancient tomb overgrown with bramble[b] which contained the body of the Patron and Apostle of Spain. A rude and hasty chappel suitable to the poverty of the Christians was immediately built by Alphoso[c] the chaste King of Leon; and in the year 876, his successor Alphonso iii erected[d] on that spot a temple more worthy of the majesty of the Saint. By the verses of Walafridus Strabo (Canis.[e] Antiq. Lecteon. Tom vi p 661)[16] who died in 849, and by the Martyrologies of Ado and Usuard it is evident that before the end of the ixth Century the tomb of St James was celebrated throughout Europe; nor was it difficult to frame a legend which accounted for the conveyance of his body from the country where he had suffered martyrdom to the country where he had preached the Gospel. The solitude of Compostella was insensibly changed into a flourishing City which acquired the Episcopal and even the Metropolitan honours of the deserted sees of Iria Flavia, and Merida. During the tenth and the succeeding centuries, the Spaniards, the French the Germans and the Flemings resorted in pilgrimage to the shrine of St James of Compostella, and such was the ardour of their zeal, that quarrels

[a] *I.* pass   [b] *II.* brambles *Entry published MW 1814, v. 494–5*   [c] *II.* Alphonso
[d] *I.* dedicated   [e] *II.* Cænis.

and even murders very frequently happened while the several nations contended for the privilege of watching before the Altar. (Innocent iii Epistol edit Baluz. L x p 43).[17] On this new theatre the Apostle of Spain soon displayed his miraculous powers for the relief of his friends and the punishment of his enemies. The former experienced his aid in the most imminent dangers, and the most desperate diseases.; and the Arabian General Almanzor[18] who had dared to violate the sanctuary of Compostella lost the greatest part of his army by the effects of the dysentery. (Sampirus Asturicensis in Edit Sandoval[a] p 70. Roderic Toletan L v C 16.)[19] In the wars between the Christians and the Moors it was impossable that St James could remain an indifferent spectator[b] and the Spanish soldiers, particularly the military order which, under his patronage, was founded in the twelfth Century devoutly invoked his aid as that of a good and valiant Knight. Strange as that title might appear for a Saint who probably had never been on horseback in his life (See Monachus Siliensis apud Francisc. de Berganza Antiquit Hispan. p 543)[20] it was soon justified by nocturnal visions which prepared the minds of the Spaniards for the belief of a more public and visible apparition. At first it seems probable that they contented themselves with celebrating the miraculous aid which he had given to their ancestors, and we may observe that his exploits in the battle of Clavigium so pompously described by Mariana[21] (L vii. C 13) and Roderic of Toledo (L iv. C13) are unnoticed by the more ancient writers: But as the[c] habits of faith were insensibly confirmed by time and by repeated acts of credulity the warriors of the twelfth and thirteenth Centuries could persuade themselves and their contemporaries, that, with their own eyes, they had seen their heroick Apostle mounted on a white horse, leading them to battle and to victory. (See Lucas Tudensis[22] ad ann. 1230. Tom iv Hispania Illustrat. p 114). In succeeding Ages, St James displayed his prowess in Italy, Flanders India, and America (see a curious circumstance in Robertson's History of America Vol ii p 448)[23] and his influence was felt, even when his presence was invisible. The day of his festival was auspicious to the arms of Spain, according to the admirable observation of Grotius "diem quem Hispani felicem sibi credunt et credendo sæpe faciunt. ["] Charles the V chose for the invasion of Provence that holy day which in the preceding year had been crowned by the conquest of Tunis but on this occasion

---

[a] *II*. Sandooul   [b] *I. om.* spectator   [c] *I*. their

St James and the Emperor were obliged to retire with disgrace: (See a fine passage in the Memoires de du Bellay quoted by the Abbe d'Artigny Melanges d'histoire &c Tom ii p 290.[24]

The Bollandists by whom I have been guided have laboured the article of St James with indefitagable [sic] diligence. Act. Sanctor. Mensis Jul. Tom vi p 1-124.

The pleasing and even Philosophical fiction of the seven sleepers[25] who in the year 250 retired into a cave near Ephesus to escape the persecution of Decius, and who awoke one hundred and eighty seven years afterwards (see Asseman. Bib. Orient. Tom i p 338). has been received with universal applause. It is remarkable enough that this prodigy should be related by James Sarugi who was born only fifteen years after it is supposed to have happened; and who died Bishop of Batnæ in the year 521. (Asseman. Tom i p 289). From the legends and offices of the Church of Syria the^a tale was soon adopted by the Christian World: by the Latins (Gregor Turon.[26] de glor. Martyr. L i. C 95 passio eorum, quam Syro quodam interpretante in Latinum transtutimus) by the Greeks (Phot. Cod. 253) by the Russians. (Menologium Slavo-Russicum)[27] and by the Abyssians (Ludolf. p 436). Mahomet had probably heard it with pleasure when he conducted the camels of his mistress Cadigiah to the fairs of Syria. He inserted it in the Koran, and the story of the seven sleepers is related and embellished by the Arabs the Persians and all the nations who profess the Mahometan Religion. (Renaudot Hist Patriarch Alexandrin. p 38. 39). The seven sleepers who were^b discovered in a cave in Norway, (Paul. Warnefrid L i C4. Olaus Magnus L i C 3)[28] may serve as a proof how forcibly this fable had affected the imagination of the rudest Nations of the North. The festival of the seven sleepers is observed by the Church of Rome: but even Baronius (Annal Ecclesiast. ad ann 853) has ventured to deny their existence, which the Bollandists very feebly maintain. See Acta Sanct. mens Julii Tom vi. p 375-387

The Greeks the Latins and the Russians revere St Christopher, and we are well assured that before the seventh Century, Churches and monasteries were consecrated under his name. (Eulog. de memorialè SS L ii C 4.10. in Hisp. Illustr. Tom iv. Gregor. Epistol. viii 33). The Acts of this extraordinary Saint represent him as a

^{a} I. it ^{b} I. om. were

Giant eighteen feet high with a human body and a dog's head, born in an island of Cannibals, who was miraculously endowed with speech, reason, and faith; and who converted 48.111 souls[a] before[b] he suffered martyrdom under King Dagnus supposed to the Emperor Decius. If we reject these Acts, we must content ourselves with remaining in total ignorance. See the Bollandists. Acta SS. mens. Julii. Tom vi p 125–149.

Tacitus[c] describes the site of Jerusalem with his accustomed brevity and precision. "duos *colles* immensum editos claudebant *muri* per artem obliqui['']" (Hist. v. ii) See likewise Josephus de B J. L vi. C 6.

The hill situated to the south was called Sion and originally constituted the ancient or upper City. The northern hill called Acra, was gradually covered by the Temple, by the buildings of the new or lower city and in modern times by those which surround the modern sepulchre. Jerusalem has insensibly moved towards the North and the hill of Sion is long since deserted. By the comparaison of the measures taken on the spot by Des Haies and Maundrell, it appears that the actual circumference of Jerusalem amounts to 2000, or 1960 French Toises

According to the measurement of a Syrian Engineer (Euseb.[29] Prep. Evangel. L ix C 36) the circumference of ancient Jerusalem was 27 Stadia which gives us 2550 Toises, and agrees perfectly with the nature of the ground as represented in Des haies's plan. It results from the best authorities and the most accurate measures, that the enclosure of the great Mosque of Jerusalem, (supposed to contain the whole ground of the ancient temple[)] is about 215 Toises in length and 172 in breadth. and consequently about one Roman mile or eight Stadia in circumference. But if we deduct the waste ground allotted for the court of the Gentiles, the temple itself formed a square each side of which was equal to 500 Hebrew cubits or 142 French toises. (A curious dissertation of M. d'Anville sur l'ancienne Jerusalem. Paris. 1747. pp. 75. It is now out of print and was lent me by that Geographer himself[30]

The Generality of Burgundy contains 2432 parishes. and 144.203 *Feux*: computing the latter at five persons to each *feu*, we should find 721.015 inhabitants.[d] But it is probable that this is far below

[a] *I.* persons   [b] *I.* to the   [c] *Entry published MW 1814, v. 496–7*   [d] *I.* p

the real number. According to the Memoirs of M. Ferrand Intendant of Burgundy, the population in the year 1700 amounted to 1.266.359 persons. and according to a denombrement, which the Abbè d'Expilly[31] received de tres bonne main it consisted of 1.273.357 persons. In that case we might assign about 500 persons to a parish. Dictionaire des Gaules. Tom i. p 787.788

Population of Switzerland

1	Zurich town 10.616.	175.009.
	canton 164.393	
2	Bern town 13.681.	336.689.
	canton 323.008	
3.	Lucern. — — —	100.102
4.	Uri — — —	25.528
5.	Scheitz —	21.500
6.	Underwald — —	20.000
7.	Zug — —	20.000
8	Glaris — —	20.000.
9.	Basil — —	28.453.
10.	Friburg. — —	72.800.
11.	Soleurre. — —	45.000
12	Schaffausen — —	30.000.
13.	Appenzel. Protestants 38.000[a]	
	Catholics 13.100[b]	51.100.

The thirteen Cantons.	946.141
The Subjects of the Swiss.	350.900
The Allies of the Swiss.	544.500
Total	1.841.531
Catholics.	829.330
Protestants.	1.012.207

Among the Allies.

The three Leagues of the Grisons. with their subjects of the Valteline &c	250.000
The Abbot territory and free City of St Galt.	100,150.
The Republic of Valais.	90.000.
Geneva $\begin{cases} \text{town. 24.000} \\ \text{country 16.000} \end{cases}$	40.000
Neufchatel and Valengin —	33.330

[a] I. 18.642   [b] I. 6.406

These curious details (the greatest part of which must however be considered only as probabilities and approximations) were furnished by M. Thormann d'Oron. formerly Secretary to the Œconomical Society of Bern, to the Abbè Expilly who published them in his Dictionnaire des Gaules. Tom vi p 1034–1051

After establishing with some probability that the Gultones of Pythias who occupied a space of 6000 stadia among the Œstuaries of the Ocean were the Goths of Sweden, Olaus Rudbeck[32] continues, quanquam autem hæc omnia videantur ex Historiis Norvagorum Islandorum et nostris planissima esse nulla tamen ratio potior illa quam suppeditant LL Uplandicæ veteres. Tit ii S 9. "Tum Rex regno legitime admotus censetur Up-suinoum, puta Suderinanum Guttorum et Gothorum et omnium Smalandorum. *Atlantica Vol i C 12. p 452.*

Fuitque semper Rex Upsalensis Rex totius Sueoniæ a tempore Attini usque ad Agnari divitis mortem. Inde divisum fuit regnum in certas quasdam portiones (*probably ten*) quarum singulas singuli pire hæreditaris sibi adquisiverunt: crevitque hoc pacto Regum hæc loca numerus. Fuit tamen Rex Upsalensis superior habitus reliquis. Snorro p 25 ap. Rudbeck Tom i C vii p 208.

As late as the time of St Olaus of Norway the King of Upsal disdained the alliance of the inferior Kings. Rudbeck p 209. The right of election is explained in the law of Upland or Upsal. Tit de jure Regn. C i. S 1. In eligendo Rege 3 Sueoniæ regionum primæ partes sunt. Penes judicem Uplandiæ primum ad Upsalam esto suffragium Regis inaugurandi; sine vitio sequentibus cæteris. . . . . . . Ostrogothia . . . Westrogothia &c.

Pæderasty

Familiar to the ancient inhabitants of Palestine, the Canaanites &c whose colonies filled the coasts of the Mediterranean: Fable of Sodom (*Genesis xix.* 5); extreme[a] but indiscriminate rigour of the law of Moses (*Leviticus xviii 22. xx. 13*) Story of the Levite. (*Judges xix. 22*) Absolute silence of Homer from my own[b] attentive examination of the Iliad and Odyssey.

Four Dissertations of Maximus of Tyre (*xxxiv. xxv xxvi. xxvii. p. 283–333. Edit. Davis and Markland London 1740*)[33] on the

---

[a] *I.* parti   [b] *I.* accurate and

Socratic love. The language of Socrates is suspicious and scandalous (*p. 287*) but he may be defended by. 1 The silence of his accusers and of the Comic writers (*p. 291. 293*). 2 The loose and amorous style of Homer, Hesiod, Sappho Anacreon &c (*p 293-299*). 3 The purity of his intentions; he *hunted* the youth of Athens for the possession not of their bodies but of their souls. (*p. 301*): human beauty an emanation and image of the το καλον. (p 329-331) Maximus himself correct and vehement. ὡπάντων ἀνθρώπων ἀνσητότατε νεκρὸν ἀνορύττεις· οὐ γὰρ ἂν ᾿Ετλης θίγειν σαρκὸς ἄρρενος, ἀθικτου χρήματος σαρκὶ ἄρρενι. ἄδικος ἡ μίξις, ἄγονος ἡ δυνουσθια &c.

(*p. 319. 321*).

A creed most uncommonly orthodox for a *Greek*! Yet he acknowledges the power of this sensual passion; Actæon of Corinth[a] was torn peacemeal by his lovers (*p 283*). The unfortunate lovers of Locri hanged themselves (*p 319*). The Thebans, Cretans Spartans are praised as *honourable* lovers; but the Eleans were infamous (p. 285. 317).

Lex Scantinia[34] or rather Scatina contra Venerem *nefandam* says the honest German (*Heineccius. Hist Jur. Civ.* 1. *n° 108*) *aversam* says the Polite Italian (*Gravina .Opera. p.432.3*). The *date* of it AUC. 601 (*Pighius Annal. Tom ii p 435*); The *author*. M. Scatinius Aricinus who perhaps desired to efface the ignominy of one of his name (*Val. Max. L vi. C 1: N° 7*) who, for[b] an attempt on his own son had suffered by an extraordinary judgement of the people (AUC. 527 *Pigh. Tom. ii p 116*); another extraordinary judgement AUC. 466 against a creditor[c] who attempted to abuse his debtor a youth the son of a Consul. (*Frensheim. Supplement*[35] *L iv. xi. 25*[)] The *object* molle et effeminatos qui ipsi sponte muliebria paterentur, aut pueris vim inferrent (*Ernesti. Clav. Ciceron*). The *penalty* x mill. nummum (*Quintilian iv. 2. vii 4*); *ridiculed* (Cælius *in Cicer Epist ad Fam. viii. 12. 14*); *enforced* (*Sueton in Domitian C. 8*) *alleged*, but as almost obselete (*Juvenal. Satir ii. 44*).

The hardy and martial education of the Cretan Youth which was imitated by Lycurgus—It was a disgrace not to have a lover.—

---

[a] *I*. Thebes   [b] *I. om.* for   [c] *I*. deb

Rapes, possession of sixty days, civil and religious honours &c
Strabo Geog. L x p 739. 740.—Esteem of the Cretan laws. Ib. p 731

The virtuous, but almost incredible loves of the Spartans, without sensual desire or jealousy of rivals. Xenophon de Resp. Lace-
dæm. p 678 Edit Leunclav. Franckfort 1596. Plutarch in Lycurg.
p. 93. 94. Edit in 12° Henr. Stephan. The danses and exercises of
naked virgins (p 87) might be instituted to promote the cause of
Nature.

Ingenuum stupravit, et stupratus se suspendit; non tamen idem
stuprator capite ut causa mortis punietur sed x mill. quæ pœna
stupratori constituta est dabit.— —Interdum quasi damnemus ipsi.
Vis te dicam vino impulsum errore lapsum nocte deceptum, vera
sunt ista fortasse. tu tamen ingenuum stuprasti, solve x millia.
Quintil. Institut. L iv. C 2. p 336.7. Edit. Burman. he again states
the question. L vii. C 2. p 635.6.

Montesq.[36] L xii C 6. condemns the tyrannical laws against[a]
pæderasty. trust to the genial influence of nature.

finished p 200. April 28th 1783[37]

[a] I. of

Miscellanea.

Petrarch speaks of the use[a] of Gun-powder nuper rara, nunc communis. de Remed. utruisq. fort. L i. Dial 99. ad Azzonem Corregium principem Parmensensem, who sold Parma. AD 1344. Murator. Antiq. Ital. Tom ii Diss. 26. p. 505–6.[1] NB. Yet the Princeps. Parm. might be a compliment of the Orator, or an addition of the Scribe. The treatise should be sifted

[b]Henry, a Protestant, an Anabaptist an Apostate monk, a wandering preacher, speciem pietatis habens, cujus virtutem penitus agnegavit. His gains were spent ludendo aleis, aut in usus turpiores. Frequenter siquidem post diurnum populi plausum, nocte insecutâ cum meretricibus, inventus est et interdum etiam cum conjugatis. Inquira[c] si placet vir nobilis, quomodo de Lausana civitate exierit. &c St Bernard. Epist. 242. Tom i. p 239. Edit Mabillon. Venet. 1750.[2]

[d]Juxta lacum etiam Lausanensem totius diei itinere pergens penitus non attendit aut se videre non videt. Cum enim vespere facto de eodem lacû socii colloquerentur, interrogabat eos, ubi lacus ille esset, et mirati sunt. universi.[3] St Bernardi. Vita secunda auctore Alano. (a monk and Bishop of Auxerre. he died at Clairvaux. AD 1181[e]) C 16. N°. 45. Opera. Tom vi p 1383. 1ma Vit.[f] iii. 2. Tom vi p 1232. One of his disciples Amadeus was Bishop of Lausanne.[4] Vita 1ma L ii. C 8. 1225. ii: C 20 p 1388.

Feuille de la Blancherie. 30. Aout 1786. An Arabic MS. found in the Monastery of St Martin at Palermo containing[g] the public correspondence between the Great Emir and the Mouleis, composed A.H. 375 in the 162d. year of the Conquest. It is written on Bamboo leaves, and is now printing at Palermo, with a Latin version and notes of the Abbé Villa.[5]

Pliniana.

L i. in præfat. a lost passage of Livy. satis gloriæ, jam posse desinere, ni animus inquies pasceretur opere. Pliny scolds him. 20.000 facts

[a] MS. of the use of the use   [b] *Entry published in MW 1814, v. 523–4*
[c] *II.* inquire   [d] *Entry published in MW 1814, v. 524*   [e] *II.* 1183   [f] *II.*
Vet.   [g] *I.* and

in the 36 Books of Pliny from 2000. Vol. ex 100 exquisitis auctoribus. Fabricius or Ernesti (Bibliot Latin. Tom ii p 183) too boldly reads 500: the epithet confines the list to the leading authors *Auctor.* pro scriptor prompts Hardouin to doubt the preface as spurious.[6]— Ενκυκλοπαιλια[a] *Faciebat* not *fecit.* modest Apelles or Polycletus except twice or thrice

[a] *I.* Encycl

[1787 Fragments for Volumes V and VI]

Vol v[a]

1. Charlemagne in Bouquet.[1]
Mecca poems by Jones.[2]
Instruction of Moaviyah. in Otter. Mem.[3]

$\left\{\begin{array}{l}\text{Greek fire. two writers, an Arab}\\\text{a Catalan. apud. Jul. Scaliger}\\\text{contra Cardan. (Isaac Voss. Observat}\\\text{Variæ C. 15. Le Beau. xiii 104}^{4}\end{array}\right.$

Andreæ Schott. Script. Hispan.[5]

$\left\{\begin{array}{l}\text{Genealogy of Basil. by}^{b}\text{ [(]Ducange Fam. Byz. p 138}^{c}\text{[)] Photius,}\\\text{Fleury}^{6}.\\\text{Marriage of Henry i (1051) with}\\\text{the daughter of Russia in Bouquet}^{7}.\end{array}\right.$

$\left\{\begin{array}{l}\text{de Varangis. in Bayer Mem. Petropol.}\\\text{(iv. 275. ix. x)}^{8}\text{ Saxo. Grammaticus}\\\text{perhaps Langebek. Dan. Ducange}\\\text{in Alexiad. et Villehardouin.}^{9}\end{array}\right.$

William. Norman. a lamb, lyon, angel.
perhaps Ordericus Vit.[10]

$\left\{\begin{array}{l}\text{Fabrotti. Basilic}\omega\nu\text{ LX. Paris 1647.}\\\text{Reitz in Meerman. Tom v}^{11}\end{array}\right.$

Glaber of pilgrims. in Bouquet.

$\left\{\begin{array}{l}\text{Miraculous fire of Jerusalem.}\\\text{in Mosheim. Dissert.}^{12}\end{array}\right.$

Saracens in France in Bouquet[13]

Vol vi.

$\left.\begin{array}{l}1\\2\\3.\\\end{array}\right\{\begin{array}{l}\text{French authors of the 1}^{st}\text{ ii}^{d}\text{ and iii}^{d}\\\\\text{Crusade in Duchesne.}^{1}\end{array}$

4. William of Malmsbury. p 130–154.[2]

---

[a] *I.* iv   [b] *I.* in   [c] *I. om.* Ducange . . . p. 138. *Added in bottom margin. Insertion mark apparently after deleted "in."*

5 {English authors of the Crusades.
6 {Richard 1. Edward 1[3]
7. Assises de Jerusalem.[4]
8 Rhamnusius. de bello. C.P.[5]

9. {Dugdale   {of the house of
   {Ezra Cleavland   {Courtenay.
   {Dictionaire d'Expilly[6]

Spanish. history of the Catalan War[7]
Leo Allatius de consensione. Græc.[8]
Adelais or Irene of Brunswick[9]

{Nicephor. Greg {de Genuens.
{Petrarch[10]

Mamalukes. Volney 1. 89–187.[11]
Ransom. of St Louis. Dissert xx.
800[m] Bezans. 400[m] Livres. 100[m] Marks[12]
Haithon. de regn. Orient.[13]
Script. Hung. de Tartaris[14]
Marcus Paulus. Venetus[15]
Yasa. or Yacksa. Timour (Institutions
de) p 61. 121–396. abolished by
Sharock. Arabshah.[16]
Spanish Embassies to Timour[17].
Moscow. not pillaged by Timour
Lesveque. a Note in Vie. 1. p 64.–67.[18]
Knolles.[19]
Marshals of France[20]
Sagredo.[21]
Philelphus de laud. Mahomet ii[22]
Laurus Quirinus to Pope Nic v. (Hody
p 192) MS in Cotton library.[23]
Leonardus Chiensis[24]
Crusii Turco. Græcia.[25]
Lenglet de Fresnoy.[26]

[Other Fragments]

de Bello C. Pano Historia Petri[a] Ramnusii. Editio altera. Venetus
1634[b]. in folio. Villehardouin ad unguem est secutus other authors
common—no Archives. Habuit autem classis universa (ut annales
Veneti tradunt.) naves 480.

[a] *DF corrects to* Paulo   [b] *DF corrects to* 1635

Nam præter triremes numero 50. Venetis classiariis militibus remigibusque refertas quas ab initio Dandulus Gallis liberaliter, putatis studio pollicitus fuerat, 310 oneraries instructæ dicuntur in quarum 240 quæ sine remigiis quadratis velis agebantur[a] externus miles est impositus, reliquis 70 commeatus et cætera impedimenta deportabantur, quum hippagogis 120 omnis Cataphractorum equitatus deveheretur. L i. p 33. He names the 50 Captains of the gallies, all Venetian nobles. p 38.

Pantaleon Barbus, a patriot opposed the election of Dandulus. (L iii p 137 ut tradunt annales Veneti [)][1]

1. Representation du procedé tenu en l'instance faicte devant le Roi par Messieurs de Courtenay pour la conservation de l'honneur et dignité de leur maison branche de la Royalle[b] maison de France à Paris 1613 in 8°.

2. Representation du subject qui a porté MM de Salles et de Fraville de la maison de Courtenay à se retirer hors du Royaume 1614. in 8°

3. De stirpe et origine domût de Courtenay. addita sunt responsa celeberrimorum Europæ. Jurisconsultoram Paris. 1607 of[c] 20. of Italy and Germany who all agree for the fact and right.[c] Esme in 1603. xiii[th] from Peter. In their poverty, they retired, veiled their rank. served as soldiers—first legal demand in 1603. injuriously provoked to prove their noblesse.

low condition of Joseph and Mary no bar to their being acknowledged of the race of David.

Esme de Courtenay had killed the Baron de la Riviere 1609[d] he [demanded][e] a tryal as a prince—The parliament prosecuted him as a private man. His letter from Thionoille May 8. 1610. was not received till after Henry iv's death. princes for private crimes have no occasion for a pardon under the great seal. theirs with yellow wax not green[f].[2]

Pope published that Manuel refused to worship an image of Christ. wrote against him. Hist pol. p 1[3] Had the Emp. been known, a captive p. 12.[4] new settlers from Mesembria, Selybria Heraclea, Adrianopole &c. received from Mahomet houses at CP. lands, and slaves and bought many valuables cheap. p 13[5] At the end of five

---

[a] I. ab   [b] I. maison Royalle   [c] I. om. of . . . right.   [d] I. om 1609
[e] I. demanded a free pardon or a tryal ("demanded" deleted accidentally)   [f] I. white

days, the Great Duke. Great domestic; Protostrator (fil Cantac
μεσαζοντος[6]) put to death. p 12. 13.[7] Gallies over land p. 9.[8]
Hist politicæ. CP. 1391–1478 in Crusii Turco-Græcia. p 1–43.[9]
Theodos. Zygomala Epist ad Martin Crusium AD 1581 p 74–98.
de CP. periculis. de Græcia statu[10] Hist Patriarch. post captam urbem. L v. p 106–184. Emanuel.
Malaxus scrips. in Græc. vulg.
Mahomet invested with the crosier.[11] Leonard. Chiensis from Chios.
16 August. 1453[a]. Hist à Turca CP. p 108 20 leaves. Norimbergæ
1544. in 4° 300.000 Turks. 15.000 Janizaries. greatest cannon broke.
second drawn 150 yoke of oxen—ball lapidem qui palmis undecim
ex meis ambibat in gyro.[12] Greeks wanted powder their ordance
less heavy. Walls could not support the great ones the Turks
covered[b] by ruins, yet sometimes homines et tent. extermin.[13]

four ships from Chios, three[c] Genoese, one Imp. with corn from
Sicily[14] last speech. more to the Latins.

Justinian. gloriæ, salutis, Suique oblitus[15]

At[d] indies doctiores nostri paravere contra hostes machinamenta
quæ tamen avare dabantur. Pulvis erat nitri, modica exigua; tela
modica Bumbardæ[e] si aderant, incommoditate loci primum hostes
offendere maceriebus[f] alveisque tectos non poterant. Nam siquæ
magnæ erant, ne murus concuteretur noster quiescebant.[16]

> Ad quæ marmoreas præstabat Roma columnas,
> Quasdam præcipuas pulchra Ravenna dedit.
> De tam longinquâ poterit regione vetustas
> Illius ornatum, Francia, ferre tibi.

Poeta Saxonicus (he lived under Arnoul) de rebus Gestis Caroli
magni L v. 437–440 in Bouquet Tom v. p 180. He copies Eginhard
and the monk of S[t] Gall.

Extruxit etiam Aquisgrani basilicam plurimæ pulchritudinis ad
cujus structuram a Roma et Ravenna columnas et marmora devehi
fecit Sigebert in Chron. Bouquet Tom v. p 378[17]

[a] I. om. from . . . 1453   [b] I. by   [c] I. one G   [d] I. Nor
[e] DF bombardæ   [f] I. non poterant maceriebus

[Codice Diplomatico]

Codice Diplomatico della Sicilia sotto il governo degli Arabi, publicato per opera e studio di Alfonso Airaldi Arcivescovo di Eraclea, Giudice dell'Apostolica legazione, e[a] della Regia Monarchia nel Regno di Sicilia. Tom. ii. Parte 1ma Parte ii[da] (two Volumes in 4°. pp. 564, 661.). Palermo della Regia stamperia. 1790.[1]

These Acts extend from the year 296 to 375 of the Arabic Æra of Mahomet. in 300 (P. i p. 92. 93) The Archbishop approaches with conscious shame the Hegira[2] yet he still maintains an Arabic solar year which begun in March as the Greek in September. The text translated and medals explained by the Abbate Giuseppe Vella,[3] intendissimo de caratteri Arabo-Occidentali, called[b] to the Academy of Naples (p xxvi) his divina peritea is praised by Olaus Gerardus Tychsen in Univ. Rostock Prof. ling. Oriental. ad calcem P. i.

Airoldi gives in his preface a tolerable history of the Aglabites and Fatimites.[4]—has given in the two first Tomes l'intiero primo Codice Martiniano, promises in the third tutte le altre Memorie, from another Cod. Mart, and from Fez and Morocco (p xxvi[)]

Part ii. p 528–534

In the year 364 e morto l'Arcivescovo de Balirmu, che era huomo assai buono et era mio[c] amico: a Christian priest the friend of the Great Emir!

The claim of the Patriarch of CP rejected by the Emir and Caliph— The Archb[ishop][d] of Palermo consecrated by the Bishops of Sicily. that of ordaining him at CP, probable enough (Thomassin Discipline de l'Eglise. Tom i L i. C 10. Tom ii L ii. C 8. 19): but the inheritance of Bishops a last usurpation of Rome or rather Avignon in the great schism. (Tom iii L ii. C 57. Was Palermo an[e] Archb. in 976?[)]

In 883 Sicily once Roman now Greek had cum insulis minoribus twenty two Bishops of whom Syracuse was Metropolitan and Panormus the seventh only. (Notitiæ Episcopat Græc. a Leone

[a] *I.* et   [b] *I.* a member of   [c] *I.* il   [d] *I. om.* The Archb . . . Sicily
[e] *I.* and

Sapiente ad Andronicum Palæslogun. a Jacob. Goar (Script. Byz. Tom 18. p 303. Edit Venet.)

In 1071. Archiepiscopus Panormitanus. Græcus timidus .. ab impiis dejectus in paupere Ecclesiâ Sᵗⁱ Cyriaci. restored by the Normans to the Cathedral. BMV. Gaufred Malaterra Hist. Sicula. L ii. C 45. in Muratori Script rerum. Italic.⁵ Tom v. p 574.

A Latin Archb. Alcher. till 1109, Gregory vii s bull in 1083. Fleury. Hist. Eccles. xiii. p 537 from Rocch. Pyrrhus. Tom i. p 100.

AH. 347 or rather 351 a grand circumcision of 15.000 Sicilian boys beginning by the sons and brothers of the Emir. The African Lord gave 100.000 pieces of silver and 50 bales of new cloathing for the new Moslems (Abulfeda Annales. Tom ii p 447. a Reiske et Adler. Scio habedin in Excerpt. Hist. Saracenico-Siculæ a Carusio in Muratori. Script. rerum Italic. Tom i. Part ii p 252.)⁶

The Codice Diplomatico. Tom ii P ii p 329 employsᵃ the fact and the Emir himself writes that he circumcised his own son a new born infant, of whom his wife (la mia moglie, had he but one?) was delivered a few days before.

Yet the Mahometans do not circumcise their children, till they are at least six years old, till they can repeat, There is but one God and Mahomet is his prophet. (Sale's preliminary discourse to the Koran. p 106) Ah you thought of the Jews!

Zanklah, and Stamboul,⁷ old Greek, and new Turkish!

Basilian monks: yes now there are Benedictines Franciscans &c.

In Catana or Katine.⁸ 200.000, or 230.000 inhabitants (Tom ii P. i p 64. P ii. p 140)

ᵃ *I.* employed

Materials for a Seventh Volume

Substantive Changes, *Decline and Fall*, B.M. Shelf-Mark C. 60 m. 1

I, 1. (first paragraph; Bury i. 1) [Substitution of "times" for "empire" in "prosperous condition of their empire". Marginal comment]: Should I not have given the *history* of that fortunate period which was interposed between two Iron ages? Should I not have deduced the decline of the Empire from the civil Wars, that ensued after the fall of Nero or even from the tyranny which succeeded the reign of Augustus?[1] Alas! I should: but of what avail is this tardy knowledge? Where error is irretrievable, repentance is useless.

I, 2. (first paragraph; Bury i. 1) [Substitution for "to deduce the most important circumstances of its decline and fall; a revolution which will ever be remembered, and is still felt by the nations of the earth"]: to prosecute the decline and fall of the Empire of Rome: of whose language, Religion and laws the impression will be long preserved in our own, and the neighbouring countries of Europe. [marginal comment] N.B. Mr. Hume told me that in correcting his history, he always laboured to reduce superlatives, and soften positives. Have Asia and Africa, from Japan to Morocco, any feeling or memory of the Roman Empire?

I, 2. (second paragraph; Bury i. 1) ["a rapid succession of triumphs" underlined. In margin] EXCURSION 1, *on the succession of Roman Triumphs*

I, 3. (third paragraph; Bury i. 2–3) [new note to "the advice of confining the empire within those limits, which Nature seemed to have placed as its permanent bulwarks and boundaries"] Incertum metû an per invidiam (Tacit. Annal. I. 11) Why must rational advice be imputed to a base or foolish motive? To what cause, error, malevolence or flattery shall I ascribe this unworthy alternative? Was the historian dazzled by Trajan's conquests?

Note 15, to I, 6. (Bury i. 5, n. 16) [Addition] Julian assigns this Theological cause of whose power he himself might be conscious[a] (Caesares p 327.) Yet I am not assured that the Religion of Zamolxis

[a] *I.* conscious himself

subsisted in the time of Trajan, or that his Dacians were the same people with the Getæ of Herodotus. The transmigration of the Soul has been believed by many nations,[a] warlike as the Celts, or pusill-animous like the Hindoos. When speculative opinion is kindled into practical enthusiasm, its operation will be determined by the prævious character of the man or the nation.

I, 7. (eighth paragraph, Bury i. 6) [Substitution of "minds" for "characters" in "the thirst for military glory will ever be the vice of the most exalted characters"; additional note] The first place in the temple of fame is due and is assigned to the successful heroes who had struggled with adversity; who, after signalizing their valour in the deliverance of their country have displayed their wisdom and virtue in foundation or government of a flourishing state[.] Such men as Moses, Cyrus Alfred, Gustavus Vasa Henry iv of France &c.[2]

I, 7. (eighth paragraph; Bury i. 6) [Substitution for second sentence] Late generations, and far distant climates may impute their calamities to the immortal author of the Iliad. The spirit of Alexan-der was inflamed by the praises of Achilles: and succeeding Heroes have been ambitious to tread in the footsteps of Alexander. Like him the Emperor Trajan aspired to the conquest of the East; but the Roman[b] lamented with a sigh &c

I, 11. (thirteenth paragraph; Bury i. 9) [Additional note to "climates of the North over those of the South"] The distinction of North and South is real and intelligible; and our pursuit is terminated on either side by the poles of the Earth. But the difference of East and West is arbitrary, and shifts round the globe. As the men of the North not of the West the legions of Gaul and Germany were superior to the *south*-eastern natives of Asia and Egypt. It is the triumph of cold over heat; which may however and has been sur-mounted by moral causes.

I, 15. (sixteenth paragraph; Bury i. 12) [Additional note to "corre-spondent number of tribunes and centurions".] The composition of the Roman officers was very faulty. 1. It was late before a Tribune was fixed to each cohort. Six tribunes were chosen for the entire legion, which two of them commanded by turns (Polyb. L vi p 526 Edit Schweighæuser)[3] for the space of two months. 2. Our long subordination from the Colonel to the Corporal was unknown.

[a] *I.* other nations   [b] *I.* he lamen

I cannot discern any intermediate ranks between the Tribune and the Centurion the Centurion, and the Manipularis or private legionary. 3 As the Tribunes were often without experience, the Centurions were often without education, mere soldiers of fortune who had risen from the ranks (eo immitior, quia toleraverat. Tacit. Annal 1.20). A body equal to eight or nine of our battalions might be commanded by half a dozen young gentlemen and fifty or sixty old serjeants Like the legion, our great ships of war may seem ill-provided with officers: but in both cases the deficiency is corrected by strong principles of discipline and vigour.

Note 53 to I, 17. (Bury i. 14, n. 55) [Substitution for "As . . . Agricola"] Quôd mihi pareret legio Romana Tribuno. (Horat Serm. L i. vi, 45); a worthy commander, of three and twenty from the schools of Athens! Augustus was indulgent to noble birth, liberis Senatorum . . . militiam auspicantibus non tribunatum modo legionum, sed et præfecturas alarum dedit (Sueton. C 38).

Note 86 to I, 32. (Bury i. 26, n. 94) [Addition to note, after underlining "a league and a half above the surface of the sea"] More correctly, according to Mr Bouguer, 2500 Toises (Buffon Supplement Tom. V p 304).[4] The height of Mont Blanc is now fixed at 2426 Toises. (Saussure Voyage dans les Alpes Tom i p 495):[5] but the lowest ground from whence it can be seen is itself greatly elevated above the level of the sea. He who sails by the isle of Teneriff, contemplates the entire Pike, from the foot to the summit.

II, 353. (Chapter XXII, last paragraph; Bury ii. 430) [New note to "But the personal merit of Julian was, in some measure, independent of his fortune"] το τεχνιον πασα γαια τρεφει was the boast and comfort of Nero the musician (Sueton. C 40). But the applause of venal or trembling crowds was dispelled by the first manifesto of the Rebels, which pronounced him a most execrable performer; (C 41)[a] and could he have survived his descent from the throne, it is more than probable, that he would have been hissed from the stage. The present King of N[aples][6] is satisfied that, in case of a revolution, he could subsist by the trade of a fisherman or a pastrycook. Perhaps he would be disappointed. The amusement of a hour must not contend with the labour of a life. Frederic[7] alone, of the monarchs of the age, was capable, like Julian, of making his own fortune

---

[a] *I. om.* (C 41)

IV, Preface, iv. (Bury i. xii) [Substitution of "[ha]ve been silent, as long [as] he" for "should be silent, if he still" "dispensed the favours of the crown." Addition] In the year^a 1776 when I published the first Volume, in 1781 when I published the second and third, Lord North[8] was first Lord of the treasury. I was his friend and follower, a Member of parliament and a Lord of trade: but I disdained to sink the Scholar in the politician.

V, 367. (Chapter LI; Bury v. 475) [Substitution re "Algezire" for "that advances into the sea" in "they bestowed the name of the Green island, from a verdant cape that advances into the sea"]: and small isle on the western side of the bay of Gibraltar.

VI, 209. (Chapter LXI; Bury vi. 444, and n. 87) [Deletion of second sentence of note 67, which is renumbered 67[4]; addition in text after "Each pilgrim was ambitious to return with his sacred spoils, the relics of Greece and Palestine; and each relic was preceded and followed by a train of miracles and visions."] A cross, or a crown of thorns might be easily transported; since the house of the Virgin Mary was carried through the air two thousand miles, from Nazareth to Loretto[67], a perpetual monument[67²] of priestly fraud, and popular credulity.[67³]

[At end of paragraph: 67[4]][9]

VI, 291 (Chapter LXIV, second to last sentence, third paragraph; Bury vii. 4) [Substitution in the text, after "The reason of Zinghis was not informed by books; the khan could neither read nor write; and, except the tribe of the Igours," for "the greatest part of the Moguls and Tartars were as illiterate as their sovereign"]: the præceptors of the North, his native subjects were as illiterate as their sovereign.

VI, 292 (Chapter LXIV, last sentence, third paragraph; Bury vii. 5–6) [Substitution of "the Mogul" for "their domestic" annals; addition of "Japanese[7²]" to beginning of the list; addition to the sentence]: The zeal [17²] and curiosity[17³] of Europe soon explored the Empire of the Great Khan; and the monuments of Tartar history have been illustrated by the learning of modern times.[18] [vi. 293][10]

VI, 567 (Chapter LXX, third sentence first paragraph; Bury vii. 255) [Substitution of "judgement" for "taste" in "the taste of a learned nation."][11]

^{a} I. years

Vol 1   Supplement
                             to
                       the History
                            of
        the decline and fall of the Roman Empire

[p. 85. 1 19-.][a1] I here confound the maternal with the paternal
descent of Augustus. His mother was indeed of Aricia, a municipal
alliance which Cicero[(1)] very properly defends against the noble
insolence of Antony. But the *Octavian* family belonged to *Velitræ*
an ancient city of Latium,[(2)] which had been worthy to suffer for
its brave resistance to the arms of Rome. The opposite reports of
friends and enemies are honestly and doubtfully stated by Suetonius.[(3)] I much fear that the great-grandfather of Augustus was
a freedman and a rope-maker: the grandfather was content with the
enjoyment of wealth and the obscure honours of his corporation;
and his long life was more innocent and happy than[b] that of his
grandson. The father of Augustus was the first Senator and Prætor
of his family: his provincial administration of Macedonia is crowned
by the impartial praise of Cicero[(4)]; and death alone could have
blasted his hopes of the Consulship[.]

[1.c] Philippic iii. 6   [2] See Cluver. Ital. Antiq Tom ii L iii p 1015 &c.
[3] Sueton in Octav. C 1-4   [4] ad Quintum fratrem. L i Ep. 1. 2.[2]

1[rst] Period[1]

*From the accession of Nerva to the
death of Marcus Antoninus*

Marcus Cocceius Nerva

[Vol. i. p. 91][d2]

[A D 96 — — September 18.][e] After the murder of Domitian, Nerva
a venerable Senator was invested with the purple. His wishes rather

---

[a] *In margin of MS. unbracketed*   [b] *MS. that*   [c] *MS. has notes in right-
hand margin. Note numbers, both here and in text, are Gibbon's.*   [d] *In right-hand
margin of MS. unbracketed*   [e] *Dates Gibbon's but in margin of MS. unbracketed.*

than his actions, his virtues rather than his powers announced to the Romans, the first dawn of the Golden Age.

[AD. 97[a] October. 28] Oppressed by the vices of the times, and the insolence of the Prætorian Guards, Nerva supplied his own weakness by the adoption and association of Trajan who commanded the legions of the lower Germany. The manly vigour and military[b] powers of the *son*, secured the public peace during the three last years of the *father's* reign

Marcus Ulpius Trajanus

[A D. 98 January 27 A D. 100 &c —] -Emigration of the Huns from the confines of China westward. The more savage Hords pitched their tents along the Volga, while the Euthalites, or Indo-Scythæ, or white Huns occupied the cities of Sogdiana, and the banks of the Indus.

[A D 100 September. 1] Pliny the Consul pronounced in the Senate the Panegyric of Trajan; who listened during three unblushing hours to the sound of his own praise.

[AD. 103. —] First Triumph of Trajan over the Dacians, and the first which Rome ever extorted from that warlike nation. The suppliant Ambassadors of their King Decebalus were referred by the General to the Senate.

[A D 105 —] The dependent Kingdom of Arabia Petræa was reduced into a province. The cities of Petra and Bostra dated from that event the æra of their felicity.

[A D 108 — —] Second triumph of Trajan over the Dacians whom he finally subdued after five years War. Decebalus escaped by a voluntary death from the shame of being led a captive. The Roman province of Dacia was an evidence of conquest more certain, though less durable than the column at Rome or the bridge over the Danube.

[AD 110 —] The Imperial provinces of Bithynia and Pontus were delegated to Pliny the younger: his Epistle with Trajan's rescript is the most ancient and authentic record of the progress and persecution of the Christians. The martyrdom, at Rome of Ignatius Bishop of Antioch may be placed about this time

[AD 112.] Trajan was near sixty years of age, when he marched into

---

[a] *I.* 98   [b] *I.* public tranquility (*replaced by* military powers)

the East against the Parthians, and ambitiously aspired to emulate the conquests of Alexander.

[AD 116 — —] After the reduction of Armenia, Mesopotamia, and Assyria, the victorious Emperor gave a King to the Parthians; and indulged his pride and curiosity by sailing down the Euphrates and Tigris into the Persian gulph.

[AD. 117. August 10.] In his return homewards Trajan died at Selinus in Cilicia from him surnamed Trajanopolis. In his last moments the arts of the Empress Plotina obtained or supposed the adoption of his cousin Hadrian.

Publius Ælius Hadrianus.

[August 11 — — AD 120 — —] After the evacuation of the Eastern conquests of Trajan, the active Genius of Hadrian undertook a series of itinerant labours far superior to those of Hercules

> Nec vero Alcides tantum telluris obivit.

But it would be difficult to measure the steps or to mark the dates of his circuits of the Roman World, every province of which he regulated[a] and adorned

[AD 121 —] A wall or rampart of turf was erected by Hadrian from the Solway to the Tine to protect the Roman province of Britain against the inroads of the Caledonians.

[AD 130 —] Hadrian visited Egypt: the temple and city which he consecrated to the beautiful Antinous are the monuments of his shame and grief.

[A D 132 —] The perpetual Edict was composed and published by Salvius Julianus the Prætor of the year and the most eminent lawyer of the age. This civil Code and the Imperial constitutions of Hadrian himself gave a new form to the Roman Jurisprudence.

[AD 133 —] Amidst his civil and military labours, Hadrian reposed himself at least[b] for the third time in the groves of the Academy. The Emperor accepted the annual office of Archon, listened to the Christian Apologies, was initiated to the Eleusinian mysteries, finished the temple of the Olympic Jupiter, and deserved the names of Benefactor and lawgiver of Athens.

[a] *I*. b   [b] *I*. the least

[A D 135.] A rebellion of the Jews, who had followed their Messiah Barchochebas was suppressed by the Lieutenants of Hadrian. Five hundred and eighty thousand were slain, Palestine was depopulated, Jerusalem was profaned. Since this irrecoverable blow the Jews have never presumed to erect a national standard.

[AD 138. January 1.] The death of Lucius Ælius Verus, the adoptive son of Hadrian, and the first who enjoyed the title of *Cæsar*, as a dignity subordinate to that of *Augustus*

[July 10ᵗʰ] The death of Hadrian himself. The impatience of sickness betrayed him into some acts of cruelty: but the verses to his departing soul bespeak a happy composure; and he deserved the gratitude of posterity by the adoption of [a] a son and a grandson, of the elder and the younger Antonine.

TITUS ANTONINUS PIUS

[AD 140 — —] A wall or rampart of turf between the firths of Clyde and of Forth was erected by Lollius Urbicus Governor of Britain, who afterwards stretched his conquests on the Eastern side of Scotland as far as Inverness. But this remote and useless acquisition, the province, as it is called of Vespasiana was doubtfully held, and speedily lost.

[A D 147 — —] The younger Antonine, Marcus Aurelius, was invested with the Tribunitian and Proconsular powers. From this time the merits of their auspicious Government may be divided between the Father and the son; but they enjoyed without a division the inimitable concord of virtue and friendship the unsuspecting confidence of authority and obedience.

The Secular games were celebrated at the close of the ninth Century of Rome; nor did that festival ever present so fair a picture of the public felicity.

[A D 161 March 7.] Antoninus Pius, the[b] Numa of Imperial Rome, died at the age of seventy five. During a reign of twenty three years the master of the World was unconscious of a foreign or[c] domestic enemy.

---

[a] *Page Gibbon numbered* 3 *began here* (293ʳ)   [b] *I.* died   [c] *I.* of

Marcus Aurelius Antoninus Philosophus
Lucius Cejonius Commodus Verus.

After the association of Verus, the Roman Empire beheld for the first time two *Augusti* invested with equal supremacy. The dissolute life of Verus was unstained with blood; but his only merit was a grateful reverence for the [*sic*; unfinished][3]

[AD 167 —] The two Emperors triumphed for the Parthian victories which had been obtained under their auspices by their Lieutenants. While they fought in Armenia and Babylonia, Marcus was detained at Rome by duty, and Verus was amused at Antioch by pleasure. The ruin of Seleucia and Ctesiphon, and the importation of the plague were the fruits of the Parthian War.

[A D 168. —] At the head of a barbaric confederacy which spread from the Ocean to the Euxine, the Marcomanni and Quadi threatened Italy, and summoned the two Emperors to the Upper Danube.

[AD 169.] The death of Verus, whose vices displayed and disgraced the philosophy of his wiser Colleague.

[A D 174.] A seasonable storm of rain, hail, and lightening which refreshed the Romans and dismayed the Barbarians was improved into a miracle: and the miracle might be variously ascribed to Egyptian magic, to Jupiter and Mercury, or to the God of the Christians.

[A D 175.] The Revolt of Avidius Cassius in Syria. The single Rebel of the age was obliged to report the Emperor's death, and to affect the restoration of the Commonwealth Yet his dream of Royalty lasted only three months, and Marcus enjoyed the exquisite pleasure of the forgiveness of injuries.

[A D 176 November 27.] The[a] Philosophic Marcus bestowed the title of Augustus on his son Commodus a boy of fifteen, and the character of Goddess on his departed wife, the wanton Faustina: a fond parent, and a blind husband!

[December 23.] The two Emperors triumphed over the Marcomanni and Quadi; a præmature triumph for an imperfect victory!

[A D 178 August 5.] The two Emperors were summoned to the Upper Danube by a rebellion of the Marcomanni and Quadi, whom they again vanquished in several engagements.

[A D 180 March 17.] Marcus Antoninus at the age of fifty nine died

---

[a] *Page Gibbon numbered 4 began here (293[v]). Gibbon did not number f. 292*

at Vienna on the Danube. His virtuous spirit, according to every good system of Religion must have been received with open arms by the Father of the Universe

The Limits of the Roman Empire

In the first chapter of my history I have given the state of the Roman provinces. During this period the Emperors acquired the stony[a] confines of Arabia,[4] and the ample province of Dacia. Some debatable land in Britain was alternately gained and lost. The conquests of Trajan beyond the Euphrates passed away like a shadow.

[Vol. vi. p 200.]

Vol. vi. p 200. Not. 51.[1] Historia susceptionis coronæ spineæ J.C. quam Ludovicus Rex a Balduino. Imperii C.P hærede obtinuit ac Parisus reportavit. AD 1239. auctore Galtero Cornuto Archiepiscopo Senonensi—[1.]

Louis had disapproved and stopped the donation of Courtenay[2] to the Prince of Achaia and Baldwin acquiesces and even rejoyces in this opposition which preserves the family estate as a jointure for his wife. tanta inopia et paupertatis angustiâ tenebamur oppressi, quòd[b] penitus ignorabamus quo ire aut quid facere deberemus.[2]

Baldwin offers his niece to the Sultan of Iconium[3] and presses Queen Blanche[4] to obtain her from her parents. The Sultan is the richest and most powerful of the Pagans, a friend of Baldwin, an enemy of Vataces.[5] He engages by treaty 1. To allow the princess her Religion, Chappel, Clergy &c 2. To rebuild and protect the Christian Churches. 3. To oblige the Bishops to obey the Latin Patriarch. His Emir insinuated a distant hope of his conversion.[3.]

[1][c] Duchesne[6] Historiæ Francorum scriptores. Tom v. p 407-411.
[2.] *Vol. vi. p 197[d].* Duchesne Tom v. p 423-424.
[3] *Vol. vi. p 197[d].* Duchesne Tom v. p. 424-426

[The Sabatic year and the Jubilees]

The Sabatic year and the Jubilees a demonstration of the Divine legation of Moses?[1]—an argument in two parts the first unsupported by reason, the second contradicted by facts.[1]

Petavius doubts whether the Jews observed the Jubilees and Sabatic years during the periods of Idolatry and servitude[2.]

[a] *I.* r   [b]*I.* ut   [c] *Notes in right-hand margin of MS.*   [d] *Actually 199.*

During the Babylonish captivity the land was left uncultivated, till the number of Sabatic years had been fully repaid. As[a] we reckon 52 or 70 years the neglect will carry us to the years 952 or 1096 before Christ, and the latter æra coincides with the government of Samuel.[(3.)]

The Jubilees of Palestine revived at Rome; the name rather than the institution.[(4.)]

1.[b] Lettre d'un anonyme dans le Tom xxx. p 83–115 de la Bibliothéque

2 de Doctrina temporum. L ix. C 27. Tom ii p 31. Antwerp. 1703.

3. Prideaux Connections. A.B.C. 536. he quotes ii. Chronicles. xxxvi. 21.

4 *Vol. vi. p 559*[2]

Memoranda

Forest at C.P.— {Voyages de la Motraye[1] Tom i. p 267–273. 410. 411 422

View of C.P. {Letters of Baron Fabricius xiv. p 56. 57. English. Edition.[2]

Act of Union at Florence {Bibliotheque Critique de Richard Simon. Tom i C v. p. 52–56.[3]

Supplemental notes to the six Volumes of the History of the decline and fall of the Roman Empire[c]

(1)[d] *Vol vi. p 508.* View of C. P—— Letters of Baron Fabricius. xiv. p 56.57. English translation.[1]

(2) *vi. 412 Not. 72.* Act of Union in the Synod of Florence——— Bibliotheque Critique de Richard Simon. Tom i. C 5. p 52–56[2]

(3) *vi. 120.* Ruins of S[t] John d'Acre—Memoires du Chevalier d'Arvieux Tom i. p 269–280[3]

[a] *I.* If by Gibbon.
[b] *MS. page divided in half; text on left half; notes on right. Numbered*
[c] *MS. rectos only*
[d] *Numbers superscript in MS.*

(4) *iv. 327* The plague in the East—Capper's Observations on the passage to India. p 230.231[4]

---

(5) *V. 287*.[5] Population of Bassora——Capper's Observations &c. p 228.

---

(6) *1.66.67*[6] Communication between Egypt and India— — — Capper's Observations &c p 45–61, and passim Introduction and letter

(7) *Vol. iv. 126 Nº 4*.[7] Speedy passage from England to India— Capper's Introduction p xxvi

---

(8) *V. 562.* Harold the Varangian. — Torfæi. Hist. rerum Norvegicarum P. iii. p 202 255–372. Mallet. Hist. de Dannemarc. Tom ii p 273–276. Tom iii p 193–214 (in 12°), who quotes Annalist Saxon. apud Eccard Corpus Hist. Tom i. col. 496 Pontoppidan. Gesta Danorum extra Daniam. Tom i. p 32–34[8]

---

(9) *vi. 64*.[9] Danes and Norvegians in the Holy land ——Pontoppidan Gesta Danorum &c. Tom i. p 37–57

---

(10) *V. 562. vi. 64*.[10] Crusade of Sigurd King of Norway A D 1107— Torfæi. Hist. Norveg. rerum Tom iii p 447–460

---

(11) *vi. 209* House of Loretto—Geddes's Miscellanies Vol iv. p 97–155[11]

---

(12) *V. 538.* Servetus—Chauffepié: Dictionaire Critique Tom iv. p 219–245 ₶[a] Intolerance of the reformers and Apology of Calvin- Bibliotheque Raisonnée. Tom i p 366–400. Tom ii p 93–176, perhaps by M. de la Chapelle[12]

---

(13) Vol. v. p 368. Force again Gibraltar-Drinkwater's Hist. of the siege of Gibraltar[13] p 281 ff Ammunition-p 353

---

[a] *A signal to the printer? See below Gibbon's notes 14–16.*

(14) *iv. 153. № 33.* Ecclesiastes, Sceptic or Saducean.—Calmet. preface ‖. Salvation of Solomon. Dissertations[14] Tom ii. p 178–192

---

(15) *III. 525.526* Ruins of the Church and monastery of St Simeon Stylites—Drummond's travels into Asia[15] p 195–198 ‖‖ .about 40 miles east of Antioch, 26. NE of Aleppo—Map and Itineraries. p 288.289

---

(16) *Vᵃ. 292 N⁰ 7².* Invasion of Japan by the Moguls——Kæmpfer's Hist. of Japan. L ii. C 5 p 187 ‖‖‖ from the national annals, Nippon Odaiki, and Nippon Okaitsû, both in Sʳ Hans Sloane's museum[16]- Introduction p xlvii

---

(17) *iv. 616.* A parrot's creed — Buffon. Hist Naturelle[17] Tom xxi (des oiseaux vi) p 104

---

(18) *iv. 411.* De jure libertatis P.R. judicium——Cicero in Verrem. Actio ii. L i. C 5. et Hottoman Paul. Manutium &c in locum[18]

---

(19) *iv. 325.* The King of Portugal fired a pistol at the Comet of 1664.—Memoirs of Fremont d'Ablancourt. p 150. English translation[19]

(20.) *iv. preface.* The Leman lakes denominated by the ancients, lake of Lausanne——Hadrian Vales. Notitia Galliarum. p 265 d'Anville Notice de la Gaule. p 406. Antonin Itinerar. p 378. Edit. Wesseling. Loys de Bochat. Memoires sur l'hist. ancienne de la Suisse. Tom iii p 601. *vi. p 84. № 30²⁰*

---

(21) *V.ᵇ 384.385.* The wife's claim of property to her husband's testicles—is gravely related by the *Reverend* Dʳ Joseph Warton Essay on the Genius and writings of Pope Vol. i. p 322. 324. first Edition—Quære whether it be not left out in the second?[21]

(22.) *vi. 83 N⁰ 29*—Clairvaux has lately bought and buried a learned library of the President Bouhier—d'Alembert. Memoires des Academiciens. Tom v. p 306.307[22]

ᵃ *Actually VI.*   ᵇ *Actually IV.*

(23.) *iv. 68.* ὡς καλον εστιν ενταφιον ἡ τυραννις — Isocrates in Archidamo. Tom ii p 40 Edit Auger, the saying of a friend of Dionysius.[23]

(24.) *ii. 531.* A town of Cannibals lately between Surat and Ahmedabad, foolish! ———— Voyages de Thevenot. Part iii. L i. C 4. p 19[24]

(25.) iv. 547. A million of Jews in Egypt, credat Judæus!— Philo adv. Flacc. p 523 l 30 apud Heyne Opuscul. Tom i p 134[25]

(26.) v.[a] p 343. N° 116. Fabulis similia..fide Abulpharagii[26]——
Heyne Opuscul. Tom i. p. 129. de genio sæculi Ptolemæorum.

(27.) v. 113. Privilege of Elis—Αρχιδαμος Ηλειοις μαλον ἡσυχια, Plutarch. Apothegm. Laconica. Tom i. p 387. Edit. Hen. Stephani. p 29. Edit Mattaire in 4° Lond. 1741[27]

---

(28) vi. 307.[28] The same God, like the Indian fig-tree propagated from the Brahmines to Siam, Pegu, China and Japan—Kæmpfer's Hist of Japan Vol. i. p 241

(29.) v. 428. Astronomy preserved[b], but not improved by the Arabians————Bailly. Hist. de l'Astronomie moderne. Tom i. p 221[29]

Augerii Gislenii Busbequii Omnia quæ extant, Lugd. Batavorum, ex officinâ Elzeviriana. 1633. in 12°

The travels of Busbequius consist of four Epistles, and contain the narrative of his two Embassies from Ferdinand i King of the Romans and afterwards Emperor to the Ottoman Porte. (November 1554–November 1562). In the first he describes his journey from Vienna to Amasia: the second includes the events and observations of a seven years residence or rather imprisonment at C.P.—It was

---

[a] *I.* Quæ de novissima ejus clade capta ab   [b] *I.* observed

his duty and his amusement to study the characters of Soliman ii and his ministers, the policy of the Government, the discipline of the Camp, and the virtues and vices of the most formidable enemies of Christendom. The tragic adventures of Mustapha and Bajazet are told with the spirit and dignity of an historian.[1] His ears or those of his interpreters were always open to the reports of foreign countries, of Crim Tartary, Mingrelia and Cathay; we are indebted to his curiosity for the first copy of the marbles of Ancyra, and the most ancient MS. of Dioscorides,[2] and he viewed with the eyes of a Naturalist the numerous collection of animals that enlivened his solitude—Busbequius is my old and familiar acquaintance, a frequent companion in my post chaise. His Latinity is elegant, his manner is*a* lively his remarks are judicious[.]

a I. om. is

Part IV

LAST WORKS, 1789–1793

INTRODUCTION

In one of his memoranda (Add. MSS. 34882, f. 175^r), Gibbon has recorded the dates of composition of the last three volumes of his history:

The ivth Volume of the History of the decline and fall of the Roman Empire   begun March 1^{rst} 1782 ended June. 1784.

The vth Volume——begun. July 1784.—ended May 1^{rst} 1786.

The vith Volume—begun. May the 18th 1786—ended June 27th 1787.

These three Volumes were sent to press. August 15th 1787 and the whole impression concluded April.[1]

From the *Memoirs* (pp. 181–2) we learn of Gibbon's additions to his manuscript and correcting of his proofs while these volumes were being printed, and we learn that publication was delayed to coincide with his fifty-first birthday, 8 May 1788. But after that 'double festival' how did the historian occupy himself?

At the end of July 1788 he returned to Lausanne and his library: 'My Seraglio was ample, my choice was free, my appetite was keen. After a full repast on Homer and Aristophanes, I involved myself in . . . Plato . . . but I stept aside into every path of enquiry which reading or reflection accidentally opened' (*Memoirs*, p. 183). The brief note on music and 'Homer' may be a fragment from that 'full repast'; it is definitely in Gibbon's late hand.[2]

But the delights of literary pottering were dimmed by the illness, and effectually ended by the death (5 July 1789) of Gibbon's friend, Deyverdun. He had promised himself 'a year of jubilee' (Preface,

DF iv. vi); Deyverdun's will had secured Gibbon's continued possession of their house in Lausanne, with all its comforts; but he felt 'alone in paradise' (*Memoirs*, p. 184). Perhaps that is why he began to wish or to expect to undertake some less aimless literary activity. There were several possibilities.

As we have seen (Part III above), one project that presented itself to him was the composition of a new volume for his history, but that notion was soon abandoned, or at least postponed. Another was the composition of the history of his own life.[3] G. A. Bonnard's definitive edition of the *Memoirs*, together with the full texts of the six drafts as published by Sir John Murray (*The Autobiographies of Edward Gibbon* (London, 1896)), provide the student with all[4] the materials needed for the study of this undertaking, with the small exception of some fragmentary notes for a 'separate annotation' on the antiquity of the English universities, to which Gibbon alludes in the *Memoirs* (p. 48). These materials, which are printed below, may have been written as early as spring, 1789, when Gibbon was drafting the first version of his memoirs that contains an account of his Oxford years.[5]

The 'Notes on John Philpot' are in Gibbon's late hand, and some of them occur on the same sheet with some of the notes about Oxford (Add. MSS. 34882, f. 218). They were, therefore, probably made about the same time, and may illustrate how Gibbon played first with the idea of his memoirs, then with his 'Historical Excursions',[6] and then with the memoirs again. If they were written after Gibbon had read Sir Samuel Egerton Brydges's genealogical notes about the Gibbon family, however (*Gentleman's Magazine*, lviii. 698; lix. 584; lxii. 519), they may instead represent Gibbon's reaction to Brydges's speculation that the Elizabeth Philpot who was Gibbon's great-great-great-grandmother was descended from this John Philpot. In that event, Gibbon's notes were made not earlier than 1792, when he first saw Brydges's pieces.

We can obtain valuable information about these 'Historical Excursions' from Gibbon's letter to M. Ernest Langer, librarian to the Duke of Brunswick, dated Rolle, 12 October 1790. After thanking Langer for procuring for him a copy of the *Origines Guelficae* of Leibnitz, Gibbon says:

Votre curiosité, peut-être Votre amitié desirera de connoitre mes amusemens, mes travaux, mes projets pendant les deux ans qui se sont écoulés depuis la derniere publication de mon grand ouvrage. Aux questions indiscrètes qu'on se permet trop souvent vis-à-vis de moi, je répons avec une mine renfrognée et d'une manière vague; mais je ne veux rien avoir de caché pour Vous et pour imiter la franchise que Vous aimez, je Vous avouerai naturellement que ma confidence est fondée en partie sur le besoin que j'aurai de votre secours.—Après mon retour d'Angleterre, les premiers mois ont été consacrés à la jouissance de ma liberté et de ma bibliothèque, et Vous ne serez pas étonné, je crois, si j'ai renouvellé une connoissance familière avec nos auteurs Grecs. . . . Le souvenir de ma servitude de vingt ans m'a cependant effrayé. . . . Il vaut bien mieux, me suis je dit, choisir dans tous les pays et dans tous les siecles des morceaux historiques que je traiterai separément suivant leur nature et selon mon goût. Lorsque ces Opuscules (je pourrai les nommer en Anglais, *Historical Excursions*) me fourniront un volume, je le donnerai au public: ce don pourroit etre rénouvellé, jusqu'à ce que nous soyons fatigués, ou le public ou moi. . . . (*Letters*, iii. 203)

Despite Gibbon's graceful remark (below) that 'Brunswick' was the first of these excursions, it is probable that the essay called by Sheffield 'On the Position of the Meridional Line and the Supposed Circumnavigation of Africa by the Ancients' (*MW* 1814, v. 170–208) was prompted by this re-reading of the Greek authors—specifically, of Herodotus. Perhaps this essay was alluded to by Gibbon as early as 11 February 1789, when he wrote to his publisher, Thomas Cadell: 'Since my return I have been, as I promise in the preface [of 1788], very busy and very idle in my library: several ideal works have been embraced and thrown aside . . .' (*Letters*, iii. 142–3).

The conjecture that re-reading Herodotus prompted this essay— I have called it 'The Circumnavigation of Africa'—is founded on the extensive marginal comments Gibbon made in the copy he was using. Some of these marginalia are obviously preliminary to part of the 'Circumnavigation of Africa', as can be seen by comparing 'Marginalia from Herodotus' with pp. 388–97 of that essay. One of Gibbon's notes in the essay itself cites an edition of Tiraboschi dated 1790, but the text could have been written before 1790, as Gibbon had access to the work in question early enough to quote it several times in the *Decline and Fall*. Sheffield dated the essay '1790 or 1791'; I suggest 1789–90. It should be noted that the sections of this essay seem to me to have been incorrectly ordered by Lord Sheffield. My arrangement, therefore, differs from his, as will be explained in my notes.

The major purpose of the letter to Langer, however, as Gibbon implies, was to solicit the librarian's aid in another historical project, an account of the ancient house of Brunswick, from which the Hanoverian kings of England were, of course, descended. The letter continues:

Dans ce projet je ne vois qu'un inconvenient: un objet interessant s'étend et s'aggrandit sous le travail. . . .
Ces soupçons ont été vérifiés dans le choix de ma première *Excursion*.

. . . Dans mon histoire j'avois rendu compte de deux alliances illustres, du fils de Marquis Azo d'Este avec la fille de Robert Guiscard, et d'une princesse de Brunswick avec l'Empereur Grec. Un premier apperçu de l'antiquité et grandeur de la maison de Brunswick a excité ma curiosité.
. . . Mes recherches, en me dévoilant la beauté de mon sujet, m'en ont fait voir l'étendue et la difficulté. L'origine des Marquis de Ligurie, et peut-être de Toscane a été suffisament éclaircie par *Muratori* et *Leibnitz*; l'Italie du moyen age, son histoire et ses monumens me sont très connus, et je ne suis pas mécontent de ce que j'ai déjà écrit sur la branche cadette d'Este, qui est restée fidèle à garder les cendres casanières. Les anciens Guelfs ne me sont point étrangers, et je me crois en etat de rendre compte de la puissance et de la chute de leurs héritiers les Ducs de Baviere et de Saxe. La succession de la maison de Brunswick au trone de la Grande Bretagne sera très assurément la partie la plus intéressante de mon travail . . . et un Anglois devroit rougir, s'il n'avoit pas approfondi l'histoire moderne et la constitution actuelle de son pays. Mais entre le prémier Duc et le prémier Electeur de Brunswick il se trouve un intervalle de quatre-cent cinquante ans. . . . Comme je me propose de crayonner des Mémoires et non de composer une histoire, je marcherois sans doute d'un pas rapide, je présenterois des résultats plutôt que des faits, des observations plutôt que des récits: mais vous sentez combien ce tableau général exige de connoissances particulières; combien l'auteur doit être plus savant que son ouvrage. Or cet auteur, il est à deux cents lieues de la Saxe, il ignore la langue, et il ne s'est jamais appliqué à l'histoire de l'Allemagne. [J'ai besoin d'un] correspondant exact, un guide eclairé, un oracle enfin. . . . Par Votre caractère, Votre esprit, Vos lumieres, Votre position, Vous êtes cet homme précieux et unique que je cherche. . . . (*Letters*, iii. 204–5)

It is obvious that Gibbon had already written all or part of the first book he proposed for this work, 'The Italian Descent'. Indeed, as I will show in the notes to that essay, he may already have written two drafts of parts of it. But the second section, to have been called 'The German Reign', was completed only through the account of Henry the Lion, who died in 1195, and includes nothing of the four hundred and fifty years between the first Duke of Brunswick and Luneberg and the first Elector of Hanover; nothing of the forty years that intervened between Henry the Lion and Frederic II's creation of the first Duke of Brunswick (1235), and nothing of the Electors of Hanover and Kings of Great Britain.

Lord Sheffield published this work in his 1796 edition and augmented it in 1814, but he deleted certain passages (see below, pp. 469–70), and he neglected both another draft of certain portions of the account (Add. MSS. 34880, f. 331, ff. 350^v–353^v) and some notes to 'L i C i' which had been written on a separate sheet (now in Add. MSS. 34881, f. 249). There is evidence that the version he chose was not always Gibbon's latest draft and that his ordering of the separate short pieces in what he called 'Section IV' (*MW* 1814, iii. 479–554) did not always make the best possible sense. The headnote and notes to the present edition will explain how and why the version printed here differs from Sheffield's.

In general, under the title *Antiquities of the House of Brunswick*, I have tried to assemble a version representing Gibbon's latest revisions of Chapter I, 'The Italian Descent' (in three sections), and Chapter II, 'Accounts of the German Branch'. For Chapter I, Section III, however, there are no revisions, and he himself had not assembled the revised materials or given them a final collective form. For that reason I have also included, in 'Other Drafts', all the material omitted in my version from the first section of the draft published by Sheffield and the whole of 'Section II' of that draft, as well as an unpublished set of fragmentary preliminary notes, now separated from the Brunswick materials though in the same volume of manuscripts (Add. MSS. 34880, f. 278).

At some point not earlier than 1 March 1792, Gibbon made or copied[7] a 'Habsburgica', an elaborate genealogical table of the Habsburgs, and commented on it briefly. This table is obviously connected with the last sentences of the remarks on knowing one's ancestors in an isolated autobiographical fragment (Add. MSS. 34874, f. 129) included in Gibbon's *Memoirs* (p. 5)—but whether the autobiographical fragment led to the genealogical interest or vice versa cannot now be determined. The 'Habsburgica' can be dated because it lists Francis II as emperor, and he did not become emperor until 1792. The table and remarks were not published by Sheffield.

The last two productions of Gibbon's life require no elaborate explanation. They are the essay on the publication of the English historical documents, 'An Address &c', and the marginalia in Harwood's *View of the Various Editions of the Greek and Roman Classics*, both written in the summer of 1793. Both show that Gibbon retained his critical sense and his gift of phrase even in the last months of his life. And they permit us to compare the forty-first year of the historian's working life with the first. When we consider that his whole lifetime was less than fifty-seven years, that we have here only the by-products of his two major works, and of those by-products, only the ones that were written in English, we can more fully appreciate both the man and the scholar.

HOMER

About the 26th or 33d Olympiad, Terpander of Lesbos composed the νομοι, the airs or tunes proper for singing to the Cithara the verses of Homer in the public games. See the treatise of Plutarch on Music with the remarks of Burette in the Memoires de l'Academie[1] Tom. x. p 116. 213–224

[Notes on Philpot]

[1377.][a] John Philpot Alderman, Orator of London at the head of a deputation to invite the future King (R. 2[)] from Kingston to London. Holl. Vol. iii p 415 16

[1378.] supplied the weakness of Gov. fitted out a fleet at his own charge. fought John Mercer the Scot,[1] and fifteen Spaniards, took them with much treasure recovered[b] the Scarborough fleet, quæstioned for his presumption but dismissed. p. 419. 20 discovered a conspiracy. p 428.

[1381.] stood with King and Mayor. knighted the first of the four Citizens after Walw. and Ralph. Standish[2]. girded with the girdle of knighthood. before the arrival of London succours. p 433.

A plan of Sir Nicholas Walwort. Mayor to attack the Rebels, drunk and asleep. The City (with some Knights and soldiers) could have mustered 8000 well armed men. The mob was but 60000: but milder counsels prevailed. nine Aldermen for the King three for the Rebels. (Chronicle of Froissard. fol. 261 vers. of John Bouchier Lord Berners.[3] Part 1.

Tower &c—Extreme danger of the King in Smithfield. The Mayor came with twelve horsemen well armed under their coats. Philpot perhaps one of these perhaps one of the good men who hastened from their friends and servants. Froissard does not notice his Knighthood. fol. 263. vers.

---

[a] *All dates Gibbon's, but in margin of MS., unbracketed.*   [b] *I. om.* recovered the Scarborough fleet

[Notes on the Antiquity of the English Universities]

Theobaldus. Archiep. Cant. consecratus AD. 1138. obiit. 1161. Canonicus Lichfeldensis in Wharton. Anglia Sacra. Tom i. p 110

AD 1187. Topographiam et expugnationem Hiberniæ scripsit. Wharton Anglia sacra. Tom ii p. 374.

Nosse enim vos pro certo volui, quod transactis annorum curriculis triginta vel pluribus, cum circiter editionem dictæ topographiæ primam, et libri recitationem in publicâ Cleri audientiâ per triduum solempniter Oxoniæ factam. (Giraldus Cambrensis Epistola ad Capitulum Herefordense. de libris a se scriptis. p 439.

Thus far Giraldus himself, his three days feast to the Doctors, Scholars &c of Oxford is attested only by his biographer[a] who must have written after his death (1220. Anton. à Wood Hist. et Anti-quitates[b] Universitatis[c] Oxoniensis. L i p 55. 56 [)] who places this event in 1183. He quotes thus 4[d] ut in Vita Sylv. Girard. ad finem. Libri 4 distinct. MS, et in alio Exemplari ejusdem vitæ in Bib. Cotton. C 28. p 38

Giraldus Cambrenis (Barry)

Cave. Hist. Litteraria p 617. Very poor Biographia Britannica Vol i p 645 second Edition, an elaborate but ill-tempered article probably by an Irishman Fabricii Bibliotheca Latina[e] medii et infimi ævi. Tom iii p 62–65 Edit Mansi. very correct. The small treatises of Giraldus are published in Wharton's Anglia sacra. Tom ii Catalogus brevior librorum suorum. p 445. de Rebus a se gestis. Libri iii p 457.

Item de Topographia Hibernica, liber sc. de sitû terræ. illius, et mirabilibus ejusdem multis exaratus, apud Oxoniam per tres dies continuous in publicâ *Cleri* audentiâ recitatus. Nicholson. Irish Hist. Library p 2. they are the words of the Catalogue. This recital is placed by the Biog. in 1187. It is said that he feasted on the first

---

[a] I. biographers   [b] *Last word on Add. MSS. 34882 f. 217 verso.*   [c] *First word on Add. MSS. 34882 f. 218 recto.*   [d] *MS. very obscure.*   [e] *I. om.* Latina

day the poor, on the second the masters and principal students, on the third the scholars, soldiers and townsmen of Oxford. On what evidence? The Biograph. slides in this fact between two quotations from the de rebus, and Mr Warton (Hist of English poetry Vol i Diss ii) who had seen the originals appeals only to Antony Wood. Hist et Antiq. Oxon. I suspect some trick.[1]

Gervasius Dorobernenjis or Cantuariensis

He lived about 1200 a Benedictine monk—in the Vitæ. Archiepisc. Cant. We read, Magister Vacarius . . . in Oxenfordia legem docuit. Selden. Judicium de decem Script. in Opp. Tom ii. p 1169. 1173. The date is certain, 1149. the place doubtful, Selden owns his ignorance and believes Vacarius was an itinerant teacher (Diss. ad Fletam. Opp. Tom ii p 1082–1085. Gervase wrote sixty years afterwards when Oxford was doubtless a *Studium*; or the words in Oxenfordia, might easily slip from the margin into the text. John of Salisbury (Policratii viii.[)] mentions Vacarius, Vacario nostro indictum silentium. but he does not favour any Oxford lectures. Leges Romanas in Britanniam. *Domus*. VP. *Theobaldi* Britanniarum Primatis asciverat. much more probable.[2]

Robert Pulein venit Oxenfordiam (1144) ibique scripturas Divinas quæ per idem tempus in Anglia obsoluerant præ Scholasticis quippe neglectæ fuerant per quinquennium legit MS Contin. Bedæ in Bibliot Bodleian. fol 275 Vid. Antiq. Oxon. L i. p 49. Cave. Hist Literaria p 582. Fabric. B. L medii ævi. Tom vi. 106.[3]

Ld Lyttleton (Hist Vol. ii p 327)[1] observes how little is known of Oxford in the reign of Henry. ii[.] Age of learning—Weigh the siege of Oxford under Stephen, and the fabulous silence of Jeffrey of Monmouth.

Matthew Paris Hist. Major Lond. 1684. gives the first historic titles of the Oxford studies. In 1209, the Clerks applied[a] *Artes liberales*: they lodged three or four together in *Hospitia*, hired[b]. Provoked by an act of injustice, recesserunt[c] ab Oxoniâ ad tria millia Clericorum, quam magistri quam discipuli, ita quod nec

---

^a *I and II.* applied to   ^b *I.* hired to   ^c *I.* they recesserunt

unus ex omni *universitate* remansit. some went to Cambridge others to Reading. villam*ᵃ* Oxoniæ vacuam reliquerunt. p 191.

In 1252. Convocatâ scholarium universitate quæ de diversis Mundi partibus illic studuit, &c. p 740 In 1257. Statuta Universitatis *antiqua* et approbata... Oxon Univers. schola secund Ecclesiæ. p 811

The series of Chancellors of the University begins in 1233. Ayliffe's Hist of Oxford Vol. ii p 278. The first charter of Henri iii is in 1244 (Appendix p vi*ᵇ*) but it supposes the prævious state of the *University*.

1. Prudens antiquitas (ut in annalibus nostris legitur) hanc urbem etiam Britanniæ sæculo musis consecravit. Cambden. Britannia. p 267. The Greek Philosophers came to Cricklade with Brutus. Sir*ᶜ* John Spelman Æfrid. Vit. p 137. monstrum Græcolada. a G. P ut aliqui facile credunt quos Hist. Oxon. ibi Academiam instituisse prodit quæ postea Oxon. translata. Cambden*ᵈ* p 176.

2. Asser. Menevins. de Reb. Ælfrid gestis in Camden. Anglica Norman. Hibern. p 16. Francofurte. 1603. The Asser &c announced by Cambden (in præfat) as a republication of Archb. Parker's Edition (1575) quos denuo cum exemplaria in Angliâ varius inveniantur. Claudius Marnius e suo prelo nunc edit. Yet this Oxford. passage does not exist in Parker'[s] Edition, nor in his original MS in Saxon characters venerandæ antiquitatis ... Æfredo superstite descriptum *now*ᵉ *in the Cotton library* (Parker in præfat). This inconsistency strongly urged by Spelman p 141. 142. 143. and feebly answered by Obadiah Walker. Cambden in his Britannia p 267–268. inserts this passage ut legitur in Optimo MS. Asserii: but he had never seen it, says his friend Archbishop Usher. Brittanic. Ecclesiarum Antiq. p 184. Neque enim ipse exemplar ejusmodi unquam viderat. why *optimo*, ubi latet. an evident tack.

3*ᶠ* Primum Westmonasteris*ᵍ*, postmodum Oxoniensi studio traditus eram. Ingulphi Historia p 73 in Tom i Rerum Anglicarum Script. a Fell et Gale. Oxon. 1684. Some have doubted, but the Editors have found this passage in all MSS. (Gibson's Cambden Vol. i. p 305) Ingulphus[2] boasts of his proficiency in Aristotle and Tully's Rhetoric: yet in 1048, Aristotle was unknown, Oxford lay in ruins; had neither Cathedral nor Monastery to which the studies were confined. The Divinity lectures of Robert Pulein*ʰ* in the Abbey of Oseney (1129–1135) I consider as the punctum saliens of the University. Cambden ubi supra. Nicholson (English library) p 150–152.) is free learned and lively.

3*ⁱ* In 1109. Joffrid Abbot of Croyland sent a colony of monks who opened public schools at Cambridge of Grammar Logic, Rhetoric and Theology, after the manner studii Aurelianensis, Ex ista*ʲ* fonte videmus..totam Angliam factam frugiferam per plurimos magistros et doctores de Cantabrigiâ exeuntes. (Petri Blesenis Continuatio Ingulphi. in Script rerum Anglicar. Tom i. p 114. 115. he died circa 1200).—Curious but spurious: *frater* Terricus (frater is properly*ᵏ* as*ˡ* mendicant *fryar*) acutissimus sophista, logicam Aristotelis juxta. Porphyrii Aviroiz*ᵐ* Isagogas et commenta adolescentionibus tradidit.—But Averroes was not born till 1131, he interpeted Aristotle 1187–1192 and died after 1200. d'Herebelot p 715. Bayle Tom 1. p 384–91. Saxius places him at 1198

ᵃ II. villani   *ᵇ II.* 6   *ᶜ I.* p. 1   *ᵈ I.* p.   *ᵉ I.* om. *now in the Cotton library*   *ᶠ Superscript in MS.*   *ᵍ II.* Westmonasteriensi   *ʰ I.* Robert de Puleyne   *ⁱ II. om. number. Placement of number ambiguous in MS. Seems intended to indicate continuation of note 3, already numbered.*   *ʲ II.* isto   *ᵏ II.* probably   *ˡ II.* a   *ᵐ II.* Averoiz

[Marginalia in Herodotus]

[p. iii][a]

His native dialect, the *Doric* was coarse vulgar and obscure; and the example of Herodotus (who preferred the smoother *Ionic* for an elegant general history) has been followed by other Dorians, Timæus Philistus, Diodorus Siculus, Dionysius of Halicarnassus who all[b] *repudiated their vernacular idiom*. (Bentley against Boyle p 316. 317. 330 &c) But the Doctor is strangely mistaken in adding the name of Ephorus, an *Æolian* of the City of Cumæ. (Strab Geog. L xiii. p 923. 924 Edit Amstel.[c] 1707).

[p. 1; i. 1]

This is not surely the first page of history. Were these fabulous rapes the original cause of the Persian War? Were the distant Barbarians of Asia, the Phœnicians, the Colchians,[d] and the Trojans engaged in *one common* cause of rapine and revenge against the Greeks of Europe? The word *Barbarians* cannot be found in the poems of Homer.

[p. 3; i. 4]

This reflection is true in every age: the name and privilege of a rape cannot be applied to the elopements of Medea, and Helen; and if Europa was deceived by a bull, she soon rejoyced in the discovery of a God. Herodotus may claim[e] the merit of fairly representing the Greeks as the agressors.

[p. 4; i. 8–12]

The conduct of fond husbands and virtuous[f] wives should not perhaps be weighed by reason, and historical probability: yet I much suspect that this story of the Queen (who is justified by S[t] Jerom) was invented by the poet Archilochus as a satire on female modesty. The whole fable or history[g] of Gyges is discussed by the Abbé Sevin and M Freret (Mem. de l'Acad. des Inscriptions. Tom v. p 254. 280 &c).[1]

---

[a] *Page unnumbered. Signature***.   [b] *I. om.* all   [c] *I.* Amstd   [d] *I.* T
[e] *I.* likewise claim   [f] *I.* the actions of lovers (*replaced by* virtuous wives)   [g] *I.* G

[p. 11; i. 24]

An odd digression, and most unphilosophical fable! Since it supposes the friendship of a man and a Sea-fish (a sort of porpess Pennant's British Zoology Vol iii p 48),[2] and the exquisite sensibility of a *deaf* animal to the sound of the Lyre.

[p. 13; i. 30–33]

Plutarch (in Solone. Tom 1 p 204) who fondly embraces this moral tale, derides the vain opposition of *Chronological Canons* (see Marsham p 582). If the[a] interview, in itself, appear probable, we may easily antedate the reign of Crœsus, and suppose that Solon was elected Archon (Olymp[b] xLvi. 8) several years before he gave laws to the Athenians. Such an hypothesis would be more consistent with the lives, both of the King, and of the Philosopher.

[p. 17; i. 32]

Voltaire (Tom xiv. p 320) has ridiculed the observation of Solon, which is clear and judicious, that we[c] should not calculate the good and evil incident to any human life, till[d] death has finally closed the account.[3] A metaphysian may perplex himself by contrasting[e] apparent happiness, or misery, with secret pain[f] or pleasure: yet, even in this fallacious light, Solon destroyed the felicity which he denied. The actual sensation of the King of Lydia must have been exquisitely painful, at the moment, when his pride was disappointed[g] and mortified. Solon's examples of real happiness, are worthy of a sage, and a freeman, and the[h] historian relates them in a style of elegant simplicity.

[p. 23; i. 50]

The παλαιστη, or smaller palm is a fourth part of the Greek or English foot (d'Anville Mesures Itineraires p 21 &c).[4] The Talent is equiponderant to seventy pounds Troy weight (Hooper's ancient measures &c p 37–64). These ἡμιπλινθια, therefore, or wedges were either nine or eighteen inches in length,[i] and three inches in height;[j] their thickness indefinite; their weight, one hundred and forty or one hundred and seventy five pounds: their

---

[a] *I.* this   [b] *I.* several   [c] *I.* if we calculate (*replaced by* we should not calculate)   [d] *I.* we should expect, (*replaced by* till ... closed the account.)   [e] *I. a.* confounding *I. b.* comparing   [f] *I.* pleasur   [g] *I.* disappointment   [h] *I.* he rel   [i] *I.* length;   [j] *I.* breadth

value great, but various and unknown; since only four were[a] of pure gold, and the[b] remaining one hundred and thirteen,[c] of a paler colour, and baser alloy. They seem to have been piled longitudinally, as the basis or pedestal of the Lyon, of pure and mossy gold, which weighed seven hundred pounds, and cannot be appreciated at less than £28.000 sterling, exclusive of the workmanship. When the temple of Delphi was pillaged two hundred years afterwards (Olymp. cviii. 2), the gifts of Crœsus still formed the most conspicuous part of the Holy treasure. The total amount, in Gold and silver was then valued at 10.000 silver talents, above two millions sterling (Diodor. Sicul. Tom ii L xvi. p 126. Edit Wesseling).

[p. 34; i. 69]

From this example, and many similar facts (Bentley against Boyle p 529–533) we may learn that Gold was extremely scarce among the Greeks. Yet the gift of the Spartans asserted a superiority[d] of art and genius, more valuable than the wealth of the Barbarians. Candaules had purchased a picture of Bularchus (the sack of Magnesia) by covering it with gold. (Plin. Hist Natur. vii. 39).

[p. 46; i. 91]

A dangerous mode of defence! Neither Philosophy nor Religion will admit this mixture of *necessary* and *contingent* events. If the fall of Crœsus was irrevocably decreed, the time and manner must have been equally determined. The smallest links are essential to form the perfect continuity of the great chain. The words of the Oracles themselves have been attacked with irresistible impudence by Oenamaus the Cynic (Vandal. de Oraculis p. 330 &c), who demonstrates that such fatal ambiguity to a generous benefactor must have proceeded, either from the ignorance, or[e] the malice, of Apollo. I should like to know, how much Herodotus received from the priests of Delphi.

[p. 49; i. 95]

Opposite[f] witnesses must be balanced; and we can only deduct the surplus of credibility. But when each weight is positively light, this comparative surplus must be extremely minute.

---

[a] *I.* of these wedges were   [b] *I. om.* the   [c] *I.* fourtee   [d] *I.* nobler superiority   [e] *I.* of   [f] *I.* Contradictory

[p. 49; i. 96–119]

Rousseau has wisely observed (Emile. Part. i p 281) that the most incredible narratives of Herodotus may be esteemed as moral lessons. In this doubtful history of the Medes we may trace the progress of Civil society. They renounced their freedom to escape the evils of anarchy: their slavery was confirmed and alleviated by the selfish arts, and specious virtues of their first King; but his son was a conqueror, and his great-grand-son a tyrant.

[p. 54; i. 107–8]

About the same period the dreams of the King of Babylon were equally strange and mysterious. Yet the river or the vine, that issued from the secret charms of Mandane excite only our derision: while Nebuchadnazzar's image[a] of gold, silver, brass iron and clay (Daniel ii 31–45) still exercises the faith and learning of the present age.

[p. 55; i. 110]

We sometimes detect a Romance by the easy, though wonderful[b] annihilation of time and space.

Herodotus places these mountains, where Cyrus should have been exposed, in the neighbourhood, both of Ecbatana, and of the Euxine sea. Elsewhere (C 123) he supposes that a man on foot might carry a fresh hare from Ecbatana to Pasargada, the residence of Cyrus and his family (C 125) Ecbatana, the modern Hamadan, is distant, at least, 600 miles, from Pasargada. and from the Euxine sea.

[p. 62; i. 117–18]

I cannot understand why the guilt or merit of preserving the infant Cyrus[c] should have been ascribed to Harpagus; since *he* had given the most peremptory instructions for his death, which must have taken place, if Harpagus himself had not been deceived by the herdsman.

[p. 68; i. 135]

How coolly he mentions this Greek taste among the *indifferent* fashions which they learned from foreign nations![5]

[p. 80; i. 170]

Had the Ionians removed to Sardinia, that fertile island (obscure and barbarous in every age) might have become the seat of arts, of

---

[a] *I. om.* image   [b] *I.* wonderful,   [c] *I. om.* Cyrus

freedom, and perhaps of Empire. Such a powerful colony might have oppressed the infant fortune of Rome, and changed the history of mankind.

[p. 84; i. 178]

These dimensions, which have been devoutly swallowed by the voracious[a] herd, are gigantic and incredible. A brick wall, at least, 100 yards high, and 30 yards thick must have inclosed an *Area* of 200 square miles, and thirteen Cities of the size of Paris might have stood within the precincts of Babylon. Messieurs Freret and d'Anville have attempted to apply smaller measures (Mem. de Acad. des Inscriptions Tom xxiv p 441. 552. Tom xxviii p 253). But the positive declaration of Herodotus himself seems to exclude their officious kindness. I much doubt whether he ever saw Babylon. We may recollect the Greek historian (Lucian de conscribend. hist Tom ii p 38 Edit Reitz), who had travelled into Armenia, without stirring from Corinth.

[p. 94; i. 201-2]

The most decisive circumstances prove this Araxes to be the Oxus, or Gition: Yet the name and source may seem to indicate the Armenian river; and the islands, as large as Lesbos, with their savage inhabitants are much more suitable to the Volga. The ideas of Herodotus were not clear or consistent. See the opinions of M M. de la Nauze[6] de Guignes, and d'Anville (Memoires de l'Acad. des Inscriptions Tom xxxvi. p 69-85).

[p. 96; i. 203]

It is not easy to ascertain or verify this vague computation But Herodotus has the merit of discovering two important truths, which were disregarded by the false science of succeeding Geographers: that the Caspian sea is a lake, without any communication with the Ocean; and that it is much more extensive from north to south, than from East to West. (Examen des historiens d'Alexandre p 181-193. Esprit des Loix. L xxi. C 9.)[7].

[p. 101; i. 214]

If Cyrus died in the seventieth year of his age, (Dionon in Persicis apud Ciceron de Divinat i.[b] 23) he was born, at least, six years before

---

[a] *I.* com   [b] *I.* ii

the reign of Astyages; and the long romance of his infancy melts into air.

[p. 104; ii. 2]

The story is perfectly absurd, since it implies, that the pronunciation of articulate sounds, the knowledge of an arbitrary language, and the desire of an artificial food are all innate to the mind of children, without the aid of instruction, or example.

[p. 106; ii. 6–9]

The *Schœnus* was equal to four *Roman miles*, each of which contained fifteen of the smallest *Stadia*. Herodotus extends the coast of Egypt 40 miles to the eastward of the Pelusiac,[a] and somewhat more to the westward of the Canopic, mouth of the Nile. His[b] computation justly leaves 160 miles for the basin of the Delta, which advances into the Sea between Pelusium and Canopus. The sides of the triangle, from the sea to the point near Heliopolis, accord with the measure of 100 miles. From the point of Delta to Syene, under the Tropic the long, narrow valley of the Nile runs 475 miles from north to south, and the average breadth may be liberally esteemed 12 miles, between the Arabian, and the Libyan, chains of mountains The whole surface of Egypt (of[c] habitable land) contains no more than 2100 square leagues, a *twelfth* part only of France This calculation, which refutes some extravagant fables, renders the authentic facts more truly marvellous. (d'Anville Description de l'Egypte p 1–31).

[p. 144; ii. 107]

According to Manetho (apud Joseph in Apion L i C 15. Tom ii p 447 Edit Havercamp), Armais, or Danaus, fled from the just resentment of his brother, the great Sethosis or Sesostris, King of Egypt, and Conqueror of the East.[8] This royal consanguinity, of which Herodotus was ignorant, is highly incredible. A private adventurer, of ancient Egypt, or modern Europe, might lead a Colony to some newly discovered lands; but I have never read that any fugitive prince of England or France has sought a refuge and a Kingdom among the Savages of America. The design of Manetho, who flourished in the Court of Ptolemy Philadelphus, was obvious, though artful. The Ptolemies derived their maternal or illegitimate

[a] *I.* Ca   [b] *MS. ambiguous. Possibly changed to* This   [c] *I.* inh

descent (Quint. Curt. L ix. C 8, Pausanias L i p 14. 15 with the notes of their Editors), from the Kings of Macedonia, and consequently from Hercules and Danaus. After a long abscence the genuine race of the Egyptian monarchs, expelled the usurpers, and claimed their lawful inheritance. Yet I am satisfied that Manetho would not have supposed this identity, unless the reign of Sethosis had coincided, in his Dynasties, with the Greek Æra of Ægyptus and Danaus, about fifteen Centuries before Christ (Marsham Canon. Chron. p 82. 113. 125)

[p. 159; ii. 121]

This foolish story, so unworthy of a grave historian is neatly and agreably told; and the reader is tempted to forget, that this *first* of men is no more than a paltry thief, whose boldness and cunning might be easily matched or surpassed in the annals of the Old-Bailey.

[p. 163; ii. 124 ff.]

If fame was the object of the Egyptian Kings who erected the Pyramids, never was vanity more compleatly disappointed. Their useless and ostentatious tyranny has been justly condemned by the sentence of Egypt, and of posterity: but the names of the[a] founders and the time of the foundation are involved in doubt and darkness. (Greaves's Pyramidographia (p 1–58.

[p. 164; ii. 124]

The basis of the great Pyramid is a regular square, and each of the four sides, which truly correspond with the four cardinal points, measures in length about 700 Greek or English feet. Four equilateral triangles gradually ascend, (by a flight of 207 steps),[b] and mutually incline till they meet, as it were, in a point, at the perpendicular height of 500 feet from the smooth and solid rock, which rises 100[c] feet more above the level of the plain. This massy edifice covers eleven acres of ground, the precise area of Lincoln's Inn fields, as it was quaintly designed by Inigo Jones. (Greaves's Pyramidographia in his works Vol i p 91–107 and his life by D[r] Birch p xii–xxv) Greaves (p 108–138) describes the inside of the great pyramid, the entrance on the north side at the height of 38 feet, the narrow

---

[a] *I.* fou   [b] *I. om.* (by a flight of 207 steps),   [c] *I. Either* 101 *or* 107 (*MS. obscure*)

shelving descent, the three galleries, the deep well (mentioned by Pliny), and the two sepulchral chambers. Maillet (who might read the Pyramidographia in the Recueil of Thevenot) adds little more than mistakes, conjectures, and fables (Description de l'Egypte p 215–261); that the Pyramids were built before the flood, that they were covered with silk, or incrusted with marble, that they were never opened before the reign of the Khalifs. The French Consul, or his editor the Abbé Mascrier,[9] appears to be vain, ignorant, and credulous, in almost every part of his elaborate description of Egypt.

[p. 173; ii. 142]

This vague and traditional report of the Greeks, deserves much less credit than the national Chronology of the priest Manetho, who digested the xxxi Dynasties of the Kings of Egypt from Menes to Alexander the great. According to the text of Africanus, and the computation of Joseph Scaliger (Canon. Isagog. p 124–135), they form a series of 5355 Julian years, which[a] begins 5684 years before the Christian Æra. A philosophic mind will not hastily receive or reject this extreme antiquity of the Egyptians.

[p. 298; iv. 42]

The circumnavigation of Africa[10] has been treated as doubtful or fabulous by some of the[b] gravest writers of antiquity, Polybius, Strabo, Pliny Ptolemy &c who either profess their ignorance of the Torrid zone, or boldly unite the African, with the Indian, Continent. (Robertson's Hist. of America Vol i p 354 8º Edit. d'Anville Mem. de l'Academie. Tom xxxii p. 612). The modern discoveries have restored the credit of Herodotus; and his prævious knowledge of a Geographical truth has been admitted to prove the reality of an ancient voyage, by which alone it could be ascertained. In my opinion this evidence is inconclusive. 1. The Phœnicians of Herodotus do not remark any new and characteristic facts, which were afterwards verified by the Portuguese; the extent of Africa (which Herodotus still believed to be smaller than Europe), the form of the land, the nature of the sea, or the men, animals, plants and constellations of the southern Hemisphere. Antiquity must have known, that it was either *possible*, or *impossible* to circum-navigate Africa. Herodotus chose the affirmative; and the affirmative has happened to be true. 2. The Portuguese, inspired by the genius

[a] *I.* fro   [b] *I. om.* the

of Prince Henry, directed by the Compass, and impelled by a strong commercial interest, sailed round the Cape of Good Hope, after the laborious perseverance of fourscore years. Does their success render it more probable, that the Phœnicians, to gratify the curiosity of a King of Egypt, atchieved the same discovery in the term of about eighteen months, which was all they spent in actual navigation?

Listen to the Spirit of the Cape, the dark sublime phantom created by the fancy of Camoens (Lusiad L v p 211 Mickle's translation).

> Nor[a] Roman prow, nor daring Tyrian oar
> Ere dash'd the white wave foaming to my shore;
> Nor Greece nor Carthage ever spread the sail
> On these my seas to catch the trading gale.
> You, you alone have dared to plough my Main;
> And with the human voice disturb my lonesome reign

I would take the Ghost's word for a thousand pounds.[11]

[p. 299; iv. 43]

Yet one of the Magi,[12] who might accompany, as Chaplain, the unfortunate Sataspes assured Gelon[b] of Syracuse that *he* had actually sailed round Africa (Heraclid. Pont. apud Posidonium, apud Strab. Geograph L ii p 155). The imperfect, if real, attempts of Hanno (Periplus in Geograph. Minor. Hudson Tom i p 1–6), and of Eudoxus[13] (Strab. Geograph L ii p 155–160) have likewise been magnified into successful circumnavigations. (Plin Hist. Natur ii. 67).

[p. 300; iv. 45]

Yet the division is convenient enough; and some unknown trifling circumstances might easily suggest these appellations to the Greek or[c] Phœnician navigators. The fourth part of the Globe has been unworthily occupied or rather stolen, by a Florentine pilot (Robertson's hist. of America Vol. i p 380). But posterity is just; and each generation repeats, that Columbus discovered *America*, without recollecting the obscure name of *Amerigo* Vespucci

---

[a] *MS. has 2 vertical lines alongside the remaining portion of this entry, including the last sentence.*   [b] *I.* H   [c] *I. om.* or Phœnician

[p. 321; iv. 86]

The shameful error of Laurentius Valla[14] (who translates, "centum ac decem millia Orgyanem, et centum" instead of "Centum et undecim myriades) should not[a] have escaped Gronovius[15] Wesseling &c. But the Geographical error of Herodotus himself is more important than[b] this verbal mistake. His numbers, (they[c] perfectly coincide,) produce 11.100 Stadia, which, if equal to 1387½ Roman miles, are almost double the real length of the Euxine. M. d'Anville would instantly solve the problem by the calculation of smaller Stadia; but the acurate measures of the Bosphorus, the Propontis and the Hellespont require the common, large, Olympic Stadium of eight to the Roman mile. It is more likely that Herodotus was deceived by adding the eight *longest nights* to the nine *longest days*. Nine days navigation, each of sixty or seventy miles may naturally fill the space from the Bosphorus to the Phasis: and such were the terrors of the Euxine, that the unskillful Greeks were more inclined to cast anchor, than to hoist sail in the night.

[p. 509; vii. 8 ff.]

Without absolutely condemning the composition of speeches so familiar to the ancients, I shall presume to impose the three following laws on this species of historical fiction. 1 That the truth of the leading fact, of the council, debate, orations &c be positively ascertained. 2. That some natural means be suggested through which, the historian (who cannot plead the inspiration of the Muses,) might derive his intelligence. 3. That the language and ideas be strictly adapted to the national and personal characters of his Dramatic speakers. On these principles it would not be easy to justify the orations of Xerxes, Mardonius, and Artabanus.

[p. 515; vii. 11]

δουλων των εμων δουλος, would have been more expressive of contempt and less repugnant to history. The Achemenidæ had never been the sovereigns of Pelops; but Phrygia is numbered (Diodor. Sicul. Tom i L ii p 115 Edit Wesseling) among the provinces of the Assyrian Empire which was subverted by the Medes and Persians.

---

[a] *I.* should have (*replaced by* should not have)   [b] *I. om.* than   [c] *I.* which

[p. 515; vii. 12 ff.]

Such a fable, which at the Olympic games might be crowned by the applause of the Greeks disgraces the serious history of an important War. The præternatural, though deceitful vision of Xerxes is evidently borrowed from the dream of Agamemnon in the second book of the Iliad; and the *envious* temper of the Deity is a first principle in the Theology of Herodotus himself.

[p. 519; vii. 20]

This interval of *ten* years is so accurately true, that the two battles of Marathon and Salamis were fought in the month of September of the respective years 490 and 480, before the Christian Æra. The date of the latter is ascertained by an Eclipse of the Sun. (Freret in the Acad.*a* des Inscriptions Tom xviii Hist. p 134. Tom xxvi. Mem. p 161. 183)

a *I*. Mem. de l'Acad. (*Gibbon marked out* Mem. de l')

[The Circumnavigation of Africa]

[On the Canary Islands]

By the Greek[1] and Arabian Cosmographers the first meridian was [1][a]
loosely placed at the Fortunate or Canary[b] Islands: the true position
of the isle of Ferro has been determined by modern observation;
and the degrees of longitude proceed with singular propriety from
the western limit of the old Hemisphere. The absurd vanity of the
Spaniards and Dutch, the French and English has variously transported this ideal line from a common and familiar[c] term: the
longitudes of Madrid and Amsterdam of Paris and Greenwich must
now be compared, and the national diversity of speech and measure
is aggravated by a new source of perplexity and confusion. The
prince of Geographers, the celebrated d'Anville has shewn his
judgement and impartiality by adhering to the old style.

It was the duty of the Greek poets, who described the residence
and rewards of departed Heroes to adorn *their*[d] fortunate islands
with the gifts of perpetual spring and spontaneous plenty. A remote
and hospitable land has often been praised above its merits by the
gratitude of storm-beaten mariners. But the real scene of the
Canaries affords, like the rest of the World, a mixture of good and
evil; nay even of indigenous ills and of foreign improvements. Yet,
in sober truth, the small islands of the Atlantic and Pacific Oceans
may be esteemed as some of the most agreable spots on the Globe.[1]
The sky is serene, the air is pure and salubrious: the meridian heat
of the Sun is tempered by the sea-breeze: the groves and vallies,
at least in the Canaries, are enlivened by the melody of their *native*
birds; and a new climate may be found, at every step, from the
shore to the summit, of a mountainous ascent.

In the Atlantic or Fortunate islands of Plutarch[2] we acknowledge
with some hesitation the first features of the Canaries to which
Sertorius was desirous of escaping from the horrors of Civil War.
The description of Pliny[3] is more accurate and distinct; and his
knowledge was derived from the discoveries and writings of Juba[4],

---

[a] Gibbon's page number in right-hand margin of MS. II. om.   *[b] I. om. or Canary*
[c] I. convenient   *[d] I.* the (*no italics*)

the most learned King that ever reigned over the Moors. The names of the Canary islands, their number of six or seven, and their respective distance are marked, though with some uncertainty. The plenty of the Orchilla Weed, so useful to the dyers will justify the appellation of the Purple isles, and the use of a Manufacture which Juba intended to establish. A multitude of dogs and goats, with the ruins of some stone buildings announced the more early visits perhaps of the Phœnicians: but these islands appear to have been destitute of inhabitants, and I must assign to a later age, the arrival of the Getulian emigrants who preserved their idiom, and soon lost the imperfect art which had conveyed them over a narrow sea. The Kingdom of Juba was reduced into a province: but the Romans were satiated with Empire, and they disdained or feared to plant a Colony in the Atlantic Ocean. It is less easy to account for the neglect of the Mahometans: they were Conquerors fanatics and Merchants; nor could the great[a] desert protect from their ambition the black nations of the Niger. Yet the Arabian Geographers are content to repeat the fables of Ptolemy; and Abulfeda's ignorance[5] is betrayed by the wild supposition that the Fortunate islands had been overwhelmed by the waves.

While Abulfeda deplored their loss they were given by Pope Clement vi[6] (1344) with the title of Kingdom to Lewis de la Cerda the rightful though banished heir of Castille. The[b] title was vain, the grant ineffectual: the Canaries which had been recently discovered by the Genoese[7], were infested by some roving pyrates from Catalonia and Biscay, but the first serious idea of conquest was entertained and executed by William de Bethancourt a Gentleman of Normandy who sailed from la[c] Rochelle in search of these Fortunate islands. Deserted by his country which was unwilling or unable to support a naval enterprize, he implored the aid and acknowledged the sovereignty of the King of Castille, his hopes and possessions were transferred by sale and inheritance to the Spaniards, and their blood and language soon predominated in the new settlements. In the space of eight years (1400–1408) William de Bethancourt had compleatly reduced and imperfectly[d] planted the four smaller Canaries, Lancerota, Fuerteventura, Gomera and Ferro[8]: but the natives of[e] the three larger islands of Canaria, Palma and Teneriff resisted above seventy years the private adventurers of Spain: nor was it till the close of the fifteenth century that they

  [a] *I.* S   [b] *I.* But   [c] *I.* the   [d] *I.* imperfectedly   [e] *I. om.* the natives of

finally yielded (1495) to the fleets and armies, the artillery and the missionaries of Ferdinand and Isabella.[9] Their weapons were unequal but they used the advantage of the ground; their generosity could spare a suppliant enemy, and they reserved for their[a] own defeat the precipice of despair. The remains of the old inhabitants are now incorporated with the Conquerors: the population of the Canaries may amount[b] to near two hundred thousand souls who enjoy[c] under the yoke of civil and ecclesiastical tyranny, the blessings of peace and the arts of commerce, which were unknown 2[d] to the savage liberty of their predecessors.

---

1. The ignorance of Ptolemy. (L iv C 7 in Bertii Threatrum[e] Geographiæ antiquæ Tom i p 127)[2] has ranged the *six* Fortunate islands under the same meridian line, the most northern point of which is sunk as low as the latitude of the Cape de Verd islands.

2. Plutarch in Sertorio. Tom iii p 312. Edit. Bryan. Yet some circumstances are fabulous, and others would[f] more easily adapt themselves to the Madeiras. If we prefer the Canaries, Lancerota and Fuerteventura the nearest to the African shore, must be the two islands of Plutarch.

3. Pliny (Hist. Natur. vi. 37) had likewise consulted the Periplus of Statius Sebosus. The Geographer will be satisfied with d'Anville (Geographie ancienne Tom iii p 116) and Cellarius (Geographia Antiqua Tom ii P ii p 141): but the idle scholar may consult the texts of Mela, Ælian and Solinus with the Commentaries of Isaac Vossius, Perizonius and Salmasius

4. See the life and[g] writings of Juba King of Mauritania by the Abbé Sevin in the Memoires de l'Academie des Inscriptions. Tom iv. p 457.

5. Abulfed. Geograph. Tabula. v p 230. Vers. Reisk.

6. Vie de Petrarque Tom i p 199.–205. I have disdained a silly and groundless story that the English Ambassadors at Avignon were alarmed by the grant of the *fortunate* Islands, a title which according to their prejudice could belong only to those of Britain.

7. Petrarch. de Vitâ solitariâ. L ii. Sect vi C 3. p 277. Edit Basil. The Abbate Tiraboschi (Istoria della letteratura italiana. Tom iv. p 111) maintains this national discovery against the national jealousy of a Spanish Critic

8. See a small but valuable treatise of Pierre Bergeron de la Navigation &c (C. 6. 7. 29-35[h]) which introduces the Voyages principalement en Asie &c La Haye. 1735. 2 Vol. in 4°.

9. The History and description of the Canary Islands by George Glass. (London 1764) are drawn partly from a Spanish MS. composed at Palma, and partly from the reading and experience of the Author. But he had not, nor have I, seen the copious[i] work of a native of the Canaries (Josephi de Viera Y Clavijo Noticias de la Historia General de les Islas[j] de Canaria Madrid 1762 &c. iv Vol. in 4°) Clavijo is the unfortunate man[k] who has been dishonoured, perhaps unjustly by the wit and malice of Beaumarchais.[3]

---

[a] *I.* themselves (*replaced by* their own defeat)   [b] *I.* may now amount
[c] *I.* who now enjoy   [d] *Gibbon's page number in right-hand margin of MS. II. om.*
[e] *II. corrected to* Theatrum   [f] *I.* to   [g] *I. om.* and writings   [h] *II.* 6,
7—29—35   [i] *I.* comp   [j] *II.* Isles   [k] *I.* manner

[The Circumnavigation of Africa]

I

From the designs of Prince Henry to their final accomplishment by Vasco de Gama, the Portuguese discoveries of Africa and India have been the theme of many historians: but the copious stream which uniformly flows in the same channel is derived from a muddy and penurious source. The inquisitive Ramusio (1550) deplores the negligence of the Kings of Portugal, who should[a] have required and preserved the fresh memorials of each successful expedition. That no more than four persons had survived to commemorate the acts of their countrymen is the complaint of Castaneda (1553) a laborious historian, who might converse with Gama himself, and who had exhausted the original archives of Lisbon, and Goa. The narrative of the two African voyages of Cadamosto the Venetian is the only composition of the fifteenth Century which has reached my know-ledge:[1] that curious navigator describes the scenes in which he was personally engaged; his fancy was not inflamed by patriotism; nor could his judgement be affected by any subsequent events. From this contemporary monument, I shall extract the purest idea of the primitive designs and discoveries of Prince Henry and his associates.

From his castle on the shores of the Atlantic, near Cape Lagos in Portugal Prince Henry encouraged and improved the art of Navigation, without trusting his person to the Ocean. The trade between Italy and Flanders passed before him and Mosto[b] himself is an example how liberally he engaged the service of the most skillful seamen, and the bravest[c] spirits of the Age. His original[d] motives were Religion and Chivalry: the master of the order of Christ was bound by the injunction of a dying father to pursue the Moors on the sea as well as[e] on the land: but his zeal was soon directed by curiosity and his curiosity was rewarded with the first-fruits of commerce. His *caravels* which annually infested the coast of Azafi and Messa were urged by his powerful voice beyond the tremendous capes of Non and Boyador, they slowly moved along[f] a sandy desert of a thousand miles, which drinks the waters of the Atlantic, and explored the Senegal[g] and the Gambia, that separate the countries of the whites and the Blacks. From the fertile[h] and

---

[a] *I.* might [b] *II.* Cadamosta [c] *I. and II.* bravest spirit *MS.* bravests spirit *s added by Gibbon in revision* [d] *I.* first [e] *MS. second* well as *added in margin by Gibbon* [f] *I.* a lon [g] *I.* mouths [h] *I.* banks of

populous banks of these rivers they still[a] advanced to the south; but the Sierra Leone appears to be the most remote discovery of Prince Henry, who in the labour of forty years did not attain the term of the navigation of Hanno. But the Canaries or Fortunate islands had emerged from the darkness of the middle age, and the vessels of Portugal were driven by the winds or guided by the compass to the more distant isles of Madeira and Cape Verd. The commercial profits of Prince Henry and his associates which sometimes exceeded one thousand per cent were derived from various sources. The settlement of Madeira had been rapid and useful; and the four Colonies of the Island consisted of eight hundred Christians, of whom one hundred were qualified to serve on horseback. A large quantity of Cedar and Rose-wood was annually exported, the sugar-canes, which Prince Henry introduced, surpassed in[b] their produce those of Cyprus and Sicily, and the vines of Candia derived a new flavour from the soil and climate. A plentiful fishery attoned in some degree for the barrenness of the desert: Arguin was enriched by the inland trade; and the land of the Negroes afforded a fair promise of gold-dust, ivory and slaves.

It is curious to observe how[c] strongly in this first interview the superiority of the *Whites* was felt and acknowledged by the Blacks. The Portuguese sails as they swelled to the wind were mistaken by the Azenaghis for enormous bird[s]: when the ships lay at anchor near the shore they assumed the form of sea-monsters, and in their rapid motions they were likened to the spirits of the air and deep. The Negroes trembled at the sound and effect of the muskets and cannon, one of which, as it was said, could destroy an hundred enemies at a single blast. They admired the dress and music, the arts, the luxury, the riches of the Europeans, who enjoyed their paradise in this World, and who surpassed in power and knowledge the magicians and perhaps the Deities of Africa. But an opinion prevailed on the banks of the Gambia, that the black slaves who were embarked in the foreign vessels, supplied with a grateful food the polite Cannibals of Europe. If we follow the fate of these unhappy men, this false suspicion is rather favourable than injurious to Christian humanity

---

[1.] See the Italian original of the narrative of M. Aluise da ca[d] da Mosto in the Collection of Ramusio Tom i. folio. 104-121, a Latin Version in the Novus Orbis of

---

[a] *I.* a [b] *I.* in goodness [c] *I.* in [d] *II.* Cadamosta

Grynæus and a French abstract in the Histoire Generale des Voyages Tom ii p 285–321. Mosto[a] left Venice August the 8th A D 1454. at[b] the age of twenty two: he performed his two Voyages in the years 1455 and 1456, and he finally quitted Portugal the 1[rst] of February. 1463

II

The African trade of the Portuguese, as it is described by Mosto may afford some glimpses into the inland Geography of that vast continent, an obscure scene which has been less invisible to the Arabian Moors[1] than to any other nation of the ancient or modern World.

By the care of Prince Henry the little island of Arguin near Cape Blanco was settled and fortified: but he gave a monopoly of ten years to his own exclusive Company. After some hostilities against the Azenaghis the last shade between the whites and blacks, their alliance was found to be more conducive to the interest of trade and even of Religion. They pitched their tents from Mount Atlas to the Senegal: their hard and wandering life qualified them to be the carriers of the desert; and Hoden a station in their country was in the road of the Moorish caravans. Six days journey from Hoden, Teggazza possessed a mine of rock-salt, which was greedily purchased and used by the natives of the torrid Zone to preserve, as they believed, their blood from putrefaction. The camels laden with salt travelled in forty days from Teggazza to Tombuto, in thirty more from Tombuto to Melli, a city and Kingdom whose place our ignorance cannot ascertain[2]: but such were the difficulties of the way that of an hundred camels not more than twenty five were expected to return. Melli was frequented by the Mahometans of Egypt and Barbary; and the silk of Grenada was often exchanged for the gold and slaves of the most inward Africa. This valuable cargo was distributed in three different channels. The Eastern caravan, the merchants of Grand Cairo repassed an[c] unknown desert from the Niger to the Nile. The western caravan after moving in a body from Melli to Tombuto was separated in the two streams of Tunis and Morocco. The latter approached the sea coast of Arguin: the manufactures of Europe intercepted some portion of the gold-dust, and seven or eight hundred blacks were annually exported for the use of the Portuguese. Ramusio whose views of commerce are just and enlarged, exhorts the nations to invade the monopoly of salt; to lade their ships at the islands of Cape Verd,

---

[a] *II.* Cadamosta   [b] *I.* he   [c] *I.* the

and to penetrate by the Senegal and the Gambia into the Golden regions of Africa. But the negligence of the Europeans or the invincible obstacles of Nature have hitherto prevented the execution of this splendid design

But the exchange with an invisible people of salt for gold is described by Mosto on the faith of the itinerant Arabs. From Melli the salt was transported on mens shoulders as a great lake or river of fresh water where it was left without a guard on the shore. The merchants of Melli and some unknown strangers who arrived in large boats had their respective hours for visiting this solitary market: the heaps of gold-dust which the purchasers deposited were proportioned to the value of the salt; and as soon as the scales were equal, the price was accepted, the merchandize was removed, and the whole transaction was concluded without seeing each others faces, but without a suspicion of fraud or violence. It is added that a King of Melli indulged his curiosity to know these mysterious traders: but that a captive who had been surprized in an ambuscade, obstinately rejected all food, and died on the fourth day without having[a] shewn the power or inclination to speak. The singularity of the transaction some circumstances of gross fable, and the silence of Leo Africanus[3] may provoke a legitimate doubt: but this mode of invisible traffic is reported by Herodotus[4], whom the Venetian had never read, and by the Moors of Barbary who had never heard of the Venetian.[5]

---

1. I have before me the Latin Version of the Sherif al Edrisi so foolishly styled the Geographia Nubiensis by the Maronites (Paris 1619 in 4°), and the Italian original of Leo Africanus first published by Ramusio (Tom i fol. 1–104) The English translations from these writers in Moore's travels into Africa (Appendix p 1–79) are executed by no vulgar hand.

2. D'Anville's great Map of Africa[4] affords not any traces of Meli, which is however described by Leo. (P. vii fol. 84. verso[b]) and which seems to be the Malel of Edrisi (Geograph. Nubiens. Clim. i. P ii p 10)

3. Yet we may[c] prove from Leo or Edrisi the scarcity of salt, the plenty of gold, and the fresh-water lakes in the midst of Africa.

4. Herodot L iv. C 196. He gives indeed this trade to the Carthaginians and places the invisibles on the sea-coast

5. Shaw's travels p 239. This[d] learned traveller appears himself unacquainted with the original passage of Herodotus, or the narrative of Mosto[e]

---

a MS. have   *b* II. om. verso   *c* I. p   *d* I. Though a scho
e II. Cadamosta

III

Before the arrival of the Portuguese, before[a] the age of Mahomet, under the reign of Adrian[1], the commerce and even the dominion of[b] the Arabs was spread along the Eastern shores[c] of Africa on either side of the Equinoctial line. After a long and lucrative traffic, the Mahometans of Arabia were tempted by the nakedness of the people and the richness of the land, but in the ninth century, Zanguebar, the coast of the Zenghis was still savage and idolatrous. The northern position of Magadoxo and Brava points them out as the most ancient settlements (A H. 320 AD 932); the kingdom of Quiloa was founded (A H 400 AD 1009) by a Persian prince of the race of the Sultans of Shiraz; Melinda Monbaza[d] and Sofala flourished in the twelfth Century; these maritime colonies were encreased by vagrant Bedoweens and Negro proselytes, and the reign of Islam extended to the isle of Madagascar and the tropic of Capricorn.[2]

The contrast of the Savage Africans may have embellished the portrait of the Arabians of Zanguebar, but the features of a rich and civilized people are not easily mistaken. According to the heat of the climate and the fashion of the East they were cloathed in loose garments of silk or cotton; their turbans were of fine linnen; nor did they neglect the elegant luxury of gold and gems. These ornaments might be brought from a distance, but the state of the colonies marked an high degree of wealth and improvement. The cities were populous and regular, the public and private buildings were of hewn stone or painted wood; the gardens were filled with the plants of India; the adjacent lands were cultivated with skill and care, and the inhabitants possessed great numbers of cattle and domestic animals. The Ironworks of Melinda, the gold-mines of Sofala were at once the monuments of their art, and the sources of their opulence. In War they employed the arms of Antiquity, bows and arrows scymetars and lances; the horsemen of Monbaza, and the archers of Melinda were renowned: but they were ignorant of the invention of Gunpoweder, and the use of canon. These maritime colonies could not forget the art of navigation: they traded with Aden and Ormuz, with Cambaye and Calicut; but their course was directed by the Monsoons; and they never ventured beyond the Cape of Currents in the twenty fourth degree of southern

---

[a] *I.* fo   [b] *I. om.* of the Arabs   [c] *I. a.* coast *I. b.* side   [d] *I.* Melinda and Monbaza

latitude. The Government of their petty states was loosely balanced by the Royal and Aristocratical powers: the Koran was the bond of Union, but the rival sects of Omar and Ali excommunicated each other on this lonesome coast. The Arabians had introduced their language, and the rudiments of letters; but they were ill-provided with books, and it is only in the Lusiad, that a King of Melinda could be familiarized to the names of Homer and Ulysses.[3.]

From the Senegal to the cape of Currents Vasco de Gama had seen no vessels on the Ocean except his own. After passing that cape, the canoes of the Negros, their artificial trinkets and their vague reports announced his approach to a civilized, perhaps to an Indian, World. The first interview of the two nations was in the isle of Mozambique; the[a] thundering[b] arms of the Portuguese astonished the Arabians, and applauded the Hero who had emerged from the storms and darkness of the south. But Gama could not long dissemble that he was a Christian, the enemy of their faith, and the invader of their commerce: he abhorred the Moors, and the belief that all Mahometans were Moors has propagated that[c] African name to the extremities of Asia. The open or secret enmity which laboured to destroy his ship and intercept his return is more easily explained than the hospitable wellcome, and important aid which he received from the princes of Melinda. In twenty three days he traversed without care or danger an Ocean of seven hundred leagues from Melinda to Calicut. His trusty pilot an Indian of Guzarat steered the well-known course by a compass, a quadrant and a marine chart[d], and his experience or prejudice despised the Astronomical instruments of Europe.

According to the most liberal computation Vasco de Gama discovered no more than twenty degrees of southern latitude from the Cape of Good Hope to Mozambique. But a thin veil separated[e] Lisbon and India, and the last adventurer by whom it was removed has usurped the sole[f] honours of the circumnavigation of Africa. Yet Gama might boast that by him alone the Equinoctial line had been crossed four times; and that he had atchieved in two years the longest Voyage which had been performed by the sons of men[4]

---

1. Arrian in his Periplus of the Red sea, is illustrated by d'Anville. Memoires de l'Academie Tom xxx p 88 &c

---

[a] I. and the   [b] MS. thunderings   [c] II. the   [d] I. car   [e] I. by   [f] I. fame of those who had prepared his way. Yet Gama (replaced by sole honours. . . . Yet Gama)

2. See the Arabians (Geograph. Nubiensis, p^a 27. 28 Abulfeda. Geograph. Tab·
xxvii p 355. 356. and Yakouti in the Notices des MSS de la Bibliotheque du Roi Tom
ii p 395.) whose knowledge seems to have decayed with time. The Abbé Renaudot
(Anciennes relations des Indes p 303–308) is most instructive.

3. The English translator of Camoens justifies this impropriety by an old Syriac
version of Homer: But the fact is doubtful, and the inference ridiculous. (Mickle's
Introduction.[)]

4. Osorius de rebus Lusitanicis L i. Mariana Hist. Hispan L xxvi. C 17–20. Tom iii
p 217–228. Hist. Generale des Voyages. Tom i.

IV

Of the maritime nations of Europe the French have had the
smallest share in the fame and benefits of the great naval discoveries.
Yet their authors pretend, that they were the first, after the fall of
the Roman Empire, who sailed along the coast of Africa beyond the
southern limit of the World. Before the year 1364 the ships of
Normandy had penetrated as far as Cape Verd, the river Senegal
and the mountains of Sierra Leone: and in the month of September
1365, an act of association was signed between the merchant
adventurers of Dieppe and Rouen. The joint efforts of this trading
company produced a rapid encrease of wealth and knowledge: the
domestic names of Paris and Dieppe were applied to the new
factories on the coast of Guinea; and a French title is maintained
to the original foundation (1383–1386) of the well-known fort and
settlement of St George de la Mina. But the civil confusions of
France were soon renewed by the insanity of Charles vi (1392); the
spirit of commerce and navigation evaporated; the sons of opulent
traders aspired to the rank of Gentlemen and soldiers; their African
colonies were^b deserted or destroyed, and this French discovery
vanished like a dream from the coast of Guinea, and the memory of
men.[1]

It is indeed a dream—. I will not deny that the Normans of the
fourteenth Century frequented the Atlantic Ocean; that their ships,
returning with a cargo of Spanish wines might be driven far away to
the southward, and that the conquest of the Canary islands was
first undertaken by a private gentleman of Normandy. But this
offspring of national vanity, this fable of a Senegal and Guinea
Company may be annihilated by some short and simple reflections.
1 Less than thirty years (1334–1364) cannot decently be assigned
for the first and most laborious steps of the Atlantic navigation, and

^{a} *I.* Abu ^{b} *I.* vani

these years must fall on the calamitous reigns of Philip of Valois and his son John. The military strength of the Kingdom was lost in the fields of Creçy and Poitiers: two hundred and thirty ships and thirty thousand seamen were destroyed in a naval engagement: Normandy was invaded by the English, Caen was pillaged; the miseries of War and faction aggravated each other; the wealth of France was drained for a King's ransom; and the great plague swept away the third part of the human race. And was this a time?

——2. The writers of the age are ignorant, (and they could not have been ignorant) of these African discoveries. Such exploits would have been enrolled by the historian of Charles v[5] among the peaceful triumphs of his reign. Would not the archives of France and England afford some acts of regulation or favour to the Norman company? Must not the new commodities of Guinea Gold-dust, Ivory and Negroes have been soon noticed in the market of Bruges? Could the curious and vagrant Froissard[6] never meet a talkative mariner who had sailed beyond the Tropic? The fourteenth Century might be inattentive to the benefits of trade; the genuine or specious miracles of an Atlantic Voyage would have been transcribed and read as eagerly as a romance of Chivalry or the legend of a Saint. 3. The Portuguese may assert the faith of their own historians: but the Venetian Cadamosto[a] was a contemporary and a stranger: and Cadamosto[a] affirms that their discoveries were long checked by the supposed impossibility of passing Cape Boyador. Could such an impossibility have been supposed, if the French vessels had been seen within the memory of man steering an annual course to their Guinea settlements above twenty degrees southward of the impassible Cape? 4. This pile of improbabilities is raised on an airy basis. I might peruse with attention the original act of association in the Archives of Dieppe: but alas! these archives have been consumed by fire (1694). I *will* smile at the reference to some anonymous Manuscripts in the library of a town lawyer whose name is discreetly suppressed. Nor shall I deign to examine the collateral proofs, a vague appellation, a broken date and the old attachment of the Negroes for the French nation. 5. The motive of this idle fiction may be easily detected. In the beginning of the seventeenth Century, the Senegal[b] and Guinea trade was actually exercised by the African Company of Dieppe and Rouen. These Merchant Adventurers were prompted by interest as well as pride to magnify the antiquity

---

[a] *II*. Cadamosta   [b] *I*. tra

of their house to claim the inheritance of the Golden coast, and to urge, against the Portuguese, a prior right of discovery and possession.

---

1. See two works of Pere Labat. L'Afrique Occidentale. Tom i. p 6–16 and Voyage en Guinée. Tom i p 133. 238 &c. and likewise l'Histoire Generale des Voyages. Tom. ii p 424. Tom iv p 2 &c.

V

A question naturally arises whether Prince Henry explored the Atlantic, the sea of darkness as it was styled by the Arabs, in search of a southern passage to the spicy regions of India. The views of Cademosto[a] do not seem to reach[b] beyond the fame and profit of his immediate discoveries: but the views of a soldier are not those of his general, and the largest designs are most worthy of a Hero who was deeply skilled in the Cosmography of the Age. I can admit that he cherished a secret and distant hope of circumnavigating Africa: nor shall I arraign the gratitude of posterity, which has placed on his head the naval crowns of his successful disciples. Their ardour was chilled, about twenty years, under the reign of his nephew Alphonso v,[7] a reign of foreign and domestic war; but the African Voyage[c] was prosecuted by the industry of John ii, and finally atchieved by the fortune of Emanuel. Their Royal efforts directly pointed to India and the Spicy trade: the spirit of the court encouraged the Portuguese to press forwards on the Ocean, with a brave disdain of prejudice at home and danger abroad. The Genius of Columbus tormented Europe, and awakened Spain: but Vasco de Gama was a chosen servant who executed with prudence and resolution the commands of his Sovereign.

The thirty seven years (1460–1497) between the decease of Henry, and the voyage of Gama, had opened a[d] more extensive sphere of Theory and practise. The study of the ancients had been revived: the copies of their writings were[e] multiplied; and before the accession of John ii (1481), the original text of Pliny, and the Latin versions of Herodotus and Strabo had been repeatedly printed at Rome and Venice[(1)]. The circumnavigation of Africa by the Phœnicians and Persians, by Hanno and Eudoxus became the favourite theme of discourse; and the fabulous or doubtful tales of

---

[a] *II.* Cadamosta   [b] *I.* have   [c] *I.* Vor   [d] *I.* opened both in Theory
and practise a   [e] *I.* had been

Antiquity rekindled the courage and promoted the discoveries of the modern Argonauts. A Planisphere or map of the World[2] was delineated in[a] the convent of Murano at Venice: the[b] Kings of Portugal employed and rewarded the ingenious monk; and the most perfect edition of his work was long exhibited in a Benedictine Abbey in the neighbourhood of Lisbon. Marine Charts, such as may be still extant in our libraries, were drawn by Italian artists and distributed to Portuguese commanders; and the outline of old knowledge, and recent conquest announced the subject or at least the field of enquiry. The Mathematicians of John ii, two Physicians of Jewish names, and a German Cosmographer, the famous Martin Behaim of Nuremberg[8] invented the Astrolabe and calculated tables of declination[3]: the art of navigation was improved, and instead of creeping along the shore, the mariners of Europe gave themselves to the deep. The eastern direction of the coast of Guinea seemed to open a speedy prospect of India: but when the African continent again pointed to the south, the hopes of the Portuguese were blasted[c]; they viewed[d] with astonishment the stars of a new Hemisphere; and long hesitated on the verge of the Equator. The thirty five degrees of southern latitude from the line to the southern promontory were discovered in two successive voyages by the Captains of John ii: the promontory was turned; and a just confidence in the powers of man imposed on the Cape of Tempests, the more auspicious name of CAPE OF GOOD HOPE.

I am told, but I do not believe that the King of Portugal received from Congo the first intelligence of the Christian Empire of Abyssinia: the unknown space between the Nile and the Zayre is oc[cu]pied[e] by deserts and savages; and a more easy mode of intercourse[f] may be found in the common pilgrimage of Jerusalem. The curiosity of John ii was imperfectly qualified: his first messengers returned after a feeble and fruitless effort: his second Ambassadors were more worthy of their trust; but Payva died in Abyssinia, and his associate Covigliam was detained a perpetual exile in that solitary land.[9] Yet before his captivity, the intrepid Covigliam had transmitted home[g], an account of his first labours. From the red sea, he had visited the coasts of the Ocean, as far as Calicut on the Indian and Sofala on the African side. At Calicut he had seen the great market of Oriental spices; at Sofala he had

---

[a] *I.* at Mura [b] *I.* near [c] *I.* were again blasted [d] *I.* were
[e] *MS. om. letters at line division* [f] *I.* co [g] *I.* on

learned from the Arabian mariners, that the southern Ocean is boundless and navigable, and he justly concluded that the Caravels which traded to Guinea might explore their way to the isle[a] of Madagascar and the shores of Malabar[4]. Columbus plunged into the sea of darkness: but the merit of Gama is somewhat abated by the previous inspiration[b] of hope and knowledge.

---

1. See the Greek and Latin *Bibliothecæ* of Fabricius and the Annales Typographici of Mattaire

2. Tiraboschi. Istoria della letteratura Italiana. Tom vi P. i p 216. Modena 1790. For the planisphere of Murano he quotes the Annales Camal. (of the Camaldoli) Tom vii p 252. Mr Senebier p 211 describes some maps of the xv[th] Century in the library of Geneva.

3. Geddes' Church history of Æthiopia. p 39.

4. Covigliam himself related his adventures to Francesco Alvares[10] who found[c] in Abyssinia (1520) after an exile of thirty years (Viaggio[d] della Ethiopia. C 103 in Ramusio Tom i. fol 254.[)]

VI

While the liberality of Gelo and his brother Hiero attracted every stranger who could amuse or instruct the court of Syracuse, a Persian *Mage* related to[e] the former of those princes that he himself had circumnavigated the whole continent of Africa.[1] An event of such magnitude cannot be lightly received on the single credit of a wandering priest, whose Religion and country afford the fairest grounds of suspicion. The Magi abhorred the art of navigation which tended to sully the purity of one of the sacred elements[2]; the Persians never aspired to the fame of a maritime people, and a voyage of distant discovery, though not incredible, must be deemed in their character, a very singular adventure. It is certain however that in the time of Gelo and Xerxes[3] they *once* attempted the circumnavigation of Africa, and the exagerated tale of the *Mage* of Syracuse must be tryed and reduced by the authentic relation of Herodotus, who derived his intelligence from the report of the Carthaginians.[4]

Under the reign, and in the court of Xerxes, his kinsman Sataspes was condemned to be impaled for the crime of ravishing a noble Virgin. But a mother, the sister of Darius interceded for the guilty youth, on whom she promised to inflict a punishment not less

---

[a] *I.* sho　　　[b] *I.* possession　　　[c] *II.* was found　　　[d] *I.* Descrittione Viaggio
[e] *I. om.* to the former of those princes

terrible than death itself; and he accepted as the condition of his pardon the task of sailing round Libya, and returning home by the Red sea. After preparing his ship and mariners in Egypt, Sataspes sailed beyond the columns of Hercules, and coasted along the African shore to the promontory of Soloe, (Cape Boyador), from whence he steered his southern course in the Atlantic Ocean. The natives whom he saw were of a diminutive stature: their[a] garments were composed of the leaves[b] of the Palm tree: they were affrighted by the aspect of a naval monster, and wheresoever he landed, they fled into the Country, abandoning their villages and cattle to the rapacious strangers. But Sataspes, who was not endowed with the spirit of discovery beheld with anxious despair the prospect of an endless sea, and his complaint that his ship was stopped, that it would advance no farther may be imputed to the dead calms, that prevail in the neighbourhood of the line. The dangers and fatigues of his expedition and return might have expiated the crime of love: but the justice or revenge of Xerxes was inexorable: Sataspes was impaled according to the rigour of his first sentence; and his misfortunes, though not his Character may afford a faint similitude of our countryman Sir Walter Raleigh.[1] After the death of Sataspes one of his Eunuchs escaped to the isle of Samos with a large sum of money, of which he was defrauded by the perfidy of a Samian, whose name is forgotten by the tenderness of the father[c] of history. The Asiatic Greeks maintained a free and frequent intercourse with Sicily: and a *Mage*, who had served as chaplain in the Libyan voyage, might accompany the Eunuch's flight, and abuse the privilege of a traveller

---

1. This *Mage* had been introduced in one of the Dialogues of Heraclides Ponticus a disciple of Plato and Aristotle (Vossius de Historicis Græcis L i. C 8. 9.) But his voluminous writings are now lost as well as those of Posidonius by whom this passage had been quoted and we are now reduced to the testimony of Strabo (Geograph. L ii. p 155. 158.).

2. Plin. Hist Natur. xxx. 7.

3. This Synchronism lasted seven years (485–478 before Christ[)]: but the Egyptian rebellion will not permit us to place the Voyage of Sataspes before the third year (482) of the reign of Xerxes. (Herodot L vii. Diodor. Sicul L xi).

4. See Herodot. L iv C 43. p 298[d]. 299 Edit Wesseling, and the excellent French version of Mr[e] Larcher[12] with his learned notes. Tom iii p 156. 405.

---

a I. the   *b I.* st   *c I.* G   *d II.* 398   *e II.* M.

VII

By the command of the Senate of Carthage, two Admirals, Himilco and Hanno were sent at the same time to navigate the northern and southern parts of the Atlantic Ocean. HANNO sailed from Carthage with a fleet of sixty large ships carrying a multitude of men, women, and children, which has been magnified to the incredible number of thirty[a] thousand persons. In twelve days from the streights of Gibraltar he reached the small island of Cerne or Arguin: planted seven cities or colonies for the benefit of trade, and fixed his last station at Cerne itself, which has since been occupied, disputed and abandoned by the modern powers. As he advanced he discovered a large river, most probably the Senegal, well-peopled with Hippopotami and Crocodiles: and his course was directed first to the South and afterwards to the East along the coast of Guinea. A chain of mountains, the Sierra-Leone overlooked the Ocean; and burning[b] Volcanos poured into its waves their torrents of liquid fire. In the heat of day all was silent: but the forests blazed with nocturnal lights, and re-echoed with the joyous sound of flutes timbals[c] and drums. In some slight encounters the arms of the Carthaginians must prevail over the wandering natives, who spoke a language unknown to the Moorish interpreters By their speed of foot the savages escaped: but the hairy skins of three female captives were exhibited as trophies at Carthage; and, though Hanno mistook for women these mute and perverse animals, it is more probable that they were *Pongos*,[13] the large monkey of human shape. The cape of *tres Puntas* in Guinea five degrees north of the Equator appears[d] to have been the term of this whole Atlantic navigation of thirty eight days: the scarcity of provisions compelled Hanno to return; nor does he seem to have detached any light vessels to prosecute the line of southern discovery. The date of his Voyage rests or rather floats on a period of four centuries (700 to 300 years before Christ); but, for various reasons I am inclined to sink it as low as the prosperity of the Republic of Carthage will permit.

The Journal or Periplus of Hanno[1] is still extant in a Greek version, nor can I agree with the idle suspicions of Dodwell that it has been changed or corrupted since its first appearance soon after the age of Aristotle.[2] This concise narrative was translated or

---

[a] *I.* sixty   [b] *I.* their burning   [c] *II.* cimbals   [d] *I.* was

abstracted from a Punic inscription on a plate of brass or marble in the temple of Saturn at Carthage: the practise of these ancient records is acknowledged; and most of the proper names may be reasonably derived from the Hebrew or Phœnician idiom.[3] The *Libyc* books, the wanderings of Hanno were indeed exposed on the Athenian stage as notorious fables; but the Greeks were at once credulous and sceptical; and even the ridicule attests the existence of the books and the fame of the Voyage.[4] The trade and colonies of Carthage along the shores of the Atlantic and the Libyan deserts are firmly established: yet it must be allowed that one of our best witnesses the Geographer Scylax denies the possibility of navigating beyond Cerne in a shallow and muddy Ocean.[5]

A much longer Voyage of Hanno, the entire circumnavigation of Africa from the streights of Gibraltar to the Red sea will not be supported by the single and hasty assertion of the elder Pliny. In the course of a work as extensive and various as Nature itself, his critical attention is often bewildered; and while he believes the most singular, he rejects the most simple, circumstances of the Periplus of Hanno.[6]

---

1. See the Periplus of Hanno in the first Volume of Hudson's Geographi minores with Dodwell's dissertation. Mariana. Hist. Hispan. Tom i. L i. C 22. p 32. 33. Pomponius Mela. L iii C 9 p 401 cum observat. Isaac Vossii. Bougainville sur le Voyage d'Hannon in the[a] Memoires de l'Academie des Inscriptions. Tom xxvi p 10–46 Tom xxviii p 260–318.

2. Aristot. περι θαυμασιων ακουσματων C xxxv. p 77. Edit. Beckman. Gotting. 1786. This collection of wonderful stories is drawn from the writings of Aristotle, and may be ascribed to one of his first disciples.

3. Bochart. Canaan. L[b] i. C 37. in Opp. Tom i p 639–644.

4. Athen. Deipnosophist. L iii. C 7. p 83. Aristides in Oratione Ægyptiacâ. in Opp. Tom ii p 356. Edit. Jebb.

5. Scylacis Caryandensis Periplus. p. 53. in Geograph. min. Tom i.

6. Plin. Hist. Natur. ii[c]. 67. v. 1. vi. 36.

VIII

"In the time of our grandfathers (it was said in the reign of "Claudius), a certain Eudoxus flying from the wrath of Ptolemy "Lathyrus King of Egypt embarked on the Red sea and sailed "round to Cadiz in Spain". This passage is extracted by Pomponius Mela[1] from the writings of Cornelius Nepos who lived in the time of the same Ptolemy, and deserved the friendship of Cicero and

a II. om. the   *b I.* L iii   *c I.* L ii C 3

Atticus.[2] A witness of a respectable character, who affirms a recent and notorious fact will naturally engage the public confidence: this African circumnavigation has been unanimously[a] admitted[b], and I must conceal my suspicions, could I not produce from the philosopher Posidonius, a writer of equal age and authority, the true and accurate state of the voyages of Eudoxus.[3] His eye might be deceived by the unnatural distortions, and monstrous dresses of the southern savages, he might find some tribes ignorant of the use of language and fire: but that he returned by a new road to the northern hemisphere

Ignotum per iter, gelidas enavit ad Arctos

I positively deny.

Under the reign of the second Euergetes, who died one hundred and seventeen years before the Christian Æra, Eudoxus of Cyzicus a priest a linguist, and a mariner arrived in Egypt and gained the favour[c] of the prince and people. A new field of riches and knowledge was opened to the Ptolemies by the shipwreck of an Indian on the red sea. With this guide, who had soon learned the Egyptian tongue Eudoxus sailed to India on his first Voyage of discovery, but the cargo of spices and precious stones with which he returned, exposed him to the avarice of the Tyrant. After his death under the regency of his widow Cleopatra, Eudoxus was again employed. In his second voyage he was driven on the coast of Æthiopia; among the hospitable natives he distributed the unknown blessings of corn, wine and dry figs, while his own curiosity was gratified with a catalogue of their barbarous words; and the prow of a foreign ship, inscribed with horse[d], which had been cast on their shore by the western winds.[4] In[e] the port of Alexandria this fragment was recognized by the merchants of Cadiz who even named the ship, a fishing vessel which some years before was supposed to be lost beyond the river Lixus on the western coast of Africa. Eudoxus now held the thread of discovery, but fear or indignation urged him to leave the unworthy court of Ptolemy Lathyrus the son of Cleopatra. I slightly mention his return home, the sale of his estate, his visit to Italy and Marseilles and his final departure from Cadiz with a great ship and two brigantines to explore the Atlantic Ocean. Fired with the hope of reaching India he supported the

---

^a I. om. unanimously   ^b I. admitted by critics and philosophers   ^c I. confidence   ^d II. horses   ^e I. The

murmurs[a] of his crew, and the loss of his vessels, built a small galley of fifty oars and continued his route till he heard on the Western[b] the same language which he had found on the Eastern, side of the continent of Africa. On his return to the river Lixus he offered himself and his discoveries to the Moorish King, but the timid Bogud was apprehensive of opening his dominions to unknown enemies, and had not Eudoxus escaped to the Roman province of Spain, the dangerous secret might have been extinguished with his life. His second voyage from Cadiz was prepared with more prudence and skill: the form of his vessels was adapted to the seas and shores: and instead of an useless train of singing-girls and physicians, he enlisted a laborious company of husbandmen and artificers, resolving to winter on[c] a verdant island, which he had discovered in the Ocean——It is here, at this critical moment that Posidonius disappoints our curiosity referring his readers to the Spaniards of Cadiz, as the most likely to be informed of the failure or success of the voyage[d] of Eudoxus, against the reality of which the Geographer Strabo has raised some idle and envious objections.

---

1. Mela de sitû Orbis. L[e] iii C 9. p 402 403. 405 Edit Voss. The same passage of Cornelius Nepos is quoted by Pliny. (Hist. Natur. L[e] ii. C 67)

2. See[f] Aulus Gelius Noctes Atticæ. L[e] xv. C 28. We have some fragments of the letters of Cicero to Cornelius Nepos, who has composed a life of Atticus which is still exstant

3. Posidonius apud Strabon. Geograph. L ii p 155–160

4. According to Pliny a similar wreck was found by Caius Cæsar the grandson of Augustus in the Red sea. Such stories could not have been entertained had the ancients formed any just idea of the size of Africa, of the cape which advances near thirty five degrees into the southern hemisphere.

IX

Of the four circumnavigations of Africa, three have been disproved, and the overthrow of Sataspes, Hanno, and Eudoxus must disturb the easy and early triumph of the Phœnicians of Nechus. Nor are these doubtful or[g] fabulous expeditions attested by the consent of ages. The spirit and perhaps the records of naval enterprize were lost in the destruction of Tyre and Carthage; and their conquerors were unwilling to believe, even the real atchievments, which they were unable to imitate. The World of the Greeks

---

[a] *I.* 1   [b] *I.* Eastern   [c] *I.* in   [d] *I.* enterprize   [e] *II.* lib.   [f] *I.* Posidonius apud S   [g] *I.* exped

the Romans and the Arabians was circumscribed within a narrow out-line. Some Geographers, accidentally stumbling on the truth, affirm or rather suspect that Africa, except in the Isthmus of Suez, is encompassed by an open and navigable sea. But a large majority, in weight as well as in number, represent the Climates beyond the Equator*a* as unknown or impervious; a torrid zone in which no mortals can breathe, a shallow and muddy Ocean in which no vessels can move or an interposing tract of land which joins in a southern latitude the continents of Æthiopia and India. By all who raised such insuperable barriers, the *possibility*[b] of a circumnavigation was denied: but the few who admitted that it was *possible* might doubt or disbelieve that it had ever been actually performed.

Arrian[1] or the nameless author who under the reign of Adrian has composed a description of the Red sea, embraces, according to the style of Antiquity the Persian and Arabian Gulphs with a part of the Ocean between India and Africa. He runs the African coast to the city and promontory of Rhapta, which is placed by Ptolemy in the eighth degree of southern latitude. From thence continues Arrian, the land turns to the west, and the surrounding Ocean WHICH HAS NEVER BEEN EXPLORED, at length mingles with the waters of the Atlantic. Under a Roman Emperor the task of discovery might have been shortened, if his subjects had sailed in friendly correspondence from his ports of Egypt and Spain. But Adrian was not ambitious of conquest; his curiosity did not grasp the knowledge of the Globe; and the endless promontory of the south would have soon exhausted the skill and patience of his mariners.

Above the crowd of vulgar Geographers, Eratosthenes and Ptolemy exalt their heads, as the great masters of Cælestial and terrestrial Science. Eratosthenes[2] was the first who dared to measure and delineate the Earth: but in his erroneous system, a burning and desolate Zone extends twelve degrees on either side of the Equinoctial line. The land of Cinnamon on the eastern coast of Africa is situate within the twelfth degree: it might be superfluous to add that none had ever*c* penetrated beyond this term of *our* habitable world, but the sentence is of damning weight from an universal scholar to whom Herodotus was familiar, and who commanded the treasures of the Alexandrian library.[3] The Geographical sphere of Ptolemy[4] was enlarged by the Roman discoveries, and his own propensity to magnify space and distance beyond their

a *I*. lin   *b* *I*. possible   *c* *I*. even

real proportions. His promontory of Prasum, a Cape Verd on the Eastern coast[a] of Africa is forced as low as the fifteenth degree of southern latitude: but he draws, from the neighbourhood of this cape, the line of an unknown continent[b], which is finally united with the country of the Asiatic Sinæ. Ptolemy reigned near fourteen centuries on Earth, as well as in Heaven; nor was the Greek Oracle ever confuted by the experience of the Arabians.

In[c] the sublime fiction of Camoens,[5] the spirit of the Cape, arising from his stormy waves at once accuses and applauds the Portuguese, the first of men who had explored their way round the southern promontory of Africa.

> Nor Roman prow nor daring Tyrian oar
> Ere dashed the white wave foaming to my shore:
> Nor Greece nor Carthage ever spread the sail,
> On these my seas to catch the trading gale.
> You, you alone, have dared to plough my main,
> And with the human voice disturb my lonesome reign.

I[d] WILL TAKE THE GHOST'S WORD FOR A THOUSAND POUNDS![14]

---

1. Arrian. Periplus maris Erythræi. p 150. Edit. Blancard.

2. Eratosthenis Geographicorum Fragmenta. L[e] ii p 63 &c L iii p 193. Gotting. 1789.

3. It is generally agreed among scholars that Eratosthenes was styled βητα not from being the second in every science but as the second Keeper (239–194 years before Christ) of the Alexandrian library (Fabricius Bibliot. Græc. Tom ii p 471)

4. Claud. Ptolemæus. L iv C 9. L vii C 4. in Bertii Theatrum[f] Geographiæ veteris Tom i p 131. 212

5. Mickle's Lusiad p 211. 212. An Englishman must praise the versification; the Portuguese acknowledge the fidelity of this elegant translation.

X

Nechus King or Pharoah of Egypt, who reigned six hundred years before the Christian Æra is mentioned in the Hebrew[g] Chronicles[1] as well as by the Father of Grecian history[2]. The mind of Nechus was susceptible of every kind of ambition: the Jews and Syrians fell before his arms: he entered Jerusalem in triumph; his Empire was bounded by the Euphrates; and the ships of War which he built commanded the Mediterranean and the Red[h] sea. The execution of his canal from the Nile to the last mentioned sea

[a] *I. om.* coast   [b] *I.* country   [c] *I.* N   [d] *II. treats as separate paragraph*
[e] *II.* lib.   [f] *I.* G   [g] *I.* Jewish   [h] *I.* gulph of Arabia.

might have changed the commerce of the World, but after expend-
ing the lives of an hundred and twenty thousand of his subjects,
the King of Egypt was alarmed by an oracle, and turned his[a]
thoughts to the fame and advantage of naval discoveries. At his
command, and in his vessels a chosen band of Phœnicians penetrated
from the Arabian gulph into the southern Ocean returned in[b] the
third year by the streights of Gibraltar and proved for the first time,
that, except in the isthmus of Suez, the continent of Africa is on all
sides encompassed by the sea. In the autum of the first and second
year, these bold navigators landed on some convenient spot, committed their seeds to the ground, patiently waited the returns of the
next harvest, and resumed their voyage with a fresh supply of
provisions. The Phœnicians reported that in[c] sailing round Africa
they had seen the Sun on their right-hand, "a phænomenon says
"Herodotus, which to some, may seem[d] less incredible than it does
"to me."

Since the modern discoveries of the Portuguese we know the
possibility and we suppose the *reality* of an ancient circumnavigation
of Africa. The reign of Nechus is accurately fixed in the last and
most authentic period of the history of Egypt: his father Psam-
metichus had opened the country to the Greeks, and his death did
not happen more than one hundred and sixty years before the
travels of Herodotus. An inquisitive spirit forms the character of
the[e] historian whose authority has been fortified by the improvement
of criticism and science: he had visited Egypt before the chain of
tradition was buried in the ruins of the temples and sacerdotal
Colleges: he investigated[f] the remains of the docks or arsenals
which Nechus had built; and the Pharoah after the example of
Solomon might reasonably entrust his Vessels to the most skillful
navigators of the East. The ignorance of the Greek might tempt
him to deny but his impartiality forbade him to dissemble the
Astronomical fact, which, in our eyes, is the surest pledge of his
veracity. As soon as they had passed the line, the Sun would appear
on the right-hand of the Phœnicians.

I have allowed full weight to these specious probabilities, but I
must object with equal fairness that Herodotus was a stranger in[g]
Egypt, who saw with his own eyes, but who heard with the ears of
his careless or credulous interpreters. The priests were ambitious

---

[a] *I.* this   [b] *I.* into   [c] *I.* th   [d] *I. om.* seem   [e] *I.* an   [f] *I.* visite
[g] *I. om.* in Egypt

of impressing the minds of strangers with a splendid idea of their cœlestial and terrestrial science; and in the observatories of Thebes and Heliopolis the astronomers could safely calculate the motions and aspects of the planets. A journal of the Voyage of the Phœnicians, which Herodotus had never seen, must have demonstrated it's truth or falsehood: their adventures would be measured by the standard of probability, and the seas and lands, the winds and seasons, the plants and animals would be compared with the genuine and unalterable face of Nature. But a southern communication between the Indian and Atlantic Ocean might be affirmed or denied: the chance was equal; and a lucky guess may have usurped the honours of actual discovery. My surprize and suspicion are excited by the successful agriculture[a] of the strangers in unknown climates and new soils; by the seeds of the temperate Zone which yield their encrease between the Tropics: nor can I persuade myself that these infant navigators sailed round Africa in three summers to amuse the curiosity of a King of Egypt. The Compass was in the hands of the Portuguese: they were stimulated by the spirit of Chivalry, fanaticism, and avarice: yet after seventy years of labour and danger, their fruitless efforts were still repelled by THE CAPE OF TEMPESTS[.]

---

1. These Chronicles, the reigns of Pharaoh-Necho and the contemporary history of the East are illustrated in[b] the learned writings of the Christian Chronologists, in the Animadversions of Scaliger, in the Annals of Archbishop Usher, in Prideaux' Connections in Sir John Marsham's Canon Chronicus, in an Essai sur l'histoire Orientale in the Monde primitif of Mr Court de Gebelin. By these and by many more the Phœnician Voyage round Africa is reported without a shadow of suspicion.

2. Herodot. L ii. C 158. 159. p 181. 182. L iv. C 42 p 298. In every quotation of Herodotus I use[c] the Greek Edition of Wesseling with his learned notes, and those of Mr[d] Larcher, the French translator, a scholar and a Critic.

---

[a] *I.* navigation of the   [b] *I.* by   [c] *I.* wish   [d] *II.* M.

ANTIQUITIES[a]
OF
THE HOUSE OF BRUNSWICK

CHAPTER 1[b]

SECTION 1[c]

[Section I]

The curiosity of an English subject[d] may be tempted to enquire into the Antiquities of a family which after an alliance with the daughters of our Kings has been called by a free people to the legal inheritance of the Crown. The illustrious house of Brunswick is now divided into two branches: Charles Duke of Brunswick enjoys the right of primogeniture: George iii Elector of Hanover and King of Great-Britain is distinguished by the superiority of title and dominion. For their common parent in the sixth and seventh degree, they both acknowledge Duke Ernest the Confessor, who[e] lived at the time of the Reformation; and Ernest is the ninth in lineal descent from Otho the child, the first Duke of Brunswick and Luneburgh (1235). A princely illustration of five or six hundred years might be drawn without dishonour from an adventurous soldier, a faithful client, whose services had been rewarded by the Emperor. But the fief which Frederic ii imposed, had been a free and patrimonial estate; the gift which Otho accepted was the last remnant of a more splendid fortune.[1] His grandfather Henry the Lyon had united with his Slavic conquests the powerful Dutchies of Bavaria and Saxony. From the shores of the Baltic to the banks of the Tyber that ambitious prince and his father Henry the proud[f] were obeyed, or respected, or feared; and in the great quarrel[g] of the Guelphs and Ghibelines the former appellation was derived[h] from the line of their female ancestry.

---

[a] *I.* MEMOIRS   [b] *I.* BOOK THE FIRST   [c] *I.* CHAPTER 1   [d] *I. om.* o̤
an English subject   [e] *I.* and who   [f] *I.* superb   [g] *I.* quarrels   [h] *I.* drawn

But the male pedigree of the house of Brunswick must be explored beyond the Alps: the majestic tree which has since overshadowed Germany and Britain, was first rooted in the Italian soil. Our[a] most skillful guides, Muratori and Leibnitz, ascend with equal confidence and truth to the Marquis Albert-Azo Lord of Este, and one of the most conspicuous personages of the eleventh Century. Guelph[b] Duke of Bavaria and grandfather of Henry the proud was the eldest son of the Marquis by his[c] first wife Cuniza or Cunegonde, the heiress of the ancient Guelphs. His second wife Garsenda, of the Counts of Maine in France, was the mother of Fulk and Hugh: and the descendants of Fulk, were the Marquisses of Este, and the Dukes of Ferrara and Modena; who, after a long succession of princes, are now merging, by a last daughter[2]; in the Austrian family.[d] The fair anticipation of the name of ESTE-BRUNSWICK may denote the venerable stem before it's separation into the German and Italian branches.

A generation of mankind, the common interval between the birth of a father and that of his son is fixed by Herodotus at the term of about thirty three years, at the computation of three generations for one Century. The experience of modern times has confirmed the reckoning of the Greek historian: and, though a royal marriage may be hastened for the important object of succession, yet the same rule has been verified in the families of sovereigns and subjects.[(1)] It is strictly just in the twenty two generations and[e] the seven hundred and sixty six years (996–1762) which have elapsed from the birth of the Marquis Azo to that of the Prince of Wales; and if the collateral lines of Brunswick and Modena[f] afford no more than twenty one, and twenty generations, the difference might be explained by some peculiar circumstances of their respective history.

Twenty two generations, seven or eight hundred years, occupy a small place even[g] in the historical period of the World. But all greatness is relative: and there are not many pedigrees, in Europe or Asia, which can establish, by clear and contemporary proofs, a similar antiquity. If the ancestors of the Marquis Azo are lost, as they must be finally lost, in the darkness and disorder of the middle ages; it will be remembered that the use of hereditary names and

[a] *I*. The   [b] *I*. Henry the superb Duke of Saxony and Bavaria is the unquestionable great-grandson   [c] *I*. Cun   [d] *I*. *om.* in the Austrian family.
[e] *I*. or   [f] *I*. Ferrara   [g] *I*. in the period

armorial ensigns was unknown; that the descent of power and property was frequently violated; that few events were recorded, and that few records have been preserved. Yet human pride may draw some comfort from the reflection that the authors of the race of Este-Brunswick can never be found in a private or plebeian rank: their first appearance is with the dignity of princes; and they start at once, perfect and in arms, like Pallas, from the head of Jupiter

---

1. See Herodotus. L ii C 142. and his justification by Freret. Histoire[a] de l'Academie des Inscriptions. Tom xiv. p 15-20

This short review may explain and justify the threefold division of these memoirs which appropriates a separate book to i THE ITALIAN DESCENT, ii THE GERMAN REIGN, and iii THE BRITISH SUCCESSION of the house of Brunswick. The obscure interval from the first Duke to the first Elector will be connected on either side with the more splendid scenes of their ancient and modern history. The comparative date and dignity of their pedigree will be fixed by a fair paralel with the most illustrious families of Europe. Even the flowers of fiction so[b] profusely scattered over the cradle of the princes of Este disclose a remote and decreasing light which is finally lost in the darkness of the fabulous age. But it will be prudent, before we listen to the rude or refined tales of invention, to erect a strong and substantial edifice of truth on the learned labours of Leibnitz and Muratori.

The Genius and studies of Leibnitz[1] have ranked his name with the first Philosophic names of his age and country: but his reputation, perhaps would be more pure and permanent, if he had not ambitiously grasped the whole circle of human science. As a *Theologian*, he successively contended with the Sceptics who believe too little, with[c] the Papists who believe too much, and with the Heretics who believe otherwise than is inculcated by the Lutheran confession of Augsburgh.[2] Yet the[d] Philosopher betrayed his love of union and toleration: his faith in Revelation was accused while he proved the Trinity by the principles of Logic, and in the defence of the attributes and providence of the Deity he was suspected of a secret correspondence with his adversary Bayle.[3] The *Metaphysician* exspatiated in the fields of air: his præ-

---

[a] *I.* Memoires   [b] *I.* which have been   [c] *II.* and with   [d] *Ia.* in the midst of Religious warfare he embraced the counsels of union and toleration: he was ac *Ib.* under this mask the Philosopher

established harmony of the soul and body might have provoked the jealousy of Plato; and his Optimism the best of all possible Worlds seems an idea too vast for a mortal mind. He was a *Physician* in the large and genuine sense of the word[a]: like his brethren he amused himself with creating a globe, and his *Protogæa* or primitive earth has not been useless to the last hypothesis of Buffon which prefers the agency of fire to that of Water.[4] I am not worthy to praise the *Mathematician*: but his name is mingled in all the problems and discoveries of the times; the masters of the art were his rivals or disciples and if he borrowed from Sir Isaac Newton the sublime method of fluxions, Leibnitz was at least the Prometheus who imparted to mankind the sacred fire which he had Stolen from the Gods.[5] His curiosity extended to every branch of Chymistry, Mechanics, and the arts; and the thirst of Knowledge was always accompanied with the spirit of improvement. The vigour of his youth had been exercised in the schools of *Jurisprudence*; and while he taught, he aspired to reform the laws of Nature and Nations of Rome and Germany. The annals of Brunswick, of the Empire, of the ancient and modern World, were present to the mind of the *historian*; and he could turn from the solution of a problem to the dusty parchments, and barbarous style[b] of the records of the middle age. His Genius was more nobly directed to investigate the origin of languages and nations; nor could he assume the character of a *Grammarian* without forming the project of an universal idiom and alphabet. These various studies were often interrupted by the occasional *politics* of the times; his[c] pen was always ready in the cause of the princes and patrons to whose service he was attached: many hours were consumed in a learned correspondence with all Europe: and the Philosopher amused his leisure in the composition of French and Latin *poetry*. Such an example may display the extent and powers of the human understanding: but even *his* powers were dissipated by the multiplicity of his pursuits. He attempted more than he could finish; he designed more than he could execute: his imagination was too easily satisfied with a bold and rapid glance on the subject which he was impatient to leave; and Leibnitz may be compared to those heroes whose empire has been lost in the ambition of universal conquest.[6]

When he was about thirty years of age (1676) the merit of Leibnitz was discovered and adopted by the Dukes of Hanover, at whose

[a] *I.* World   [b] *I.* fanc   [c] *I. and II.* and his

court he spent the last forty years of his life in free and honourable
service. In this station he soon became the author or at least the
architect of a monument which they were ambitious of raising to
the glory of their name. With the view of preparing[a] the most
authentic documents for the history of the house of Brunswick, he
travelled over the provinces of Germany and Italy, their[b] ancient
seats. In this learned pilgrimage, he consulted the living and the
dead, explored the libraries, the archives, the monasteries and even
the tombs; and diligently collected or copied the books, the manuscripts and the charters of every age. As the curiosity of the
historian had not been limited to the proper[c] bounds of his subject,
the various treasures which he had imported were published in
several Volumes,[7] with as much speed and care as the multitude
of his avocations would allow; and it may be[d] deemed either a
praise or a reproach, that the raw materials are often less valuable
than the observations, and prefaces of the Editor himself. In the
year 1695 the nuptials of the prince of Modena with a princess of
Hanover engaged him to dispell the errors and fables of preceding
Genealogists, and to restore[e] the true connection of the Kindred
branches, which were thus united, after a separation of more than
six hundred years. This occasional pamphlet[8] was designed as
the prelude of the great Latin work, which he meditated on the
Brunswick Antiquities. With a Genius accustomed to draw lines
of communication between the most distant sciences, he traced in
his Introduction the revolutions of the country and its inhabitants;
of the country from the natural remains of fossiles and petrifications,[f]
of the inhabitants from the national vestiges of language and
manners. The story of a province[g] and a family swelled in his
capacious mind into the annals of the Western Empire: the origins
of the Guelphs of Bavaria and the Marquisses of Este would have
been[h] interwoven in their proper place; and the narrative would
have been deduced from the reign of Charlemagne (AD 769) to the
last Emperor of the Saxon line (1025). But the term of an ante-
diluvian life would have been scarcely adequate to the labours and
projects of Leibnitz: the imperfect manuscript of his Annals was
buried in the library of Hanover; and the impression though long
since promised is still refused to the curiosity of the public. But

---

a I. collecting the most authentic materials   *b* I. an   *c* I. narrow
d I. bee   *e* I. establish   *f* II. petrifactions   *g* I. provinces   *h* I. om.
been

the ideas and papers of that great man were freely communicated to his disciple and successor, Eccard,[9] and the researches more[a] peculiarly belonging to the house of Brunswick have formed the basis of the *Origines Guelficæ*, which were compiled by the industrious historiographer. The rashness of Eccard[10] who changed his service and religion condemned his work, till envy and malevolence had subsided, to a long oblivion; nor was it till many years after his decease that the Origines Guelficæ were printed in five Volumes in folio, by the care of the Electoral librarians.[b] The hands of the several workmen are apparent; the bold and original spirit of Leibnitz, the crude erudition[c] and hasty conjectures of Eccard, the useful annotations of Gruber, and the critical disquisitions of Scheid the principal Editor of this Genealogical history.[11]

In the construction of this domestic monument, the Elector of Hanover, ten years after the return of Leibnitz, had[d] dispatched a second Missionary (1700) to search the archives of his Italian kinsmen. Their archives[e] were in the most deplorable state: but the princes of Este were awakened by shame and[f] vanity; and their subject Muratori was recalled from Milan to reform and govern the Ducal library of Modena. The name of Muratori[12] will be for ever connected with the litterature of his country: above sixty years of his peaceful life were consumed in the exercises of study and devotion: his numerous writings on the subjects of history, antiquities religion, morals and criticism are impressed with sense and knowledge, with moderation and candour: he moved in the narrow circle of an Italian priest; but a desire of freedom, a ray of philosophic light sometimes breaks through his own prejudices and those of his readers. In the cause of his prince, he was permitted and even encouraged[g] to explore the foundations, and to circumscribe the limits, of the temporal power of the Bishops of Rome: and his[h] victorious arguments in the dispute for Commachio,[3] accustomed the slave to an erect posture and a bolder step.[13] One of his antagonists the learned Fontanini had been provoked in the heat of controversy to cast some reflections on the family of Este, as if they had been no more than simple citizens of Padua, who in the thirteenth Century were invested by the Popes with the title and office of Marquis of Ancona. Truth and honour required an answer to this invidious charge; and the firmest answer was a

---

[a] *I.* which more peculiarly belonged   [b] *I. om.* by . . . librarians   [c] *I.* 1
[d] *I. om.* had   [e] *I. om.* archives   [f] *I.* and fear an   [g] *I.* pr   [h] *I.* the su

simple and genuine exposition of facts. The courts of Brunswick and Modena were joyned in the same family interest; and their trusty librarians, Leibnitz and Muratori corresponded with the confidence of allies, and the emulation of rivals.[14] But the speed of the German was outstripped in[a] the race by the perseverance of the Italian: if the conjectures of Muratori were less splendid his discoveries were more sure; and he could examine with the leisure of a native the monuments and records which his associate had formerly viewed with the haste of a traveller. After a diligent enquiry of three years, both at home and abroad, he gave to the World the first Volume of the *Antichità Estense*, a model of Genealogical criticism;[15] and in the second Volume which was delayed above twenty years, he continues the descent and series to his own times. The more strenuous labours of his life were devoted to the general and particular history of Italy. His Antiquities,[16] both in the vulgar and the Latin tongue, exhibit a curious picture of the laws and manners of the middle age; and a correct text is justified by a copious Appendix of authentic documents. His Annals[17] are a faithful abstract of the twenty eight folio Volumes[18] of original historians; and whatsoever faults may be noticed in this great collection,[19] our censure is disarmed by the remark that it was[b] undertaken and finished by a single man. Muratori will not aspire to the fame of historical Genius: his modesty may be content with the solid though humble praise of an impartial critic and indefatigable compiler.

With such guides, with[c] the materials, which they have provided, and with some experience of the way[d] I shall boldly descend into the darkness of the middle age: and while I assume the liberty of judgement, I shall not be unmindful of the duties of gratitude.[e]

L i. C i

1. Leibnitz born at Leipsic June 23. 1646. died at Hanover. 14 November. 1716.—Eloge. Oeuvres de Fontenelle Tom V. p 447–506—sa Vie par le Chevalier de Jaucourt. Essais de Theodecèe Tom i p 1–312. Leibnitii Vit. a Bruckero. Opp. Tom i p liv–ccix.—His own life to Pelisson. Opp. I. 716–[sic] A loss! an example.

2. Gothofred Gul. Leibnitii in vi. Tom in 4°. Geneva 1768 apud fratres de Tournes by Louis Dutems imperfect[f], where Monody, where Neufchatel why the Theodicèe in Latin? Why the letters not Chron? Have we all to Bernouilli B. R.[4]

---

[a] *I.* on th   [b] *I.* is the   [c] *I.* and with   [d] *I. om.* and with some experience of the way   [e] *MS.* gratitude.[1] *See Introduction, Part IV.*   [f] *I. om.* imperfect . . . B.R.

3. A Deist. Fontenelle p 504. Pfaff knows[a] Le Clerc believes, cum Baylis sentire. Bibl. Act M. Tom xv. p. 179. 180.–pious or decent Apology of Dutems. Præf. gen. p vii.–xiv

4. See Opp. Tom ii. P ii. p 181–240. Compare Theorie de la Terre. H N. Tom i with Epoques. Suppl. Tom V.[5]

5. Prometheus of Eschylus. wonderful. the second part of the three. solution in Horat. L i. Od. ii.

6. Beautiful allusion of Fontenelle.—of Leibnitz himself the arma Dei, and mortalis mucro. Virgil xii. 739.

7.[b] Codex J. G. diplomat. fol. Han. 1693. with the Mantissa. fol. 1700—Accessiones historicæ 2 Vol. 4° Lips et. Hans. 1698—Scriptores rerum Brunswicensium. 3 Vol. fol. Han. 1707. 10. 11.

8. Lettre[c] sur la connexion des maisons de Brunswic et d'Este. Opp. Tom iv. P ii p 80–85.

9. This plan given by Eccard. Opp. Tom iv P ii p 78–79. from thence Font. and Jaucourt, but why do they call the five Saxons, de la maison de B?

10. Leibnitz to Muratori. p 108—see two zealous letters in B. G.[6] Tom ix. p 194.–203. half a madman half a knave, his works numerous. retired to Wurtzbourg without paying his debts, no Religion, stole books. &c.

11. Origenes Guelficæ. præeunte G G. Leibnitio stylo J G. Eccardi literis consignatum, a J D Grubero novis probationibus instructum jam vero in lucem admissum a Christ. L Scheidio. Han. in fol. Tom i. 1750. ii. 51. iii. 52. iv. 53. in 1780 the v. with Index by Jungius

12. Vita del Pro. L A M. by his nephew. 4°. Ven. 1756. born 1672. Oct. 21. at Milan 1695. at Modena 1700. died there 1750. Januar 23. Curious but en beau.[7]

13. See last Diss. on Saints, Relicks, monks &c. Il Voto sanguinanō, a pleasant controversy. Vita. p 109–129. judgement. p 208–212.

14. xxi letters from Leibnitz to Mur. in Opp. Tom iv[d] P. ii. p 89–112. from 1709–1716. in 1707 when he published 1st Vol. he knew nothing before Azo. see præfat ad Bereng. Panyg. Epist. M. ad L. Tom iii S. R. B.[8]

15. Antichità Est. ed Italiane. Tom i Modena 1717 in folio. The MS a whole year in Leibnitz s hands. Ant. Este. Tom ii Modena. 1740.

16. Antiquitates It. medii Ævi. Tom vi fol. Mediol. 1738–1743. Dissertazione sopra le Antichità Italiane. 3 Vol in 4°. Milano (Venezia) 1751[e] posthumous

17. Annali d'Italia. Milano (Venezia) xii Vol 4° 1744–1749. Ibid 1753. in 8. xviii Vol which I use.

18. Scriptores rer Ital. in folio. 25 Tom. (the three first each of two Vol.) Milano. 1723–1751 by the Palatine Socii. must not be confounded with the ridiculous Thesaurus of 45 Vol. of Grævius Burman &c.[9]

19. See the extract or criticism of Maffei a secret enemy. In the Osservazione litterarie Tom i p 79–121. Want of a Chron. Concordance.

In those happy times, when a Genealogical tree could strike its 1[f] root into every soil, when the luxuriant plant could flourish and fructify without a seed of truth, the ambition of the house of Este-

[a] I. believes   [b] MS. number 5. All subsequent notes to this section have been renumbered in the present edition. The notes were written on a long sheet, folded, as follows: 249ʳ, upper fold, 1–6; 249ʳ, lower fold, 5–10; 249ᵛ, upper fold, 11–16, with two notes numbered 13. Notes 17–23 (below, p. 510) were on 249ᵛ, lower fold.   [c] I. Lettres [d] I. iii   [e] I. om. 1751   [f] II. om. Gibbon's page number.

Brunswick was easily gratified with a Roman pedigree. The name of *Azo*[a] or *Atto* so familiar to the Italian line was deduced as a manifest corruption from the Latin Original of *Attius* or *Accius* or *Actius*:[b] and this fanciful identity an article of faith in the court of Ferrara, was not disputed in the sixteenth century by the rudeness of foreign criticism.

In a visit to Venice (1685) Ernest Augustus Duke and afterwards Elector of Hanover accepted with a gracious smile the Manuscript of Theodore[c] Damaidenus a Belgic Abbot, and the *Augusta Decora Romano-Brunsvicensia*[1] were[d] honourably placed among the archives of his family. This splendid folio is decorated with the luxury of medals, inscriptions and Classical authorities; but the historian spins from his own bowels and from those of his blind or fallacious guides,[e] an unbroken thread of two thousand four hundred and thirty six years. The first of the Duke' ancestors whom Damaidenus pretends to know is Actius Novus one of the companions[f] of Romulus, whose services were rewarded with a statute by the founder of the City. His great-grandson is the famous Augur who divided a stone with a razor in the presence of the elder Tarquin. The *Attii* or *Actii* are enrolled as Senators while all the Senators were Patricians: they continued to serve in all the Wars of the Republic, but their civil ambition seldom aspired above the office of Edile. In the age of the Antonines they migrated from Rome to Ateste, their riches and merit promoted them to the honours of the colony, and about four hundred years after Christ Caius Actius the thirty third in lineal descent from the companion of Romulus was chosen by his countrymen their protector and prince. But if the Prætor M. Attius Balbus, a real personnage of the seventh Century of Rome could have any possible affinity with our fabulous series, the genuine lustre of the Accii would be derived from their union with the human and Divine glories of the Julian race[.] Julia the sister of Julius Cæsar was the wife of the Prætor Attius, and by their daughter Attia, their grandson Augustus himself might be claimed as a kinsman by the Duke of Modena, and the King of Great-Britain. A prudent Advocate may repeat with pleasure the verses of the Æneid that celebrate the youthful command of the Trojan Atys, the founder, according to Virgil of the Atian family.

Alter Atys, genus[g] unde Atii duxere Latini

---

[a] *I.* Att　　[b] *I. om.* or Actius　　[c] *I.* the A　　[d] *I.* This Sp　　[e] *I. om.* and from those . . . guides,　　[f] *I.* Dukes c　　[g] *I.* unde genus La

Parvus Atys, pueroque puer dilectus Iulo

but he will dissemble the reproach of Antony, and the apology of Cicero, which may leave a stain on the maternal descent of Augustus.[2]

From the fifth Century of the Christian Æra, the fables of Damaidenus are grafted on the Romance, rather than the history, of[a] Pigna,[3] who had[b] been content to deduce from that period the succession of the Accian family and the princes of Este. The first of these princes Caius Actius was called to the glorious labour of defending Italy against[c] the Goths, and his grandson the more illustrious Foresto opposed in arms the great invasion of Attila and the Huns. On the intelligence of the siege of Aquileia he marched from Este and Padua with a chosen band of subjects and allies, cut his way through the Barbaric host, and displayed the standard of the white Unicorn in every action of defence and attack till he was mortally wounded by a Scythian arrow. Eloquent in council, invincible in the field, an Hero in his life, a Christian in his death, the glory of Foresto would be compleat, if such a man had ever existed in the World. After the fall of Aquileia, the honour of his son Acarinus is saved by a prudent retreat; and the fugitives of Este withdraw at his command, and found a new city in the morasses of Ferrara. In the subsequent revolutions of Italy, the imaginary descendants of these ideal chiefs, are often oppressed and always emerge: in the cause of loyalty or patriotism they sometimes support and sometimes resist the[d] Kings of Lombardy, and Emperors of the West; and in the light of the twelfth Century, a fabulous Rinaldo is created to save Milan, and defeat the armies of Frederic Barbarossa. The lust of fiction is punished by the contempt of truth, and if some corrupt traces may [be] discerned of the separation of the German and Italian lines, the Genealogist is ignorant of the fame and fortunes of the house of Este-Brunswick.

Yet this history, so pregnant with falsehood,[e] was composed by a man of learning and character, in a knowing age and a polite court, by the accomplished John Baptista Pigna, Secretary of State to Alphonso ii Duke of Ferrara.[4] But the artful courtier was disposed to shut his eyes and to follow his leaders. The imperfect papers of Count Faleti who first discovered the Roman Attii, and[f] explored[g] in Germany a long-lost branch of the family[5] were given into his hands, and he used with equal confidence[a] the[b] Manuscript remains of Pelegrino Prisciano.[6] The *War of Attila*, a Provençal Romance of the fourteenth Century appeared in his eyes a genuine and contemporary work of Thomas the Scribe of Nicetas Patriarch of Aquileia.[7] He was probably deceived by the lives of the Emperors which the Count Boyardo, with more than poetic licence has imposed as an Italian Version of the Latin original of Ricobaldus[8]. The spurious fragments had been gradually consolidated by the public credulity: fictions were changed into facts, traditions[c] into truths, and conjectures into realities. The materials were prepared; and while he added the last varnish to the pleasing tale the conscience of Pigna might applaud without much scruple his own veracity and innocence.   2[d]

I am fatigued with the repetition of fables, but an illustrious race must always be crowned with its proper Mythology. After fixing on the Earth the solid foundations of the house of Este-Brunswick, I am desirous of proving that we are not less able to build in the air.

---

1. I can only be acquainted with the MS. work of Damaidenus by the learned preface of Scheidius to the first Volume of the Origines Guelficæ. p 19-33.

2. Ignobilitatem objicit, says the Orator (Philippic iii. 6) and we may learn from Suetonius (in Octavio. C 2.) that Antony was still more severe on the paternal ancestors of Augustus. The Emperor himself allowed that his father was the first Senator of the family.[10]

3. Historia de Principi di Este di Gio: Battista Pigna In Vinegia 1572 in 4°. I possess likewise a Latin Version of the same work Ferrariæ 1585 in folio It extends from the fall of the Roman Empire to the year 1476 Pigna promised, but has only promised a second Volume.[11]

4. Pigna, the friend of Tasso, is the sage Elpino of the Aminta. See his various merits in the Italian Observations on that Pastoral Drama by Menage (p 160-164).[12]

5. From Pigna's dedication I collect, that he himself signified (1560) the Duke's orders to Count Girolamo Faleti whose MSS.[e] annals at the time of his death had been only carried down to Azo ix (1216-1240).

6. Pellegrino Prisciano, keeper of the Archives to Hercules i[f] (1495) had collected and written many Volumes concerning the house of Este. Muratori who praises his fidelity complains that the far greater part of his MSS.[g] had been shamefully consumed in fire-works (Antichita Estense Tom i C ix. p 69

7. See Muratori's preface to the Antichità Estense p. xix. I have neither the Provençal romance which is preserved in MS. in the library of Modena, nor the Italian abridgement printed in 1568. But Pigna (L i. p 11-30 has extracted the most important and least improbable circumstances

8. After much hesitation Muratori has published in the ix[th] Volume of his Scriptores rerum Italicarum (p 279-423) this work of Ricobaldus or Boyardo. The mention of the

---

[a] *I.* freedom	[b] *I.* the bold guesses of Falletus who first discovered the Atti
[*deleted*] Roman Attii, and	[c] *I.* error [d] *II. om. Gibbon's page number*
[e] *II.* MS. [f] *I.* ii	[g] *I. om.* of his MSS.

Garter may prove that it was not composed till Hercules i Duke of Ferrara had been invested with that order by Edward iv King of England.

Before[a] the name of Atys was invented by Virgil, before the I[b] Attian family was propagated to modern times, a fabulous tradition had connected the princes[c] of Troy with the Dukes of Ferrara and Brunswick. But the manufactures even of the Italians in the thirteenth Century were coarse and clumsy, and they could only devise that Marthus an unknown Trojan besieged Milan, and founded, after his own name, a small city in the Milanese; and that, of four brothers who sprang from this[d] Chief, the eldest was the father of the future Marquisses of Este[(1)]. It was not till after the year fourteen hundred that the romances of French Chivalry passed the Alps and the Pyrenees; and I am inclined to adopt the sentence of Cervantes[(2)], who wishes to forgive the lyes of Archbishop Turpin, Charlemagne and his twelve Peers, from the grateful reflection that they afforded the first hints to the invention of Boyardo, from which the *Christian* Poet, Ludovico Ariosto has so finely composed his inimitable Web. Such a Magician as Ariosto can annihilate time and space: and he dispenses, by the prerogative of Genius, with the laws of history, Nature and his own art.

According to the wild though delightful fictions of the Italian bards[(3)] the house of Este-Brunswick is descended from the race of the Trojan Kings. Astyanax the son of Hector was saved by an artifice from the victorious Greeks: Sicily gave him a retreat and a Kingdom; and the valiant youth avenged on Argos and Corinth the injuries of his country. Polydore the son of Astyanax fixed his residence in Calabria, and Flovian the grandson of Polydore (a brief Chronology!) was the first of the race of Hector who settled at Rome. By his two sons two noble branches arose from the same stem: the one is decorated by the Imperial titles of Constantine and Charlemagne; the other after a long and splendid succession is illustrated by the name of Ruggiero or Roger the favourite Hero of Ariosto and his readers. In the spirit of chivalry his strength and valour are his first virtues: the adverse ranks of battle are pierced by his lance or[e] shivered by his sword; and the effects of his resistless charge are compared to the explosion of the Gran Diavolo a thundering piece of ordnance in the arsenal of Ferrara. In more equal combat he stands invincible against the foremost[f] Paladins

[a] *Begins f. 328[r] ; f. 327[v] blank.*   [b] *II. om. Gibbon's page number*   [c] *I.* Trojan princes   [d] *I.* that   [e] *I.* of   [f] *I.* fur

of France; and the two Pagan champions, Mandricardo the Tartar, and Rodomonte the African are slain after two desperate encounters by the hand of Roger. These martial terrors are softened by youth and beauty, by the generosity of his temper, his courteous manners and the tenderness of his heart. He burns with a pure and honourable flame for the fair Amazon, Bradamante, and if he is seduced by the arts of Alcina, if he is fired by the naked charms of Angelica, his affections are constantly fixed on his noble spouse, the destined[a] mother of the house of Este. Their *White Eagle* was depicted on his shield as the hereditary symbol of the Trojan line: the *Arms of Hector* he possessed by the double claim of inheritance and conquest; and if his horse *Frontin*, and his sword *Balisarda* were obtained by less worthy means, Roger was guiltless of the theft, and they became his own since he was able to defend them. But the Hero disdained the use of supernatural aid; and indignantly cast into Well,[b] the magic shield which dazzled the eyes, and benumbed the senses of all beholders.

By his mother, a Saracen princess, the unborn Roger was transported from[c] Italy to Africa, and the helpless infant was saved educated[d] by the Enchanter Atlas. His first arms were pointed against the monsters of the desart, and he passed the sea under the Imperial standard of Agramante who invaded France with all the powers of the Pagan or Mahometan World. The destinies of the house of Este require his conversion: but the event is artfully delayed and the trembling balance is suspended by the master-hand of the poet.[e] Tender of his life, and careless of his fame the African Magician presumes to oppose the decrees of Heaven; secludes his pupil from the World fascinates his eyes, sends him to wander through the air on a Hippogrif, and dissolves his courage in the isle of Luxury and love. The example of his Christian ancestors is a weighty argument for an illiterate soldier; and he assures his mistress that for her sake he is ready to undergo a baptism not only of water but of fire. But a man of honour, a loyal Knight is apprehensive of the reproach of deserting his benefactor and his party, an unfortunate benefactor, and a falling party. A seasonable wound allows the Christians to vanquish under the walls of Paris: but a single combat which must determine the WORLD'S DEBATE, the lover of Bradamante is forced to encounter her brother Rinaldo, till he is delivered

---

[a] *I.* futur   [b] *II.* a well   [c] *I.* into   [d] *II.* and educated   [e] *I.* Italian poet

from[a] the fatal conflict by[b] the treachery and flight of the African Monarch. A shipwreck, a desart island, an Hermit and a prophecy assist the operation of Grace: every scruple is satisfied, every duty is accomplished, every obstacle is removed; and the poem concludes[c] with the nuptials and last victory of the Christian Hero.

But as the poet has used and abused the privilege of anticipation, he displays in a variety of pictures the fortunes of Roger and his descendants. Seven years after his baptism the Paladin will be slain by a perfidious assassin: his widow will be delivered of a son in the fruitful country between the Adige and the Brenta; and the warlike Youth, after he has avenged his father, will be invested by the Emperor with the Lordship of Este, and accepted as their native 2[d] prince by the remaining Trojans of the Colony of Antenor. The visionary forms of her future progeny pass in rapid succession before the eyes of Bradamante, and a friendly sage foretells their names and actions in a mixed strain of history and fable. According to the popular opinion[(4)], the establishment of the Saxon branch is ascribed to the marriage of Albert-Azo, in the tenth Century with[e] an imaginary daughter of the Emperor Otho the great.[13] The Italian states of the princes of Este are described, Ferrara, amidst the waters of the Po, the soft Reggio, and the turbulent Modena; their Wars against the Venetians and the Popes are discreetly announced; and the prospect is always closed by the fame the virtues and the fraternal union of Alphonso i and Cardinal Ippolito. The Duke was the sovereign, the Cardinal affected to be the patron, of Ariosto: they will live in the everlasting life of their poet "Myriads, perhaps "of heroic names, are plunged by time into the stream of oblivion: "whilst a few are saved by the grateful and melodious swans, and "honourably deposited in the temple of Immortality."

---

1. Muratori. Antichità Estense. Tom i C ix. p 67. 68. This tradition of Paulus Marrus (1280) is preserved by Gualvan de la Flamma (1320) in his great Chronicle of Milan, which Muratori (Tom xi p 534) disdained to publish among his Scriptores rerum Italicarum.

2. See Don Quixote Part i C vi p 55 of the small edition of Madrid. The most grateful incense is the praise which one man of Genius bestows on another; we are[f] sure that he feels the merit that he applauds. Yet I do not clearly conceive the epithet of *Christiano* as it is applied to the most pleasing but least Christian of Poets.

3. The original pedigree is recorded, and perhaps invented by Count Matteo Boyardo. (Orlando Inamorato L iii Canto v) but I cannot gravely refer to all the passages of Ariosto who should be familiar to every reader of taste.

---

[a] *I. om.* he is delivered from   [b] *I.* is dissolved   [c] *I.* of Aristo   [d] *II. om.*
Gibbon's page number   [d] *MS.* with with   [f] *I.* shall

4. See Ricobaldo or rather Boyardo (Tom ix. p 314 Scriptor. rerum Italic.) and Pigna (L i*ᵃ* p 73–76). Yet Pigna had learned from Count Faleti the true descent of the Dukes of Saxony and Brunswick.

The Marquis Otbert I and his father Adalbert are the undoubted ancestors of the house of Este-Brunswick: but the slumbers of Leibnitz and Muratori were still tormented by the question "Who are the ancestors of Adalbert?" The German Philosopher, more ardent, and more*ᵇ* artful than his associate, inculcates, in*ᶜ* his private letters[1], the propriety of their holding the same opinions: and the two Librarians, of Hanover and Modena, agreed to adopt the Marquisses or Dukes of Tuscany, whose hereditary splendour shines through the darkness of the ninth and tenth Centuries[.][2]

In this Hypothesis, which has obtained the sanction of Genius and learning, the noble family of Este-Brunswick ascends four or five additional steps, and unfolds a pedigree of a thousand years. Under the reign of Charlemagne (812–813), Boniface i,[14] of the Bavarian nation,*ᵈ* appears with the titles of Count and Duke: Lucca was his residence, Tuscany his province, and his merit may be presumed from the choice of the Emperor. His son and successor Boniface ii[15] fullfilled the duties of chivalry, by the deliverance of the Empress Judith, and a crusade against the Saracens of Africa. The defence of Tuscany and the isle of Corsica was entrusted to the Marquis: he assembled his subordinate Counts, armed a fleet, cleared the sea, and pursued the Africans to their own shores. His camp, between the ruins of Carthage and Utica, was five times assaulted by a numerous host of Barbarians: they fell or fled; and the Moors might fear, the Christians might imitate, the example of his bold invasion and successful return. (828). The fame of Adalbert i[16] is less pure; he turned his arms against the Vicar of Christ: yet the pillage of Rome (878)*ᵉ* is the act of no vulgar robber; and a sentence of excommunication records the power and spirit of the Marquis or Duke of Tuscany. The virtues of Adalbert ii[17] are inscribed on his tomb; the sceptre of Italy was alternately given and resumed by his policy or passion: but he deserved the epithet of the *Rich*: and a monarch whom he sumptuously entertained in his palace of Lucca was heard to exclaim "The Marquis is indeed a King, and "it is only in a vain title that I am superior to my Vassal[.]"[18] After his decease*ᶠ* (917) his two sons Guido and Lambert successively

ᵃ I. om. L i   *ᵇ I.* most   *ᶜ I.* the pro   *ᵈ I.* of Bavarian race
ᵉ I. om. (878)   *ᶠ I.* death

reigned: but Guido was snatched away by an early death; and the unhappy Lambert, after his victory in a judicial combat, was deprived, by the Tyrant of Italy, of the Tuscan[a] principality his liberty and his sight (931). In a cultivated age the eyes of the body may be supplied by those of the mind: but a[b] Barbarian incapable of managing an horse and wielding a lance is dead to all the offices of civil life.[19]

The princely families of Tuscany and Este-Brunswick are not unworthy of each other: but the connection between them is founded on presumptive, rather than positive, evidence. The name of Adalbert and the title of Marquis were common to both; the *Terra Obertenga* in the Counties of Arezzo, Pisa and Lucca preserved[c] for ages the appellation[d] of the Marquis Otbert i; and his descendants were possessed of various estates in the province of Tuscany, and the isle of Corsica. If the Genealogist, like the modest Muratori, will accept a disposition to believe that Otbert descended from a younger branch of the house of Tuscany, I embrace the probable conjecture; and the change of law and nation was so familiar to the Italians, that the transformation of a Bavarian into a Lombard will lightly weigh in the opposite scale. But the absolute decree of Leibnitz that Adalbert the father of Otbert i was the son of Guido Marquis of Tuscany provokes the opposition of a free-born Critic. The silence, almost the testimony, of the historian Liutprand, denies that filial relation; nor will the order of Nature confine two perfect generations within the compass of thirty five[e] years (925–960). The good faith of Leibnitz is not exempt from suspicion: but as a Monarch, from his lofty throne, is apt to confound the inferior ranks of society, a mathematician may not discriminate the several degrees of moral proof, which fall short of his favourite Demonstration.

A prudent, though tender, regard for the honour of the house of Este-Brunswick will rather decline than press this Hypothesis of Leibnitz. The supposition of the two sons of Adalbert ii and Berta is indeed an idle and malicious[f] calumny: but it is somewhat unlucky that Marozia the wife of Guido himself should burn with all the fires of Venus[(3)]; that his mother Berta[20] should enlist an army of lovers[(4)]; and that his grandmother Rotilda should be styled a *Whore*[(5)] by the successor of the Apostles. In these ages of military license, the chastity of the women was less immaculate than the valour of the men: nor could the noble blood of the Dukes and Marquisses of Tuscany be conveyed, with certainty and clearness, in a descent through such polluted channels.

---

1. Leibnitz. Opera. Tom iv. P ii. p 89-112. Edit Dutems.
2. See the Antichita Estense. Tom i C xxii-xxvi. p 205-264. and the Origines Guel-ficæ. Tom i. L ii. and the History of Liutprand
3. Meretrix impudentissa Veneris calore succensa. (Liutprand L ii. C 13. p 440)
4. Hymenæi exercitio dulcis nonullos sibi fidelis effecerat. (Idem. L ii C 15. p 441)
5. *Mœcha*. Epist. Johannis viii. 84. 85. apud Muratori. Annali d'Italia. Tom vii p 231.

[SECTION ii]

The researches of Muratori and Leibnitz[a][1] have added four generations to the authentic pedigree of the house of Este-Brunswick: the four immediate ancestors of the Marquis Azo, their common parent, have been rescued from the Dæmon of oblivion who had nearly devoured them. In some genuine and venerable parchments the names and descents of Adalbert, of Otbert i, of Otbert ii and of Albert-Azo i are still visible to the curious eye. Their civil acts of sale and purchase, of donation and testament affirm the extent and variety of their landed property; and sometimes insinuate their liberal disposition, the dignity of their fiefs and the number of their followers. The seat of their power can no longer be defined, but the ancestors and kinsmen of Azo ii are distinguished by the rare and princely titles of Count and Marquis; and in the tenth and eleventh centuries, these titles were appropriated to the hereditary Governors of cities and provinces. They profess themselves of the law and nation of the Lombards, who, after the sceptre had been transferred to the French and Germans, were still deemed the true and indigenous Lords of the Kingdom of Italy.

The sole recommendation of the Marquis Adalbert is to have lived[b] in the beginning of the tenth century, a remote æra, which *scarcely* any other family in Europe can fairly maintain on the firm ground of historical evidence[.] But the son of Adalbert is conspicuous in the great revolution which adjudged to the German name the titles[c] and prerogatives of Emperors of Rome and Kings of Italy. When the first Otho was solicited to pass the Alps and chastise the tyranny of Berengarius,[21] Otbert, the *illustrious* Marquis Otbert[2]

---

[a] *I. om.* and Leibnitz   [b] *I. om.* lived   [c] *I.* title

accompanied the Apostolical Nuncios and stood before the Saxon throne (960) as the representative and advocate of his noble Peers. The desertion of a sovereign, perhaps a benefactor, the appeal to a foreign jurisdiction, the introduction of an army of strangers may expose him to the reproach of ingratitude and treason, and there is always a strong presumption that private rather than public interest directs the measures of a statesman. But the crimes of Berengarius would justify a revolt; by a formal treaty Otho had been acknowledged the Judge of the King and the Protector of the people, and his bloodless*a* conquest of Italy abundantly proves that Otbert thought and acted with a large majority of his countrymen. The virtues of Otho ensured a reign of justice and peace, and a mortal may be excused if he was incapable of unrolling the book of Fate. After the victory, the services of Otbert were rewarded by the Emperor with the office of Count of the sacred Palace, the supreme Judge and principal minister of the Kingdom of Italy. In the close of life, Otbert i retired from the World to the Cloyster: and the same diligence, perhaps the same pride which he had displayed in the government of nations was employed in the humble task of collecting and feeding the hogs of the monastery.

In a period of forty years, the rapid succession of the three Othos ended in the grave (962–1002). The Germans claimed their dominion, the Italians asserted their independence: and the Iron crown was disputed by Henry the Saxon, and Arduin the Lombard till after a civil or rather social War of twelve years, the fortunate Henry obtained the honours of Emperor, and Saint. Among the champions of national freedom, the first to erect the standard and the last to bow the knee, were the Marquis Otbert ii, his four sons and his grandson Azo ii who*b* was then (1016) about twenty years of age.*c* The distance of their fields of battle will shew the extent of their influence and the obstinacy of their struggle: they made a vigorous stand in the neighbourhood of Pavia, they raised a dangerous insurrection at Rome: they were vanquished and made prisoners in the plains of Apulia. According to the law of Lombardy the*d* six Marquisses had incurred the penalties of forfeiture and death: the crime and sentence are recited in a judicial act: but, after a short pause, their lives were spared, and the greatest part of their estates was restored. That they were generous and grateful I am willing to believe; but after the decease of their benefactor, they

a I. rapid   *b I.* th   *c I. om.* of age   *d I.* they made a fruitless attempt to place the King of France; or the Duke of Aquitain on the Italian throne.

The courtly and even poetic art of an English Laureat has introduced in one of his Odes[3] the father of the Brunswick line: and the Genius of the Alps announces to the first Otbert a long descent of Heroes and Kings.

> Proceed. Rejoyce. Descend the vale,
> And bid the future Monarchs, hail.
> Hail! all hail! the Hero cry'd
> And Echo on her airy tide
> Pursu'd him murmuring down the mountain's side.

---

1. See the Antichitá Estense Tom i C x–xxi p 70–205 and the Origines Guelficæ. Tom i. L ii p 103–388.

2. Illustris Marchio Otbertus[a] cum Apostolicis cucurrerat Nunciis ab Othone . . .[b] consilium auxiliumque expetens. Liutprand. Hist. L vi C 6.

3. Whitehead's works.[22] Vol ii p 263–266. We must forgive the poet some historical and geographical errors. 1 Not a drop of the thousand rills from the Julian Alps can ever fall into the Po. 2. Ateste or Este was never in the possession of Otbert i. 3. His road lay over the Rhœtian not the Julian hills. 4. He never *left* Italy as an attendant on the Emperor Otho.

In the Epistles of Gregory vii the Marquis Azo[1] is recommended **1**[c] as the most faithful and best-beloved of the *Princes* of Italy, as the proper channel through which a King of Hungary might convey his petitions to the Apostolic throne. That prince in the long quarrel of the crown and the mitre was the Champion and counsellor of the Pope, who appeared to vindicate, with[d] the same arms, the liberty of the Catholic Church and the Italian Republic. But the Statesman[e] was not a prophet: nor did he foresee, that, after the fall of the Emperors, their great Vassals would soon be oppressed by the wealth and numbers of the rising Democracy. As the father of the house of Este-Brunswick[f] the importance of Azo[23] is magnified in our eyes; and 1 his Titles. 2 his Riches, 3 His alliances, and 4 His long life may each deserve a separate consideration.

1. In all public and private writings, Azo subscribes his name with the addition of *Marquis*, but without declaring the province or city to which it was applied. By some historians of the times he is loosely denominated, *of Liguria*: in a renewal of the grant to his grandson Obizo[g] i (1184) he is more correctly styled Marquis of

---

[a] *I.* cum Otbertus   [b] *Ellipsis Gibbon's.*   [c] *II. om. Gibbon's page number.*
[d] *I.* by   [e] *I.* P   [f] *I.* B   [g] *I.* of

Milan and Genoa; he exercised in those turbulent cities the last acts (1045, 1048) of an expiring jurisdiction; and a Milanese tradition commemorates the Golden age, in which the Government of his family was sincerely praised by the blessings of the weak and the curses of the wicked. Under the new Republic his office was superseded; the elder branch of his descendants was content with the character of Dukes of Saxony and Bavaria, but those of the younger who adhered to the Lombard law, possessed among themselves an equal right of succession. They preserved and almost appropriated the title of Marquis, and such was their acknowledged rank, that even in the Imperial presence, they expected the first salutations without veiling their bonnets to the proudest Lords.[2] Before the end of the twelfth Century this vague and floating Marquisate had settled on the name of ESTE, which appears to have been the inheritance of Azo's mother Valdrada, the daughter of Peter Candianus Doge of Venice, and the niece of Hugh the great, Marquis of Tuscany.[3] *Ateste*, or *Este*, at the distance of fifteen miles to the south-west of Padua, had formerly been a Roman colony: the estate was ample, the fief noble, the situation commanding, the castle strong. In the Wars of the Guelphs and Ghibelines, Este was besieged by the Tyrant Eccelin (1249): he battered the walls with fourteen military engines, the largest of which threw stones of twelve hundred pounds weight, while a subterraneous passage was opened, by his Carinthian miners, into the heart of the place.[4] With more courage than success the Marquisses defended their local honour against the forces of Verona and Padua: but the town and castle of Este are lost, since the beginning of the fifteenth Century in the Venetian State.

2. From his contemporaries the Marquis Azo deserved and obtained the ambiguous epithet of the *Rich*. A single rent-roll has accidentally preserved the names of eighty three of his manours or estates: the landed property which he possessed by descent or marriage appears to have been diffused from the Venetian to the Tuscan sea, and after it had been repeatedly divided among his children and grandchildren, their separate fortunes were still adequate to the dignity of their birth. But Italy, before the revival of freedom[a] and industry, was overspread with forests and morasses: Agriculture was exercised, without skill or spirit, by the hands of reluctant slaves: the produce was uncertain and insufficient[b], and

[a] *I.* for   [b] *I.* unce

as a market was distant and doubtful, a large proportion was consumed on the spot. In these ages of violence and superstition, his defence in this World, his salvation in the next, his priests and soldiers, his castles and monasteries, reduced the income, and often injured the patrimony, of a feudal Lord. His pride, on some rare festival,[5] might display a vain and tasteless magnificence: but the daily comforts of life, the arts of elegant luxury were unknown in the courts of princes; and they purchased at an exorbitant price the manufactures of Greece and Egypt, and the spices of the East. Under these disadvantages the œconomy of Azo had accumulated respectable treasures; which were exhausted however by a fruitless expedition into France, to vindicate their inheritance of Maine for the sons of his second marriage.

3. His successive alliances in Germany and France[a] establish the political and personal importance of Azo, which was fortified in Italy by a domestic union with the invincible Normans of Apulia; by the marriage of his son Hugh with a daughter of Duke Robert, a sister of the Greek[b] Empress[c]. *The Noble Lombard[d] Marquis*, (says a contemporary writer[6]) was present with many of his nobles at the celebration of the nuptials: the bridal portion was paid, as that of an eldest daughter, by a feudal subsidy; and a fleet was equipped in the Apulians harbour to waft[e] the illustrious pair over the Adriatic sea. Had the Marquis been able to struggle with the levity of the Barons of Maine, the disaffection of an obstinate Bishop, and the arms of William the Conqueror, either Hugh or his brother Fulk might have founded in France a new Dynasty of the house of Este. But Azo enjoyed the satisfaction of beholding his eldest hope, the representative of the ancient Guelphs invested with the Dutchy of Bavaria. The perfect harmony of the *father* and *son* gave strength to each other, and during the matrimonial connection of the *grandson* with the Countess Matilda, their triple alliance supported the Pope and opposed the Emperor, from the Rhine and Danube to the heart of Italy.

4. But the most remarkable circumstance in the life of the Marquis Azo is it's long duration: since at the time of his decease (1097) he was upwards of an hundred years of Age. In the annals of mankind it would not be easy to find a second example of a person illustrious by his merit or fortune who has thus exceeded the term

---

^a *I.* Italy deleted.   ^b *I. om.* Greek   ^c *MS. of followed by* Constantinople; *latter*
^d *I.* M   ^e *I.* convey   ^f *II. om. Gibbon's page number*

of an entire Century: eminence and longevity are the high prizes[a] in the lottery of life, and it is a still more extraordinary[b] chance, that both the lucky tickets should be drawn by the same adventurer. In his last years, Azo appears with dignity as a soldier and a statesman; and if a good[c] constitution be the gift of Nature, the long continuance of health and strength is commonly the reward of moderation and temperance. I remember a Persian tale of three old men,[d] who were successively met and questioned by a traveller. The youngest brother was præmaturely sinking into the grave under the load of a wife and numerous offspring. The second a childless widower, was far less decrepit and infirm. But the last, at an incredible age, still maintained the vivacity and vigour of the autumnal season: he had always persevered in a life of celibacy. Yet this moral cannot be applied to the present case: Azo was thrice married, he left three sons and one daughter; and his peace of mind might be wounded by some domestic anxiety. The reputation of Cunegonde is guarded by her virtue or our ignorance. But the dissolution of a former marriage had sullied the honour[e] of Garsenda: her subsequent behaviour was not exempt from reproach: the absence of her Lord was supplied by a French lover[(7)]; and her son Hugh, whom the Apulian princess had renounced, basely degenerately from the valour of his race. Matilda the third wife of the Marquis was a widow of noble birth: their affinity in the fourth degree awakened the inexorable justice of Gregory vii, a sentence of divorce was fulminated from the Vatican; but, whatsoever idea may be formed of Azo's vigour,, at the age of seventy eight, he might patiently submit to the Canons of the Church[.]

---

1. See the Antichità Estense of Muratori. Tom i C 4-8. 27. 28. and the Origines Guelficæ. Tom i. L ii C 10. p 206-212.

2. Gerardus Maurisius who gives a curious instance of this prerogative (apud Leibnitz. Scriptores Brunswicenses. Tom ii p 30. Muratori.[f] Script. rerum Italicarum Tom viii p 20) is the historian of the Eccelins of Romano, the hereditary foes of the Marquisses. But Muratori slides over another passage which would prove that Azo vi (1209) attempted an assassination, and refused two challenges.

3. Origines Guelficæ Tom i L ii. C 9. S. 6. p 184. 185

4. Rolandin. Hist. Patavin. L vi. C. 6. in Muratori. Script. Tom viii. p 259.

5. Such as the nuptials of Boniface Marquis of Tuscany with Beatrice mother of the Countess Matilda. The horses were shod with silver, wine was drawn from wells, spices were ground in mills &c. (Donizon. Vit. Mathildis. L i. C 9 in Muratori Script. Tom v. p. 353.

---

[a] I. princes   [b] I. luck   [c] I. stron   [d] I. om. of three old men,
[e] I. re   [f] I. L

6. Gulielmus Appulus. L iii. in Muratori. Script. Tom v.[a] p 267 See the History of the decline and fall. Vol. v. p 609.

7. Tutor et quasi maritus. . . .[b]propter illicitam familiaritatem quæ jam inter eos male succreverat. (Ex Gestis Episcoporum Cenomanensium in the Historians of France[24] Tom xii p 540). Such are the fatal words, which the reader would vainly search in the Courtly collections of Muratori, Leibnitz and Eccard. Garsenda is the mother of the Dukes of Modena.[c]

Section iii

The eldest of the three sons of the Marquis Azo, the fortunate Guelph, was transplanted from his native soil to become the root of the German, and in the fullness of time, of the British line of the family of Este. By his two younger brothers Hugo and Fulk, the Italian succession was propagated: but the race of Hugo expired in the second degree; the posterity of Fulk[d] still survives in the twentieth generation. The ancestors of Guelph on the father's and the mother's side, and the series of his descendants in Bavaria and Saxony form the antiquities of the house of Brunswick and the proper subject of this historical discourse: but our curiosity will naturally embrace the collateral branch of the princes of Este, Ferrara and Modena who have not been unworthy of their first progenitors, and more powerful kinsmen. Without confining myself to the rigid servitude of annals, without resting on every step of a long pedigree, I shall concisely display the most interesting scenes of their various fortunes.

As the right of female succession began to prevail in the feudal system of France, Garsenda the second wife of Azo might claim the Dutchy or[e] County of Maine which had been successively possessed by her father, her brother and her nephew. Her pretensions were legitimate; but the heiress of Maine had been married into a distant land: her arms were feeble; her vassals factious, her neighbours unjust. William Duke of Normandy, a famous name, was tempted by the prospect of a fertile and adjacent territory: he muttered some pretence of a gift or alliance: but ambition was his only motive, and his only title was superior strength. Four years the Cenomani, the people of Maine reluctantly bowed under his Iron sceptre; but after the forces of Normandy had been transported beyond the sea, they were encouraged by the absence rather than awed by the

---

[a] *I. vi*   [b] *Gibbon's ellipsis*   [c] *Remainder of 353ᵛ blank*   [d] *I. Hug*
[e] *I. of*

success and glory of the Conqueror of England. They solicited the Marquis of Liguria to assert the rights of his wife and son. Azo listened to their call: after the expulsion or massacre of the Normans, the cities and castles were delivered into his hands, the[a] Bishop escaped to the English court, and his new subjects admired the riches and liberality of their deliverer. But in a short time the reign of a stranger became odious and contemptible to the haughty Franks: they discovered that his treasures were exhausted; he perceived that their faith was wavering, and Azo fondly imagined that all discontents would be appeased, and that all parties would be reconciled by his own departure. In the vain hope that the Cenomani would be attached to the daughter and the heir of their ancient princes he left Garsenda and her infant Hugo under the care of a powerful Baron, the guardian of his son, and the husband, as it were of his wife. But this suspicious or scandalous connection provoked the indignation of the people; the young prince was dismissed to Italy; Garsenda disappears; and the County of Maine was torn by domestic feuds, till the presence of the Conqueror united his rebels in the calm of servitude. Azo still retained a bitter remembrance of his loss and disgrace; and his enemy the Bishop on a pilgrimage to Rome was arrested by the revenge, and released by the piety of the Ligurian Marquis. The death of King William and the discord of his sons revived[b] the spirit of the Cenomani: and their deputies invited the sons of Azo to resume the peaceful possession of their lawful inheritance. Hugo again passed the Alps; but the first acclamations again[c] degenerated into the[d] murmurs of the people and the anathemas of the Clergy. The new Count was destitute of every ressource, that could reward the service, engage the esteem or enforce the obedience of his turbulent Vassals. The honour of his alliance with the daughter of Robert Guiscard had been soon obliterated by the shame and scandal of a divorce; his countrymen exposed him with pleasure to the toils and dangers of a Transalpine reign; and the warlike natives of Gaul despised the effeminate manners of an Italian Lord. His fears were encreased and his flight was hastened by the artful eloquence of a rival, who insinuated that his mild and moderate temper was ill-formed to struggle with the furious passions of the Barbarians. The son of Garsenda trembled at the approach or the sound of an hundred thousand Normans; sold his

[a] I. a [b] I. again revived [c] I. were again [d] I. murmer and dis-content; and the

patrimony for a sum of ten thousand[a] pounds; and escaped to Italy, where he soon lost a battle and an army in the service of the Countess Matilda.[25] A writer of the times who has preserved the memory of this ignominious event, contrasts the treason or cowardice of the man with the nobility of his race. I must retract the assertion that all the princes of Este have[b] been worthy of their name and ancestry: Hugo is an exception; but in the space of seven hundred years, Hugo is a single exception.

After the decease of his father Azo, the star of the house of Este appears "shorne of its beams": their riches and power are visibly diminished; and the *Marquisses* of that name no longer stand foremost in the revolutions of Italy. In the annals of the twelfth Century their actions[c] are seldom recorded: and as this oblivion coincides with the encreasing light of history, we must seek the probable causes in the division of their property, and the ascendant of the municipal Republics. 1. After the acquisition of the Dutchy or rather Kingdom of Bavaria, Guelph the son of Azo might have generously waved the right of primogeniture, and resigned to his younger brothers, the Italian estates of the family as an equivalent for the loss of their Gallic inheritance. But such generosity is seldom found in the selfish conduct of princes or brothers; and instead of offering or accepting an equal and equitable partition, he claimed as his own the entire property of their common parent. If Guelph were an hypocrite, he might colour his avarice by a pious attachment to the relicks of his fathers: and a demand so repugnant to the maxims of natural justice seems however to have been supported by the matrimonial contract of his mother Cunegonda which had left no provision for the children of a second marriage. In that lawless age a civil process was decided by the sword. Hugo and Fulk had the advantage of actual possession and personal influence and the latter of these princes was the heir, the sole heir of the courage of their ancestors: they armed their vassals, occupied the passes of the Alps, and opposed the descent of the Duke of Bavaria, though he was assisted by the allied powers of the Duke of Carinthia and the Patriarch of Aquileia. The sons of Garsenda yielded at length to the weight of numbers, but their resistance procured more[d] favourable conditions. They preserved a rich domain from the banks of the Mincius to the Adriatic sea; they resigned the ample estates of Lombardy and Tuscany to their elder kinsmen, the German

[a] *I.* po   [b] *I.* wer   [c] *I.* names   [d] *I.* a more

Guelphs, and their supreme dominion was acknowledged by the Marquisses of Este, till the yoke was lightened and removed by time, and distance, and the rapid downfall of Henry the Lyon. The law of the Lombards which was still professed in the Italian branch disclaimed all right of primogeniture: and the portion of Hugo and Fulk was again divided in equal lots among their eight sons. In the beginning of the thirteenth century these collateral lines were indeed united in the person of Azo vi the great grandson of Fulk; but he was far from uniting[a] the whole inheritance of his[b] ancestors. Many feudal possessions had devolved on the failure of heirs male to the superior Lord: many allodial estates had been conveyed by marriage into strange families. Much wealth had been consumed, much land had been alienated to supply the expences[c] of luxury and war: and of all that had been consecrated to pious uses, not an atom could revert to the temporal successor. 2. As I am not writing the history of Italy, I shall not here attempt to delineate the rise and progress of the Republics, which revived in that country the spirit of popular freedom, and commercial industry. Their revolt against the Cæsars of Germany was embraced as a national cause: in the successful war again[st][d] Frederic Barbarossa their independence was maintained by the authority of the Church and the arms of the nobles; and among the Nobles the Marquisses of Este were still conspicuous in their decay. Obizo the youngest, but the last survivor of the five[e] sons of Fulk, appeared at the congress of Venice with a retinue of an hundred and eighty followers [AD 1177][f]: he had been engaged in the league of Lombardy; and such was his patriotic guilt, that when the Emperor had yielded every thing in the peace of Constance, the pardon of the Marquis Obizo was one of the last acts of his clemency [AD. 1183]. As we may not suspect these feudal Lords of any tender regard for the liberties of mankind, it may be fairly supposed that they acted from the passion or the interest of the moment, without discerning that they themselves would be trampled under the feet of the plebeian conquerors. Their pride was insulted and their poverty was exposed by the private and public luxury of trade: their subjects of the open country were encouraged to rebell or tempted to desert; and as soon as the prejudice of rank had been dissolved, the scale of power was rudely weighed down by the last and most[g] numerous class of society. Even the inhabitants of Este,

---

[a] *I.* united   [b] *I.* th   [c] *II.* expense   [d] *So in II; MS.* again
[e] *I. om.* five   [f] *Square-bracketed dates in margin of MS.*   [g] *I.* more

his peculiar patrimony, presumed to dispute the jurisdiction of the Marquis: and at the distance of fifteen miles they found an example, and a support in the populous city of Padua, which was able to levy an army and to support a loss of eleven thousand of her sons. The institution of the University must have contributed to the wealth and perhaps the improvement of Padua: from the provinces of Italy, from the Kingdoms of France, Spain, and England many thousand students were annually attracted by the reputation of the various professors; and more than five hundred houses were requisite for the accommodation of the strangers. The lessons of the schools might serve only to perpetuate the reign of prejudice, but the inhabitants were enriched and enlightened by a familiar intercourse with the nations of Europe. In this city the haughty ancestors of Obizo i had erected their tribunal, as the Lieutenants of the Emperor[a]: but Obizo[b] himself was honoured by the choice of a free people, who elected him their *Podesta* or supreme magistrate. In the time of his great-grandson Aldobrandino, a dispute had arisen between the City of Padua and the Marquis of Este. The Paduans raised an[c] army, summoned their allies of Vicenza, invaded his territory, besieged[d] the Castle of Este, battered the walls and even the palace with their military engines; and imposed the terms of a hard and humiliating capitulation. The Marquis was reduced to adopt the name and obligations of a simple burgher, to swear that he would faithfully obey, the laws and ordinances of the commons, and to reside some[e] months or weeks of every year within the walls of a democracy in which the lowest magistrate was his superior, and the poorest fellow-citizen his equal. The shame of this temporary submission could only be alleviated by the example of his equals: the Patriarch of Aquileia with two suffragan Bishops had solicited the honour of being admitted among the citizens of Padua: and the Count of the sacred palace, the immediate representative of Imperial Majesty was detained as a captive and a subject within the walls of Pavia. The popular states of Lombardy triumphed in the fall of the Aristocracy: and the Marquis of Montferrat was the only Noble who had strength and courage to maintain his hereditary independence.

Liberty had raised the minds of the Italians; but faction, her ugly and inseperable sister corrupted the peace and prosperity of the growing Republics. They fought against the Emperor against

---

[a] *I.* Emperors   [b] *I.* the Marquis him   [c] *I.* and   [d] *I.* batter
[e] *I.* a stated time in every year

their neighbours, against themselves: the necessity of order and discipline compelled them to name a foreign Dictator; and the nobles, most eminent in arms, in policy, in power often became the Captains and sometimes the tyrants of the independent cities. The Marquisses of Este, and the Eccelins of Romano were the two leading families of the Trevisane or Veronese March: the memory of their ancestors and the habits of command inspired that lofty and martial[a] demeanour which struck the plebeian with involuntary awe; and they were sure to gain the hearts of the multitude when they softened their pride into artful and popular condescension. The first Eccelin[b] was a gallant Knight and a dextrous politician: in Palestine and Lombardy he was elected Standard-bearer or General of the confederate armies, and in the great rebellion against Frederic i, he deserved the confidence of the Cities without forfeiting the esteem of the Emperor.[26] The civil and military virtues of his son Eccelin the second were adorned with the gifts of eloquence: he was the public and private adversary of the house of Este, and as soon as the Marquis Azo vi had declared himself Chief of the Guelphs, the Ghibelline faction acknowledged the Count of Romano for their Leader. When the Emperor Otho iv descended into Italy, his Court was attended by the rival chiefs; and their interview describes the manners of the time. Eccelin complained that in a neutral city, in a moment of truce or friendship his life had been treacherously attacked. "I was walking said he, with the "Marquis of Este on the place of St Mark at[c] Venice. On a sudden "I was assaulted by the swords and daggers of his followers: my "friends were slain or made prisoners in my sight; and it was with "extreme difficulty that I could disengage my right arm from the "strong grasp of my perfidious companion" The Marquis explained or denied the fact: but in these hostile altercations, Azo twice declined a challenge of single combat. He could not draw his sword again[st][d] Eccelin without violating the majesty of the Imperial presence, and among his Vassals he had many more noble than Salinguerra. His reasons might be good, his courage was unquestionable, but—Azo twice declined a challenge of single combat. The next day as the two leaders were riding on either side of the Emperor, he commanded them to salute each other "Sir Eccelin salute the "Marquis; Sir[e] Marquis salute Eccelin" and the command was given in the French tongue, which even in that age, appears to have

[a] I. warlike   [b] I. Ezzelin   [c] II. in   [d] So II. MS. again   [e] I. sa

been the fashionable dialect. They obeyed: but the superior dignity of the Marquis was maintained by his receiving and returning the compliment without vailing his bonnet to the humble salute of Eccelin. They soon joyned in familiar converse, and before they had rode two miles, the suspicious Emperor, who had been alarmed by their discord began to be apprehensive of their union. His apprehensions were groundless; and their deadly feuds, in council, in the field, in the cities, continued to rage with alternate success, till they both slept in the tranquillity of the grave. Their possessions and their quarrels were inherited by their sons Azo vii and Eccelin the third, but in a contest of forty years, the Marquis of Este was long oppressed by the genius and fortune of his rival. The excommunication of Frederic ii[27] exasperated[a] and justified the hostilities of the two factions. From a sermon, a bull or a crusade, the Chief of the Guelphs, the[b] friend of the Pope might derive some occasional aid: but the leader of the Ghibellines was more strongly supported by the power and often by the presence of a warlike prince who filled the Trevisane March with his armies of Germans and Saracens. By the authority of the Emperor, his own arts, and the assistance of foreign troops, Eccelin became the Captain, and Tyrant of the cities of Verona, Vicenza, Padua, Trevigi, Feltri, Belluno, Trent, and Brescia: after the loss of his patron, he maintained ten years his independent reign; and proudly boasted that since Charlemagne,[c] no prince had possessed such absolute sway over the Lombard states. The utmost efforts of his malice and revenge were directed against the Marquis of Este "Strike the head of the serpent and you are master of the body" was his frequent exhortation. From an hill near Padua, he pointed to the towers of Este, and shewed the Emperor the hostile territories[d] which were spread over the plain. Destitute of strength and succour Azo was compelled to solicit pardon, to swear fidelity and to purchase a precarious respite by the captivity and[e] perhaps the death of Rinaldo his only son,[f] who was delivered as an hostage into the hands of Frederic the second. The town and castle of Este were at length besieged by the forces of Eccelin: his artillery consisted of fourteen great battering engines; which cast stones of twelve hundred pounds weight; and his pioneers, who were drawn from the silver mines of Carinthia opened a subterraneous passage for the entrance of five hundred soldiers.

[a] I. embittered and   [b] I. mi   [c] I. the e   [d] I. which w   [e] II. om.

[f] I. who

The garrison capitulated, and instead of a total ruin, the fortifications were repaired by Eccelin who affected to reverence the dignity of the place. He had been praised as an heroe, he was gradually and at length generally abhorred as a tyrant. The seeming virtues of his youth were stained by the jealous and unrelenting cruelty of his old age: and whatsoever deductions may be allowed on a list of fifty thousand victims, his name will be for ever recorded with the savage monsters of Sicily and Rome. The hatred of mankind began to prevail over their fears, and after a long persecution, and a firm resistance, Azo found the moment of victory and revenge. His odious rival had been invited by one of the factions of Milan: the conspiracy was discovered, the enterprize failed: but, on his return to Brescia, in the passage of the Adda, at the well-known bridge of Cassano, he was intercepted by the troops of Mantua Cremona, and Ferrara under the banner of the Marquis of Este. After a short combat, the valiant Eccelin, (he deserves that praise was wounded in the foot, and taken prisoner: the[a] few remaining days of his life were embittered by the insults of the multitude, and the more insulting pity of the Conqueror. Azo vii was hailed as the saviour of Lombardy: but he derived more glory than advantage from the Tyrant's fall. The cause of the Ghibellines revived under new Leaders: the cities of the Trevisane march were[b] usurped by by the new families of Scala, and Carrara, and instead of asserting their ancient right to the government of Milan, the rising ambition of the Visconti was promoted by the arms and alliance of the Marquisses of Este.

It was in the state of Ferrara, that they first established a princely dominion on the basis and finally on the ruins of a popular government. The flat country which is intersected by the branches of the Po had formerly been a wild[c] morass impervious to the Roman highways. About the middle of the seventh Century, twelve solitary villages coalesced into a fortified town on the banks of the river: the safe and convenient situation attracted a crowd of settlers; their[d] labours were rewarded by the conversion of the fens into rich and productive land; and the rising colony was distinguished by the seat of a Bishop and the privileges of a city. After the death of the Countess Matilda, Ferrara tasted the blessings and the mischiefs of liberty: the Patricians and plebeians,[e] the Guelphs and Ghibellines[f]

---

[a] *I.* and the   [b] *I.* r   [c] *I.* desolate   [d] *I.* the l   [e] *II.* the plebeians
[f] *II.* the Ghibellines

disputed in arms the command of the Republic: thirty two towers of defence were erected within the walls, and in forty years, the factions were ten times alternately expelled. Among the thirty four noble families of Ferrara, the pre-eminence of wealth and power was claimed by the rival houses of the Adelardi and Taurelli. About the year one thousand one hundred and eighty, the former were reduced to an infant daughter: the proposal of a conciliatory marriage was rejected to[a] their adherents: the heiress was delivered into the hands of Obizo[b] the first[c]: and his grandson Azo vi was elected as the future husband of the maid, and the future chief of the name and party of the Adelardi. Marchesella died at the age of eight years, before nature would allow her to produce a child, or the law would permit her to subscribe a will: but the whole inheritance of her fathers was yielded to the Marquis of Este, and his gratitude[d] or ambition distributed the fiefs among his friends and followers. By this step he acquired a commanding influence at Ferrara: Azo vi was declared perpetual Lord and Governor of the Republic [AD 1208] and the act which is still extant betrays the madness of party by the grant of absolute and unconditional power. From this power his son was degraded to the humiliating permission of an annual visit; a popular and prosperous state was again established by the Ghibellines, and it was not till after thirty two years of revolutions, that the sovereignty of the house of Este was fixed by the valour and conduct of the seventh Azo. At the head of the confederate[e] forces of the Pope, of Venice and of Bologna he marched against Ferrara[f] [AD 1240]: but a humane conqueror might lament that the[g] revolution was effected by the calamities of a siege, and condemned by the retreat of fifteen hundred citizens. These evils were indeed compensated by the wisdom and justice of twenty four years: his funeral [AD 1264] was honoured by the tears of the opposite faction; and at the age of seventeen, his grandson Obizo ii succeeded to the office or rather the inheritance of his father. The reputation of Obizo ii engaged the turbulent republics of Modena and Reggio to accept him for their prince; and at the time of his decease three populous cities with their ample territories were subject to the sway of the Marquisses of Este. Modena and Reggio were indeed lost by the imprudence of his son the levity of the people and the arts of the Ghibellines, and the separation lasted

[a] *II.* by   [b] *I.* Azo   [c] *II.* I.   [d] *I.* prud   [e] *II.* confederated
[f] *I.* V   [g] *I.* his victory was atchieved by

thirty years, in the one, and an hundred in the other, before the rebellious children were reconciled to their parent. But the submission of Ferrara was pure and permanent; and the lapse of time insensibly erazed the forms and maxims of the old Republic. After the death of Azo viii [AD 1308], whose last will preferred a bastard to a brother, Ferrara was oppressed by the avarice of the Venetians, the ambition of the Pope, and the Catalan mercenaries of the King of Naples: but the spirit of patriotism and loyalty still lived in the hearts of the Citizens, and they soon rose to the delivrance and defence of their country under the banner of the *White Eagle*. This constant affection is at once the praise of the subject and sovereign. This[a] praise is the more precious, as it must, almost, be confined to the subjects of the marquisses of Este. They were ranked among the princes of Italy at a time when the families which afterwards emerged to greatness were confounded with the meanest of the people. They were the first who, after the twelfth Century, acquired by popular election, the dominion[b] of a free City. And they still subsist with splendour and dignity, while the tyrants, more conspicuous in their day have left only a name, and for the most part an odious name in[c] the annals of their country.

The states of Ferrara, Modena and Reggion were fairly won and recovered by the labour and fortune of the Marquisses of Este. But the liberality of the Popes and Emperors was an easy and profitable virtue: they granted the right to those who had the actual possession; bestowed the title, where the substance was lost, and confirmed their pretensions by resigning to others what they were unable to obtain or to hold for their own use. The court of Rome was informed of the merit and reputation of Azo vi; and he accepted from the two Sovereigns of Christendom, from Pope Innocent iii, and the Emperor Otho iv a double investiture of the Marquisate of Ancona, which extended over twelve Dioceses and Counties between the Adriatic and the Apennine. But this splendid gift was no more than the right, without the power of subduing a warlike people

---

[a] *For next 4 sentences, I. had*: The dignity and virtues of the Marquisses of Este was [deleted] were compared with the vices and crimes of the low born tyrants of Lombardy: the princes of Ferrara were seldom rapacious or cruel; and in an age of assassination and poison, theirs was perhaps the only family, in which a brother, without danger or suspicion, might seat himself at his brother's table. I will not dissemble that in the *Hell* of Dante, the Marquis Obizo ii is himself chained among the tyrants, by the side of Alexander and Dionysius: but it may surely be questioned whether the justice of the poet, or the malevolence of the Ghibelline pronounced the sentence of eternal damnation   [b] *I.* government of   [c] *II.* to

in strong opposition to the Church and the Empire. This enterprize, which might seem above the strength of Azo, was vigourously prosecuted by his eldest son the Marquis Aldobrandino, who raised the supplies of the war, by pawning his younger brother to the usurers of Florence. The war was suspended by his untimely death, the conquest was never atchieved; the pledge[a] was never redeemed; and in[b] the third generation[c] the vain title of Marquis of Ancona was silently dismissed. The fens of Ferrara might have been included within the limits of the Exarchate, the successors of S[t] Peter might alledge the donations of Constantine, of Pepin, of Charlemagne and of the Countess Matilda: but in the first Century after their election, the Marquisses of Este acknowledged no superior, save[d] God and the people. It was in a moment of distress and exile, that they accepted from Clement v the title of Vicars of the Church: that they submitted to hold the feudatory possession of Ferrara by an annual payment of ten thousand gold Florins. They regained their Sovereignty without the aid, and against the efforts of the Court of Rome: the treaty was however ratified, and if the tribute suffered some occasional abatement, they could never break the chain of feudal dependence which was at length fatal to the house of Este. After the recovery of Modena and Reggio they obtained on more easy terms, the title[e] of Vicars of the Empire: and the natives of Italy[f] like those of India continued to reverence the seal and subscription of their impotent King. Before the end of the fourteenth Century, the German Emperors who had been accustomed to the traffic of avarice and vanity were tempted to revive in Italy the long forgotten title of Duke [AD 1395]: and at the price of an hundred thousand gold florins the Visconti of Milan were exalted above the heads of their equals. Twenty two years afterwards, the exclusive dignity of the Dukes of Milan was somewhat impaired by the similar honours of the Dukes of Savoy [AD 1417] The third candidate was Borso Marquis of Este, the twelfth in lineal descent from the old Marquis Albert Azo the second: his reign was wise and fortunate, and the proverb[g] which he left behind him "This is "not the time of Duke Borso" is far more glorious than all the trappings of mortal[h] pride. In the year one thousand four hundred and fifty two, by the Emperor Frederic the third, he was created Duke of Modena and Reggio [AD 1452[i]]: eighteen years afterwards, the

---

[a] I. pledged   [b] I. at the en   [c] I. generations   [d] I. but excep

[e] I. titles   [f] I. Indi   [g] I. praise w   [h] I. hum   [i] II. om. this date

ambitious imitation of Pope Paul the second conferred on Borso the superior title of Duke of Ferrara [AD 1470[a]]: and the crowns, the mantles, and the sceptres used in these pompous investitures, were second only to the majesty of Kings. In the sixteenth Century, a Duke was imposed on the Republic of Florence by the arms and authority of Charles v: and the Genius of the great Cosmo soon gave him a rank in the political system of Europe. A dispute for precedency arose between the Dukes of Ferrara and Florence: and if the Este[b] could boast the nobility of their race and the priority of their creation, the Medici might plead the wealth, the extent, and perhaps the independence of the state over which they reigned. The courts of Rome and Vienna long balanced their respective claims without risquing a final sentence: and the dispute could only be appeased[c] by the invention of the new title and prerogatives of Grand Duke of Tuscany [AD 1569]. In this frivolous contest the powers of France and Spain were interested; and, had it been decided by arms, such a war would have added[d] a chapter to the annals of human vanity.

While the honours of the Este[e] were multiplied by Popes and Emperors, a Republic insulted and almost oppressed the Dukes of Ferrara. Had Venice been prudent, Venice would have been content with the riches of commerce and the command of the sea. But this maritime Empire served only to stimulate the ambition of Italian[f] conquest: discipline and wealth obtained an easy victory over weakness and discord; and in the fifteenth Century, the provinces of *Terra firma* were added to the dominions of St Mark. Nicholas the third Marquis of Este, and Lord of Ferrara made a feeble effort to assist the Carrara princes, and[g] to save the important barrier of Padua [AD 1405]. The Venetians instantly filled the Po with armed vessels; his territories were ravaged; his capital was starved, till he left his allies to their fate; implored the mercy of the Senate; and resigned himself to such conditions as resentment[h] and avarice could impose. After a servitude of fourscore years, his son Hercules i was accused of a generous or criminal revolt: the superior forces of Venice encompassed Ferrara[i] by sea and land, and if a league of the Italian powers protected him from total ruin, the Duke was bound, by the[j] new treaty in a closer and more weighty chain [AD

[a] *II. om. this date*   [b] *I.* form   [c] *II.* could be appeased only   [d] *I.* been the last triumph of human vanity   [e] *II.* House of Este   [f] *I.* i; *II.* an Italian   [g] *I.* princes his allies,   [h] *I.* pride   [i] *I.* him   [j] *I.* a n

1482-1484.]. 1. A superior title, and more ample sway might compensate for the loss of property and command in the neighbourhood of Padua. But ESTE was still dear and sacred to the princes of that name: the transient recovery of the castle, the town, and the fief [AD 1389] had delighted their hereditary pride, and it was not without regret that they beheld that ancient possession, the source of their title, for ever melted into the Venetian state. The *Polesine* or island of Rovigo, which had once been mortgaged for sixty thousand Ducats to the Venetians, was irrecoverably ceded by Hercules I: and not a vestige remained of the patrimonial estates to the north of the Po, which had been[a] acquired five hundred years before by the marriage of Albert Azo i. 2. The goods and persons of the Venetians who descended the Po were exempt from all tolls and duties whatsoever: every stranger was shielded under that respectable name; and even the peasants of[b] the borders began to claim the immunities of S[t] Mark. The same grievance which impaired the revenue, attacked the sovereignty of the Duke of Ferrara, since he was forbidden to raise any forts or barriers which might [obstruct][c] a free passage through his territories by[d] land or water. 3. With the avarice of a trading power Venice aspired to a monopoly of salt in the Adriatic gulph. The Duke was rigorously deprived of the use and profit of his salt-works of Commachio; and his subjects were compelled to purchase in a foreign market one of the necessaries of life, which Nature had so profusely scattered on their own shores. 4. A citizen of Venice resided at Ferrara with the title of *Vicedominus*; he was the proper Judge of his countrymen: but the arrogance[e] of his behaviour insulted the Prince,[f] his[g] daily usurpations interrupted the course of justice: and his last act was the imprisonment of a native and a priest. Peace was oppressive; but War might have been fatal to the house of Este. The three last sovereigns of Padua, a father and his two sons, had been strangled in the prisons of Venice, the remains of the Carrara and[h] Scala families were proscribed: and the deliberate cruelty of the Senate was justified by the examples of ancient Rome.

Twenty five years after the last treaty of Hercules i, his son and successor Alphonso i embraced the fairest hope of liberty and revenge. In the league of Cambray [AD 1509], the four great poten-

[a] *I.* contin been inherited   [b] *I.* be   [c] *So II. Nothing in MS.*
[d] *II.* either by   [e] *I.* insolence   [f] *I.* sovereign   [g] *I.* and his
[h] *I.* family

tates of Europe united their arms, against a single Republic; the Pope, Julius ii; the Emperor, Maximilian of Austria; Lewis xii, King of France and Duke of Milan; and Ferdinand King of Arragon and Naples. Each of the allies had suffered some injuries, had lost some territories, and they all considered the prosperity of Venice, with the same sentiments of indignation and envy which are excited in the breast of a noble by the luxury and insolence of a wealthy merchant. While Maximilian delayed, while Ferdinand dissembled, while the Pope pronounced his excommunications, the King of France, at the head of his invincible cavalry had passed the Alps, and, on the banks of the Adda, the mercenary bands of Sta Mark were trampled under their horses feet.[b] The firmness of Rome, after a great defeat, was not imitated by the Senators of Venice: they despaired of the Republic, evacuated in a day the conquests of an age, and abandoned to the confederates the division of the spoil. Under the wing of these confederates, Alphonso Duke of Ferrara had acceded to the league of Cambray, and accepted the office or[c] rather the title of Standard-bearer or General of the Church. The first act of hostility was to vindicate his independence: the County of Rovigo yielded to his attack; and he received from the Emperor the investiture of Este. In this public shipwreck, Venice was saved by the zeal of her Nobles, and the fidelity of her subjects: the nobles sacrificed their lives or at least their fortunes in their own cause; the subjects without speculating on the theory of government had long enjoyed, and now regretted the wisdom and justice of a parental Aristocracy. The Metropolis was impregnable and rich, the transmarine provinces were untouched; the navy was entire, new armies were purchased; the allies began to feel suspicion and to affect pity; and the delivrance of Padua announced the rising fortunes of the Republic. While the Venetians strove to resist or disarm their more formidable enemies, the rebel Alphonso (such was the style of the Senate) was marked as the object of vengeance to which his situation exposed him on every side. Against the advice of the wisest counsellors, their Admiral Angelo Trevisano with eighteen Gallies and a train of brigantines and privateers,[d] entered the mouth of the Po, spread desolation on either bank, and prepared with forts and bridges the passage of the army and the siege of Ferrara. But the army was called away by a seasonable diversion; and the fleet was destroyed by the valour and conduct of the Duke

---

[a] I. the Republic   [b] I. h   [c] I. of   [d] II. *om.* and privateers

himself and his brother the Cardinal Hippolito. Under the shelter of the dykes they had planted their long batteries which supported an incessant fire: and the affrighted Venetians were suddenly oppressed by the armed vessels which issued from the City. The Admiral ignominiously fled with the great standard of St Mark, two gallies escaped, three were burnt or sunk and the remaining thirteen followed the triumph of the Conqueror who immediately assaulted[a] and demolished all the works of the siege. His victory might be ascribed to his superior artillery, and that superiority was the effect of his own skill and industry. Three hundred Canons were cast in his foundery and deposited in his arsenal: he liberally entertained the best engineers; and the well-adapted fortifications of stone, of earth and of water had rendered Ferrara one of the strongest places in Italy. The French who served with their ally, celebrate the politeness the knowledge, the magnificence of the Duke: and Alphonso expended above three hundred thousand Ducats to reward the service, and secure the friendship of the Gallic chiefs.

But their friendship soon became dangerous to the house of Este: when the same confederates who had joyned with France for the destruction of Venice, conspired with Venice for the expulsion of the French [AD 1510]. The new league was formed and sanctified by Julius ii who secretly aspired to deliver Italy from the Barbarians: and the fidelity of the Duke of Ferrara to his first engagements exasperated the fiercest and most ambitious of the[b] successors of St Peter. Alphonso was degraded from the rank of a vassal and a Christian: his rich forfeiture was devoured by the avarice, perhaps, of a papal nephew, and his sentence of condemnation was extended to both worlds. Against [him][c] the temporal and spiritual arms of Rome were equally directed: his city of Modena was occupied [AD 1511]: in the depth of a severe winter the presence of Julius animated the troops, and the aged father of the Christians pressed the siege of Mirandola with the vigour of a youthful soldier. Ferrara however was saved by it's own strength and the Gallic succours: the army of Lewis xii invaded the Ecclesiastical state under the command of his nephew the valiant[d] Gaston of Foix: in the battle of Ravenna [AD 1512] the fury of the French cavalry was encountered by the firmness of the Spanish infantry, and the success of the day might be attributed in some degree to the Duke of Ferrara who led

---

[a] *I.* att   [b] *I.* Popes   [c] *So II; not in MS.*   [d] *I.* valour

the vanguard and directed the infantry. But after the loss of Gaston, the strange retreat of the victorious army, and the rapid evacuation of Italy, the solitary and humble client of France remained without defence under the hand of a mercyless oppressor. While he waited as a suppliant in the Vatican his city of Reggio[a] was surprized and stolen: he was insulted by the proposal of yielding Ferrara for a poor and precarious exchange, and even the validity of his safe conduct was questioned by a perfidious court. The liberty and perhaps the life of Alphonso were rescued by the grateful friendship of the Colonna: they forced the Lateran gate, lodged him in their[b] castle of Marino, and watched over his escape in the various disguises of an[c] huntsman, a servant, and a fryar. A single event could suspend his ruin; and by that event was his ruin suspended. Julius ii expired [AD 1513]: his passions were buried[d] in his tomb: but his policy with a milder aspect still reigned in the councils of his successors[.] Leo x was too generous to be just; and the ambition of his family was concealed by the sacred veil of the honour and interest of the Church. After the victory[e] of Marignan [AD 1515], Francis i might have discharged his obligations by an act of equity and power: but instead of commanding he negociated with the Court of Rome. The restitution of Modena and Reggio to his long-suffering ally was often promised and as often eluded: the failure of a secret conspiracy provoked the Roman Pontiff to thunder a new sentence of excommunication and forfeiture, and one of the medals of Alphonso attests his miraculous delivrance from the *Lyon's* paw. Adrian vi had a conscience, a faculty long dormant in the Vicars of Christ: but his scruples were removed by the Italian casuists; and he found it more easy to absolve the sins than to restore the states of the house of Este. Clement vii, an illegitimate son, adopted the politics of the[f] Medici; and had his arts been successful, Machiavel who was still alive, might have been proud of his disciple. After a tedious and treacherous delay the sword of Alphonso vindicated his own rights; and his prudence seized the fortunate moments of the conclave and the captivity of Clement vii. The gates of Modena and Reggio were joyfully opened to their native prince: and on a payment to the Pope of an hundred thousand Ducats, his succession was confirmed by the sentence of the Emperor Charles v, whose interest prompted him to establish the

---

[a] *I.* Modena was   [b] *II.* the   [c] *II.* a   [d] *I.* si   [e] *I.* battle
[f] *I.* his

peace of Italy. During these revolutions, the Duke of Ferrara concluded a truce, and finally a treaty with the Venetians: his patrimonial estates of Este and Rovigo were for ever lost: but he no
longer felt or feared the tyranny of a Republic, which had been
trained to moderation in the school of adversity.

Among the noble marriages of the Este, two princes, Azo viii
and Hercules i had been allied to the crown of Naples in[a] the rival
houses of Anjou and Arragon. But these lofty[b] connections had not
been productive of any solid benefit, and the Venetians signified
their displeasure, that the Duke of Ferrara had preferred the daughter
of a King instead of chusing a Senator for his father[c] and patron.
In[d] the next generation the house of Este[e] was sullied by a sanguinary and incestuous race; by the nuptials of Alphonso i with
Lucretia, a bastard of Alexander vi, the Tiberius of Christian Rome.
This modern Lucretia might have assumed with more propriety the
name of Messalina; since the woman who can be guilty, who can
even be accused, of a[f] criminal commerce with a father and two
brothers, must be abandoned to all the licentiousness of venial[g]
love. Her vices were highly coloured by a contempt for decency: at
a banquet in the Apostolical palace, by the side of the Pope, she
beheld without a blush the naked dances and lascivious postures of
fifty prostitutes: she distributed the prizes to the champions of
Venus, according to the number of victories which they atchieved
in her presence. Hercules i was unwilling to accept such a consort
for his eldest son: but he was apprehensive of the bulls and daggers[h]
of the Borgia[i] family: he was tempted by the sum of one hundred
and twenty thousand Ducats, the city and district of Cento, and
the reduction of his annual tribute to a slight[j] quit-rent of an hundred
florins: the marriage-articles were signed; and as the bed of Lucretia
was not then vacant, her third husband, a royal bastard of Naples,
was first stabbed and afterwards strangled in the Vatican. Perhaps
the youth of Lucretia had been seduced by example; perhaps she
had been satiated with pleasure; perhaps she was awed by the
authority[k] of her new parent and husband: but the Dutchess of
Ferrara lived seventeen years without reproach, and Alphonso i

---

[a] *I.* b in the su   [b] *I.* splendid   [c] *I.* pa   [d] *Next 6½ sentences, through
his fidelity was rewarded, added by Gibbon on separate sheet. I.* The nuptials of the son
of Alphonso the first were still more illustrious;   [e] *I.* eldest   [f] *I.* th
[g] *II.* venal [*Sheffield marked this passage "better omitted" (f. 317ʳ) from "since the
woman who can" through "atchieved in her presence" but it is printed in II.*]   [h] *I.* the
daggers   [i] *I.* Borgias: he   [j] *I.* tr   [k] *I.* dignity of her new father

believed himself to be the father of three sons. The eldest, his successor Hercules ii, expiated this maternal stain by a nobler choice; and his fidelity was rewarded by mingling the blood of Este with that of France. By his second marriage with Anne Dutchess of Brittany, Lewis xii left[a] only two daughters: Claude the eldest became the wife of his successor Francis i, and Renée her younger sister, who had once been promised to Charles v, was betowed on Hercules ii, hereditary prince, and after his father's decease, Duke of Ferrara. Her portion of two hundred and fifty thousand crowns[b] was paid in a territorial equivalent the Dukedoms of Chartres and Montargis: but Renée was perhaps the true heiress of Brittany, since the agreement which secured the perpetual independence of the Dutchy might be applied with as much reason to a second daughter as to a second son. The French princess, whose mind was more beautiful than her person continued above thirty years to adorn the Court of Ferrara: her liberal understanding was improved by the learning of the age; nor was it *her* fault, if, in the learning of the age, she discovered and studied the vain science of Astrology. During a long exile she cherished a tender remembrance of her native country: every Frenchman, according to his degree, who visited Ferrara either praised her magnificence[c] or blessed her charity: and the relicks of a Neapolitan expedition, ten thousand naked and hungry fugitive[d] were relieved by the profuse alms of the Dutchess. When her treasurer represented the enormous expence "They are my countrymen, Renée generously replied, and had God "given me a beard, they would be now my subjects." But these virtues were the splendid sins of an[e] heretic. From her cradle, and in her marriage the daughter of Lewis xii, the daughter-in law of Alphonso i had learned to hate the tyranny of the Pope: her firm and curious understanding was not afraid of Religious enquiries; and she listened to the new teachers who professed to revive the old truths of the Gospel. Clement Marot, and John Calvin were hospitably entertained at Ferrara [AD 1535]; in the conversion of the Dutchess the eloquence of the preacher was seconded by the wit of the poet; and the Apostle of Geneva was proud to spread his conquests on the verge of the realm of Antechrist. But this spark which might have kindled a flame in Italy was quickly extinguished by the diligence of the Inquisitors, and Hercules ii was apprehensive of the temporal, as well as the spiritual, punishment of the guilt of

---

[a] *I.* ha   [b] *I.* p   [c] *II.* munificence   [d] *II.* fugitives   [e] *II.* a

heresy. Calvin and Marot fled beyond the mountains: Renée heard with sullen constancy the sermons of the Popish doctors; but, after suffering the dismission of her French servants, and the hardships of a prison, she submitted with a sigh to wear the mask of dissimulation. A more open profession of Calvinism after her husband's death determined and hastened her departure from Ferrara; and the last fifteen years of Renée of France were spent in her native country. In the bloody scenes of persecution and war the Dutchess maintained her dignity and protected her brethren. Her castle of Montargis near Paris was a sure azylum for the Huguenots; and when it was threatened with a siege, she boldly replied "The Catholics "may assault my residence: they will find me standing in the breach, "and prepared to try whether they will fire on the daughter of a "King of France." She was the daughter of a King: but the wife of her son, Alphonso ii, was the daughter and sister of two Emperors, of Ferdinand i and Maximilian ii of the house of Austria.

The five Dukes of Ferrara, Borso, Hercules i, Alphonso i, Hercules ii, and Alphonso ii, seem to have been magnified in the eyes of Europe, far beyond the measure of their wealth and power. Their merit was superior to their fortune; they supported with firmness the calamities of War; they improved and enjoyed the prosperity of peace. Near a century before the end of their reign, Alexander vi in his bull of investiture applauds the useful labours of Hercules i; which had encreased the numbers and happiness of his people, which had adorned the city of Ferrara with strong fortifications and stately edifices, and which had reclaimed a large extent of unprofitable waste. The vague and spreading branches of the Po were confined in their proper channels by moles and dykes; the intermediate lands were converted to pasture and tillage; the fertile district became the granary of Venice; and the corn exports of a single years[a] were enchanged[b] for the value of two hundred thousand Ducats. The triangular island or *Delta* of Mesola at the mouth of the Po had been recovered from the waters by Alphonso ii, who surrounded it with a wall nine miles in circumference: a palace with its dependencies of stables and gardens arose in this new creation, and it was reserved by the founder for his[c] favourite amusements of hunting and fishing. Ferrara became one of the most flourishing of the Italian cities: the walls and buildings have survived the loss of the inhabitants which are now reduced from

[a] *II*. year   [b] *II*. exchanged   [c] *I*. th

fourscore thousand to a tenth part: the works of superstition were enriched by each generation: the Arsenal, in a long peace was succeeded by theatres and palaces; and if the hand of the princely architect be most conspicuous, many[a] vacant houses are the monuments of private opulence and taste. Modena and Reggio more favourably treated by Nature were not abandoned by the house of Este: the course of the Po opened much inland and some foreign trade,[b] and a colony of Flemish exiles attempted to revive the declining arts of the loom. I am not instructed to define the revenue of the Dukes of Ferrara: but it is the praise of Alphonso i that he left a treasure without encreasing his taxes; it is the reproach of Alphonso ii, that with an encrease of taxes he left behind him a considerable debt. The court of these princes was at all times polite and splendid: on extraordinary occasions a birth, a marriage, a journey, a festival, the passage of an illustrious stranger, the strove to surpass their equals and to equal their superiors; and the vanity of the poeple was gratified at their own expence. Seven hundred horses were ranged in Borso's stables: and in the sport of hawking, the Duke was attended to the field by an[c] hundred falconers. In[d] his Roman expedition to receive the Ducal investiture, his train of five hundred Gentlemen, his Chamberlains and pages, one hundred menial servants, and one hundred and fifty mules were cloathed according to their degree in brocade[e] velvet or fine[f] cloth: the bells of the mules were of silver, and the dresses, liveries and trappings were covered with gold and silver embroidery. The martial train of Alphonso ii in his campaign in Hungary consisted of three hundred Gentlemen, each of whom was followed by an Esquire, and two *Arquebusiers* on horseback; and the arms and apparel of this gallant troop were such as might provoke the envy of the Germans and the avarice of the Turks. Did[g] I possess a book printed under the title of the *Chivalries of Ferrara*, I should not pretend to describe the nuptials of the same Duke with the Emperor's sister: the balls the feasts, and turnaments of many busy days; and the final representation of the Temple of Love which was erected in the palace-garden with a stupendous scenery of porticos and palaces of woods and mountains. That the last shew should continue six hours without appearing tedious to the spectators is perhaps the most incredible circumstance In each

---

[a] *I.* th [b] *I.* na [c] *II.* a [d] *I.* When [e] *I.* brocades [f] *I.* the
[g] *I.* W

generation of the house of Este, a younger brother with the rank of Cardinal held some of the richest*a* Bishopricks, and Abbies in Italy and France. These noble and wealthy Ecclesiastics were the patrons of every art: the *Villa Estense* at Tivoli near Rome is the work of Cardinal Hippolitus brother to Hercules*b* ii: the palace gardens and water-works exhibit in their present decay the spirit of a prince and the taste of the age.

A philosopher, according to his temper may laugh or weep at this ostentatious and oppressive splendour; nor will he be disarmed by the patronage and perfection of the finer arts which flourished in Italy in the sixteenth century. But he will approve the modest encouragement of learning and Genius an expence which can never drain the treasures of a prince. An university had been founded at Padua by the house of Este, and the scholastic rust was polished away by the revival of the litterature of Greece and Rome. The studies of Ferrara were directed by skillful and eloquent professors, either natives or foreigners: the Ducal library was filled with a valuable collection of manuscript and printed books, and as soon*c* as twelve new comedies of Plautus had been found in Germany the Marquis Lionel of Este was impatient to obtain a fair and faithful copy of that ancient Poet. Nor were these elegant pleasures confined to the learned world. Under*d* the reign of Hercules i, a wooden theatre, at the moderate cost of a thousand crowns, was constructed in the largest court of the palace; the scenery represented some houses, a sea-port and a ship; and the Menechmi of Plautus which had been translated into Italian by the Duke himself was acted before a numerous and polite audience. In the same language and with the same success, the Amphitryon of Plautus, and the Eunuch of Terence was*e* successively exhibited, and these classic*f* models which formed the taste of the spectators, excited the emulation of the poets of the Age. For the use of the court and theatre of Ferrara, Ariosto composed his Comedies[28] which were often played with applause, which are*g* still read with pleasure: and such was the enthusiasm of the new art,*h* that one of the sons of Alphonso i did not disdain to speak a prologue on the stage. In the legitimate forms of dramatic composition the Italians have not excelled: but it was in the Court of Ferrara, that they invented and refined the *pastoral comedy*, a romantic Arcadia which violates the truth of manners, and

---

a I. best Abbies   *b I.* A   *c I.* a   *d I.* In   *e II.* were   *f I.* anci
g I. may be   *h II.* arts

the simplicity of Nature; but which commands our indulgence by the elaborate luxury of eloquence and wit. The *Aminta*[a] of Tasso was written for the amusement and acted in the presence of Alphonso ii; and his sister Leonora might apply to herself the language of a passion which disordered the reason, without clouding the Genius of her poetical lover. Of the numerous imitations the *Pastor Fido* of Guarini, which alone can vie with the fame and merit of the original, is[b] the work of the Duke's Secretary of State: it was exhibited in a private house at Ferrara: but the retreat of the author from the service of his native prince has bestowed on Turin the honour of the first public representation. The father of the Tuscan muses, the sublime but unequal Dante had pronounced that Ferrara[c] was never honoured with the name of a Poet: he would have been astonished to behold the chorus of bards, of melodious swans (their own allusion) who now peopled the banks of the Po. In the court of Duke Borso and his successor, Boïardo[d] Count of Scandiano was respected as a noble, a soldier, and a scholar: his vigorous fancy first celebrated the loves and exploits of the Paladin Orlando; and his fame has at once been preserved and eclipsed, by the brighter glories of the continuation of his work. Ferrara may boast that on her classic ground, Ariosto and Tasso lived and sung; that the lines[e] of the *Orlando Furioso*, and the *Gierusalemme liberata*, were inscribed in everlasting characters under the eye of the first and second Alphonso. In a period of near three thousand years, five great Epic poets have arisen in the World: and it is a singular prerogative that two of the five should be claimed as their own by a short age and a petty state.

But the glory of Ferrara, and perhaps the *legitimate* race of the Este expired with Alphonso ii [AD 1597. October 27][.] As he left neither children nor brothers, his first cousin Don Cæsar the son of a younger son of Alphonso i was the next in the lineal order of descent. His claim to the succession was ratified by the will of the late Duke, who had obtained from the Emperor, though not from the Pope, the privilege of chusing an heir in[f] his own family. And the Senate of Ferrara, which still preserved a semblance of election, presented him, with apparent loyalty, the sword of[g] Justice and the[h] sceptre of dominion. The people submitted to a prince who seemed

[a] *I.* immortal *Aminta*   [b] *I.* was   [c] *I.* never was a poet born at Ferrara
[d] *I.* was   [e] *I.* immortal lines   [f] *I.* and   [g] *I.* and sceptre
[h] *I.* power

to unite the[a] various titles of birth, of[b] donation, and of the public choice, the accession of Don Cæsar was announced to the courts of Italy and Europe, and his reign might have been peaceful and prosperous had not the ambition of Clement viii revived the design of restoring[c] Ferrara to the Ecclesiastical state. In the confidence of right or at least of power, the Roman Pontiff sternly rejected the Ambassador and obedience of a pretended Duke who had not expected the approbation of the Holy see. A monitory or summons to appear in fifteen days was affixed on the Church-doors; and the Apostolical chamber demanded the possession of the fief till the vassal should have cleared his birth and title in the court of his supreme Lord. It was in vain that the Duke of Ferrara solicited a delay; that he provoked an enquiry, that he negociated a compromise, that he submitted his cause to the arbitration of a neutral judge. "The honour and interest of the Church (said the inexor-"able Pontiff) must not be deserted. In the vindication of St Peter's "patrimony, I will sell the last chalice of the Altar; I am ready to "march in person against the sacrilegious rebel; and I would dye "in the ditch of Ferrara with the Holy Sacrament in my hands." This generous resolution was applauded by the Cardinals, and they protested that if Clement viii should be taken from the World they would impose by a common oath the same obligation on the future Pope. Some forms of Judicial proceeding were hastily dispatched; and before two months had elapsed from the death of Alphonso ii, a tremendous bull of forfeiture, excommunication and interdict was thundered against the pretended Duke and his impious adherents. At the same time the military preparations were urged with incessant vigour and an army of[d] sixteen thousand horse and foot, which fame had soon magnified to twenty five thousand was assembled near Faenza under the command of Cardinal Aldobrandini the Pope's nephew and Legate. The state of Europe was most favourable to the ambition of Rome; and the prospects of Don Cæsar were on all sides black[e] and comfortless. The Emperor Rodolph ii might be a well-wisher to the house of Este; but his remote and insufficient forces were occupied by the Turks in Hungary. If the rival monarchs of France and Spain should deign to interfere in this Pygmy war, the enmity of the one would not ensure the support of the other. Henry iv had been persuaded by a selfish agent to prove the sincerity of his conversion in the sacrifice

---

[a] *I.* so man   [b] *II. om.* of   [c] *I.* uniting   [d] *I.* near   [e] *I.* d

of an old and faithful ally. Philip ii, the Dæmon of the South was now anxious to leave his son and his dominions in peace: but the revolution was consummated before he could signify his intentions: and the Spanish ministers in Italy were suspected of a secret conspiracy against the Imperial fiefs of Reggio and Modena. The Italian[a] princes balanced between fear and envy: Venice was least desirous of the neighbourhood and least apprehensive of the resentment[b] of the Pope: but her words were ambiguous and her actions were slow. Don Cæsar had been left without troops or treasures; the fortifications of Ferrara were neglected in a long peace: the people was aggrieved by taxes; the Clergy was seduced[c] by the[d] prejudice of conscience or the hopes of preferment; the emissaries of Rome were busy and persuasive: and the ancient loyalty to the house of Este was corrupted by the promise of a Golden age.

But the instant cause of his ruin was in the character of the Duke himself. Had Don Cæsar been endowed with the spirit[e] and constancy of his ancestors, he might have been saved by the resolution to fall. Had he listened to the advice of a veteran, a bold sally on the half-formed camp of Faenza might have dissipated the Pope's soldiers who would cease to be formidable, when they ceased to be feared. The siege of Ferrara was an arduous enterprize: courage would have given him time, time would have given him friends; the Venetians would have armed for his interest and their own; many brave adventurers of France and Italy would have drawn their swords in his quarrel; and the novelty of danger, the lassitude of war, the weight of expence, the chances of mortality would have inclined his enemies to a safe and honourable peace. Far different were the feelings of the successor of Alphonso: he had been educated, remote from[f] the council and the field, in the bosom of luxury and devotion: his mild and timid disposition was astonished by the thunder of spiritual and temporal arms; nor could he expect from others the support which he denied to himself. When he entered the Cathedral, the priests interrupted their rites and fled from the Altar;[g] his venal ministers exagerated the danger, and concealed the ressources; he was alarmed each hour by the intelligence of secret treason; and a Jesuit persuaded him, that Modena and Reggio, that his life, that[h] even his soul could only be saved by an immediate

[a] *I.* Italians   [b] *I.* P   [c] *I.* a   [d] *I.* prejudice or hope,   [e] *I.* courage
[f] *I.* from arms and government   [g] *II.* altars   [h] *II.* and

capitulation. The terms were dictated in the camp by the imperious
Legate. That Don Cæsar should deliver his eldest son as an hostage,
resign the Ducal sceptre in the presence of the Magistrate, divide
his artillery with the Pope, and surrender the *possession* of the
Dutchy of Ferrara with all it's dependencies. And that in return
for his submission he should be absolved from all Ecclesiastical
censures, and permitted to enjoy the Diamond palace with the
personal effects, and allodial estates of the house of Este. After the
conclusion of the treaty the Conqueror was eager to reign and the
exile was anxious[a] to depart. On the twenty eighth of January one
thousand five hundred and ninety eight, Don Cæsar evacuated a
city in which his ancestors had reigned near four hundred years.
A splendid, but mour[n]ful procession of his family and household
passed slowly through the streets: the Duke of Modena (his remaining title) was seated in an open coach; his eyes were cast down
on a letter which he seemed to read, as if desirous of escaping the
view of those objects which he must see no more. The minds of
the people were already changed: their curiosity was melted into
pity: they had neglected the defence, they deplored the loss, of their
native prince;[b] and the first evening of his departure, five thousand
persons were deprived of the[c] daily bread which they received
from the charity or magnificence[d] of the Ducal court. These
melancholy reflections were suspended by the triumph of the Legate,
and the speedy visit of Clement viii who was impatient to behold
his new conquest. But as soon as the festival of the Revolution had
subsided, Ferrara was left to the solitude and poverty of a provincial town,[e] under the Government of priests: a citadel was
erected to fix the inconstancy of the inhabitants, and within seventeen years after the death of Alphonso ii, a fourth of his capital was
already in ruins. Nor were the losses of Don Cæsar confined to
the sacrifice of Ferrara: the territory, salt-works and fishery of Commachio, an Imperial fief, were seized by the hand of power: his
allodial property was diminished and disputed by the chicanery of
law. Even the Dutchy of Chartres and the mortgages[f] of the house
of Este in France were withheld from the heir and creditor under
the[g] pretence that he was a foreigner: it was a just observation of
the Grand Duke of Tuscany, that his brother-in law Don Cæsar
might have resisted his enemies, if the million and a half of gold,

---

[a] *I.* eager   [b] *II.* price   [c] *II.* their   [d] *II.* munificence   [e] *I.* city
[f] *I.* estates   [g] *II. om.* the

which his predecessors trusted to the most Christian King, had been safely deposited in the treasury of Ferrara.

In this singular transaction ambition and avarice were the motives of Rome. Her forms of Judicial proceeding were precipitate and violent: without evidence or tryal, she judged in her own cause, she pronounced in her own favour and she forcibly seized for her own use the valuable object in dispute. But as it is possible, and barely possible that truth and justice may be supported by the means most adverse to their Nature, I shall freely examine the descent[a] of Don Cæsar and his right of succession without[b] any[c] interest to corrupt or any prejudice to mislead the equity of my decree. After the decease of Lucretia Borgia his second wife, Alphonso i who[d] was still in the manly vigour of life, embraced a decent mode of satisfying his passions without injuring his family. Instead of seeking a third alliance in the courts of Europe he purchased a maiden of Ferrara, of obscure parentage and exquisite beauty. Laura was entertained several years in the state of a concubine: but this illegal union might, in some degree be excused by the dignity of her lover, and her own imitation of conjugal virtue. She became the mother of two sons, Don Alphonso, and Don Alphonsino, a title and a name which had been lately introduced into Italy by the prevailing influence of the Spaniards. Their birth is acknowledged to have been illegitimate;[e] in[f] the testament of their father which is dated fourteen[g] months before his death they simply are styled the children of a free man by a free woman; nor did he add, in his last illness of several weeks, any clause or codicil to declare a[h] change of their condition. That, according to the laws of the Church and state, these bastards were legitimated by a subsequent marriage is supposed by their advocates, but the supposition cannot be justified by the regular proof of a contract, a certificate or a witness In default of such evidence, Muratori produces a large body of presumptions and circumstances; with an artful suggestion that much more would have been found by a more early scrutiny: but it was the interest as well as the duty of Laura to establish her own marriage and the legitimacy of her sons, and if her neglect be not ascribed to conscious guilt it [must][i] not however militate as an argument in her behalf. Her faithful champion, the librarian of Modena has collected many testimonies of poets,

---

orators, historians and genealogists, some of whom could not mistake the truth and others could[a] not have any temptation for falshood: and from their consent he infers the belief and tradition of the times, that the concubine of Alphonso i was finally promoted to the rank of his wife. The same favourable conclusion may[b] be drawn from the honours which she was permitted to enjoy near forty years[c] under the reigns of his successors; the appellation, dress and attendance of his relict or widow; the guardianship of her children; the princely style of most excellent and illlustrious; and above all the family name of Este which she subscribed on all public and private occasions. The title of Dutchess of Ferrara was alone wanting; and when pride and envy were no more, that title was bestowed in the solemn pomp of her funeral, which was attended by the Duke Alphonso ii, his brother the Cardinal, the court the Clergy, and the *arts* or corporations of the City. The five sons of Alphonso i, with the sole distinction of primogeniture, were educated as equals and companions Don Alphonso the first-born of Laura was treated as a prince, both at home and abroad: he was invested with the Marquisate of Montecchio, and the French order of St Michael; and his wife the mother of Don Cæsar, was the daughter of the reigning Duke of Urbino. The same honours were transmitted to Don Cæsar himself: he obtained an alliance still more splendid, the sister of the Grand Duke of Tuscany: and both in his life-time and at his death Alphonso ii acknowledged[d] him as his cousin and successor. Could we divest our minds of a secret suspicion, arising from the indulgence which in so many courts and countries has been lavished on the bastards[e] of princes, such presumptions might amount to the moral, if not the legal, proof of a legitimate descent. But the interest, though not the honour of the Dukes of Modena reposes on a firmer basis, which would not be shaken by the[f] quality of their female ancestor. The Popes are pleased to forget that they first granted the Dutchy of Ferrara to Borso a natural son of the Marquis Nicholas iii; and that the bull of Alexander vi extends the right of succession to all the descendants whatsoever of Hercules i. They were compelled to renounce the possession of Ferrara, but they have never ceased to assert the justice of their claim: the arguments which the court of Rome has disdained, may one day be heard in the louder tone of the Austrian canon; and a severe

---

a I. h   *b I.* might   *c I. om.* near forty years   *d I.* considered
e I. chi   *f I.* their

account may be required of the arrears and damages of two hundred years.

The abdication of Don Cæsar is related by Muratori, a loyal servant, under the name of the tragedy of Ferrara: and in the melancholy tale I have myself[a] been affected by the sympathy which we so generously indulge to the real or imaginary distresses of the great. Yet on a cooler survey I am inclined to doubt whether the last Duke of Ferrara was the most unfortunate of men. His life and liberty were safe: he was neither beheaded on a[b] public scaffold; nor dragged at the chariot-wheels of the Conqueror, nor cast into a deep and perpetual dungeon. By the soldiers and statesmen of the age he was indeed despised for the feeble defence and hasty desertion of his ancient seat. But as contempt is seldom deserved where it is felt, it is seldom felt where it is deserved: Don Cæsar was unconscious of the public reproach, and the[c] orators of his reign reserved their panegyric for the milder virtues of discretion and patience. He had lost the most precious jewel of his family: but an easy Journey of two days conveyed his court from the palace of Ferrara to that of Modena, where he lived in prosperity and peace above thirty years: by the Tuscan princess he became the father of six sons and three daughters and the reigning Duke is the[d] fourth in descent and the sixth in succession from the eldest of his sons. In this last period of decline the house of Este[e] has still preserved the external advantages of rank, riches and power: and these advantages were illustrated by the antiquity of their name and.[f] At the beginning of the seventeenth Century, an Emperor and six Kings were respected as the chiefs of the Christian Republic: but the Dukes of Modena maintained an honourable place in the second class of the princes of Europe. Their pride was seldom mortified by the presence of a superior: as long as the isles of Sicily and Sardinia were attached to the Spanish monarchy, Italy was not dignified with a regal title; a profane layman was not degraded by kneeling to the Pope, or yielding the precedence to his cardinals: nor was the native pre-eminence of hereditary rank[g] disputed by the ministerial honours of a Doge or a Viceroy. After the loss of Ferrara, the successors of Alphonso ii continued to reign over the united dutchies of Modena and Reggio, and their[h] territory about thirty leagues in length,

---

about ten in breadth was afterwards enlarged by the Lordship of
Corregio,*a* and the Dutchy of Mirandola. Their revenue is vaguely
computed at one hundred*b* thousand pounds sterling, a sum inadequate to the extraordinary demands of War, but which might support
with decent œconomy the expences*c* of the*d* Court and government.
Perhaps the latter were sometimes sacrificed to the former. When
Addison traversed the principalities of*e* Modena and Parma he was
scandalized by the magnificence of those petty courts: "he was
"amazed to see such a profusion of wealth laid out in coaches, trap-
"pings tables, cabinets, and the*f* like precious toys in which they*g*
"are few princes in Europe who equal them, while at the same time
"they have not had the generosity to make bridges over the rivers
"of their countries for the convenience of their subjects as well as
"strangers"[29] Yet the annals of Modena describe many public
works of use as well as ornament: the plenty of gold and silver is
expressed in a single coinage of Francis i of near half a million*h*
sterling: but I am ignorant whether the two*i* hundred and*j* thirty
thousand*k* Ducats, and the two hundred thousand Spanish Doub-
loons, which were paid to the Emperor for the investitures of
Corregio and Mirandola should be placed to the account of treasure
or of debt. In the narrow sphere of their dominions the Este princes
were absolute: nor do I find any example of resistance to their
reason or passion. The vanity of the human heart is*l* flattered by
the degree, rather than by the extent, of authority: and if the Sovereign was*m* conscious of his duties the man might tremble at accepting the trust of an*n* hundred and fifty thousand of his equals. His
equals by Nature, they were many of them his superiors in merit:
the natives of Modena were distinguished in the Arts and sciences;
and like the pastoral comedy, the mock-heroic*o* poetry of the Italians
was invented by Tassoni*p* a subject of the house of Este. The
state of such a prince would perhaps be the most desirable in
human life, if it were accompanied with that domestic security
which a wealthy nobleman enjoys under the protection of a great
Empire[30] The long peace of Italy in the*q* seventeenth Century was
interrupted only by some short and bloodless hostilities: but in
the three great wars between the Austrian and Bourbon powers,

a I. F	*b* I. th	*c* I. personal expences	*d* II. a	*e* I. he was sc
f I. such	*g* II. there	*h* I. millions	*i* I. twen	*j* I. thousand
k I. *om.* thousand		*l* I. w	*m* I. is	*n* II. one	*o* I. burlesq
p I. *om.* Tassoni		*q* I. the [*deleted*]; *om.* Italy in the			

the Duke of Modena has been thrice reduced[a] to the alternative of slavery or exile. His[b] neutrality was violated, his dominions were occupied by foreign troops, his subjects were oppressed by military contributions, and the mischievous expence of fortifications only served to expose his cities to the calamities of a siege.

I have long delayed, and I should willingly suppress, three disgraceful anecdotes, three criminal actions, which sully the honour of the name of Este: of these the first and the third are piously dissembled by the Librarian of Modena. I. In his descent to the infernal regions, in the ninth circle of Hell, the poet Dante beheld the condemnation of sanguinary and rapacious men: they were deeply immersed in a river of blood, and their escape was prevented by the arrows of the Centaurs. Among the Tyrants he distinguished the ancient forms of Alexander, and Dionysius: of his own countrymen he recognized the black Eccelin, and the fair Obizo of Este, the latter of whom was dispatched by[c] an unnatural son to his[d] place of torment. This Obizo can be no other than the second[e] Marquis of that name, who died [AD 1293 February 13[f]] only seven years before[g] the real or imaginary date of the *Divine Comedy* (AD 1300): his[h] life does not afford the character of a Tyrant: but[i] he was one of the pillars[j] of the Guelph faction; and were he not associated with a Ghibelline chief, we might impute[k] his sentence to the prejudices rather than the justice of the Tuscan bard. But the parricide of his son, a crime of a much deeper dye is attested by the commentary of[l] Benvenuto of Imola who[m] observes, from an old Chronicle, that Azo viii was apprehensive of the same treatment which he had inflicted on his father. It must be added that this commentary on Dante, which was composed only fourscore years after the event, is dedicated to Nicholas ii Marquis of Este and great grandson of Obizo ii, who tacitly subscribes to the guilt of his ancestors. ii Under the reign of Nicholas iii [AD 1425 March[n]], Ferrara was polluted with a domestic tragedy. By the testimony of a maid, and his own observation, the Marquis of Este discovered the[o] incestuous loves of his wife Parisina, and Hugo his bastard son, a beautiful and valiant youth. They were beheaded in the castle by the sentence of a father and husband who punished his shame, and survived their execution.

---

[a] *I.* exposed   [b] Th   [c] *I.* to h   [d] *II.* this   [e] *I.* third   [f] *II. om.* A D 1293 February 13   [g] *I.* only before   [h] *I.* but his   [i] *I.* and   [j] *I.* columns of   [k] *I.* imputed   [l] *I. om.* the commentary of   [m] *I.* one of   [n] *II. om.* March   [o] *I.* an

He was unfortunate if they were guilty: if they were innocent he was still more unfortunate: nor is there any possible situation, in which I can sincerely approve the last act of the justice of a parent.[31]

iii. Guicciardini the gravest of the Italian historians records a bloody scene which, in his own time [AD 1505], had[a] sullied the court of Ferrara; the[b] deed might revive the memory of the Theban brothers,[32] and the motive was still more frivolous, if love (says he) be a more frivolous motive than ambition. The Cardinal Hippolito was enamoured of a fair maiden of his own family: but her heart was engaged by his natural brother, and she imprudently confessed to a rival, that the beauteous eyes of Don Julio were his most powerful attraction. The deliberate cruelty of the Cardinal measured the provocation and the revenge: under a pretence of hunting he drew the unhappy youth to a distance from the City, and there compelling him to dismount, his eyes, those hated eyes were torn[c] from his head by the command and in the presence of an[d] amorous priest who viewed with delight the agonies of a brother. It may however be suspected that the work was slightly performed by the less savage executioners, since the skill of his physicians restored Don Julio to an imperfect sight. A denial of Justice provoked him to the most desperate counsels: and the revenge of Don Julio conspired with the ambition of Don Ferdinand against the life of their sovereign and eldest brother Alphonso i. Their designs were prevented, their persons seized, their accomplices were executed: but their sentence of death was moderated to a perpetual prison, and in their fault the Duke of Ferrara acknowledged his own.—These dark shades in the annals of the house of Este must not be excused by the example of the Italian tyrants; whose courts and families were perpetually defiled with lust and blood, with incest and parricide; who mingled the cruelty of savages with the refinements of a learned and polite age. But it may be fairly observed, that single acts of virtue and of vice can seldom be weighed against each other: that it is far more easy to fall below, than to rise above, the common level of morality: that three or four guilty days have been found in a period of two hundred years: and, that in the general tenor of their lives, the Marquisses of Este were just temperate and humane, the friends of each other, and the fathers of their people.

In a more superstitious age I should boldly oppose to the sins of

---

twenty generations the monastic virtues of Alphonso iii, the son and successor of Don Cæsar. Yet even these virtues were produced by the blind impulse of repentance and fear. The nature of Alphonso was impetuous and haughty: and a deep indignant regret for the loss of Ferrara[a] was the first sentiment of his childhood. As soon as he had released himself from the authority of a governor whom he hated, and a father whom he despised, the hereditary prince became the slave of his passions and the terror of Modena: his appetite for blood was indulged in the chace and the city, and he soon considered the life of a man and of a stag as of equal value. One of the most considerable private families in Italy, (such is the dark language of Muratori) was provoked by some secret motive to form a design of assassinating Alphonso. Their dagger was turned aside from his breast; their chief was sacrificed to his justice, he threatened to extirpate the whole race: nor could the intercession of princes, or of the Pope himself avert the rage of persecution and revenge. The only voice that could soothe the passions of the savage was that of an amiable and virtuous wife the sole object of his love, the voice of Donna Isabella, the daughter of the Duke of Savoy, and the grand-daughter of Philip ii King of Spain. Her dying words sunk deep into his memory: his fierce spirit melted into tears, and after the last embrace [AD 1626 August 22.], Alphonso retired into his chamber to bewail his irreperable [*sic*] loss and to meditate on the vanity of human life. But instead of resolving to expiate his sins and to seek his salvation in the public felicity, he was persuaded that the habit and profession of a Capuchin were the only armour that could shield him from Hell–fire. The two years from the death of his wife to the decease of his father [AD 1628 December 11[b]], were dedicated to prayer and pennance, and no sooner had Alphonso attained the rank of a sovereign than he aspired to descend below the condition of a man. With the approbation and blessing of the Pope who might possibly smile at this voluntary sacrifice, the Duke of Modena, after[c] a reign of six months, resigned the sceptre to Francis his eldest son, a youth of nineteen years of age, and secretly departed to a Franciscan convent among the mountains of Trent [A D 1629.[d]]. By a special privilege his noviciate and profession were consumated in the same day: the austere and humble fryar attoned[e] for the pride and luxury of the prince, and

---

[a] *I*. Modena   [b] *II. om.* A D 1628 December 11   [c] *I.* in   [d] *II. om.*
A D 1629   [e] *I.* expiated the

it was the wish of brother John-Baptist of Modena to forget the World and to be for ever forgotten. But^a obedience was now his first duty, and the noble captive, for the honour of the order and of Religion, was exhibited to the Emperor, the Archdukes, and the people of the Austrian provinces by whom he^b was contemplated with curiosity and devotion. Three^c years he wandered between Venice and Vienna as an intinerant preacher: he had the pleasure, in one of his journies to be half drowned in a river, and half starved on a rock: and he vainly^d hoped to convert the heretics of the north, or to receive from their hands the crown of martyrdom. During the last twelve years [AD 1632-1644] he was stationed in the convent of Modena, the humble slave of the subjects of his son: the city and country were edified by his missions and sermons; and as often as he appeared in^e the pulpit, the contrast of his dignity and dress most eloquently preached the contempt of this world. The conversion of the Jews, the reformation of manners the maintenance of the poor afforded a daily exercise to the zeal of the abdicated Duke: but that zeal was always^f chargeable, often troublesome, and sometimes ridiculous: his death was a relief to the court and people; nor have the princes of Este been ambitious of adorning their family with the name and honours of a Saint. The Capuchin might behold, perhaps with pity, and perhaps with envy, the temporal prosperity of his son. In peace and war, in Italy and Spain, in the Austrian and French alliance, the Duke of Modena supported the dignity of his character: and Francis i [AD 1629-1658], in a larger field would have ranked among the Generals and statesmen of an active age.

The name of Rinaldo, a name immortalized by Tasso, in Epic song, had been applied to the youngest son of Duke Francis i: he might faintly remember the last days of his^g father, and the short government of his brother Alphonso iv; but he was no more than seven years of age, when his infant nephew^h Francis the^i second, succeeded^j to the Ducal title. In his early youth Rinaldo was proposed as a candidate for the crown of Poland, a wild, and had it not failed a ruinous attempt: the example of so many of his Kinsmen suggested a more rational pursuit; and in the thirty second year he was promoted to the dignity of Cardinal at the request of James ii King of Great Britain who had married his niece. The long reign

---

^{a} *I.* The wisdom or vanity of his superiors exhibited this edifying [*deleted*] pious spectacle to the Emperor, ^{b} *I.* it ^{c} *I.* He wandered ^{d} *I. om.* vainly
^{e} *I.* an ^{f} *I.* af ^{g} *I.* th ^{h} *I.* brother ^{i} *II.* II ^{j} *I.* was

and short life of her brother Francis ii was an helpless state of minority and disease: he died without children, and had the right female*ª* succession prevailed, the unfortunate race of the Stuarts might have found a safe and honourable refuge in the inheritance of Modena. But as the order of investiture preferred*ᵇ* the more distant males, Cardinal Rinaldo ascended without a question the vacant throne of his nephew. The*ᶜ* resignation of his hat was accepted by the Po[pe]*ᵈ*; but he might marry without a dispensation a princess of Brunswick his cousin in the nineteenth degree; and this alliance was soon dignified by the nuptials of her sister with Joseph King of the Romans, the son and successor of the Emperor Leopold. The life of Rinaldo i Duke of Modena was extended beyond the term of eighty three years: in the various fortunes of his long reign, he supported a double exile with fortitude and patience; and in the intervals of peace, the country was restored by a wise and paternal government. His son Francis iii was of a more active spirit. He signalized his valour in the wars of Hungary: followed the standard of the house of Bourbon commanded or seemed to command in several battles and sieges; and extorted the confession, that had his advice been [followed]*ᵉ* the events of the war would have been more successful. His wife was a princess of Orleans, the daughter of the Regent: she was noble, beautiful, and rich; but in the true estimate of honour, the meanest virgin among his subjects would have been a more worthy consort. Their son Hercules iii, the reigning Duke acquired a valuable and convenient territory with the heiress of Massa Carrara. Their only daughter, by the command of his*ᶠ* inexorable father was delivered to the Archduke Ferdinand the Emperor's brother;[33] the marriage has been fruitful in children of both sexes, and the Dutchies of Modena, Reggio and Mirandola will soon be the patrimony of a younger branch of the new family of Austria. In the decline of life, Hercules iii is the sole remaining male of the house of Este, and the long current of their blood must speedily be lost in a foreign stream.

[Accounts of the German branch]

The nuptials of Azo had transplanted the Este family from Italy*ᵍ* to Germany, from the Po to the Danube. His grandson Henry the

ª II. of female   *ᵇ I.* gave a   *ᶜ I.* For   *ᵈ So II. MS.* Po;   *ᵉ So*
II. Not in MS.   *ᶠ I.* the   *ᵍ I.* German

black, and his great-grandson Henry the proud, acquired by marriage, new and ample possessions on the Elb, and Weser; and Henry
the Lyon the heir of these possessions is the first of his race[a] to
whom the title of BRUNSWICK can be strictly appropriated. The
Lyon was the tenth male in lineal descent from the Marquis Adalbert: and his maternal pedigree might be derived from the *Dukes*,
the *Emperors*, and the *Hero*, of Saxony[(1)]

I. The Genius of Henry the fowler might govern the Kingdom
of Germany with one hand, and the Dutchy of Saxony with the
other; and the arts and cities of that savage region are ascribed to
his political institutions. Otho i, by a rare felicity was not inferior
in personal merit to his father: but the majesty of a Roman Empire
appeared incompatible with the office of a provincial Duke; the
pursuit of Italian realms carried him far away to the south; and his
ancient patrimony was left exposed to the inroads of the Slavi and
the Danes. It became necessary to station a soldier on the banks of
the Elb; nor would that soldier have been obeyed by the Saxon[b]
chiefs, unless the splendour of his birth, and the extent of his
property had already given him a leading influence in the Country.
About the middle of the ninth Century the noble race of Billing, an
indigenous Chieftain or *prince* emits the first ray of historic light:
his blood was mingled with that of the French conquerors

— ——Francorum clarâ de stirpe potentûm

and his daughter Oda is celebrated as the grandmother of Henry
the fowler, The valiant Herman the son of the second, and the
great-grandson of the first, Billing was appointed military Governor,
and at length[c] created hereditary Duke of Saxony by his cousin
Otho the great (960): and four descents, Bernard i, Bernard ii,
Ordulph, and Magnus, continued the lineal succession till the
beginning of the twelfth Century. In their wars against the northern
Barbarians, these Dukes were seldom successful: but they asserted
their own prerogatives and the liberties of the nation; their independence sometimes provoked the jealousy of the Emperors; nor did
the royal maids of Norway and Hungary disdain the alliance of
such[d] powerful vassals. The male line of the Billings was extinct in
Duke Magnus: (1106) his eldest daughter Wulfilda had been given
to Henry the black, afterwards[e] Duke of Bavarians[f]: the modern

---

[a] *I. om.* of his race   [b] *I.* Saxons   [c] *I.* create   [d] *I.* these   [e] *I.* after
[f] *II.* Bavaria

Dutchies of Luneburgh and Saxe-Lawenburgh were her princely inheritance: and her children, of the family of the Este-Guelphs, succeeded to these territories on either side of the Elb, which are still enjoyed by the Electoral branch of the house of Brunswick.

ii. From their original patrimony the five Saxon Emperors, Henry the fowler, the three Othos, and Henry the Saint may be styled without impropriety, of the ancient house of Bru[n]swick. But their connection with the Este-Guelphs can be found only in female alliances; and their blood may have been transfused by three streams of imperfect clearness. Their common source is derived from Henry the fowler, the King, at least, of Germany, and the son and grandson of the Dukes of Saxony, Otho (880) and Ludolph. (858). Otho enjoyed the glory of refusing the Crown; and of Ludolph it may be sufficient to affirm, that he was the sole hope and honour of an illustrious race; that his birth was equal to his fortune, his virtue to his birth, and his beauty to his virtue. We have reason to believe, though we have not a right to assert, that his uncle Ecbert was sanctified in the chaste embraces of St Ida;[2] that his father Bruno is the founder of Brunswick (*Brunonis vicus*); and that^a his grandfather an elder Bruno was the friend of Witikind, with whom he fought under the standard of freedom, and with whom he yielded to the God of the Christians. In^b the fifth ascending degree the proselyte must^c be the progenitor of a Saint, of Bruno Archbishop of Cologne and brother of the Emperor Otho i. His domestic^d Biographer thus describes the merits of this Saxon family. "As far as "reaches the memory of man, the grandsires of the grandsires are "all most noble: nor would it be easy to find an obscure or degener- "ate member in the whole series.[3]"

I now return to the three channels of communication between the old and the new house of Brunswick, between the Saxon Emperors and the Este-Guelphs. 1 According [to] the monk of Weingarten, the father of Cunegonde, Guelph iv was the son of Count Rodolph of Altorf and of his wife Itha the daughter of Richlinda daughter of the Emperor Otho i. But the children, alas! of the great Otho are conspicuous in history; Richlinda is invisible; and her existence can only be saved by degrading her to the rank of an illegitimate daughter whose alliance,^{e} however, might be an object of ambition to the proudest vassal of Germany. 2. The matrimonial conquests^f

---

^{a} *I. om.* that ^{b} *I.* The fifth ^{c} *I.* wa ^{d} *I.* cont ^{e} *I.* nuptials
^{f} *II.* conquest

of Henry the Black had extended over Luneburgh and the Elb; Brunswick and the Weser were embraced by those of his son Henry the proud, whose nuptials with Gertrude the daughter of Richenza and the Emperor Lothaire ii (1126) enriched and illustrated the Guelphic line. Richenza the female parent of an Heiress was herself an heiress and the daughter of an heiress. From her father Duke Henry she claimed the county or principality of Nordheim in the southern part of the Electorate of Hanover, from her mother Gertrude she derived the city and country of Brunswick which had been enjoyed by[a] four successive generations of her ancestors. Gertrude[b] alone represented her childless brother Ecbert ii Margrave of Misnia and Brunswick: he was the son of Ecbert i, of Ludolph of Bruno ii, and of Bruno i; whose pedigree would emerge into a brighter day, as the younger son of Henry Duke of Bavaria, a younger brother of the Emperor Otho i. This highest step trembles indeed under our[c] feet: yet the evidence of local chronicles must not be despised: inheritance is the most natural mode of possession; and in the tenth Century the Margrave Bruno i possessed the patrimonial estate of the ancient house of Brunswick. 3 Our last and best dependence is on the maternal grandfather of Henry the Lyon; on Lothaire ii, who was successively Count of Supplingeburgh, Duke of Saxony, King of Germany, and Emperor of the Romans. His father Count Gebehard fell in battle (1075),[d] and is numbered among the slain with the first princes of the Empire. It is *almost* certain that he was the son of Otho Duke of Swabia: it is *absolutely* certain that the father of Duke Otho was Ezo Count Palatine, a noble courtier, who obtained in marriage Matilda the daughter of the Emperor Otho ii, by the fortune, as it is fabled, of a game at dice. The slight defect in the Genealogy of Lothaire ii is overbalanced by the general consent[e] of the twelfth Century that he was the heir, as well as the successor, of Otho the great; and the three probable connections of the ancient and new houses of Brunswick will be consolidated into one rational belief. It may not be superfluous to add that the Empress Theophano the consort of Otho ii, was a Greek princess of the Basilian or Macedonian Dynasty; which held the sceptre of Constantinople, and derived a splendid and specious origin from the royal race of the Arsacides of Parthia. Reason[f] may suspect, and fancy will pronounce, that

---

[a] *I.* since the middle of the tenth century [b] *I.* She [c] *I.* of [d] *I.* an
[e] *I.* belief [f] *I. om.* Reason . . . Crassus.[3]

the French colours, on the field of Minden were presented to the descendant of a King, who had received the Roman eagles, after the defeat of Crassus. [3]

iii. After a brave resistance and a prudent submission, Witikind the Saxon Hero ended his life in the bosom of peace and Christianity. His son Wicbert was not less eminent in the Church than in the State: his grandson Walbert was educated in the manners, and promoted to the dignities of the French court. After a chasm of one or two generations, four brothers of the race of Witikind appear with the title of Count[a] in his native country of Westphalia. Among these Theodoric is illustrated by the temporal and spiritual honours of his daughter St Matilda, the Queen of Henry the fowler, and the mother of the Saxon Emperors. [4] By this female descent the Este-Guelphs and many other noble families participate of the blood of Witikind: but his male-posterity is extinguished or lost; and in the tenth, eleventh, and twelfth centuries, I cannot discover any name, which is connected by the writers of the time, with the name of the Hero. Yet some fabulous claims were cherished in silence and four hundred years after his death the Chronicle of a French monk[b] deduces from the four brothers, the father and uncles of St Matilda, the nobility of *all* Saxony, Italy, Germany, Gaul, Normandy, Bavaria, Swabia, Hungary, Bohemia, Tuscany and Poland[5]; a strange profusion, which much debases the value of the gift! Vanity may grasp these ideal trophies: the Electors of Saxony and the Dukes of Savoy may embrace the shades of their visionary fathers; but the hundred heads of the male children of Witikind dissolve into air, as soon as they are touched by the spear of criticism. [34]

Our accurate knowledge of the origin, establishment, and alliances of the Este-Guelphs may now smile at the errors and fables of a darker age. After the separation of the house of Este by the two marriages of the Marquis Azo, the two diverging branches of his posterity insensibly became strangers and aliens to each other: the intercourse of the distant nations of Europe was rare and hazardous; and the fall of the Empire had separated the Worlds of Italy and Germany. A tradition still survived in the court of Ferrara that in some remote age, an Hero of their blood had transported his hopes and fortunes[c] beyond the Alps: but the date, the characters and the consequences of his emigration[d] were soon obliterated by

---

^{a} *I.* Counts ^{b} *So II. MS.* monks ^{c} *II.* fortune ^{d} *I.* transmigration

ignorance and supplied by fiction.[6] In the tenth Century the valiant Azo an Italian noble attended the standard and deserved the esteem of Otho the great. Alda a natural daughter of the Emperor was the reward of his services: she was endowed with the imaginary fief[a] of Fausburch or Friburgh in Saxony, and the twins, Fulk and Hugo, were the offspring of their marriage. Hugo returned to his native country, and propagated the race of the Marquisses of Este, Dukes of Ferrara and Modena; while Fulk remained in Germany, supported the[b] falling house of Saxony[c] and transmitted to his descendants[d] *some* great County or Dutchy [in][e] the unknown regions of the North. The Dukes of Brunswick on the other hand, preserved a faint remembrance of their Italian origin: the title of their ancestors was familiar to their ear; but they had forgotten the name of Este, and their misguided tenderness confounded the *Marquisses* of Montferrat or Mantua with their real kinsmen.[7] About the middle of the sixteenth century the mist was in some measure dispelled by the enquiries of Count Faleti who had been sent into Germany by Hercules ii Duke of Ferrara and the perfect connection of the two branches was finally restored by the faithful service of Leibnitz and Muratori

---

1. For these Saxon genealogies, see the Dissertations of Eccard with the annotations of Scheidius in the iv[th] Volume of the Origines Guelficæ, and the Prolegomena of the latter especially. Tom iii p 10 &c.

2. The original life of St Ida is published by Leibnitz (Script. Brunswic. Tom i p 175-184.

3. [2f] History of the decline and fall of the Roman Empire. Vol. v[g]. p 148.[35]

4. Vita. S[ctae] Mathild. in Leibnitz. Script. Bruns. Tom i. p 194.

5. Alberic. trium fontium. Chron. in Leibnitz. Accessiones Historicæ. Tom ii. p 257.

6. Ricobaldo. in Muratori. Script. rerum Italic. Tom ix. p 315. 317. 321.

7. Leibnitz. Opp. Tom iv. P ii. p 83. Edit. Dutems.

According to the Philosophers who can discern an endless involution of *Germs* or organised bodies, the future animal exists in the female parent; and the male is no more than an accidental cause which stimulates the first motion and energy of life. The Genealogist who embraces this System should confine his researches to the female line, the series of mothers; and scandal may whisper, that this mode of proceeding will be always the safest and most assured.

[a] *I.* castle   [b] *I.* the greatness of   [c] *I. om.* of Saxony   [d] *II.* descendant
[e] *So II. Om. in MS.*   [f] *Thus in MS. I.* 4   [g] *I.* Tom

But the moral connection[1] of a pedigree is differently marked by the influence of law and custom:[a] the male sex is deemed more noble than the female; the association of our idea pursues the regular descent of honours and estates from father to son; and their wives, howsoever essential, are considered only in the light of foreign auxiliaries. This rule indeed will be sometimes broken by an exception: the sole remaining daughter of an ancient and powerful family will assume the character of a son, and her children who inherit the fortunes, may be assimilated to the name, of her own ancestors. The origin of her less conspicuous husband may gradually disappear; but if she be married to an equal, their common posterity will celebrate the union of two illustrious houses.

This last remark may be applied to the family of ESTE-BRUNSWICK which so prosperously grafted the fruits of Italy on a German stem. The antiquity and importance of the Guelphs to whose name and possessions they succeeded is acknowledged in the twel[f]th Century (1152) by Otho Bishop of Frisingen[2]. "In the Roman Empire "(says that contemporary writer) two famous families have flourished "till the present time on the confines of Gaul and Germany; the "Henrys of Gueibelinga and the Guelphs of Altdorf, the one pro- "ductive of Emperors, the other of great Dukes. By the contests of "such men, armed with power, and ambitious of renown, has the "peace of the Republic been often endangered" An equal opposition to the Franconian and Swabian Emperors must redound to the honour of a subject family, and the praise is the less questionable, as the historian himself was issued from the rival house. This curious passage unfolds the seeds of the two factions of the Church and the Empire; and it likewise appears that the name of Guelph, as well as of Henry, was no more than a personal and Christian appellation, the frequent use of which might denote in the language of posterity, the succession of an entire Dynasty. Between the ascending and descending series of the Guelphs the connection is formed by the marriage of Cunegonde the daughter of the first, and the mother of the second, race. The nobility and riches of Azo were not inferior to those of his consort; but, after their sons and grandsons had been invested with the Dutchies of Bavaria and Saxony, the distant fame of an Italian Marquis was gradually lost; and, these princes, adhering to their maternal ancestors, assumed the more popular character of native Germans.

[a] *II.* customs

About the end of the twelfth Century, a short chronicle was composed by a monk of Weingarten to immortalize in this World, as well as in the next, the Lords of Altdorf, the founders and bene-factors of his convent.[3] After a diligent search into such chronicles and charters as were then exstant, he fairly confesses that his visible horizon is bounded by the age of Charlemagne, by the well-known Welf[a] or Guelph the father of the Empress Judith. But he is persuaded that the ancestors of his first Hero were men of valour and renown

Vixere fortes ante Agamemnona

that, for ages, before the introduction of Christianity, they flourished in riches and honours; that they governed their own people, and that their name went forth into foreign lands. Such presumptions are more satisfactory to a rational mind, than his romance of a Trojan colony and descent, than an absurd marriage with Kathilina the daughter of a Roman Senator, whose name might be[b] trans-lated into *Whelp* in the German or English idioms. The conjectures of Leibnitz or his disciple Eccard are follies of a graver kind: they build without materials an edifice of characters and adventures, and grasping some shadowy[c] semblances, they forcibly derive the Guelphs from a brother of Odoacer King of the Heruli, who extin-guished the Roman Empire (476) in Italy and the West. From the beginning of the historic period the Chronicle of Weingarten enumerates only six[d] generations, Guelph the father of Judith, Ethico, Henry, Rodolph, and the[e] two last Guelphs the father and brother of Cunegonde; a number scarcely sufficient for an interval of two hundred and fifty years. The probable chasms have indeed been supplied by the industry of Leibnitz and Eccard.[f] The names of Guelph or Welf i, Ethico i, Welf or Wolfhard ii, Ethico ii, Henry, Rodolph i the brother of St Conrad, Welf iii, Rodolph ii, Welf or Wolfhard iv, and Welf v are enrolled in their list: but a descent of ten generations reverses the difficulty, and the scene is now crowded by the new Actors. At the two extremities, the chain of the ancient Guelphs is strongly rivetted in truth: but the

---

a I. om. Welf or   *b I.* signify a   *c I.* shadowing   *d I.* five
e For remainder of this sentence, I. Guelph the father of Cunegonde a number scarcely sufficient for an interval of two almost three hundred [*in margin*] hundred and fifty years.   *f MS.* (A) *Next lines preceded by* (A) *in margin* (The names of . . . ten generations) *I.* but their addition of two Guelphs, of a second Rodolph Henry, and a second Rodolph

intermediate links cannot be discriminated with clearness and certainty[4]

---

1. Hume' Essays. Vol. ii p 192. 193.
2. Otho. Frisingensis L ii. C 2 in Muratori. Script. rerum Italic. Tom vi. p 699. 700.
3. Chronicon Weingartense. from the Vienna MS. in Origines Guelficæ Tom v. p 31. 32. 33. It had been published less correctly by Canisius and Leibnitz
4. See the first and[a] fifth Books of the Origines Guelficæ

Of the first Guelph the rank is ascertained and the name is illustrated by the marriage of his daughter Judith with the Emperor Lewis the pious, the son and successor of Charlemagne.[1] The magnitude of the French Empire had almost excluded the choice of a foreign princess: nor could the Leaders of a warlike nation disdain the alliance of the Peers whose judgement had raised them to the throne. The father of Judith was of the noblest race of the Bavarians: the nobility of her Saxon mother was equally conspicuous; Guelph[b] is indifferently described by the style of Count, or Duke or Prince; and the more honourable appellation of Freeman (*Vir egregiæ libertatis*) may be applied to the situation as well as the character of the independent Chief. After the decease of his first wife, Lewis the pious invited the fairest and most noble Damsels: the heart or rather the heart of the Emperor was disputed in these nuptial games; and the beauty of Judith was rewarded with a fond and feeble husband, whom she continued to govern till the last hour of his life. The loud praises of her wit and learning her courage and piety announce at least the pretensions of the Empress; and she might excuse the invectives that were pointed against the dangerous seduction of her graces and charms During ten years (819–830) of specious prosperity the daughter of Guelph enjoyed and embellished the feasts of an itinerant Court. But the vices of the state and the calamities of the age were gradually ascribed to her influence: Bernard Duke of Septimania was known to be her favourite, and was believed to be her Lover; she wished to provide a Kingdom for her infant Charles; and the three sons of Lewis by his first wife conspired against the Stepmother whom they had provoked. By the successful rebels she was twice torn from the Palace, and immured, under the monastic veil, in the Cloysters of Poitiers, and Tortona. (830–834)[c] The Emperor was twice restored: he embraced his wife with the credulity of love: Judith and her

[a] *I.* book of th   [b] *I.* a   [c] *I. om.* (830–834)

Q

favourite asserted their innocence with oaths and challenges: her days were concluded (843) in peace and honour; and the posterity of Guelph reigned in France (840-987) till the sixth Generation.

Conrad and Rodolph two of the sons of Guelph had abandoned their paternal seat to share the prosperous and adverse fortunes of their sister. When she was degraded to a nun they were shaven as priests: but they stood beside the throne as princes of the blood. Conrad i had two sons Conrad ii and Hugh, from his Ecclesiastical benefices, surnamed the *Abbot*. Their ambitious spirit maintained their hereditary rank, and they appears*a* conspicuous in the government of provinces, and in the annals of peace and war. According to some learned Antiquaries Conrad i left a third son the famous Robert the strong, the father of the Kings of France of [the]*b* third race. Their opinion will not sustain the rigour*c* of critical enquiry: but the text of an original Chronicle is alledged in it's favour; and a series of an hundred Kings still hangs by the various reading of a single vowel.(2)

Yet a Kingdom may be found to which the purest history will assert the title of the Guelphic line. Conrad ii and his son Rodolph were Dukes or Marquisses of the Trans-Jurane Burgundy which includes the *Pays de Vaud*, and the happy spot where I am now writing. In the shipwreck of the Carlovingian Monarchy (888), Rodolph, with the applause of his Bishops and Nobles assumed a Royal crown at the Abbey of S*t* Maurice; his sceptre was the Martyr's lance enriched with a nail of the true Cross, and the second Kingdom of Burgundy which he founded subsisted one hundred and forty four years, in a lineal succession of four princes. The independence of Rodolph i (888-912) was confirmed by two victories, and finally acknowledged in a Diet of the German Empire. His son Rodolph ii (912-937) twice attempted the conquest of Italy and his retreat was purchased by a fair equivalent. his dominion extended over the French or western part of Switzerland, Franche-Comté, Savoy, Dauphiné, and Provence; and the country between the Rhône and the Alps adopted the new appellation of the Kingdom of Arles. The long reign (937-993) of Conrad the son of Rodolph ii was glorious and pacific, and the friendship of the great Otho was the firmest bulwark of his throne. His*d* son Rodolph iii surnamed the lazy was the spectator perhaps the cause of the decay and dissolution of his government (993-1032). After his death, the Sovereignty

a II. appear   *b II. supplies* the   *c I*. test   *d I.* R

of the Kingdom of Arles or Burgundy devolved, as a fief or legacy to his nephew the Emperor Conrad the Salic; the effective power was usurped by the Vassals: but the Regal titles of this collateral line may reflect some dignity on the fathers of the house of Brunswick.[3]

---

1. The Chronological and Alphabetical indexes of the vi[th] Volume of the Historians of France will direct the more curious reader to all the original texts which speak of the Empress Judith. The best proofs of the nobility of Guelph are the testimonies of Thegan (p 79) of the Astronomer (p 102) of the Annals of Eginhard (p 178), of those of St Bertin (p 207) and of the Saxon Chronicle (p 219)

2. Fratres or Fatris is the question; of which the opposite sides are strongly argued by Foncemagne (Memoires de l'Academie des Inscriptions Tom xx p 558–567) and Scheidius (Præfat ad Origin. Guelfic. Tom ii. p 24–43.)

3. See the iv[th] Book of the Origines Guelficæ. (Tom ii.) and the Baron de Zurlauben (Hist. de l'Academie. Tom xxxvi. p 142–159.)

While the ancestors of the Kings of Burgundy pursued the path of ambition, their kinsmen, the elder branch of the Guelphs, preferred a life of independence in the free possession of their allodial estates of Bavaria and Swabia. From Guelph the father of the Empress Judith these estates descended to the first or second Ethico whose lofty spirit is commemorated in a curious tale by the Monk of Weingarten.[1] As soon as Henry the son of Ethico had attained the age of manhood, the aspiring Youth without his father's privity or consent attached himself to the Emperor, obtained his favour, deserved his esteem, and attended with assiduous zeal the long circuits of the court and army. By the advice of the princes, and at the solicitation[a] of his Sovereign, the son of Ethico consented[b] to receive a fief or benefice of four thousand *Mansi*[c] or measures of land in the Upper Bavaria, and to perform the hommage of a faithful client. Henry, surnamed of the golden chariot, long flourished in the wealth and dignity of the palace: but his father was deeply wounded by this sacrifice of honour to interest, by this base abdication of the Nobility and freedom of the Guelphic name. After pouring a complaint into the bosom of his friends, the high-minded Ethico resolved to conceal his shame from the World. He quitted (says the Monk) his Regal edifices, and rich possessions, retired with only twelve companions to the solitary mansion of Ambirgo, amidst the mountains, and there ended his days without

---

[a] *I.* u   [b] *I.* contented   [c] *I.* farms (*replaced by Mansi* or measures of land)

seeing or forgiving his degenerate son. The acquisition, in the ninth Century, of such a fief as Ethico disdained, would satisfy the pride of the noblest family in Europe.

Had a rent–roll of the Guelphic possessions been preserved, an uncouth list of castles and villages which have long been transferred to new owners, would offend the ear, without informing the mind of the English reader. The authors of the family were of Bavarian extraction: but their principal seat was in Swabia in the neighbour- hood of the lake of Constance, and the Austrian Præfecture of Altorf and Ravensperg[(2)] is derived from the ancient Guelphs, who according to the fashion of the times had abstained from the use of any local denominations. Their various Estates as they might be acquired by donation, marriage, or purchase were scattered over the wide extent of Bavaria and Swabia, from the mountains of Tirol to the plains of Alsace; and several free communities of the Grisons were once the slaves of these powerful Landlords. In their house- hold they displayed the pomp and pride of Regal œconomy; and the domestic offices of Stewards, Butlers, Marshals Chamberlains, and Standard-bearers were exercised by Counts, or by Nobles of an equal rank. Their first Officer, the *Advocate* represented their person and maintained their cause in the Imperial or Ducal court; and they enjoyed the singular privilege of protecting, without effusion of blood, all persons who were legally proscribed till they had answered or satisfied the demands of Justice. The Episcopal churches of Frisingen, Augsburgh, Constance and Coire, and the monasteries of popular sanctity were endowed by their devotion with liberal grants of lands and peasants. Even the humiliating tribute which the Kings of Burgundy and the Guelphs of Altorf were bound to offer at the shrine of S[t] Othmar was an[a] annual commemoration of the antiquity of their house. They made attonement for the guilt of their ancestors, who, in the eighth Century had governed the Dutchy of Alemannia, and had abused their power in the persecu- tion of the Saint.

The darkness of German history in the ninth and tenth Centuries has cast a veil over the lives and characters of the ancient Guelphs. But it may be presumed that they were illiterate and valiant; that they plundered Churches in their youth and restored them in their old age; that they were fond of arms, horses and hunting; and that they resisted with equal spirit the exercise of arbitrary and legal

[a] *MS.* an an

power. St Conrad, $^{(3)}$ alone of his race (892–976) by seeking a place in Heaven, has deserved a memorial on Earth. After his education in the school, and his service in the chapter, of Constance, he was raised by a free election to the Episcopal chair (934) which he continued to fill forty two years. The Church was enriched by his patrimony and defended by his kindred: the Bishop of Constance did not affect the austere life of an Hermit; and his temperate manners were those of a German noble: but his chastity was immaculate from sin or scandal, he was assiduous in prayer, and his religious merits were crowned by the pilgrimage of Jerusalem. $^{(4)}$ The miracles^a of St Conrad are fancied with some degree of taste: he voided harmless, a spider which he had bravely swallowed in the Communion-cup; and he delivered two souls, who, in the form of birds were enduring their purgatory in the water-fall of the Rhine. But the most marvelous scene was exhibited at the Church and Abbey of Einsidlen, the Loretto of Switzerland, which under the name of our Lady of the hermits is annually visited by many thousand pilgrims$^{(5)}$. The Clergy, Nobility and people had flocked to the feast of the dedication: (948); but at the midnight hour of the Vigil, the Bishop of Constance was favoured with an extraordinary Vision. The Heavens were opened: Jesus Christ arrayed in the Episcopal habit, accompanied by the Virgin Mary, and attended by a Choir of Angels, descended from on high to officiate at his own altar: the Saints and Martyrs assumed the characters of Priests and Deacons, and the whole consecration was performed according to the ritual of the Church. In the morning the Bishop arose: he related his dream; a voice, from the sky or the roof, announced that the place was already Holy; and this visionary act has been acknowledged by the decrees of Rome. One hundred and forty seven years after his death Conrad was canonized by Pope Calixtus ii (1123): the Guelphic name was honoured by this cælestial kinsman, and the liberal devotion of Henry the black Duke of Bavaria declared him the worthy nephew of the Saint

As soon as St Conrad was received into Heaven he should have secured an act of indemnity for the obsolete sins of his family. But St Othmar was still inexorable, and the effects of his revenge were felt by the tenth generation of the Guelphs. By the grand-daughter, perhaps, of the Emperor Otho i, Rodolph ii of Altorf had two sons, Henry and Guelph. The eldest, an impatient Youth denied the

^{a} I. f

annual payment of his sin-offering; but the denial was soon followed by his untimely death. After hunting the roe-buck in the mountains, he reposed his wearied limbs under the shadow of a rock: an huge fragment fell on his head; and the vindictive Saint might behold him rolling down the precipice. The submission of his brother Guelph iv was rewarded with a longer and more glorious life. Rich in lands, and potent in arms he long tormented his neighbour the Bishop of Frisingen, attended the Emperor to his coronation at Rome, and afterwards joined against him in a successful rebellion. His nuptials with Imiza, daughter of the Count of Luxemburgh, and niece of the Empress St Cunegonde, were productive of two children; of Guelph v who succeeded his father, and of Cunegonde or Cuniza the future heiress of her family, who was given in marriage to the Marquis Azo, with eleven[a] hundred or[b] eleven thousand *Mansi* of land[6] in the valley of Elisina in Lombardy[c][7]. The portion appears to have been worthy of a prince; but the situation, the measure, and the value of the Estate cannot, now, be exactly defined.[d]

After Europe was moulded into the feudal system an independent Chieftain would have stood naked and alone: the fear of injury was stimulated by the ambition of favour, and the descendants of Ethico and Henry were more inclined to follow the example of the son, than to sympathize with the feelings of the father. Guelph v the brother of Cunegonde was invested with the Dutchy of Carinthia, and the Marquisate of Verona (1047);[e] an important province, which included the country of Tirol, and commanded the passage of the Rhætian Alps. But the servant of Henry iii maintained the vigour of his character, and the pride of his birth. An Italian Diet was summoned, according to custom, in the plain of Roncaglia. Guelph, at the head of his[f] vassals waited three days without seeing, or hearing from, the Emperor: on the fourth he sounded the trumpet of retreat; and, though he met Henry on the way, neither threats, nor prayers nor promises could prevail on him to return. An arbitrary tax of a thousand marks had been imposed on the Citizens of Verona: their Marquis, in arms flew to their relief, and the concessions of the Emperor could scarcely purchase an ignominious escape. This act of patriotism or rebellion for which he is said to have testified some remorse concludes the story of the Duke of Carinthia. He died (1055) childless in the prime of life, the

---

[a] *I.* the Elsine valley of valley of Elisina in Lombardy   [b] *I. om.* eleven hundred or   [c] *I. om.* in the   [d] *I.* defined.[6]   [e] *I. om.* (1047)   [f] *I.* the

last male of his*a* family. Desirous*b* of exchanging the temporal goods which he was about to lose for an everlasting possession in Heaven Guelph*c* endowed the Abbey of Weingarten with the rich gift of his estate*d* and vassals. Two of his principal servants accepted the testament; but, after his funeral, they were resisted in the execution of this rash and unjust deed, which offended even the prejudices of the Age. Imiza his mother was not ignorant that her daughter*e* Cunegonde had left a son: she dispatched messengers into Italy; and the youth, on his arrival, annulled the donation, and asserted his own right, as the true and legitimate heir of the ancient Guelphs.

---

1. In this imperfect review of the history of the Guelphs, the Chronicle of Weingarten (Origines Guelficæ Tom v p 32–35) may be considered as the text, and the Origines*f* Guelficæ (Tom ii. L iv and v) as the commentary.

2. See Geographie de Busching. Tom vii p 130–137 and Tom viii. p 644–647.

3. The life of S*t* Conrad (Leibnitz. Scriptores rerum Brunswicensium Tom ii p 1–14) may be illustrated by the Origines Guelficæ (Tom ii p 206–212) and the proofs or documents of the v*th* Book (N°. 7.8.9.)

4 From the word *tertio* in the life of S*t* Conrad (C vi).*g* it is supposed that he thrice visited Jerusalem. I am more inclined to suspect*h* that *mense* has been dropt by a careless transcriber: three pilgrimages are useless and improbable.

5 *One hundred thousand* according to the *moderate* calculation of Mr Coxe![36] The*i* English traveller lashes our Lady of the Hermits with the spirit of a protestant rather than of a philosopher; and his excellent translator corrects him with the enthusiasm not of a bigot, but of a poet.

6. From the customs and charters of Lombardy Muratori attempts to determine the usual *Mansus* (Antichità Estense Tom i p 3–5): and his evaluation would produce two hundred, or more probably twenty, thousand English acres. But he finds that some *Mansi* were of more ample dimensions; and I could acquiesce in the loose definition of as much land as will maintain a peasant with his family.

7. Leibnitz understands the Val d'Elsa in Tuscany and his opinion is approved by Eccard and Fontanini. (Origines Guelficæ Tom ii p 223, 224). But Gruber dissents from his text; and Muratori wishes to read *Vallis Lusina*, the village and manour of Lusia in the Veronese territory which soon afterwards appear in the possession of the Marquis Azo.

Two streams of noble blood the two families of Este, and the Guelphs were united in the son of Azo and Cunegonde who obtained the maternal name of his grandfather and uncle. By the marriage settlement which seems to have excluded the younger children Guelph vi was assured of the patrimony of his father: he already possessed the inheritance of his mother (1055): his fortune was

---

a *I.* the ancient family of the Guelphs of Altorf changing *and before remainder of this page in margin.*
b *MS. signal* (A) *after* ex-
c *I.* he   *d* *II.* estates
e *I.* son Cu   *f* *I.* Of   *g* *I. om.* (C vi)   *h* *I.* suspected   *i* *I.* Our

adequate to his birth, and his warlike ambitious spirit soared above his fortune. An Italian by nature and education he was a German by adoption; and from the age of manhood the Lord of Altorf had fixed his residence and his hopes in the country that was the seat of government. In the diet of Goslar (1071) he was invested by the Emperor Henry iv with the Dutchy of Bavaria which in that age extended to the confines of Hungary, and his nuptials were celebrated with Judith the daughter of Baldwin Count of Flanders and the widow of a titular King of England.[1] These titles are illustrious: but the Brunswick princes, who are lovers of truth and freedom will permit me to observe that they were dearly purchased by the sacrifice of virtue. His first wife was Ethelinda the daughter of Henry Duke of Bavaria: their alliance was consecrated by oaths, and while Fortune smiled Guelph was a tender husband and a pious son. But after Henry, in the storms of faction had been proscribed by[a] the Emperor, the Lord of Altorf deserted the father, repudiated the daughter, and basely solicited the spoils of a friend with whom it was his duty to fall. Gold and silver are the idols of a venal court, the Guelphic patrimony was injured by his profuse ambition; and his ascent to one of the most eminent dignities of the Republic was disgraced by the public reproach of ingratitude and perjury[2]. By the early and obstinate revolt of the Duke of Bavaria against his Imperial Benefactor these reproaches will be tinged with a blacker dye, if the defence of the Church does not absolve from all moral obligations. Whatsoever were his sins they were expiated however by a[b] pilgrimage to the Holy land: the greater part of his army was buried in the plains of Asia minor; and he died on his return at Paphos in the isle of Cyprus. (1101). His life had been prolonged to an advanced period: yet he survived only four years the longevity of his father the Marquis Azo. The articles of settlement were rigorously exacted by the Bavarian Duke: but, the sons of the second marriage, Fulk and Hugh opposed their elder brother in the passes of the Alps, and his insatiate avarice yielded to a more equal treaty of partition.

By the Queen Dowager of England, the first Guelphic Duke of Bavaria had two sons, Guelph vii and Henry, surnamed the *black*. The eldest at the age of seventeen (1089) was sent[c] into Italy and commanded by his parents to ascend the nuptial bed of Matilda

---

[a] *I.* the   [b] *I* an ex   [c] *I.* married by his father and grand-father to the famous Matilda Countess of Tuscany, at that time in her forty third year.

the Great Countess of Tuscany who had attained the autumnal ripeness of forty three years. This Heroine the spiritual daughter of Gregory vii was twice married: but interest rather than love directed her choice, and her virginity was twice insulted by a crooked dwarf, and an impotent boy. The[a] first and the second night had been cold and inefficient: but as young Guelph still complained of some artifice or enchantment, the fairest tryal was offered him on the morning of the third day. The Countess (I soften the words of a Dean[3]) spread herself on a table; and after striving to raise the husband by the display of her naked charms and lascivious motions, she dismissed him from her presence with a blow of contempt. Their conjugal union was hopeless;[b] but six years (1089–1095) elapsed between the marriage and the divorce; and the government of Tuscany was administered in their joint names, till the imperious temper of Matilda provoked[c] the grandson of Azo to reveal a secret which her pride would have concealed from the World. On his father's decease[d] Guelph[e] vii succeeded to the Dutchy of Bavaria (1101) of which he had already obtained the reversion: his power ranked him among the first princes of Germany; and when he represented the majesty of the Empire, a sword of state was carried before him. The Bavarians applauded the mildness of his sway, and his paternal care in the education of the noble youth. At Rome he appeared with dignity as the mediator between the Emperor and the Pope The French who saw him at Troyes, at the head of a great Embassy were astonished by the huge corpulence and sonorous voice, which, in his person, however were not the attributes of manhood. After a reign of nineteen[f] years he died, (1120) most assuredly, without children; and his younger brother Henry the black, reunited all the subordinate fiefs, and allodial estates of the family in Germany and Italy[4]

---

1. Of Tostus son of Earl Godwin and younger brother of Harold against whom, with a Norwegian army he had unsuccessfully disputed the crown

2. Cunctis detestantibus, quod clarissimam et inopinatissimam in Republicâ dignitatem tam fœdâ ambitione polluisset, says Lambert with a sense and style far above the xi[th] Century

3. Cosmas[g] Dean of the Church of Prague, whom I only know by the Abregé Chronologique de l'histoire d'Italie of the most accurate St Marc (Tom iv p 1253). Some faults

---

[a] II. substitutes asterisks for the next two sentences. Cf. J. E. Norton, A Bibliography of the Works of Edward Gibbon (Oxford, 1940). p. 194.   [b] II. inserts note reference here.   [c] I. con   [d] I. deceased   [e] I. he   [f] I. twenty   [g] II. For more particular information see Cosmas

and fables may weaken his credit, but of the impotence of Guelph vii, I cannot entertain a doubt

4. See the two first Guelphs of Bavaria in the vith Book of the Origines Guelficæ.
(Tom ii).

Till the beginning of the twelfth Century the provincial honours
of the Marquisses of Este, the Lords of Altorf, and even the Dukes
of Bavaria were those of a private though illustrious family: and the
series of their names and actions must be painfully extracted from
the occasional hints of charters and chronicles. During a subsequent
period of an hundred years the Este-Guelph,[a] the princes of the
Brunswick line are the first actors in the revolutions of the Empire:
their lives and characters are deeply impressed on the annals of the
times; and our loose memorials will assume the tone of an historical
narrative.[37]

After the death of his elder brother, Henry the black, son of
Guelph vi and grandson of the Marquis Azo had[b] succeeded to the
Dutchy of Bavaria and the estates of the family. He survived only
six years (1120-1126): but his political weight on a vacancy of the
throne contributed to fix the right of election in the German Aristocracy. The royal funeral, of Henry v was solemnly performed; and
the Duke with the sacerdotal and noble attendants, subscribed a writ
of summons which speaks the language of liberty and resentment.
The Diet was held in the neighbourhood of Mentz: the separate
tribes, the Franks, the Swabians, the Bavarians encamped on
either side of the Rhine, and the immediate Vassals with their
numerous and warlike followers composed an assembly or rather
army of sixty thousand soldiers and freemen. But the Archbishop,
a dextrous statesman, removing the scene from the camp to the
cathedral, transferred the right of voting from the many to the few,
and as the comparative few were still too many in his eyes, the
prævious nomination of an Emperor was devolved on a select com-
mittee of ten princes and prelates, the first rudiments of the Electoral
college. Three candidates, Leopold Marquis of Austria, Lothaire
Duke of Saxony, and Frederic Duke of Swabia were unanimously
named: and the two former after a modest refusal for themselves
engaged to support the choice of the Majority. The evasions of the
Duke of Swabia betrayed a secret and offensive presumption of
hereditary right. He was the son of Frederic of Stauffen, a soldier
of fortune: but his mother Agnes was the daughter and sister of the

[a] *II*. Este-Guelphs   [b] *I. om.* had

two last Emperors, he shared with his brother Conrad the rich inheritance of the Ghibeline[a] or Franconian house, and his ambition might be coloured by the examples of the preceding reigns. These examples and this ambition the[b] Electors had resolved to crush by the free choice of Lothaire of Saxony: but the attempt was dangerous, as long as the Bavarian Duke might cast into the opposite scale the votes of his dependent Bishops, and the swords of his military Vassals. His[c] personal attachment, for he had given his sister to Frederic, insensibly yielded to stronger arguments of public or private interest. Henry the black appeared in the Cathedral of Mentz, and no sooner had he assented to the wishes of the majority, than the Saxon was proclaimed in triumph, and the Swabian fled in despair.

The difference of an hereditary or elective Monarchy is of small moment to a dying man; nor did Henry survive many months the diet of[d] Mentz. In his last moments (1126) the fears of superstition prevailed: but he contrived to expire in the habit of a monk, and thus disappointed the infernal spirits who might have formed some pretensions to the soul of the Duke. The devotion of Conrad his eldest son is[e] far more edifying and meritorious. The noble youth embraced the solitary life of a priest; renouncing a princely inheritance, the pride of the World, the[f] exercise of arms, and the hope of posterity. His birth and virtue must have raised him to the Archbishoprick of Cologne, had he not escaped from this new temptation to[g] the Abbey of Clairvaux in France, where he pronounced the vow of a Cistercian monk under the austere discipline of S[t] Bernard. Even this discipline was too soft for his encreasing fervour: he undertook a pilgrimage to the Holy land, and buried himself in the cell of an hermit of the desart. The decay of his health, which had been broken by immoderate pennance, compelled him to return: he found a grave at Bari on the sea-coast of Italy; his memory is still revered by the people; and in the present century (1722) the relicks of S[t] Conrad have been carried in procession to obtain from Heaven the blessing of seasonable rain.[h]

As the eldest son was dead to the World, the feudal and allodial estates[i] were divided between the two surviving brothers, Henry

---

^a *I. and II.* Ghibelline   ^b *I.* and the   ^c *I.* The perso   ^d *I.* Election
^e *I.* wa   ^f *II. om.* the   ^g *I.* had he not   ^h *I. no paragraph. MS. in*
margin, Gibbon's hand: a new paragraph   ⁱ *I.* property was (*replaced by* estates
were)

the proud and Guelph viii; but the right of primogeniture was considered, and Henry alone in his twenty fifth year,[a] succeeded to the title and office of Duke of Bavaria. His character may be estimated by the first acts of his government in the provincial diet of Ratisbon: every complaint was heard, every wrong redressed, every crime punished; and the civil judge was protected by the military Commander. In a circuit round the province he reconciled the quarrels of his vassals, and exacted the most effectual sureties of oaths and pledges for the suspension of private war: the castles of the disobedient were demolished, their persons were proscribed, and Bavaria enjoyed a respite of ten years (1126–1136) from the disorders of the feudal system. The Duke had levied a tax on the citizens of Ratisbon, but the produce was surely inadequate to the expence of a stone bridge of fifteen arches which he constructed over the deep and rapid stream of the Danube. Churches and convents are the monuments of the middle age; and a work of public use attests the sense as well as the riches of the founder.

The marriage of Gertrude the daughter and heiress of the Emperor Lothaire with Henry the proud[b] was not accomplished till after his father's death; but it may be presumed that his desertion of a brother in law for a stranger was purchased by the hope or promise of this valuable alliance. The nuptial feast was celebrated, in the summer, (1126[])[c] on the banks of a pleasant river: the spacious meadows were covered with tents, and edifices of timber, and the scene[d] might have presented a pleasing and pastoral image if the sound of arms, the riot of intemperance, and the pride of rank could have been excluded from an assembly of German nobles. A general invitation attracted twenty or thirty thousand guests; the princes, barons and Knights, their numerous retinues, and the crowd of meaner spectators; and the festival was continued several weeks by the profuse hospitality of the bridegroom who bore away the prize in all the tournaments of chivalry. In the rising troubles of the Empire the services of the Duke of Bavaria recommended him to the confidence and gratitude of his *August* father (1126–1135). The Ghibeline[e] brothers rose in arms against the successful candidate, and Conrad accepted the title of King: their adherents were numerous in Italy and Germany, and they seduced the fidelity of Albert Archbishop of Mentz the master-mover in the election

---

[a] *I. om.* in . . . year   [b] *I.* proud Du   [c] *I. om.* (1126   [d] *I.* rural scene
[e] *I.* Swabian brothers

of Lothaire. "Embrace the Prelate (says Henry in a private letter) "but trust him not. Honey is on his lips; but his heart is filled with "the blackest gall." The sword of the Duke of Bavaria was not less useful than his political sagacity: and Lothaire stimulated his courage by exhorting him to march, like Judas Machabæus against the enemies of the Lord. Their power extended from the Upper-Danube to the lower Rhine: the artificial strength of the province had suggested a vulgar saying that the Dukes of Swabia never moved without a castle at their horse's tail; but their best reliance was on the firm and faithful support of the cities of Spires and Ulm. The reduction of these cities may be ascribed to the valour and conduct of the Guelphic prince: he surprized and vanquished his uncle Frederic who was advancing to the relief of Spires; and the walls even the buildings of Ulm were levelled to the ground by his irresistible assault. After a series of losses and defeats the Ghibeline brothers resigned their pretensions and implored their pardon, and Lothaire, without a rival, was acknowledged sole Monarch of the German Empire.

From Lothaire ii and his consort Richenza, the inheritance of Brunswick would legally descend to their daughter whose husband the Duke of Bavaria already enjoyed in right of his mother the Saxon patrimony of the house of Billing. Before his accession their Ducal office had been exercised by the Emperor himself: he now wished to devolve it on some faithful client; and what client could be more faithful than his adoptive son? The Guelphs by their female alliances[a] possessed a natural[b] command on the banks of the Elb and Weser: the genius of Henry the proud was equal to the double administration of Saxony and Bavaria: precedents might be found of a similar union; and the complaint of pluralities was over-ruled by affection and silenced by authority. Few Christian Kings in the twelfth Century could vye with the power and dominion of the Duke of Saxony and Bavaria, supreme Governor of the Danish, Slavic, and Hungarian borders; nor was a fair occasion neglected[c] of restoring an Italian province to the elder branch of the Marquisses of Este and perhaps of Tuscany. As the representative of the Cæsars, and the King of the Lombards, Lothaire ii contested the illegitimate donation of the Countess Matilda to the Roman Church: but he accepted, as a compromise the investiture of her patrimony which was widely diffused from the Adriatic and the Po to the Tyber

^{a} *II*. alliance ^{b} *I*. comm ^{c} *I*. om

and the Tuscan sea. An annual quit-rent of one hundred marks of silver declared the supremacy of the Pope, and the reversion was granted to Henry the proud on condition that he should swear fidelity and perform hommage to the Apostolic see. The fortunate Henry was now raised above the level of a subject: he is addressed by his august father as the presumptive heir of the Monarchy: and had Lothaire returned victorious from the Apulian war, a loyal diet might have gratified his wish in the election of a successor. The house of Brunswick might at this day be seated on the throne of Germany; and if the sense and spirit of the Guelphs had kept inviolate their hereditary domains, they might have rekindled the lustre of the Imperial crown, and asserted the prerogatives of Otho and Charlemagne.

While Lothaire ii accomplished the indispensable pilgrimage of his Roman coronation his son in law was left behind to maintain peace or to prosecute war in the Teutonic Kingdom. (1133). In a second expedition, the Emperor prepared to vindicate the altar and the throne from the schism of an Anti-pope, and the rebellion of a King of Sicily. The powers of Germany obeyed his summons (1136): fifteen hundred Knights and men at arms marched under the banner of the Duke of Saxony and Bavaria: Henry the proud appeared as the second person in the host[a]; the Italians beheld their future sovereign; and instead of the cold service of a vassal or mercenary he displayed the active consciousness that he was labouring for himself. On the first descent from the Rhætians Alps the great-grandson of the Marquis Azo stormed the castles of the lakes and mountains, visited the patrimony of his fathers, and granted as the superior Lord the fief of Este to his cousins of the younger branch. From Verona to Turin and from Turin to Ravenna he led or followed the Royal standard; oppressed the proud, interceded for the prostrate; and subscribed the feudal laws, which Lothaire promulgated in the diet of Roncaglia. After celebrating the festival of Christmas, the Emperor (1137) divided his forces: with the main body he marched along the Adriatic coast into the heart of Apulia, while Henry the proud passed the Apennine at the head of three thousand German horse. The Bishops and Magistrates who had been expelled by popular insurrection were reinstated by his arms: Florence was

---

[a] I. army

besieged, Lucca was pardoned: he inflamed the territory and burst
the gates of Sienna: the province[a] was reduced; and to his Saxon
and Bavarian honours Henry added a third title; of Duke of Tuscany.
As the Vassal of S[t] Peter he conducted Pope Innocent ii from the
Synod of Pisa to the siege of Bari, a march of five hundred miles
through[b] a schismatic people, an hostile country, a line of fortified
towns, and the garrisons of Normans and Saracens in the service
of Roger King of Sicily. The powers of Henry were inadequate to
the siege of Rome: but in his progress to the south, the Abbey of
Mount Cassin, the principality of Capua, and the Ecclesiastical
province[c] of Beneventum were compelled to acknowledge their
lawful Governors.[d] In the most perilous assaults his Germans were
guided, and rallied, and checked by the hand of a master, and against
the Pontiff himself his vassal presumed to vindicate the rights of
conquest and of the Empire. After the interview of Lothaire and
Innocent, the Teutonic army moved from the Upper to the lower
sea; the prudent valour of the Duke was equally conspicuous in the
successful sieges of Bari and Salerno, and he might claim an ample
share in the glory of his father, whose epitaph proclaims, that he had
driven the Infidels from the continent of Italy.

But these conquests were preserved only in the epitaph which was
speedily to be inscribed on the sepulchre of Lothaire. An Apulian
summer had melted the strength of the hardy Germans; their retreat
was spiritless and slow, and the Emperor who felt the decay of life,
had scarcely descended from the Alps when he expired (December[e]
3: 1137) in[f] a nameless village of Bavaria, leaving the possession of
Saxony and the hope of the Empire to his adoptive son. The claims
of Henry were founded on the superior advantages of merit and
fortune. But the epithet of the *proud* betrays a vice in his character
most offensive to a free-born people: and his monopoly of power
alarmed the jealousy of his peers who were apprehensive that the
Lord of so many provinces might subvert the balance of the constitution. The conspiracy of the Ecclesiastical and secular princes
was encouraged by the policy of Rome alike unmindful of ancient
injuries and recent services. The Guelphs who represented the
house of Saxony were sacrificed to the heirs of the Ghibelline or
Franconian line, and the ambitious Conrad who had abdicated the
Royal title again ascended the steps of the throne. (1138) An hasty,

---

[a] *I*. provinces *II*. provinces were   [b] *I*. from the   [c] *I*. state   [d] *I*. master
[e] *II*. Dec.   [f] *I*. at

irregular, meeting, anticipated the summons and the forms of election, but their choice was ratified by the consent of the nation. The Empress Dowager Richenza and her Saxon vassals were compelled to attend the Diet, and to renounce the cause of their own candidate. Even Henry himself desisted from the fruitless contest; and the Imperial ornaments which he had received from his dying father were delivered[a] with many a sigh, after many a delay, into the hands of a rival. A barbarous people is attached to visible symbols: nor could the Germans acknowledge their lawful Sovereign unless they[b] beheld the crown and scepter, the sword and the lance, which had been consecrated by ancient use and popular superstition.

But the pride and power of Henry could neither stoop to obey nor expect to be forgiven. The question was agitated whether two Dutchies could legally be vested in the same person, and it was soon decided in the negative by those who wished to oppress, and those who aspired to succeed the reigning Duke. Perhaps Henry might have been allowed to retain either Saxony or Bavaria: but his spirit scorned the ignominious option: his refusal was interpreted as a crime; by the sentence of revenge, envy and avarice assembled in a diet, he was stripped of *all* his possessions, and the head of the rebel was proscribed with the tremendous ceremonies which accompany the Ban of the Empire. The Dutchies of Saxony and Bavaria were respectively granted to their first and most powerful Vassals, to Albert the Bear Margrave of Brandenburgh and to Leopold margrave of Austria. Leopold was the half-brother of the Emperor, and as the father of Albert had married[c] a younger daughter of Duke Magnus he disputed with the Guelphs the inheritance of the house of Billing. Bavaria, from the impulse of fear or affection submitted on the first approach of the Austrians, and so rapid was the revolution, so universally was he deserted that Henry the proud, with only four followers escaped from the banks of the Danube to those of the Weser and the Elb. There indeed he made a vigorous and successful stand. Richenza embraced her daughter, and appealed to her fathers: the Saxons were impatient of a foreign master, the allodial estates of Brunswick and Luneburgh poured forth a swarm of soldiers; and no sooner had they recovered from their first astonishment than the Guelphic vassals of Swabia and Bavaria resorted in crowds to the standard of their Lord.[d] The son in law of Lothaire found an army, and that army had a General: his pride

---

[a] *I.* transmitted   [b] *I.* he   [c] *I.* marriage   [d] *I.* hereditary Lord

was stimulated by shame and resentment; the Bear fled before the Lyon (I use the quaint language of the age), and Albert of Brandenburgh sought a refuge in the court of his benefactor. Exasperated by this haughty defiance, Conrad himself marched against the rebel at the head of a royal army: but on a nearer survey of his strength the Emperor halted, doubtful of the event; a parley was sounded, a negociation was opened, a diet was announced. In a general perhaps a more impartial assembly, Henry prepared to defend the justice of his cause by arguments, as well as by arms, when, after a short illness in his thirty seventh year (1139) his worldly contentions were terminated by the hand of death. A death thus præmature thus sudden, thus seasonable might awaken suspicions[a] of prison: and these suspicions have been propagated and believed by the zeal of party: but they are not justified by the character of the times, of the nation, or of the personal adversaries of the Duke of Saxony. The Germans of the twelfth century might be often cruel, but they were seldom perfidious

---

After the decease of Henry (1139) the proud,[b] the eldest hope of the Guelphic line reposed on his only son, the third Henry, an orphan of ten years of age, who afterwards claimed the royal appellation of the LYON, either from his father, his[c] character or his armorial ensigns. The personal resentments which had been excited by the pride of the late Duke might be disarmed by the tender innocence of his successor: but political enemies, and some of them were Bishops, are rarely moved by generosity or compassion, and the young Lyon must have been caught in the toils had not his brave and faithful Saxons defended with persevering arms the child of the nation. His grand-mother Richenza, a woman as it should seem of sense and spirit possessed the affection, and assumed the regency of the Country: but her daughter Gertrude a blooming and impatient widow was too soon (1141) persuaded to form an hostile connection, and her second[d] marriage with Henry Margrave of Austria the brother and successor of Leopold appeared to countenance his[e] usurpation of Bavaria. Yet this alliance was productive of a truce and a treaty, and the son of Gertrude renouncing by his mother's advice the Bavarian Dutchy was acknowledged

---

[a] *I.* the suspicion   [b] *II.* Henry the Proud, (1139)   [c] *I.* from his
[d] *I.* mar   [e] *II.* the

as Duke of Saxony by the Emperor and the[a] Empire, a specious act which[b] ensured some years of domestic peace, without any material injury to the right of the minor. The education of Henry the Lyon was that of a Saxon and a soldier, to support the inclemency of the seasons, to disdain the temptations of luxury, to manage the horse and the lance, to contend with his equals in the exercise of military and even civil virtues, and to disguise the superior gifts of fortune, perhaps of Nature by the winning graces of modesty and gentleness. At eighteen[c] (1147) the Duke of Saxony, and as he still deemed himself of Bavaria was introduced at the diet of Frankfort into an assembly of men and princes; and the recent institution of Knighthood supplied the national custom of delivering the sword and spear to a noble Youth. Europe was then agitated by the preparations of the second Crusade: the Emperor Conrad and[d] the King of France had[e] listened to the voice of S[t] Bernard, and while the flame of enthusiasm was kindled in every martial bosom the spirit of Henry would prompt him to march and might lead him to perish in the dangerous adventure. But the northern states of Germany with their allies of Denmark and Poland preferred an holy Warfare less remote more beneficial and equally meritorious against the idolatrous Slavi of the Baltic coast; and one hundred and sixty thousand soldiers of Christ were speedily enrolled to convert or exterminate his enemies. The Duke of Saxony, with a numerous body of his vassals[f] and subjects unfurled the banner of the Cross; and, although this first campaign was neither successful nor glorious, he shewed himself on a splendid theatre to the Christians and Pagans of the North After the return of the Emperor from the Holy land, Henry the Lyon endeavoured without success to wrest Bavaria from his Austrian competitor; but while he was detained on the Danube, a messenger announced that Conrad had entered Saxony with a great army. "Command my vassals (replied the "dauntless chief) to assemble at Brunswick on[g] Christmas-day; they "shall find me at their head" The term was short, the distance was long, the passes were guarded; yet the Duke was faithful to his appointment. Disguising his person, with only three attendants, he darted swift and secret through the hostile country, appeared on the fifth day in the camp of Brunswick, and forced his Imperial adversary to sound a precipitate retreat. (1150)

[a] *II. om.* the   [b] *So in II; MS.* with   [c] *MS.* the eighteen   [d] *I. om.* and
[e] *I.* and th   [f] *I.* subject   [g] *I. om.* on Christmas-day

During the minority of Henry a valiant uncle, Guelph viii asserted in arms the cause of his nephew: but if the proscription of the father and the renunciation of the son were admitted as legal acts, he claimed Bavaria as the patrimony of his ancestors. His reasons were specious, his troops were drawn from the hereditary estates of Swabia and Italy; the subsidies of the Kings of Sicily and Hungary fomented the rebellion; he often prevailed in the battles and sieges of a ten years war; and if Guelph was sometimes crushed by the weight of Imperial power, his invincible spirit rose more terrible from every defeat. It was it one of these battles, that the contending shouts of *Hye Guelph! Hye Ghibelline!* produced the names of the two factions, so famous afterwards and so fatal in the annals of Italy. It was in one of these sieges, that a splendid example was displayed of conjugal tenderness and faith. As an offended Sovereign, Conrad had refused all terms of capitulation to the garrison of Winesberg: but as a courteous Knight he permitted the women to depart with such of their precious effects as they themselves could transport. The gates of the town were thrown open; and a long procession of matrons, each bearing a husband, or at least a man, on her shoulders passed in safety through the applauding camp. This moral story, which is told (if I am not mistaken) by the Spectator,[38] may be supported however by ancient evidence: but the wife of Guelph, the Dutchess Ita must be excluded from the honourable list; since her husband was actually in the field attempting with insufficient forces the relief of Winesberg. After seven campaigns (1140–1147) these destructive hostilities were suspended by the engagement of the rival chiefs in the second Crusade: but no sooner had they reached Constantinople, than Guelph, under the pretence of sickness, deserted the service[a] of the holy sepulchre. He[b] returned by sea; and, after a secret conspiracy with the King of Sicily, and the Senators of Rome, passed through Italy, descended from the Alps, and resumed an impious war, against the absent servants of the Cross. In the battle of Flocberg (1150),[c] against[d] Henry the son of Conrad, he strove to cover the retreat of his fainting troops: their heavy armour protected them from mortal wounds: but three hundred of his Knights were made prisoners; the treatment of their leader, a supposed captive, was debated in the Emperor's council, and his triumph was announced to the East and West. The captive alas was still free and

---

[a] *I.* holy service.　　[b] *I.* After a sec　　[c] *I. om.* (1150)　　[d] *I.* he str

vigorous and obstinate. instead of sueing for pardon, he stipulated a treaty (1151); and the favours of the court were the reward of his long opposition. But the mind of Guelph was still hostile to the persecutors of his family, and he joined with his peers, who refused to attend their unpopular sovereign, in his Roman pilgrimage.

After the decease of Conrad, the unanimous election of his nephew Frederic Barbarossa (1152) appeared to open a new prospect of concord and peace. The aspiring Monarch who already grasped the Kingdoms of Italy, embraced the Margrave of Austria and the Guelphic princes as his friends and Kinsmen, and sincerely laboured to terminate their Bavarian quarrel by an amicable compromise or a judicial sentence. The claimant pressed a speedy decision; but the actual possessor interposed so many evasions and delays, that the final settlement was postponed till the Emperor should return from his Roman coronation. Frederic passed the Alps[a] with a court and army not unworthy of the successor of Charlemagne. (1154): the uncle and the nephew were desirous of shewing their power and proving their loyalty, and the gallant squadrons that marched under the banner of the *Lyon* were equal in number to those of the Emperor himself. From the siege of Tortona and the camp of Milan in which the name of Henry is mentioned with honour, I hasten to the Vatican (1155). A transient harmony prevailed between the spiritual and temporal Monarchs of Christendom: but the Imperial crown had scarcely been placed on the head of Frederic, when the alarm-bell rang from the Capitol, and the august rites were disturbed by an assault of the Romans from the bridge S[t] Angelo. The Germans stood in arms, and battle-array, after a conflict of some hours, they slew or drove into the river a thousand rebels, without losing a single man; and the glory of the day was ascribed to the Duke of Saxony who fought in the foremost ranks. At his entreaty the Pope relaxed the strictness of Ecclesiastical discipline: the Emperor declared him the firmest pillar of his throne; and as Frederic was young and brave he might express the genuine feelings of affection and esteem. On his first entrance into Italy, Henry had exercised the rights of primogeniture and dominion in renewing the pre-cedings[b] grants to his cousins the Marquisses of Este. The son of Cunegonde was many years older than the children of Garsenda: and the descendant of the former was already in the fourth, while

---

[a] *I.* arm   [b] *II.* preceding

the posterity of the latter was only in the second, degree from their common parent[.]

Without involving Germany in a civil War, the restitution of Bavaria could no longer be delayed. The Emperor had pledged his word, the Diets had pronounced their sentence, and the performance was imperiously urged by the arguments, the services and the power of Henry the Lyon who[a] had received the hommage of the Nobles, and the oaths and hostages of the city of Ratisbon. A fair compensation however was yielded to his father-in law, the uncle of Frederic Barbarossa as soon as he desisted from a possession of eighteen years; and the agreement, which had been discussed in many private assemblies, was consummated by a public ceremony in the plain of Ratisbon (.1156) Henry Margrave of Austria resigned the seven banners or symbols of the Bavarian Dutchy into the hands of the Emperor who delivered them to Henry the Lyon: but the Guelphic prince immediately returned two of these banners which were used by Frederic in the investiture of his uncle. The Margrave of Austria was created an independent Duke; his territories, with the addition of three neighbouring Counties were for ever enfranchised from the dominion of Bavaria: the right of succession was extended to his female heirs, and his extraordinary privileges seemed to raise him above a subject of the Empire. By this act the circle of the Duke of Bavaria was circumscribed: but the Bishops of the province still attended his courts; and he stretched a real, or nominal jurisdiction over the three remaining Marches of Tyrol, Styria and Istria, as far as the shores of the Adriatic gulph.

After his return to allegiance Guelph viii had been content with the vague appellation of Duke till it was fixed an[d] realized by the acquisition of the Italian provinces in which his elder brother, his uncle, and perhaps his more distant ancestors had formerly reigned. From the liberality of his nephew Frederic Barbarossa (1153) he received the titles and possessions of Duke of Spoleto, Marquis of Tuscany, Prince of Sardinia, and Lord of the house or patrimony of the Countess Matilda against whose donation, as the heir of her second husband, he might lawfully protest. Her allodial estates on either bank of the Po, on either side of the Appennine had been dilapidated by waste and rapine: but the power of the Emperor, and the prudence of Guelph[b] reduced them into the form of a

---

[a] *I. om.* who . . . Ratisbon   [b] *I. a.* his Lieutenant   *I. b.* the Duke

well-regulated and productive domain. At the head of a strong army he performed the circuit of the Dutchy and the Marquisate; invested seven Counts with as many banners; garrisoned the Castles with his faithful Vassals, dictated his charters to *his own* Notaries, revived[a] in his Parliaments the authority of the Royal laws, and bridled, with a firm hand, the ambitious independence of the Tuscan cities. Pisa alone was a free and flourishing republic: but the Pisans, in every division, adhered to the Emperor: they respected the dignity of his Lieutenant; and it was only through the medium of their maritime conquests, that Guelph could assume the title of Prince of Sardinia

---

In the portraits of the uncle and the nephew, of Guelph viii, and Henry the Lyon a contemporary (1158) has presumed to borrow the pencil of Salust; and Radevic observes with satisfaction, that the sublime characters of Cæsar and Cato had been revived in his own age. Such indeed was the difference of the times and the countries that the comparison could not be very perfect or precise: the Cato of the twelfth Century could not be animated by the patriotism of a citizen and the philosophy of a Stoic: nor could the new Cæsar possess the universal genius which aspired and deserved to be the first of mankind. Yet the milder Guelph might be endowed with an amiable facility of giving and forgiving, while the more rigid Henry affected the useful virtues of patience, constancy and justice. The tone of panegyric, the propensity of human Nature, and the lives of the two Heroes will even prompt[b] a suspicion that their dissimilar merits degenerated into the opposite faults; that the boundless indulgence of the uncle was often careless and profuse; and that the inflexible severity of the nephew was not always exempt from harshness and pride. By those who may have seen Henry the Lyon he is described with black eyes and hair, of a majestic countenance, middle stature and muscular strength. His nobility, riches and power were extraneous accidents; but the Duke of Saxony and Bavaria stood near[c] thirty years (1150–1180) in a lofty station, the second only in dignity and renown to one of the most illustrious of the German Emperors.

In the rudeness of the middle Age the task of Government required rather a strong than a skillful hand. Servile labour and

---

[a] *I.* and revived   [b] *I.* jus   [c] *I.* twenty four years (1156–1180)

blind obedience were imposed on the people: the Clergy exercised a separate jurisdiction; and the nobles demanded only a judge and a leader, who himself followed the court and the standard of his supreme Lord. The provinces of Henry the Lyon extended to the foot of the Alps and the shores of the Baltic; his civil and religious duties transported him beyond the mountains, and the sea: yet[a] so rapid was his motion, so vigorous his command, that the absent prince was still present to the hopes of his subjects and the fears of his enemies. His valour had been signalized at Rome: in the second expedition of Frederic into Italy, the distress or at least the difficulties of the Emperor were relieved by the wellcome arrival of the Guelphic troops: The Tuscans and Swabians of the uncle, the Bavarians and Saxons of the nephew almost doubled his army: and their seasonable succour determined the success of the siege of Crema, one of the most desperate actions of the War of Lombardy. Henry visited Bavaria as often as he[b] was called (and he was often called) to redress injuries and pacify tumults; and the foundation of Munich is a flourishing proof of his discernment and munificence. But Henry kept his principal residence in Saxony: Brunswick was his capital: the statue of a Lyon commemorates his name and dominion; he fortified the city with a ditch and, wall; and, according to the balance of attack and defence, such fortifications might afford a respectable protection. The silver mines of[c] the Hartz which have been improved by his successors were already worked by his peasants, and in the scarcity of precious metals, this singular advantage rendered him one of the richest sovereigns in Europe. Jealous or envious of his greatness, the Ecclesiastic and secular princes conspired on all sides against the Saxon Duke: from Bremen and Cologne to Magdeburgh they successively fell before him; and a sentence of the Diet pronounced the injustice of their fallen arms (1168.). A King of Denmark was expelled by two competitors: he had acknowledged the supremacy of the Empire; and the eloquence of prayers or of gold prevailed on Henry to vindicate his cause. The Duke passed the wall of the limits (1156), pillaged the city of Sleswick and advanced fourteen days march into the Country: the approach of the Danes, the want of provisions, or the holy season of Lent compelled him to retreat, but the vassals of his Slavic subjects transported Sweno to the isles, and the fugitive was reinstated in a third part of his Kingdom. After the reunion of the Danish

[a] *I.* that   [b] *I.* it was neccess   [c] *I.* in

Monarchy, Henry contracted a public and private alliance with
Waldemar i: these ambitious princes had several personal inter-
views; and their confederate arms invaded by sea and land the
Slavic Idolaters of the Baltic coast.

The alternative of death or Baptism had formerly been proposed
to the Saxon ancestors of Henry the Lyon. He[a] presented the same
alternative to the Idolatrous Slavi, and a superstitious age applauded
the triumph of the Catholic Hero. At the end of ten years (1160–
1170) of an holy War, interrupted however by some truces, the
powerful and obstinate tribe of the Obotrites, who occupied the
present Dutchy of Mecklenburgh were reduced to accept the laws
and religion of the Conqueror. In the open field, in fair battle they
could not struggle with the arms and discipline of the Germans;
and such rude bulwarks as[b] the natives could raise were soon overthrown by the engines that had been used in the sieges of Italy.
But they often prevailed in the surprize and stratagems of excursive
hostility; and the traces of their footsteps were lost in the impervious
woods and morasses which overspread the face of the Country. On
the sea they were dextrous and daring pyrates; and unless the
mouths of the rivers were carefully guarded, they manned their
light brigantines, and ravaged with impunity the isles of Denmark
and the adjacent coasts. To the first summons, Niclot King or
great prince of the Obotrites returned an answer of ironical submission, that he would adore Henry, and that Henry, if he pleased
might adore his Christ; a profane mockery since the Pagans themselves reconciled the worship of Idols with the belief of a supreme
Deity. After the failure of a sally, the Barbarian upbraided the
effeminacy of his two sons: it was incumbent on him to upbraid
them by his own success; but he fell in the rash attempt; his head
as a grateful present was sent to the Danish King; and a third son
who served in the Christian army, applauded with savage zeal the
justice of his father's punishment. The two brothers, Pribislaus and
Wertislaus succeeded to the command, and, delayed[c] the servitude
of the nation. In the siege of their most important fortress the elder
hovered round the Saxon camp, while the younger assumed the
more dangerous task of defending the place. After refusing an
honourable capitulation, Wertislaus threw himself on the mercy of
the Conqueror who sent the Royal captive to Brunswick ignominiously bound in fetters of iron. A treaty soon placed him in

    [a] *I.* The sa   [b] *I.* and as   [c] *I.* for a while uphe

the more responsible situation of an hostage: the Obotrites, perhaps by his secret instigation, again rose in arms; but Wertislaus himself was the victim of rebellion, and as soon as the Duke of Saxony entered the Slavic territory, he shewed the King hanging on a gibbet. This act of cruelty may perhaps be justified by the maxims of war or policy: but if the Duke appealed to the recent massacre of Mecklenburgh, the rebels perhaps might plead the retaliation of some prior injuries. The fortune of the younger brother was less disastrous: after a brave defence of his country and his gods, Prisbislaus submitted, like Witikind, to the yoke of necessity, and embraced with apparent sincerity the religion and manners of the victorious Germans. Henry who esteemed his valour restored to the Christian vassal[a] the greatest part of the dominions which he had wrested from the Pagan adversary; and the reigning family of the Dukes of Mecklenburgh is lineally descended from Pribislaus, the last King of the Obotrites. The Slavic provinces beyond the Elb were possessed by Henry the Lyon, not as a portion of the Germanic Empire; but as an absolute and independent conquest which he alone had been able to atchieve. The Guelphic Duke was styled the Prince of princes, and legislator of nations, and the three new bishops of the Obotrites received from his hand their pastoral crosier, a prerogative which Rome had denied to the Emperors themselves.

I observe with a mixture of pain and pleasure the beneficial consequences of War[b] and persecution. The improvement[c] of Agriculture and the arts alleviated in some degree the servitude of the Christian proselytes. The Saxon castles of Henry and his Vassals were gradually incorporated into flourishing towns. By the institutions of Churches and convents the first rays of knowledge were diffused: and from Holland Flanders and Westphalia, the vacant desert was replenished with industrious colonies who have almost extinguished the manners and language of the Slavic race. The foundation of Lubeck is a mermorable event in the history of commerce. Near the mouth of the river Trave that falls into the Baltic that convenient station hade been discovered and used by some Christian merchants: but their infant settlement was repeatedly destroyed by fire, and the sword of the Pagans: and its progress was discouraged by the[d] jealousy of Henry the Lyon, till he had

---

[a] *I. and II.* vassals [b] *I.* servitude [c] *I.* introduction [d] *I. om.* the jealousy of

acquired (1157)[a] from his vassal the Count of Holstein the absolute and immediate property of the soil. Under the shadow of his power, Lubeck arose on a broad and permanent basis: the establishment of a mint and a customhouse declared the riches and the hopes of the Sovereign: the seat of a Bishop was transferred to the rising City; and the grant of a municipal government secured the personal, and prepared the political liberty of the burghers. The proclamation of the Duke of Saxony to the Danes, and Norwegians the Swedes and Russians discovers a liberal knowledge of the advantages of trade and the methods of encouragement. They are invited to frequent his harbour of Wisby with the assurance that the ways shall be open and secure by land and water; that they shall be hospitably entertained and may freely depart; that the imposition of duties shall be light and easy: that[b] their persons and property shall be guarded from injury; and that in case of death the effects of a stranger shall be carefully preserved for[c] the benefit of his heirs. The charter of Henry to the merchants of the isle of Gothland is still exstant, the[d] first outline of the maritime Code of Wisby as famous in the Baltic as the Rhodian laws had been formerly in the Mediterr[an]ean. This judicious policy was rewarded with a large and rapid encrease: but the arts of cultivation have far less energy[e] and effect than the spontaneous vigour of Nature and freedom. The commerce and navigation of his favourite colony encreased with her growing independence, and before the end of the thirteenth Century, Lubeck became[f] the metropolis of the sixty four cities of the Hanseatic league. That singular Republic, so widely scattered, and so loosely connected, was in possession, above two hundred years, of the respect of Kings, the naval dominion of the Baltic, the Herring fishery, and the monopoly of a lucrative trade. Novogorod in Russia, Bergen in Norway, London in England, and Bruges in Flanders were their four principal factories or staples. The large ships of their numerous and annual fleets exported all[g] the productions of the North; and sailed homewards richly laden with the precious commodities and manufactures of the southern climates. Lubec, an Imperial City, was soon enfranchised from the dominion of the house of Brunswick; but Henry the Lyon was revered as a founder; and his great-grandson Duke Albert[h] obtained from Henry iii (1266) the first English charter of the Hanseatic towns.

[a] *I.* om. (1157)   [b] *I.* and that   [c] *I.* from   [d] *I.* an ou   [e] *I.* vigour
[f] *I.* wa   [g] *I.* or   [h] *I.* Albert i

The baptism or the blood of so many thousand Pagans might have expiated the sins of the Catholic Hero: but his conscience was still unsatisfied, his salvation was still doubtful; and it was in the fairest season of victory and peace (1172) that he accomplished the fashionable devotion of a pilgrimage to the Holy land. His first attendant Pribislaus King of the Obotrites exhibited to the World his own faith and the fame of the Conqueror: the Bishop of Worms the Imperial Ambassador accompanied him as far as Constantinople: several eminent persons of the Clergy and Nobility imitated his example; their followers were numerous: a train of horses and waggons transported the bagage and provisions, and the camp was guarded by twelve hundred Knights or soldiers exercised in the use of arms. After leaving Ratisbon and the confines of Bavaria the Guelphic Prince was kindly entertained by Henry Duke of Austria: their former differences were buried in oblivion; and they mingled their tears at the tomb of a mother and a wife. Hungary was the Kingdom of a Christian ally; and the journey was continued by land and water from Vienna to Belgrade: the Duke preferred the more easy though perilous navigation of the Danube; but his progress was measured by the march of the Caravan which joined him every evening on the banks of the River. From Belgrade to Nissa he painfully[a] advanced through the woods and morasses of[b] Servia and Bulgaria whose wild inhabitants, the nominal subjects[c] of Christ and the Greek Emperor, were more inclined to claim the privilege of Rapine, than to exercise the laws of hospitality: they attacked his camp in the night; their feeble arms were repelled by his vigilance, and his genuine piety disdained the temptation of revenge. In the journey between Nissa and Constantinople, the way-worn pilgrims enjoyed the comforts of a civilized and friendly province, and the Emperor Manuel who had sent an embassy to Brunswick, received Henry as the equal of Kings. The wealth and luxury of the Byzantine court were ostentatiously displayed, and after the pleasures of the chace and banquet, the Saxon or his chaplains disputed with the Greeks on the procession of the Holy Ghost. The friendship of the two princes was confirmed by mutual gifts, and the Russian furs were perhaps overbalanced by the horses and arms, the scarlet cloth and fine linnen of Germany. A stout ship was provided for the Duke and his peculiar retinue, and the Voyage from Constantinople to St John of Acre on the coast of

---

[a] *I.* tr   [b] *I. om.* of Servia and Bulgaria   [c] *I.* servants

Palestine was disturbed by a storm, and is embellished by a miracle. After a short journey [by][a] land he reached Jerusalem, and was saluted in solemn procession by the Patriarch and the military orders. Henry the Lyon visited the Holy sepulchre and all the customary places of devotion in the city and country: the churches were adorned with the silver of the Saxon mines; and he presented the Templars with a thousand marks for the service of their perpetual crusade. Palestine applauded his liberal and magna[ni]mous spirit, and had he not been prevented by secret jealousies, his valour might have been felt by the Turks and Saracens.

In his return by a different way the Duke of Saxony was actuated by motives of convenience rather than of curiosity. He followed the sea-coast of Syria to the northward: from the harbour of Seleucia or S[t] Simeon the vessels of the prince of Antioch transported[b] him over the gulph to the river of Tarsus in Cilicia; and by this short passage he escaped the territories of a[c] faithless Emir. From Tarsus to Constantinople his march intersected in a diagonal line the extent of Asia minor: the mountains were of laborious ascent; the sandy plain was destitute of water and provisions; the more populous country was full of danger, suspicion, and Mahometan zeal: and Henry was the only pilgrim who, as a peaceful traveller, proceeded in safety through the Turkish dominions. But the Sultan of Iconium Kilidge[d] Arslan[e] ii of the race of Seljuk watched over his safety, embraced him as a friend, praised his Religion, and claimed, on the mother's side a distant affinity with the house of Saxony. His presents, in the Oriental style, were adapted to the accomodation and amusement of the noble stranger; a *Caftan* or flowing robe of silk embroidery, the choice for[f] himself and his followers of eighteen hundred horses, of whom thirty most sumptuously caparisoned were selected for his peculiar use; six tents of felt, and six camels to carry them; two well-trained Leopards with the proper horses and servants for that singular mode of hunting. Such gifts might be accepted without a blush; some precious gems, more precious for the workmanship than the materials might be honourably received from the Greek Emperor: but the Duke rejected the gold and silver of the Byzantine Court, declaring in a tone of lofty politeness that of such metals[g] his own treasury was sufficiently provided. The avarice of Henry was confined to the

[a] *II. supplies* by   [b] *II.* transplanted   [c] *I.* the   [d] *I. om.* Kilidge . . .
Seljuk   [e] *I.* Arl   [f] *I.* of eighteen hunte hundr   [g] *I.* treasur

acquisition of Holy relicks, and of these he imported an ample store from Palestine and Greece: but the reformation has annihilated their ideal value; the bits of wood or bone have been thrown away; and the empty cases alone are preserved for their curious and costly ornaments. The[a] Journey from Constantinople to Ratisbon and Brunswick is not marked by any accident or event. On his return home, after a year's absence (1173) the Duke of Saxony found his name illustrious, his servants faithful, his enemies silent, his dominions in a peaceful and prosperous state: and to the merits of his pilgrimage he would reasonably impute this fair prospect of public and private felicity.

Henry the Lyon was twice married: but his first wife Clementia of the Ducal house of Zæringen gave him only a daughter, who, after being long considered as an heiress was reduced to comfort herself on the throne of Denmark. His desire of male posterity, the wish of vanity and ambition at length determined Henry to solicit a divorce; some bar of remote and invisible consanguinity afforded the pretence: every defect of law or evidence was supplied by the all-sufficient oath of the Emperor: the sentence was pronounced (1163) by the spiritual court of Constance: and, without any stain on her own honour or her daughter's legitimacy Clementia found a second husband in the princely family of Savoy. The policy of Frederic Barbarossa had eagerly solicited the separation; he wished to connect himself and his friend with the most powerful and illustrious of our English Kings; and the Imperial Ambassadors demanded Matilda eldest daughter of Henry ii, for the Duke of Saxony and Bavaria. The fame of Henry the Lyon, of his birth and merit, his riches and dominion obtained from the father an easy consent and an ample dower: the Princess Royal of England embarked for Germany with a splendid train: the marriage ceremony was performed (1168) at Minden in Westphalia; as[b] the bride was no more than twelve years of age, the consummation was delayed but[c] she remained pregnant at the departure of her husband for the Holy Land. In his absence the Dutchess kept her court at Brunswick, and administered a nominal regency, under the guard and guidance of his most faithful servants: but her private virtues were her own; the[d] genuine lustre of meekness, purity and benevolence was[e] enhanced in the popular esteem by devout prayers, and frequent

<hr>

^a I. om. The Journey   ^b I. but as   ^c I. till after the pilgrimage of her husband to (replaced by but . . . for)   ^d I. and the   ^e I. wer

masses; and "she was beautified (says an historian with some ele-
"gance) by the comeliness of Religion" After the return of Henry
her riper age soon blessed him with a numerous progeny. Besides
two, or perhaps three daughters, Matilda became the mother of
four sons, Henry, Lothaire, Otho and William, from the youngest
of whom all the princes of Brunswick are lineally derived. By this
alliance they number among their ancestors the Plantagenets Counts
of Anjou, the Dukes of Aquitain*a* and Normandy, the Kings of
Scotland whose origin is lost in a Highland mist, and the Kings of
England the*b* descendants of the Saxon conquerors, who drew their
fabulous pedigree from the God Woden. The male posterity of
Henry ii soon*c* withered, almost to the root: the eldest son of the
princess Matilda was the presumptive heir of his*d* uncle King
John; and after the birth of Henry iii no more than a single life,
the precarious life of a boy, stood between his title and the throne
of England. According to the probable order of events the children
of Henry the Lyon should have reigned over us five hundred years
before the accession of the Hanover family.

The prosperity of Henry the Lyon had now reached it's summit;
and he might justly fear the revolution of the descending wheel. A
sovereign, the most opulent and fortunate of his age was reduced
to the state of a culprit, a suppliant, an exile; and the last fifteen
years of his life (1180–1195) exemplified the sage remark of antiquity,
that no man should be pronounced happy before the hour of his
death.[39]

To the resentment, legitimate or unjust, of the Emperor Frederic
Barbarossa the cause of his ruin must be ascribed. The long union
of these princes had been apparently cimented by a singular conformity: they had both passed the middle season of life without any
male posterity. On both sides they entertained and encouraged a
fond hope of surviving and inheriting; but amidst their professions
and professions, each was tempted to hate and despise the other for
indulging the same wish which he secretly cherished in his own
bosom. The Duke of Saxony was first awakened from this dream of
ambition; and his prospects were blasted by the birth (1165) of a
royal infant who at the age of four years was crowned King of
Germany and heir apparent of the Roman Empire. Such a natural

a I. om. Aquitain and   *b I.* wh   *c I.* was   *d I. om.* his uncle

event, such a just exclusion might disappoint a presumptive successor: but he could loudly complain of the avarice and treachery of his friend who grasped with disingenuous arts the inheritance of their common uncle. I have already enumerated the titles and possession[a] of Guelph viii, who reigned in the middle provinces of Italy, and aspired to found in its native soil a second dynasty of the house of Este-Brunswick. His designs were seconded by the fair promise of a son the ninth and last of his respectable name. The youth was educated in the arts of policy and war: during his father's absence beyond the sea or the mountains, he supported the weight of government: and his firm humanity protected the Italian subjects against the rapine and violence of the German soldiers. But this new Marcellus was only shewn to the World: The father had returned to the banks of the Danube apprehensive of losing the merit of a pilgrimage in the guilt of a schism: the son was permitted to lead his forces and to follow the Emperor: but Guelph ix perished in this unfortunate campaign, a præmature victim not of the enemy's sword, but of the[b] epidemical disease which swept away so many thousands at the siege of Rome. After this irreperable loss the Tuscan prince considered Henry the Lyon as the sole representative of the Guelphic name: a will was drawn in favour of his nephew; but as the Cæsar of the twelfth century was always prodigal, and often poor he required for the assurance of so many provinces the grateful retribution of a gift a loan or a fine. The demand could not be refused, but the ill-timed parsimony of the new Cato so long hesitated, that the peevish old man was offended by the hesitation which bespoke a doubt of his honour or the expectation of his speedy death. So fair an opportunity of supplanting his cousin was seized by the vigilant and dextrous Frederic: he stepped forwards with an immediate offer of the money: the offer was eagerly accepted: the pride of family yielded to the impulse of passion; and Guelph viii surrendered to a Ghibelline heir all his feudal and allodial estates in Italy and Swabia reserving only the enjoyment of them during his own life. The mortification of Henry was embittered by a tardy sense of his own folly: his wounded spirit was inflamed by fresh injuries and new suspicions; and he accused the Emperor of tampering with his servants to betray[c] their trust and deliver his castles, as soon as they should hear of their master's death in[d] his pilgrimage to the Holy land.

[a] _II_. possessions   [b] _I_. an   [c] _I_. de   [d] _II_. or

While this deep animosity rankled in his breast Henry the Lyon was summoned (1174) to attend the Emperor beyond the Alps and to draw his sword against the rebels of Lombardy. He disobeyed[a] the summons and his disobedience might be justified by the spirit of the times and of the constitution. The strict military duty of a vassal was confined to the defence of Germany and the Imperial coronation at Rome. At the coronation of Frederic, the Duke had signalized his valour and fidelity. In a second, *voluntary*, expedition he had freely exposed his person and his troops: but he could not submit to be the perpetual slave of obstinacy and ambition, to joyn in the oppression of an innocent and injured people, to persecute a Pope who was acknowledged by the greatest part of Christendom, and to prepare by the conquest of Italy the future servitude of his country. The complaint of age and infirmity may seem ill-adapted to the ripe manhood of forty six years: but a soldier might express no dishonourable fear of the climate the disease and perhaps the poison which had been fatal to the bravest of his nation and family. The government of the two great Dutchies of Saxony and Bavaria engaged the full attention of Henry the Lyon: and his Slavic labours in war and peace were an ample discharge of his debt to the Church and State. Such reasons are specious, such scruples might be sincere: but he debased[b] their value by offering to accept as the reward[c] of his military service the city of Goslar which would have given him the exclusive command of the silver mines. Frederic disdained to pay this exorbitant price, but he soon repented of his disdain: Milan had arisen from its ashes, the league of Lombardy was powerful and united; a ruinous winter was consumed in the siege or rather blockade of Alexandria; his Germans fainted his Bohemians retired, and his spirit was reduced to implore the aid of an enemy who smiled at his distress. The two princes had an interview at Chiavenna near the lake of Como: Henry was still cold and inexorable, and after trying every mode of argument and prayer, the Emperor, such is the meanness of ambition, threw himself at the feet of his vassal. The unrelenting vassal, with secret joy and apparent confusion raised his[d] sovereign from the ground; but he listened without displeasure to a[e] loud whisper of one of his attendants "Suffer, dread Sir, the Imperial crown to lye at your "feet; speedily it must be placed on your head" Some vague

---

[a] *I.* refused to obey [b] *I.* diminished their weight [c] *I.* price [d] *I.* him
(*replaced by* his sovereign) [e] *I.* the

professions of loyalty faintly coloured the denial and departure of the Duke, and the Empress who had been an indignant witness of the scene addressed her husband in the vehemence of female passion "Remember what has passed, and God will remember it "one day!" The admonition was needless, at least for the temporal Monarch. All his subsequent misfortunes, the failure before Alexandria (1175), the loss of the battle of Lignano, (1176) the ignominious treaty of Venice (1177) were imputed to the desertion of Henry the Lyon; and the Emperor accused him in a public assembly of an indirect conspiracy against his life and honour.

After the revolt of Italy the genius and fortune of Frederic still commanded the obedience of the Germans; and the ruin of the Guelphic house was the first aim of his policy and revenge. The pride of Henry has been arraigned for refusing an act of oblivion at the moderate price of five thousand marks of silver: but such a fine would have been a confession of guilt rather than a pledge of safety: and the artful Ghibelline after sacrificing his private resentments, would have maintained the character of an inflexible Judge. The*a* subjects of the Empire appealed to his tribunal: his duty compelled

[Other Drafts]

SECTION*b* 1

An English subject may be prompted by a just and liberal curiosity to investigate the origin and story of the house of Brunswick; which, after an alliance with the daughters of our Kings, has been called by the voice of a free people to the legal inheritance of the Crown. From George the first and his father the first Elector of Hanover we ascend in a clear and regular series to the first Duke of Brunswick and Luneburgh, who received his investiture from Frederic the second about the middle of the thirteenth Century. If these ample possessions had been the gift of the Emperor to some adventurous soldier, to some faithful client, we might be content with the antiquity and lustre of a noble race, which had been enrolled near*c* six hundred years among the princes of Germany. But our ideas are raised, and our prospect is opened by the discovery, that the first Duke of Brunswick was rather degraded than adorned

---

a II. om. these last twelve words; MS. ends abruptly. Remainder of f. 345 blank
b II. SECT. I (After full title)   *c* II. nearly

by his new title, since it imposed the duties of feudal service on the
free and patrimonial estate, which alone had[a] been saved in the
shipwreck of the more splendid fortunes of his House. His ancestors
had been invested with the powerful dutchies of Bavaria and
Saxony, which extended far beyond their[b] limits in[c] modern
Geography: from the Baltic sea to the confines of Rome they were
obeyed or respected or feared; and in the quarrel of the Guelphs
and Ghibellines, the former appellation[d] was derived from the name
of their progenitors in the female line. But the genuine masculine
descent of the princes of Brunswick must be explored beyond the
Alps: the venerable tree which has since overshadowed Germany
and Britain was planted[e] in the Italian soil. As far as our sight can
reach we discern the first founders of the race in the Marquisses
of Este, of Liguria, and perhaps of Tuscany. In the eleventh
Century the primitive stem was divided into two branches; the elder
migrated to the banks of the Danube and the Elb, the younger more
humbly adhered to the neighbourhood of the Adriatic: the Dukes
of Brunswick, and the Kings of Great Britain are the descendants
of the first; the Dukes of Ferrara and Modena were the offspring of
the second.

[Here the continuous draft had pp. 400-4 above: "This short
review. . . . the duty of gratitude."]

An old charter of the reign of Charlemagne and the beginning
of the ninth Century, has casually preserved the memory of
BONIFACE the Bavarian; the Count or Governor of Lucca, the father
of the Marquisses of Tuscany, and the first *probable* ancestor of the
house of Este and Brunswick. His name[f] and country, his title and
province I shall separately consider: and these considerations will
explain the state of Italy in his time and that of his immediate
descendants.

1. In the origin of human speech, a method must have been
wanted and sought and found of discriminating the several individuals of the same tribe, who were mingled in the daily offices even
of savage life. In every language the invention[g] of proper and
personal names[17] must be at least as ancient as the use of appellative
words. The truth of this remark is attested by the ancient continent

---

from India to Spain: from the lakes of Canada to the hills of Chili, the same distinctions were familiar to the inhabitants of the new World; and our navigators who have recently explored the islands of the South-sea add their testimony to the general practise of mankind. As soon as a new-born infant has enjoyed some days,[18] and begins to promise some years of life, he is distinguished as a social being from his present and future companions: the friends of the family are convened to gratulate the parents and to welcome[a] the stranger; and the festival has been usually connected with some religious ceremony, the sacrifices of the Greeks, Romans and Barbarians,[19] the circumcision of the Jews, and the baptism of the Christians. The primitive choice of every word must have had a cause and[b] a meaning: each name was derived from some accident or allusion or quality of the mind or body;[20] and the titles of the savage Chiefs announced their wisdom in council, or their valour in the field. Such in the book of Nature and antiquity are the heroes of Homer; and the happy flexibility of the Greek tongue can express in harmonious sounds all possible combinations of ideas and sentiments. But in the lapse of ages and idioms, the true signification was lost or misapplied: the qualities of a man were blindly transferred to a child, and chance or custom were the only motives that could direct this arbitrary imposition. The Christians of the Roman Empire were a mixture of Jews, of Greeks, and of Latin provincials: their profane names were sanctified by baptism; those of the Bible were respectable and familiar: and the casual affinity with an Apostle or Martyr might encourage the pious youth to imitate his virtues. But in the three centuries which preceded the reign of Charlemagne the western world was over-whelmed by a deluge of German conquerors. After their conversion to Christianity they long adhered, from pride or habit to the idiom of their fathers: and their Teutonic appellations with a softer accent and a Latin termination[21] were almost exclusively used in the baptism of princes and nobles.[22] Till the tenth or twelfth Century,[c] the Old, was abandoned to the Jews, and the new, testament to the people and clergy: Adam and David, Peter and Paul, John and James George and Francis[23] were neglected as unknown or despised as plebeian; and *Boniface* is the only name of Ecclesiastical origin, which the Chiefs of Barbaric race condescended to assume. This honourable exception may be justly ascribed to the fame and

a *I.* hai   *b* *I.* or   *c* *I. om.* Century

merit of St Boniface the first[24] Archbishop of Mentz or Mayence, the Missonary of Rome, the reformer of France and the Apostle of Germany, who lost his life in preaching the Gospel to the Frisians. He was born in England, and in his own baptism he had been styled Winfrid: but with the Episcopal character the Saxon received[a] the more Christian appellation of Boniface, which had been illustrated by a Martyr and a Pope. Of the Hessians, Thuringians, and *Bavarians*, whom[b] he reclaimed from Idolatry, many were ambitious even of a nominal conformity with their patron: and, from his age and country the Count[c] of Lucca might be one of the fortunate infants, who were baptized by the Apostle of Bavaria.

ii[d] The Christian priests who subdued the Conquerors of the West had inculcated the duty of damning their Idolatrous[e] ancestors, and persecuting their dissenting subjects. But the toleration which they denied to Religious prejudice, was freely extended to the institutions of civil or barbaric life. The Romans of Italy, the great body of the Clergy and people, were[f] still directed by the Codes of Theodosius and Justinian: the laws of the Lombards were promulgated for their own use; after the fall of their kingdom they still preserved their national jurisprudence; and the victorious Franks enjoyed the benefit, without imposing the obligation, of the Salic and Ripuarian Codes. The three great nations who successively reigned in Italy were every where mingled and every where separate: a similar indulgence was granted to the smaller colonies of Goths, Alemanni, or *Bavarians*; and so perfect was the practise of civil toleration that every freeman, according to his birth or choice, might embrace the law, by which he himself and his family would be tryed. In the acts, which have escaped to our time, Count Boniface and his descendants profess[g] to live according to the nation and law of the Bavarians: but this profession rather defines the origin of his blood, than the place of his nativity; and it is possible that some generations of his ancestors might have already[h] felt the milder influence of climate and religion. The name of the Bavarians first rises into notice amidst the dying agonies of the Western[i] Empire: but the tribe or troop of adventurers which assumed that[j] name soon swelled to a powerful Kingdom, and covered the province of Noricum from the Danube to the Alps.

[a] *I.* had received   [b] *I.* whom he proselytes   [c] *I.* Governor or Count
[d] *II.* 2.   [e] *I.* an   [f] *I.* was   [g] *I.* professed   [h] *I. om.* already
[i] *I.* Roman   [j] *I.* their

The vicinity of Italy provoked their desires; the alliance of the Lombards encouraged their hopes: they joyned the standard of the invader; and on the confines of Modena and Tuscany, the memory of their ancient settlement is not totally extinct. If we compare, however, the smallness of the Colony with the numbers of the nation, it may seem more probable that Count Boniface was born in Bavaria, perhaps of noble and idolatrous parents; and that his services were rewarded by Charlemagne with the government of an Italian province. The eye of the vigilant and sagacious Emperor pervaded the vast extent of his dominions: and the merit of every subject, in whatsoever country or condition he had been cast, was assigned to the station most beneficial for himself and the state. While the Kingdoms of the West obeyed the same sceptre, a native Frank might command on the banks of the Tyber; the frontiers of Brittany were guarded by a loyal Lombard and the Saxon proselyte would signalize his new zeal for Christianity against the Saracens of Spain. Charlemagne affected to consider all his subjects with the impartial love of a father: but he was not unwilling to transplant a powerful chief into a foreign soil; and he cherished a secret preference of the men and the nations whose sole dependance was on the royal favour. The Franks^a were jealous of the elevation of an equal; the Lombards might not easily forgive the triumph of a conqueror: but the Alemanni and Bavarians, who had been long oppressed, were devoted by loyalty and gratitude to the service of their benefactor.

iii^b I am ignorant of the parents of Boniface the Bavarian: of his character and actions I am likewise ignorant. But his official title describes him as one of the principal ministers and nobles of the Kingdom of Italy. The Latin^c appellations of Dukes and Counts were transferred with the latitude of foreign words to the Judges and leaders of the Barbarians: these different titles^d were applied to the same person or station: they varied according to the fashion of the age and country; and it was [not]^e till after the ninth Century that the Dukes, assuming a clear pre-eminence of dignity and power stood foremost on the steps of the throne. In the vulgar and legal idiom, the temporal peers (I anticipate the expression of more recent times) were styled *Princes*, and in their families the Kings and Emperors of the West might solicit a wife or bestow a daughter

---

^{a} *I.* Fren ^{b} *II.* 3. ^{c} *I.* appelati ^{d} *I.* persons we ^{e} *II. supplies* not

without degrading the majesty of their rank. It was at once their privilege and their duty to attend the national council: nor could any law acquire[a] validity or effect without the consent and authority of these powerful nobles. In their respective districts, of ample or narrow limits, each Duke or Count was invested with the plenitude of civil and military power, and this union of characters must be ascribed rather to the imperfection of the arts than to the talents of the men. They presided in open[b] courts of justice, and determined all civil[c] and civil causes with the advice of their plebeian assessors their *Scabini*, who were somewhat less illiterate than the Judge himself. At the Royal summons, they reared their standard, assembled their freemen and vassals, and marched at their head on every occasion of danger and honour. Such taxes as could be levied on a rude and independent people were shared between the supreme and the[d] subordinate chief, and there exists an agreement by which a Lombard Duke was permitted to reserve a moiety of the revenue for his public and private use. The prerogative of appointing and recalling these provincial magistrates was esteemed a sufficient pledge of their obedience; and the servants[e] of Charlemagne might obey without reluctance the first of mankind. But the memory of a favour was lost in the grant of an office; and the grant of an office was insensibly consolidated into the right of a freehold possession. The Counts and Dukes were amenable to the circuits of the *Missi* or Royal Inquisitors: but they were more able to maintain than willing to suffer an act of injustice: and it was gradually admitted as a constitutional maxim, that they could not be deprived of their dignity without a charge, a tryal and a conviction of felony. The founder of the Western Empire might sometimes reward the[f] son by the gift or the reversion of his father's province; a dangerous reward, which was often extorted from the fears rather than the[g] bounty of succeeding princes. They could not despoil the legitimate heir of his lands his followers, and his popular name; and it was deemed more prudent to secure the public peace by the[h] indulgence of his private ambition.

iv[i] The province entrusted to the vigilance of Count Boniface is one of the most fertile and fortunate spots of Italy. It is bounded

---

[a] *I.* acquired   [b] *I.* their open *in margin, but not in Gibbon's hand.*   [c] *II. corrects to* criminal. *MS. has* criminal   [d] *II. om.* the   [e] *I.* offi   [f] *I.* or encourage the   [g] *II.* from the   [h] *I.* gratifying (*replaced by* the indulgence of)   [i] *II.* 4.

by the rivers Magra and Arno, by[a] the sea and the Apennine[b]; and in the old days of independence this tract of country had been the debateable land between the Ligurians and Etruscans; till it was finally annexed by Augustus to the region of Etruria. The harbour of Luni is capable of sheltering the navies of Europe; the circumjacent hills of Carara have supplied an inexhaustible store of white marble for the noblest works of sculpture and architecture; and Lucca itself is situate almost on the banks of the Ausar or[c] Serchio, a river which flowing ten miles farther to the South is finally lost under the walls of Pisa, in the waters of the Arno. In the best age of the commonwealth, the sixth century of Rome, an allotment of sixty[d] thousand acres was divided among two thousand citizens who were soon associated with the ancient natives; but the colony of Lucca finally preferred the title and privileges of a municipal town. After suffering some injury from the Barbaric storm, Lucca appears to revive and flourish under the Lombards, as the seat of a Royal mint, and the metropolis of the whole province of Tuscany. The Republic, less extensive as it should seem, than the command of Boniface[e], now contains one hundred and twenty thousand inhabitants who are enriched by the exportation of oil and silk. But their riches are the fruits of industry, and their industry is guarded by liberty[f] and peace. I am inclined to believe that this small and happy community is more wealthy and populous than was formerly the Tuscany of Charlemagne; and, that,[g] even in its decay, the state of Tuscany still possesses more inhabitants and more treasure, than could have been found in the disorderly and desolate Kingdom of the Lombards.

From the interposition of Ildeprand[h] Count of Lucca, it may be suspected that at the time of his father's decease Boniface the second had not acquired sufficient strength and maturity for the vacant office. But these friends or rivals who had exercised the government of Lucca were soon superseded by the establishment of the lawful heir; and the youth approved himself worthy of his name and honours. The example and impunity of treason could never tempt his loyalty; and while the Empire of Lewis the pious was relaxed by weakness or agitated by discord, Boniface asserted the glory of the French, and the Christian, arms. He had been entrusted with the defence of the maritime coast and the isle of Corsica againt the

---

[a] *I. om.* by   [b] *I.* Ligurian   [c] *II.* and   [d] *I.* thir   [e] *I.* Leopold
[f] *I.* freedom   [g] *II. om.* that,   [h] *II.* Ildenrand

Mahometans of Africa, and his right to command the service of the neighbouring Counts, may entitle him to the appellation of Duke or Marquis of Tuscany which was assumed by his descendants. With a small fleet he sailed from Pisa in search of the robbers of the sea; they had vanished on his approach: he cast anchor on the friendly shores of Corsica, and after providing himself with expert pilots, he steered his intrepid course for Africa, and boldly landed on the coast between Carthage and Utica. The Aglabites who reigned in Africa as the nominal Vicegerents of the Caliphs were astonished and provoked by the insolence of the Christians whose valour had been hitherto confin ed to a*a*defensive war. Their camp was immediately surrounded by a formidable host of Arabs and Moors: five times did they mount to the assault: they were repulsed five times with slaughter and shame. The field was covered with the bodies of their slain; in*b* the hot pursuit some adventurous Franks became the victims of their own rashness: But the more prudent chief was satisfied with victory: he embarked the troops; the captives and the spoil, and returning in triumph to the port of Luni or the mouth of the Arno, left an example of successful enterprize which was long remembered by the Moslems of Afric and seldom imitated by the Christians of Italy. The birth character and adventures of the Empress Judith will be introduced with more propriety in the*c* story of the Guelphs: and I shall only observe that after his abject fall and fortunate restoration, Lewis the pious might still tremble for the safety of a beloved wife. She was confined in a monastery at*d* Tortona in the power of a rebellious son; and if the ambition of Lothaire was disappointed, the blood of a stepmother might be a grateful offering to his revenge. Boniface*e* with some loyal subjects perceived her danger and flew to her relief: by their celerity and courage, Judith was rescued from prison, and they guarded her passage over the Alps, till she met the embraces of an impatient husband. This gallant act which deserved the gratitude of the Emperor exposed the Count of Lucca to the displeasure of Lothaire who was still master of the Kingdom of Italy; and who denied the investiture of their fiefs to all the accomplices of the escape of Judith. Boniface retired to France, where his exile was alleviated by the most honourable employments: in the civil wars, after the death of Lewis, he might secure*f* his pardon, without

a *I.* th   *b* *I.* but in   *c* *I.* another   *d* *II.* of   *e* *I.* Count Boniface
f *I.* deserve

forfeiting his allegiance, and there is reason to believe that he ended his days in the Government of Tuscany. The sword of Chivalry was consecrated to the service of Religion and the fair: and the African Victor, the Deliverer of the Empress had fulfilled the duties of a perfect Knight.

His son and successor Adalbert the first has a more unquestionable right to the appellations[a] of Duke and Marquis of Tuscany. The title of Marquis or rather Margrave was introduced into Italy by the French Emperors: the Teutonic etymology of the word implies the Count or Governor of a *March* of a frontier province: his station gave him at least a military command over several of his equals: and in the division of the Monarchy, the number and importance of these hostile limits was continually multiplied. Yet the life of Adalbert is much less pure[b] and illustrious than that of his father[c]: either an historian was wanting[d] to his actions or his actions afforded no materials for history; and it is only by the glimmering of old charters, that, during thirty years his existence is visible. The decay of Genius and power in each Imperial generation had confirmed the independance of the hereditary Governors; till the failure of the eldest branch in the person of Lewis the second concluded a century of domestic peace, and opened an endless series of Revolutions. The election of the Kings of Italy was decided by the voices and by the swords of the factious Nobles: they chose the object the measure, and the term of allegiance and the name of the candidate whom they supported was a sufficient apology for every act of violence and rapine. A Pope of an active and ambitious spirit, John viii most bitterly complains of the two Marquisses or Tyrants of Lambert of Spoleto, and Adalbert[e] of Tuscany who were brothers in alliance, in arms, and in sacrilege. They solicited the aid of the miscreant Saracens, invaded the Ecclesiastical state, entered the City, profaned the Churches, extorted an oath of fidelity from the Romans, and dared to imprison the successor of S[t] Peter. After the departure of these public robbers, as they are styled without[f] much injustice by the Pontiff, he affected to display their guilt and his own danger: the sacred relicks were transported from the Vatican to the Lateran palace: the altar was clothed in sackcloth, and the doors of the temple were inhospitably shut against the devotion of the pilgrims. By the

---

[a] *II.* appellation   [b] *I. om.* pure and   [c] *I.* par   [d] *II.* wanted
[e] *II.* of Adalbert   [f] *I.* by the

apprehension of a second insult, John viii was driven from the Apostolical seat: he fled by sea to the usual azylum of France, offered the two Worlds to whosoever would avenge his quarrel, and in the synod of Troyes proclaimed the vices and pronounced the excommunication of the two Marquisses of Spoleto and Tuscany, the enemies of God and man. Some political events gave a new turn to his interest and language; *the most glorious* Adalbert and his wife (so[a] lately a robber and an adulteress) are recommended in his Epistles to the love and protection of the friends of the Church. From such invective and such praise, it might be inferred that calumny is a venial sin, or that every sin is obliterated by a reconciliation with the Pope. A Casuist less indulgent, I shall not so easily absolve the sacrilegious Marquis of Tuscany: he lived in an age of the darkest superstition, and his assault on the Vatican is truly criminal, since it was condemned by the prejudices of his own conscience.

In the dignity of Duke and Marquis of Tuscany he was succeeded by his son the second Adalbert who has been only distinguished from the first by the nice microscope of Chronological criticism. Such and so great was the pre-eminence of his wealth and power, that he alone among the princes of Italy was distinguished by the epithet[b] of the *Rich*; an epithet of ambiguous praise, since it expresses the liberality of fortune rather than of Nature. He[c] married Berta the daughter of Lothaire King of Austrasia or Lorraine who was the great-grandson of Charlemagne: a distinction rather honourable than singular: since many of the princes of the Age were descended by the females from the Imperial stem. His independence was built on the ruins of the Empire of Charlemagne: the failure of lawful heirs enlarged the scene of contention: the sceptre was alternately won and lost in a field of battle: and the Italians from a maxim of policy, entertained the competition of two Kings. The Dukes of Friuli and Spoleto long disputed the crown; and while Berengarius reigned at Verona, his rivals Guido and Lambert were seated on the throne of Pavia. These princes the father and son were the uncle and cousin of Adalbert: but[d] he supported or deserted their standard with licentious perfidy, and one of his attempts did not much redound to the honour or advantage of the Marquis of Tuscany. He marched to surprize Lambert who hunted

[a] *I. om.* so lately   [b] *I.* appelatio   [c] *I. om. this sentence*, He . . . stem.
[d] *I.* an

without suspicion in a forest near Placentia: but he forgot that discipline and sobriety are most essential to secret enterprize. The tents of the Tuscans, who deemed themselves secure of their royal game, resounded with drunken and lascivious songs; their intemperance subsided in sleep; and at the dead of night they were surprized[a] by the vigilant Lambert at the head of no more than one hundred horse. The Marquis who could neither fight nor fly, was dragged from his shelter among the mules and asses of the bagage, and his shame was embittered by the rude pleasantry of the Conqueror. "Thy wife Berta, said he had promised that thou "shouldst be either a King or an ass. A King thou art not, but[b] thy "second title I shall not dispute: and wisely hast thou chosen a "place of refuge among the animals of a similar species" The death of Lambert restored the Captive to liberty and dominion: but the character of Adalbert was still the same, and the state of Italy long fluctuated with the vicissitudes of his interest or passions. Berengarius who was oppressed by his service, sometimes accused and sometimes imitated the example of his ingratitude.[c] A new pretender, Lewis King of Arles was defeated, and dismissed, and recalled, and again established, and again dethroned, as he was the friend or[d] enemy of the Marquis of Tuscany. In a moment of seeming concord the new Sovereign visited Lucca, where he was entertained with the ostentation of[e] expence, which vanity will often extort from avarice and hatred. As Lewis admired the numerous and well-dressed ranks of the Tuscan soldiers, the attendance of the palace, and the luxury of the banquet, he softly whispered "This "Marquis is indeed a King, and it is only in a vain title, that I am "superior to my vassal." By the diligence of flattery or malice this whisper was reechoed: the pride of Berta was offended, her fears were alarmed; she alienated her husband's mind; he conspired with the disaffected nobles; and a hasty perhaps an[f] harmless saying deprived the unfortunate King of Arles, of the crown of Italy and his eyes. Adalbert the second died at Lucca in a mature age, and his real or imaginary virtues are inscribed on his tomb. We are solicited to believe, that he was formidable to his enemies, liberal to his soldiers, just to his subjects and charitable to the poor; that his memory was embalmed in the tears of a grateful people; and that the public happiness was buried in his grave. An epitaph is a

---

[a] *I.* themselves surprized   [b] *I. om.* but thy second title I shall not dispute:
[c] *I.* perfi   [d] *I.* an   [e] *I.* wh   [f] *II.* a

feeble evidence of merit; yet an epitaph on the dead may prove somewhat more than a panegyric on the living

Adalbert the second left behind him three children, two sons Guido and Lambert, the eldest of whom was acknowledged as Duke and Marquis of Tuscany, and one daughter Hermenegarda, who married and survived a prince of equal rank on the confines of Piémont. The pride and power of Berta were not impaired by her husband's death; and to her passions I should impute[a] an unequal contest with the Emperor and King of Italy who, by fraud or force, imprisoned the mother and her son in the fortress of Mantua. But her faithful clients refused to surrender the cities and castles committed to their trust: a treaty was negociated; the captives were released: their possessions were restored; and I must applaud the moderation, perhaps the courage of Guido who sincerely submitted to forgive and to be forgiven. Of the death of the Emperor Berengarius, who was stabbed in his palace by a private villain, Guido was neither the author nor accomplice[b]: but in the subsequent election his voice had a free and decisive weight: and the laudable motives of filial and[c] fraternal tenderness might prompt him to gratify his mother by supporting the claim of Hugh or Hugo Count of Provence her son by a former husband. The Marquis commanded the sea-ports of Tuscany: his sister an[d] active and popular widow could shut or open the passes of the Alps: a Royal pretender, Rodolph of Burgundy was chased beyond the mountains; by the unanimous choice of the Nobles,[e] Hugh was invited and proclaimed: he landed at Pisa: and the sons of Adalbert were proud to salute their brother as King of Italy. But this event which seemed to consolidate the fortunes was the immediate cause of the downfal of their house. The new Monarch insensibly betrayed a faithless and ungrateful character: his vices were scandalous, his talents mean, and if his ambition was sometimes checked by fear, it was never restrained by humanity or justice. The death of Berta dissolved the union between the children of her first and her second nuptials: the mild and moderate Guido expired in the prime of life: the[f] Dutchy of Tuscany was occupied by Lambert: but in an[g] hasty and indecent marriage with Marozia his brother's widow; the King of Italy trampled on the prejudices of mankind.[h] Hugh was already conscious of the public hatred and contempt: he might

---

[a] *I.* imputed [b] *II.* the accomplice [c] *II.* or [d] *I.* co [e] *I.* It
[f] *I.* Lamber occu It [g] *II.* a [h] *I.* his su

justly dread the courage, the ambition, the popularity of the Marquis; and his avarice was stimulated by the hopes of a rich forfeiture. Regardless[a] of a mother's fame, he invented or encouraged the report, that the obstinate barrenness of the wife of Adalbert had tempted that impious woman to procure and substitute two male infants whom she educated as her own: and the arbitrary sentence of the King who disclaimed Lambert[b] as a brother must have denied his right to the succession of Tuscany. Had this cause been argued before a tribunal of law and reason, the advocate for the Marquis would have pleaded the long and tranquil possession of his name and state; and have deprecated[c] the injustice of a charge which was not advanced till after the decease of both[d] his parents. The Orator would have painted in the most lively colours the absurdity of the supposition; the difficulty of fascinating the eyes and silencing the tongues of a jealous court; and the strong improbability that the Dutchess of Tuscany should have *twice* risqued the danger and shame of a discovery. He would have authenticated the circumstances of her pregnancy and delivery, and after establishing his defence on argument and fact he might have tryed to awaken the tender and indignant feelings of the Audience. Instead of such a tedious process the intrepid Lambert cast down his gauntlet and challenged to single combat the false accuser of his own and his mother's fame. The challenge was accepted; a champion arose; the lists were opened; and such was the goodness of his cause or the vigour of his arm, that the Marquis obtained an easy victory in the Judgement of God. Even this judgement was not respected by the Tyrant. Instead of embracing his genuine brother, he loaded[e] the conqueror with irons, confiscated his dominions, and deprived him of his eyes: while the nobles of Italy who so often resisted the execution of the laws, most basely acquiesced in this act of cruelty and injustice. The unhappy[f] prince survived his misfortune many years: but he was already dead to his enemies and the World In a civilized society, the mind is more powerful than the body: and the influence of strength or dexterity is far less extensive than that of eloquence and wisdom. But among a people of Barbarians, the blind Warrior, who is no longer capable of managing an[g] horse, or of wielding a lance must be excluded from all the honours and offices of public life.

---

[a] *Thus II. MS. has* A Regardless   [b] *I.* he   [c] *I.* er   [d] *I.* his
[e] *I.* cast   [f] *I.* unfortunate   [g] *II.* a

Such were the five descents in the Bavarian line, of the Counts of Lucca, and Marquisses or Dukes of Tuscany. The fourth generation of the posterity[a] of Boniface co-incides with the age of the Marquis Adalbert[b] who may be styled the third of that name, if we can safely rivet this intermediate link of the Genealogical chain. After a long hesitation and various tryals, the active curiosity of Leibnitz subsided in the opinion that Adalbert the third, the unquestionable father of the house of Este and Brunswick was the son of the Marquis Guido, and the grandson of Adalbert the second: and that his right of succession to the Dutchy of Tuscany, which had been superseded by his tender years was finally lost in the calamity of his uncle. In a mind, conscious of its powers, and indulgent to its[c] productions this idea struck a deep and permanent root: As an historian Leibnitz[d] was acquainted with the stubborn character of facts: as a critic he was accustomed to balance the weight of testimony: as a mathematician he would not prostitute the name of demonstration: but he affirmed that his opinion was *probable* in the highest sense and the philosopher could not patiently tolerate a Sceptic. These historical enquiries he compared to the labour of an Astronomer who frames an hypothesis such as can explain all the known phænomena of the Heavens: and then exalts his hypothesis into truth by exposing the errors of every other possible supposition. From the library of Hanover, the discovery was transmitted to that of Modena with an earnest desire of litterary or at least of political union; and the pedigree of Adalbert the third was ratified by the consent of Leibnitz and Muratori. Yet in this dark and doubtful step of Genealogy, impartial criticism may be allowed to pause: and even the silence of a contemporary writer may[e] incline the scale against many loose and floating atoms of modern conjecture. The first fifty years of the tenth Century are illustrated by the labour and eloquence of Liutprand Bishop of Cremona who exposes with a free and often satyrical pen the characters and vices of the times. He relates the death of Guido and the succession of Lambert, without insinuating that the former left any children, or that the latter was appointed guardian of their minority. He deplores the fate of Lambert without informing the reader of the escape of his nephew; by what resources of flight or defence, of prayer or negociation, he escaped the cruelty of the tyrant, and lived to propagate the glories of his race. The Marquis Otbert the undoubted

[a] *I.* descen   [b] *II.* d'Adalbert   [c] *I.* his powers   [d] *I.* he   [e] *I.* many

son of Adalbert the third, is honourably mentioned: and it might be reasonably expected that some hint should have been given of his lineal descent from the Tuscan princes whose names and actions had been already celebrated in the history of Liutprand. Nor can the order of time, that infallible touchstone of truth be easily reconciled with the hypothesis of Leibnitz. Guido Marquis of Tuscany, was the third husband of the insatiate Marozia: her second was killed in the year nine hundred and twenty five; and ten or twelve months must be granted for the shortest widowhood, the term of pregnancy, and the birth of her son Adalbert. No more than thirty six years after his birth, *his* son the Marquis Otbert appears in the World as a statesman and a patriot. Such a precipitate succession which crowds two generations into one is repugnant to the whole experience of ages: a fact so strange and improbable could only be forced on our belief by the absolute power of positive and authentic evidence.

In this enquiry I should disdain to be influenced by any partial regard for the interest or honour of the house of Brunswick: but I can resign without a sigh the hypothesis of Leibnitz which might seem to exhibit the *nominal* rather than the *natural* ancestors of the son of Guido. This doubtful*a* expression is not founded on the absurd and malicious fable that*b* the two last Marquisses of Tuscany were stolen in their infancy from an obscure and perhaps a plebeian, origin: Berta was their genuine mother, and their pedigree would not be tainted with suspicion, if the right of the father could be ascertained with the same clearness and certainty. But in these barbarous times, the valour of the men appears to have been maintained with more high and jealous care than the chastity of the women: and such was the peculiar infelicity of the Marquis Guido that his wife, his mother and his two grand-mothers are all accused in their respective generations, of a slight or scandalous deviation from the line of virtue. In the Pontifical epistles, the wife of Adalbert i is branded with the opprobrious name of Adulteress; and without insisting on*c* the Pope's infallibility, it may be fairly urged, that as the character of a public robber was applied to the sacrilegious enemy of Rome, the vices of Rotilda must have afforded some ground or colour for private reproach The mother of Berta, the famous Valdrada, long fluctuated between the state of a wife, and the shame of a concubine. She might be innocent in the judgement

a I. suspicion (*replaced by* doubtful expression)   *b* I. were suppos   *c* I. of

of conscience and reason: but her pretended marriage with Lothair King of Lorraine was[a] repeatedly annulled by the sentence of the Roman[b] Pontiff. By an obstinate resistance her fame might have been preserved: a false and fruitless penitence could only aggravate her sin: and she became alike guilty in the eyes of the Church and the[c] public, when she continued to dwell in the embraces of her lover, after a lawful Queen had been restored to the honours of his throne and bed. The pleasures of Berta were subservient to her ambition, and Adalbert ii[d] appears to have been endowed with the patient virtues of an[e] husband. By the liberal freedom with which she imparted to the nobles of Tuscany every gift in her power to bestow the Dutchess secured their grateful attachment in the hour of danger: and at the age of threescore[f] she might be justly vain, that her favours were precious, her lovers fond, her friends and clients still mindful of their past obligations. As the infidelity of Hermenegarda could sully only the blood of another family it is almost needless to mention that the daughter of Berta most faithfully copied the example of her mother. But the satyrical eloquence of Liutprand is unable to paint the vices of Marozia wife of the Marquis Guido; from her early youth, exclaims the Bishop she had been inflamed by all[g] the fires of Venus: and again and[h] again did she exact from her lovers the payment of their debts. Her family was powerful at Rome: by the corruption of Marozia, of her mother, and of her sister, the Church and state were polluted[i] and oppressed: their favourites and their[j] children were successively promoted to the throne of St Peter: and in the spiritual Babylon, the city of the seven hills, a more inquisitive age would have detected the scarlet whore of the Revelations. The son of Marozia the grand-son of Berta, the[k] great-grandson of Rotilda might be perplexed in the discovery or the choice of his true progenitors.

The Hypothesis that Adalbert iii was the son of the Marquis Guido will not endure the test of a critical enquiry: but I am disposed to embrace the general opinion of Leibnitz and Muratori, and to believe with them that the families of Este and Brunswick are descended from a younger branch of the house of Tuscany. A charter commemorates the name of Boniface son of Adalbert i and brother of Adalbert ii: his existence is certain; his marriage

[a] I. had   [b] I. Church   [c] II. of the   [d] II. the Second   [e] II. a
[f] I. om. score   [g] So II; MS. the all the   [h] I. om. second and again
[i] I. ins   [j] I. bastards   [k] II. and the

probable, and according[a] to the custom of nations, the respectable name of a grand-father and uncle would be naturally repeated in the person of his son. In the last years of the ninth Century we may fix the birth of Adalbert iii, who will stand in the corresponding degree as first[b] cousin to the Marquis Guido: the order of Nature will be restored, and, in the succeeding generation a sufficient space will be left for the growth and maturity of Otbert 1. By this early separation from the original stem we avoid the more scandalous vices of Berta and Marozia. The silence of Liutprand will no longer surprize or embarass the Critic: Boniface and his son Adalbert iii[c] were neither the Sovereigns nor the heirs of Tuscany: their private[d] fortunes were less splendid and more secure than those of the Marquisses their elder kinsmen; and their names, not conspicuous perhaps by crimes or virtues might escape the memory or the pen of the general historian. As[e] the objections diminish the presumptive proofs of a connection between the houses[f] of Tuscany and Este leave[g] a deeper impression on the mind. The repetition of the name of Adalbert has already been noticed as a family-feature. In the Kingdom[h] the name of Adalbert was less rare however than the title of Marquis of such recent use and such local application, but which was uniformly used from the tenth to the fifteenth Century as their hereditary and proper style by the princes of Este. The military governors who commanded in the Alpine or Greek limits do not suggest any traces of conformity, and our ignorance of the province which was ruled by Adalbert iii and his immediate descendants will be tempted to believe that the vague appellation of Marquis which was common to all, might be cherished by their vanity as a perpetual attribute, and memorial of the longlost dominion of Tuscany. But the circumstance of the clearest and most substantial presumption arises from the rent-roll of their ancient estates which were spread over the heart of Tuscany, the Counties of Lucca and Luna, and even the isle of Corsica a remote dependance of the Government of Boniface ii.[i] Tradition has preserved the name and limits of the *Terra Obertenga*, so often cited in old charter[j]; the[k] lands of the Marquis Otbert 1: and if he received them from his father, it will not be difficult to suppose that they were originally granted to Boniface iii as the portion or patrimony

---

[a] *I.* the re   [b] *I. and II.* the first   [c] *II.* the Third   [d] *I.* po
[e] *I.* In   [f] *I.* families   [g] *I.* acquire po   [h] *MS. has insertion mark here but no insertion.*   [i] *I.* th   [j] *II.* charters   [k] *II.* as the

of a younger brother. The perfect and easy coalition of the Marquisses of Tuscany and Este is resisted[a] only by a single obstacle, and the resistance is less insuperable than it may appear at the first glance: the former adhered to the law and nation of the Bavarians, while[b] the nation and law of the Lombards was professed by the latter. But we must not forget that in the barbaric Jurisprudence of Europe, a national character might be either conveyed by descent or adopted by choice; and that each family, each individual might select and renounce the name and institutions of these political sects. The Bavarians, a minute colony, were almost invisible in the mighty kingdom of the Lombards: their decreasing numbers could not secure a regular supply of Judges and witnesses: an Italian prince would be desirous of obliterating the remembrance of his foreign origin; and the smaller rivulets were gradually lost in the master-stream. Such a change of law and nation[c] is agreable to reason and practise: but in this particular instance, it may not be presumed, it cannot be proved: and the objection must be allowed to counterbalance some grains of probability in the opposite scale.[d]

17. Ὁι ανωνυμοι εισιν μουνοι ανθρωπων. των ἡμεις. ιδμεν. Herodot. iv. 18 a Libyan tribe Atlantes? corrupt or uncertain. See Valkenaer[40] ad locum.-New Holland.

18. Ἀμφιδρομια. 5th day. name day the 10th. Meursius has exhausted in Græcia Feriata. Opp. Tom iii. p 793-796. quotes Aristophan. and Schol. Isæus, Demosthenes, Suidas Hesychius, Harpocration. the Author of M. E. some I have read all possess, yet he is my benefactor.[41]

19. Macrobius. Sat. L i. C 16. Dea Nundina, dies lustricus ninth for boys. 8th for girls.

20. Grotius ad. Lucam. 1. 59. The father chose the name[42]

21.[e] L'Abbé B. (Voyage d'Annacharis raises a foolish laugh. (C. 66). proper from appelative, but why these read from Plato (in Cratyl) to Desbrosses Gebelin. much learning. more fancy, some truth.[43]

22. Before the conquest all our Kings, Saxon. since of thirty three, two and twenty German[f] eleven foreign, all the women.

23. St Francis of Assise son of a Merchant, his first name John. from his fluent French language the boy was surnamed Franciscus the little Frenchman. Fleury. Tom xvi. p 205. From thence to Kings, millions &c. Voltaire[g] need not have been scandalized.

24. St Boniface martyr. 11 June 755. born at Crediton or Kirton in Devonshire in 680. For his life see Baronius, Pagi, Fleury.

---

[a] I. resistance   [b] II. whilst   [c] I. changes of law and national   [d] Next sentence originally continued without a break, but Gibbon drew a line and wrote in margin the label SECTION ii.   [e] I. om. note 21. Gibbon changed numbers of original 21-3 to 22-4 when he inserted the new note.   [f] I. Germany   [g] I. From

Section ii

A judicious critic may approve the Tuscan descent of the families of Este and Brunswick: but a sincere historian will pronounce that the Marquis Adalbert is their first unquestionable ancestor; that he flourished in Lombardy or Tuscany in the beginning of the tenth Century: that his character and actions are buried in oblivion; and that his name and title alone can be placed at the head of an illustrious pedigree.

This pedigree is animated by his son the Marquis Otbert i, and his life is connected with the revolutions of Italy. If the records or the times were more numerous they might confirm the probability of his descent from the Marquisses of Tuscany, since the earliest date of his name and honours coincides with the fall of their oppressors and the first year or even month of a new reign. The tyrant Hugh had fled beyond the Alps, loaded with the curses and treasures of the Italians: his son[a] Lothair a feeble youth had passed away like a shadow: and after a vacancy of twenty four days, the Marquis Berengarius, grandson of[b] the Emperor of[c] the same name was exalted to the throne. A grant of four castles was made to the Bishop of Modena and in the original deed of gift, the new monarch is pleased to declare, that the advice and request of his trusty and well-beloved the Marquis Otbert had moved him to this act of liberality or devotion. His power at court may be ascribed to the recent merits of the election; and the advocate on the behalf of others would not be mute or unsuccessful in his own cause. Of the favours which he received, or the services which he performed I am alike ignorant: but at the end of nine years the counsellor and favourite of Berengarius was transformed into a fugitive and a rebel; who escaped to the Saxon court, inflamed the ambition of Otho, and soon returned with an army of Germans[d] to dethrone a sovereign, perhaps a benefactor of his own choice. His conduct appears at the first glance to be tainted with ingratitude and treason, and his guilt may be aggravated by the reflection, that he[e] imposed a foreign yoke on his country, and prepared the long calamities of tyranny and faction. At the distance of eight[f] centuries I shall not vindicate the pure and rigid patriotism of the father of the house of Brunswick. According to the experience of human nature we may calculate an[g]

[a] *I.* L   [b] *I. and II.* to   [c] *I.* Berengarius   [d] *I.* strangers   [e] *I.* Otbert
[f] *I.* thr   [g] *II.* a

hundred, nay a thousand chances against the public virtues of a statesman: the*a* Marquis viewed the King of Italy first as an equal and afterwards as an enemy: and in the loose governments of the feudal system, the duties of allegiance were proudly violated by the members of an armed and lawless aristocracy.

Yet our imperfect view of the history of the times will afford some apology and may allow some praise for the flight and rebellion of the*b* Marquis Otbert. 1. The patriot who in the cause of political freedom is false to gratitude and honour offends against the natural feelings of mankind, but if those feelings are violated by a Tyrant, they applaud the sword of the rebel, or even the dagger of the conspirator.[44] Berengarius was a bad subject and a worse prince: and the most opposite vices were reconciled in the dissolute and flagitious character of his wife Villa. From the revenge or justice of his predecessor he had been saved by the blind humanity of Lothaire the son of Hugh who cherised the faithless enemy of his crown and life. His suspicious death was followed by the persecution of his widow Adelais the sister of the King of Burgundy. At the age of eighteen a beautiful and innocent princess was stripped of her lands*c* her jewels, and her apparel, exposed to the brutal repetition of blows, and insults, and cast into a subterraneous dungeon, where she endured above four months the last extremities of distress and hunger A pleasing and pathetic tale might be*d* formed of her miraculous escape with a damsel and a priest; of their concealment among the rushes of the lake Benacus, where*e* they were supported many days by the charity of a fisherman: and of her rescue by a generous Knight who conducted the princess to his impregnable fortress of Canossa; and defied the vengeance of the King of Italy. The romance would conclude with the arrival of a victorious lover, a royal deliverer: the nuptials of Otho and Adelais were celebrated at Pavia, and her singular adventures were a prelude to the future glories of the Empress and the Saint. The arms of Otho had been seconded by the revolt of the Italians, but in this revolt the name of Otbert is not mentioned and we should rather accuse than admire the patient loyalty of the Marquis. Before he renounced his obedience and*f* gratitude the unrepenting Tyrant had accomplished the measure of his sins; the church and state, the rich and the poor were the indiscriminate victims of the cruelty and avarice of

---

a *I.* he   *b* *II. om.* the   *c* *II.* land   *d* *I. om.* be   *e* *I.* and where
f *I. om.* and gratitude

Berengarius. 2. In his first victorious expedition the prudence or magnanimity of Otho had declined the rigour of absolute conquest, and was content to be styled the protector of an injured nation. A prostrate enemy was spared and forgiven: after waiting three days before the palace-gates, Berengarius was admitted to the royal presence and the golden sceptre of the Kingdom of Italy was again delivered to his hand[a]. But he pronounced an oath of fidelity, a solemn engagement, that he would be ready in council and in the field to obey the commands of his sovereign; and that he would govern his people with more equity and mildness than he had hitherto[b] displayed. By this unequal treaty the right of Otho was established to judge and punish the crimes of his feudatory: the Marquis Otbert is no longer a rebel who solicits[c] the aid of a foreign prince; and all the Vassals of Italy might lawfully appeal from their immediate, to their supreme, Lord. 3. The appeal was urged by the most respectable deputies of the Church and State, and their voice was the voice of[d] the kingdom of Italy. The Roman Pontiff dispatched his Apostolical legates to complain of the temporal and spiritual wrongs which St Peter and St Paul had long suffered from the tyranny of Berengarius. An Archbishop of Milan stood[e] before the King of Germany to deliver the sentiments of the oppressed Clergy: the *Illustrious* Marquis Otbert (I copy the words of the historian)[45] spoke in the name and in the cause of his peers; and the powers of these Ambassadors were ratified by the secret letters and messengers of almost all the Counts and Bishops of Italy. 4. In the second, as in the first expedition, Otho yielded to the call of justice and freedom: but in the passes of the Trentine Alps his march was stopped a day and a-night by the seeming opposition of sixty thousand Italians. The suspicions of Berengarius[f] had been appeased by their ready obedience to his summons, and in this martial assembly, they were the masters of the throne and the representatives of the people. A temperate negociation was however proposed: the timely abdication of the father might have softened their hatred; and they had consented to acquiesce under the government of his son Adalbert. The obstinate despair of the old King provoked them to abjure his name and family: they[g] sheathed their swords and opened their gates: an[h] hundred banners waved round the Royal standard of Saxony: the deliverer was

---

[a] *II*. hands   [b] *I*. th   [c] *I*. implores   [d] *I. om*. of the kingdom
[e] *I*. appeared   [f] *I*. the Tyrant   [g] *I*. their sw   [h] *II*. a

saluted King of Italy, and he[a] received the *Iron crown* in the Cathedral of Milan. The Pope confirmed the revolution, and after a vacancy of twenty eight years, the title of Emperor of Romans[b] was[c] revived in the person of Otho the great. 5. The benefits or mischiefs which might arise from the union of Italy and Germany could be decided only by experience: nor could the foresight of the Marquis Otbert anticipate the experience of three hundred years. It was enough for a mortal statesman to obey the wishes, and consult the happiness of the present generation by placing in the hands of wisdom and power, the sceptre of the Italian Kingdom.

In one of the annual Odes, which still adorn or disgrace the birth-days of our British King, the Laureat with some degree of courtly and even poetic art, has introduced the founder of the Brunswick race.

> When Otbert left th'Italian[d] plain
> And soft Ateste's green domain,
> Attendant on Imperial sway
> Where fame and Otho led the way,
> The Genius of the Julian hills,
>   (Whose piny summits nod with snow,
> Whose Naiads pour their thousand rills
>   To swell th'exulting Po)
> An eager look prophetic cast,
> And hail'd the Hero as he past

By a lofty prediction of fame and Empire, this[e] benevolent Genius exalts the courage of the Hero, and displays the[f] future greatness of his posterity from the nuptials of Azo to the succession of British Kings.

> Proceed. Rejoyce. Descend the vale
> And bid the future Monarchs hail!
>   Hail, all hail, the Hero cry'd
> And Echo on her airy tide
> Pursu'd him murmuring down the mountain's side

I shall not presume to enquire whether such distinct and distant views of futurity may not surpass the prescience of a mountaini[g]

---

[a] *I.* Otho   [b] *II.* the Romans   [c] *I.* war   [d] *II.* the Italian
[e] *I.* the   [f] *I.* in   [g] *II.* mountain

God: but I am compelled to vindicate my own accuracy by observing some Geographical and historical errors of the mortal bard. The possessions of Otbert were not situate in the Venetian plain but among the mountains of Tuscany, and we shall soon discover that the green domain of Este or Ateste was acquired by the marriage of his grandson. In his attendance, where fame and Otho led the way, he would have passed not the Julian but the Rhætian Alps: he must have followed the high road of Verona and Trent, the great and customary passage between Italy and Germany. The name of the Julian Alps is confined to a low range of hills soon bounded by the north-eastern extremity of the Adriatic, and which opposed in the tenth Century a feeble barrier*a* to the inroads of the wild Hungarians. The streams which issue from those hills are lost in the sea, or intercepted by the neighbouring rivers and of their thousand rills not a drop can be mingled with the waters of the Po. Even the motive and the date of the passage of Otbert are wantonly corrupted. The patriot entrusted with the cause of Italy is degraded into an adventurer who seeks his fortune in the Emperor's service: and he bids an everlasting farewell to the country, which he was most impatient to revisit and deliver. The poet may deviate from the truth of history; but every deviation must*b* be compensated by the superior beauties of fancy and fiction

Among the followers of his triumphal car, the servants of his fortune, Otho could distinguish the patriot fugitives, who had risqued their lives and estates to*c* assert his rights and the freedom of*d* Italy. The most illustrious of these the Marquis Otbert was rewarded with riches and honours, and there is some reason to believe that his vague title was applied to the province of Liguria, which according to the Roman Geography included the cities of Milan and Genoa. But the descendant of Adalbert 1 might advance an equitable though not a legal claim to the Dutchy of Tuscany: and some suspicion will taint the pedigree of a favourite who neglects to ask, or fails to obtain the restitution of a patrimonial dignity. Our surprize will be encreased and removed by the discovery of the same fact. Hugh King of Italy had granted the Tuscan Dutchy first to his brother, and then to his bastard; it was inherited by the son of that bastard; and succeeding Monarchs, the tyrant Berengarius, and the German Otho respected the possession of these fallen and unpopular princes. So strange an indulgence

a *I.* inroad t   *b* *II.* ought to   *c* *I.* in his   *d* *I.* of Liberty

must have been founded on some secret but powerful motive, and the same motive, could it now be revealed might explain either the modest indifference or the unavailing request of Otbert himself. But the Marquis (shall I say?) of Liguria was invested with an office, far more worthy of his abilities, and far more expressive of the royal confidence: The[a] Count of the sacred palace was the prime minister of the Kingdom of Italy, and it was observed in Classic style that the Dukes, the Marquisses and the Counts submitted to the pre-eminence of his Consular Fasces. In an age when every Magistrate was a noble and every noble was a soldier, the Count Palatin often assumed the command of armies; but in his proper station he represented the judicial character of the Emperor;, and pronounced a definitive sentence as the Judge of all civil and criminal appeals. The City of Pavia, and the Castle of Lomello were his ordinary residence: but he visited the provinces in frequent circuits, and all local or subordinate jurisdiction was suspended in his presence. This important office was exercised above twelve years by the Marquis[b] Otbert: the public acts (the few that have escaped) announce the proceedings of his tribunal, at Lucca, Verona &c; and he continued to deserve and enjoy the favour of the Emperor. If in[c] the decline of life the lassitude of Camps and Courts had tempted him to seek a cool and independent solitude, I should praise[d] the temper of the philosopher: but the firmest minds are enslaved by the prejudices of the times, and the retreat of Otbert was inspired by the basest superstition. Under the monastic habit in a Benedictine[e] abbey which he had richly endowed, the Marquis laboured to expiate the sins of his secular life. Pride[f] and ambition are the vices of the World: humility is the first virtue of a monk; and the descendant of princes, the favourite of Kings, the Judge of nations was conspicuous among his brethren in the daily labour of collecting and feeding the hogs of the monastery. His sanctity was applauded: but if he listened to that applause, the penitent was entangled in a more subtle snare of the Dæmon of Vanity

After the resignation of the Count Palatin his office was given to favour or merit: but his patrimonial estates were inherited by the Marquis Otbert, who can only be distinguished by the epithet of

---

[a] *I.* As Count   [b] *I.* D   [c] *I.* the l   [d] *I.* applaud   [e] *I.* a convent (*replaced by* a Benedictine abbey)   [f] *I. om.* Pride and ambition are the vices of the World:

the second from the similar name and title of his father. The life of the second Otbert was tranquil or obscure: he was rich in lands, in vassals, and in four valiant sons, Azo, Hugh, Adalbert, and Guido: but their valour embittered his old age and involved the family in treason and disgrace. The reigns of the three Otho[s],[a] a period of forty years, had been a transient season of prosperity and peace. But on the failure of their direct line, the Germans maintained the[b] right of conquest, the Italians revived the claim of independence; and both were ambitious and resolute to establish a King of their own nation and choice. The princes and Lords of Italy were all of Barbaric origin; but as it happens in the progress of nobility, the strangers of the second were despised by those of the third or fourth generation: and the old settlers who could boast some ages of usurpation, esteemed themselves the ancient natives, the true proprietors of the soil. In the hostile diets of Mentz and Pavia, two rival Kings were elected, Henry[c] the Saxon, and Arduin the Lombard; and they disputed the Iron crown in a civil or rather social[d] War of ten years. The German invaders were long checked and sometimes defeated in the passes of the Alps: but their strength and numbers finally prevailed: The[e] fortunate Henry obtained the title of Emperor, and afterwards of Saint; Arduin was degraded and saved by the Monastic habit: and his adherents were pardoned or punished according to the measure of their guilt or power. Among these adherents, the first to erect the standard, and the last to bow the knee were the Marquis Otbert ii, his four sons and his grandson Azo ii, the immediate founder of the lines of Brunswick and Este. The distance of their fields of battle may prove the extent of their influence and the obstinacy of their struggle: they made a vigorous stand in the neighbourhood of Pavia; they raised a dangerous insurrection at Rome; and they were vanquished and made prisoners in the plains of Apulia. A judicial act recites their crimes, and pronounces their condemnation. The six Marquisses were convicted by[f] the law of the Lombards of conspiring against the King's life: and such conspiracy was punished according to the same law with confiscation and death. Their collateral offences, murder, rapine and sacrilege are the inevitable consequences of civil war: but the violation of some oath which had been extorted in the hour of distress exposed them to the more ignominious reproach of treason

---

[a] *MS.* Otho [b] *II.* their [c] *I.* and they disputed [d] *II.* a social
[e] *I.* Arduin [f] *I.* ac

and perjury. Yet their lives were spared by the clemency of the pious Emperor: the portion of their lands which had been dedicated to pious uses, he could not restore: but he generously forgave the ample forfeiture which had devolved to the state; and when they resumed their seats in the assembly of their[a] peers, they professed themselves the grateful and loyal servants of their benefactor

But as the Saxon Henry left neither children nor kinsmen to inherit their obedience and gratitude, the sons of Otbert ii used or abused their freedom; and again opposed the election of Conrad, the first Emperor of the Franconian line. In the hope of foreign aid they offered the Iron crown and promised the Roman[b] Empire to Robert King of France; and the Marquis Hugo, the second brother was intrusted with this important Embassy. But the son of Hugh Capet was of an inactive temper: his new Kingdom was unsettled; and with his approbation the Italian deputies transferred their offer to William of Aquitain, a vassal not less powerful than his Sovereign. The Duke of Aquitain behaved on this momentous occasion with a just temperance of courage and discretion. He accepted the crown for his family,[c] protesting that under his reign, Italy should enjoy such days, as she had never known: his foremost troops were dispatched beyond the Alps, and he visited Rome under the pretence of a pilgrimage. But on a nearer prospect of the scene the Duke of Aquitain was satisfied that he could neither[d] encounter his antagonist nor confide in his party. The temporal peers were inclined to his cause; but the Archbishop of Milan, and the most important prelates had been promoted by the house of Saxony: they were steady to the German interest; and William rejected the sole effectual measure, that of filling their vacant seats with his own Ecclesiastics. He prudently withdrew from the unequal and ruinous contest: in a farewell epistle he acknowledges the truth and constancy of *one* Italian Lord, and this singular expresses[e] involves the sons of Otbert in the national reproach of levity or falshood. During his Embassy in France the Marquis Hugo had been pressed by the Monks of Tours to restore some Abbey-lands which he had usurped in the neighbourhood of Milan. At the distance of six hundred years and six hundred miles, the[f] superstitious Rebel was subdued by the apprehension of the vengeance of St Martin.

By such exploits the memory or at least the name[g] of the four

[a] *II.* the   [b] *I.* roya   [c] *I.* families   [d] *I.* never   [e] *II.* expression
[f] *II.* that   [g] *II.* names

sons of Otbert ii has been preserved from oblivion. Azo i the eldest brother propagated the race; and by his first marriage with the niece of Hugo Marquis of Tuscany, that chief acquired a rich patrimony and a commanding influence in the Venetian province The character of Hugo, his power and his long reign had given him a respectable place among the princes of the times: but the title of *Great*, the title of Alexander, Pompey, and Charlemagne, becomes ridiculous when it is necessary to ask, and difficult to find the reason of the appellation. From the upper to the lower sea his command extended over the middle regions of Italy: with the right he grasped the Dutchy*a* of Tuscany, with the left that of Spoleto; till on the voluntary or compulsive resignation of the latter, he contracted his domain within the limits of hereditary sway. In the exercise of arms Hugo was strong and fortunate, and the*b* siege and chastisement of Capua, he appeared with dignity as the minister of Imperial justice: but the same sword might be turned against his sovereign; and Otho iii is said to have betrayed a secret satisfaction when death delivered him from so formidable a vassal. Far different were the feelings of the Clergy and people of Tuscany. The former bewailed an humble votary and a liberal benefactor: a*c* convent at Florence in which his tomb has been long shewn, is one of the seven monasteries which he richly*d* endowed with lands, slaves, and gold and silver plate for the service of the Altar. In the opinion of the age these virtues were more pleasing to the Deity, than the justice and humanity which he displayed in his temporal administration. The*e* Marquis of Tuscany loved praise, and hated flattery: a nice touchstone which discriminates vanity from the love of fame. In the chase, on*f* a march, he often rode away from his attendants; visited the cottages; conversed with the peasants and passengers to whom his person was unknown; questioned them freely concerning the character and government of their prince; and enjoyed the sincere and simple effusions of their gratitude and veneration. The birth of Hugo may at once be styled base and illustrious; since he was the doubtful offspring of the bastard son of the King of Italy of the same name; but his life was deemed of such importance to mankind, that the knowledge of its approaching term was communicated from heaven to*g* earth by a special revelation. After his decease, the Dutchy of Tuscany were delegated to a stranger, but a female might

---

a I. Tuscany   *b* II. in the   *c* I. and a   *d* I. founded, and richly
e I. Hugo (*replaced by* The Marquis of Tuscany)   *f* I. in on th   *g* I. by

succeed to his private estates; and his sister had married Peter
Candianus the fourth Doge or Duke of Venice of his name and
family. In that early[a] period of the Republic the Magistrates were
arbitrary and feeble, and the elective Dukes were alternately the
tyrants and victims of a tumultuous democracy. By his[b] connection
with the Tuscan Marquis the pride of Candianus was elated: he
assumed the manners of a feudal Lord: levied a body of Italians,
and insulted a free city with the arms and licentiousness of his
mercenary guards.[c] A furious multitude encompassed his palace:
the gates and the soldiers resisted their assault: they fired the
adjacent houses; and in the attempt to escape the Duke and his
infant son were transpierced with a thousand wounds. Such scenes
were then frequent at Venice: they may reconcile our[d] minds to
the silent and rigid order of the modern Aristocracy. The duties
of the widow of Peter Candianus were to revenge an husband and
to educate a daughter of the same name as her own. The daughter
Valdrada became the wife of the Marquis Albert[e] Azo the first;
and it[f] is apparent from the date of the birth of their eldest son,
Albert[g] Azo ii that these nuptials were consummated in the lifetime and approved by the consent of a wealthy and childless uncle,
who could only hope to live in the posterity of his niece.

The north-eastern region of Italy which began to be vivified by
the rising industry and splendour of Venice extends from the shores
of the Adriatic to the foot of the Alps. Had experience confirmed
the prolific virtues of the climate, did the Venetian hens lay one or
two eggs every day; did the ewes drop their lambs twice or thrice
in a year; were the women delivered of two or three infants at a
birth, the land must soon be over-stocked and exhausted. After
translating the Greek fables into simple truth, we shall still
acknowledge one of the most pleasant and plentiful regions of Italy,
a soil productive of grass, corn and vines,[h] a generous breed of
horses, and innumerable flocks of sheep more precious by the
fineness of their wool. Padua the[i] first of the fifty cities of Venetia
had been so often trampled by the passage of the Barbarians, that
few vestiges remained of the ancient splendour, which in the tide
of human affairs, she afterwards recovered and surpassed. Fifteen
miles to the South of Padua, Albert Azo the[j] first fixed his perman-

---

[a] *I.* earth   [b] *II.* this   [c] *II.* guard   [d] *I.* of   [e] *I. om.* Albert
[f] *I.* fr   [g] *I. om.* Albert Azo ii   [h] *I.* w   [i] *I.* one (*replaced by* the first)
[j] *I.* i

ent and principal seat in the castle and town of Ateste or ESTE, formerly a Roman colony of some note: and an*a* harmless anticipation we may apply to his descendants the title of Marquis of Este, which they did not however assume till the end of the twelfth century From Este, their new estates, the inheritance of Hugo the Great extended to the Adige the Po, and the Mincius,: Their farms and cattle were scattered over the plain: many of the heighths, Montagnana, Monselice &c were occupied by their forts and garrisons; and they possessed a valuable tract of marsh land, the island (as it may be styled) of Rovigo, which almost reaches to the gates of Ferrara. The first step in the emigrations of the family was from the neighbourhood of the Tuscan to that of the Adriatic sea.

The name and character of the Marquis Albert-Azo the second shine conspicuous through the gloom of the eleventh Century. The most remarkable features in the portrait are 1. His Ligurian Marquisate. ii*b* His riches iii His long life. iv His marriages v. His rank of nobility in the public opinion. The glory of his descendants is reflected on the founder; and Azo ii claims our attention as the stem of the two great branches of the pedigree, as the common father of the Italian and German princes of the kindred lines of Este and Brunswick.

1 The fair conjecture that the two Otberts, the father, and son, commanded at Milan and Genoa with the title and office of Marquis acquires a new degree of probability for Azo i, and ascends to the level of historic truth in the person of Azo ii. Before the middle of the eleventh century, the*c* ruins of Genoa had been restored; it's active inhabitants excelled in the arts of navigation and trade: their arms had been felt on the African coast, and their credit was established in the ports of Egypt and Greece. Their riches encreased with their industry, and their liberty with their riches. Yet they continued to obey or at least to revere the majesty of the Emperors: in*d* an act, as it should seem of the year one thousand and forty eight, the Marquis Albert Azo presides at Genoa in a court of Justice, and his assessors, the magistrates of the City are proud to style themselves the Consuls and Judges of the sacred palace. The royal dignity of Pavia was gradually eclipsed by the wealth and populousness of Milan, the first of the Italian cities that dared to erect the standard of independence. The government of Milan was divided between

a II. by an   *b* II. *substitutes Roman numerals for MS. Arabic.*   *c* I. Genoa
had   *d* I. and, as late as the year 1048, in a ju

the two representatives of St Ambrose and of Cæsar. The veneration of the flock for the shepherd was fortified by the*a* temporal state and privileges of*b* the Archbishop; and his*c* annual revenue of fourscore thousand pieces of gold supplied an ample fund for benevolence or luxury. The civil and military powers were exercised by the Duke or Marquis of Milan, (for these titles were promiscuously used), and the voice of tradition is clear and positive that this hereditary office was vested in the ancestors of the house of Este. Some of the prerogatives which they assumed are expressive of the rigour of the feudal system: they were the heirs of all who died childless and intestate, and a fine was paid on the birth of each infant who defeated their claim: their officers levied a tax on the markets, and their minute inquisition exacted the first loaf of bread from each oven, and the first log of wood from every cart-load that entered the gates. Yet an old historian more forcibly affected with the calamities of his own days, deplores the long-lost felicity of their golden age which had been equally praised by the blessings of the feeble*d* and the curses of the strong. They drew their swords for the service of the prince and people, but their reign was distinguished by long intervals of prosperity and people.*e* The distant possessions and various avocations of the Duke or Marquis often diverted him from the exercise of this municipal trust: his powers were devolved on the Viscounts and Captains of Milan; these subordinate tyrants formed an alliance or rather conspiracy with the *Valvassors* or nobles of the first class, and the people was afflicted by the discord or the union of a lawless oligarchy. A private insult exasperated the patience of the plebeians: they rose in arms, and their numbers and fury prevailed in the bloody contest. The Captains and nobles retired; but they retired with the*f* spirit of revenge: collected their vassals and peasants of the adjacent country, encompassed the City with a circumvallation of six fortresses, and in a siege or blockade of three years reduced the inhabitants to the last extremes of famine and distress. By the interposition of the Emperor and the Archbishop the peace of Milan was restored: the factions were reconciled: they wisely refused a garrison of four thousand Germans; but they acquiesced in the civil government of the Empire. The Marquis again ascended his tribunal, and that Marquis is Albert Azo the second. A judicial act of the year one

a *I.* his   *b* *I. om.* of the Archbishop;   *c* *I.* a   *d* *I.* weak   *e* *II.* peace
f *II.* a

thousand and forty five attests his title and jurisdiction, and, as the representative of the Emperor[a] he imposes a fine of a thousand pieces of gold. The progress of Italian liberty[b] reduced his office to the empty name of Marquis of Liguria, and such he is styled by the historians of the age. In the next century his grandson Obizo i is invested by the Emperor Frederic i with the honours of Marquis of Milan and Genoa as his grandfather Azo held them of the Empire; but this splendid grant commemorates the dignity without reviving the power of the house of Este.

ii[c] Like one of his Tuscan ancestors Azo ii[d] was distinguished among the princes of Italy by the epithet of the *Rich*. The particulars of his rent-roll cannot now be ascertained: an occasional though authentic deed of investiture enumerates eighty three fiefs or manours which he held of the Empire in Lombardy and Tuscany, from the Marquisate of Este to the County of Luni: but to these possessions must be added the lands which he enjoyed as the vassal of the Church, the ancient patrimony of Otbert (the *Terra Obertenga*) in the Counties of Arezzo, Pisa, and Lucca, and the marriage-portion of his first wife, which according to the various readings of the manuscripts may be computed either at twenty, or at, two hundred thousand English Acres. If[e] such a mass of landed property were now accumulated on the head of an Italian nobleman, the annual revenue might[f] satisfy the largest demands of private luxury or avarice, and the fortunate owner would be rich in the improvement of agriculture, the manufactures of industry, the refinement of taste, and the extent of commerce. But the barbarism of the eleventh Century diminished the income and aggravated the expence of the Marquis of Este. In a long series of war and anarchy, man and the works of man had been swept away; and the introduction of each ferocious and idle stranger had been overbalanced by the loss, of five or six perhaps, of the peaceful, industrious natives. The mischievous growth of vegetation, the frequent inundations of the rivers were no longer checked by the vigilance of labour; the face of the country was again covered with forests and morasses; of the vast domains which acknowledged Azo for their lord, the far greater part was abandoned to the wild[g] beasts of the field and a much smaller portion was reduced to the state of constant and productive husbandry. An adequate rent may be obtained from the

---

[a] *I*. Co   [b] *I*. in   [c] *II*. 2   [d] *II*. the Second   [e] *I*. Were

[f] *I*. woul   [g] *I*. beasts o

skill and substance of a free tenant who fertilizes a grateful soil, and enjoys the security and benefit of a long lease. But faint is the hope and scanty is the produce of those harvests, which are raised by the reluctant toil of peasants and slaves condemned to a bare subsistence, and careless of the interest[a] of a rapacious master. If his granaries are full, his purse is empty; and the want of cities or commerce, the difficulty of finding or reaching a market, oblig him to consume on the spot a part of his useless stock which cann be exchanged for merchandize or money. The member of a well-regulated society is defended from private wrongs by the laws, and from public injuries by the arms, of the state; and the tax which he pays is a just equivalent for the protection[b] which he receives. But the guard of his life, his honour and his fortune was abandoned to the private sword of a feudal chief; and if his own temper had been inclined to moderation and patience, the public contempt would have rowzed him to deeds of violence and revenge. The entertainment of his vassals and soldiers, their pay and rewards, their arms and horses surpassed the measure of the most oppressive tribute; and the destruction which he inflicted on his neighbours was often retaliated on his own lands. The costly elegance of palaces and gardens was superseded by the laborious and expensive construction of strong castles on the summits of the most inaccessible rocks: and some of these, like the fortress of Canossa in the Apennine, were built and provided to sustain a three-years siege against a royal army. But his[c] defence in this world was less burthensome[d] to a wealthy lord than his salvation in the next: the demands of his chappel, his priests, his alms his offerings, his pilgrimages were incessantly renewed; the[e] monastery chosen for his sepulchre was endowed with his fairest possessions and the naked heir might often complain that his father's sins had been redeemed at too[f] high a price. The Marquis Azo was not exempt from the contagion of the times: his devotion was amused and inflamed by the frequent miracles which were performed in his presence; and the monks of Vangadizza who yielded to his request the arm of a dead saint, were ignorant of the value of that inestimable jewel. After satisfying the demands of war and superstition, he might appropriate the rest of his revenue to use and pleasure. But the Italians of the eleventh century were imperfectly skilled in the liberal and mechanic arts:

[a] *II.* interests   [b] *I.* inju   [c] *I.* the   [d] *I.* cho   [e] *I.* an a
[f] *I.* two

the objects of foreign luxury were furnished at an exorbitant price
by the merchants of Pisa and Venice: and the superfluous wealth
which could not purchase the real comforts of life was idly wasted
on some[a] rare occasions of vanity and pomp. Such were the nuptials
of Boniface Duke or Marquis of Tuscany, whose family was long
afterward[b] united with that of Azo by the marriage of their children.
These nuptials were celebrated on[c] the banks[d] of the Mincius
which the fancy of Virgil[46] has decorated with a more beautiful
picture. The princes and people of Italy were invited to the feast
which continued three months, the fertile[e] meadows which are
intersected by the slow and winding course of the river, were
covered[f] with innumerable tents, and the bridegroom displayed and
diversified the scenes of his proud and tasteless magnificence. All
the utensils of service were of silver, and his horses were shod with
plates of the same metal, loosely nailed, and carelessly dropt to
indicate his contempt of riches. An image of plenty and profusion
was expressed in the banquet: the most delicious wines were drawn
in buckets from the well; and the spices of the East were ground in
water-mills, like common flour. The dramatic and musical arts were
in the rudest state: but the Marquis had summoned the most
popular singers, harpers, and buffoons. to[g] exercise their talents on
this splendid theatre: their exhibitions were applauded; and they
applauded the liberality of their patron. After this festival I might
remark a singular gift of the same Boniface to the Emperor Henry
iii, a chariot and oxen of solid silver which were designed only as
the[h] vehicle for a hogshead of vinegar. If such an example should
seem above the imitation of Azo himself, the Marquis of Este was
at least superior in wealth and dignity to the Vassals of his Compeer.
One of these vassals the Viscount of Mantua presented the German
Monarch with one hundred falcons, and one hundred bay horses,
a grateful contribution to the pleasures of a Royal sportsman. In
that age, the proud distinction between the nobles and *princes* of
Italy was[i] guarded with jealous ceremony: the Viscount of Mantua
had never been seated at the table of his immediate lord: he yielded
to the invitation of the Emperor: and a stag's skin filled with pieces
of gold was graciously accepted by the Marquis of Tuscany as the
fine of his presumption.

iii.[j] The temporal felicity of Azo was crowned by[k] the long

---

[a] *I.* r   [b] *II.* afterwards   [c] *I.* wh   [d] *I.* bat   [e] *I.* rich
[f] *I.* crowned   [g] *I.* their exhibi   [h] *II.* a   [i] *I.* with   [j] *II.* 3   [k] *I.* wi

possession of honours and riches: he died in the year one thousand and ninety seven, aged upwards of an hundred years; and the term of his mortal existence was almost commensurate with the lapse of the eleventh Century. The character as well as the situation of the Marquis of Este rendered him an actor in the revolutions of that memorable period: but time has cast a veil over the virtues and vices of the man, and I must be content to mark some of the Æras, the mile-stones of his life which measure the extent and intervals of the vacant way. Albert-Azo the second was no more than seventeen when he first drew the sword of rebellion or patriotism, when he was involved with his grand-father, his father, and his three uncles in a common proscription. In the vigour of manhood, about his*a* fiftieth year, the Ligurian Marquis governed the cities of Milan and Genoa as the minister of Imperial authority. He was upwards of seventy when he passed the Alps to vindicate the inheritance of Maine for the children of his second marriage. He became the friend and servant of Gregory vii, and in one of his epistles[47] that ambitious Pontiff recommends the Marquis Azo as the most faithful and best-beloved of the Italian princes, as the proper channel, through which a King of Hungary might convey his petitions to the Apostolic throne. In the mighty contest between the crown and the mitre the Marquis Azo, and the Countess Matilda led the powers of Italy, and when the standard of S*t* Peter was displayed neither the age of the one, nor the sex of the other could detain them from the field. With these two affectionate Clients, the Pope maintained his station in the fortress of Canossa, while the Emperor, barefoot on the frozen ground, fasted and prayed three days at the foot of the rock: they were witnesses to the abject ceremony*b* of the pennance and pardon of Henry iv, and in the triumph of the Church, a patriot might foresee the deliverance of Italy from the German Yoke. At the time of his*c* event, the Marquis of Este was above fourscore; but in the twenty following years he was still alive and active amidst the revolutions of peace and war. The last act which he subscribed is dated above a century after his birth: and in that act the venerable chief possesses the command of his faculties, his family, and his fortune. In*d* this rare prerogative of longevity, Albert-Azo the second*e* stands alone, nor can I recollect in the *authentic* annals of mortality a single example of a King, or prince, of a statesman or general, of a philosopher or poet whose

a I. the   *b I.* hu   *c II.* this   *d I.* A   *e II.* II.

life has been extended beyond[a] the period of an hundred years. Nor should this observation which is justified by universal experience be[b] thought either strange or surprizing. It has been found that of twenty four thousand new-born infants, seven only will survive to attain that distant term: and much smaller is the proportion of those who will be raised by fortune or Genius, to govern, or afflict or enlighten their age or country. The chance that the same individual should draw the two great prizes in the lottery of life will not easily be defined by the powers of calculation.[48] Three approximations which will not hastily be matched, have distinguished the present century, Aurungzeb, Cardinal Fleury, and Fontenelle. Had a fortnight more been given to the philosopher he might have celebrated his secular festival; but the lives and labours of the Mogul King, and the French minister were terminated before they had accomplished their ninetieth year. A strong constitution may be the gift of Nature, but the few who survive their contemporaries must have been superior to the passions and appetites which urge the speedy decay[c] and dissolution of the mind and body. The Marquis of Este may be presumed from his riches and longevity to have understood the œconomy of health and fortune.

iv.[d] I remember a Persian tale of three old men who were successively questioned by a traveller as he met them on the road. The youngest brother, under the load of a wife and a numerous family was sinking into the grave before his time. The second though much older, was far less infirm and decrepid: he had been left a widower and without children. But the last and eldest of the three brothers still preserved, at an incredible age, the vigour and vivacity of the autumnal season: he had always preferred[e] a life of celibacy. The enjoyment of domestic freedom could not, however contribute to the longevity of the Marquis Azo; he married three wives; he educated three sons; and it is doubtful whether chance or prudence delayed his first nuptials till he had at least accomplished the fortieth year of his age. These nuptials were contracted with Cuniza, or Cunegonda a German maid; whose ancestors, by their nobility and riches were distinguished among the Swabian and Bavarian Chiefs; whose brother was invested by the Emperor Henry iii with the Dutchy of Carinthia and the Marquisate of Verona on the confines of the Venetian possessions of the house of Este. The marriage of Azo and Cunegonda was productive of a son, who

[a] I. by   [b] I. a   [c] I. dissolu   [d] II. 4   [e] I. l

received at his baptism the name of GUELPH to revive and perpetuate the memory of his uncle, his grandfather, and his first progenitors on the maternal side. I have already defined the ample domain which was given as a marriage-portion to the daughter of the Guelphs: but, on the failure of heirs male, her fortunate son inherited the patrimonial estates of the family, obtained the Dukedom of Bavaria; and became the founder of the eldest or German branch of the house of Este, from which the Dukes of Brunswick, the Electors of Hanover, and the Kings of Great-Britain are lineally descended. After[a] the decease of Cunegonda, who must have departed this life in the flower of her age, the Marquis of Este solicited a second alliance beyond the Alps: but his delicacy no longer insisted on the choice of a virgin; the widower was content[b] with a widow; and he excused the ambiguous stain which might adhere to his bride by a divorce from her first husband Her name was Garsenda the daughter and at length the heiress of the Counts of Maine: she became[c] the mother of two sons, Hugo and Fulk, and the[d] younger of these is[e] the acknowledged[f] parent of the Dukes of Ferrara and Modena. The same liberal fortune which had crowned the offspring of the first, seemed to attend the children[g] of the second, nuptials of the Marquis Azo: but *their* fortune was hollow and fallacious; and after the loss of their Gallic inheritance, the sons of Garsenda reluctantly acquiesced in some fragments of their Italian patrimony. Matilda, the third wife of Azo was another widow, of noble birth, since she was his own cousin, in[h] the fourth degree; but this consanguinity provoked the stern and impartial justice of Gregory vii. His friend was summoned to appear before a Synod at Rome: the inflexible priest pronounced a sentence of divorce; and whatsoever idea may be formed of the Marquis's vigour, at the age of seventy eight he might submit without much effort to the Canons of the Church. Besides his three sons, Azo had a daughter named Adelais who was educated in the family of the Countess Matilda. But the damsel is only mentioned to attest the miraculous virtue of Anselm Bishop of Lucca: she was relieved, in the night from a violent fit of the cholic by the local application of a pillow, on which the Saint had formerly reposed his head.

[a] I. The origin of the ancient Guelphs, and the eventful history of their successors will be the proper and interesting theme of the following book. [b] II. contented [c] I. bore [d] I. from the younger [e] I. I shall deduce in the next chapter, the descent and series of (*replaced by* is the acknowledged parent of) [f] II. knowledged [g] I. sons [h] I. but this

V. A wealthy Marquis of the eleventh century must have commanded a proud hereditary rank in civil society. In the judgement of the Pope, the Emperor, and the public Albert-Azo ii[a] was distinguished among the princes, and the first princes of the Kingdom of Italy. His double alliance in[b] Germany and France may prove how much he was known and esteemed among foreign nations, and he strengthened his political importance by a[c] domestic union[d] with the[e] conquerors of Apulia and Sicily. I shall not repeat the story of the Norman adventurers: nor shall I again delineate the character and exploits of Robert Guiscard; which to the readers, shall[f] I say to the many readers, of the history of the decline and fall of the Roman Empire are sufficiently familiar.[49] But as Duke Robert had four daughters, the choice of his other three sons in law may serve as a test, a touchstone of the comparative weight and value of the house of Este. Michael Emperor of the Greeks was the first name in the Christian World: Raymond Count of Barcelona was the independent sovereign of a warlike people; and the meanest of the three a French Baron of military renown, was the cousin of the Kings of France and Jerusalem, the brother in law of the King of Navarre and Arragon. Such were three of the sons, by alliance of the Norman conqueror, who had previously rejected a proposal for the eldest son of the Emperor Henry iv: the marriage of a fourth daughter will be most accurately represented in the words of the Apulian poet: "While the Hero resided within the walls of the "Trojan city, he received the visit of a certain noble Lombard "Marquis, accompanied by many nobles of his country. Azo was "his name. The object of his journey was to request that the Duke's "daughter might be granted as a wife to Hugo his *illustrious* son. "The Duke convened an assembly of his Chiefs; and with their "consent and advice the daughter of Robert was delivered to the "son of Azo. The nuptial rites were solemnized in due form, and "the festival was celebrated with gifts and banquets. After the "consummation of the marriage, the Duke solicited his Counts and "powerful Vassals to bestow a free gift which might grace the "joyful departure of the bride and bridegroom; and he enforced "his demand by reminding them that no subsidy whatsoever had "been given to her sister the Greek Empress. The demand of a "tribute was entertained with a[g] murmur of surprize and discontent:

---

[a] *II. om.* ii   [b] *I.* with the   [c] *I.* his   [d] *I.* connection   [e] *I.* a
II. om. shall I say to the many readers,   [g] *I.* so

"but all opposition was fruitless, and they presented their sovereign
"with mules and horses and various offerings. He bestowed them
"on the husband of his daughter with an addition from his own
"treasures: a fleet was prepared; and both the father and son were
"transported with great honour to their native shores." This
evidence of a contemporary poet or rather historian who had no
temptation to flatter the princes of Este would alone be sufficient to
establish the nobility and splendour of their family, the family of
Brunswick, beyond the distant term of seven hundred years. If the*a*
Marquis Azo were the first of his race whose name and memory
had been preserved we might acquiesce in our ignorance with a
just*b* persuasion of the dignity and power of his unknown ancestors.
Of these illustrious ancestors the zeal and diligence of Leibnitz and
Muratori have discovered four probable*c* and four certain degrees.
After the*d* examination of their proofs, a scrupulous critic may
suspect, that in deriving the Marquisses of Este from those of
Tuscany "the ascent of reason has been aided by the wings of
"imagination".⁵⁰ but he must confess that since the beginning
of the tenth century the series of generations flows in a clear and
unbroken stream

[Fragments]

Cynthii Joannis Baptistæ Gyraldi, Nobilis Ferrariensis, Illustrissimi
ac Excellentissimi Herculis Atestini ii, Ducis Ferrariensium iv, ab
Epistolis, de Ferrariâ et Atestinis principibus Commentariotum.
Ferrariæ 1556. In Thesaur. Antiquitat. Italiæ. Græv. et Burman.⁵¹
Tom vii P. I. Actius or Azo the son of Hercules in Gaul. p 4–5.
Forestus charged Attila with 500 horse, his death, sack of Padua,
Este &c.

Albert Azo favourite and son-in law of Otho I.—Count of Friburgh,
his two sons Fulk and Ugo, the former acquires Saxonum regnum,
and yields to his brother Este &c. p. 7–8.

The Adelphi of Terence was acted by the sons and daughters of
Hercules ii, before Paul iii and the Roman Court at Ferrara. p 62.

---

a *I. om.* the Marquis   *b* *I.* fu   *c* *I.* hi   *d* *I.* weighing (*replaced by*
the examination of)

Alphonsi Cagnacini. Fagmentum. Historicum Antiquitatis Ferrariæ.

Hippoliti Angelerii de Antiq. urbis Atestinæ Actia gens, (C. Actius) AD 403 florere incepit et patriæ principatum adepta est. Amidst the invasions of the Goths &c he was elected first Decurio, and then prince of Ateste. p 17–18

HABSBURGICA

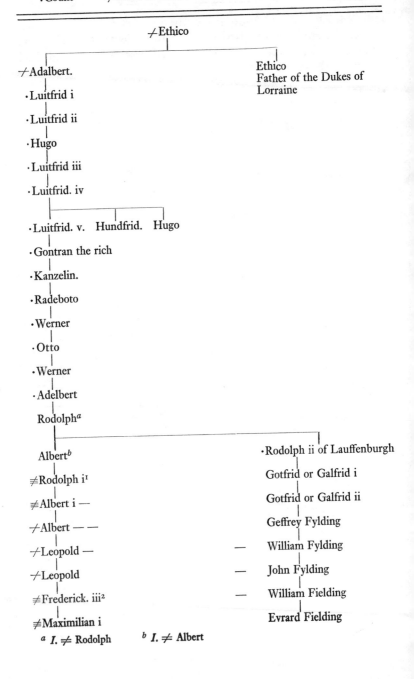

.Count   ⊬Duke or Arch-Duke   ≢King   ≢Emperor

⊬Ethico

Ethico
Father of the Dukes of
Lorraine

⊬Adalbert.

·Luitfrid i

·Luitfrid ii

·Hugo

·Luitfrid iii

·Luitfrid. iv

·Luitfrid. v.   Hundfrid.   Hugo

·Gontran the rich

·Kanzelin.

·Radeboto

·Werner

·Otto

·Werner

·Adelbert

Rodolph[a]

Albert[b]   ·Rodolph ii of Lauffenburgh

≢Rodolph i[1]   Gotfrid or Galfrid i

≢Albert i —   Gotfrid or Galfrid ii

⊬Albert — —   Geffrey Fylding

⊬Leopold —   —   William Fylding

⊬Leopold   —   John Fylding

≢Frederick. iii[2]   —   William Fielding

≢Maximilian i   Evrard Fielding

[a] *I.* ≢ Rodolph   [b] *I.* ≢ Albert

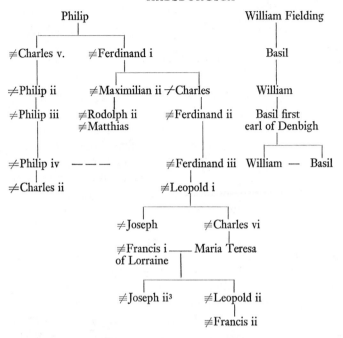

HABSBURGICA

Philip iii the 118th from Adam according to Sandoval—False Berosus of Annius[4] of Viterbo —Hunnibald of the Abbot Trithemius[5]— From Sigibert lawful heirs of France according to Valdes[6]—Duke of Lerma 121st from Adam —heir to Britain by Brutus according to Pegnefiel Contreras of Grenada.[7]

Oeuvres de la Mothe le Voyer. Edit de Pfœrten 1756. Tom iv. P i. p300.–305.—laughs at the Spanish folly as a philosopher and Frenchman

Two favourite systems. from the Anicii and Petro-Leones of Rome—from the Merovingians—Rodolph i Charles v, Leopold for the 1[rst], Maximilian i, Ferdinand i for the 2[d].

Schæpflin Alsatia Illustrata. Tom ii p 460–462

Guilleman. is obliged to attack them—ascribes the 1[rst] to Albertus Argentinensis,[8] the 2[d] to Trithemius—

Habsburgica L i. p 1–9.

An Address &c

That History is a liberal and useful study, and that the history of our own country is best deserving of our attention are propositions too clear for argument, and too simple for illustration. Nature has implanted in our breasts a lively impulse to extend the narrow span of our existence, by the knowledge, of the events that have happened on the soil which we inhabit, of the characters and actions of those men from whom our descent, as individuals or as a people is probably derived. The same laudable emulation will prompt us to review[a] and to enrich our common treasure of national glory: and those who are the[b] best entitled to the esteem of posterity are the most inclined to celebrate the merits of their ancestors. The origin and changes of our Religion, and government[,] our[c] arts, and manners afford an entertaining and often an instructive subject of speculation; and the scene is repeated and varied by the entrance of the victorious strangers, the Roman and the Saxon, the Dane and the Norman, who have successively reigned in our stormy isle. We contemplate the gradual progress of Society from the lowest ebb of primitive barbarism to the full tide of modern civilization. We contrast the naked Briton who might have mistaken[d] the sphere of Archimedes for a rational creature[1], and the contemporary of Newton, in whose school Archimedes himself would have been an humble disciple. And we compare the boats of osier and hydes that floated along our coasts, with the formidable navies, which visit and command the remotest shores of the Ocean. Without indulging the fond prejudices of patriotic[e] vanity, we may assume a conspicuous place among the inhabitants of the Earth. The English will be ranked among the few nations, who have cultivated with equal

(1)[f] I allude to a passage in Cicero (de Naturâ Deorum. L ii. C 34) Quod[g] si in Britanniam sphæram aliquis tulerit hanc, quam nuper familiaris noster effecit Posidonius, cujus singulæ conversiones idem efficiunt in Sole, et in Lunâ, et in quinque stellis errantibus, quod efficitur in Cœlo, singulis diebus et noctibus: quis in illa barbarie dubitet quin ea sphæra sit perfecta ratione.

---

    a *I.* compute   *b* *II. om.* the   *c* *II.* of our   *d* *I.* gazed with blind wonder on the sphere of Archimdes[1] (*replaced by* mistaken the sphere of Archimedes for a rational creature[1])   *e* *I.* National   *f* *All notes in margin of MS.* *Numbered by Gibbon*   *g* *I.* Si quis in

success the arts of War, of learning[,] and of commerce: and Britain, perhaps, is the only powerful and wealthy state, which has ever possessed the inestimable secret of uniting the benefits of order with the blessings of freedom.

It[a] is a maxim of our law, and the constant practise of our Courts of Justice never to accept any evidence, unless it is the very best, which under the circumstances of the case, can possibly be obtained. If this wise principle be transferred from Jurisprudence to Criticism the inquisitive reader of English history will soon ascend to the first Witnesses of every period, from whose testimonies the moderns, however sagacious and eloquent must derive their whole confidence and credit. In the prosecution of his enquiries he will lament that the transactions of the middle ages have been imperfectly recorded and that these records have been more imperfectly preserved: that the successive Conquerors of Britain have despised or destroyed the monuments of their predecessors; and that[b] by their violence or neglect so much of our national antiquities has irretrievably perished. For the losses of history are indeed irretrievable: when the productions of fancy or science have been swept away, new poets may invent, and new philosophers may reason; but if the[c] inscription of a single fact be once obliterated, it can never be restored by the united efforts of Genius and industry. The consideration of our past losses should excite[d] the present age to cherish and perpetuate the valuable relicks which[e] have escaped[.] Instead of condemning the MONKISH HISTORIANS (as they are contemptuously styled) silently[f] to moulder in the dust of our libraries, our candour and even our justice should learn to estimate their value, and to excuse their imperfections. Their minds were infected with the passions and errors of their times; but those times would have been involved in darkness, had not the art of writing, and the memory of events been preserved in the peace and solitude of the Cloyster. Their Latin style is far removed from the eloquence and purity of Salust and Livy, but the use of a permanent and general idiom has opened the study and connected the series of our ancient Chronicles from the age of Bede to that of Walsingham.[1] In the eyes of a philosophic[g] observer these Monkish historians are even endowed with a singular though accidental merit; the unconscious simplicity with which

---

[a] *II. fails to paragraph.*
[b] *I. om.* that
[c] *I.* a si
[d] *II.* incite
[e] *I. om.* which have escaped
[f] *I.* To m
[g] *I.* contemporary

they represent the manners and opinions of their contemporaries: a natural picture, which the most exquisite art is unable to imitate.

Books, before the invention of printing were separately and slowly copied by the pen; and the transcripts of our old historians must have been rare, since the number would*a* be proportioned to the number of readers capable of understanding a Latin work and curious of the history and antiquities of England. The gross mass of the Laity from the Baron to the mechanic were more addicted to the exercises of the body, than to those of the mind: the middle ranks of society were illiterate and poor: and the Nobles and Gentlemen, as often as they breathed from War, maintained their strength and activity in the chace or the tournament. Few among them could read, still fewer could write, none were acquainted with the Latin Tongue; and, if they sometimes listened to a tale of past times, their puerile love of the marvellous would prefer the Romance of Sir Lancelot or Sir Tristram to the authentic narratives most honourable to their country and their ancestors. Till*b* the period of the Reformation the ignorance and sensuality of the Clergy were continually encreasing: the ambitious prelate aspired to pomp and power; the jolly Monk was satisfied with idleness and pleasure, and the few students of the Ecclesiastical order perplexed, rather than enlightened, their understandings, with occult science, and scholastic Divinity. In the Monastery, in which a Chronicle had been composed, the original was*c* deposited, and perhaps a Copy; and some neighbouring Churches might be induced by a local or professional interest to seek the communication of these historical memorials. Such manuscripts were not liable*d* to suffer from the injury of Use; but the casualty of a fire, or the slow progress of damp and worms would often endanger their limited and precarious existence. The Sanctuaries*e* of Religion were sometimes profaned by Aristocratic oppression, popular tumult[,] or military license; and, although the cellar was more exposed than the library, the envy of ignorance will*f* riot in the spoil of those treasures which it cannot enjoy.

After the discovery of printing, which has bestowed immortality on the works of man, it might be presumed that the new art would be applied without delay to save and to multiply the remains of our National*g* Chronicles. It might be expected that the English, now

---

a I. must have been *b I.* The ignorance *c I.* Manuscript was
d I. exposed *e I.* most holy Sanctuaries *f I.* (*for remainder of sentence*) is
gratified by extinguishing the light of learning *g I.* domestic

waking from a long slumber would[a] blush at finding themselves
strangers in their native country and, that our princes, after the
example of Charlemagne, and Maximilian i, would esteem it their
duty and glory, to illustrate the history of the people over whom
they reigned. But these rational hopes have not been justified by
the event. It was in the year 1474 that our first press was established
in Westminster Abbey by William Caxton: but in the choice of his
authors that liberal and industrious artist was reduced to comply
with the vicious taste of his readers; to gratify the Nobles with
treatises on Heraldry, Hawking, and the game of Chess. and[b] to
amuse the popular credulity with romances of fabulous Knights,
and legends of more fabulous Saints. The father of printing expresses
a laudable desire to elucidate the history of his Country; but instead
of publishing the Latin Chronicle of Radulphus Higden, he could
only venture on the English version by John de Trevisa: and[c] his
complaint of the difficulty of finding materials for his own continuation of that work, sufficiently attests that even the writers,[d] which
we now possess of the fourteenth and fifteenth Centuries, had not
yet emerged from the darkness of the Cloyster. His successors, with
less skill and ability were content[e] to tread in the footsteps of Caxton:
almost[f] a Century elapsed without producing one original edition of
any old English historian. and[g] the only exception[h] which I recollect
is the publication of Gildas (London 1526) by Polydore Virgil, an
ingenious foreigner. The presses of Italy, Germany, and even
France might[i] plead in their defence, that the minds of their
Scholars, and the hands of their workmen were abundantly exercised
in unlocking the treasures of Greek and Roman Antiquity: but the
World is not indebted to England for one *first* Edition of a Classic
author. This delay of a century is the more to be lamented, as it is
too probable that many authentic and valuable monuments of our
history were lost in the dissolution of Religious houses by Henry
the eighth.[2] The protestant and the patriot must applaud our
deliverance; but the Critic may deplore the rude havock that was
made in the libraries of Churches and Monasteries by the zeal, the
avarice and the neglect of unworthy[j] reformers.

Far different from such reformers was the learned and pious
Matthew Parker, the first Protestant Archbishop of Canterbury in

---

[a] *II.* should   [b] *I. om.* and to amuse . . . more fabulous Saints.   [c] *I.* he
[d] *I.* Chronic   [e] *I.* constrained   [f] *I.* and almost   [g] *I.* The (*replaced by* and
the)   [h] *I.* con   [i] *I.* may   [j] *I.* licentious

the reign of Queen Elizabeth. His Apostolical virtues were not in-compatible with the love of learning: and while he exercised the arduous office not of governing but of founding the Church of England, he strenuously applied himself to revive the study of the Saxon tongue and of English Antiquities. By the care of this respectable Prelate, four of our ancient historians were successively published; the *Flores* of Matthew of Westminster (1570) the *Historia Major* of Matthew Paris (1571), the *Vita Ælfridi Regis* by Asserius, and the *Historia brevis* and *Upodigma Neustriæ* by Thomas Walsingham.[3] After Parker's death this national duty was for some years abandoned to the diligence of foreigners. The Ecclesiastical history of Bede had been printed and reprinted on the continent as the common property of the Latin Church; and it was again inserted in a Collection of British writers (Heidelberg 1587) selected with such critical skill that the romance of Jeffrey of Monmouth and[a] a Latin abridgement of Froissard are placed on the same level of historical evidence[.] An edition of Florence of Worcester by Howard (1592) may be slightly noticed; but we should gratefully commemorate the labours of Sir Henry Saville, a man distinguished among the scholars of the age by his profound knowledge of the Greek language and Mathematical sciences. A just indignation against the base and plebeian authors of our English Chronicles had almost provoked him to undertake the task of a general and legiti-mate history: but his modest industry declining the character of an architect was content to prepare materials for a future edifice. Some of the most valuable writers of the twelfth and thirteenth Centuries were rescued by his hands from dirt and dust and rottenness (e sitû, squalore, et pulvere) and his Collection under the common title of *Scriptores post Bedam* was twice printed first in London (1596) and afterwards at Frankfort (1601) During the whole of the seventeenth and the beginning of the eighteenth Centuries the same studies were prosecuted with vigour and success: a miscellaneous Volume of the *Anglica Normannica* &c (Frankfort 1603), and the *Historia Nova* of Eadmer (London 1623)[b] were produced by Cambden and Selden to whom literature is indebted for more important services. The names of Wheeloc[c] and Gibson, of Watts and Warton of[d] Dugdale and Wilkins should not be defrauded of their due praise: but our attention is fixed by the elaborate Collections of Twysden

---

[a] *I. om.* and   [b] *I. om.* (London 1623)   [c] *II.* Wheeler   [d] *I. om.* of Dugdale and Wilkins

and Gale: and their titles of *Decem* and *Quindecim Scriptores* announce that their readers possess a series of twenty five of our old English historians. The last who has dug deep in[a] the mine was Thomas Hearne, a Clerk[b] of Oxford poor in fortune and indeed poor in understanding. His minute and obscure diligence: his voracious and undistinguishing appetite, and the coarse vulgarity of taste and style have exposed him to the ridicule of idle wits. Yet it cannot be denied that Thomas Hearne has gathered many gleanings of the harvest; and[c] if his own prefaces are swelled[d] with crude and extraneous matter, his editions will be always recommended by their accuracy and use.

I am not called upon to enquire into the merits of foreign nations in the study[e] of their respective histories except as far as they may suggest an[f] useful lesson or a laudable emulation to ourselves. The patient Germans have addicted themselves to every species of literary labour; and the division of their vast Empire into many independent states would multiply the public events of each country, and the pens, however rude, by which they have been saved from oblivion. Besides innumerable editions of particular historians I have seen (if my memory does not fail me) a list of more than twenty of the voluminous Collections of the *Scriptores rerum Germanicarum*. Some of these are of a vague and miscellaneous Nature; others[g] are relative to a certain period of time; and others again are circumscribed by the local limits of a principality or a province. Among the last I shall only distinguish the Scriptores rerum Brunswicensium, compiled at Hanover in the beginning of this Century by the celebrated Leibnitz. We should sympathize with a kind of domestic interest in the fortunes of a people to whom we are united by our obedience to a common sovereign: and we must explore with respect and gratitude the origin[h] of an illustrious family, which has been the guardian, near fourscore years of our liberty and happiness. The antiquarian who blushes at his alliance with Thomas Hearne will feel his profession ennobled by the name of Leibnitz. That extraordinary Genius embraced and improved the whole circle of human science; and after wrestling with Newton and Clarke in the sublime regions of Geometry and Metaphysics, he could descend upon earth to examine the uncouth characters, and barbarous Latin of a Chronicle or Charter. In this as in almost every other active

---

[a] *II.* into [b] *I.* poo [c] *II.* but [d] *II.* filled [e] *I.* studies [f] *II.* a
[g] *I.* some [h] *I.* antiquities

pursuit Spain has been outstripped by the industry of her neighbours. The best collection of her national historians was published
in Germany: the recent attempts of her royal Academy have been
languid and irregular; and if some memorials of the fourteenth and
fifteenth Centuries are lately printed at*a* Madrid,[4] her five oldest
Chronicles after the invasion of the Moors still sleep in the obscurity
of provincial*b* Editions (Pameplona 1615. 1634. Barcelona 1663.).
Italy has been productive in every age of Revolutions and writers,
and a complete series of these original writers from the year five
hundred to the year fifteen hundred are most accurately digested
in the *Scriptores rerum Italicarum* of Muratori.[5] This stupendous
work which fills twenty eight folios and overflows into the six
Volumes of his*c* *Antiquitates Italiæ medii ævi* was atchieved in
              years[6] by one man; and candour must excuse some
defects in the plan and execution which the discernment and
perhaps the envy of criticism has too rigorously exposed. The
Antiquities of France have been elucidated by a learned and ingenious people: the original historians which Duchesne had undertaken to publish, were left imperfect by his death: yet he*d* had
reached the end of the thirteenth Century; and his additional
Volume (the sixth) comes home to ourselves, since it celebrates the
exploits of the Norman*e* Conquerors and Kings of England. About
              years[7] ago the design of publishing *les Historiens des
Gaules et de la France* was resumed on a larger scale and in a more
splendid form: and, although the name of Dom Bouquet stands
foremost, the merit must be shared among the veteran Benedictines
of the Abbey of S*t* Germain des prez at Paris. This noble collection
may be proposed as a model for such national works: the original
texts are corrected from the best manuscripts; and the curious
reader is enlightened without being oppressed by the perspicuous
brevity of the prefaces and notes. But a multitude of obstacles and
delays seems to have impeded the progress of the undertaking*f*;
and the *Historians of France* had only attained to the twelfth Century
and the thirteenth Volume, when a general deluge overwhelmed
the country, and its ancient inhabitants.[8] I might here conclude
this enumeration of foreign studies if the *Scriptores rerum Danicarum*
of Langebek and his successors which have lately appeared at
Copenhagen,[9] did not remind me of the taste and munificence of a

---

a *I. om.* at Madrid   *b* *I.* a provincial edition (*replaced by* provincial editions)
c *II.* the   *d* *II. om.* he   *e* *I.* Normans   *I.* understanding

Court and Country, whose scanty revenues might have apologized for their neglect

It is long, very long indeed, since the success of our neighbours, and the knowledge of our ressources have disposed me to wish that our Latin memorials of the middle age, the[a] *Scriptores rerum Anglicarum* might be published in England, in a manner worthy of the subject and of the country. At a time when the decline and fall of the Roman Empire has intimately connected me with the first historians of France, I acknowledged (in a note) the value of the Benedictine Collection,[10] and expressed my hope that such a national work would provoke our own emulation. My hope has failed, the provocation was not felt; the emulation was not kindled, and I have now seen without an attempt or a design near thirteen years[b] which might have sufficed for the execution. During the greatest part of that time I have been absent from England: yet I have sometimes found opportunities of introducing this favourite topic in conversation with our literary men and our eminent booksellers. As long as I expatiated on the merits of an undertaking, so beneficial to history, and so honourable to the nation I was heard with attention; a general wish seemed to prevail for its success. But no sooner did we seriously consult about the best means of promoting that success, and to[c] reducing a pleasing theory into real[d] action, than we were stopped at the first step by an insuperable difficulty, the choice of an Editor. Among the Authors already known to the public, none, after a fair review could be found, at once possessed of ability and inclination; unknown or at least untryed abilities could not inspire much reasonable confidence: some were too poor, others too rich; some too busy others too idle: and we knew not where to seek our English Muratori in the tumult of the metropolis or in the shade of the University. The age of Herculean diligence which could devour and digest whole libraries is passed away; and I sat[e] down in hopeless despondency, till I should be able to find a person endowed with proper qualifications, and ready to employ several years of his life in assiduous labour, without any splendid prospect of emolument or fame.

The man is at length found: and I now renew the proposal in a higher tone of confidence[f]; The name of this Editor is Mr John

[a] *I.* might be   [b] *I. om.* years   [c] *II.* of   [d] *II.* a real action   [e] *I.* sh
[f] *I.* (*before next sentence, continued*) since I can now recommend both the workman. On the zeal and abilities of the Editor of my choice, I boldly and considerately stake whatsoever credit I may have obtained from the public opinion.

Pinkerton: but as that name may provoke some resentments and revive some prejudices it is incumbent on me for his reputation to[a] explain my sentiments without reserve: and I have the satisfaction of knowing, that he will not be displeased with the freedom and sincerity of a friend. The impulse of a vigorous[b] mind urged him at an[c] early age to write and to print before his taste and judgement had attained to their maturity. His ignorance of the World the love of paradox and the warmth of his temper betrayed him into some improprieties; and those juvenile sallies which candour will excuse, he himself is the first to condemn, and will perhaps be the last to forget. Repentance has long since propitiated the mild Divinity of Virgil against whom the rash youth, under[d] a fictitious name had darted the javelin of criticism. He smiles at his reformation of our English tongue, and is ready to confess that in all popular institutions the laws of custom must be obeyed by reason herself. The Goths still continue to be his chosen people; but [he] retains no antipathy to a Celtic savage; and without renouncing his opinions and arguments, he sincerely laments that those litterary arguments have ever been embittered, and perhaps enfeebled by an indiscreet mixture of anger and contempt. By some explosions of this kind the volatile and fiery particles of his Nature have been discharged, and there remains a pure and solid substance endowed with many active and useful energies. His recent publications, a treatise on Medals and the edition of the early Scotch Poets discover a mind replete with a variety of knowledge, and inclined to every liberal pursuit; But his[e] decided propensity, such a propensity, as made Bentley a critic and Rennel a Geographer[11] attracts him to the Study of the history and antiquities of Great Britain; and he is well qualified for this study, by[f] a spirit of Criticism, acute discerning and suspicious. His edition of the original lives of the Scottish Saints has scattered some rays of light over the darkest age of a dark country: since there are so many circumstances in which the most daring legendary will not attempt to remove the well-known landmarks of truth. His Dissertation on the origin of the Goths with the Antiquities of Scotland are in my[g] judgement elaborate and satisfactory works: and were this a convenient place I would gladly enumerate the important questions on[h] which he has rectified

---

[a] *I.* and my own to   [b] *I. a.* An irresistible impulse *I. b.* powerful impulse
[c] *I.* a very early   [d] *I.* th   [e] *I.* but he   [f] *I.* by a love of truth most scrupulous and accurate   [g] *I.* jud   [h] *II.* in

my old opinions concerning the migrations of the Scythic or German nation from the neighbourhood of the Caspian and the Euxine to Scandinavia[a] the eastern coast[b] of Britain and the shores of the Atlantic Ocean. He has since undertaken to illustrate a more interesting period of the history of Scotland; his materials are chiefly drawn from papers in the British Museum, and a skillful judge has assured me after a perusal of the Manuscript that it contains more new and authentic information than could be fairly expected from a writer of the eighteenth Century. A Scotchman by birth, Mr Pinkerton is equally disposed and even anxious to illustrate the history of England: he had long without my knowledge, entertained a project similar to my own; his twelve letters, under a fictitious signature, in the Gentleman's Magazine (1788)[12] display the zeal of a patriot and the learning of an antiquarian. As soon as he was informed by Mr Nichol the bookseller of my wishes and my choice: he advanced to meet me with the generous ardour of a volunteer, conscious of his strength, desirous of exercise[c] and careless of reward: we have discussed in several conversations every material point that relates to the general plan and arrangement of the work, and I can only complain of his excessive docility to the opinions of a man much less skilled in the subject than himself. Should it be objected that such a work will surpass the powers of a single man, and that industry is best promoted by the division of labour, I must answer that Mr Pinkerton seems one of the children of those Heroes whose race is almost extinct: that hard assiduous study is the sole amusement of his independent leisure; that his warm inclination will be quickened by the sense of a duty resting solely on himself, that[d] he is[e] now in the vigour of age and health, and that the most voluminous of our historical Collections was the most speedily finished by the diligence of Muratori alone. I must add that I know not where to seek an associate; that the operations of a society are often perplexed by the division of sentiments and characters and often retarded[f] by the degrees of talent and application; and that the Editor will be always ready to receive the advice of judicious Counsellors and to employ the hand of subordinate Workmen.

Two questions will immediately arise concerning the title of our historical collection, and the period of time in which it may be circumscribed The first of these questions whether it should be styled the *Scriptores rerum Britannicarum*, or the *Scriptores rerum Anglicarum* will be productive of more than a verbal difference: the former imposes the duty of publishing all original documents that relate to the history and antiquities of the British islands; the latter is satisfied with the spacious though less ample field of England. The ambition of a conqueror might prompt him to grasp the whole British World and to think with Cæsar that nothing was done while any thing remained undone.

Nil actum reputans dum quid superesset agendum.

But prudence soon discerns the inconvenience of encreasing a[a] labour already sufficiently arduous, and of multiplying the volumes of a work which must unavoidably swell to a very respectable size. The extraneous appendages of Scotland, Ireland and even Wales would impede our progress, violate the unite[b] of design and introduce into a Latin text a strange mixture of savage and unknown idiom. For the sake of the Saxon Chronicle; the Editor of the *Scriptores rerum Anglicarum* will probably improve his knowelge [of] our mother tongue; nor will he be at a loss in the recent and occasional use of some French and English memorials[.] But if he attempts to hunt the old Britons among the islands of Scotland, in the bogs of Ireland and over the mountains of Wales, he [must] devote himself to the study of the Celtic dialects without being assured that his time and toil will be compensated by any adequate reward. It seems to be almost confessed that the Highland Scots do not possess any writing of a remote date; and the claims of the Welsh are faint and uncertain. The Irish alone boast of whole libraries which they sometimes hide in the fastnesses of their country and sometimes transport to their Colleges abroad: but the vain and credulous obstinacy with[c] which amidst the light of science they cherish[d] the Milesian fables of their infancy may teach us to suspect the existence, the age and the value of these Manuscripts, till they shall be fairly exposed to the eye of profane Criticism. This exclusion however of the Countries which have since been united to the crown of England must be understood with some latitude[:] the Chronicle of Melross is common to the borderers of both Kingdoms; the Expugnatio Hiberniæ of Giraldus Cambrensis contains the interesting story of *our* settlement in the Western isle; and it may be judged proper to insert the Latin Chronicle of Caradoc

---

[a] *I.* the   [b] *II.* unity   [c] *I.* wh   [d] *I.* still

(which is yet unpublished, and the Code of native laws which were abolished by the Conqueror of Wales.[13] Even the[a] English transactions in peace and war with our[b] independent neighbours, especially those of Scotland will be best illustrated by a fair comparison of the hostile narratives. The second question, of the period of time which this Collection should embrace admits of an[c] easier decision; nor can we act more prudently than by adopting the plan of Muratori and the French Benedictines who confine themselves within the limits of ten Centuries from the year five hundred to the year fifteen hundred of the Christian Æra. The former of these dates coincides with the most ancient of our national writers; the latter approaches within nine years of the accession of Henry viii which Mr Hume considers as the true and perfect Æra of modern history. From that time we are enriched and even oppressed with such treasures of contemporary and authentic documents in our own language; that the historian[d] of the present or[e] a future age will be only perplexed by the choice of facts and the difficulties of arrangement. *Exoriatur aliquis!* a man[f] of genius at once eloquent and philosophic who should accomplish in the maturity of age, the immortal work, which he had conceived in the ardour of youth[.]

---

[a] *I.* our (*replaced by* the English)   [b] *I.* these   [c] *I.* an i   [d] *I.* modern historian   [e] *I.* age is (*om.* or a future age)   *I.* Geni

[Annotations in Harwood]

HOMER, B.C. 850. The positive age of Homer is of less moment than the relative distance between the author and his work. After three or four centuries he might expatiate in the fields of fiction: but if Homer lived within fourscore years of the Trojan war (Mitford's History of Greece, vol. i, p. 166, &c.) he might converse with the last companions of Ulysses and Æneas, and the probable human part of his narrative may be almost read as the history of his own times.

HOMERI OPERA inter Poetas Græcos Heroici Carminis ab Henr. Stephano.

HOMERI ILIAS, Gr. cum veteribus Scholiast. a Johan. Baptist. Gaspar d'Anse de Villoison. Venet. 1788, in folio.—The vain man had promised a standard Homer, an ancient variorum from the editions of Alexandria, Athens, Marseilles, &c. but—parturiunt montes!

VITA HOMERI, inter Opuscula a Gale, p. 118. A loose Essay on his Universal Knowledge.[1]

VITA HOMERI, ad calcem Herodoti. Some genuine traditions are perhaps mingled with the low tales of a grammarian.

APOTHEOSIS HOMERI, a Gisberto Cupero, Amstel. 1683, in 4to. A curious and learned interpretation of an ancient monument.

ANTIQUITATES HOMERICÆ, ab Everhard. Feithio[a] Argentorat. 1743, in 12mo. A poor sketch of a noble subject.

GNOMOLOGIA HOMERI, a Jacob. Duport. Cantab. 1660, in 4to.

The moral sentences of Homer, with a copious and entertaining collection of imitations, allusions, applications, parodies, &c. The Abbé de Longuerue[b], a tasteless pedant, valued Feithius[c] and Duport more than Homer himself.

GEOGRAPHIA HOMERI, ab H. Schlichthorst. Gotting. 1787, in 12mo.[2]

GEOGRAPHIA HOMERI, ab Aug. Gul. Schlegel. Hanover, 1788, in 12mo.—The tasks of two German students.

AN INQUIRY INTO THE LIFE AND WRITINGS OF HOMER. London,

---

[a] *MW 1814.* Feilhio   [b] *MW 1814.* Longuerve   [c] *MW 1814.* Feilhius

1735, in 8vo, by Blackwell[a] of Aberdeen, or rather by Bishop Berkley.[3] A fine though sometimes fanciful effort of genius and learning.

AN ESSAY ON THE ORIGINAL GENIUS AND WRITINGS OF HOMER, by Robert Wood, Esq. London, 1775, in 4to. Pompous and superficial, the scholar, the traveller, and politician! Yet not without taste and merit.

THE ILIAD AND ODYSSEY OF HOMER, BY ALEXANDER POPE. London, 1771, 9 volumes in crown 8vo. The most splendid poetical version that any language has produced.

AN ESSAY ON POPE'S ODYSSEY, by Spence. London, 1747, in 12mo. Pleased Pope, and can please none else; dry and narrow!

ILIAS ET ODYSSEA, BY BARNES, 2 vols. 4to. 2*l*. 2*s*. Cantab. 1711.

When BARNES'S HOMER appeared at Cambridge, Dr. Bentley expressed his contempt for the edition and the editor, who understood (he said) as much Greek as a Greek cobbler. Barnes is indeed a vulgar critic, and surely much inferior to Lucian's Micyllus.[4]

ILIAS ET ODYSSEA, Gr. 2 vols. fol. Glasg. 1758.

As the eye is the organ of fancy, I read Homer with more pleasure in the Glasgow folio. Through that fine medium the poet's sense appears more beautiful and transparent. Bishop Louth has said that he could discover only one error in that accurate edition, the omission of an *iota* subscribed to a dative. Yet how could a man of taste read Homer with such literal attention?

HOMERI OPERA, A BERGLERO. 2 VOLS. 12MO. 5*s*. AMST. 1707.[5]

DR. CLARKE'S EDITION. 2 VOLS. 4TO. ILIAS, LONDON, 1729; ODYSSEY, 1740.

Though not a Bentley, Dr. Clarke was a scholar and a critic. Even his metaphysical genius was usefully employed on the nice distinctions of grammar and language. His edition of Homer deserves much esteem.

ERNESTI'S EDITION OF HOMER. 5 VOLS. 8VO. LIPS. 1759.

Ernesti's Homer is a republication of Clarke's edition, with some improvements of his own. But the more original labours of Heyne of Gottingen have raised, and will doubtless answer the public expectation.

A HYMN TO CERES, *attributed to* HOMER, *has very lately been discovered by a German, in a Library at Moscow, and published by Rhunkenius in Holland. Lugd. Bat. 1780, in 8vo.*

[a] *MW 1814.* Blackwall

I am by no means ungrateful for the discovery of this mythological hymn; yet I should be far more delighted with the resurrection of the *Margites* of Homer, the picture of private life, and the model of ancient comedy. What an universal genius! We may think indeed of Shakespeare and Voltaire.

HESIOD, B.C. 870. If Hesiod, according to Velleius Paterculus, lived about the first Olympiad, 120 years after Homer, his rustic simplicity will only mark the different state of Bœotian and Ionic civilisation.

HESIODI OPERA ET DIES inter Poetas Gnomicos, BRUNCK. His only genuine work (without the Invocation to the Muses) according to his countrymen near Mount Helicon. (Pausanias, l. ix. p. 771, Edit. Kuhn.) In the Theogony I can discern a more recent age; yet it passed for Hesiod's in the time of Herodotus.

The GNOMICA, or Moral Poems of Theognis, Phocylides and Solon in the *Poetæ Heroici* of *Henry Stephens*, and the *Analecta and Poetæ Gnomici of Brunck*.

PINDAR, *inter Poetas Græcos Lectii.*

THE ODES OF PINDAR, translated into English Verse, with a Dissertation on the Olympic Games, &c. by Gilbert West. London, 1750. 2 vols. in 12mo. West has learning, good sense, and a tolerable style of versification; but Gray and Dryden alone should have translated the Odes of Pindar, and they did much better than translate.

In the Greek Poets of Henry Stephens and Lectius, and in the Analecta and Poetæ Gnomici of Brunck, we may read the fragments yet extant of CALLINUS, ARCHILOCHUS, ALCMAN, MELANIPPIDES, IBYCUS, TELESTES, MIMNERMUS, ALCÆUS, SAPPHO, ERINNA, STESICHORUS, SIMONIDES, PANYASIS, BACCHYLIDES. The shipwreck of lyric poetry is the heaviest loss the Grecian literature has sustained. How delightful would it be to glow with the free-born ardour of Alcæus, and to melt with the amorous passions of Sappho! Yet Pindar still survives, the last, but, according to the ancients, the greatest of the lyric choir. The dearest objects of my regret are the better *Iambics* of Archilochus, (whose inventive genius has been compared with that of Homer himself,) and the pathetic elegies of Simonides, of which such an exquisite specimen[6] has escaped the injuries of time.

The fragments of the martial Tyrtæus, (and they are indeed martial,) which are contained in the *Analecta et Poetæ Gnomici of Brunck*, have been published in separate editions.

SPARTAN LESSONS, or the praise of valour, by TYRTÆUS, in Greek. Glasgow, 1759, in 8vo.

TYRTÆUS, Greek and Latin; a Christian. Adolpho Klotzio. Altenburg, 1767, in 8vo.

LE THÉATRE DES GRECS, PAR LE PÈRE BRUMOY; Amsterdam, 1732. 6 vols. in 12mo. and the last improved edition, Paris, 1785—89. 12 vols. in 8vo. Like most of the Jesuits, Brumoy was a literary bigot, and a superficial scholar. Instead of studying the original, he uses and abuses the Latin version (μυριοι, sexcenti, six cent.) Yet on the faith of this worthy interpreter, many a French critic has talked about the Greek theatre.

L'ŒDIPE DE SOPHOCLE, et les OISEAUX D'ARISTOPHANE, traduites par Boivin le Cadet: one of the best scholars that France ever produced. Paris, 1729.

HISTOIRE D'HÉRODOTE TRADUITE DU GREC, PAR M. LARCHER, avec des Notes, &c. Paris, 1786. 7 vols in 8vo.[7]

The version is clear and correct; the notes are learned and judicious; and a scholar will only regret that Larcher has not published an improved edition of the Greek text. Yet this is the man whom Voltaire made the object of his ridicule.

RECHERCHES ET DISSERTATIONS SUR HÉRODOTE, *par le President Bouhier*. Dijon, 1746, in 4to.

THE SPEECHES OF ISÆUS, translated, with notes, by *William Jones*. London, 1778, in 4to.

XENOPHONTIS MEMORABILIA SOCRATIS, ab Ernesti, Gr. Lipsiæ, 1755, in 12mo.

XENOPHON'S EXPEDITION OF CYRUS, by *Edward Spelman*. London, 1747, 2 vols. 8vo.

One of the most accurate and elegant prose translations that any language has produced. It is enriched with many notes, and Forster's Geographical dissertation.

L'EXPÉDITION DE CYRUS, traduite par LARCHER. Paris, 1778, 2 vols. in 12mo.

Histoire des Animaux, par ARISTOTE, en Grec et en François, par Camus, Paris, 1783. 2 vols. in 4to. Camus is a scholar and a naturalist. The first volume contains a pure text; the second is an elaborate parallel between Aristotle's knowledge and the discoveries of the moderns.

Aristoteles de Mirabilibus Auscultationibus. Gr. et Lat. Gotting. 1786, in 4to. This collection of strange stories, which may be drawn from Aristotle's works, is illustrated by the copious and curious notes of *John Beckman*,[a] the editor.

APOLLODORI ATHENIENSIS Bibliotheca, Greek et Lat. cum notis Chr. G. Heyne. Gotting. 1782, 1783. 4 vols. in 12mo. The text is comprised in the first volume: the three last are a mine of mythological erudition.

POLYBII MEGALOPOLITANI Historiarum quicquid superest, Gr. et Lat. recensuit, digessit, illustravit Johannes Schweighæuser.[b] Lipsiæ, 1789-1793. 6 vols. (yet unfinished) in 8vo. This accomplished edition, both for the text and notes, will soon extinguish the preceding ones. The fragments are disposed in such lucid order, that we seem to have recovered the forty books of the history of Polybius.

The General History of POLYBIUS, translated from the Greek, by *Hampton*. London, 1772, 1773, 4 vols. in 8vo. The English translator has preserved the admirable sense, and improved the coarse style of his Arcadian original. A grammarian, like Dionysius, might despise Polybius for not understanding the structure of words; and Lord Monboddo might wish for a version into Attic Greek.

L'Histoire de POLYBE traduite du Grec par le Père *Vincent*

---

[a] *MW 1814.* Beekman   [b] *MW 1814.* Schleighæuser

Thuillier, avec un Commentaire Militaire par le Chevalier *de Folard*, Amsterdam, 1753—1759, 7 vols. in 4to. The mixed offspring of a monk ignorant of tactics, and a soldier ignorant of Greek. Language and history are tortured to support the *column*; but in his modern anecdotes and observations, Folard is lively, interesting, and authentic.

DIODORUS SICULUS.—Histoire Universelle de DIODORE DE SICILE, traduite par l'Abbé Terasson, Paris, 1756. 7 vols. in 12mo. The execution is tolerable, but the design was singular for a mathematician, who despised history and the ancients.

APOLLONII Sophistæ Lexicon, Iliad et Odyss. ab HIERONYM. TOLLIO, Lugd. Bat. 1788, 2 vols. 8vo.
NOVUM LEXICON GRÆCUM IN PINDARUM ET HOMERUM A CHRIST. TOBIA DAMM. BEROLINI, 1774. 4to. If we compare these two Lexicons, the Greek in his long language must veil his bonnet to the German, a most useful interpreter of Homer.

EDITOR'S NOTES

PART I

Introduction

1. All references to Gibbon's memoirs will be to *Memoirs of My Life*, ed. G. A. Bonnard (London, 1966).

2. See Geoffrey Keynes, *The Library of Edward Gibbon* (Oxford, 1940), *passim*.

3. D. M. Low suggests that Gibbon may have done some of this reading later than he thinks, e.g. at Oxford. See *Edward Gibbon 1737–1794* (London, 1937), p. 32, n. 3, and J. W. Swain's similar argument in *Edward Gibbon the Historian* (London, 1966), pp. 13–15.

4. Bonnard, notes to *Memoirs*, pp. 290–1, supplies the information and theory about Gibbon's source for 'Kishen', in a different context.

5. See, e.g., *Essai*, note to Chapter XXXVIII.

6. Lord Sheffield published the chronological table (dated 13 January 1758) that Gibbon made to accompany his French essay on Newton (*MW* 1814, iii. 150); in it, the date of the conquest of Egypt by the Hyksos is given as follows: Newton 1440, Marsham 1643, Usser 2184. In item xxx above, Gibbon gives the date as 2082. Compare *DF* (Chapter VIII), i. 238, n. 1; Bury i. 195–6, n. 2, where Gibbon gives 2184 B.C. as the date of the reign of Ninus, which is 1968 in the chronology we are considering.

7. See *Memoirs*, p. 252.

8. In a pencil note in B.M. Add. MSS. 34880, f. 6$^\text{v}$. Similarly f. 7$^\text{v}$, etc.

9. Published in *Miscellanea Gibboniana* (Lausanne, 1932).

10. Published in J. E. Norton, *The Letters of Edward Gibbon* (New York, 1956), i. 14–19, 25–30, 38–44, 49–53, 58–64, with translations; and appendix by D. M. Low (*Letters*, i. 387–90).

11. *Gibbon's Journal to January 28th, 1762*, ed. D. M. Low (London, 1929), hereafter cited as *Journal A*.

12. Really thirty, as he says at the end of the essay.

13. Table of Contents, *MW* 1814.

Chronology 1st Period

The Roman numerals are all certainly or probably lower case, except the I's, all of which are small capitals. Lord Sheffield did not print this chronology, which is apparently a fair copy in Gibbon's best hand. It is written on both rectos and versos of ff. 280–2 of B.M. Add. MSS. 34880. That there is a difference of one year between Gibbon's date and that given by modern sources for some events, e.g. 2781 B.C. for the beginning of a Sothic period in Egypt, as against 2782 B.C. in Gibbon, might enable the student of the history of chronology to determine whose authority Gibbon was adopting. The extent of Gibbon's youthful studies in chronology is indicated in *Memoirs*, pp. 42–3, 55–6, and Bonnard's notes, pp. 249–52, 260–1.

In the manuscript the left-hand column of each page is labelled in the margin 'Years/Before the/Christian Æra'. This label is replaced in the present edition by the heading printed above the column of dates.

1. All Biblical events are dated as in Usher (the dates then listed in the Authorized Version), unless Gibbon has otherwise noted.

2. Cf. *DF* (Chapter XV, n. 62), i. 562 (Bury ii. 23, n. 63).

3. Agrees with date of Kaliyuga given in modern sources.

4. See *DF* (Chapter XXVI, n. 23), ii. 575; Bury iii. 80, n. 23. The epoch was fixed 'by the authority of the present emperor', i.e. Ch'ien Lung.

5. See *DF* (Chapter VIII, n. 1), i. 238; Bury i. 197, n. 2, which accords with this date.

Common Place Book of 1755

The English notes in this commonplace book appear on ff. 5–21 and f. 38 of B.M. Add. MSS. 34880. Gibbon numbered the pages of this book with a different number for the recto and verso of each sheet. Lord Sheffield published the note on Giannone in *MW* 1814, v. 512–13. The other notes have not been published before.

Each sheet of the commonplace book is divided so as to leave room on the left for a heading (here printed in the body of the text as a sub-head) and references to sources (here printed at the end of each entry). The source that he himself had used Gibbon underlined; the authorities cited by his source were also listed, but not underlined. Though he had been in Lausanne for more than a year and a half, he began his entries with translations into English of material from French sources. After English entries on the title of 'highness' and on duels, Gibbon quotes, in Latin, Caesar on Druids. Then he considers knighthood, in English; the chimaera, in French (his sources are the Abbé Banier, Pliny the Naturalist, and Servius's comments on Virgil); knighthood again, but this time, using Giannone, in French; 'Christianisme' according to Julian the Apostate (La Bletterie's *Vie de l'empereur Julien* is mentioned in *Memoirs*, p. 79, as one of the three books read at this period that most influenced Gibbon's later career), and the success of Corneille's *Le Cid*, both the latter also in French.

English notes on Don Antonio, the 'Algonkin' language, and Arragon are interrupted by a French note on Ambrones (from M. de Bochat, Caesar, and a learned journal). These titles, and those following, suggest a rough alphabetical scheme: 'Austria, Don Juan de' (English) is preceded by Arlaud (from his works in the *Bibliothèque Germanique*) and followed by Marcus Aurelius (from Spanheim's edition of Julian's *Caesars*) and Auspices (from Dacier's Horace), all in French. Then there is a series of entries beginning with *p*; those not in English are on Pierre of Argon (Giannone again), 'Pliny Junior', Pierre. Pertius (M. de Bochat), and Philosophie (from yet another learned journal). The first sentence of the note on Pliny is in English: 'Pliny Junior says he will mark all his uncle's treatises, and that even in the order in which they were written.' Discussing the mistakes in the French translation of Pliny's letters, Gibbon uses not only the Latin text of Pliny, but several other Latin writers and scholars.

After a lengthy note on the Council of Constance, five French notes, mostly from Giannone and dealing with Church history, and all on subjects beginning with *c*, follow; but we then return to *p*—and the pages were numbered by Gibbon, so this cavalier treatment of the alphabet is not the fault of Lord Sheffield or the British Museum binders. It may be attributed rather to the manufacturers of the notebook Gibbon was using, who provided a form for making an index to one's entries by entering the numbers of the page(s) on which one had made notes according to the first letter and the first *vowel* thereafter in the heading. Gibbon has in fact filled in the page numbers from this commonplace book in the form provided. He allowed two facing pages for each letter combination, and if that were inadequate, he simply continued on another pair of pages somewhere else in the book. Hence, after his 'Co' notes he could turn the page and begin 'Po' notes without fear of confusion.

The long English note on the Pope is followed by short Latin notes on Pompey (from Sallust) and Pompeianus (Caesar). So much for that pair of letters. For the next entry, which begins the 'De' page, we return to Voltaire and English with 'Despotism,' continuing with l'Abbé Banier and Ovid for a French note on destiny, and then Latin again for a note from a current journal on Demetrius Soter. Finally, English notes on Guelfs, Frizeland, Iroquois, and Fra Paolo Sarpi begin new entry pages and complete the substantially English section of the commonplace book.

The biographical note on Sarpi condenses a thirty-page notice in the *Bibliothèque raisonnée*, and the one on Bochat introduces a little essay (in French and not made at the time of the original entry, judging from the difference in ink) on the errors young Gibbon had detected in the works of that eminent scholar of Lausanne. The other four scattered notes substantiate several of the particular interests that Gibbon mentions (in the *Memoirs*) in his reading at this period. The reference to Marsham, the chronologist, shows a continuation of the interest in the 'order of time and place' that had led to the *Age of Sesostris*, the book he tried to write at the age of fifteen. As for the others, he 'occasionally consulted the most interesting articles of [Bayle's] Philosophic dictionary', and 'Giannone's Civil history of Naples' is another of the 'three particular books, [which] may have remotely contributed to form the historian of the Roman Empire' (*Memoirs*, p. 79).

The note from Giannone is a little essay, but most of the English notes are more dependent on the text of Gibbon's source. Some, indeed, 'digest' the source largely by selection, translation, and omission—see, for example, the material from Amelot de la Houssaie quoted below as a note to the first entry.

1. The second sentence of this saying of Pliny's is quoted in *Memoirs* (p. 97), with *ex* before *aliquâ*. Bonnard neatly gives Gibbon's precise source: 'The elder Pliny's maxim is known from what his nephew, the younger Pliny, says of his

uncle's studious habits in a letter to Marcus (Pliny's *Letters*, iii, 5)' (*Memoirs*, p. 284).

2. *Mémoires historiques, politiques, critiques et littéraires*, 1722. The other sources listed by Gibbon are those cited in Amelot de la Houssaye, except that the reference to Lenglet du Fresnoy is independent. In volume i. 53 ff., Amelot de la Houssaye has the following entry:

Altesse

Autrefois le titre d'Altesse ne se donnoit qu'aux Rois, aujourd'hui il est devenu si commun, que toutes les grandes Maisons se l'attribuent. Tous les Grans, dit un Moderne, veulent être confondus avec les Princes, & font prêts de donner ateinte aux Privilegés de la Dignité Royalle. Nous en formes déja a *l'Altesse*; l'orgueil de nos descendans usurpera la *Majesté*. . . .

Filippe II. envoyant Don Juan, son frére naturel, à la guerre de Grenade, lui ordonna de ne prendre que le titre d'*Excellence*; mais Don Juan ne laissa pas de soufrir, que la Ville de Grenade le traitât d'*Altesse*, ne croyant pas contrevenir aux ordres du Roi en recevant un honneur qu'il n'éxigeoit point.

3. See p. 15.

4. *Trattato del titolo regio dovuto alla Serenissima Casa di Savoja, con un ristretto delle rivoluzioni del Reame de Cipri ragioni della Casa di Savoja sopra di esso*, Turin, 1633.

5. *Guerra de Granada hecha por el rey de España Felippe II contra los Moriscos de aquel reino sur rebeldes*, Madrid, 1610.

6. *Felipe II Rey d'España*, Madrid, 1619.

7. *Méthode pour étudier l'Histoire*, Paris, 1735. Later edition in Keynes, but this one more fully cited in a subsequent French entry in this commonplace book (*MW* 1814, v. 515; B.M. Add. MSS. 34880, f. 46ᵛ).

8. Beheaded for duelling.

9. Of France.

10. Jacques de Levis, Comte de Quelus, and his seconds, MM. de Maugiron et de Livarot, were 'mignons' of Henri III; Charles d'Entragues and his seconds (MM. de Schomberg et de Riberac) were 'favoris du duc de Guise'. Schomberg and Maugiron died on the spot, Riberac died that afternoon, Quelus died thirty-three days later. *NBG*.

11. *Germania*, c. 31.

12. Crowned king of the Romans 1248.

13. *c.* 1461.

14. 1515.

15. Oudart de Biez, maréchal in 1542; knighted Henri II in 1544.

16. *Intra* in Amelot de la Houssaye.

17. *Condidit* in Amelot de la Houssaye.

18. *Magnanimitatis* in Amelot de la Houssaye.

19. Moderns appear to disagree with Amelot de la Houssaye's rejection of Barbara Blomberg's claim to be the mother of Don Juan of Austria. See *BU*.

20. Andrew Morosini, *Historia Veneta, ab anno 1521 ad annum* 1615, Venice, 1623.

21. *DF* (Chapter XLIX), v. 167–8; Bury v. 309–10.

22. 1753.

23. Cf. *DF*, e.g. (Chapter XLIX) v. 152–3; Bury v. 296–7.

24. Cf. *DF* v. 155, n. 134; Bury v. 299, n. 142.

25. First of the 'Saxon Emperors'.

26. *DF* v. 162; Bury v. 304.

27. 1254.

28. Modern Vlie and Texel.

29. 'Je me sers de la 6ᵐᵉ Edition de cet Ouvrage. impriméé a Londres en 1693' (B.M. Add. MSS. 34880 f. 47ᵛ).

30. Cf. *DF* (Chapter XXXVIII), iii. 613; Bury iv. 147.

31. Uncle (by marriage) of Gibbon's friend Georges Deyverdun.

32. Bayle's *Dictionnaire*, article 'Bellarmin', especially remarks M and X, with notes 46, 47, 79, and 85, is Gibbon's source. The sources cited are Bayle's. Jacopo Fuligatti, *Vita del Cardinale Bellarmino della Compagnia di Giesù*, Rome, 1624. Edwin Sandis, *Relation de l'Église et de l'état*, 1642. James I of England published an *Apology for the Oath of Allegiance* (1606) answering two breves of Pope Paul V and a letter of Bellarmin's. Conrad Vorst, *Anti-Bellarminus Contractus...*, 1610. Johann Friedrich Mayer, *de fide Baronii et Bellarmini ipsis pontificiis ambigua eclogae*, Amsterdam, 1697.

33. Gibbon extracts from Bayle's notes 109, 116, and 118. François Garasse, *La Doctrine curieuse des beaux esprits de ce temps...* Paris, 1623. François Ogier *Jugement et censure de la doctrine curieuse du P. Garasse*, Paris, 1623.

34. Gibbon's own source. Courayer is the primary source of the thirty-page account in the *Bibliothèque*. The other sources are also mentioned in that article.

35. Pietro Giannone, *Istoria civile del Regno di Napoli* (1723), French translation published Geneva, 1742, but see Appendix.

36. Gibbon's edition of Cicero was then that of Isaac Verburgius, *Ciceronis opera quae supersunt omnia...*, Amsterdam, 1724. See *Memoirs*, p. 75, and Bonnard's note, p. 274.

Petersfield Speech

A printed copy is in B.M. Add. MSS. 34881, f. 251. Also in *Journal A*, Appendix II, pp. 242–4.

1. Presumably William Jolliffe. *Journal A*, n. 3, pp. 23–4.

2. Presumably 'one Barnard of Alresford', *Journal A*, p. 23. See April 1ʳˢᵗ entry, p. 24. Sir John Barnard retired from public life 1758, died at Clapham, 29 August 1764.

Hurd on Horace

This essay is written on thirty folio pages, B.M. Add. MSS. 34880, ff. 189–218, rectos only except for long notes, cued in Gibbon's text with square brackets, while he uses round brackets in the text to cue page references, which he has placed in the margin. In the present edition these marginal references are inserted into Gibbon's round brackets, while numbers are supplied in his square brackets for the long notes, which are printed at the end of the essay.

On p. 35, after 'The Chorus ... bearing a part in it, gives it', Gibbon changed notebooks, and the next page is headed, in his hand, 'Continued from Vol. I, p. 44'. Lord Sheffield published this essay, with numerous small changes (indicated in the apparatus criticus), in *MW* 1796, ii. 27–50, and *MW* 1814, iv. 113–54.

1. William Warburton. See 'Critical Observations on the Sixth Book of the Aeneid', p. 159.

2. *Les Aventures de Télémaque*. Cf. 'Critical Observations on ... the Aeneid', p. 142.

3. See *Memoirs*, p. 76, and Bonnard's note, p. 275; see also 'Index Expurgatorius', p. 107.

4. About which of them invented the calculus.

5. Chapter 19.

6. Gibbon refers to his writing of this essay several times in *Journal A*: pp. 45, 49, 198.

PART II

Introduction

1. See Low, p. 199.

2. Except the *Mémoire justicatif* (1779), a state paper written at the request of the Secretary of State and the Lord Chancellor; see *Memoirs*, pp. 160–1; Low, 281–2.

3. Gibbon mentions the abstract in his account of his preparatory studies for the *DF*, after his discussion of his attempted Swiss history and his 'Critical Observations on the Sixth Book of the Aeneid'. The next date he mentions (p. 149) is 1770. No doubt that is why Sheffield assigns the date 1770 to the Blackstone abstract. Gibbon himself seems to place it as late as 1768, though he mentions no date.

4. In *Edward Gibbon the Historian* (London, 1966), pp. 122–3.

5. Compare an early essay included in the *Decline and Fall* (iii. 629–40; Bury iv. 160–9, and for date, Appendix 6, p. 529). Called 'General Observations on the Fall of the Roman Empire in the West', it was written, according to Gibbon, prior to the accession of Louis XVI, i.e. before May 1774 (*Memoirs*, p. 175).

Abstract of Blackstone

Lord Sheffield printed excerpts from this work in *MW* 1814, v. 545–7, as follows: his first paragraph is Gibbon's note [1] (p. 63 above); his second is Gibbon's *second* paragraph. Then he prints notes [4], [5] (omitting the last sentence), and [7]. The notes, which I have numbered, were written by Gibbon on the backs of the main sheets, parallel to the passages in the text to which they pertain. He headed the first such sheet of notes 'Remarks'. He discontinued this practice after the seventh folio. I have inserted his first five 'remarks' at the end of the 'Introduction', and the last two after the chapters to which they pertain.

Sheffield says that he omits the remainder of this essay because it is 'principally extracts' (v. 547). Though the information and even the point of view is usually Blackstone's, the language, the arrangement (within sections), and the emphases are Gibbon's; this is certainly not just a set of paraphrases and quotations. At first Gibbon follows Blackstone more closely than is his later practice, but a comparison of Gibbon's seventh paragraph with its source in Blackstone may show us how far from being merely 'extracts' Gibbon's abstracts are, even when they are relatively close to their original.

Blackstone says (page references to the edition Gibbon cites):

> The judges in the several courts of justice [are] bound by an oath to decide according to the law of the land. Their knowledge of that law is derived from experience and study; . . . and from being long personally accustomed to the judicial decisions of their predecessors. And indeed these judicial decisions are the principal and most authoritative evidence, that can be given, of the existence of such a custom as shall form a part of the common law. (69).
>
> The reports are extant in a regular series from the reign of king Edward the second inclusive (71).
>
> Besides these reporters, there are also other authors, to whom great veneration and respect is paid by the students of the common law. Such are Glanvil and Bracton . . . with some others of antient date, whose treatises are cited as authority; and are evidence that cases have formerly happened in which such and such points were determined, which are now become settled and first principles. One of the last of these methodical writers in point of time [is Sir Edward Coke]. (72)

Gibbon's own description of the relationship between what he has done and Blackstone seems more apt than Sheffield's: 'a copious and critical abstract of that English work [i.e. Blackstone] was my first serious production in my native language' (*Memoirs*, p. 148).

Traces of Gibbon's own views and interests will be found throughout, e.g., paternal power, English and Roman; property qualifications for voting; slavery. The abstract is found in Add. MSS. 34881, ff. 217–41, rectos only, except for 'Remarks'. It can be dated 1765 (or early 1766), because Gibbon says 'we have only the first Volume', but the second volume was published in 1766. Gibbon's page-references to Blackstone, in the right-hand margin of the manuscript, are here printed in square brackets at the beginning of the relevant section.

1. Habeas Corpus Bill, 1679.

2. The Triennial Act, 1694; set maximum length of a parliament at three years, lengthened to seven years in 1716.

3. 1689.

4. Act of Settlement, 1701.

5. i.e. from 1066 to 1603.

6. Bill of Rights, 1689.

Hints

Each of the seventeen small sheets in this set (B.M. Add. MSS. 34882, ff. 187–203) was headed 'Hints' No. I, II, etc., but the number was the number of the sheet, not of the entry. Instead, Gibbon indicated divisions between entries with a line across the sheet. I have retained Gibbon's horizontal rules, as usual, and also the hint numbers. My placement of these cannot correspond exactly to his however, so I have used a vertical rule to indicate the division between manuscript sheets. Gibbon used the rectos only, except that notes appear on the verso of the sheet to which they pertain. I have inserted the notes to each item at its conclusion.

The comments 'on the character and conduct of Brutus', 'Hints' No. XIV and XV, are clearly preliminary to the formal essay on Brutus (pp. 96–106), and references within those hints will be explained only where they are not duplicated in the completed essay. The Hints were published by Lord Sheffield in *MW* 1814, v. 536–44. As discussed above, the Mably reference ('Hints' No. III) shows that the Hints cannot be earlier than 1765. On general principles, we can perhaps date these miscellaneous historical notes 1765–8, when Gibbon had not yet settled down to the preparation of his great work.

1. Re civil wars, cf. *DF* (Chapter V), i. 146; Bury i. 118.

2. Cf. 'Brutus' essay, p. 98.

3. Cf. *Memoirs*, p. 42.

4. For Pharamund see *DF* (Chapter XXXI), iii. 221–2, n. 168; Bury iii. 350–1, n. 174.

5. For Salic Law, see above, p. 184 and *DF* (Chapter XXXVIII), iii. 583–4, n. 67; Bury iv. 122, n. 71.

6. Cf. *Memoirs*, p. 170.

7. Of France.

8. See *DF* (Chapter XXXVIII), iii. 569; Bury iv. 110.

9. *Epistles to Several Persons*, Epistle I, to Sir Richard Temple, Lord Viscount Cobham. Gibbon blends lines 174–6:

> Search then the Ruling Passion: There, alone,
> The Wild are constant, and the Cunning known;
> The Fool consistent, and the False sincere. . . .

(The Twickenham Pope, III. ii. 31, ed. F. W. Bateson).

10. Molière's *Comtesse d'Escarbagnas*, 1671; Shakespeare's *Merry Wives of Windsor*, c. 1600–1.

11. Cf. *DF* (Chapter XXVIII), iii. 102, notes 89 and 90; Bury iii. 215, notes 96 and 97.

12. Plutarch, non-Christian, non-prelate; Bellarmin, Catholic cardinal; Tillotson, Anglican archbishop. Cf. *Vindication*, p. 277.

13. i.e., Le Sage's *Bachelier de Salamanque*.

14. All Gibbon's sources for these notes on Brutus are also cited in the completed essay, except Guischardt, whom Gibbon read in May 1762 (*Journal A*, pp. 71–5).

15. Corneille's *La Mort de Pompée, c.* 1643.

16. Thucydides, admiral; Guicciardini, ambassador and governor.

17. Joseph Warton.

Digression on the Character of Brutus

This essay, in the hand of a copyist but with autograph corrections, may be found in B.M. Add. MSS. 34880, ff. 264–72. Lord Sheffield published it in *MW* 1814, iv. 95–111. It should be compared with its rough draft in 'Hints' above, pp. 93–4. Gibbon's copyist followed Gibbon's own practice of beginning each line of a quoted passage with another quotation mark; I have done so also, though naturally I could not preserve the exact location of these marks.

1. With this remark, compare a passage in Gibbon's planned revision of *DF* i. 7, p. 339 above. Timoleon, deliverer of Sicily, 344–337 B.C. Lucius Junius Brutus, legendary first consul of Rome, deliverer of Rome from the Tarquins. Andrea Doria, deliverer of Genoa in 1528. Gustavus Vasa, deliverer of Sweden from the Danes in 1521–3. The four princes of Orange, presumably, are the successors of William I: Maurice, Frederick Henry, William II, and William III (of England). For the 'three peasants' see Gibbon's note 4.

2. Cf. 'Hints', No. II, p. 88 above.

3. For Tschudi, see Bonnard's reference in *Memoirs*, p. 307, i.e. in G. von Wyss, *Geschichte der Historiographie in der Schweiz*, Zurich, 1895, pp. 196–202. Gibbon read and marked Tschudi's *Chronicon helveticum* with his friend Georges Deyverdun in the summers of 1765–7 (*Memoirs*, p. 141).

4. Not identified.

5. Middleton considered the Brutus letters genuine; Tunstall and Markland disagreed with him.

6. In addition to the editions cited in Keynes, Gibbon may have used the quarto *Essays* of 1758. See 'Index Expurgatorius', No. 3.

Index Expurgatorius

The entries in the 'Index Expurgatorius' were numbered and provided with an alphabetical listing by Gibbon. They are written on both sides of Add. MSS. 34882, ff. 29–48, and were printed by Sheffield in *MW* 1814, v. 548–79, except that numbers 4 and 15 were omitted, and the item numbers were altered suitably in both text and index list. The lines between items are Gibbon's. He sometimes omits them, when the end of an entry coincides with the end of a sheet. The works cited, especially Buffon's index (I.E. 40) and *Monthly Review*, August 1767 (I.E. 35), suggest 1768–9 as a probable date for the 'Index Expurgatorious'. Some of the entries—Lardner, Warburton's *Divine Legation*, Frederick the Great—deal with subjects also dealt with in the *Mémoires littéraires de la Grande Bretagne pour l'an 1767 (1768)*, on which Gibbon collaborated with Georges Deyverdun. As the index is written in English, it is not likely that Gibbon thought of it as possibly publishable in one of the volumes of *Mémoires littéraires*. But reading for the journal might well have occasioned his discovery of the errors he here indexes, or discovering the error may have led him to decide to review some work in the journal.

1. In 1762 Gibbon read and wrote a critical abstract of this work by Richard Hurd; see above, pp. 27–53. Warburton, especially in his *Divine Legation*, was a favourite target of Gibbon's irony: cf., e.g., in Draft E of his memoirs, 'The Divine Legation of Moses is a monument, already crumbling into dust, of the vigour and weakness of the human mind' (Murray, p. 305; Add. MSS. 34874, f. 98ʳ). François Catrou is mentioned as one of the scholars young Gibbon consulted in his classical studies, *Memoirs*, p. 76.

2. Hume's *Essays* in 4° were issued in 1758 and in 1768; according to Keynes, Gibbon *owned* the latter edition. If Gibbon has given the date incorrectly here, this reference is further evidence that the 'Index Expurgatorius' should be dated no earlier than 1768. Gibbon shows more confidence in Hume and Wallace as authorities on population in note 87 to Chapter IX, *DF* i. 288; Bury i. 236, n. 90.

3. Perhaps Sheffield decided to suppress the note because Gibbon was personally acquainted with M. de Beaufort and complimented him in the *Memoirs* (p. 87), or perhaps Sheffield made the decision while preparing *MW* 1796, before M. de Beaufort's death, even though the 'Index Expurgatorius' was not published until *MW* 1814.

4. Pierre-Julien Rouillé worked with Catrou on an *Histoire romaine (BU)*.

5. To live up to Gibbon's standards of elementary chronological literacy we must remember that dates A.U.C. start 753 B.C. For Gibbon's view of Brutus, see above, pp. 96–106.

6. There is no record of Gibbon's having owned this work by William Guthrie. It had four editions between 1744 and 1758 (*DNB*).

7. Guischardt's *Mémoires militaires*, first published in 1757, were read by Gibbon in May 1762 (*Journal A*, pp. 71–5). Gibbon read a dissertation upon the Roman Calendar on 25–6 August 1761 (*Journal A*, pp. 33, 166–9).

8. Cluverius's *Italia antiqua* had been Gibbon's constant companion while preparing for his Italian journey. See *Journal B* and Georges A. Bonnard, *L'Importance du deuxième séjour de Gibbon à Lausanne* (Lausanne, 1944).

9. Gibbon approved highly of both Photius: cf. *DF* (Chapter LIII), v. 512–3; Bury vi. 104–5, and Muratori: cf. *DF* (Chapter LXX), vi. 618, n. 98; Bury vii. 300, n. 110. Re Salmasius, see Gibbon's *Essai sur l'étude de la littérature* and *DF* (Chapter XL), iv. 72, n. 64; Bury iv. 229, n. 65.

10. Apuleius, *Metamorphoseon libri XI*, ed. John Price, Paris, 1635 in Gibbon's library. Lucian, *Opera*, ed. Jean Bourdelot, Paris, 1615; Saumur, 1619.

11. It is ironic that Gibbon himself was later to take romance for history in writing of Mohammed (Bury, *DF* 'Introduction', i, p. xlvii).

12. In editions of Pope's works of 1726 and later, new ll. 5–10 were added, and this 'verse 6' became the twelfth line (*Minor Poems*, ed. John Butt, Twickenham Pope, vi. 205–6). The correction was apparently not made in the edition of Addison from which Gibbon quotes.

13. See *DF* (Chapter XVI), i. 646–7; Bury ii. 92–3.

14. In *DF* (Chapter XLVII), iv. 598, n. 118; Bury v. 150, n. 121, Gibbon remarks, 'The inscription of Siganfu, which describes the fortunes of the Nestorian Church from the first mission A.D. 636 to the current year 781, is accused of forgery by La Croze, Voltaire &c. who become the dupes of their own cunning while they are afraid of a Jesuitical fraud.'

15. For Gibbon's distrust of Porphyry, see 'Index Expurgatorius' No. 26; he thought the work cited was spurious. Prudentius, like Lactantius, was presumably disqualified as a witness because of his Christian prejudices.

16. Harmodius and Aristogeiton killed Hipparchus, one of the tyrants of Athens, and were themselves killed as a result (514 B.C.). Cf. 'Brutus' essay above, p. 104.

17. Cf. *DF* (Chapter LI, notes 69 and 71), v. 314–15; Bury v. 429, n. 81, and 431, n. 85.

18. Re Bérénice, cf. *DF* (Chapter XLIV), iv. 382, n. 133; Bury iv. 482, n. 134 and *DF* v. 491, n. 60; Bury vi. 86, n. 66.

19. Tillemont was an important aide to Gibbon in the first four volumes of the *DF*—cf. note 79 to Chapter XLVII (iv. 577; Bury v. 132, n. 81).

20. *Royal and Noble Authors* (1758).

21. Jean-Baptiste de la Curne de Ste. Palaye, *Mémoires sur la Chivalrie*, Paris, 1759–81. Cf. *DF* (Chapter LXVIII), vi. 514, n. 93; Bury vii. 206, n. 124.

22. Ulisse Aldrovandi, *Histoire naturelle*, 13 vol. fol., 1599–1606.

23. Contrast *DF* (Chapter XLI), iv. 157, n. 44; Bury iv. 297, n. 52, and see *DF* (Chapter L), v. 175, n. 11; Bury v. 315, n. 12.

24. *BU* agrees that the translator was Bernard Tscharner. Jean-Jacques Leu, *Dictionnaire universel de la Suisse*, 20 vol. 4°, 1746–63.

Critical Observations on the Sixth Book of the *Aeneid*

In his *Memoirs*, Gibbon speaks of this pamphlet as 'an accidental sally of love and resentment; of my reverence for modest Genius, and my aversion for insolent pedantry' (p. 144). He continues

The learning and abilities of [Warburton] had raised him to a just eminence; but he reigned the Dictator and tyrant of the World of Litterature. The real merit of Warburton was degraded by the pride and presumption with which he pronounced his infallible decrees; in his polemic writings he lashed his antagonists without mercy or moderation:

and his servile flatterers . . . assaulted every modest dissenter who refused to consult the oracle, and to adore the Idol. In a land of liberty, such despotism must provoke a general opposition . . . *I* too without any private offence was ambitious of breaking a lance against the Giant's shield: and in the beginning of the year 1770, my Critical observations on the sixth book of the Æneid were sent without my name to the press. In this short Essay, my first English publication, I aimed my strokes against the person and the Hypothesis of Bishop Warburton. . . . But I cannot forgive myself the contemptuous treatment of a man, who, with all his faults, was entitled to my esteem; and I can less forgive, in a personal attack, the cowardly concealment of my name and character. (144–6)

The edition of 1770 is the only authority for the text of this essay. There is no manuscript, and a reprint of 1794 for one Thomas Green was made after Gibbon's death and without any revision by him (see J. E. Norton, *A Bibliography of the Works of Edward Gibbon*, Oxford, 1940, pp. 20–1). Sheffield included this essay in *MW* 1796, ii. 497–525, and *MW* 1814, iv. 467–509 (changing the title to 'Critical Observations on the Design' &c.).

The success of Gibbon's argument has been discussed by Low, pp. 204–5; Norton, *Bibliography*, pp. 20–1; Bonnard, notes to *Memoirs*, p. 311. According to Low, the issue was still a matter of scholarly debate in 1937. I do not know that thirty more years have sufficed to settle it. For the general reader, the vigour of the mind revealed and the language revealing it, and particularly the enthusiastic delight that Gibbon allowed himself to feel and to express with regard to literature, in contrast to his zealous avoidance of zeal in politics and religion, make the essay of enduring interest.

1. i.e. William Warburton, in *The Divine Legation of Moses demonstrated* and in 'A Dissertation on the Sixth Book of Virgil's Aeneis', in Virgil's *Works* trans. Pitt and Warton. See Gibbon's first note.

2. *Marmora Arundeliana* (1624) of John Selden. The Arundel Marbles, i.e. the collection of Thomas Howard, Earl of Arundel, included the Parian Chronicle.

3. These authors are obviously diverse in kind as well as in time. For Sanchoniatho and Orpheus, see *OCD*, under Philo (5) and *Orphic Literature* respectively. Gibbon expresses his view of Zaleucus and Charondas later in his note. He regarded Porphyry's oracles as spurious (see 'Index Expurgatorius', No. 26, above) and calls Geoffrey of Monmouth's history of England, which introduces the exploits of King Arthur, a 'romance' (see p. 538 above). Thus Gibbon was highly sceptical of the historical authority of all the authors he lists in this sentence.

4. 'A heap of learned rubbish', according to Gibbon's 'Index Expurgatorius', No. 26.

5. Perhaps the 'learned Catholic' is Jean Bourdelot, whose edition of Lucian is cited by name in 'Index Expurgatorius', No. 15.

6. Warburton had appealed specifically to Book I, Epistles 9 and 16 of the *Epistles to Atticus*.

7. In his *Lucian*, published at Amsterdam in that year.

8. Voltaire expresses his disappointment in the latter half of the *Aeneid* in 'Virgile' in his 'Essai sur la poésie épique'. I do not find the exact phrase Gibbon

quotes from Warburton's quotation, in modern editions of this essay, but that is perhaps because Voltaire first wrote it in English (1726), and its first appearance in French was in a translation not by Voltaire himself, but by the Abbé Desfontaines. When Voltaire reprinted the French version, in 1731 and 1733, he corrected its faults, the latter revision being especially thorough. It is possible that Warburton was not using Voltaire's latest revision.

9. *Rambler*, No. 176 (Saturday, 23 November 1751).

10. The edition of *Les Aventures de Télémaque* that Gibbon owned at this time has not been identified (Keynes, p. 123). Cf. above, 'Hurd on Horace', p. 41.

11. Wechel was the printer of Amyot's Plutarch.

12. Gibbon no doubt alludes to such lines as the first three in the 'Hymn' in Thomson's *Seasons*:

> These, as they change, Almighty Father, these
> Are but the varied God. The rolling year
> Is full of thee.

13. Cf. *DF* i. 6; Bury i. 5, and p. 339 above.

14. Cf. *Aeneid*, vi. line 751. But this is quoted from Pope, 'Messiah,' l. 90.

15. Or, as Yeats was to put it, 'How can we know the dancer from the dance?'

16. Robert Lowth.

17. See Gibbon's next note 7.

18. *Satyricon*, 118, 5. 'Dr. Warton' is Thomas Warton the younger.

19. Richard Hurd. See above, Part I, pp. 27–53.

20. *Le Virgile travesti* (1648), Book VI.

21. James I of England, in *Demonology, in Form of a Dialogue* (1597), argued that witches, demons, etc., exist.

Outlines of the History of the World

This essay, probably to be dated 1771 (see above, p. 57), may be found in B.M. Add. MSS. 34880, ff. 239–59. Lord Sheffield printed it in *MW* 1796, ii. 405–37, and *MW* 1814, iii. 1–55. Differences between Gibbon's knowledge and priorities here and those of the final two volumes of the *DF* are obvious. His values and value judgements, however, show relatively little change in the same period (1771–88).

The editor's notes direct the reader to parallel passages in the *DF*. Passages not annotated deal with matters not treated (or treated only incidentally) in the history. There are a number of chapters in the *DF* v and vi to which no references are made below. These chapters contain materials either unknown to, or neglected by, Gibbon, in this earlier survey. Even the page references in the *DF*, moreover, may serve to show how the neat division into centuries and sovereigns broke down as Gibbon surveyed some 800 years of the Eastern empire, 'a tedious and uniform tale of weakness and misery', but '*passively* connected with the most splendid and important revolutions which have changed the state of the world. The space of the lost provinces was immediately replenished with new colonies and rising kingdoms: the active virtues of peace and war deserted from the vanquished to the victorious nations; and it is in their origin and conquests, in their religion and government, that we must explore the causes and effects of the decline and fall of the Eastern empire' (*DF* (Chapter XLVIII) v. 2, 4; Bury v. 169, 171).

Dates and certain headings placed by Gibbon in the left-hand margin of his manuscript are in the present edition inserted into the text in square brackets.

1. *DF* (Chapter LII), v. 452–3; Bury vi. 51–2.

2. *DF* v. 432–8, 443–55; Bury vi. 34–40, 44–54.

3. *DF* v. 447–9; Bury vi. 47–8.

4. *DF* v. 449–52; Bury vi. 48–51.

5. *DF* (Chapter XLIX), v. 146–8; Bury v. 291–3.

6. *DF* (Chapter LII), v. 423–30; Bury vi. 27–34.

7. *DF* (Chapter LIII), v. 471–9; Bury vi. 68–75.

8. *DF* v. 511–17; Bury vi. 103–8.

9. Contrast *DF* (Chapter XLIX), v. 147–8; Bury v. 292–3.

10. *DF* (Chapter LVI), v. 588; Bury vi. 173–4.

11. *DF* (Chapter XLIX), v. 148–9, 157–8; Bury v. 293–4, 300–1; and (Chapter LV), v. 557; Bury vi. 144–5.

12. *DF* (Chapter LII), v. 416–17; Bury vi. 21–2.

13. *DF* v. 417–18, 458; Bury vi. 22, 56.

14. *DF* v. 456–8; Bury vi. 55–6.

15. *DF* v. 458–63; Bury vi. 56–61.

16. *DF* (Chapter XXXVII), iii. 519; Bury iv. 69.

17. *DF*, Chapter LVII.

18. *DF* (Chapter XLIX), v. 151–9; Bury v. 296–302.

19. *DF* (Chapter LVI), v. 598–603; Bury vi. 184–8.

20. *DF*, Chapter LVIII.

21. *DF*, Chapter LV.

22. *DF* (Chapter LXIX), vi. 518–28; Bury vii. 209–18; vi. 544–50; Bury vii. 233–9.

23. *DF*, Chapter LXIV.

24. *DF* (Chapter LIX), vi. 108–10; Bury vi. 354–6.

25. *DF* vi. 110–12; Bury vi. 356–8.

26. *DF* vi. 113–17; Bury vi. 358–62.

27. *DF* (Chapter LXIV), 319–23; Bury vii. 31–5.

28. *DF*, Chapter LXV.

29. *DF* (Chapter LXVI), vi. 419, 431–3; Bury vii. 119, 129–31.

30. *DF*, Chapter LXVIII.

31. *DF* (Chapter LXX), vi. 604–6; Bury vii. 288–90.

32. *DF* vi. 608; Bury vii. 291.

Second Commonplace Book

These notes were written on ten sheets numbered by Gibbon in the upper left corners (odd numbers) and the upper right corners (even numbers), now in B.M. Add. MSS. 34882, ff. 207–16. Gibbon's even-numbered pages are blank, except his 14 (f. 214ʳ), which completes a note begun on 13. His odd numbers are the versos of the B.M. volume, except that ff. 210 and 216 are inserted so that Gibbon's 7 precedes his 6, his 20 precedes his 19—6 and 20 are blank, of course.

Each page contains entries on only one subject, which Gibbon labelled in the left-hand margin. The labels are here printed as subheads. He provided volume and page references to his authorities in the right-hand margin. In the present edition these references are listed at the end of each entry. Note numbers in round brackets or without brackets are Gibbon's; those in square brackets have been supplied here by the editor.

The heading 'common place book' and some additional notes on Mexico from a detached sheet (see above, Part III, p. 318) were added in pencil by Sheffield or one of his assistants. The references to Raynal, whose history was first published in 1770, and the lack of a reference to Robertson's *History of America* (see note one below) make it possible to date these notes between 1770 and 1777, probably about 1774. They were printed in *MW* 1814, v. 529–35.

1. Chiapa = modern Chiapas. As Las Casas is treated at length in William Robertson's *History of America* (i. 218–36), published in 1777, and as Robertson's work was immediately read and admired by Gibbon (see *Letters*, ii. 152–3), this entry tends to confirm the hypothesis that this commonplace book should be dated prior to 1777, for if it had been possible, Gibbon would almost certainly have referred to Robertson as well as Raynal.

2. The edition cited, though in Gibbon's library, was not listed in his Bentinck Street catalogue compiled in 1777.

3. In *DF* (Chapter L), v. 254–5, n. 164, Bury, v. 380, n. 177, Gibbon summarizes these accounts of Hercules's feat, apropos of Mohammed. He omits there the reference to Arnobius. The *DF* editions of the works cited are evidently the same ones cited here, except for Apollodorus (see below).

4. In *DF* reference, cited as L. i. eleg. iii, not L. iii ep. 1.

5. The Apollodorus in Keynes is cited in *DF*. But the page-reference differs, so Gibbon cannot have used that edition for this note.

6. See Part IV, p. 367 above.

7. Not listed as in Gibbon's Bentinck Street Library.

On 'L'Homme au masque de fer'

The manuscript of this essay is not in Gibbon's hand. It is in B.M. Add. MSS. 34880, ff. 261–3, on both sides of the folios. As there are very few corrections in the manuscript, and those consist of insertion or deletion of single letters, we cannot be sure whether Gibbon proofread this copy or not. Sheffield included the essay in *MW* 1814, v. 41–7, and in the first edition of *MW* ii. 527–30.

1. 1752.

2. 1770–2.

3. For François de Vendome, Duc de Beaufort, see *BU*.

4. Louis de Bourbon, Comte de Vermandois, natural son of Louis XIV and the Duchesse de la Vallière; legitimized 1669. See *BU*.

5. James Scott, Duke of Monmouth, natural son of Charles II; created Duke of Monmouth in 1663.

6. Henri Griffet, S.J., wrote a *Journal du règne de Louis XIV* in his edition of Daniel's *Histoire de France* (1755–8). In 1770 he published *Réponse de M. de Sainte-Foix . . . et recueil de tout ce qui a été écrit sur le prisonnier masqué.* He was not Confessor to the Bastille until some years after 1703, however. See *BU*.

PART III

Introduction

1. The third edition was the first in which the notes were printed at the foot of the page. See J. E. Norton, *A Bibliography of the Works of Edward Gibbon* (Oxford, 1940), pp. 46–7.

2. In 'Preface' to Edward Gibbon, *Vindication* (Oxford, 1961), p. viii.

3. See Georges A. Bonnard, 'Gibbon at Work on his *Memoirs*', *English Studies*, xlv. 210–11.

Notes on Modern Europe

As shown above, p. 209, the notes below must have been made during May–October 1777. They are found in B.M. Add. MSS. 34882, ff. 224–52. Sheffield published two of the notes about Russia and one brief note about France (indicated as they occur), in *MW* 1814, v. 525–9. The primary interest of these notes is perhaps the concern Gibbon shows in them for economic data—populations, percentages of persons in religious life, amounts and sources of revenue, military establishments. Various notes deal with Spain, Poland, Sweden, Prussia, and Italy, as well as Russia and France. Although Gibbon used the material about the population of France in *DF* (Chapter XVII), ii. 68, and n. 182 (Bury ii. 196, and n. 191), much of his interest in this material can be attributed not to the needs of the history, but to his concern about the events of his own time, and to his increasing awareness, sometimes underestimated by readers of the *Decline and Fall*, of the influence of economic facts on historical events. On the other hand, he also condescends to record some tidbits of scandalous gossip.

The two notes numbered in square brackets were written by Gibbon on the back of the facing sheets and not cued by him to any specific spot in the text.

1. i.e. the Opéra, the Comédie Française, and the Opéra-Comique.

2. *livres*. In 1753 a *livre* was worth about 10½*d*. (see *Memoirs*, p. 269 n., and Magdalen College Library MS. 359, i. 1).

3. Joseph II of Germany became Holy Roman Emperor in 1765; travelled incognito in France in April 1777.

4. Conseiller d'État 1775.

5. —de la Reyniere, *fermier général*. See A. B. L. Grimod de la Reynière, son and grandson of *fermiers généraux* (*NBG*).

6. Jacques Necker, Gibbon's friend since 1765, became Director General of Finance for France in June 1777.

7. Jules François de Cotte became Président in 1745. (François Bluche, *Les Magistrats du Parlement de Paris au XVIIIᵉ siècle* (*1715–1771*), Paris, 1960.) He was elected an honorary member of the Academy of Architecture in 1777 (*Répertoire de la Gazette de France*, by the Marquis de Granges de Surgères, 1902–6).

8. For Count Sergius Soltikov, see *BU*, at Soltikov, Peter.

9. Count Alexis Grigorievich Orlov, called 'le balafre', according to Rulhière, cited in R. N. Bain, *Peter III*, Appendix I, London, 1902.

10. Theodore Bariatinsky was the murderer, according to Bain, loc. cit.

11. Prussian minister to Versailles, 1772.

12. Not further identified.

13. Rive's catalogue, Part I, appeared in Paris in 1783, 3 vols.; Part II, Paris, 1788.

14. Stanislaus II.

15. Could this M. Garnier, clerk in the Contrôle Générale in 1777, possibly be Germain Garnier, economist and politician, who was created comte by Louis XVIII? Germain Garnier, after successful but not extraordinary law studies in Paris, 'se trouva procureur au Châtelet avant trente ans', i.e. *c.* 1783–4 (*BU*).

16. M. Le Clerc de Septchênes, who translated *DF* i into French in 1776 'feebly though faithfully' (*Memoirs*, p. 194), was the son of a French treasury official, but no Le Clerc, 'premier Commis de tresor Royal', is listed in *BU* or *NBG*.

17. Ivan Sergievitch Bariatinsky, ambassador to Paris under Catherine II.

18. Obviously the first Partition (1772), not the second (1793).

19. For Piotr Maurycy de Glayre see *Polski Słownik Biograficzny*, Instytut Historii, 1935– .

20. By Jean-George Canzler.

21. 1718.

22. Ambassador to Paris 1766–83.

23. De Fleury's ministry 1726–43.

24. *Contrôleur général* in 1763.

25. For Ludovicus Sextius de Jarente, Bishop of Orleans 13 March 1758, see *Hierarchia Catholica Medii Ævi et Recentioris Ævi*, Patavii, 1958, vi. pp. 107, 196.

26. Ambassador to France 1770–80.

27. Frederick II.

Materials for corrections and improvements for the 1ʳˢᵗ Vol. of my History

These 'materials' are unpublished. They may be found in B.M. Add. MSS. 34882, ff. 176–9, rectos only. This manuscript is unusually difficult to read; I may easily be mistaken about details of punctuation, capitalization, and even spelling, in proper names. Departures from normal modern spelling are Gibbon's, however—not mine. As the page-references to the *Decline and Fall* fit the pagination of the editions in which the notes are placed at the foot of each page, instead of in an appendix at the end, the paper must have been written after 1777, when the third edition, the first in which the notes were so placed, appeared (see Norton, *Bibliography*, p. 43). The material from Jerome about the size of Palestine is referred to, but not quoted, in Gibbon's *Vindication*, p. 247 above. Gibbon's fullest use of a particular point or source is usually his first; he tends to condense, rather than to expand, his references. Furthermore, if he were listing 'improvements' brought to mind by the writing of the *Vindication*, i.e. writing after its completion, he would have included the one improvement he promised there (p. 270) to make in future editions of his history. But that improvement is not included in this paper. Consequently, I conclude that these materials were collected before the *Vindication* was written, i.e. 1777–8.

1. i.e. of *DF* i, third and subsequent editions in quarto; Bury i. 197–8.

2. Nicolaus of Damascus, in *Excerpta de Virtutibus et Vitiis* (from Polybius), ed. Henri de Valois, in 1634.

3. Ctesias calls founder Arbaces; Herodotus, Deioces.

4. 'The first Universal History written in Latin, a work completed by Pompeius Trogus in 9 A.D. . . . has only survived in the abridgement . . . drawn up by Justin' (Sandys, i. 189).

5. In B.M. Add. MSS. 34880, f. 289, item 36, Gibbon lists '*Vita et res gestæ Saladini auctore Bohadine. Edidit et Latine vertit. Albertus Schultens in fol. Lugdan. Batav. 1755.*' His reference here is to the geographical index of that work.

6. Volume and page references for both d'Anquetil du Perron and Foucher are to Académie des Inscriptions et Belles-Lettres, *Mémoires de littérature*.

7. Clement of Alexandria, λόγος προτρεπτικὸς πρὸς ῞Ελληνας.

8. In addition to the edition cited in Keynes, Gibbon owned 'Edit. Græc. Rob. Stephani, Paris 1544' (*Vindication*, p. 302 above).

9. See *DF* (Chapter LI), v. 383, n. 199; Bury v. 487, n. 231.

10. Actually 1537.

A Vindication &c.

Despite the 'vollies of . . . Ecclesiastical ordnance' (*Memoirs*, p. 160) that Gibbon's fifteenth and sixteenth chapters produced as soon as they were published (17 February 1776), he did not attempt to answer his attackers (as he explains here) as long as they raised 'literary Objections'. When, however, in 1778, twenty-one-year-old Henry Davis, armed with plentiful gall, a new Balliol B.A., and erudition acquired largely from Gibbon's own notes, raised 'criminal Accusations' of plagiarism and misrepresentation against him, Gibbon at last felt obliged to defend his work. The public should perhaps be grateful to Mr. Davis, for provoking so brilliant a reprimand. Furthermore, the *Vindication* contains many of Gibbon's explicit statements about his views of the craft of writing history. Part I, Section XII, pp. 264–5, and Part II, I–IV, pp. 276–81, are particularly interesting in this respect, as well as the second section of Gibbon's answer to the 'Confederate doctors' (Chelsum and Randolph), pp. 298–307.

In a letter to the *Gentleman's Magazine* (54. 968–9), one G. J. Leslie summarized the controversy in a way with which posterity can cheerfully agree:

I cannot help esteeming the 'laboured and artful Vindication' [Davis's view] as an additional and splendid proof of the talents and erudition of its admirable author. The very face of that Examination carries strong marks of its being the production of a vain young man, confined and illiberal in his notions of religion and philosophy, and flattered into print by friends less knowing than himself. . . .

Leslie goes on to say: 'Mr. Davis's book, however, contains some few remarks which bear hard upon Mr. Gibbon's particular deductions, or general principles, of which I have endeavoured to point out the most conclusive', listing some nine or ten points. Shelby T. McCloy, *Gibbon's Antagonism to Christianity*, London, 1933, Chapters I–IV, examines all the early attacks on Gibbon's fifteenth and sixteenth chapters. The *Vindication* can be read with pleasure, however, without any knowledge of the attacks. Judging from those I have read myself, I consider that a fortunate circumstance.

The *Vindication* was printed twice in 1779 and not thereafter during Gibbon's lifetime. There is no manuscript. My copy text is the first edition, but I have placed substantive changes from the second edition in my text, indicating the reading of the first edition in the apparatus criticus. Marginal subheads in the eighteenth-century editions are here printed as subheads in the text.

Lord Sheffield printed the *Vindication* in *MW* 1796, ii. 551–629, and *MW* 1814, iv. 515–648, from a copy of the second edition. The following changes occur *passim* and therefore will not be individually noted:

1. Gibbon editions number notes; Sheffield uses printers' devices.

2. Sheffield freely alters the placement of note references with respect to punctuation marks.

3. Both Sheffield and Gibbon use the author's name for the first reference on a page and Id. for later references on the same page. I have restored the actual reading of Gibbon's editions, even though my pagination, like Sheffield's, differs from Gibbon's.

4. Sheffield usually abbreviates a reference *within* a note here *to* a *DF* note as 'N.' Gibbon usually writes out the word 'Note'. I follow Gibbon without specifying Sheffield's choice in each case.

5. I shall not notice regular substitutions of italic for roman and roman for italic in notes and quotations. Sheffield's practice is exactly the inverse of Gibbon's.

In the apparatus criticus, '*I.*' will as usual mean 'Gibbon first wrote,' i.e. in this case, 'the first edition read'. . . . '*II.*' will mean, as usual, 'Sheffield has'. . . . But it will also occasionally be necessary, where my text has the reading of Gibbon's first edition, to indicate variants in his second edition. These will be signalled by 'B.'

1. The full title was *An Examination of the fifteenth and sixteenth chapters of Mr. Gibbon's history of the Decline and Fall of the Roman Empire In which his view of the PROGRESS of the CHRISTIAN RELIGION is shewn to be founded on the MISREPRESENTATION of the AUTHORS he cites AND Numerous Instances of his Inaccuracy and Plagiarism are produced.*

2. See *Letters* and *Memoirs* for Gibbon's friendship with William Robertson.

3. 'Epistle II. From Oxford', of *Epistles to Mr. Pope, concerning the Authors of the Age* (1730):

> At that tribunal stands the writing tribe,
> Which nothing can intimidate or bribe:
> *Time* is the judge; *Time* has nor friend nor foe;
> False fame *must* wither, and the true *will* grow.
> Arm'd with this truth, all critics I defy;
> For if I fall, by my *own* pen I die.

4. Davis, in his *Reply*, took up this challenge and (pp. 14–16) objects to the vagueness of Chapter XV, notes 59, 65, 68, 69, and 152; Chapter XVI, n. 103. He also objects to the form of notes 8, 14, 22, 31, 32, 61, 71, 79, 85, 98, 102, 103, 124, 135, 139, 142, 149, 155, 168, 177, 180, 193 of Chapter XV, and notes 7, 10, and 15 of Chapter XVI. Apparently, with the best will in the world he can find no fault in the others 351 notes to the two chapters. Though Gibbon's documentation certainly is not always so precise or so consistent as the modern scholar might wish, it is both quantitatively and qualitatively far superior to that of any of his contemporary historians.

5. Of Justin Martyr, Gibbon says (p. 260) that he owns *Opera*, fol., Paris, 1742, ed. Benedictines of St. Maar, as well as the edition of the *Apologiae* in Keynes.

6. Of these five reasons, Davis says, 'the *first* of them is at best but a confession of plagiarism . . . the last gives ample liberty to father any opinion on any writer of credit' (*Reply*, p. 16). The charitableness of Davis's critical approach as it is

here demonstrated, and the profundity of his understanding of scholarly method, are typical of him.

7. 'Vespae', however, is the reading of the fourth and subsequent editions of *DF* i, where editions I–III have 'apes'. In effect, then, Gibbon *did* enjoy the services of Davis as corrector of the press, albeit without Davis's co-operation.

8. *Histories* L. V, C. 8.

9. So corrected in Gibbon's fourth and subsequent editions.

10. i.e. Antiochus Sidetes' siege of Jerusalem (135 B.C.), and Pompey's conquest of Judaea (65 B.C.).

11. For the Reverend East Apthorpe, see *Memoirs*, p. 160, and note, *Memoirs*, p. 316. For the 'Gentleman without a Name' see pp. 310–12.

12. Re Calvin and Servetus, see *DF* (Chapter LIV), v. 538, n. 36 (Bury vi. 127, n. 43).

13. Gibbon's critics might be forgiven for not accepting Templeman's testimony at face value, for in note 89 to his first chapter, Gibbon himself had remarked, 'See Templeman's Survey of the Globe: but I distrust both the doctor's learning and his maps.'

14. Cf. above, 'Materials for . . . the 1ʳˢᵗ Vol. of my History', p. 228. Gibbon apparently owned Erasmus's first edition of St. Jerome, that of Basle, 1537.

15. Corrected in fourth and subsequent editions of *DF*.

16. Also corrected. For Gibbon's considered opinion of Le Clerc as church historian, see *DF* (Chapter XLVII, n. 1), iv. 533; Bury v. 97.

17. Page-reference given in *DF* is 34, not 84.

18. In Gibbon's subsequent editions, Jerome reference is given as 'tom. i. p. 284'. Bury adds 'c. 53.' (ii. 27, n. 73).

19. As Gibbon expressly speaks of Sulpicius' *complaint*, Davis's objection seems unusually obtuse, even for Davis. It is depressing to observe Davis's continuing to argue this point in his *Reply*, pp. 76 ff.

20. Actually p. 584.

21. Pliny the younger is earlier than St. Cyprian and St. Dionysius of Alexandria by almost two centuries. More reasonable critics than Davis have objected to Gibbon's mixing evidence from different periods to complete a single picture. What Davis objects to, however, is all drawing of inferences.

22. In Davis's *Reply*, p. 23, he confesses to not having finished the passage; it 'was owing to my not having read to the end of the section, which happened to be a very long one'. All the relevant material in Mosheim is found on two quarto pages, 912 and 913.

23. Cf. 'Hints' No. 11 and 12 above.

24. Davis, *Examination*, p. 168:

It will appear evident, even to a demonstration, that our historian has not only the same chain of thoughts, but often that his very *expressions* are borrowed. . . . My reader may, perhaps, be surprised that I should mention *a similarity of thoughts* as a proof of *plagiarism*: But if we consider that Mr. G's talents shine most conspicuously in the elegance of language, we must naturally imagine, that he would not constantly adopt *the very words* of the author, as he could so easily set off the sentiments in new and more graceful expressions, which would at the same time, serve to disguise the plagiarism.

Davis continues, p. 169, note,

Our author, in a note makes an observation with respect to these words of Middleton, though he is far from acknowledging that he borrowed any thought from him; hoping, no doubt, by this indirect method, to which he frequently has recourse, to evade the accusation of being *a plagiary*.

And, with italics to mark what seem to him very close resemblances, p. 110, Davis says,

Middleton . . . says, 'These forged books are frequently cited and applied to the defence of Christianity, by the most eminent Fathers, as true and genuine pieces, *and of equal authority with the scriptures themselves.*

Mr. G. speaking of these spurious books says, almost in Middleton's words, 'These *pious forgeries were obtruded* on the Gentiles *as of equal value* with the genuine inspirations of heaven.'

Finally, in *Reply*, p. 41, Davis says, 'Can there be a more evident proof of his wilful mutilation, misrepresentation, and plagiarism? he inserts or leaves out, at his pleasure, the account of the author whom he pretends to follow faithfully.' In other words, Gibbon 'plagiarizes' names and facts and 'mutilates' when he leaves out interpretations.

25. Cf. 'Hints', p. 92 above.

26. In *Corpus Byzantinæ Historiæ*, presumably edit. Louvre, which was in Gibbon's library at Bentinck Street. Cf. *DF* iv. 49; Bury iv. 210, notes 13 and 14 to Chapter XL.

27. In *DF* ii (Chapter XIX), 135, n. 23; Bury ii. 252, n. 26, Gibbon suggests that the Thebaean legion could inspire more than one kind of absurdity: 'The zeal of M. de Voltaire, to destroy a despicable though celebrated legend, has tempted him on the slightest grounds to deny the existence of a Thebæan legion in the Roman armies.'

28. *Tartuffe* 1664; revised 1669.

29. Henri de Valois edited Eusebius in 1659 and 1668.

Materials for the fourth Vol. . . . *November* 8th 1781

With this summary of the state of Procopius' text, we may compare Gibbon's note 14 to *DF*, Chapter XL (the second chapter of the fourth volume), iv. 49 (Bury iv. 210, n. 14):

The literary fate of Procopius has been somewhat unlucky. 1. His books de Bello Gothico were stolen by Leonard Aretin, and published (Fulginii, 1470. Venet. 1471. apud Janson. Mattaire, Annal. Typograph. tom. i. edit. posterior, p. 290. 304. 279. 299.) in his own name (see Vossius de Hist. Lat. l. iii, c. 5. and the feeble defence of the Venice Giornale de Letterati tom. xix. p. 207.). 2. His works were mutilated by the first Latin translators, Christopher Persona (Giornale, tom. xix. p. 340–348.) and Raphael de Volaterra (Huet de Claris. Interpretibus, p. 166.), who did not even consult the MS. of the Vatican library, of which they were præfects (Aleman. in Præfat. Anecdot.). 3. The Greek text was not printed till 1607, by Hoeschelius of Augsburgh (Dictionaire de Bayle, tom. ii. p. 782.). 4. The Paris edition was imperfectly executed by Claude Maltret, a Jesuit of Tholouse (in 1663), far distant from the Louvre press and the Vatican MS. from which, however, he obtained some supplements. His promised commentaries, &c. have never appeared.

Lord Sheffield did not publish this paper. It is in B.M. Add. MSS. 34882, f. 180 r and v. According to Gibbon's own memorandum (Add. MSS. 34882, f. 174), the fourth volume of the *Decline and Fall* was begun on 1 March 1782, and completed in June 1784.

1. Gibbon summarizes Procopius' career in *DF* iv. 48–50; Bury iv. 210–11. His account is substantiated and supplemented by Bury, Appendix 1 to volume iv, 513–17.

2. Lodovico Antonio Muratori, *Rerum Italicarum Scriptores* (*A.D. 500–1500*), *quorum potissima pars nunc primum in lucem prodit*, 28 vol. fol., Milan, 1723–38, 1751, is so listed in *DF* vi. 618, n. 98 to Chapter LXX, q.v. (Bury vii. 300, n. 110). Listed as purchased by Gibbon in his bookseller's account for 1785, B.M. Add. MSS. 34715, f. 5.

Cosmas

Lord Sheffield, or one of his assistants, has written at the top of these sheets (B.M. Add. MSS. 34880, ff. 275–6), 'The substance of this paper is introduced and even repeated in Gibbon's 4th Volume.' That is an exaggeration. Some of this material, however, appears almost verbatim in the *DF*, enough to make probable the inference that this paper was preliminary, not supplementary, to the history. Lord Sheffield did not publish the essay. It is written on both rectos and versos.

1. See *DF* (Chapter XLVII), iv. 596–7, n. 116 (Bury v. 148, n. 119), and (Chapter XL), iv. 79, n. 77 (Bury iv. 234–5, n. 78). The second *DF* note cited above says in part, 'he [Cosmas] refutes the impious opinion, that the earth is a globe . . . this work . . . displays the prejudices of a monk, with the knowledge of a merchant.' See also n. 95 to Chapter XLII: *DF* iv. 266; Bury iv. 385, n. 105.

2. *DF* (Chapter XL), iv. 76, with note 72; Bury iv. 233, n. 73. 'The subjects of the great king exalted, without a rival, his power and magnificence; and the Roman, who confounded their vanity by comparing his paltry coin with a gold medal of the emperor Anastasius, had sailed to Ceylon, in an Æthiopian ship, as a simple passenger.'

3. *DF* iv. 71, n. 73; Bury iv. 233, n. 74.

4. 'Along the African coast, they penetrated to the equator in search of gold, emeralds, and aromatics' (iv. 77; Bury iv. 233) and iv. 107, n. 133; Bury iv. 257, n. 133: the emeralds of the white Huns 'were purchased from the merchants of Adulis who traded to India (Cosmas, Topograph. Christ. l. xi. p. 339.).'

5. *DF* iv. 77 (Bury iv. 257). The Louvre edition of Procopius is in the *Corpus Byzantinæ Historiæ*. See above, 'Materials for the fourth Vol. . . .', p. 314.

6. Gibbon discusses the silk and spice trade iv. 73–6; Bury iv. 230–3 and n. 72 (Bury n. 73).

7. *DF* (Chapter XLVII), iv. 596–7, n. 116 (Bury v. 148–9, n. 119). 'The pepper coats of Malabar, and the isles of the ocean, Socotora and Ceylan, were peopled with an encreasing multitude of Christians.'

Mexico

This list of points about Mexico, from Add. MSS. 34882, f. 206 r and v, was published by Lord Sheffield as if it were a continuation of quite a different set of notes—see above, Second Commonplace Book, p. 199—in *MW* 1814, v. 529–30. The references within these notes show that they cannot be dated earlier than 1782. The handwriting is very similar indeed to that used for the notes on Busbequius (above, pp. 351–2).

1. François-Xavier Clavigero. His *Storia antica del Messico* first appeared in 1780–1.

2. Pope, *Essay on Man*, Epistle I, apropos of the 'poor Indian's' expectations of the afterlife, had written: 'He asks no Angel's wing, no Seraph's fire;/ But thinks, admitted to that equal sky, / His faithful dog shall bear him company' (ll. 110–12).

3. Volume xxi of Buffon's *Histoire naturelle* was published in 1779.

Notes / Gibbon

The small notebook bound in red Morocco that contains the following materials is in the Pierpont Morgan Library, New York City (Morgan V-10-B 'Original Manuscript Note Book for his History of Rome'). Gibbon wrote 'Notes' and his last name on the cover. Inside, white sheets are alternated with grey blotter sheets. Ordinarily Gibbon wrote only on the rectos of the white sheets, with references to his sources on the versos if necessary. The entry on paederasty, however (pp. 327–9), was written on both front and back of the twenty-second and twenty-third sheets. There are eleven blank sheets at the end of the 34-sheet book.

Divisions between entries are indicated by Gibbon either by leaving the remainder of the sheet blank, or by a solid line drawn across the page. At the end of the last entry (f. 23ᵛ) Gibbon wrote 'finished p 200. April 28ᵗʰ 1783.' Presumably he refers to page 200 of the fourth volume of the *Decline and Fall*, which he had begun on 1 March 1782, according to his own memorandum (B.M. Add. MSS. 34882, f. 174).

Sheffield published the first four entries (though without the headings that indicated that Gibbon thought of them as additional notes for his completed volumes) and the sixth entry, in *MW* 1814, v. 489–97. The other notes have not been published before.

1. In discussing the reasons for the general reception of the Apocalypse as canonical now, when it was not listed among the canonical books by the Council of Laodicea, Gibbon says, 'The Greeks were subdued by the authority of an impostor, who, in the sixth century, assumed the character of Dionysius the Areopagite' (*DF* (Chapter XV), i. 564, n. 67; Bury ii. 25, n. 68). Perhaps Gibbon meant to add this information to that note, or at least to associate the material here with that reference. He would not have objected to the ironic ambiguity of the first sentence of this entry in that context.

2. 'Certain works of "Dionysius [the Areopagite]" had been sent by pope Paul I to Pepin-le-Bref between 758 and 763, and a splendid MS of his mystical writings had subsequently been presented to Louis the Pious by the Byzantine emperor, Michael the Stammerer (827). The author was regarded as the patron-saint of France'—the convenient summary is Sandys's, i. 492. Gibbon may be less than just to Hilduin's sincerity.

3. The translation of 'Dionysius the Areopagite', by Johannes Scotus Erigena, was published 858–60.

4. From 845. For Gibbon's opinion of Hincmar, see *DF* (Chapter XXXVIII), iii. 565, n. 28; Bury iv. 106, n. 31.

5. Cf. *DF* (Chapter XXIII), ii. 402–4, especially n. 125; Bury ii. 470–2, n. 127.

6. See, in Appendix, Dupin.

7. Cf. *DF* (Chapter XXIII), ii. 404, n. 123; Bury ii. 472, n. 125.

8. For Procopius see above, 'Materials for the fourth Vol. . . .', p. 314. Venantius Fortunatus and Gregory of Tours were read by Gibbon in Bouquet's *Recueil des historiens des Gaules et de la France*. Pope St. Gregory I is discussed at length in *DF* (Chapter XLV), iv. 456–63; Bury v. 33–8.

9. Glaber is in Bouquet, op. cit.; William of Tyre in *Gesta Dei per Francos*.

10. Robertus Monachus (see Bury vi. 525), in *Gesta Dei*. Petrus Tudebode's chronicle is in André Duchesne, *Historiae Francorum scriptores* (5 vols., 1636–49), which Gibbon did not own. See *DF* (Chapter LVIII), vi. 9, n. 19; Bury vi. 266, n. 20.

11. John Cantacuzenus, historian and emperor; see *DF* (Chapter LXIII), vi. 272–8; Bury vi. 498–506.

12. In *DF* (Chapter XXXIII), iii. 352, n. 46; Bury iii. 414, n. 48, Gibbon describes the 'Acta Sanctorum of the Bollandists' (i.e. Joannes Bollandus, continued by Godefridus Henschenius and other Belgian Jesuits): 'This immense calendar of saints, in one hundred and twenty-six years (1644–1770) and in fifty volumes in folio, has advanced no farther than the 7th day of October. The suppression of the Jesuits has most probably checked an undertaking, which, through the medium of fable and superstition, communicates much historical and philosophical instruction.'

13. Cf. *DF* (Chapter XV), i. 610–11, n. 176; Bury ii. 63, n. 177. Flavius Dexter, *Omnimoda Historia*, found at Saragossa in 1619, a forgery. Marcus Maximus, Bishop of Saragossa in 592. Julien Petri (Perez), supposed chronicler.

14. *Opera*, ed. Erasmus, Basle, 1537, cited in *Vindication* above, p. 266.

15. Noel Alexandre, *Histoire ecclésiastique*, 24 vols., 1676–86.

16. Henricus Canisius, *Antiquae lectionis*, first published 1601–8, in 6 volumes. Better known in *Thesaurus monumentorum ecclesiasticorum et historicorum sive Henrici Canisii Lectiones Antiquae*, of Jacques Basnage, Antwerp, 1725.

17. For the letters of Innocent III, see *DF* (Chapter LXI), vi. 177, n. 6; Bury vi. 415, n. 7: 'the collection in 2 vols. in folio, is published by Stephen Baluze.'

18. 'Al-Mansur' means 'the Victorious' and consequently was a designation accorded to or claimed by many Moslem generals. The most famous was Mohammad Amir Almansur, regent of Cordoba.

19. Sampiro, Bishop of Astorga, ed. by Fray Prudentio de Sandoval. Roderic Toletan, i.e. Roderique de Rada Ximenès, Archbishop of Toledo in 1209, is in what Gibbon calls 'Elmacin'. See Appendix. See also *DF* (Chapter LI), v. 371, n. 179; Bury v. 478, n. 211.

20. The Chronicon (*c.* 1103) by a Monk of Silos (a Benedictine Abbey in Old Castille) (Ulysse Chevalier, *Répertoire des sources historiques du Moyen Âge: topo-bibliographie*). For Francisco de Berganza y Arce, author of *Antiquedades de España propugnadas*, see *NBG*.

21. Cf. *DF* (Chapter LI), v. 364, n. 166; Bury v. 472, n. 198.

22. Lucas of Tuy, suffragan of the archdiocese of Santiago (q.v. in *Catholic Encyclopedia*), compiled a 'Chronicon de España', which is in Ludovicus Nonius (Nuñez), in *Hispaniæ Illustratae*, ed. Andreas Schott, fol., Frankfurt, 1603–8. See, however, Appendix, Nuñez.

23. William Robertson, *History of America*, 2 vol. 4°, London, 1777. Robertson had sent a copy to Gibbon (see *Letters*, ii. 152–3—14 July 1777).

24. Antoine Gachet d'Artigny, *Petit réservoir contenant une variété de faits historiques et critiques*, 5 vols., La Haye, 1750.

25. See *DF* (Chapter XXXIII), iii. 350–2; Bury iii. 412–14.

26. Gregory, Bishop of Tours, 'in Max[ima] Bibliothecâ Patrum' according to *DF* iii. 350, n. 43; Bury iii. 412, n. 45. ? *Maxima Bibliothecâ Veterum Patrum et Antiquorum Scriptorum Ecclesiasticorum* primo quidem a M.[Margarinus] de la Bigne in lucem edita, 28 vols. fol., Leyden, Geneva, 1677, 1707.

27. See 'Mavrokordato' in Appendix.

28. Olaus Magnus, *Historia de gentibus septentrionalibus* (1555). For Paul, son of Warnefrid, see Chevalier, *Répertoire des sources historiques du Moyen Âge: bio-bibliographie*.

29. 'Edit. Græc. Rob. Stephani, Paris 1544' cited in *Vindication* (above, p. 302).

30. Cf. *DF* (Chapter XXIII), ii. 382–3, n. 60; Bury ii. 454, n. 61.

31. Jean Joseph d'Expilly, *Dictionnaire géographique historique et politique des Gaules et de la France*, published (to the letter *S*) in 6 vols. fol., Avignon, 1762–70.

32. In *DF* (Chapter IX), i. 264, n. 15; Bury i. 217, n. 16, Gibbon speaks of this work as 'uncommonly scarce' and cites Bayle's extracts from it in *République des Lettres*, Janvier et Février 1685.

33. Cf. *DF* (Chapter XLIV), iv. 407–10, especially n. 192; Bury iv. 504–6, n. 197.

34. A law, according to the *Cambridge Ancient History*, 'of uncertain date punishing paederasty' (ix. 880).

35. Johannes Freinsheim, *Supplement* to Titus Livy (1654).

36. *Esprit des Loix*, l. xii, c. 6: *DF* iv. 409, n. 199; Bury iv. 506, n. 204.

37. Presumably of *DF* iv, probably somewhere during or at the end of the account of Justinian (Chapters XL and XLI).

Miscellanea

These notes, which may be found on four narrow slips (similar to those used for the fragmentary notes for the *DF* in 1787, see below) in B.M. Add. MSS. 34882, ff. 220–3. The date 30 August 1786 is mentioned within one of the entries. Two of the entries, indicated in the apparatus criticus, were included in *MW* 1814, v. 523–4. One of these, and one other appear in substance in the *DF*, as indicated in the editor's notes. One entry deals with an alleged Arabic manuscript. It turned out to be a forgery (see editor's notes to the entry), the product of the man also responsible for the 'Codice Diplomatico' on which Gibbon was making notes and comments in or after 1790. Those notes are printed above, pp. 336–7.

1. Cf. *DF* (Chapter LXV), vi. 376, n. 92; Bury vii. 81, n. 106.

2. St. Bernard. His works are not in Keynes, but the edition is cited in full in n. 28 to Chapter LIX, *DF* vi. 83; Bury vi. 332, n. 32.

3. *DF* (Chapter LIX), vi. 84, n. 30; Bury vi. 333, n. 34: 'The disciples of the saint... record a marvellous example of his pious apathy. [He quotes the passage here, repunctuated.] To admire or despise St. Bernard as he ought, the reader, like myself, should have before the windows of his library the beauties of that incomparable landskip.'

4. St. Amadeus of Hauterive, Bishop of Lausanne.

5. Giuseppe Vella, 'faussaire littéraire' (*BU*). Sheffield, or one of his assistants, has written on the manuscript below this entry, 'This book has been published and the arguments against its Authenticity are so strong, that it is generally considered as a Forgery.'

6. For Jean Hardouin see *BU* (or Sandys, ii. 298–9): he had a habit of regarding the classics as thirteenth-century forgeries—Pliny was one of the few who generally escaped his censure.

1787 Fragments for Volumes V and VI

These mysterious fragments, B.M. Add. MSS. 34882, ff. 160–7, and headed only 'Vol. v' and 'Vol. vi', become clear when they are compared with the *Decline and Fall* v and vi. Most of the references can be found in the notes, which presumably were more easily changed in proof than was the text proper. The two lists headed by volume numbers are comparable to the fragmentary notes for draft F of Gibbon's memoirs (see Bonnard's notes, *Memoirs*, where he cites and expands many of these fragments). It seems clear, then, that Gibbon's preliminary reminders to himself habitually took this form; even for references, it would seem that his characteristic method of composition was to 'suspend the action of the pen, till I had given the last polish to my work' (*Memoirs*, p. 159), for these fragments are not the drafts of notes, but mere memoranda. They are written on narrow slips longer than the sheets used for the 'Index Expurgatorius' or the 'Hints'.

In the material on ff. 163–7, to which I have given the subheading 'Other Fragments', we have a glimpse of Gibbon's methods when he wished to make direct quotations from, or extensive reference to, a work he did not own. It is instructive to compare these passages with their counterparts in the *Decline and Fall*. Clearly either Gibbon or his printer felt perfectly unconcerned about maintenance of the accidentals of his source.

The date of these fragments, as shown above, pp. 210–11, must be August 1787–April 1788, though not all of these notes were the result of newly acquired sources. While revising, Gibbon obviously took the opportunity to correct other sins of omission as well as those that had previously been unavoidable.

The fragments have not been printed before, except as revised and inserted in the *Decline and Fall*.

Vol. v

1. *DF* (Chapter XLIX, n. 95), v. 136; Bury v. 283, n. 100. 'But I have likewise examined the original monuments of the reigns of Pepin and Charlemagne, in the vth volume of the Historians of France.' See, in Appendix, Bouquet.

2. *DF* (Chapter L, n. 41), v. 188 (Bury v. 325, n. 44): 'The seven poems of the Caaba have been published in English by Sir William Jones; but his honourable mission to India has deprived us of his own notes, far more interesting than the obscure and obsolete text.'

3. *DF* (Chapter LI, n. 138), v. 349; Bury v. 459, n. 158. 'My conquest of Africa is drawn from two French interpreters of Arabic literature, Cardonne . . . and Otter (Hist. [Bury corrects to Mem.] de l'Academie des Inscriptions, tom. xxi. p. 111–25. and 136.). They derive their principal information from Novairi, who composed, A.D. 1331, an Encyclopædia in more than twenty volumes.'

4. 'Greek fire' is discussed in Chapter LII, v. 402–3 (Bury vi. 9–12), but only n. 23 (Bury n. 25) seems relevant, and it does not mention Scaliger, Voss, or Le Beau. Gibbon mentions the 'neat and concise abstract of Le Beau (Hist. du Bas–Empire)' in note 34 (Bury n. 35) to Chapter LIII, v. 481; Bury vi. 77.

5. André Schott edited two collections of Spanish writings, published at Frankfurt, one in 1603–8, and one in 1608.

6. Gibbon discusses Basil I's family (Chapter XLVIII) v. 38–49; Bury v. 201–11. He mentions Photius as the educator of Basil's son, but gives no references to his sources in notes. Cf. (Chapter LII), v. 435, n. 30; Bury vi. 37, n. 89. Charles du Fresne, sieur Du Cange; his *Familiæ Byzantinæ* is frequently cited in the *DF* and was consulted by Gibbon in the Venetian edition of the Byzantine history.

7. *DF* (Chapter LIII), v. 494–5, n. 66; Bury vi. 89, n. 72. 'Henricus primus duxit uxorem Scythicam, Russam, filiam regis Jersoslai. . . . in the year 1051. See the passages of the original chronicles in Bouquet's Historians of France (tom. xi. p. 29. 159. 161. 319. 384. 481.).'

8. *DF* (Chapter LV), v. 561, n. 46; Bury vi. 148, n. 58. 'Theophil. Sig. Bayer de Varagis (for the name is differently spelt), in Comment. Academ. Petropolitanæ, tom. iv. p. 275–311.' Bayer is described by Gibbon, three notes earlier, as 'a learned German, who spent his life and labours in the service of Russia'.

9. *DF* (Chapter LV), v. 563, n. 48; Bury vi. 150, n. 62. 'Ducange has collected from the original authors the state and history of the Varangi at Constantinople (Glossar. Med. et Infimæ Græcitatis, sub voce βαραγγοι. Med. et Infimæ Latinitatis, sub voce *Vagri*. Not. ad Alexiad, Annæ Commenæ, p. 256, 257, 258. Notes sur Villehardouin, p. 296–299.). . . . Saxo Grammaticus affirms, that they spoke Danish; but Codinus maintains them till the fifteenth century in the use of their native English.' Jakob Langebek was the first of the editors of the *Scriptores rerum Danicarum*, a collection of Danish historical documents.

10. Gibbon's source for this description of William the Conqueror is given by him as follows, in note 25 to Chapter LVI, v. 593; Bury vi. 179, n. 33: 'Gulielm. Appulus, l. ii. c. 12. according to the reference of Giannone (Istoria Civile di Napoli, tom. ii. p. 31.), which I cannot verify in the original.' Gibbon knew that Ordericus Vitalis had described the departure of English refugees from the Normans, who served the Greek emperor, for he refers to that account in note 70, v. 615; Bury vi. 198, n. 88. William of Apulia's poem was begun *c.* 1099, finished by 1111, according to Bury vi. 552. Gibbon found it in Muratori's *Scriptores rerum Italicarum*—see n. 15 to Chapter LVI, *DF* v. 587; Bury vi. 173, n. 16.

11. *DF* (Chapter LIII), v. 465, n. 5; Bury vi. n. 5. 'On the subject of the *Basilics*. . . . XLI books of this Greek code have been published, with a Latin version, by Charles Annibal Fabrottus (Paris, 1647), in seven tomes in folio; IV other books have since been discovered, and are inserted in Gerard Meerman's Novus Thesaurus Juris Civ. et Canon. tom. v.' (1751–4).

12. *DF* (Chapter LVII), v. 681, n. 70; Bury vi. 255, n. 78: 'Per idem tempus ex universo orbe tam innumerabilis multitudo cœpit confluere ad sepulchrum salvatoris Hierosolymis. . . . (Glaber. l. iv. c. 6. Bouquet, Historians of France, tom. x. p. 50.).' v. 679, n. 63 (Bury vi. 253, n. 70): 'In his Dissertations on Ecclesiastical History, the learned Mosheim has separately discussed this pretended miracle (tom. ii. p. 214–306.), de lumine sancti sepulchri.'

13. *DF* (Chapter LII), v. 405, n. 25; Bury vi. 12, n. 27. 'For the invasion of France, and the defeat of the Arabs by Charles Martel. . . . The texts of the chronicles of France, and lives of saints, are inserted in the collection of Bouquet (tom. iii.).'

Vol. vi

1. *DF* (Chapter LVIII), vi. 9, n. 19; Bury vi. 266, n. 20. '. . . It was late before I could obtain a sight of the French historians [of the crusades] collected by Duchesne.' (He enumerates them.) Gibbon did not own André Duchesne's *Historiæ Francorum scriptores* (5 vols., 1636–49).

2. *DF* (Chapter LVII), vi. 39–40, n. 77; Bury vi. 293, n. 79. 'William of Malmsbury (who wrote about the year 1130) has inserted in his history (l. iv. p. 130–154.) a narrative of the first crusade: but I wish that, instead of listening to the tenue murmur which had passed the British ocean (p. 143.), he had confined himself to the numbers, families, and adventures of his countrymen.'

3. *DF* (Chapter LIX), vi. 118, n. 106; Bury vi. 363, n. 120. 'See Carte's History of England, vol. ii. p. 165–175. and his original authors, Thomas Wikes and Walter Hemingford (l. iii. c. 34, 35.), in Gale's Collection (tom. ii. p. 97. 589–592).' Richard I is the subject of vi. 103–8, especially n. 80; Bury vi. 350–4, n. 89. For Gale, see above, Part IV, 'An Address', p. 539.

4. *DF* (Chapter LVIII), vi. 66, n. 132; Bury vi. 317, n. 140. 'The Assises de Jerusalem, in old law French, were printed in Beaumanoir's Coutumes de Beauvoisis (Bourges and Paris, 1690, in folio), and illustrated by Gaspard Thaumas de la Thaumassiere, with a comment and glossary.' Used by Gibbon as authority for valuing war-horses, under feudalism, three times as much as serfs.

5. *DF* (Chapter LX), vi. 173, n. 103; Bury vi. 412, n. 120.

I shall conclude this chapter with the notice of a modern history, which illustrates the taking of Constantinople by the Latins; but which has fallen somewhat late into my hands. Paolo Ramusio, the son of the compiler of voyages [i.e., Giovanni Battista Ramusio], was directed by the senate of Venice to write the history of the conquest; and this order, which he received in his youth, he executed in a mature age, by an elegant Latin work, de Bello Constantinopolitano et Imperatoribus Comnenis per Gallos et Venetos restitutis (Venet. 1635, in folio). Ramusio, or Rhamnusius, transcribes and translates sequitur ad unguem, a MS. of Villehardouin, which he possessed; but he enriches his narrative with Greek and Latin materials, and we are indebted to him for a correct state of the fleet, the names of the fifty Venetian nobles who commanded the gallies of the republic, and the patriot opposition of Pantaleon Barbus to the choice of the doge for emperor.

See Gibbon's original notes for this note, pp. 333–4. 'Rhamnusius' is printed 'Rhamnusus', but Gibbon so corrected it in his own copy of the *DF* (British Museum C. 60 m. 1).

6. Gibbon does not mention the *Dictionnaire des Gaules* of the Abbé Jean Joseph d'Expilly in the notes to his 'Digression on the Family of Courtenay', *DF* (Chapter LXI), vi. 211–20; Bury vi. 446–54, but he frequently refers to Ezra Cleaveland (e.g., n. 70; Bury n. 90), and Sir William Dugdale, e.g. notes 70, 80, and 83 (Bury notes 90, 100, and 103).

7. *DF* (Chapter LXII), vi. 252–3, n. 50; Bury vi. 483, n. 66. Ducange 'quotes an Arrogonese history, which I have read with pleasure, and which the Spaniards extol as a model of style and composition (Expedicion de los Catalanes y Arragoneses contra Turcos y Griegos; Barcelona, 1623, in quarto; Madrid, 1777, in octavo. Don Francisco de Moncada, Conde de Osona, may imitate Cæsar or Sallust; he may transcribe the Greek or Italian contemporaries: but he never quotes his authorities, and I cannot discern any national records of the exploits of his countrymen.'

8. *DF* (Chapter LXII), vi. 240, n. 33; Bury vi. 472, n. 43. The *DF* text deals with the reconciliation of the (Greek) emperor Michael Palæologus, with the Latin church. 'This curious instruction, which has been draw with more or less honesty by Wading and Leo Allatius from the archives of the Vatican, is given in an abstract or version by Fleury (tom. xviii. p. 252–258.).' In 1651, Leo Allatius published the χρονικὴ συγγραφή of George Acropolites, who 'represented the Greek Emperor at the Council of Lyons' and whose history 'embraces the period from 1203 . . . 1261' (Bury, Appendix 1, vi. 518). Fleury's abstracts are praised by Gibbon in *DF* (Chapter LXVI), vi. 379, n. 1; Bury vii. 83, n. 2.

9. *DF* (Chapter LXIII), vi. 265–6; Bury vi. 494, mentions Andronicus III (reigned 1328–41): 'his two wives were chosen in the princely houses of Germany and Italy. The first, Agnes at home, Irene in Greece, was daughter of the duke of Brunswick.' See also note 14.

10. *DF* (Chapter LXIII), vi. 285, n. 50 and 286, n. 54; Bury vi. 512–13, n. 55, n. 59, re the victory of the Genoese over the Venetians and Greeks, 1352: '50The events of this war are related by Cantacuzene (l. iv. c. 11.) with obscurity and confusion, and by Nic. Gregoras (l. xvii. c. 1–7.) in a clear and honest narrative. The priest was less responsible than the prince for the defeat of the fleet.' '54The Abbé de Sade (Memoires sur la Vie de Petrarque, tom. iii. p. 257–263.) translates this letter, which he had copied from a MS. in the king of France's library. Though a servant of the duke of Milan, Petrarch pours forth his astonishment and grief at the defeat and despair of the Genoese in the following year (p. 323–332.).'

11. *DF* (Chapter LIX), vi. 118, n. 105; Bury vi. 363, n. 119: 'The expence of each Mamaluke may be rated at 100 louis; and Egypt groans under the avarice and insolence of these strangers (Voyages de Volney, tom. i. p. 89–187.).'

12. *DF* (Chapter LIX), vi. 116, n. 98; Bury vi. 361, n. 110. 'For the ransom of St. Louis, a million of byzants was asked and granted; but the sultan's generosity reduced that sum to 800,000 byzants, which are valued by Joinville at 400,000 French livres of his own time [Jean de Joinville lived *c*. 1224–1317], and expressed by Matthew Paris by 100,000 marks of silver (Ducange, Dissertation xx. sur Joinville).'

13. *DF* (Chapter LXIV), vi. 292, n. 10; Bury vii. 5, n. 13. 'Haithonus, or Aithonus, an Armenian prince, and afterwards a monk of Premontré (Fabric. Bibliot. Lat. medii Ævi, tom. i. p. 34.), dictated in the French language, his book de *Tartaris*, his old fellow-soldiers. It was immediately translated into Latin, and is inserted in the Novus Orbis of Simon Grynæus (Basil, 1555, in folio).' For the prince, see *Hayton* in *BU*.

14. *DF* vi. 293, n. 16 (Bury vii. 6, n. 19): 'I should quote Thuroczius, the oldest general historian (pars ii. c. 74. p. 150), in the ist volume of the Scriptores Rerum Hungaricarum, did not the same volume contain the original narrative of a contemporary, an eye-witness, and a sufferer (M. Rogerii, Hungari, Varadiensis Capituli Canonici, Carmen miserabile, seu Historia super Destructione Regni Hungariæ, Temporibus Belæ IV. Regis per Tartaros facta, p. 292–321.): the best picture that I have ever seen of all the circumstances of a Barbaric invasion.' See in Appendix, Schwandtner.

15. *DF* vi. 293, n. 17; Bury vii. 6, n. 20. 'From motives of zeal and curiosity, the court of the great Khan, in the xiii^th century, was visited by two friars . . . and by Marco Polo, a Venetian gentleman. . . . the Italian original or version of the third (Fabric. Bibliot. Latin. medii Ævi, tom. ii. p. 198. tom. v. p. 25.) may be found in the ii^d tome of Ramusio.'

16. *DF* (Chapter LXV), vi. 361, n. 68; Bury vii. 69, n. 76: 'Arabshah (tom. ii. c. 96. p. 801. 803.) reproves the impiety of Timour and the Moguls, who almost preferred to the Koran, the *Yacsa*, or Law of Zingis (cui Deus maledicat): nor will he believe that Sharokh [Timour's son] had abolished the use and authority of that Pagan code.' Gibbon gives the full reference for Arabshah in note 5, vi. 332; Bury vii, 43, and adds, 'This Syrian author is ever a malicious, and often an ignorant, enemy: the very titles of his chapters are injurious; as how the wicked, as how the impious, as how the viper, &c.' See *DF* vi. 332, n. 3 (Bury vii. 43), for Gibbon's comment on his editions of the *Institutes.*

17. *DF* (Chapter LXV), vi. 359, n. 64; Bury vii. 67, n. 72. 'Sherefeddin (1. vi. c. 24.) mentions the ambassadors of one of the most potent sovereigns of Europe. We know that it was Henry III. king of Castile; and the curious relation of his two embassies is still extant (Mariana, Hist. Hispan. l. xix. c. 11. tom. ii. p. 329. 330. Avertissement à l'Hist. de Timur Bec, p. 28–33.).'

18. *DF* (Chapter LXV), vi. 338, n. 20; Bury vii. 49, n. 25. 'M. Lévesque (Hist. de Russie, tom ii p. 247. Vie de Timour, p. 64–67. before the French version of the Institutes) has corrected the error of Sherefeddin, and marked the true limit of Timour's conquests. His arguments are superfluous, and a simple appeal to the Russian Annals is sufficient to prove that Moscow, which six years before had been taken by Toctamish, escaped the arms of a more formidable invader.'

19. Gibbon's note 41 to Chapter LXIV (*DF* vi. 312; Bury vii. 24, n. 66). 'In one of the Ramblers, Dr. Johnson praises Knolles (A General History of the Turks to the present Year. London, 1603) as the first of historians, unhappy only in the choice of his subject. Yet I much doubt whether a partial and verbose compilation from Latin writers, thirteen hundred folio pages of speeches and battles, can either instruct or amuse an enlightened age, which requires from the historian some tincture of philosophy and criticism.' Rambler No. 122 (Saturday, 18 May 1751).

20. *DF* (Chapter LX), vi. 136, n. 31; Bury vi. 379, n. 37; or perhaps Chapter LXVI, vi. 392, n. 25; Bury vii. 94, n. 26.

21. *DF* (Chapter LXVIII), vi. 516–17, n. 96; Bury vii. 208, n. 127. 'For the reign and conquests of Mahomet II. I have occasionally used the Memorie Istoriche de Monarchi Ottomani di Giovanni Sagredo (Venezia, 1677, in 4to). In peace and war, the Turks have ever engaged the attention of the republic of Venice. All her dispatches and archives were open to a procurator of St. Mark, and Sagredo is not contemptible either in sense or style. Yet he too bitterly hates the infidels; he is ignorant of their language and manners; and his narrative . . . becomes more copious and authentic as he approaches the years 1640 and 1644, the term of the historic labours of John Sagredo.'

22. *DF* (Chapter LXVIII), vi. 465; Bury vii. 160: 'his own praises in Latin poetry[4] . . . might find a passage to the royal ear'. Note 4: Francis Philelphus 'by

a Latin ode, requested and obtained the liberty of his wife's mother and sisters from the conqueror of Constantinople. . . . (see his Life by M. Lancelot, in the Memoires de l'Academie des Inscriptions, tom. x. p. 718. 724, &c.).'

23. *DF* vi. 505, n. 72; Bury vii. 198, n. 97. 'See Ducas (c. 43.), and an epistle, July 15th, 1453, from Laurus Quirinus to pope Nicholas V. (Hody de Græcis, p. 192. from a MS. in the Cotton library).'

24. *DF* (Chapter LXVIII), vi. 498, n. 58; Bury vii. 191, n. 81. 'In the severe censure of the flight of Justiniani, Phranza expresses his own feelings, and those of the public. . . . the words of Leonardus Chiensis express his strong and recent indignation, gloriæ salutis suique oblitus.' See p. 335 for other fragments. Leonardus Chiensis is identified in vi. 468, n. 11; Bury vii. 463, n. 12.

25. *DF* vi. 510, n. 82; Bury vii. 202, n. 112. 'The fact [that the Sultan delivered the staff of office to the Patriarch Gennadius] is confirmed by Emanuel Malaxus, who wrote, in vulgar Greek, the History of the Patriarchs after the taking of Constantinople, inserted in the Turco-Græcia of Crusius (l. v. p. 106–184).' See other fragments, p. 335.

26. Gibbon owned and read various works by Nicholas Lenglet du Fresnoy from 1755 on. I have found no particular reference in these passages, however.

Other Fragments

1. See again Gibbon's note 103 to Chapter LX, *DF* vi. 173, quoted above, p. 581, note 5; and in his text, vi. 147, with n. 54; Bury vi. 390, n. 67.

2. *DF* (Chapter LXI), vi. 215–16, and n. 76; Bury vi. 450, and n. 96:

> The more adventurous embraced without dishonour the profession of a soldier: the least active and opulent might sink, like their cousins of the branch of Dreux, into the condition of peasants. . . . It was not till the end of the sixteenth century . . . that . . . the question of the nobility, provoked them to assert the royalty, of their blood. They appealed to the justice and compassion of Henry the fourth; obtained a favourable opinion from twenty lawyers of Italy and Germany, and modestly compared themselves to the descendants of king David, whose prerogatives were not impaired by the lapse of ages or the trade of a carpenter[76].
>
> [76]Of the various petitions, apologies, &c. published by the *princes* of Courtenay, I have seen these three following, all in octavo: [he lists these three works, without the comment on 'De Stirpe . . .' and in the order 1. De Stirpe, 2. Représentation du Procedé, and 3. Représentation du subject; then adds] It was an homicide, for which the Courtenays expected to be pardoned, or tried, as princes of the blood.

3. *DF* (Chapter LXVI), vi. 390; n. 21; Bury vii. 93, n. 22:

> The Roman pope was offended by this neglect [Manuel's, of the plenary indulgence available when he visited Italy in a jubilee year]; accused him of irreverence to an image of Christ; and exhorted the princes of Italy to reject and abandon the obstinate schismatic[21].
>
> [21]This fact is preserved in the Historia Politica, A.D. 1291–1478, published by Martin Crusius (Turco Græcia, p. 1–43.). The image of Christ, which the Greek emperor refused to worship, was probably a work of sculpture.

4. *DF* (Chapter LXVIII), vi. 499, n. 61; Bury vii. 193, n. 85: 'Leonardus Chiensis very properly observes, that the Turks, had they known the emperor, would have laboured to save and secure a captive so acceptable to the sultan.'

5. Cf. *DF* VI. 509; Bury VII. 201:

the population was speedily renewed; and before the end of September, five thousand families of Anatolia and Romania had obeyed the royal mandate, which enjoined them, under pain of death, to occupy their new habitations in the capital.

6. 'Dicti qui in Aula Imperatoris primas obtinent.' Du Cange, *Glossarium*.

7. See vi. 507–8, with n. 79; Bury vii. 199–201, n. 106:

After [Constantine's] decease, Lucas Notaras, great duke[79], and first minister of the empire, was the most important prisoner. . . . [The Christians] adorn with the colours of heroic martyrdom the execution of the great duke and his two sons; and his death is ascribed to the generous refusal of delivering his children to the tyrants lust.

[79]Phranza was the personal enemy of the Greek duke. . . . Ducas is inclined to praise and pity the martyr; Chalcocondyles is neuter; but we are indebted to him for the hint of the Greek conspiracy.

8. *DF* (Chapter LXVIII), vi. 491 and n. 48; Bury vii. 184, n. 65:

The genius of Mahomet conceived and executed a plan of bold and marvellous cast, of transporting by land his lighter vessels and military stores from the Bosphorus into the higher part of the harbour. . . . the . . . fact . . . is recorded by the pens, of the two nations[48].

[48]The unanimous testimony of the four Greeks is confirmed by Cantemir (p. 96.) from the Turkish annals: but I could wish to contract the distance of *ten* miles, and to prolong the term of *one* night.'

9. As in note three above, vi. 390, n. 21.

10. *DF* (Chapter LXVIII), vi. 468, n. 11; Bury vii. 163, n. 12 mentions 'a tract of Theodosius Zygomala, which he addressed in the year 1581 to Martin Crusius (Turco-Græcia, l. i. p. 74–98. Basil, 1584).'

11. vi. 510, n. 82; Bury vii. 202, n. 112, quoted above.

12. *DF* vi. 468, n. 11, also gives the full reference for Leonardus Chiensis.

Historia C.P. a Turco expugnatæ. Norimberghæ, 1544, in 4to, 20 leaves. . . . the earliest in date [of the 'standard texts'], since it was composed in the isle of Chios, the 16th of August 1453, only seventy-nine days after the loss of the city, and in the first confusion of ideas and passions.

The particular passages are cited in note 24, vi. 476; Bury vii. 169, n. 26: 'Leonardus Chiensis measured the ball or stone of the *second* cannon: Lapidem, qui palmis undecim ex meis ambibat in gyro', and vi. 479, with n. 30; Bury vii. 173, n. 34, which gives the numbers of Turks and Janizaries.

13. *DF* (Chapter LXVIII), vi. 484–5; Bury vii. 178. In n. 37 (Bury n. 46), the passage from which Gibbon draws these particulars and of which he made a Latin note is quoted with the comment, 'This passage of Leonardus Chiensis is curious and important.'

14. In vi. 486, n. 42; Bury vii. 180, n. 53, Gibbon remarks that 'it is singular that the Greeks should not agree in the number of these illustrious vessels', but he himself speaks of four ships in his marginal guide and five in his text.

15. *DF* vi. 498, n. 58; Bury vii. 191, n. 81 quoted above.

16. *DF* vi. 485, n. 37; Bury vii. 178, n. 46; repunctuated.

17. *DF* (Chapter LXXI), vi. 630, n. 30; Bury vii. 310, n. 39. 'I shall quote the authentic testimony of the Saxon poet (A.D. 887–889), de Rebus gestis Caroli magni, l. v. 437–440. in the Historians of France (tom. v. p. 180.).' He quotes 'Ad quæ. . . . Francia ferre tibi.' Then he continues, 'And I shall add, from the Chronicle of Sigebert (Historians of France, tom. v. p. 378.),' and he quotes 'Extruxit . . . fecit.' In the *DF* version, both quotations differ in accidentals from those recorded in his manuscript and printed here.

Codice Diplomatico

This set of notes, to be found in B.M. Add. MSS. 34880, f. 277 r and v, must have been written in or after 1790. The 'Codice Diplomatico' with which they deal was a forgery. Airoldi was the dupe of Vella, who persuaded him to write a Latin version of what he claimed was an Italian translation of an Arabic original. Except for Tychsen, mentioned here, Orientalists of the time were soon suspicious. Gibbon seems at first to be taking the work as genuine, but he seems by the end of the piece to be highly sceptical. Cf. 'Miscellanea,' above, p. 330. These notes have not been published before.

1. Alfonso Airoldi, Archbishop of Heraclea, was only the dupe of Vella (see below), according to *BU*. *NBG* lists him, but only with reference to this work.

2. The Hegira was 16 July A.D. 622. See *DF* (Chapter L), v. 225, n. 118; Bury v. 356, n. 127. Hence, to convert dates A.H. to dates A.D., add 622, and vice versa.

3. Giuseppe Vella, 'faussaire littéraire'. See *BU* for an account of his elaborate hoaxes.

4. Dismissed in a sentence in *DF* (Chapter LII) v. 438; Bury vi. 40:

But the caliphs of Bagdad had lost their authority in the West; the Aglabites and Fatimites usurped the provinces of Africa; their emirs of Sicily aspired to independence; and the design of conquest and dominion was degraded to a repetition of predatory inroads.

5. For Gaufred Malaterra, see *DF* (Chapter LVI), v. 587, n. 15; Bury vi. 173, n. 16. For Muratori's *Rerum Italicarum Scriptores* see above, p. 574, note 2. For Nicodême, Bishop of Palermo 1065–88, see Richard et Giraud, *Bibliothèque sacrée*, Paris, 1824.

6. Cf. *DF* (Chapter LII), v. 438, and note 85; Bury vi. 40, n. 101.

7. Modern Messina (NE. Sicily) and Istanbul, respectively.

8. Modern Catania, E. Sicily (population 1960: 301, 682).

Materials for a Seventh Volume

These fragments seem to me either certainly or probably part of Gibbon's abortive attempt at a seventh, supplemental volume for the *Decline and Fall*, about which he wrote to his publisher on 17 November 1790 (see above, Introduction, p. 211). On 5 February 1791 Gibbon wrote again to Cadell, from whom he had not heard, saying, 'I am curious to know your opinion concerning the nature and value of a seventh or supplemental Volume of my history: but I much doubt whether any prospect of advantage will now tempt me to undertake a work which cannot be productive either of amusement or reputation to the author.' (*Letters*, iii. 211).

During this short period, however, he had gone through the first chapter of his history as if for a rather full supplement and planned the location of 'Excursion 1', its subject one he had already treated in French. These notes, and others he had made in five of the six volumes of his personal copy of the *Decline and Fall*, now in the British Museum (Shelf-mark C. 60 m. 1), are the first item below.

Similarly the 'Supplemental notes to the six Volumes' (B.M. Add. MSS. 34882, ff. 181–6), the 'Supplement to the History' (Add. MSS. 34880, f. 291), and the chronology of the '1ʳˢᵗ Period/ From the accession of Nerva to the death of Marcus Antoninus' (Add. MSS. 34880, ff. 291–2) are certainly designed for such a volume. They are readily associated with two of the categories Gibbon mentioned to Cadell, supplements, and chronological tables.

Probably, but not certainly, the notes on 'The Sabatic years' (Add. MSS. 34882, f. 171), the 'Memoranda' (all repeated in the 'Supplementary Notes'; in Add. MSS. 34882, f. 168), the 'Vol vi p 200 Not. 51' material (same volume, f. 170), and the assessment of Busbequius (same volume, f. 205) are also intended for 'excursions' and for his 'critical review' of his authors. The 'Vol vi p. 200' material, however, which is based on Duchesne's collection of French historical writers, consulted by Gibbon for the first time while he was correcting proofs for volumes V and VI of the *Decline and Fall* and not in his library, might belong instead with the '1787 Fragments', above p. 332.

The remaining evidence of preparation for the contemplated seventh volume is the lists of authors and places cited in the *Decline and Fall*, not in Gibbon's hand but among his papers, which he apparently caused to be drawn up by an amanuensis. Authors and places listed alphabetically occupy ff. 60–82 and 83–106, respectively, of B.M. Add. MSS. 34882, and lists in order of appearance in the *DF*, with *DF* page references, require ff. 108–37, and 138–59, of the same volume. Perhaps their very length discouraged Gibbon. The lists might have been drawn up earlier, e.g. in preparation for the index of the history, but the geographical table, in particular, seems designed specifically for the seventh volume, and of little use to an indexer of the *Decline and Fall*.

We cannot regret the loss of the seventh volume, for Gibbon's interest turned instead to the other historical essays (above, Part IV) and the autobiography. But these materials, not published by Lord Sheffield (except for the Busbequius note, *MW* 1814, v. 580), should certainly be of interest to readers—and to editors—of the history.

Some of the *Decline and Fall* annotations were included in Bury's introduction, though not in his text, to his edition of the history (xxxv–xxxviii). The remaining items, however, have not been published before.

Substantive Changes, *Decline and Fall*

1. By 'deduced', Gibbon means 'described', not 'inferred logically'. See *OED*. All these substantive changes are discussed in Patricia B. Craddock, *Studies in Bibliography*, xxi. 191–204.

2. Cf. 'Digression on the character of Brutus', above, p. 96. Alfred is called 'the most glorious of English kings' in *DF* (Chapter XXXIX), iv. 39; Bury iv. 202, and cf. 'Outlines of the History of the World', above, p. 164; for Henry IV see above, 'Hints', Nos. 4–6, and *DF* (Chapter XXXVIII), iii. 569; Bury iv. 110 and (Chapter XLI) iv. 178; Bury iv. 313.

3. See p. 550 above for Gibbon's praise of Schweighaeuser's edition of Polybius.

4. The fifth volume of the *Supplément* of Buffon's *Histoire naturelle* was published in 1778.

5. Horace Bénédict de Saussure, *Voyage dans les Alpes* (1779).

6. Ferdinand IV, King of Naples.

7. Frederic the Great, of Prussia.

8. Frederick North, Lord North, was prime minister 1770–82. This tribute to Lord North had given Gibbon some trouble; the corrected proof is in the Pierpont Morgan Library in New York City. See the illustration in J. E. Norton, *A Bibliography of the Works of Edward Gibbon* (Oxford, 1940), facing p. 60.

9. See 'Supplemental Notes to the six Volumes,' No. 11.

10. See 'Supplemental Notes. . .,' No. 16.

11. Corrected in Errata, first edition (signature $4U_1b$); overlooked by Bury.

Supplement

1. Bury i. 70.

2. With this 'Supplement' compare Gibbon's note 2 in his third set of notes to the *Antiquities of the House of Brunswick*, p. 408 above.

1^{rst} Period

1. A pencil note on the MS. erroneously says 'Inserted in the history'. No doubt this was designed to be the first of the chronological tables Gibbon suggested to Cadell (*Letters*, iii. 209).

2. This chronology applies to Chapter III—i. 91–7 (Bury i. 74–9).

3. We can complete the sentence from *DF* i. 93 (Bury i. 76): 'a dutiful reverence for his wiser colleague, to whom he willingly abandoned the ruder cares of empire'.

4. *DF* i. 4–7 (Bury i. 3–5). Cf. Bury i. 449, Appendix 3, 3.

Vol. vi. p 200

1. *DF* (Chapter LXI); Bury vi. 437, n. 64. Gautier de Cornut, Archbishop of Sens 1222.

2. Chapter LXI, n. 47; Bury vi. 435, n. 59.

3. Bury vi. 435–6.

4. Queen Blanche of Castille; mother of Louis IX.

5. John Vataces, Emperor of Nice.

6. André Duchesne, *Historiae Francorum scriptores*, 5 vols., 1636–9. Cf. *DF* (Chapter LVIII), vi. 9, n. 19, Bury, vi. 266, n. 20.

The Sabatic year . . .

1. Cf. above, 'Hints', Nos. 9 and 10, and *DF* (Chapter XXVIII) iii. 102, n. 90; Bury iii. 215, n. 97.

2. Bury vii. 247 (Chapter LXIX). Cf. also Chapter VII, i. 234, n. 56; Bury i. 193, n. 72.

Memoranda

1. Cf. *DF* (Chapter XVII), ii. 8; Bury ii. 145.

2. See 'Supplemental Notes', No. 1.

3. See 'Supplemental Notes', No. 2.

Supplemental Notes

1. (Chapter LXVIII); Bury vii. 200–1. Baron Frederick Ernest de Fabrice's *Lettres . . . pour servir à l'histoire de Charles XII* were in Gibbon's library, listed B.M. Add. MSS. 34715 f. 37^r.

2. (Chapter LXVI); Bury vii. 112, n. 74.

3. (Chapter LIX); Bury vi. 365.

4. (Chapter XLIII); Bury iv. 436.

5. (Chapter LI); Bury v. 406.

6. (Chapter II); Bury i. 54.

7. (Chapter XLI); Bury iv. 273, n. 6.

8. (Chapter LV); Bury vi. 149. Torfaeus's *Norvegica*, 2 tom., is listed in a catalogue of Gibbon's library, B.M. Add. MSS. 34715, f. 21^v. 'Eccard' and the 'Saxon annalist' are cited, and the references are expanded by Bury, two pages later—Gibbon's n. 51, Bury's n. 66. Johann Georg von Eckhart, *Corpus historicum medii aevi*.

9. (Chapter LVIII); Bury vi, 314.

10. See references for notes 8 and 9.

11. (Chapter LXI); Bury vi. 444. Cf. above, 'Substantive Changes', p. 341. In

a list of the books he owned headed 'Octavo', B.M. Add. MSS. 34880, f. 285, Gibbon listed 'Geddes's tracts 7 Vol.'

12. (Chapter LIV); Bury vi. 127.

13. (Chapter LI); Bury v. 476.

14. (Chapter XLI); Bury iv. 294, n. 41.

15. (Chapter XXXVII), Bury iv. 73–4.

16. (Chapter LXIV); Bury vii. 5–6. Cf. above, 'Substantive Changes', p. 341. Sir Hans Sloane's collection was the foundation of the British Museum.

17. (Chapter XLVII); Bury v. 165.

18. (Chapter XLIV); Bury iv. 507.

19. (Chapter XLIII); Bury iv. 434.

20. p. iii. Bury i. xii. Also (Chapter LIX); Bury vi. 333, n. 34. Cf. *Miscellanea*, above, p. 330.

21. (Chapter XLIV); Bury iv. 484–5. The 1762 edition, which Gibbon owned, *was* the second; the first volume was first published in 1756. There was a 'third edition corrected' in 1772; perhaps that was the edition Gibbon was unable to verify his reference in.

22. (Chapter LIX); Bury vi. 332, n. 33. Clairvaux bought the library of Jean Bouhier in 1781 (*DBF*); it was closed in 1790 (*Catholic Encyclopedia*).

23. (Chapter XL); Bury iv. 225.

24. (Chapter XXV); Bury iii. 44.

25. (Chapter XLVII); Bury v. 108.

26. (Chapter LI); Bury v. 453, n. 136. 'Mar Gregor of Melitene, known as BAR-HEBRAEUS OF ABULPHARAGIUS (Abū'l-Faraj), lived in the thirteenth century' (Bury v. 515, Appendix 1, q.v.)

27. (Chapter XLIX); Bury v. 264.

28. (Chapter LXIV—and n. 33); Bury vii. 20, n. 52.

29. (Chapter LII); Bury vi. 31.

Busbequius

1. Cf. *DF* (Chapter LXV), vi. 342–56 and 364–5; Bury vi. 52–64 and 71.

2. 'the famous illustrated Dioscorides' and some 240 manuscripts altogether (Sandys, iii. 377).

PART IV

Introduction

1. For the length of time available for the actual composition of each volume, see J. E. Norton, *A Bibliography of the Works of Edward Gibbon* (Oxford, 1940), p. 57.

2. Sheffield published this note (*MW* 1814, v. 244) immediately after Gibbon's journal entry for 16 August 1762. Gibbon had been reading Homer and articles by Burette, the scholar cited in the note, during that summer. But the hand of the note is utterly unlike the hand of the journal, and almost identical to the hand of the materials that can definitely be dated in the late 80s and early 90s. As Gibbon once remarked, 'If it were in my power to place the volume . . . before the eyes of every reader, I should be satisfied' (*Vindication*, p. 257).

3. See G. A. Bonnard, 'Gibbon at Work on his *Memoirs*', *English Studies*, xlv. 207–13.

4. In addition to the materials in B.M. Add. MSS. 34874, all (except a brief sketch in French) published by Murray and utilized by Bonnard as explained in his introduction, the following materials are relevant to the memoirs: Add. MSS. 34880, f. 284 (a list of autobiographers, numbered as to type—cf. *Memoirs*, p. 2); 34882, ff. 172–5 (draft for note on Thomas Newton, cf. *Memoirs*, p. 174, n. 47; and list of dates of composition of *DF* iv–vi); f. 204 (re Lord North, published *Memoirs*, 212–13); ff. 217–19 (re Gibbon arms, Gibbon's schoolmasters, and an Acton cousin—see *Memoirs*, pp. 8, 18, and 33); and ff. 253–5 (outlines of 'Sect. iv', that is, *c*. 1771–81, and 'Sect. v', *c*. 1781–11 June 1788).

5. Bonnard, 'Gibbon at Work', p. 209.

6. Gibbon might have thought of including Philpot in 'another scheme of Biographical writing' which he mentions to Sheffield in letters of January 1793: 'the lives or rather the characters of the most eminent persons in art and arms, in Church and State who have flourished in Britain from the reign of Henry VIII to the present age' (*Letters*, iii. 312). The obvious objection to this theory is that Philpot, otherwise a suitable subject, flourished well before the reign of Henry VIII.

7. Gibbon mentions a 'Habsburgica' as one of the sources for his remarks, and the genealogy that connected the Habsburgs with the Fieldings was included in Dugdale's *Baronage of England*, see Appendix and Bonnard's note, *Memoirs*, pp. 232–3.

Music in Homer

British Museum Add. MSS. 34880, f. 279. Published *MW* 1814, v. 244; *Journal A*, p. 117.

1. See *Memoirs*, p. 97.

Philpot

Add. MSS. 34880, f. 283 contains the first three notes; Add. MSS. 34882, f. 218 contains the note from Froissart, immediately after a note about the antiquity of Oxford University (see above, p. 361). All are unpublished.

1. John Mercer's son, according to *DNB*, in Philipot.

2. Sir William Walworth, Mayor. Ralph Standish not in *DNB*.

3. The Chronicles of Jean Froissart, translated by John Bourchier, Lord Berners.

[Notes on the Antiquity of the English Universities]

The materials collected here are found in two places in the British Museum volumes: Add. MSS. 34882, f. 218 v and r (the sheet is reversed), contains the passage beginning 'Theobaldus. Archiep. Cant.' and ending 'et in alio Exemplari ejusdem vitæ in Bib. Cotton. C. 28. p 38'; the other materials are from Add. MSS. 34881, f. 250 r and v. The materials on the recto, however, are Gibbon's notes to his comments on the verso, i.e. this sheet is also incorrectly bound into the volume. The bracketed note numbers in the text are supplied by the present editor, but the notes themselves were numbered by Gibbon.

The remark from Matthew Paris and the two short memoranda following it, preceded by the text of Gibbon's note number 3, were published by Lord Sheffield, *MW* 1814, v. 522–3.

1. Reviewed by Gibbon in *Mémoires littéraires de la Grande-Bretagne pour l'an 1767*, London, 1768 (*Memoirs*, p. 143).

2. Ingulphus was the secretary of William the Conqueror.

[Marginalia in Herodotus]

Gibbon owned at least three editions of Herodotus (see Keynes, p. 149), but he preferred (see 'Circumnavigation of Africa', above, p. 397) the edition of Peter Wesseling (1692–1764), *Historiarum libri ix*, Greek and Latin, fol., Amsterdam, 1763. In December 1934 Geoffrey Keynes discovered that Gibbon had made annotations in the margins of his copy of this edition (Keynes, p. 33). These annotations are here printed in full for the first time. Lengthy excerpts were published by Lord Rothschild in *The Rothschild Library* (2 vols., Cambridge, 1954). A photograph of one annotated page may be seen there and in Keynes, between pp. 32 and 33.

At the beginning of each annotation I give, in square brackets, the page number in the 1763 folio on which it occurs, followed by a reference to the book (roman numeral) and chapter (arabic numeral) in Herodotus to which Gibbon's comment is pertinent. The annotations on pp. 298–9 of the folio, pp. 371–2 above, seem to me clearly preliminary to the essay on 'The Circumnavigation of Africa by the ancients', q.v.

1. Gibbon owned St. Jerome's *Opera*, ed. Erasmus, Basle, 1537. On Archilochus of Paros, see 'Annotations in Harwood', above, p. 549.

2. It is pleasant to think that it is Herodotus, not Gibbon and Pennant, who seems to be justified by modern naturalists.

3. Compare Gibbon's allusion re 'Henry the Lyon' of Brunswick, p. 490.

4. Cf. Gibbon's own 'Principes des poids, des monnoies, et des mesures des anciens' and 'Dissertation sur les anciennes mesures . . . also Remarques sur "An Inquiry into . . . the Ancient Measures . . . by Dr. Hooper"', *MW* 1814, v. 66–169; Add. MSS. 34881, ff. 1–60.

5. Cf. 'Second Commonplace Book', above, pp. 202–3.

6. After reading another of de la Nauze's chronological studies, young Gibbon once remarked: '*Most excellent*: I never understood the Roman Calendar before' (*Journal A*, p. 33).

7. See *DF* (Chapter XXVI) ii. 575, n. 21; Bury iii. 80, n. 21, and, in Appendix, Sainte-Croix.

8. Gibbon has told us that his first effort at historical composition was called *The Age of Sesostris* and was an attempt to discover when that ruler lived (*Memoirs*, p. 55). His conclusions here differ from his conclusions at the age of fifteen.

9. Cf. 'Index Expurgatorius', No. 17, above.

10. See pp. 393–7 above.

11. Cf. *Hamlet*, Act III, scene ii.

12. See above, pp. 388–9.

13. See above, pp. 390–3.

14. Lorenzo Valla trans. Herodotus into Latin.

15. Jakob Gronov's edition of Herodotus was published in 1715 at Leyden.

[The Circumnavigation of Africa]

The remarks on various circumnavigations are not, as Lord Sheffield's edition leads us to infer, a single continuous narrative. Instead, there are eleven small essays, each with its own set of notes, Add. MSS. 34880, ff. 355–66. The two folios printed here with the title 'On the Canary Islands' occupy the recto and verso of f. 355 and continue briefly on to f. 356ʳ, which also contains the nine notes. The verso of f. 356 is blank. Then there are ten folios, each containing its own continuation and notes on the verso. Some versos are not completely filled. I have introduced Roman numerals at the beginning of each distinct essay and I have arranged them in an order that differs from Lord Sheffield's (the B.M. order). I have done so for two reasons. (1) The sheets on which the essays were written had been numbered by Gibbon. Those numbers are now inverted and at the foot of the page, but they provide a clue to the sequence of the sheets when Gibbon wrote upon them. (2) Although the essays are to some extent independent of each other, so that they can be read in various orders without serious inconvenience, I do not think the arrangement favoured by Sheffield is the one most probable from the internal evidence.

Gibbon numbered the sheets as follows:

f. no.	his nos.	position of numbers
355	25–26	inverted; lower inner corners
356	none	
365	31–32	inverted; lower inner corners
363	29–30	inverted; lower inner corners
362	27–28	inverted; lower inner corners
366	48–47	inverted; lower outer corners
364	46–45	inverted; lower outer corners;
	also, 31–30	inverted; lower inner corners
361	37–38	inverted; lower inner corners

f. no.	his nos.	position of numbers
360	35–36	not inverted; upper outer corners, crossed out
357	33–34	inverted; lower inner corners
358	42–41	inverted; lower outer corners
359	40–39;	changed to 41 inverted; lower outer corners

The sections appear below in the order in which I have just listed them. They appear in *MW* 1814, v. 170–205, in the order of the folio numbers, except that Lord Sheffield puts the notes (with typographical symbols, not numbers) at the foot of the page, and they are printed below as numbered by Gibbon at the end of each essay.

I will not try the reader's patience with an elaborate explanation of this new arrangement, especially as some of the articles could be placed elsewhere with almost equal propriety. I should remark, however, that Lord Sheffield's ordering of Gibbon's loose sheets is not necessarily founded on any more intimate knowledge of Gibbon's wishes than is mine.

1. Perhaps that is why Voltaire, as Gibbon remarks in *DF* (Chapter I) i. 32, n. 87; Bury i. 26, n. 95, 'unsupported by either fact or probability, has generously bestowed the Canary Islands on the Roman empire.'

2. Pierre Bertius, *Theatrum Geographiae antiquae*, 2 vol. fol., 1618–19, listed as in Gibbon's library in B.M. Add. MSS. 34715, f. 20ᵛ.

3. Don José Clavijo y Foxardo allegedly seduced the sister of Pierre Augustin Caron de Beaumarchais and is the subject of Beaumarchais's play *Eugénie* (1767).

4. Possibly in his *Twelve maps of antient geography* or his *Atlas ancien et moderne*.

5. Regent 1356–60; reigned 1364–80.

6. Cf. *DF* (Chapter LXIV), vi. 324, n. 61; Bury vii. 36, n. 93: 'I should not complain of the labour of this work, if my materials were always derived from such books as the chronicle of honest Froissard . . . who read little, enquired much, and believed all.'

7. Reigned 1438–81, but Prince Henry did not die until 1460.

8. His astrolabe was for use on ships, unlike earlier medieval astrolabes.

9. For both Alphonso de Payva and Pedro de Covilham, see *BU*, Covilham.

10. See *BU*.

11. Gibbon thought of writing about Raleigh (see *Journal A*, pp. 30, 44, 101–3, and 198; *Memoirs*, pp. 120–2).

12. Henri Larcher's translation of Herodotus (7 vols., 1786) is listed in Gibbon's book purchases for 1787 (B.M. Add. MSS. 34715).

13. 'Variously identified with the Chimpanzee, and the Gorilla' (*Shorter OED*).

14. Cf. *Hamlet*, Act III, scene ii, and 'Marginalia in Herodotus', above, p. 372.

The Antiquities of the House of Brunswick

Sometime before the accession of Francis II to the throne of Austria in 1792, and probably before his own letter to Ernst Langer of 12 October 1790 (quoted above), Gibbon completed a draft of what he intended to be the first of three books, or chapters, of the *Antiquities of the House of Brunswick*. This first 'book', 'The Italian Descent', which has three sections, is in B.M. Add. MSS. 34880, ff. 295–324. It was printed by Lord Sheffield in *MW* 1796, ii. 637–705, and reprinted by him, with an additional 'Section IV', in *MW* 1814, iii. 359–554.

'Section IV' was made up by publishing most of the loose sheets Sheffield had found with the Brunswick papers. Many of these loose sheets have their own notes, carefully written out and numbered by Gibbon. They are treated as a number of separate pieces by Gibbon, not as a single manuscript. He did not begin one piece at the end of a sheet incompletely filled by another; he did not number these accounts with respect to each other. Lord Sheffield omitted the ones that blatantly repeated what had already been printed, but he does not seem to have realized that some of his 'Section IV' was, in effect, a different draft of parts of the 'Italian Descent'.

The last piece he printed, for example, which begins 'The fair anticipation of the name of Este-Brunswick' (*MW* 1814, iii. 552–4), is actually part of what I believe is a second draft of Gibbon's introduction. A comparison of Add. MSS. 34880, f. 350ᵛ with the first paragraph as printed by Lord Sheffield (iii. 360) shows that one is clearly a draft of the other. I think the continuous draft, the draft printed by Sheffield, is the earlier of the two, for the following reasons. The f. 350 draft includes information not in the f. 295 draft, specifically the name of the common ancestor of the current Duke of Brunswick and George III of England, and the name and date of creation (1235) of the first Duke of Brunswick, as opposed to merely 'about the middle of the thirteenth Century'. The novelty of the material as it continues on the recto of f. 350 (the sheet is reversed in the B.M. volume) is attested by Sheffield's including it in his 'Section IV'. It is possible that this beginning was an earlier false start, rather than the beginning of a draft later than the continuous one retained by Sheffield, but it is not like Gibbon to prefer, in revising, a vague and even misleading indication of time to the simple mention of a date of which he was certain.

Furthermore, several of the pieces published in 'Section IV', and two never printed, seem to demand a context such as that provided by substitution or insertion in an earlier manuscript. For example, Sheffield prints first in 'Section IV' f. 326, which begins, 'In those happy times, when a genealogical tree could strike its root in every soil ... the ambition of the House of Este-Brunswick was easily gratified with a Roman pedigree.' The demonstrative clearly demands a referent, which is available via the last sentence of f. 295ᵛ: 'But it will be prudent, before we listen to ... invention, to erect a strong ... edifice of truth on ... Leibnitz and Muratori.' This sentence introduces three ample paragraphs on those authorities, ending with the following transition: 'With such guides ... I shall boldly descend into the darkness of the middle age: and while I assume the liberty of judgement, I shall not be unmindful of the duties of gratitude[1]' That '1', omitted by Lord Sheffield, is not a note number, as I shall show, and seems to me to invite the insertion of the short piece (ff. 326–7) labelled by Gibbon pp. '1' and '2', with its notes. Another separately numbered and annotated essay is obviously invited by the conclusion of f. 327; it is on ff. 328–9 (*MW* 1814, iii. 484–9). Its conclusion, in turn, permits an easy return to 'the first *probable* ancestor of the house of Este and Brunswick'.

For the passage fixing the probable ancestors of the House of Brunswick, however, there is also another draft, which may be reconstructed from f. 331. In the continuous draft published by Sheffield, Gibbon devotes some eighteen pages to the ancestry derived by the hypothesis that the Adalbert known to be the ancestor of the house of Brunswick was the son of Guido, Duke and Marquis of Tuscany, the descendant of Boniface, who is called 'the first *probable* ancestor'. But in both drafts Gibbon ultimately rejects that hypothesis, though he accepts the conclusion that the house of Brunswick might be descended 'from a younger branch of the house of Tuscany'. The explanation of this lesser hypothesis is clearer in the continuous draft, and that draft is much the longer of the two. But the draft on f. 331 is shorter because it is concentrated on the fortunes of the family of Boniface, rather than on the general history of Europe, in which Gibbon was of course to some extent repeating what he had said in the *Decline and Fall*, and the shorter draft has full notes. I therefore think that it too is a revision, rather than an earlier attempt.

Gibbon's 'Section II' of his first book, finally, begins with a review of the careers of the first certain members of the family, Adalbert and his son Otbert I. Again I think the loose sheets provide a later draft, because the continuous version is more concerned with the empire than with the family of Este-Brunswick, and because the loose sheets have full, not fragmentary, notes.

Lord Sheffield omitted completely the fragmentary notes to the continuous draft of Section I which Gibbon headed 'L i C i' and which are now in B.M. Add. MSS. 34881, f. 249. In some cases these notes can clearly be attached to parts of the continuous draft, but there are no note numbers in the manuscript of the draft, and the notes themselves are misnumbered by Gibbon. The '1' referred to above cannot be a reference to the first footnote, because the first nineteen notes in the list have obvious earlier references, within the accounts of Leibnitz and Muratori. Moreover, the note numbered '7' (actually 9) inquires: 'Why do they [Eccard, Fontenelle, Jaucourt] call the five Saxons [i.e. Saxon emperors], de la maison de B[runswick]?' By the time Gibbon wrote the loose sheets, he knew why, as we can see in the 'Accounts of the German Branch' above pp. 454–5. Obviously this acquisition of knowledge is further evidence that the continuous version is earlier than the loose sheets, at least if the loose sheets were, as their appearance suggests, all written at much the same time.

In addition to publishing material omitted by Sheffield, then, I have also rearranged some of the material he did publish. The table below gives the references to the British Museum volume in the order in which I have arranged them (all references to Add. MSS. 34880, unless otherwise specified) followed by the page reference in Sheffield's 1814 edition.

The Italian Descent

Section I	f. 350^v	unpublished
	f. 350^r	iii. 552–4
	ff. 295^v–297^r	iii. 361–7
34881,	f. 249^r and ^{v}	unpublished
	ff. 326^r–329^r	iii. 479–89
	f. 331	unpublished
Section II	ff. 351–3	unpublished
Section III	ff. 311–24^r	iii. 423–77

Accounts of the German Branch

ff. 332–3	iii. 492–500	
f. 330	iii. 489–92	
ff. 334–43	iii. 501–34	
ff. 346–9	iii. 539–52	
ff. 344–5ʳ	iii. 534–9	

Other Drafts

Section I	f. 295, ff. 297–303ʳ	iii. 359–60; 367–92
Notes 34881,	f. 249ᵛ	unpublished
Section II	ff. 303–11	iii. 393–423
Preliminary fragments f. 278		unpublished

Of course I have also restored material which Lord Sheffield deleted for reasons of propriety, elegance, et cetera, as the textual notes will show.

It should be noted that Gibbon supplies reference dates, sometimes in the margin, sometimes in the text. All are printed here in the text. These dates in square brackets were in the margins of the manuscript; dates in round brackets were placed so in the text by Gibbon.

This essay is undeniably incomplete. But Gibbon's method of composition, in self-contained units small enough to be manageable, makes it easy for us to enjoy the part that we have. It should be remembered that Gibbon intended this work as a historical 'excursion', not as a formal history. As a result, the tone is interestingly intermediate between the familiarity—almost intimacy—of some of the *Decline and Fall* footnotes and the solemnity of the text of the history. I think it is of value to all students of Gibbon and of eighteenth-century historiography, though I cannot speak to its value for the historian of Brunswick.

1. See pp. 417–18.

2. Maria Beatrice, daughter of Hercules III Rinaldo, married Archduke Ferdinand of Austria, third son of Francis I.

3. Territory disputed by pope and emperor—cf. *DF* (Chapter XLV), iv. 443, n. 34; Bury v. 23, n. 42.

4. Louis Dutens edited *G. H. Leibnitzii opera omnia*, 6 vol. 4°, Geneva, 1769, printed by Jean-Jacques and Jacques Detournes. Leibnitz's correspondence with Jean Bernouilli was in the Bibliothèque royale.

5. Supplément, v, *Époques de la nature*, of Buffon's *Histoire naturelle* was published in 1778.

6. *Bibliothèque germanique.*

7. *Vita del proposto L. A. Muratori*, by Gian Francesco Soli Muratori.

8. *Scriptores rerum Brunswicensium.* See Gibbon's note 7 above.

9. *Scriptores rerum Italicarum* purchased by Gibbon in 1785 (B.M. Add. MSS. 34715). See p. 574, n. 2, above. Johann Georg Graeve published 'the works of earlier scholars collected and reprinted in the three *Thesauri*, (1) *eruditionis scholasticæ* (1710); (2) *antiquitatum Romanorum*, in twelve folio volumes (1694–9); and (3) *antiquitatum et historiarum Italiæ*, in nine volumes (1704), continued by [Pieter] Burman' (Sandys, ii. 328). Cf. Other Drafts, Fragments, p. 530.

10. Cf. above, 'Supplement to the History', p. 342.

11. For Giovanni Battista Nicolucci Pigna, see *NBG*.

12. Cf. *DF* (Chapter LVIII), vi. 25–6, n. 54; Bury vi. 281–2, n. 56.

13. Cf. Accounts of the German Branch, p. 458.

14. Cf. 'Other Drafts', Section I, iii, pp. 497–8.

15. Ibid. iv., pp. 499–50.

16. Ibid., pp. 501–2.

17. Contrast ibid., pp. 502–4.

18. Lewis, King of Arles—see p. 503.

19. Cf. 'Other Drafts', Section I, iv, pp. 504–5.

20. Cf. *DF* (Chapter LIII), v. 493; Bury vi. 88.

21. Cf. *DF* (Chapter XLIX), v. 148–9; Bury v. 293–4 and Other Drafts, Section II, pp. 511–14.

22. William Whitehead, *Plays and Poems* (1774); laureate 1757–85.

23. Cf. *DF* (Chapter LVI), v. 609, n. 60; Bury vii. 193–4.

24. In Appendix, see Bouquet.

25. Cf. *DF* (Chapter LVIII), vi. 4; Bury vi. 261–2.

26. Cf. *DF* (Chapter XLIX), v. 161–2; Bury v, 304, n. 156.

27. Cf. *DF* v. 162, and n. 148; Bury v. 304, n. 156.

28. The first comedy written in Italian, Ariosto's *Cassaria*, was first performed at Ferrara, in 1508 (Sandys, ii. 156).

29. In the section called 'Bologna, Modena, Parma, Turin, etc.' of his *Remarks on Several Parts of Italy, etc. in the years 1701, 1702, 1703*.

30. Cf. the prince's non-conclusion, in *Rasselas*, Chapter XLIX.

31. Cf. above, Blackstone essay, p. 85.

32. The situation seems as reminiscent of the fate of Oedipus himself as of the rivalry of Eteocles and Polynices.

33. Brother of Joseph II, Emperor 1765–90, and Leopold II, Emperor 1790–2; but uncle of Francis II, Emperor 1792.

34. The intimacy of Gibbon's knowledge of his favourite epic poets is well illustrated in this off-hand, perhaps half-conscious, echo of *Paradise Lost*, iv. 810–12.

35. Chapter XLIX. Bury v, 293.

36. The 'thousands' included, in 1755, Gibbon himself and his tutor Pavillard. See *Memoirs*, pp. 79–80, and *Misc.*, pp. 28–32.

37. Cf. 'Outlines of the History of the World', above, with the remainder of these accounts of the German branch.

38. *Spectator*, No. 499, Thursday, 2 October 1712 (Addison).

39. The saying of Solon, according to Herodotus, as discussed by Gibbon on p. 365 above.

40. Lodewyk Kaspar Valckenaer contributed to the Herodotus folio of Amsterdam, 1763.

41. *Etymologicum Magnum* is listed as in Gibbon's library on f. 290 of B.M. Add. MSS. 34880, 'Gr. a Fred. Sylburg. 1594. fol.'

42. Grotius edited Lucan in Antwerp, 1614, and Leyden, 1626.

43. Volume 3 of the *Monde primitif* of Court de Gebelin is an *Histoire naturelle de la parole.* 'L'Abbé B' is possibly Pierre Michon, better known as 'l'abbé Bourdelot' (Jean and Edmé Bourdelot were his mother's brothers), whose 'Hist des Voyages' is listed in Gibbon's library in Add. MSS. 34715, f. 45.

44. Cf. essay on 'Brutus', p. 98, and 'Hints', pp. 93–4.

45. Cf. Gibbon's note 2, p. 416 above.

46. *Eclogues* 7. 12.

47. Cf. Gibbon's note 1, p. 419 above.

48. Cf. *Memoirs*, p. 186:

When I contemplate the common lot of mortality, I must acknowledge that I have drawn a high prize in the lottery of life. . . . The general probability is about three to one that a new-born infant will not live to compleat his fiftieth year(68). I have now passed that age. . . .

See also *Memoirs*, p. 196.

49. *DF*, Chapter LVI.

50. Not identified.

51. Cf. Gibbon's note 18, second set, Section I, above.

Habsburgica

This genealogical table, and the comments on it, are in Gibbon's late hand, in B.M. Add. MSS. 34880, ff. 273–4. The recto of 273 ends with Maximilian i and Evrard Fielding; hence, there is no line to show their connection with the Habsburgs and Fieldings on the verso. The connection between the Fieldings and the Habsburg family was, in any event, fictitious, as Bonnard explains in the notes to *Memoirs*, pp. 232–3.

Gibbon was certainly interested in the connection between the great writer and the ruling house, as his reference in the *Memoirs* (p. 5) showed. But he might have drawn up or copied this 'Habsburgica' for other reasons. The Habsburgs often come up in the affairs of Este-Brunswick, and they are, of course, important in the general history of Europe. Consequently, several of them are discussed in the Outlines of the History of the World, above, Part II, and in the *Decline and Fall*, Frederick III of Austria is mentioned as the last emperor crowned at Rome. Although Gibbon did not know it, his Habsburgica concluded with the last Holy Roman Emperor, for Francis II, who had become emperor in 1792, lost that title in 1806, contenting himself with being emperor of Austria (1804–35). Lord Sheffield did not publish this piece.

1. For Rodolph to Maximilian I, see 'Outlines of the History of the World', above, pp. 177–96.

2. Cf. *DF* (Chapter LXX), vi. 608; Bury vii. 291.

3. Joseph II (Emperor 1765–90)—cf. above, 'Notes on Modern Europe', p. 213.

4. Annius of Viterbo, i.e. Jean Nanni, was so enthusiastic about antiquities that he changed his name to give it a more ancient flavour and forged a work by 'Berosus'.

5. John Heidenberg Trithème, alleged 'Fälscher' (Chevalier, *Bio-bibliographie*).

6. Diego de Valdés, *De dignitate regum Hispaniae* (1602).

7. Unidentified.

8. Albertus Argentinensis, i.e. Albert de Strasbourg, was secretary and chaplain to the bishop of Strasburg.

An Address &c.

This 'Address' was to have been published as a prospectus recommending the publication of the early historians of England, i.e. the primary sources of English history, to which Gibbon might have contributed a series of prefaces. The whole undertaking is discussed clearly by J. E. Norton, *Bibliography of the Works of Edward Gibbon* (Oxford, 1940), pp. 179–81, and by Gibbon himself, *Letters*, iii. 341–2. Of course Gibbon's death (16 January 1794) prevented this ambitious undertaking from being realized.

It was published in *MW* 1814, iii. 559–77; in the Table of Contents it is called 'An Address recommending Mr. John Pinkerton as a Person well qualified for conducting the Publication of the 'Scriptores rerum Anglicarum,' our Latin Memorials of the Middle Ages.' Gibbon wrote at the head of the manuscript simply, 'An Address &c.' The manuscript is in B.M. Add. MSS. 34880, ff. 367–77.

1. i.e. seventh–fifteenth centuries.

2. 1536–9.

3. *Flores Historiarum*, probably Roger of Wendover.

4. Cf. *DF* (Chapter LI), v. 381, n. 195; Bury v. 486, n. 227.

5. See above, p. 574, n. 2.

6. Twenty-one (1723–43).

7. Fifty-five (1738–93).

8. The 'general deluge', obviously, was the French revolution—one of Gibbon's favourite metaphors for it.

9. The *Scriptores rerum Danicarum* appeared in 1772–6.

10. (Chapter XXXVIII), iii. 556, n. 1; Bury iv. 98, n. 1.

11. James Rennell, surveyor-general of Bengal; *Bengal Atlas* (1781).

12. LXIII. 125–7, 196–8, 284–6, 404–5, 499–501; LXIV. 591–2, 689, 777–8, 877–8, 967–9, 1056–8, 1149–51.

13. *Expugnatio Hiberniae* (1169–85). Cf. *DF* (Chapter XXXVIII), iii. 610, n. 126; Bury iv. 144, n. 133. Chronicle of Melrose (twelfth century).

[Annotations in Harwood]

According to Lord Sheffield, 'The following Notes were written by Mr. Gibbon the summer before his death, at Sheffield-Place, in an interleaved fourth edition of Harwood's View of the various editions of the Greek and Roman Classics. It is to be regretted that he did not go through the whole work as he intended; but these perhaps may be interesting to collectors of books' (*MW* 1814, v. 581).

Although it is known that this copy of Harwood was given by Lord Sheffield to a 'Mr. Woodward' (*Notes and Queries*, series XI, vi. 188), I have not been able to locate it. I therefore reprint the annotations exactly as they were printed in *MW* 1814, v. 581–9, except that I have corrected errors in names (though they may have been Gibbon's or Harwood's errors) and added editorial notes.

1. Cf. *Journal A*, pp. 125 ff.

2. Herman Schlichthorst, not in Keynes or *BU*, etc. This and one other geographical work listed in B.M. catalogue.

3. Published anonymously. Blackwell was a protégé of Berkeley's, but *DNB* cites this remark of Gibbon's as inexplicable.

4. Gibbon probably found this anecdote in the *Biographia Britannia*, for the original analogy was to a blacksmith, and the *B.B.* incorrectly says cobbler (Sandys, ii. 358).

5. Cf. Sandys, iii. 3.

6. Gibbon probably alludes to the Ode on Danaë, preserved in Dionysius of Halicarnassus.

7. Larcher and Voltaire had a number of exchanges, notably Voltaire's *La Défense de mon oncle* (1767).

APPENDIX

The works listed below are those to which Gibbon alludes or refers in his 'English essays' that are known to have been in his library and were included in Keynes's *The Library of Edward Gibbon*. The purpose of this list is to facilitate the reader's pursuit of Gibbon's references; therefore:

(1) *Only* those editions that were or might have been used by Gibbon at the time of the reference within these essays are included; many other authors, titles, and editions are included in Keynes, but if an entry in Keynes is not included here, the inference is that Gibbon cannot have referred to that work or edition in these essays. When, however, there is no way to exclude any of many editions of a work or author listed in Keynes from those possibly referred to here, the reader is simply referred to the relevant pages in Keynes.

(2) The entries are here listed under the name by which Gibbon cites them; where it differs from Keynes's entry, e.g., where Gibbon refers to a translator and Keynes lists the translation under the name of the author translated, the listing in Keynes is also given.

(3) When a single author is referred to more than once and in more than one work or edition, the order within the entries here is the order in which the references are made, i.e. roughly chronological, in the order in which Gibbon acquired and used the books.

(4) Where alternative forms or spellings of the head-word of an entry are relevant to Gibbon's reader, the alternatives are supplied here in parentheses. Personal names, however, are spelled in the language of the person named. The reader will find all Gibbon's forms in the Index, cross-referenced to standard forms.

(5) The present list differs from Keynes in usually supplying Christian names of authors, and names of editors and translators. Further, works published anonymously but of which the authors are known are listed here without comment or distinction. Keynes supplies much information about bindings, bookplates, buyers, languages, and authority for inclusion in Gibbon's library that is omitted here.

The works not listed in Keynes which Gibbon is known to have

owned or used and to which he refers or alludes in these essays are
identified in the Editor's Notes.

Abū al- Fidā. *Opus geographicum*. Latinum fecit J. Reiske. 4°. Hamburg, 1770–1.
—— *Annales muslemici*, opera J. J. Reiskii [and J. G. C. Adler]. 3 vol. 4°.
Copenhagen, 1789–91.
Académie des Inscriptions et Belles-Lettres. *Mémoires de littérature*. 43 vol. 4°.
Paris, 1736–86.
—— *Notices et extraits des manuscrits de la Bibliothèque du Roi*. 2 vol. 4°. Paris,
1787, 1789.
Addison, Joseph. *Works*. 4 vol. 4°. Birmingham (Baskerville), 1761.
—— *De la religion chrétienne*. 3 vol. 8°. Geneva, 1771.
—— *The Spectator*. 8 vol. 12°. London, n.d.
Aelianus, C. *Varia historia*, ed. Perizonius. 4°. Leyden, 1731.
—— *Varia historia et fragmenta*. 2 vol. 8°. Leipzig, 1780.
Aeschylus. *See* Keynes, p. 46.
Alberti, Leander. *Descrittione di tutta l'Italia*. 4°. Venice, 1577.
Ammianus Marcellinus. *Rerum gestarum libri xviii*. . . . fol. Augsburg, 1533.
—— —— 4°. Leyden, 1693.
—— —— 8°. Leipzig, 1773.
Annius of Viterbo (Jean Nanni). Listed in Keynes under 'Berosus'. *Antiquitatem
Italiae ac totius orbis libri quinque*. 8°. Antwerp, 1552.
Anville, J. B. B. d'. *Notice de l'ancienne Gaule tirée des monumens romains*. 4°.
Paris, 1760.
—— *Traité des mesures itinéraires*. 8°. Paris, 1769.
—— *Géographie ancienne abrégée*. 3 vol. 12°. Paris, 1768.
—— *Twelve maps of antient geography*. fol. London, 1757.
—— *Atlas ancien et moderne*. fol. n.d.
Apollodorus. *Bibliothecae libri tres*, ed. C. G. Heyne. 4 vol. 8°. Göttingen, 1782–3.
Apollonius. *Lexicon graecum Iliadis et Odysseae*, ed. H. Toll. 2 vol. 8°. Leyden,
1788.
Apostolic Fathers. Listed in Keynes under Cotlerius, J. B. *SS. Patrum qui
temporibus apostolicis floruerunt opera*. Recensuit . . . Johannes Clericus. 2 vol.
fol. Amsterdam, 1724.
Appian. *Romanarum historiarum pars prior (altera)*. 2 vol. 8°. Amsterdam, 1670.
—— *Romanarum historiarum quae supersunt*. 3 vol. 8°. Leipzig, 1785.
—— *Historia delle guerre esterni (& civili) de' Romani*. 2 vol. 4°. Verona, 1730.
Apuleius. *Metamorphoseon libri XI*. Gouda, 1650.
—— *Opera* interpretatione et notis illustravit J. Floridus (Edit. Delphin). 2 vol.
4°. Paris, 1688.
Ariosto. *Orlando Furioso*. 4°. Venice, 1556.
—— —— 4 vol. 12°. Paris, 1746.
—— —— 4 vol. 4°. Venice, 1772–3.
—— *Satires*. 8°. London, 1759.
Aristides. *Opera omnia*, ed. Jebb. 2 vol. 4°. Oxford, 1722, 1730.
Aristotle. *Liber de mirabilibus auscultationibus*, explicatus a I. Beckmann. 4°.
Göttingen, 1786.

Aristotle. *Histoire des animaux avec la traduction Françoise Par M. Camus*. 2 vol. 4°. Paris, 1783.

Arnobius. *Adversus gentes libri VII*, ed. G. Elmenhorst. 4°. Leyden, 1651.

Arrianus. *Ars tactica . . . Periplus maris Erythraei*, ed. Nicholas Blancard. 8°. Amsterdam, 1683.

Arvieux, Laurent de. *Mémoires, contenant ses voyages à Constantinople*. 6 vol. 12°. Paris, 1735.

Athenaeus of Naucratis. *Deipnosophistarum libri quindecem*, ed. Casaubon. 2 vol. fol. Lyons, 1657.

Aubigné, Theodore Agrippa d'. *Histoire universelle*. 3 vol. fol. 1616–20.

Augustan History. *Historiae Augustae Scriptores sex*, C. Salmasius recensuit. fol. Paris, 1620.

Aurelius Antoninus, Marcus. *De rebus suis*. 4°. London, 1697.

—— *Iter Britanniarum*, commentariis illustratum Thomas Gale. 4°. London, 1709.

Ayliffe, John. *The Antient and present state of the University of Oxford*. 2 vol. 8°. London, 1714.

Bacon, Francis. *Works*. 3 vol. fol. London, 1753.

Bailly, Jean Sylvain. *Histoire de l'astronomie moderne*. 3 vol. 4°. Paris, 1785.

Barnes, Joshua, ed. Listed in Keynes under Homer. *Ilias et Odyssea*. 2 vol. 4°. Cambridge, 1711.

Baronius, Cesare. *Annales ecclesiastici*. 12 vol. in 6 fol. Cologne, 1622–7.

Basnage, Jacques. *Histoire des Juifs*. 15 vol. 12°. The Hague, 1716.

Bayle, Pierre. *Dictionnaire historique et critique*. 4 vol. fol. Amsterdam, 1740.

—— *Nouvelles de la république des lettres*. [1684–7]. 8 vol. 12°. Amsterdam, 1685–7.

—— *Œuvres diverses*. 4 vol. fol. The Hague, 1727–31.

Beaufort, Louis de. *La République romaine*. 2 vol. 4°. The Hague, 1766.

Beaumarchais, Pierre Augustin Caron de. *Œuvres*. 5 vol. 8°. Paris, 1780–5.

Belon, Pierre. *Observations de plusiers . . . choses memorables, trouvées en Grece . . . & autres pays estranges*. 4°. Paris, 1555.

Bentley, Richard. *A Dissertation upon the Epistles of Phalaris. With an answer to the objections of C. Boyle*. 8°. London, 1699.

Bergeron, Pierre. *Voyages faits principalement en Asie dans les XIIe, XIIIe, XIVe et XVe siècles*. 2 vol. 4°. The Hague, 1735.

Biblia sacra, iuxta vulgata editionem, I. Benedicti industria restituta. 4°. Paris, 1552.

Bibliotheca orientalis Clementino-Vaticana . . . recensuit J. S. Assemanus. 3 vol. fol. Rome, 1719–28.

Bibliothèque germanique. 76 vol. 8°. Amsterdam, 1720–60.

Bibliothèque raisonnée des ouvrages des savans de l'Europe. 52 vol. 12°. Paris, 1728–53.

Bingham, Joseph. *Works*. 2 vol. fol. London, 1726.

Biographia Britannica. 6 vol. fol. London, 1747–66.

—— 5 vol. fol. London, 1778–93.

Blackwell, Thomas. *An Enquiry into the life and writings of Homer*. 8°. London, 1735.

Bochart, Samuel. *Opera*. 3 vol. fol. Leyden, 1712.

Bochat, Charles Guillaume Loys de. *Mémoires critiques, pour servir d'éclaircis-semens sur divers points de l'histoire ancienne de la Suisse.* 3 vol. 4°. Lausanne, 1747–9.

Boiardo, M. M. *Orlando innamorata.* 4°. Milan, 1542.

Boileau-Despréaux, Nicolas. *Œuvres.* 5 vol. 8°. Paris, 1747.

—— —— 2 vol. 12°. Paris, 1750.

Boivin, Jean de Villeneuve, trans. *L'Œdipe de Sophocle, et les Oiseaux d'Aristophane.* 8°. Paris, 1729.

Bolingbroke, Henry St. John, viscount. *Works.* 11 vol. 8°. London, 1754–83.

—— *Letters on . . . patriotism.* 8°. London, 1750.

—— *Memoirs.* 8°. London, 1752.

Bouquet, Martin, et al. *Recueil des historiens des Gaules et de la France.* 13 vol. fol. Paris, 1738–86.

Boyle, Charles. *Dr. Bentley's Dissertation on the Epistles of Phalaris and the Fables of Aesop, examin'd.* 8°. London, 1745.

Brosses, Charles de. *Traité de la formation mécanique des langues et des principes physiques d'étymologie.* 4 vol. 12°. Paris, 1765.

Brucker, Johann Jacob. *Historia critica philosophiae.* 6 vol. 4°. Leipzig, 1767.

Brumoy, Pierre. *Le Théâtre des Grecs.* 6 vol. 12°. Amsterdam, 1732.

Brunck, Richard François Philippe. Ἠθικὴ ποίησις *sive gnomici poetae Graeci.* 8°. Strasburg, 1784.

Buffon, Georges Louis Le Clerc, comte de. *Histoire naturelle.* 35 vol. 4°. Paris, 1749–88.

Busbequis. (Ogier Ghislain, seigneur de Busbecq). Listed in Keynes under Gilsenius, A. *Opera.* 12°. Amsterdam, 1732.

—— —— 12°. Leyden, 1633.

Büsching, Anton Friedrich. *Géographie.* 12 vol. 8°. Lausanne, 1776–82.

Byzantine History. *Corpus Byzantinae historiae,* edit. Louvre. 27 vol. fol. Paris, 1645–1702.

—— editio secunda. 23 vol. fol. Venice, 1729–33.

Caesar, Julius. For Gibbon's six editions, see Keynes, pp. 85–6.

Calmet, Augustin. *Dissertations qui peuvent servir de prolégomènes de l'Écriture Sainte.* 3 vol. 4°. Paris, 1720.

Camden, William. *Anglica, Hibernica, Normannica, Cambrica a veteribus scripta.* fol. Frankfurt, 1603.

—— *Britannia.* fol. London, 1607.

Camoens, Luis de. *The Lusiad,* trans. William Mickle. 4°. Oxford, 1776.

Capper, James. *Observations on the Passage to India, through Egypt, and across the Great Desert.* 8°. London, 1785.

Caradoc of Llancarfan. *The History of Wales,* Englished by Dr. Powell. 8°. London, 1774.

Cardonne, Denis Dominique. *Histoire de l'Afrique et de l'Espagne sous la domination des Arabes.* 3 vol. 12°. Paris, 1765.

Carte, Thomas. *A General history of England.* 4 vol. fol. London, 1747–55.

Catrou, François, trans. Listed in Keynes under Virgil. *Les Poésies.* 4 vol. 12°. Paris, 1729.

Cave, William. *Scriptorum ecclesiasticorum historia literaria.* fol. Geneva, 1720.

Cellarius, Christoph. *Notitia orbis antiqui.* 2 vol. 4°. Cambridge and Amsterdam, 1703, 1706.

Cervantes Saavedra, M. de. *El ingenioso hidalgo Don Quixote de la Mancha.* 4 vol. 8°. Madrid, 1782.

Chardin, Jean. *Voyages en Perse, et autres lieux de l'Orient.* 4 vol. 4°. Amsterdam, 1735.

Chastellux, François. *De la félicité publique.* 2 vol. 8°. Bouillon, 1776.

Chauffepié, Jacques Georges de. *Nouveau dictionnaire historique et critique.* 4 vol. fol. Amsterdam, 1750–6.

Chelsum, James. *Remarks on the two last chapters of Mr. Gibbon's History.* . . . 8°. Oxford, 1778.

Cicero. *Opera.* 8°. Amsterdam, 1699.

—— —— 9 vol. 4°. Paris, 1740–2.

—— —— 21 vol. 12°. Glasgow, 1748–9.

—— —— 14 vol. 12°. Paris, 1768.

—— *De natura deorum.* 8°. Cambridge, 1718. See also in Keynes, pp. 95–7.

Clarke, Samuel, ed. Listed in Keynes under Homer. [*Works*]. 2 vol. 4°. London, 1740, 1754.

Cleaveland, Ezra. *A Genealogical history of the family of Courtenay.* fol. Exeter, 1735.

Clement of Alexandria. *Opera*, ed. J. Potter. 2 vol. fol. Oxford, 1715.

Commines, Philippe de. *Mémoires.* 4 vol. 8°. London and Paris, 1747.

—— —— 12°. Leyden, 1648.

Contes Arabes. *Les Mille et une nuit, contes arabes.* Traduits par Mr. [Antoine] Galland. Listed in Keynes under Arabian Nights. 6 vol. 12°. Paris, 1745.

—— 8 vol. 12°. Paris, 1773.

Cooper, John Gilbert. *The Life of Socrates.* 8°. London, 1750.

Courayer, Pierre François le, trans. Listed in Keynes under Sarpi, P. *Histoire du Concile de Trente.* 2 vol. fol. London, 1736.

Court de Gébelin, Antoine. *Le Monde primitif analysé et comparé avec le monde moderne.* 9 vol. 4°. Paris, 1773–82.

Coxe, William. *Lettres sur l'état politique, civil, et naturel de la Suisse.* 2 vol. 8°. Paris, 1782.

Cudworth, Ralph. *The True intellectual system of the universe.* 4°. London, 1743.

Curtius Rufus, Quintus. *De rebus gestis Alexandri magni*, ed. M. Maittaire. 12°. London, 1716.

—— —— ed. H. Snakenburg. 4°. Delft and Leyden, 1724.

Cuypers, Gisbert. *Apotheosis, vel consecratio Homeri.* 4°. Amsterdam, 1683.

Dacier, André, trans. Listed in Keynes under Horace. *Œuvres.* 8 vol. 12°. Amsterdam, 1735.

Dale, Antoine van. *De oraculis veterum ethnicorum dissertationes duae.* fol. Amsterdam, 1700.

Damm, Christian Tobias. *Novum lexicon Graecum in Pindarum et Homerum.* 4°. Berlin, 1774.

Dante Alighieri. [*The Divine Comedy*]. fol. Venice, 1578.

—— *Opere.* 5 vol. 8°. Venice, 1772.

Davila, Enrico Caterino. *Istoria delle guerre civili di Francia.* 2 vol. 4°. London, 1755.

Davis, Henry E. *An Examination of the fifteenth and sixteenth chapters of Mr. Gibbon's History*. . . . 8°. London, 1778.
—— *A Reply to Mr. Gibbon's Vindication*. . . . 8°. London, 1779.
Deshaies, Louis. *Voiage du Levant*. 4°. Paris, 1645.
Diodorus Siculus. *Bibliothecae historicae quae supersunt*, ed. Peter Wesseling. 2 vol. fol. Amsterdam, 1746.
—— *Bibliothecae historicae libri xv*. fol. Basle, 1559.
—— *Histoire universelle*, trad. Terasson. 7 vol. 8°. Paris, 1758.
Diogenes, Laertius. *De vitis, dogmatibus et apophthegmatibus clarorum philosophorum*. Seorsum excusas Aeg. Menagii in Diogenem Observationes auctiores habet Volumen II. 2 vol. 4°. Amsterdam, 1692.
—— —— 8°. Leipzig, 1759.
Dio(n) Cassius. *Historiae Romanae quae supersunt*, ed. H. S. Reimar. 2 vol. fol. Hamburg, 1750, 1752.
Dion, Chrysostom. *Orationes LXXX*. fol. Paris, 1604.
Dodwell, Henry. *De veteribus Graecorum Romanorumque cyclis*. 4°. Oxford, 1701–2.
(Drinkwater) Bethune, John. *A History of the late siege of Gibraltar*. 4°. London, 1786.
Drummond, Alexander. *Travels through different cities of Germany, Italy, Greece and Asia*. fol. London, 1754.
Du Cange, C. du Fresne, seigneur. *Glossarium ad scriptores mediae et infimae Graecitatis*. 2 vol. fol. Leyden, 1688.
—— *Glossarium ad scriptores mediae et infimae Latinitatis*. 6 vol. fol. Basle, 1762.
Dugdale, William. *The Baronage of England*. 3 vol. fol. London, 1675–6.
Dupin, Louis Ellies. *Nouvelle bibliothèque des auteurs ecclésiastiques*. 19 vol. in 14 4°. Paris, Mons, Amsterdam, 1690–1715.
Duport, James. *Homeri gnomologia*. 4°. Cambridge, 1660.
Edrisi. *Geographia nubiensis*, recens ex arabico in latinum versa a Gabriele Sionita et Joanne Hesronita. 4°. Paris, 1619.
Elmacin. Listed in Keynes under al-Āmidi. *Historia Saracenica* Georgii Elmacinii opera et studio Thomae Erpenii. 4°. Leyden, 1625.
Ernesti, Johann August. *Clavis Ciceroniana*. 8°. Halle, 1757.
—— ed. Homer. *Opera omnia* ex recensione S. Clarkii. 5 vol. 8°. Lips, 1759–64.
Estienne, Henri. *Poetae Graeci principes heroici carminis et alii nonnulli*. fol. Paris, 1556.
Estratto della letteratura europea. 8 vol. 8°. Berne, 1758–60. Societas Literaria Bernensis.
Euripides. *Euripidis quae extant omnia*. Opera et studio J. Barnes. fol. Cambridge, 1694.
Eusebius Pamphili. *Quae extant historiae ecclesiasticae*. Ill. Gul. Reading. 3 vol. fol. Cambridge, 1720.
—— *Thesaurus temporum*, ed. J. J. Scaliger. fol. Amsterdam, 1658.
—— *Praeparatio evangelica*. 2 vol. fol. Cologne, 1688.
Fabricius, Franz. *Historia M. T. Ciceronis*. 8°. Büdingen, 1727.
Fabricius, Johann Albert. *Bibliotheca graeca*. 14 vol. 4°. Hamburg, 1705–28.
—— *Bibliotheca latina*, ed. Ernesti. 2 vol. 8°. Leipzig, 1773, 1774.
—— *Bibliotheca Latina mediae et infimae aetatis*, ed. Mansi. 6 vol. 4°. Padua, 1754.

Feith, Everhard. *Antiquitatum Homericarum libri IV*. 8°. Strasburg, 1743.

Feuquières, Antoine de Pas, Marquis de. *Mémoires*. 4 vol. 12°. London and Paris, 1750.

—— —— 4 vol. 12°. London, 1740.

Fleury, Claude. *Histoire ecclésiastique*. 21 vol. 12°. Brussels, 1713–26.

Fontenelle, Bernard de. *Œuvres*. 10 vol. 12°. Paris, 1758.

—— —— 11 vol. 8°. Paris, 1766.

Frederick, of Prussia. *Œuvres*. 12°. Potsdam, 1760.

—— *Mémoires pour servir à l'histoire de la maison de Brandebourg*. 3 vol. 4°. Berlin, 1767.

—— *Military instructions for the generals of his army*. 8°. London, 1762.

Froissart, Jean. *Le premier (-quart) volume de l'histoire et cronique*. 4 vol. in 1 fol. Lyons, 1559–61.

Gale, Thomas. *Rerum anglicarum scriptorum veterum*. tom. I. (Historiae anglicanae scriptores quinque. Vol. II. Historiae britannicae, saxonicae, anglo-danicae scriptores XV.). 3 vol. fol. Oxford, 1684–91.

—— *Opuscula mythologica physica et ethica*. 8°. Amsterdam, 1688.

Geddes, Michael. *Miscellaneous tracts*. 3 vol. 8°. London, 1730.

—— *Several tracts against popery*. 8°. London, 1715.

Also three other volumes in 8°.

Gellius, Aulus. *Noctes Atticae*. 18°. Amsterdam, 1651.

—— *Noctium Atticarum libri XX*. Ill. J. F. et J. Gronovii . . . commentaria ab A. Thysio et J. Oiselio congesta. 4°. Leyden, 1706.

Geoffrey of Monmouth. *The British History*, trans. Aaron Thompson. 8°. London, 1718.

Gesner, Johann Matthew. *Scriptores rei rusticae*. 2 vol. 4°. Leipzig, 1735.

Gesta Dei per Francos. fol. Hanover, 1611.

Giannone, Pietro. *Istoria civile del regno di Napoli*. 4 vol. 4°. The Hague, 1753.

Gibson, Edmund, trans. Listed in Keynes under Camden. *Britannia*. 2 vol. fol. London, 1753.

Also listed under Anglo-Saxon Chronicle. *Chronicon saxonicum*, opera & studio E. Gibson. 4°. Oxford, 1692.

Glass, George, trans. Listed in Keynes under Abreu de Galindo, Juan de. *The History of the discovery and conquest of the Canary Islands*, translated by G. Glas. 4°. London, 1764.

Godefroy, Denys. *Auctores latinae linguae in unum redacti corpus*. 4°. Geneva, 1622.

Graeve, Johann Georg, ed. Listed in Keynes under Cicero. *Epistolarum libri XVI ad familiares*. 2 vol. 8°. Amsterdam, 1676–7.

Gravina, Giovanni Vincenzo. *Opera, seu originum juris civilis libri tres*. 4°. Leipzig, 1737.

Greaves, John. *Miscellaneous Works*. 2 vol. 8°. London, 1737.

Grotius, Hugo. *Opera omnia theologica*. 3 vol. fol. Amsterdam, 1679.

—— *Historia Gothorum, Vandalorum et Langobardorum*. 8°. Amsterdam, 1655.

Grynaeus, Simon. *Nouus orbis regionum ac insularum veteribus incognitarum*. fol. Basle, 1555.

Guarini, Giovanni Battista. *Il Pastor fido*. 12°. London, 1774.

Guazzezi, Lorenzo. *Dell'antico dominio del vescovo di Arezzo in Cortona.* 4°. Pisa. 1760.

Guignes, Joseph de. *Histoire générale des Huns . . . et des autres peuples tartares occidentaux.* 4 vol. in 5 4°. Paris, 1756–8.

Guillemanus, included in Fuessli, J. C. *Thesaurus historiae Helveticae.* fol. Zürich, 1735.

Guischardt, Charles Théophile. *Mémoires militaires sur les Grecs et les Romains.* 2 vol. 8°. Lyons, 1760.

Haller, Albert von. *Poésies.* 8°. Berne, 1760.

Heinecke, Johann Gottleib. *Historia juris civilis Romani ac Germanici.* 8°. Leyden, 1740.

Herbelot de Molainville, Barthélemy d'. *Bibliothèque orientale.* fol. Paris, 1697.

Herodotus. *Historiarum libri IX*, ed. Peter Wesseling and Lodewyk Kaspar Valckenaer. fol. Amsterdam, 1763.

Heyne, Christian Gottlob. *Opuscula academica.* 3 vol. 8°. Göttingen, 1785–8.

Hirtius. Listed in Keynes under Caesar.

    C. Julii Caesaris et A. Hirtii de rebus a C. J. Caesare gestis commentarii. 12°. London, 1716.

    C. Julii Caesaris et A. Hirtii quae exstant omnia. 4°. Cambridge, 1727.

    C. Julii Caesaris et A. Hirtii de rebus a C. Julio Caesare gestis commentarii cum C. Jul. Caesar. fragmentis. 8°. London, 1736.

Hody, Humphrey. *De Graecis illustribus linguae Graecae literarumque humaniorum instauratoribus.* 8°. London, 1742.

Holdsworth, Edward. *Remarks and dissertations on Virgil, with some other Classical Observations, by the late Mr. Holdsworth, Published with several Notes and additional Remarks, by Mr. [Joseph] Spence.* 4°. London, 1768.

Homer. *[Works].* Ed. S. Clarke. 2 vol. 4°. London, 1740, 1754.

    —— —— 4 vol. fol. Glasgow, 1756–8.

Hooper, George. *An Inquiry into the state of the ancient measures.* 8°. London, 1721.

Horace. ed. Bentley. 4°. Amsterdam, 1728. For six others, and translations and individual works, see Keynes, pp. 153–4.

Huber, Michel. *Choix des poésies allemandes*, trans. Bernard Tscharner. 4 vol. 12°. Paris, 1766.

Hudson, John. *Geographiae veteris scriptores graeci minores.* 4 vol. 8°. Oxford, 1698–1712.

Huet, Pierre Daniel. *Commentarius de rebus ad eum pertinentibus.* 12°. Amsterdam, 1718.

Hume, David. *Essays and treatises on several subjects.* 4 vol. 12°. London, 1760.

    —— —— 2 vol. 4°. London, 1768.

    —— —— 2 vol. 8°. London, 1777.

    —— *Dialogues concerning natural religion.* 8°. London, 1779.

    —— *The History of England.* 8 vol. 4°. London, 1770.

    —— —— 8 vol. 8°. London, 1778.

Hurd, Richard, ed. Listed in Keynes under Horace. *Epistolae ad Pisones et Augustum.* 2 vol. 8°. Cambridge, 1757.

Hyde, Thomas. *Veterum Persarum et Parthorum et Medorum religionis historia.* 4°. Oxford, 1760.

Institutes. Timur. *Institutes political and military, translated into English* [by Major Davy and Mr. White]. 4°. Oxford, 1783.

—— —— Trad. [Par Louis Langlès]. 8°. Paris, 1787.

Isaeus. *The Speeches of Isaeus* . . . with a commentary by William Jones. 4°. London, 1779.

Isocrates. *Opera omnia*, ed. A. Auger. 3 vol. 8°. Paris, 1782.

John of Salisbury. *Policraticus*. 8°. Leyden, 1639.

Johnson, Samuel. *Rambler*. 4 vol. 12°. London, 1757.

—— *The Prince of Abissinia*. 2 vol. in one. 8°. London, 1759.

Jones, Sir William. *Poems, consisting chiefly of translations from the Asiatic languages*. 8°. Oxford, 1772.

Jortin, John. *Remarks on Ecclesiastical History*. 2 vol. 8°. London, 1767.

Josephus, Flavius. *Opera omnia*, edit. Havercamp. 2 vol. fol. Amsterdam, 1726.

—— —— trans. William Whiston. fol. London, 1737.

Julian the Apostate. *Opera*, ed. Spanheim. 3 vol. fol. Leipzig, 1696.

—— *Caesares*, ed. T. C. Harles. 8°. Erlangen, 1785.

—— *Les Césars*. 4°. Paris, 1683.

Justinus, Saint. *Apologiae pro Christianis*, ed. from the papers of Dr. Charles Ashton. 8°. Cambridge, 1768.

Juvenal. *Satyrae*, ed. C. Schrevelius. 8°. Amsterdam, 1684.

—— —— ed. H. C. Hennin. 4°. Leyden, 1695.

—— —— 4°. Leyden, 1709.

Kämpfer, Engelbert. *The History of Japan*. 2 vol. fol. London, 1728.

Kane, Richard. Listed in Keynes under *System of camp discipline*. . . . *To which is added, Kane's Campaigns of King William and the Duke of Marlborough*. 8°. London, 1757.

Klüwer, Philipp (Cluverius). *Germaniae antiquae libri tres*. fol. Leyden, 1616.

—— *Italia antiqua*. 2 vol. fol. Leyden, 1624.

Labat, Jean-Baptiste. *Nouvelle relation de l'Afrique occidentale*. 5 vol. 12°. Paris, 1728.

—— *Voyage du chevalier Des Marchais en Guinée*. 4 vol. 12°. Amsterdam, 1731.

La Bléterie, J. P. R. de. *Vie de l'empereur Julien*. 8°. Paris, 1746.

Lactantius. *De mortibus persecutorum*. 8°. Utrecht, 1663.

La Hontan, L. A. de Lom d'Arce, baron de. *Voyages dans l'Amérique septentrionale*. 2 vol. 12°. La Haye, 1706.

La Mothe le Vayer, François de. *Œuvres*. 14 vol. 8°. Dresden, 1756–9.

La Mottraye, Aubray de. *Voyages en diverses provinces de la Prusse, de la Russie, de la Pologne*. fol. The Hague, 1727–32.

La Porte, Pierre de. *Mémoires*. 8°. Geneva, 1756.

Lardner, Nathaniel. *A Large collection of ancient Jewish and heathen testimonies to the truth of the Christian religion*. 4 vol. 4°. London, 1764–7.

Le Clerc, Jean. *Historia Ecclesiastica*. 4°. Amsterdam, 1716.

—— *Bibliothèque universelle*. 26 vol. 12°. Amsterdam, 1700–13.

—— *Bibliothèque choisie*. 28 vol. 12°. Amsterdam, 1718.

—— *Bibliothèque ancienne et moderne*. 29 vol. 12°. The Hague, 1726–30.

Lectius, Jacques. *Poetae graeci veteres tragici, comici, lyrici, epigrammatici*. fol. Geneva, 1614.

Leibnitz, G. W. von. *Essais de théodicée*. 2 vol. 12°. Lausanne, 1760.

—— *Origines Guelficae*. 5 vol. fol. Hanover, 1750–80.

Le Sage, Alain-René. *Le Bachelier de Salamanque*. 3 vol. 8°. Paris, 1777.

Levesque, Pierre-Charles. *Histoire de Russie*. 8 vol. 12°. Yverdun, 1783.

Lips, Joest. *Opera*. 4 vol. fol. Antwerp, 1637.

Locke, John. *Works*. 3 vol. fol. London, 1759.

Longuerue, Louis Dufour, Abbé de. *Longueruana*. 2 vol. 12°. Berlin, 1754.

Lowth, Robert. *A Letter to the author of 'The Divine Legation of Moses demonstrated'*. 8°. London, 1766.

—— trans. *Isaiah. A new translation*. 4°. London, 1778.

Lucan. *La Pharsale*, trad. Marmontel. 8°. Paris, 1766.

—— *Pharsalia*, ed. Franz van Oudendorp. 4°. Leyden, 1728.

Lucian. *Opera*, ed. Hemsterhuys and J. F. Reitz. 3 vol. 4°. Amsterdam, 1743.

Ludolf, Hiob. *Historia Aethiopica*. fol. Frankfurt, 1681.

Luitprand. *Opera*. fol. Antwerp, 1640.

Lyttelton, George, 1st Baron Lyttelton. *The History of the life of King Henry the second*. 4 vol. 4°. London, 1767–71.

Mably, Gabriel Bonnet, Abbé de. *Observations sur l'histoire de France*. 2 vol. 12°. Geneva, 1765.

Maffei, Francisco Scipione di. *Osservazioni letterarie che possono servir di continuazione al Giornal de' letterati d'Italia*. 6 vol. 12°. Verona, 1737–40.

Maillet, Benoit de. *Description de l'Égypte*. 4°. Paris, 1735.

Maittaire, Michel. *Annales typographici*. 6 vol. 4°. The Hague, 1719–41.

Mallet, Paul Henri. *Introduction à l'histoire de Danemark*. 2 vol. 8°. Copenhagen, 1755–6.

—— *Histoire de Danemark*. 6 vol. 8°. Lyons, 1766.

Marche, Olivier de la. *Mémoires*. 4°. Ghent, 1566.

Mariana, Juan de. *Historiae de rebus Hispaniae libri triginta*. 4 vol. fol. The Hague, 1733.

Markland, Jeremiah. *Remarks on the epistles of Cicero to Brutus, and of Brutus to Cicero*. 8°. London, 1745.

Marsham, Sir John. *Canon Chronicus*. 4°. Frankfurt, 1696.

—— —— fol. London, 1672.

Maundrell, Henry. *A Journey from Aleppo to Jerusalem*. 8°. Oxford, 1721.

Mavrokordato, J. N. A. *Liber de officiis*, trans. into Latin by S. Bergler. 8°. London, 1724.

Maximus of Tyre. *Dissertationes*, ed. Davis and Markland. 4°. London, 1740.

Mela, Pomponius. *Libri tres de situ orbis*, ed. I. Voss. 8°. Frankfurt, 1700.

Ménage, Gilles. *Menagiana*. 4 vol. 12°. Amsterdam, 1713.

Meurs, Jan de. *Opera omnia*. 12 vol. fol. Florence, 1741–63.

Middleton, Conyers. *Miscellaneous Works*. 4 vol. 4°. London, 1752.

—— *The Epistles of M. T. Cicero to M. Brutus, and of Brutus to Cicero*. 8°. London, 1743.

—— *The History of the life of M. T. Cicero*. 3 vol. 8°. London, 1741.

Milton, John. [*Poetical works.*] 2 vol. 12°. London, 1753.

—— *Poetical Works*. 3 vol. 4°. London, 1761.

Mitford, William. *The History of Greece, Vol. I.* 4°. London, 1784.

Molière. *Œuvres*. 6 vol. 8°. Paris, 1773.

Monboddo, James Burnet, Lord. *Of the origin and progress of language.* 3 vol. 8°. Edinburgh, 1773–6.

Moncada, Francisco de. *Expedición de los Catalanes y Arragoneses contra Turcos y Griegos.* 8°. Madrid, 1777.

Mongault, Nicholas-Huber, trans. Listed in Keynes under Cicero. *Lettres à Atticus.* 6 vol. 12°. Amsterdam, 1741.

Montesquieu. *Considérations sur les causes de la grandeur des Romains, et de leur décadence.* 12°. Paris, 1755.

—— *Œuvres.* 3 vol. 4°. Amsterdam and Leipzig, 1758.

—— —— 3 vol. 8°. London, 1772.

Moore, Francis. *Travels into the inland parts of Africa.* 8°. London, 1738.

Moses of Chorene. *Historiae Armeniacae libri III.* 4°. London, 1736.

Mosheim, J. L. von. *An Ecclesiastical history,* trans. Maclaine. 2 vol. 4°. London, 1765.

—— —— 6 vols. 8°. London, 1782.

—— *De rebus Christianorum ante Constantinum magnum commentarii.* 4°. Helmstädt, 1753.

—— *Dissertationum ad historiam ecclesiasticam pertinentium volumen primum (alterum).* 2 vol 8°. Altona and Lübeck, 1767.

Moyle, Walter. *Works.* 3 vol. 8°. London, 1726, 1727.

Muratori, G. F. S. *Vita del proposto L. A. Muratori.* 4°. Venice, 1756.

Muratori, Ludovico Antonio. *Annali d'Italia.* 18 vol. 8°. Milan, 1753–6.

—— *Antiquitates Italicae medii aevi.* 6 vol. fol. Milan, 1738–42.

—— *Dissertazioni sopra le antichità italiane.* 3 vol. 4°. Milan, 1751.

—— *Antiquità estensi ed italiane.* 2 vol. fol. Modena, 1717, 1740.

Nepos, Cornelius. *Vitae excellentium imperatorum.* 8°. Amsterdam, 1707.

Nicholson, William. *The English, Scotch, and Irish historical libraries.* fol. London, 1736.

Notitia dignitatum Imperii Romani. fol. Geneva, 1623.

—— ex nova recensione Pierre Labbe. 12°. Paris, 1651.

Nuñez, Luis. *Hispania.* 8°. Antwerp, 1607.

Ockley, Simon. *The Conquest of Syria, Persia, and Ægypt, by the Saracens.* 2 vol. 8°. London, 1708, 1718.

Optatus Milevitanus. *De schismate Donatistarum,* ed. Dupin. fol. Paris, 1700.

Origen. *Contra Celsum. Philocalia.* G. Spencerus recognovit. 4°. Cambridge, 1677.

—— *Traité contre Celse,* trans. Élie Bouhéreau. 4°. Amsterdam, 1700.

Orosius, P. *Adversus paganos historiarum libri septem.* 4°. Leyden, 1738.

Orpheus. *Argonautica, hymni, libellus de lapidibus, et fragmenta.* 8°. Leipzig, 1764.

Ovid. *Opera omnia,* ed. P. Burman. 4 vol. 4°. Amsterdam, 1727.

Pagi, Antoine. *Dissertatio hypatico.* 4°. Lyons, 1682.

—— *Critica historico-chronologica in universos annales ecclesiasticos Baronii.* 4 vol. fol. Antwerp, 1727.

Paris, Matthew. *Historia major.* fol. London, 1684.

Pascal. *Les Provinciales.* 12°. Leyden, 1761.

Pausanius. *Graeciae descriptio,* ed. Joachim Kühn. fol. Leipzig, 1696.

Pellisson-Fontanier, Paul. *Histoire de l'Académie française.* 2 vol. 8°. Paris, 1730.

Pennant, Thomas. *British zoology*. 4 vol. 8°. London, 1768–70.

Petrarch. *Opera*. fol. Basle, 1581.

Petronius. *Satyricon quae supersunt*, ed. Pieter Burmann. 4°. Utrecht, 1709.

Phalaris. *Epistolae*. Recensuit Car. Boyle. 8°. Oxford, 1695.

Philostorgius. *Ecclesiasticae historiae libri XII*, ed. J. Godefroy. 4°. Geneva, 1643.

Photius. *Librorum quos legit Photius patriarcha excerpta et censurae*, ed. D. Hoeschel. fol. Augsburg, 1601.

—— *Myriobiblion*, ed. D. Hoeschel. fol. Rouen, 1653.

Pighius, E. W. *Annales Romanorum*. 3 vol. fol. Antwerp, 1615.

Pindar. *Olympia, Nemea, Pythia, Isthmia*, ed. R. West and R. Welsted. fol. Oxford, 1697.

—— *Odes*, trans. Gilbert West. 2 vol. 8°. London, 1753.

Pinkerton, John. *Ancient Scottish poems*. 2 vol. 8°. London, 1786.

—— *Dissertation on the origin and progress of the Scythians or Goths*. 8°. London, 1787.

—— *Enquiry into the history of Scotland preceding the reign of Malcolm III*. 2 vol. 8°. London, 1789.

—— *Essay on medals*. 2 vol. 8°. London, 1789.

Plato. See in Keynes, p. 223.

Pliny (the younger). *Epistolarum libri decem*, ed. G. Cortius and P. D. Longolius. 4°. Amsterdam, 1734.

Pliny (the Naturalist). *Historiae naturalis libri XXXVII*, ed. Harduin. 2 vol. in 3 fol. Paris, 1723.

—— —— Ill. G. Brotier. 6 vol. 12°. Paris, 1779.

—— —— trans. with observations by L. Poinsinet de Sivry. 12 vol. 4°. Paris, 1771–82.

Plutarch. *Opera*, 2 vol. fol. Frankfurt, 1599.

—— *Vitae parallelae*, ed. A. Bryan. 5 vol. 4°. London, 1723–9.

—— *Les Vies des hommes illustres*, trad. Amyot. 6 vol. 8°. Paris, 1567.

—— *Opera*. 13 vol. 8°. Geneva (H. Stephanus), 1572.

—— *Apophthegmata graeca regum et ducum, philosophorum item, ex Plutarcho et Diogene Laertio*. 12°. Geneva (H. Stephanus), 1568.

—— *Apophthegmata regum et imperatorum*. 4°. London, 1741.

Pocock, Edward. Listed in Keynes under Bar Hebraeus. *Historia Compendiona dynastiarum Gregorio Abul. Pharajo* interprete Edward Pocockio. 4°. Oxford, 1663.

Pococke, Richard. *A Description of the East*. 2 vol. fol. London, 1743, 1745.

Polybius. *Historiarum quidquid superest*, recensuit J. Schweighaeuser. 5 vol. 8°. Leipzig, 1789–92.

—— *L'Histoire de Polybe*, trad. Thuillier, avec un Commentaire Militaire par Folard. 7 vol. 4°. Amsterdam, 1753–9.

—— *The General History of Polybius*, trans. J. Hampton. 4 vol. 8°. London, 1772, 1773.

Pontoppidan, Erik. *Gesta et vestigia Danorum extra Daniam*. 3 vol. 8°. Leipzig, 1741.

Pope, Alexander. *Works*, ed. Warburton. 9 vol. 8°. London, 1751.

Pope, Alexander. trans. Homer. [*Works*]. 9 vol. 12°. London, 1771.

Prévost d'Exiles, Antoine François. *Histoire générale des voyages*. 19 vol. 4°. Paris, 1746–70.

Prideaux, Humphrey. *The Old and New Testament connected in the history of the Jews*. fol. London, 1718.

Procopius. *Historiarum libri VIII*, opera D. Hoeschelii. fol. Augsburg, 1607.

—— *Arcana historia*, ed. Nicholas Alemannus. fol. Leyden, 1623.

Propertius, S. A. *Elegiarum libri quatuor*, ed. J. van Broekhuisen. 4°. Amsterdam, 1702.

Prudentius Clemens, Aurelius. *Quae exstant*, ed. Nicholaus Heinsius. 12°. Amsterdam, 1667.

Quintilian. *Opera*, ed. P. Burman. 2 vol. 4°. Leyden, 1720.

Ramusio, G. B. *Primo (-terzo) volume delle navigationi et viaggi*. 3 vol. fol. Venice, 1550, 1559, 1566.

Rapin-Thoyras, Paul de. *Histoire de l'Angleterre*. 13 vol. 4°. The Hague, 1724–36.

Raynal, G. T. F. *Histoire philosophique et politique . . . des Européens dans les deux Indes*. 7 vol. 8°. The Hague, 1774.

Reland, Adrien. *Palestina ex monumentis veteribus illustrata*. 2 vol. 4°. Utrecht, 1714.

Renaudot, Eusèbe. *Historia patriarcharum Alexandrinorum Jacobitarum*. 4°. Paris, 1713.

—— *Anciennes relations des Indes et de la Chine*. 8°. Paris, 1718.

Retz, J. F. P. de Gondi, Cardinal de. *Mémoires*. 4 vol. 8°. Amsterdam, 1731.

—— —— 4 vol. 12°. Geneva, 1777.

Robertson, William. *The History of America*. 3 vol. 8°. London, 1788.

Rousseau, Jean-Jacques. *Collection complète des œuvres*. 17 vol. 8°. Geneva, 1782–9.

Ruhn(e)ken, David, ed. Listed in Keynes under Homer. *Hymnus in Cererem*. 8°. Leyden, 1788.

Sade, J. F. P. A. de. *Mémoires pour la vie de François Pétrarque*. 3 vol. 4°. Amsterdam, 1764–7.

Sagredo, Giovanni. *Memorie istoriche de' monarchi ottomani*. 4°. Venice, 1677.

Sainte-Croix, Guilhem de Clermont-Lodève, Baron de. *Examen critique des anciens historiens d'Alexandre-le-Grand*. 4°. Paris, 1775.

St.-Évremond, Charles de St Denis, Sieur de. *Œuvres*. 10 vol. 12°. Paris, 1740.

Saint-Marc, Charles Hugues Lefebvre de. *Abrégé chronologique de l'histoire générale d'Italie*. 6 vol. 8°. Paris, 1761–70.

Sale, George, trans. *The Koran*. 4°. London, 1734.

Sallust. *C. Sallustii Crispi quae extant*. 4°. Cambridge, 1710.

—— —— 2 vol. 4°. Amsterdam, 1742.

—— *Opera quae extant omnia*. 8°. Glasgow, 1751.

—— *C. Crispus Sallustius et L. Annaeus Florus*. 4°. Birmingham (Baskerville), 1773.

—— *Histoire de la république romaine*, ed. C. des Brosses. 3 vol. 4°. Dijon, 1777.

Sanchoniathon. *Phoenician history*, translated from the first book of Eusebius *De praeparatione evangelica* by R. Cumberland. 8°. London, 1720.

Sarpi, Fra Paolo. *Opere*. 6 vol. 4°. Helmstädt, 1761–5.

Savile, Sir Henry. *Rerum anglicarum scriptores post Bedam praecipui*. fol. Frankfurt, 1601.

Scaliger, Joseph Justus. *Opus de emendatione temporum*. fol. Geneva, 1629.

Schwandtner, Jean Georges. *Scriptores rerum Hungaricum veteres*. 3 vol. fol. Vienna, 1746–8.

Selden, John. *Opera omnia*. 3 vol. fol. London, 1726.

Senebier, Jean. *Catalogue raisonné des manuscrits dans la Bibliothèque de la Ville et République de Genève*. 8°. Geneva, 1779.

Severus, P. C. *Aetna*, ed. J. Le Clerc. 8°. Amsterdam, 1703.

Shakespeare, William. *Plays*, ed. S. Johnson. 8 vol. 8°. London, 1765.

—— *Works*, ed. Theobald. 8 vol. 12°. London, 1773.

—— *Plays*, ed. Johnson, G. Steevens, and Malone. 12 vol. 8°. London, 1778, 1780.

Shaw, Thomas. *Travels, or observations relating to several parts of Barbary and the Levant*. 4°. London, 1757.

Silius Italicus, C. *Punica*, ed. A. Drakenborch. 4°. Utrecht, 1717.

Simler, Josias. *De republica Helvetiorum*. 8°. Zürich, 1734.

Simon, Richard. *Bibliothèque critique*. . . . 4 vol. 8°. Basle, 1709, 1710.

Sirmond, Jacques. *Opera varia*. 5 vol. fol. Paris, 1696.

Solinus, C. J. Cl. *Salmasii Plinianae exercitationes in C. Julii Solini Polyhistoria. Item C. J. Solini Polyhistor emendatus*. 2 vol. fol. Utrecht, 1688, 1689.

Spelman, Sir John. *Aelfredi Magni vita*. fol. Oxford, 1678.

Spence, Joseph. *An Essay on Mr. Pope's Odyssey*. 12°. London, 1747.

Stanley, Thomas. *The History of philosophy*. fol. London, 1701.

Statius, P. P. *Sylvarum lib. V. Thebaidos lib. XII. Achilleidos lib II*. Ill. I. Veenhusen. 8°. Leyden, 1671.

—— *Silvarum libri quinque*, ed. Markland. 4°. London, 1728.

Strabo. *Rerum geographicarum libri XVII*, ed. T. J. van Almeloveen. 2 vol. fol. Amsterdam, 1707.

Struve, Burkhard Gotthelf. *Corpus historiae Germanicae*. 2 vol. fol. Jena, 1730.

Suetonius. ed. J. G. Graeve. 8°. Amsterdam, 1697.

—— 4°. Utrecht, 1708.

—— ed. Burman. 2 vol. 4°. Amsterdam, 1736.

—— ed. Ernesti. 8°. Leipzig, 1775.

Tacitus. *Opera*. See Keynes, pp. 261–2. Five editions in 3 languages before 1755.

—— —— ed. T. Ryck. 2 vol. 12°. Leyden, 1686–7.

—— —— ed. J. Gronovius. 2 vol. 4°. Utrecht, 1721.

—— —— ed. G. Brotier. 4 vol. 4°. Paris, 1771.

—— —— ed. J. A. Ernesti. 2 vol. 8°. Leipzig, 1772.

Tasso, Torquato. *Arminta*. 8°. Venice, 1636.

—— *Gierusalemme liberata*. 2 vol. fol. Venice, 1760–1.

—— —— 18°. Padua, 1763.

—— —— English translation. 8°. London, 1749.

Temple, Sir William. *Works*. 2 vol. fol. London, 1721.

Templeman, Thomas. *A New survey of the globe*. 4°. London, 1729.

Ter(r)asson, Jean. Listed in Keynes under La Vergne de Tressan, L. E. de. *Séthos*. 2 vol. 12°. Amsterdam, 1732.

Tertullian. *Apologeticus*. 8°. Leyden, 1718.

—— *Opera*. fol. Paris, 1689.

Theodosius. *Codex Theodosianus, cum commentarius J. Gothofredi.* 4 vol. fol. Lyons, 1665.

Theophrastus. *Theophrastus's History of stones*, with an English version, by John Hill. 8°. London, 1746.

Thévenot, Jean de. *Relation de divers voyages curieux qui n'ont point été publiés.* 2 vol. fol. Paris, 1696.

—— *Voyages tant en Europe qu'en Asie et en Afrique.* 5 vol. 12°. Paris, 1689.

Thomassin, Louis. *Ancienne et nouvelle discipline de l'église touchant les bénéfices et les bénéficiers.* 3 vol. fol. Paris, 1725.

Thomson, James. *The Seasons.* 12°. London, 1752.

Thou, Jacques Auguste de. *Historiae sui temporis libri CXXXVIII.* 7 vol. fol. London, 1733.

—— *Histoire universelle.* 16 vol. 4°. London, 1734.

Thucydides. ed. C. A. Dukerus ex ed. J. Wasse. fol. Amsterdam, 1731.

—— 8 vol. 12°. Glasgow, 1759.

Tillemont, L. Sébastien Le Nain de. *Histoire des empereurs.* 5 vol. 12°. Brussels, 1707.

—— —— 6 vol. 4°. Paris, 1720–38.

—— *Mémoires pour servir à l'histoire ecclésiastique des six premiers siècles.* 10 vol. 12°. Brussels, 1706.

Tillotson, John. *Works.* 10 vol. 8°. Dublin, 1739–40.

Tiraboschi, Girolamo. *Storia della letteratura italiana.* 10 vol. 4°. Modena, 1786–90.

Trublet, Nicolas Charles Joseph, Abbé de. *Mémoires pour servir à l'histoire de la vie et des ouvrages de Mr. de Fontenelle.* 12°. Amsterdam, 1759.

Tschudi, Aegidus. *Chronicon helveticum.* 2 vol. fol. Basle, 1734, 1736.

Tunstall, James. *Epistola ad Conyers Middleton, vitae M. T. Ciceronis scriptorem.* 8°. Cambridge, 1741.

—— *Observations on the Epistles between Cicero and M. Brutus, in answer to the late pretences of Conyers Middleton.* 8°. London, 1744.

Tyrtaeus. *Quae supersunt omnia*, ed. Christian Adolf Klotz. 8°. Altenburg, 1767.

Us(s)her, James. *Annales veteris et novi Testamenti.* fol. Geneva, 1722.

—— *Britannicarum ecclesiarum antiquitates.* fol. London, 1687.

Valerius Maximus. *Libri novem factorum dictorumque memorabilium*, ed. A. Torrenius. 4°. Leyden, 1726.

Valois, Adrien de. *Notitia Galliarum ordine litterarum digesta.* fol. Paris, 1675.

Velleius Paterculus. *Historiae Romanae libri II.* 12°. Paris, 1620.

—— *Quae supersunt ex Historiae Romanae voluminibus duobus*, ed. Pieter Burman. 8°. Leyden, 1719.

Vertot, René Aubert de. *Révolutions de Portugal.* 8°. Paris, 1758.

—— —— 12°. The Hague, 1769.

Vialart, Charles. *Geographia sacra*, ed. Lucas Holstenius. fol. Amsterdam, 1703.

Virgil. *Works*, trans. Christopher Pitt and Joseph Warton. 4 vol. 8°. London, 1753. See Keynes pp. 277–8.

Volney, C. F. C. de. *Voyages en Syrie et en Égypte.* 2 vol. 8°. Paris, 1787.

Voltaire. *Collection complette des œuvres.* 30 vol. 4°. Geneva, 1768–77.
—— —— 57 vol. 8°. Lausanne, 1780–1.
—— ed. Listed in Keynes under Corneille. *Le Théâtre.* 12 vol. 8°. Amsterdam, 1764.
Voss, Gerard John. *De historicis graecis.* 4°. Leyden, 1651.
Voss, Isaac. *Variarum observationum liber.* 4°. London, 1685.
Wallace, Robert. *A Dissertation on the numbers of mankind.* 8°. Edinburgh, 1753.
Warburton, William. *The Divine legation of Moses demonstrated.* 5 vol. 8°. London, 1765.
Warton, Joseph. *Essay on the genius and writings of Pope.* 2 vol. 8°. London, 1762, 1782.
Warton, Thomas. *History of English Poetry.* 3 vol. 4°. London, 1774–81.
Watson, Richard. *An Apology for Christianity in a series of Letters addressed to Edward Gibbon.* 12°. London, 1776.
Wesseling, Peter. *Vetera Romanorum itineraria; sive Antonini Augusti itinerarium.* . . . 4°. Amsterdam, 1735.
Wood, Robert. *An Essay on the original genius and writings of Homer.* 4°. London, 1775.
Xenophon. Twelve entries in Keynes, pp. 286–7. including *Opera quae extant omnia.* 5 vol. 8°. Oxford, 1700–3.
—— *De Cyri expeditione.* 12°. Glasgow, 1764.
—— *The Expedition of Cyrus,* trans. Edward Spelman. 8°. London, 1749.
—— *De Cyri expeditione,* recognovit T. Hutchinson. 4°. Oxford, 1735.
—— *Memorabilium Socratis dictorum libri IV* recensuit J. A. Ernesti. 8°. Leipzig, 1755.
Young, Edward. *Works.* 5 vol. 12°. London, 1767.
Zend-avesta, traduit (par M. Anquetil du Perron). 3 vol. 4°. Paris, 1771.

INDEX